Technology in Action
COMPLETE

13TH EDITION

Alan Evans | Kendall Martin | Mary Anne Poatsy

PEARSON

Boston Columbus Indianapolis New York San Francisco Hoboken
Amsterdam Cape Town Dubai London Madrid Milan Munich Paris Montréal Toronto
Delhi Mexico City São Paulo Sydney Hong Kong Seoul Singapore Taipei Tokyo

VP, Editorial Director: Andrew Gilfillan
Executive Acquisitions Editor: Jenifer Niles
Production and Program Team Lead: Laura Burgess
Project Manager: Holly Haydash
Program Manager: Emily Biberger
Editorial Assistant: Michael Campbell
Development Editor: Shannon LeMay-Finn
Director of Marketing: Maggie Waples
Marketing Coordinator: Susan Osterlitz
Operations Specialist: Diane Peirano
Director of Digital Studio, Worforce Readiness: Blaine
Christine

Digital Strategy: Eric Hakanson
Media Project Manager, Production: John Cassar
Art Director: Diane Ernsberger
Cover Design: Studio Montage
Cover Art: Tomas Jasinskis/Shutterstock
Full-Service Project Management: Lumina Datamatics, Inc.
Composition: Lumina Datamatics, Inc.
Printer/Binder: RR Donnelley/Menasha
Cover Printer: Lehigh-Phoenix Color/Hagerstown
Text Font: 9/11 Helvetica Neue LT W1G

Credits and acknowledgments borrowed from other sources and reproduced, with permission, in this textbook appear on the appropriate page within the text.

Microsoft and/or its respective suppliers make no representations about the suitability of the information contained in the documents and related graphics published as part of the services for any purpose. All such documents and related graphics are provided "as is" without warranty of any kind. Microsoft and/or its respective suppliers hereby disclaim all warranties and conditions with regard to this information, including all warranties and conditions of merchantability, whether express, implied or statutory, fitness for a particular purpose, title and non-infringement. In no event shall Microsoft and/or its respective suppliers be liable for any special, indirect or consequential damages or any damages whatsoever resulting from loss of use, data or profits, whether in an action of contract, negligence or other tortious action, arising out of or in connection with the use or performance of information available from the services.

The documents and related graphics contained herein could include technical inaccuracies or typographical errors. Changes are periodically added to the information herein. Microsoft and/or its respective suppliers may make improvements and/or changes in the product(s) and/or the program(s) described herein at any time.

Microsoft® and Windows® are registered trademarks of the Microsoft Corporation in the U.S.A. and other countries. This book is not sponsored or endorsed by or affiliated with the Microsoft Corporation.

Library of Congress Control Number: 2015040435

ISBN 10: 0-13-428910-2
ISBN 13: 978-0-13-428910-6

Contents at a Glance

Contents

Chapter 3

TECHNOLOGY IN FOCUS

Chapter 4

Application Software: Programs That Let You Work and Play 122

Chapter 5

System Software: The Operating System, Utility Programs, and File Management........................... 160

Chapter 6

Understanding and Assessing Hardware: Evaluating Your System.. 222

Chapter 7

Networking: Connecting Computing Devices 258

Chapter 8

Chapter 9

Securing Your System: Protecting Your Digital Data and Devices

TECHNOLOGY IN FOCUS

Chapter 10

Chapter 11

Behind the Scenes: Databases and Information Systems 450

Chapter 12

Chapter 13

Behind the Scenes: How the Internet Works 532

About the Authors

Alan Evans, MS, CPA
aevans@mc3.edu

Alan is currently a faculty member at Moore College of Art and Design and Montgomery County Community College, teaching a variety of computer science and business courses. He holds a BS in accounting from Rider University and an MS in information systems from Drexel University, and he is a certified public accountant. After a successful career in business, Alan finally realized that his true calling is education. He has been teaching at the college level since 2000. Alan enjoys attending technical conferences and meets regularly with faculty and administrators from other colleges to discuss curriculum development and new methods of engaging students.

Kendall Martin, PhD
kmartin@mc3.edu

Kendall is a professor of Computer Science at Montgomery County Community College with teaching experience at both the undergraduate and graduate levels at a number of institutions, including Villanova University, DeSales University, Ursinus College, and Arcadia University.

Kendall's education includes a BS in electrical engineering from the University of Rochester and an MS and a PhD in engineering from the University of Pennsylvania. She has industrial experience in research and development environments (AT&T Bell Laboratories), as well as experience with several start-up technology firms.

Mary Anne Poatsy, MBA
mpoatsy@mc3.edu

Mary Anne is a senior faculty member at Montgomery County Community College, teaching various computer application and concepts courses in face-to-face and online environments. She enjoys speaking at various professional conferences about innovative classroom strategies. She holds a BA in psychology and education from Mount Holyoke College and an MBA in finance from Northwestern University's Kellogg Graduate School of Management.

Mary Anne has been in teaching since 1997, ranging from elementary and secondary education to Montgomery County Community College, Gwynedd-Mercy College, Muhlenberg College, and Bucks County Community College, as well as training in the professional environment. Before teaching, she was a vice president at Shearson Lehman Hutton in the Municipal Bond Investment Banking Department.

Dedication

For my wife, Patricia, whose patience, understanding, and support continue to make this work possible … especially when I stay up past midnight writing! And to my parents, Jackie and Dean, who taught me the best way to achieve your goals is to constantly strive to improve yourself through education. **Alan Evans**

For all the teachers, mentors, and gurus who have popped in and out of my life. **Kendall Martin**

For my husband, Ted, who unselfishly continues to take on more than his fair share to support me throughout this process, and for my children, Laura, Carolyn, and Teddy, whose encouragement and love have been inspiring. **Mary Anne Poatsy**

Acknowledgments

First, we would like to thank our students. We constantly learn from them while teaching, and they are a continual source of inspiration and new ideas.

We could not have written this book without the loving support of our families. Our spouses and children made sacrifices (mostly in time not spent with us) to permit us to make this dream into a reality.

Although working with the entire team at Pearson has been a truly enjoyable experience, a few individuals deserve special mention. The constant support and encouragement we receive from Jenifer Niles, Executive Acquisitions Editor, and Andrew Gilfillan, VP, Editorial Director, continually make this book grow and change. Our heartfelt thanks go to Shannon LeMay-Finn, our Developmental Editor. Her creativity, drive, and management skills helped make this book a reality. We also would like to extend our appreciation to Jonathan Cheung and Holly Haydash, our Editorial and Production Project Managers, who work tirelessly to ensure that our book is published on time and looks fabulous. The timelines are always short, the art is complex, and there are many people with whom they have to coordinate tasks. But they make it look easy! We'd like to extend our thanks to the media and MyITlab team: Eric Hakanson, Zach Alexander, and John Cassar for all of their hard work and dedication.

There are many people whom we do not meet in person at Pearson and elsewhere who make significant contributions by designing the book, illustrating, composing the pages, producing multimedia, and securing permissions. We thank them all.

And finally, we would like to thank the reviewers and the many others who contribute their time, ideas, and talents to this project. We appreciate their time and energy, as their comments help us turn out a better product each edition. A special thanks goes to Elizabeth McBride, a wonderfully talented graphic designer who helped by creating many new graphics for this edition of the text.

Technology in Action Reviewers

Pearson and the authors would like to thank the following people for their help and time in making this book what it is over the 13 editions. We couldn't publish this book without their contributions.

Neale Adams	Iowa Central Community College	Gerald Burgess	Western New Mexico University
Paul Addison	Ivy Tech	Dave Burgett	McLennan
Afrand Agah	West Chester	Ed Bushman	Yavapai College
Jack Alanen	CSU-Northridge	Marcus Butler	West LA
Karen Allen	Community College of Rhode Island	Eric Cameron	Passaic County Community College
Ted Allen Reasoner	IUPUI	Jill Canine	Ivy Tech
Peggy Anderson	SUNY at Cortland	Gene Carbonara	Long Beach Community College
Barry Andrews	Mt. SAC	Gene Carbonaro	Long Beach City College
Lou Ann Stroup	Ivy Tech	John Carlisle	Nashua Community College
Mary Ann Zlotow	College of DuPage	Glenn Carter	Sonoma State
Sabum Anyangwe	Harford Community College	Steve Carver	Ivy Tech
Linda Arnold	HACC	Patricia Casey	Trident Tech
Adnan Atshan	Passaic County Community College	Joni Catanzaro	Louisiana State University
Adeleye Bamkole	Passaic County Community College	Afi Chamlou	NOVA Alexandria
Guarav Bansal	Wisconsin-Green Bay	Robert Chirwa	KCTCS-Bluegrass-Cooper-CIT 105
Susan Barkalow	St. Cloud State	Debbie Christenberry	Randolph Community College
Bill Barnes	Catawba Valley Community College	Desmond Chun	Chabot College
Ricky Barnes	Catawba Valley Community College	Sherri Clark	Ivy Tech
Carolyn Barren	Macomb Community College	Kevin Cleary	SUNY at Buffalo
Tony Basilico	Community College of Rhode Island	Cynthia Collings	Central AZ
Steven Battilana	West Chester	Mark Connell	SUNY at Cortland
Michelle Beets	Iowa Central Community College	Kae Cooper	BCTC/KCTCS
Kourosh Behzadnoori	Tarrant SE	Dale Craig	Fullerton College
Chris Belcher	CCAC-South	Becky Curtain	William Rainer Harper College
Elise Bell	CCSF	Juliana Cypert	Tarrant County College
Julie Bell	Delgado Cmty Clg	Paul Dadosky	Ivy Tech
Robert Benavides	Collin Cty	Enoch Damson	Akron
Garland Berry	Columbia College	James Dang	Tarrant SE
Diane Bittle	HACC	Marvin Daugherty	Ivy Tech
Burton Borlongan	Mesa Community College	John Dawson	IUPUI
Carolyn Borne	Louisiana State University	Robert Deadman	IUPUI
Gina Bowers-Miller	HACC-Wildwood	Ed Delean	NOVA Alexandria
Jeff Bowker	Montco	Mary Dermody	Chabot College
Vicki Brooks	Columbia College	Don Dershem	Mt View

Charles Dessasure	Tarrant SE
Jeanette Dix	Ivy Tech
Sally Dixon	Skagit Valley Community College
Gretchen Douglas	SUNY at Cortland
Judy Duff	Louisiana Delta College
Stacia Dutton	SUNY Canton
Donna Earhart	Genesee Community College
Ed Eill	Delaware City Community College
Pam Ellis	PA College of Technology
Sylvia Emerson	Rock Valley College
John Enomoto	East LA
Ron Enz	Chattahoochee Tech
Nancy Evans	Indiana University-Purdue University Indianapolis
James Fabrey	West Chester
Deb Fells	Mesa Community College
Pat Fenton	West Valley
Marjorie Feroe	Delaware City Community College
Beverly Fite	Amarillo
Carol Fletcher	Louisiana Delta College
Barbara Fogle, Stuhr	Trident Tech
Ann Ford Tyson coordinator)	Florida State University
Tom Foster	Chandler Gilbert Community College
Susan Fry	Boise State University
Barb Garrell	Delaware City Community College
Barbara Garrell	Delaware County Community College
Rich Geglein	Ivy Tech
Janet Gelb	Grossmont Community College
Kevin Gentry	Ivy Tech
Ian Gibbons	Hillsborough Community College-Ybor
Randy Gibson	Indian River State College
Ernie Gines	Tarrant SE
Rebecca Giorcelli	Fairmont State University
Anita Girton	PA College of Technology
Ellen Glazer	Broward Community College, South
Cathy Glod	Mohawk Valley Cmty College
Valerie Golay	Ivy Tech

Jerry Gonnella	Northern KY
Holly Gould	Ivy Tech
Deidre Grafel	Chandler-Gilbert Community College
Diedre Grafel	Chandler Gilbert Community College
Kemit Grafton	Oklahoma State University-Oklahoma City
Debra Grande	Community College of Rhode Island
Nancy Grant	CCAC-South
Wade Graves	Grayson
Natalia Grigoriants	Pierce College
Glen Grimes	Collin Cty
Toby Gustafson	UCR
Greg Hanson	Ivy Tech
A.C. Chapin	Harford Community College
	Marie Hartlein
Montco	Meng Has
Burlington County College	Lisa Hawkins
Frederick Community College	Joan Heise
Ivy Tech	Sue Heistand
Iowa Central Community College	Jessica Helberg
Northern Virginia Community College	Terri Helfand
Chaffey Community College	Jaime Hicks
Ivy Tech	Fred Hills
McLennan	Timothy Hinz
Genesee Community College	Andrew Hobbs
Delaware State University	Kristen Hockman
Univ of Missouri-Columbia	Susan Hoggard
Tulsa Community College	Don Holcomb
KCTCS-Bluegrass-Cooper-CIT 105	Terry Holleman
Catawba Valley Community College	Debbie Holt
KCTCS-Bluegrass-Cooper-CIT 105	Barbara Hotta

Lois Scheidt	Ivy Tech
Marcia Schlafmitz	New Jersey City Univ.
NAME	SCHOOL
Ken Schroeder	Ivy Tech
Todd Schultz	Augusta State University
Dick Schwartz	Macomb Community College
Francis Seidel	Frederick Cmty College
Lili Shashaani	Duquesne
Emily Shepard	Central Carolina Community College
Helen Sheran	East LA
Cliff Sherrill	Yavapai College
Lisa Simpson-Kyle	Yavapai College
Noah Singer	Tulsa Community College
Steve Singer	Kapiolani Community College
Ann-Marie Smith	Delaware City Community College
Will Smith	Tulsa Community College
Michele Smolnik	Columbia College
Ali Soleymani	NOVA Alexandria
Steve St. John	Tulsa Community College
Neal Stenlund	Northern Virginia Community College
Steve Stepanek	CSU-Northridge
Jo Stephens	University of AR Community College -Batesville
Dennis Stewart	NOVA Alexandria
Ben Stonebraker	Ivy Tech
Lynne Stuhr	Trident Tech
Alexis Stull	Fairmont State University
Denise Sullivan	Westchester Community College
Dottie Sunio	Leeward Community College
Dave Surma	IU South Bend
Michael Swafford	Tulsa Community College
Cheryl Sypniewski	Macomb Community College
Ann Taff	Tulsa Community College
James Taggart	Atlantic Cape Community College
Mel Tarnowski	Macomb Community College
Juliana.P. Cypert	Tarrant County College-NE
Joyce Thompson	Lehigh Carbon Community College
Janine Tiffany	Reading Area Comm College
Faye Tippey	Ivy Tech
Matthew Trotter	South TX College
Pam Uhlenkamp	Iowa Central Community College
Pat Vacca	El Camino College
Nelmy Vasquez	Broward Community College, South
Pete Vetere	Montco
Susie Viars-Thomas	Grayson
Gabriel Viera	South TX College
Cynthia Wagner	McLennan
Rod Waller	Indian River State College
Laurie Wallmark	Raritan Valley Community College
Kari Walters	Louisiana State University
Stacy Ward	Grafton High School
Karen Weil	McLennan
Charles Whealton	Del Tech & Community College-Dover
Deena White	Grayson
Phil Whitney	Bakersfield College
Casey Wilhelm	North Idaho College
Billie Williams	San Diego City
Melanie Williamson	KCTCS-Bluegrass-Cooper-CIT 105
Xin Xu	Georgia Gwinnett College
Thomas Yip	Passaic County Community College
Roger Young	Ivy Tech
Mary Zegarski	Northampton Community College

Letter from the Authors
Our 13th Edition—A Letter from the Authors

Why We Wrote This Book

The pace of technological change is ever increasing. In education, we have seen this impact us more than ever in the past year—the Maker movement, MOOCs, touch-screen mobile delivery, and Hangouts are now fixed parts of our environment.

Even the most agile of learners and educators need support in keeping up with this pace of change. We have responded by integrating material to help students develop skills for web application and mobile programming. We see the incredible value of these skills and their popularity with students, and have included Make This exercises for each chapter. These exercises gently bring the concepts behind mobile app development to life. In addition, there is a Solve This exercise in each chapter that reinforces chapter content while also reinforcing Microsoft Office skills. These projects help to promote students' critical thinking and problem-solving skills, which employers highly value.

Our combined 50 years of teaching computer concepts have coincided with sweeping innovations in computing technology that have affected every facet of society. From iPads to Web 2.0, computers are more than ever a fixture of our daily lives—and the lives of our students. But although today's students have a much greater comfort level with their digital environment than previous generations, their knowledge of the machines they use every day is still limited.

Part of the student-centered focus of our book has to do with making the material truly engaging to students. From the beginning, we have written *Technology in Action* to focus on what matters most to today's student. Instead of a history lesson on the microchip, we focus on tasks students can accomplish with their computing devices and skills they can apply immediately in the workplace, the classroom, and at home.

We strive to keep the text as current as publishing timelines allow, and we are constantly looking for the next technology trend or gadget. We have augmented the text with weekly technology updates to help you keep your classroom on top of the latest breaking developments and continue to include a number of multimedia components to enrich the classroom and student learning experience. The result is a learning system that sparks student interest by focusing on the material they want to learn (such as how to integrate computing devices into a home network) while teaching the material they need to learn (such as how networks work). The sequence of topics is carefully set up to mirror the typical student learning experience.

As they read through this text, your students will progress through stages and learning outcomes of increasing difficulty:

1. Thinking about how technology offers them the power to change their society and their world
2. Examining why it's important to be computer fluent
3. Understanding the basic components of computing devices
4. Connecting to and exploring the Internet
5. Exploring software
6. Learning the operating system and personalizing their computer

7. Evaluating and upgrading computing devices

8. Understanding home networking options and keeping computing devices safe from hackers

9. Going mobile with smartphones, netbooks, tablets, and laptops

10. Going behind the scenes, looking at technology in greater detail

We strive to structure the book in a way that makes navigation easy and reinforces key concepts. In this edition, we have designed the text around learning outcomes and objectives, making them a more prominent part of the chapter structure. Students will see the learning outcomes and objectives in the chapter opener, throughout the text itself, as well as in the summary so they understand just what they are expected to learn.

We continue to structure the book in a "spiraling" manner, intentionally introducing on a basic level in the earlier chapters concepts that students traditionally have trouble with and then later expanding on those concepts in more detail when students have become more comfortable with them. Thus, the focus of the early chapters is on practical uses for the computer, with real-world examples to help the students place computing in a familiar context.

For example, we introduce basic hardware components in Chapter 2, and then we go into increasingly greater detail on some hardware components in Chapter 6 and in the "Under the Hood" Technology in Focus feature. The Behind the Scenes chapters venture deeper into the realm of computing through in-depth explanations of how programming, networks, the Internet, and databases work. They are specifically designed to keep more experienced students engaged and to challenge them with interesting research assignments.

In addition to extensive review, practice, and assessment content, each chapter contains several problem-solving, hands-on activities that can carried out in the classroom or as homework:

- The **Try This** exercises lead students to explore a particular computing feature related to the chapter.

- The **Make This** exercises are hands-on activities that lead students to explore mobile app development.

- The **Solve This** exercises integrate and reinforce chapter concepts with Microsoft Office skills.

Throughout the years we have also developed a comprehensive multimedia program to reinforce the material taught in the text and to support both classroom lectures and distance learning:

- The **Helpdesk training content**, created specifically for Technology in Action, enables students to take on the role of a helpdesk staffer fielding questions posed by computer users. These have been updated to reflect the way in which users access help today.

- Exciting **Sound Byte multimedia**—fully updated and integrated with the text—expand student mastery of complex topics.

- The **Tech Bytes Weekly updates** deliver the latest technology news stories to you for use in your classroom. Each is accompanied by specific discussion topics and activities to expand on what is within the textbook materials.

This book is designed to reach the students of the twenty-first century and prepare them for the role they can take in their own community and the world. It has been an honor to work with you over the past 13 years to present and explain new technologies to students, and to show them the rapidly growing importance of technology in our world.

What's New
Technology in Action, 13th Edition

Welcome to the Thirteenth Edition of *Technology in Action!*

In this edition, we have paid special attention to incorporating clearly defined and measurable Learning Outcomes and Objectives, so that you know what students will be learning and what they will be prepared to do with this new knowledge. As has always been the case with *Technology in Action*, the quizzes, review materials, and multiple learning resources are all tied to the content and objectives of the chapter. Using the resources in the chapter, you and your students will know that the key learning objectives are being achieved. *So, explore, discover, and experience technology with the immersive and adaptive Technology in Action—the book that uses technology to teach technology!*

Technology in Action is a learning system that pushes the envelope of what is possible in technology, and what is helpful in teaching. It is a system that fits the way students are learning today and uses rich companion media to engage students in and out of the classroom while providing essential training on computer concepts.

The optimal way to experience *Technology in Action* is through MyITLab. All of the instruction, practice, review, and assessment resources are in one place, allowing you to arrange your course easily, and for students to have a consistent learning experience from chapter to chapter.

Explore the Hallmarks and New Features of *Technology in Action*, 13th Edition

INSTRUCTION: **Engage all types of learners with a variety of instructional resources**

- **Interactive e-Text** provides an environment in which students can interact with the learning resources directly and receive immediate feedback.
- NEW **Preview Videos** provide students with a quick look at what they will learn in the chapter.
- **PowerPoint Presentations** can be used in class for lecture or assigned to students, particularly online students for instruction and review.
- **Audio PowerPoint Presentations** deliver audio versions of the PowerPoint presentations—an excellent lecture-replacement option for online students.
- **TechBytes Weekly** is a weekly newsfeed that keeps your course current by providing interesting and relevant news items. The articles come with ready-to-use discussion questions.
- **Make This! Projects** address the hot area of mobile app creation! Each chapter includes activities where students build programs that run on their mobile devices. Most of the chapters use App Inventor to build Android apps that can be installed on any Android device. Even without an Android device, students can use the emulator and still get creating. By the end of the course they will have built 11 small apps. Each project includes instructions and a how-to video.

    An annotated instructor's edition provides teaching tips, homework and assessment suggestions, brief overviews of each chapter's Try This, Make This, and Solve This exercises, as well as select Sound Byte talking points and ethics debate starters.

PRACTICE: **Hands-on resources and simulations allow students to demonstrate understanding**

- **Try This Projects** are hands-on projects that students complete to practice what they are learning and demonstrate proficiency with important topics. Each project is accompanied by a how-to video.
- **Solve This! Projects** put the concepts students are learning into action through real-world problem solving using Microsoft Word, Access, and Excel. There is a grader version available for most projects in the Practice folder.
- Newly Redesigned **Helpdesks** are interactive lessons based on the chapter objectives. Students are fully engaged as they play the role of a helpdesk staffer assisting customers via a live chat, decision-based simulation.
- **Sound Bytes** provide an audio/visual lesson on additional topics related to the chapter, including a brief quiz at the end.
- **IT Simulations** provide 12 individual scenarios that students work through in an active learning environment.
- **Windows 10 high-fidelity training simulations** allow students to explore Windows in a safe, guided environment that provides feedback and Learning Aids (Watch and Practice) to assist them if they need help.

REVIEW: **Self-check resources keep learning on track**

- **Replay Videos** for Parts 1 and 2 of the chapter provide an objective-based review of what students should have learned. Videos have a short quiz and can be accessed from mobile devices for a quick review.

- **Check Your Understanding Quizzes Part 1 and 2** provide a self-check covering objectives in each part of the chapter so that students can see how well they are learning the content.
- **Adaptive Dynamic Study Modules** are adaptive flashcards that provide students with a personalized review based on their strengths and weaknesses.

ASSESSMENT: **Measure performance with ready-to-use resources**

- **Chapter Quiz** provides a way for students to test that they have learned the material from the entire chapter.
- **Critical Thinking Questions** require that students demonstrate their understanding through written answers that are manually graded.
- **Testbank Exams** provide customizable prebuilt, autograded, objective-based questions covering the chapter objectives.

In addition to these changes, all chapters have been updated with new images, current topics, and state-of-the art technology coverage. Some of the chapter changes are listed here:

Chapter 1

- Learning Outcomes and Learning Objectives have been integrated throughout the chapter and in the Chapter Review.
- Throughout the chapter, text, figures, and photos have been updated.
- New content on the political impact of technology has been added.
- Content on the use of technology in careers has been updated.
- New "Dig Deeper: Augmentative and Virtual Realities" has been added.
- New ethics section on rules for ethical conduct in a global, Internet-enabled world has been added.

Chapter 2

- Learning Outcomes and Learning Objectives have been integrated throughout the chapter and in the Chapter Review.
- Throughout the chapter, text, figures, and photos have been updated to reflect Windows 10 changes.
- The section on voice input has been updated to reflect information on the latest intelligent personal assistants (such as Siri and Cortana).
- A new Bits&Bytes, "Save Power and Avoid Eyestrain: Use Blackle," has been added.

Chapter 3

- Learning Outcomes and Learning Objectives have been integrated throughout the chapter and in the Chapter Review.
- Throughout the chapter, text, figures, and photos have been updated.

- New content about project collaboration (video conferencing, screen sharing, and project management tools) has been added.
- The Bits&Bytes "Making Safe Online Payments" has been updated by adding in biometric security measures.
- A new Bits&Bytes, "Microsoft Edge: The New Browser," has been added.
- New content on caret browsing has been added.
- A new Bits&Bytes, "Maintain Privacy while Searching the Web," has been added.
- A new Bits&Bytes, "Digital Agents and Predictive Search," has been added.
- A new ethics section on using the web ethically that includes content on intellectual property, cyberbullying, privacy, and geolocation has been added.

Technology in Focus: The History of the Personal Computer

- Learning Outcomes and Learning Objectives have been integrated throughout the Technology in Focus.
- Throughout the Technology in Focus, text, figures, and photos have been updated.

Chapter 4

- Learning Outcomes and Learning Objectives have been integrated throughout the chapter and in the Chapter Review.
- Throughout the chapter, text, figures, and photos have been updated.
- Next generation smartphone sensor technology is now covered in the "How Cool Is This?" feature.
- The section on app creation software has been updated.
- Images and text have been updated to reflect Office 2016 changes.

Chapter 5

- Learning Outcomes and Learning Objectives have been integrated throughout the chapter and in the Chapter Review.
- Microsoft HoloLens is now covered in the "How Cool Is This?" feature.
- New "How Cool Is This?" feature has been added on smartwatches.
- The Bits&Bytes "Upgrading Your Operating System" has been updated.
- A new Bits&Bytes, "OS Market Share Battle," has been added.
- The Try This now covers using virtual desktops in Windows 10.
- A new Bits&Bytes, "The Snipping Tool," has been added.

- A new Bits&Bytes, "Tips for Better Organized Files," has been added.
- A new Bits&Bytes, "Save Files in the Cloud Right from Your Apps," has been added.
- A new Bits&Bytes, "Use Cortana to Find Your Files," has been added.

Technology in Focus: Information Technology Ethics

- Learning Outcomes and Learning Objectives have been integrated throughout the Technology in Focus.
- Throughout the Technology in Focus, text, figures, and photos have been updated.
- A new section, "3D Printing: Who Is Responsible When Things Go Awry?" has been added, replacing the "International Pirates" section.
- A new section, "Human-Implanted Data Chips: Protection or Orwellian Nightmare?" has been added, replacing the "Should Employers Peer into Your Personal Life?" section.
- A new section, "Mining an Asteroid: Who Owns Outer Space?" has been added, replacing the "Geolocation: Who Knows Where You Are?" section.
- A new section, "Hacktivism: Civil Disobedience or Terrorism?" has been added, replacing the "Cyberbullying: Who Should Protect Children from Each Other" section.

Chapter 6

- Learning Outcomes and Learning Objectives have been integrated throughout the chapter and in the Chapter Review.
- Throughout the chapter, text, figures, and photos have been updated.
- New coverage of 2-in-1 devices has been added.
- The Dig Deeper content on solid state hybrid drives (SSHDs) has been updated.
- Windows 10 content has been updated.
- New "Trends in IT: USB 3.1 and USB-C" has been added.
- A new Bits&Bytes, "Tower Design," has been added.

Chapter 7

- Learning Outcomes and Learning Objectives have been integrated throughout the chapter and in the Chapter Review.
- Throughout the chapter, text, figures, and photos have been updated.
- A new Bits&Bytes, "The Rise of Wearable Technology," has been added.
- New content on the Internet of Things has been added.
- New "Trends in IT: How Smart Is Your Home" has been added.

- New "Ethics in IT: Ethical Challenges of the Internet of Things" has been added.

Technology in Focus: Under the Hood

- Learning Outcomes and Learning Objectives have been integrated throughout the Technology in Focus.
- Throughout the Technology in Focus, text, figures, and photos have been updated.

Chapter 8

- Learning Outcomes and Learning Objectives have been integrated throughout the chapter and in the Chapter Review.
- Throughout the chapter, text, figures, and photos have been updated.
- A new "How Cool Is This?" feature on continuous liquid interface production has been added.
- A new Bits&Bytes, "Photo Edit on Your Phone," has been added.
- A new Bits&Bytes, "Fly-By Drone Video," has been added.
- NFC content has been updated.
- New coverage of 2-in-1 devices has been added.
- New content on the Internet of Things has been added.

Chapter 9

- Learning Outcomes and Learning Objectives have been integrated throughout the chapter and in the Chapter Review.
- Throughout the chapter, images and text have been updated to reflect Windows 10 changes.
- The chapter has been reorganized so that all types of digital threats are covered in Part 1 and all mitigation techniques are covered in Part 2.

Technology in Focus: Careers in IT

- Learning Outcomes and Learning Objectives have been integrated throughout the Technology in Focus.
- Throughout the Technology in Focus, text, figures, and photos have been updated.

Chapter 10

- Learning Outcomes and Learning Objectives have been integrated throughout the chapter and in the Chapter Review.
- Throughout the chapter, text, figures, and photos have been updated.
- The Bits&Bytes "Hackathons" has been updated.
- A new Bits&Bytes, "Your Software Portfolio," has been added.

Chapter 11

- Learning Outcomes and Learning Objectives have been integrated throughout the chapter and in the Chapter Review.

- Throughout the chapter, text, figures, and photos have been updated.
- The "How Cool Is This?" feature now covers Circos circular charts.
- A new Bits&Bytes, "Data Warehouses Are Going to the Cloud," has been added.
- A new Bits&Bytes, "Hadoop: How Big Data Is Being Managed," has been added.
- A new "Trends in IT: Mobile Business Intelligence" has been added.
- The "Ethics in IT: Data, Data Everywhere, but Is It Protected?" has been updated.

Chapter 12

- Learning Outcomes and Learning Objectives have been integrated throughout the chapter and in the Chapter Review.
- Throughout the chapter, text, figures, and photos have been updated.

- Google's Project Sunroof and solar technology are now covered in the "How Cool Is This?" feature.
- A new Bits&Bytes, "Your Car Has a Network… So Can It Be Hacked?," has been added.
- A new Bits&Bytes, "Forget Software as a Service—Lighting as a Service Can Really Save Money!" has been added.

Chapter 13

- Learning Outcomes and Learning Objectives have been integrated throughout the chapter and in the Chapter Review.
- Throughout the chapter, text, figures, and photos have been updated.
- The "How Cool Is This?" feature now covers parallax scrolling.
- A new "Ethics in IT: Do We Really Want Strong Encryption?" has been added.
- A new Bits&Bytes, "Internet of Things Goes Shopping," has been added.

Visual Walk-Through

Topic Sequence

Concepts are covered in a progressive manner between chapters to mirror the typical student learning experience.

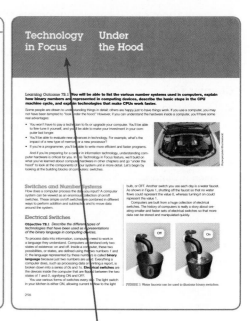

Hardware First Introduced
Chapter 2 is the first time students read about introductory hardware. It's covered at the beginning level because this is students' experience level at this point of the book.

Hardware Taught in More Depth in Additional Chapters
In later chapters, students read about hardware in greater depth because they're more experienced and comfortable working with their computers.

Technology in Focus
Four special features that teach key uses of technology today.

Clearly Defined Learning Objectives and Outcomes
Provide measurable goals for instructors and students.

Multimedia Cues
Visual integration of multimedia resources, including the Helpdesks, Sound Bytes, Preview, and Replay Videos.

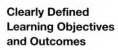

How Cool Is This?
Highlights the latest and greatest websites, gadgets, and multimedia.

Student Textbook

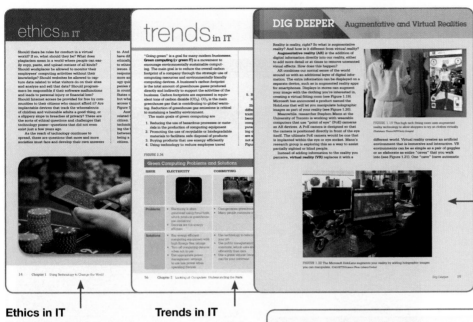

Bits & Bytes
Help make the topics immediately relevant to students' lives.

Dig Deeper
Boxes cover technical topics in depth to challenge advanced students.

Try This and Make This
Hands-on activities found between Parts 1 and 2 of each chapter.

Ethics in IT
Boxes examine the ethical dilemmas involved with technology.

Trends in IT
Boxes explore hot topics in computing.

End of Chapter Quiz
Multiple Choice, True/False, and Critical Thinking questions at the end of each chapter help students assess their comprehension of chapter material.

Solve This
Exercises that put the concepts students are learning into action using a Microsoft Office application.

Check Your Understanding quizzes provide an auto-graded, self-check covering objectives in each part of the chapter.

MyITLab

MyITLab for *Technology in Action* with the Enhanced eBook personalizes learning to help your students better prepare and learn—resulting in more dynamic experiences in the classroom and improved performance in the course. Specific features include:

- **Adaptive Learning:** *A way to enable personalized learning at scale.* Not every student learns the same way and at the same rate. MyITLab with Adaptive Learning continuously assesses student performance and activity in real time, and, using data and analytics, personalizes content to reinforce concepts that target each student's strengths and weaknesses.
- **NEW Adaptive Dynamic Study Modules,** created specifically for *Technology in Action*, 13th Edition, provide students with personalized review based on their strengths and weaknesses.

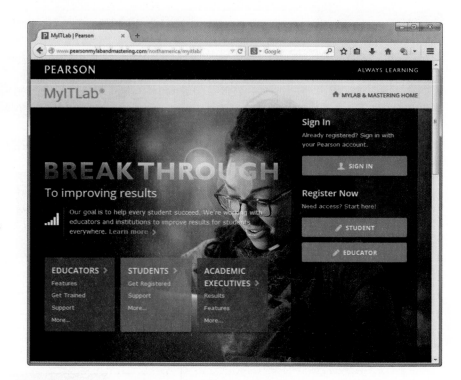

- **A powerful homework and test manager:** MyITLab lets you create, import, and manage online homework assignments, Helpdesk and Soundbyte activities, quizzes, and tests that are automatically graded. The bottom line: MyITLab means less time grading and more time teaching.
- **Comprehensive online course content:** Filled with a wealth of content that is tightly integrated with your textbook, MyITLab lets you easily add, remove, or modify existing instructional material. You can also add your own course materials to suit the needs of your students or department. In short, MyITLab lets you teach exactly as you'd like.
- **Robust Gradebook tracking:** The online Gradebook automatically tracks your students' results on tests, homework, and practice exercises and gives you control over managing results and calculating grades. And, it lets you measure and document your students' learning outcomes.
- **Easily scalable and shareable content:** MyITLab enables you to manage multiple class sections, and lets other instructors copy your settings so a standardized syllabus can be maintained across your department.

The following media is available in MyITLab, and selected items are also on the companion website.

Note: To access the premium content, including Helpdesks, Sound Bytes, and Replay Videos from the companion site, students need to use the access code printed on the card in the front of the book.

MyITLab • **The interactive eText** in MyITLab provides continuous digital learning in an interactive environment that allows students to use technology as they learn. They don't have to stop reading to find the activities such as Helpdesks, Sound Bytes, and Replay Videos—they just click on them and immediately experience the activity.

MyITLab • **IT Simulations:** These fully interactive, scenario-based simulations allow students to demonstrate their understanding of the chapter topic in an experiential learning environment.

• **Adaptive Dynamic Study Modules,** created specifically for *Technology in Action*, 13th Edition, provide students with a personalized review based on their strengths and weaknesses.

MyITLab • **Sound Bytes:** These multimedia lessons provide a multimodal approach to instruction in which topics are presented with audio, video, and interactive activities. The topics covered in the Sound Bytes expand on the coverage in the book to dive into newer technology or more depth on a specific subject.

• **NEWLY REDESIGNED and UPDATED Active Helpdesks:** These highly interactive, engaging activities provide students with a realistic experience of how help is delivered via live chat. Students play the role of a helpdesk staffer answering technology questions. These highly interactive, formative assessments provide students with a realistic, engaging experience of how support is delivered to customers today. Each Helpdesk covers core objectives in the chapter. Students play the role of a support staffer tasked with assisting customers with questions related to the content of the text. This approach allows students to apply what they are learning in a new environment. The assessment questions after each Helpdesk provide instructors with a tool to gauge and track students' progress.

• **Make This** projects address the hot area of mobile app creation! Each chapter includes a Make This mobile app project, most of which use App Inventor. By the end of the course, students will have completed 13 small projects that provide them with new skills they can use to create their own apps. And if they don't have an Android device, they can use the emulator and still learn the skills.

• **Solve This** projects put the concepts students are learning into action through real-world problem solving using a Microsoft Office application or other technology tool. For Word and Excel projects, there is also a grader version in MyITLab.

• **NEW Preview Videos:** The Preview Videos provide an author-narrated video preview of each chapter in an easy-to-use format students can view on their phones, tablets, or computers.

• **UPDATED Replay Videos:** The Replay Videos provide an author-narrated video review of each chapter part.

• **With Tech Bytes Weekly, every week is new!** This weekly newsfeed provides two timely articles to save instructors the prep time required for adding interesting and relevant news items to their weekly lectures. Tech Bytes Weekly also features valuable links and other resources, including discussion questions and course activities.

Transcript button
Used to turn transcript on or off

Sound Bytes
Multimedia lessons with video, audio, or animation and corresponding labs featuring multiple-choice quizzing.

Navigational tool

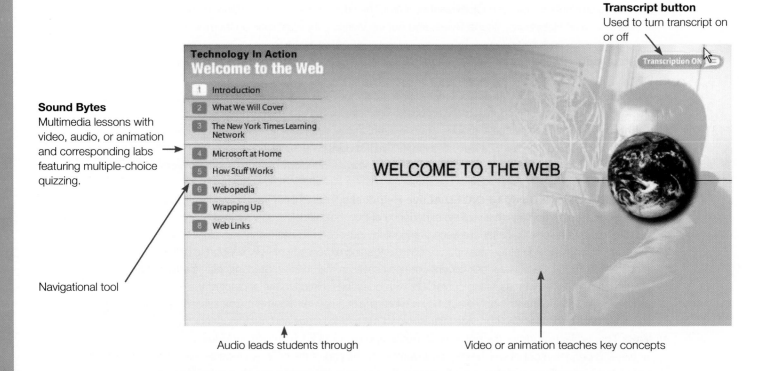

Audio leads students through

Video or animation teaches key concepts

Active Helpdesk
Interactive training that puts the student in the role of a helpdesk staffer fielding questions about technology.

Supervisor available to assist students.

Features textbook references within each Helpdesk and assessment at the end.

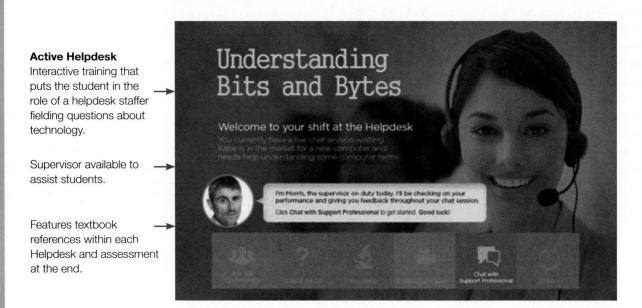

Annotated Instructor Edition

Provided with each chapter are two divider pages like the ones outlined below.

FRONT OF CHAPTER TAB

On the front side of each chapter tab, you'll find the following categories:

IN THE CLASSROOM: Activities you can use in a classroom or in online classes, including:

- **PowerPoint Presentations**
- **Discussion Exercises**
- **Active Helpdesks**
- **Sound Bytes**

HOMEWORK: Activities used out of class for assessment or preparation for the next chapter, including:

- **Web Resource Projects**
- **Active Helpdesks**
- **Sound Byte Labs**

ASSESSMENT:

- **Blackboard**
- **WebCT**
- **TestGen**
- **myitlab**
- **Student Text Test Bank**
- **Sound Byte Test Bank**
- **Helpdesk Test Bank**

The back side of each chapter tab includes notes about that chapter's Try This, Make This, and Solve This exercises.

ETHICS TAB

On the Ethics tab, you will find the following:

OPPOSING VIEWPOINTS TABLE: Outlines ethics topics that you can use to debate in the classroom.

KEYWORDS: Provides you with additional words with which to search the Internet for more information related to the ethics topic.

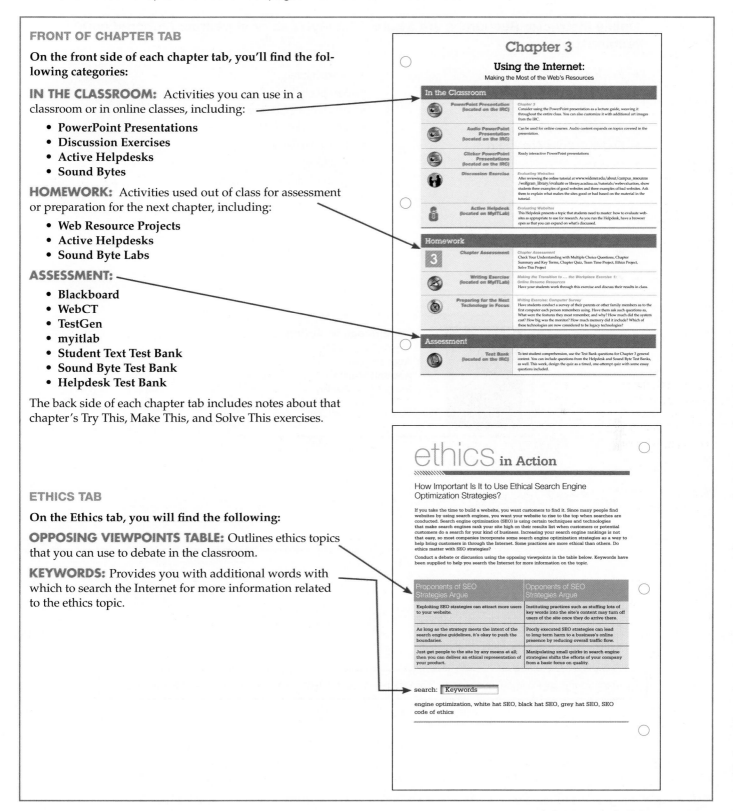

Instructor Resources

Online Instructor Resources are available in MyITLab or at pearsonhighered.com/techinaction.

- PowerPoint Presentations
- Student Text Test Bank
- Sound Byte Test Bank
- Help Desk Test Bank
- End of Chapter Answer Keys
- Rubrics
- Web Resources

- Image Library
- Sample Syllabi
- Additional Web Projects
- What's New in 13e
- Transition Guide
- TestGen

**Technology In Action
Complete, 13/E
Alan Evans
Kendall Martin
Mary Anne Poatsy**
ISBN-10: 0134289102
ISBN-13: 9780134289106

Contact your local Pearson sales rep to learn more about the *Technology in Action* instructional system.

Technology
in Action

1

Using Technology to Change the World

How Will You Put Technology in Action?

Learning Outcome 1.1 **You will be able to discuss the impact of technology on global and national issues.**

Technology on the World Stage   4

Objective 1.1 *Recognize how becoming proficient with technology can help you understand and participate in political issues in the world at large.*

Objective 1.2 *Describe how technology affects social issues in different societies.*

Technology and Our Society   7

Objective 1.3 *Describe how technology is changing our cognitive processes.*

Objective 1.4 *Explain how technology is expanding the ways we collaborate.*

Objective 1.5 *Summarize how technology has impacted the way we choose and consume products and services.*

How Will Technology Improve Your Life?

Learning Outcome 1.2 **You will be able to discuss personal impacts technology can have on your life and your career.**

Technology at Home   12

Objective 1.6 *Characterize computer literacy, and list some of its benefits.*

◀ **Sound Byte:** Questions to Ask Before You Buy a Computer

Technology and Your Career   15

Objective 1.7 *Characterize the impact computer literacy has on a variety of careers.*

Make This: MAKE: A Virtual Assistant on **page 11**

All media accompanying this chapter can be found in MyITLab.

For an overview of the chapter, watch the **Preview Video**.

HOW COOL IS THIS?

Want to **make a difference with technology**? The good news is that it has never been easier. Technology is allowing more and more of us to become **agents of change in our communities** and in the world. In London, over 20,000 school-age children are joining **Apps for Good**, a program that links students, educators, and local experts to guide students in designing and building apps to help solve problems they see around them. The **Verizon Innovative App Challenge** led students to develop apps to customize texts for students with dyslexia and apps to help connect people with causes they wanted to support with volunteer time. Civic hacking events, like one called **Random Hacks of Kindness**, are helping people create apps to track lobbyists in government, to map the location of murals in a city, and to help organize people to dig out fire hydrants after snowstorms. What kind of good can you do with technology? *(Aleciccotelli/Fotolia)*

How Will You Put Technology in Action?

Learning Outcome 1.1 You will be able to discuss the impact of technology on global and national issues.

Ask yourself: Why are you in this class? Maybe it's a requirement for your degree, or maybe you want to improve your computer skills. But let's step back and look at the bigger picture.

Technology today is not just a means for career advancement or merely a skill set needed to survive in society. It's a tool that enables us all to make an impact beyond our own lives. We've all seen movies that dangle the dream in front of us of being the girl or guy who saves the world—and gets to drive a nice car while doing it! Whether it's *The Avengers* or *Big Hero 6*, we are drawn to heroes because we want our lives and our work to mean something and to benefit others.

Technology can be your ticket to doing just that, to influencing and participating in projects that will change the world. We'd like to ask you to think about how your talents and skills in technology will let you contribute on a larger scale, beyond the benefits they will bring to you personally.

 technology on the
WORLD STAGE

Recent political and global issues are showing that technology is accelerating change around the world and galvanizing groups of people in new ways. Let's look at a few examples.

Political Issues

Objective 1.1 *Recognize how becoming proficient with technology can help you understand and participate in political issues in the world at large.*

Social Media

Social media tools enable the gathering of groups of people to connect and exchange ideas, and they have brought together people facing repression and censorship in many countries. In fact, in 2014, uprisings in the Ukraine were organized using Facebook pages. Managing control of the media is no longer simple for regimes.

Politicians worldwide have also begun to incorporate social media as part of their political strategy. In the United States, politicians like Barack Obama have Twitter and Facebook accounts that they use to communicate with their constituents. In Italy, Beppe Grillo drew the largest vote in a recent election for a single party using mainly Facebook and Twitter in place of television and newspaper ads, and in the United Kingdom politicians post over two million social media updates a year.

Social media has proven to be a very effective way of motivating people to vote. Ireland has a socially conservative heritage, decriminalizing homosexuality as recently as 1993. In the recent vote on same-sex marriage equality, Irish nationals living abroad—many young and with liberal views—were not allowed to mail in a ballot. Thousands traveled back to Ireland to cast

FIGURE 1.1 The Irish referendum on marriage equality meant many Irish living abroad traveled home just to vote, documenting their trips using #HomeToVote. *(Brian Lawless/AP Images)*

a "yes" vote in support of same-sex marriage, encouraging each other with a Twitter feed #HomeToVote (see Figure 1.1). Facebook posts for the "Yes Equality" page topped 1.6 million. With a large voter turnout, Ireland became the first country to legalize gay marriage through a popular vote.

Social media tools are providing a level of instant connection and information distribution that is reshaping the world. What can you do with social media tools that will change the future of your community?

Crisis-Mapping Tool

Another example of the interaction of technology and society is the software tool Ushahidi. Following a disputed election in

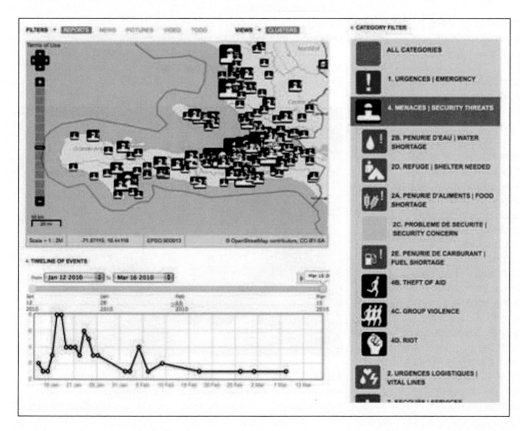

FIGURE 1.2 During a natural disaster in Haiti, Ushahidi crisis-mapping software helped identify areas of violence, helped people locate food and water, and directed rescuers to those in need. *(Reprinted with permission of Ushahidi, Inc. www.ushahidi.com)*

Kenya, violence broke out all over the country. Nairobi lawyer Ory Okolloh tried to get word of the violence out to the world through her blog, but she couldn't keep up with the volume of reports. But two programmers saw her request for help and in a few days created Ushahidi (Swahili for "testimony"). It is a **crisis-mapping tool** that collects information from e-mails, text messages, blog posts, and Twitter tweets and then maps them, instantly making the information publicly available. The developers then made Ushahidi a free platform anyone in the world can use (see Figure 1.2). So when earthquakes rocked Haiti, Ushahidi instantly told rescuers where injured people were located. When a tsunami brought Japan to the brink of a nuclear catastrophe, Ushahidi let anyone with a mobile phone find locations with clean water and food. Chile, Syria, Somalia, and the Democratic Republic of the Congo have all used this crisis-mapping software to save lives in times of political upheaval. In what other ways could technology help us face times of crisis?

Other Global Issues

Objective 1.2 *Describe how technology affects social issues in different societies.*

Political crises are not the only arena in which technology is enabling global change. Technology is impacting social issues in different countries around the world.

Health Care

Infectious diseases account for about one-fifth of all deaths worldwide. Researchers say the odds of a flu pandemic occurring in the next century are nearly 100%. Could technology help us develop and deliver vaccines in a way that saves lives? With newer scientific visualization tools, scientists are developing antibodies for flu viruses and even HIV, viruses that are difficult to target because they continually change shape. Computationally intense modeling software is helping researchers increase the pace of vaccine production, saving lives.

Retinal prosthetics are another example of global health concerns being addressed with technology. Macular degeneration and retinitis pigmentosa are two diseases that destroy the retina; they account for the majority of blindness in developing nations. Sheila Nirenberg of Cornell University is working on a microchip that can replace the function of the retina, translating incoming light into the electrical pulses the brain needs for vision. These biomedical chips could restore quality vision to the blind.

The Environment

What if every cell phone in the world had built-in atmospheric sensors? Then millions of points of air and water quality data from around the world could be constantly acquired. Tagged with geographical information, the data could alert scientists to new trends in our environment. Ideas like these are being explored by Mark Nieuwenhuijsen of the Center for Research in Environmental Epidemiology in Barcelona, Spain.

Smart Internet-connected water sprinklers are another technology that is saving water in California and other dry areas of the country. The sprinkler system checks the weather forecasts so it won't use water when rain is coming the next day. It can adjust the watering schedule based on the season and can adjust the times of watering to encourage root growth. The system is showing a 30% reduction in water usage.

Can you think of other ways you could use mobile and wearable technology to improve society?

The Digital Divide

There is a great gap in the levels of Internet access and the availability of technical tools in different regions of the world. The term coined for this difference in ease of access to technology is the **digital divide**. One danger of a digital divide is that it prevents us from using all the minds on the planet to solve the planet's problems. But this challenge created by technology is also being answered by technology.

The Next Einstein Initiative (NEI) is a plan to focus resources on the talented mathematical minds of Africa (see Figure 1.3). By expanding the African Institute for Mathematical Sciences (AIMS) across the continent, the future of Africa can be profoundly changed. Cambridge professor Neil Turok founded AIMS to bring together the brightest young minds across Africa with the best lecturers in the world. The NEI has won funding from Google's Project 10^{100}, an initiative to award $10 million to a set of five projects selected by open public voting. By capturing the enthusiasm of the world with presentations distributed

through TED (**ted.com**) and Project 10^{100}, there is now a push to create 15 additional AIMS centers across Africa.

Figure 1.4 shows additional examples of people putting technology into action to impact the world. How will you join them? ■

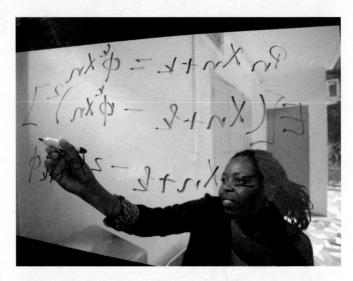

FIGURE 1.3 The Next Einstein Initiative (NEI) is rallying the support of the world to identify mathematical genius.
(African Institute for Mathematical Sciences Next Einstein Initiative (AIMS-NEI))

FIGURE 1.4

Technology in Action: Taking on Global Problems

PERSON/ ORGANIZATION	GLOBAL PROBLEM	TECHNOLOGY USED	ACTION	FIND OUT MORE ...
Peter Gabriel/ The Witness Project	Human rights abuses	Video cameras	Provide video documentation of human rights abuses; the project contributed to the arrest of warlords in the Democratic Republic of the Congo for the recruitment of child soldiers	The Witness Project: **witness.org**
SolaRoad/ Netherlands	The need for a renewable, nonpolluting energy resource	Solar cells	Solar cells are integrated into the asphalt roadway. They collect solar energy and distribute electricity all day	Netherlands' SolaRoad: **solaroad.nl**
United Nations World Food Programme (WFP)	One in seven people in the world do not get enough food to eat	GIS (geographical information systems) and mobile devices	The WFP can analyze the location and need for food, positioning food where it will help the most	World Food Programme: **wfp.org**
e-Nable	Need for inexpensive, easily maintained prosthetic hands	3D printing	This group of engineers, parents, and artists work to print and assemble hands for people they may never meet	e-Nable: **enablingthefuture.org**

technology and
OUR SOCIETY

Technology is also allowing us to redefine very fundamental parts of our social makeup—how we think, how we connect with each other, and how we purchase and consume products.

Technology Impacts How We Think

Objective 1.3 *Describe how technology is changing our cognitive processes.*

What We Think About

What do you think about in your free time? In the late twentieth century, a common trend was to think about what to buy next—or perhaps what to watch or listen to next. Information and products were being served up at an amazing rate, and the pattern of consumption became a habit. As more and more web applications began to appear that allowed each individual to become a "creator" of the web, a new kind of Internet came into being. It was nicknamed **Web 2.0**, and it had a set of new features and functionality that allowed users to contribute content easily and to be easily connected to each other. Now everyone could collaborate internationally at the click of a mouse.

Web 2.0 has fostered a dramatic shift across the world from simply consuming to having the ability to volunteer and collaborate on projects. In his book *Cognitive Surplus: Creativity and Generosity in a Connected Age*, author Clay Shirky created the term **cognitive surplus** to mean the combination of leisure time and the tools to be creative. The world's population has an estimated one trillion hours a year of free time. When coupled with the available media tools and the easy connectivity of Web 2.0, and with generosity and a need to share, projects like Ushahidi and the Witness Project (see Figure 1.4) emerge.

But why would anyone bother to work on projects like these in their free time? Modern theories of motivation show that what pushes people to apply their free time in altruistic

causes, for no money, is the excitement of autonomy, mastery, and purpose (see Figure 1.5):

- **Autonomy:** the freedom to work without constant direction and control.
- **Mastery:** the feeling of confidence and excitement from seeing your own skills progress.
- **Purpose:** the understanding that you are working for something larger than yourself.

Together, these three factors play into how we are fundamentally wired and can produce incredibly motivated behavior. The combination of motivation, technology, and a cognitive surplus is leading to powerful projects that are changing the world.

Technology Impacts How We Connect

Objective 1.4 *Explain how technology is expanding the ways we can collaborate.*

Connecting Through Music

In many societies, people connect intimately by creating and sharing music. Blend (**blend.io**) (see Figure 1.6) is a site that allows people to exchange the songs they have written as well as the electronic data and settings they used to create the song. People can explore different musical styles and techniques on the site and immediately download the components that made a song and begin to modify it. There is also a Blend blogging community that trades musical ideas among its readers. In addition, Blend is a publishing house, distributing and selling its users' digital music for them through all major outlets like iTunes,

FIGURE 1.5 Our understanding of human motivation can play a role in our use of technology to impact society. *(Bonninturina/ Fotolia, lzf/Fotolia, Vadymvdrobot/Fotolia)*

FIGURE 1.6 Blend (**blend.io**) is an example of a community that lets musicians exchange not only songs but the electronic settings and data used to create the songs. *(Stuart Hughes/Corbis)*

Spotify, and Google Play. If you can get 100 likes from the community for your song, it is qualified for release on the Blend label!

Connecting Through Business

One of the most profound ways we can connect with each other is to support other people's dreams. Kickstarter (**kickstarter.com**) helps us connect in this way by allowing people to post their ideas for community projects, games, and inventions and to ask for funding directly. Donors are given rewards for different levels of pledges, such as a signed edition of a book or a special color of a product. This style of generating capital to start a business is known as **crowdfunding**, asking for small donations from a large number of people, often using the Internet. Successful Kickstarter projects have included ice chests with integrated blenders, DNA analysis machines that could inexpensively diagnose disease, and many entertainment projects. In total, almost $2 billion of funding for businesses has been raised using Kickstarter.

Technology Impacts How We Consume

Objective 1.5 *Summarize how technology has impacted the way we choose and consume products and services.*

Technology is changing all aspects of how we decide what we'll purchase and how we actually buy goods and services—from strategies for convincing you to purchase a certain product to the mechanics of how you buy and own things.

Marketing

 New strategies in marketing are counting on the fact that most people have a cell phone with a camera and Internet access. **QR (quick response) codes** like the one shown here let any piece of print host a link to online information and video content. And studies show 82% of shoppers use their cell phone to go on the Internet before they make a purchase. They are often using so-called location-aware price comparison tools. Apps like ShopSavvy and RedLaser scan the bar code of the item and then compare prices with those of nearby stores and with the best prices available online. Techy shoppers can then get "mobile coupons" (or *mobi coupons*) delivered to their cell phones, thanks to sites like SnipSnap and Coupon Sherpa. The future promises specialized coupons created just for you based on your location and past buying preferences.

Marketers also have to be aware of the phenomenon of **crowdsourcing**—checking in with the voice of the crowd. Consumers are using apps like ScanLife to check people's verdicts on the quality of items. Forward-thinking companies are using this input to improve their products and services. AT&T, for example, has an app that lets customers report locations of coverage gaps.

Access Versus Ownership

Even the idea of ownership is evolving, thanks to new technologies. Items like cars and bikes can become "subscriptions" instead of large one-time purchases. For example, Zipcar

FIGURE 1.7 New York City's Citi Bike program uses digital technology to change our lifestyle from one of ownership to one of subscription. Riders are now taking over one million trips per month. *(Tim Clayton/Corbis)*

allows hundreds of thousands of people to use shared cars. With Zipcar, a phone call or online reservation activates your personal Zipcar. This card allows you to automatically open the door of the car you have reserved, and away you drive. GPS technology is used to track where the car is, whether it has been dropped off at the right location, and how far it has been driven. Call a Bike is a bike-sharing program in Germany. Racks of Call a Bikes are located at major street corners in large cities in the country. Simply call the phone number printed on the bike and it texts you a code to unlock the bike. When you're done riding the bike, simply relock it and you're billed automatically. The New York City version of this program, Citi Bike, has already seen riders take over seven million trips (see Figure 1.7).

These subscription-style business models are spreading now to smaller goods. **Swap.com** helps people trade books, clothes, and video games with one another using the power of peer-to-peer connections—for example, to find those who want to swap used roller blades for a baby crib.

Rachel Botsman and Roo Rogers make the case in their book *What's Mine Is Yours: The Rise of Collaborative Consumption* that the real fuel beneath these services is a shift in our acceptance of sharing. **Collaborative consumption** implies that we are joining together as a group to use a specific product more efficiently. We are so constantly connected with each other that we have again found the power of community. There are increasing opportunities to redistribute the things we have purchased and to share the services a product provides instead of owning it outright. Add in the pressure of mounting environmental concerns and global financial pressures, and we are migrating toward collaborative consumption. ■

Before moving on to Part 2:
1. **Watch Replay Video 1.1** ▷ .
2. **Then check your understanding of what you've learned so far.**

check your understanding // review & practice

For a quick review to see what you've learned so far, answer the following questions.

multiple choice

1. Which is NOT a technology that has been used to deliver assistance during times of crisis?

   a. Ushahidi

   b. blend.io

   c. social media

   d. e-mail

2. Cognitive surplus means that we now find many people with

   a. more money than free time.

   b. limited access to the Internet.

   c. excess time and free tools for collaboration.

   d. mobile devices.

3. Collaborative consumption is when people get together to

   a. find the best prices on products.

   b. exchange reviews on services and goods they have purchased.

   c. fight diseases of the respiratory tract.

   d. increase the use of a single product by sharing access to it.

4. Crowdfunding helps start-up businesses by

   a. selling stock more easily.

   b. gathering financial contributions from supporters.

   c. using QR codes to advertise and market products.

   d. replacing Web 2.0 technology.

5. Social media has been used to

   a. increase voter turnout in elections.

   b. increase communication between elected officials and their constituents.

   c. replace television and radio advertising in political elections.

   d. all of the above

 Go to **MyITLab** to take an autograded version of the *Check Your Understanding* review and to find all media resources for the chapter.

TECHBYTES WEEKLY

Stay current with the TechBytes Weekly Newsletter.

Continue

TRY THIS

Skyping Around the World

Understanding what your computer can do to improve your life is one of the benefits of being computer literate. In this exercise, we'll show you how to make a free phone call over the Internet using the desktop version of Skype, a popular Voice over Internet Protocol (VoIP) service. (Note: These instructions are for the desktop version of Skype. The interface when using Skype on a mobile device may be different.)

What You Need

WIRED INTERNET CONNECTION OR WIFI SIGNAL	A DEVICE (COMPUTER, SMARTPHONE, TABLET, SKYPE-READY TELEVISION)	A FRIEND

(Gst/Shutterstock, Dvougao/Digital Vision Vectors/Getty Images, Filo/DigitalVision Vectors/Getty Images)

Step 1 **Set Up an Account.** Go to Skype (**skype.com**), click on the **Get Skype button**, and create an account. Download the proper version for your device and install. You'll be able to call anyone with Skype and talk with just audio, with audio and video, or with free instant messaging. *(STANCA SANDA/Alamy Stock Photo)*

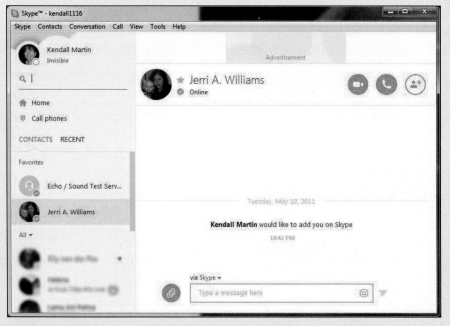

Step 2 **Build Your Contact List.** To build your list of contacts, you can add friends one at a time by clicking **Contacts**, **Add Contact**, then **Search Skype Directory** (as shown here). You can search for people using their name, their Skype name, or their e-mail address. *(Screenshot of Skype, part of Microsoft)*

(You only need to add a phone number if you plan on using Skype to call people on their *phone*, which, unlike computer-to-computer calls, is not a free service.)

For people you call frequently, drag their name up into the Favorites section.

Step 3   Make a Call. Now we're ready to call someone! Let's start by calling the people at Skype and making sure everything is hooked up properly. Under your Contacts list, click the **Echo/Sound Test Service**. Then call in by clicking the **Call button**. The Skype service will answer your call, record a short message from you, and play it back to you. You'll know everything is set to go, and you can begin calling the world for free! *(Screenshots of Skype, part of Microsoft)*

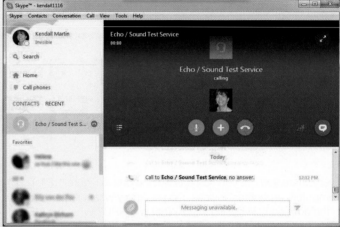

Make This ▶ TOOL: IFTTT/.com (If This Then That)

MAKE: A Virtual Assistant

If This Then That (**IFTTT.com**) is an Internet-based tool that helps you get things done automatically. By using "recipes" within this web-based tool, you can automate tasks you do during the day, such as:

- Automatically silencing your phone when you go into class
- Automatically texting your manager when you're on your way to work
- Notifying you when the president signs a new law

In this exercise, you'll explore using IFTTT to create recipes like these. *(IFTTT, Inc)*

Make the Internet work for you by knowing this one programming statement: IF THIS THEN THAT.

For the instructions for this exercise, go to MyITLab.

How Will Technology Improve Your Life?

Learning Outcome 1.2 You will be able to discuss personal impacts technology can have on your life and your career.

Technology is creating huge changes in the world as well as in how we behave socially, but it is also important to you on a more personal level. Being computer literate means being familiar enough with computers that you understand their capabilities and limitations and that you know how to use them safely and efficiently. As we discuss here, the more you understand technology, the more productive and protected you'll be at home, and the better prepared you'll be for any career.

 technology at
HOME

Everywhere you go, you see ads like the one in Figure 1.8 for computers and other devices. Do you know what all the words in the ad mean? What is RAM? What is a GPU? What are MB, GB, GHz, and cache? How fast do you need your computer to be, and how much memory should it have? If you're computer literate, you'll be a more informed consumer when it comes time to buy computers, peripherals, and technology services. Understanding computer terminology and keeping current with technology will help you better determine which computers and devices you need.

Computer Literacy

Objective 1.6 *Characterize computer literacy, and list some of its benefits.*

Let's look at a few examples of what it means to be a savvy computer user and consumer—in other words, **computer literate** (see Figure 1.9).

If you're not a savvy user now, don't worry—the following topics and more are covered in detail in the remaining chapters.

- **Avoiding hackers and viruses.** Do you know what hackers and viruses are? Both can threaten a computer's security. Being aware of how hackers and viruses operate and knowing the damage they can do to your computer can help you avoid falling prey to them.

- **Protecting your privacy.** You've probably heard of identity theft—you see and hear news stories all the time about people whose "identities" are stolen and whose credit ratings are ruined by "identity thieves." But do you

Processor:	Intel i7-5930, Factory O'Cd to 3.6GHz
RAM:	16 GB *Tri Channel* Corsair DDR4 – (2800 MHz)
Video:	AMD Radeon R9 295X2 with 8 GB GDDR5 and dual GPUs
Audio:	Creative Labs X-Fi Elite Pro; HDA 7.1 surround channel sound
Network:	Native *Gigabit* Ethernet
Storage Drive:	Hybrid drive 120 GB with 2 TB SATA-III; support for up to 5 additional drives with RAID options
Ports:	8 USB and 2 USB 3.0 2 DVI and 1 S-Video 2 IEEE 1394 1 *S/PDIF* out
Cooling:	Two-stage *liquid cooling* system
Portable Storage:	Bluetooth wireless 19-in-1 media hub with *VoIP* stereo headset

FIGURE 1.8 Do you know what all the words in a computer ad mean? Can you tell whether the ad includes all the information necessary to make a purchasing decision?

FIGURE 1.9

What Does It Mean to Be Computer Literate?

You can **avoid falling prey to hackers and viruses** because you are aware of how they operate.

You know how to **protect yourself from identity theft**.

You can **separate the real privacy and security risks from things you don't have to worry about**.

You know how to find information and **use the web effectively**.

You can **avoid being overwhelmed by spam, adware, and spyware**.

You know how to **diagnose and fix problems** with your hardware and software.

know how to protect yourself from identity theft when you're online?

- **Understanding the real risks.** Part of being computer literate means being able to separate the real privacy and security risks from things you don't have to worry about. For example, do you know what a *cookie* is? Do you know whether it poses a privacy risk for you when you're on the Internet? What about a *firewall*? Do you know what one is? Do you really need a firewall to protect your computer?

- **Using the web wisely.** Anyone who has ever searched the web can attest that finding information and finding *good* information are two different things. People who are computer literate know how to find the information they want effectively. How effective are your searches?

- **Avoiding online annoyances.** If you have an e-mail account, chances are you've received electronic junk mail, or **spam**. How can you avoid spam? What about adware and spyware—do you know what they are? Do you know the difference between those and viruses, worms, and Trojan horses? Do you know which **software** programs—the instructions that tell the computer what to do—you should install on your computer to avoid online annoyances?

- **Being able to maintain, upgrade, and troubleshoot your computer.** Learning how to care for and maintain your computer and knowing how to diagnose and fix certain problems can save you a lot of time and hassle. Do you know how to upgrade your computer if you want more

memory, for example? Do you know which software and computer settings can keep your computer in top shape?

Finally, becoming computer literate means knowing which technologies are on the horizon and how to integrate them into your own life. Can you connect your television to your wireless network? What is a media server, and do you need one? Can a USB 3.0 flash drive be plugged into a USB 2.0 port? Knowing the answers to these and other questions will help you make better purchasing decisions.

This book will help you become computer literate. In Chapter 3, you'll find out how to get the most from the web while staying free from the spam and clutter Internet surfing can leave behind on your computer. Chapter 6 shows you how to determine if your hardware is limiting your computer's performance and how to upgrade or shop for a new system. Chapter 9 covers how to keep your computer and your digital life secure. You'll be able to save money, time, and endless frustration by understanding the basics of how computers and computer systems operate. ■

 SOUND BYTE
Questions to Ask Before You Buy a Computer

This Sound Byte will help you consider important questions to ask before you buy a computer.

Should there be rules for conduct in a virtual world? If so, what should they be? What does plagiarism mean in a world where people can easily copy, paste, and upload content of all kinds? Should workplaces be allowed to monitor their employees' computing activities without their knowledge? Should websites be allowed to capture data related to what visitors do on their sites and analyze and sell that data? Should programmers be responsible if their software malfunctions and leads to personal injury or financial loss? Should Internet access be provided for free by communities to their citizens who cannot afford it? Are implantable devices that track the whereabouts of children and vulnerable adults a good thing, or a slippery slope to breaches of privacy? These are the sorts of ethical questions and challenges that technology poses—questions that did not even exist just a few years ago.

As the reach of technology continues to spread, these are questions that more and more societies must face and develop their own answers to. And because different societies and cultures have different ideas of what it means to behave ethically, there will be many different solutions to ethical questions and interpretations of ethical issues. How we navigate the different cultural responses to ethical challenges therefore becomes more and more important as the pace of technology quickens. For example, how should U.S. companies respond to censorship of their websites in countries such as China? A state in the United States can declare that online gambling is illegal, but what does that mean when its citizens have access to foreign websites hosting gambling (see Figure 1.10)?

Answering challenging ethical questions related to technology is part of being an informed citizen. This course will help you to understand technology and the ethical issues it poses. Taking the time to think deeply about the connection between technology and ethics is one step in being a more knowledgeable and thoughtful global citizen.

FIGURE 1.10 How do we enforce ethical standards in our global, Internet-enabled environment? *(John Lamb/Photodisc/Getty Images)*

technology and
YOUR CAREER

Information technology (IT) is a field of study focused on the management and processing of information and the automatic retrieval of information. IT careers include working with computers, telecommunications, and software deployment. Career opportunities in IT are on the rise, but no matter what career you choose, new technology in the workplace is creating a demand for new skill levels in technology from employees. A study from the National Research Council concludes that by the year 2030, computers will displace humans in 60% of current occupations. Having advanced skills is becoming more critical every year.

Impact of Computer Literacy on Your Career

Objective 1.7 *Characterize the impact computer literacy has on a variety of careers.*

One of the benefits of being computer literate is that you will undoubtedly be able to perform your job more effectively. It also will make you more desirable as an employee and more likely to earn more and to advance in your career. In fact, your understanding of key concepts in technology can "future-proof" you, letting you easily and quickly react to the next round of new technologies.

Before we begin looking at a computer's parts and how a computer operates in Chapter 2, let's look at a whole range of industries and examine how computers are a part of getting work done.

Retail

The amount of data generated each minute of the day is staggering (see Figure 1.11). **Big Data** is the term for this new easy accessibility to extremely large data sets. But how do businesses make sense of it? They use a technique known as **data mining**, the process of searching huge amounts of data with the hope of finding a pattern. For example, retailers often study the data gathered from register terminals to determine which products are selling on a given day and in a specific location. In addition to inventory control systems, which help managers figure out how much merchandise they need to order to replace stock that is sold, managers can use mined data to determine that if they want a certain product to sell well, they

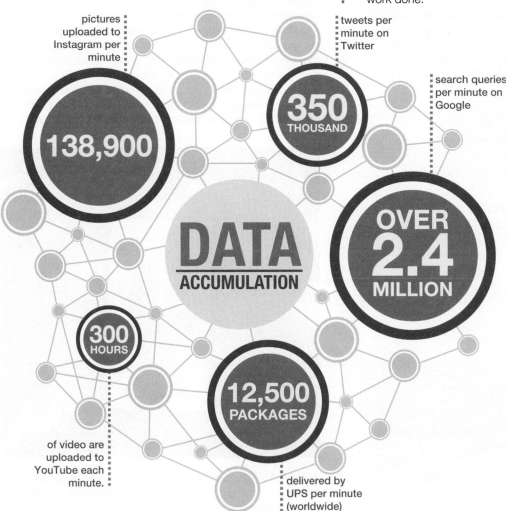

pictures uploaded to Instagram per minute

tweets per minute on Twitter

search queries per minute on Google

350 THOUSAND

138,900

DATA
ACCUMULATION

OVER 2.4 MILLION

300 HOURS

12,500 PACKAGES

of video are uploaded to YouTube each minute.

delivered by UPS per minute (worldwide)

FIGURE 1.11 Enormous amounts of data are produced every minute. Data mining is the art of translating that huge volume of raw data into useful information.

must lower its price—especially if they cut the price at one store and see sales increase, for example. Data mining thus allows retailers to respond to consumer buying patterns.

Have you ever wondered how Amazon or Netflix suggest items that fit your taste? Data mining can keep track of the purchases customers make, along with their geographic data, past buying history, and lists of items they looked at but did not purchase. These data can be translated into marketing that is customized to your shopping. This is the motivation behind the discount cards grocery stores and drugstores offer. In exchange for tracking your buying habits, they offer you special pricing. In the age of Big Data, you may be using data mining in a number of careers.

Arts

Some design students think that because they're studying art, there's no reason for them to study computers. Of course, not all artwork is created using traditional materials such as paint and canvas. Many artists today work exclusively with computers. Mastery of software such as Adobe Illustrator, Adobe Photoshop, and Corel Painter is essential to creating digital art. Eventually, you'll want to sell your work, and you'll need to showcase your designs and artistic creations to employers and customers. Wouldn't it be helpful if you knew how to create and manage a website?

Using computers in the arts and entertainment fields goes far beyond just producing web pages, though. Dance and music programs like the ones at the Atlanta Ballet and the Juilliard School use computers to create new performances for audiences. A live dancer can be wired with sensors connected to a computer that captures the dancer's movements. Based on the data it collects, the computer generates a virtual dancer on a screen. The computer operator can easily manipulate this virtual dancer, as well as change the dancer's costume and other aspects of the dancer's appearance, with the click of a mouse. This allows artists to create new experiences for the audience.

And what if you see yourself working in an art museum? Today, museums are using technology to enhance visitors' experiences (see Figure 1.12). New York's Museum of Modern Art (MoMA), for example, offers a full range of options for tech-savvy visitors: old-fashioned museum audio guides, podcasts that visitors can listen to with their smartphones, and multimedia tours that visitors download through MoMA WiFi (**moma.org**) to their own mobile device. These multimedia guides even enable visitors to listen to music the artist listened to when he or she was creating a particular work or to look at other works that reflect similar techniques or themes as those they're viewing. Developing these solutions for museums is a great career for someone with an artistic education and knowledge of technology.

Education

The education industry uses computer technology in numerous ways. Electronic textbooks are simpler to search and provide great media supports. Courses are designed around course management software such as Blackboard or Moodle so that students can communicate outside of class, take quizzes online, and find their class materials easily. The Internet has obvious advantages in the classroom as a research tool for students, and effective use of the Internet allows teachers to expose students to places students otherwise couldn't access. There are simulations and instructional software programs on the web that are incredible learning tools. For example, teachers can employ these products to give

BITS&BYTES

Computational Art

Generative design is a revolutionary new method of creating artwork, models, and animations from sets of rules, or algorithms. Artists use simple programming languages, like the free product Processing, to produce designs and animations. Try this new-age tool for self-expression! Download Processing from **processing.org** and generate your own artistic works like the one shown here.

FIGURE 1.12 Multimedia tours using mobile devices and wireless technology are commonplace in museums and galleries. *(Paul Quayle/Alamy)*

students a taste of running a global business using SimVenture (**simventure.co.uk**) or experience an amazing tour of the human body (see Figure 1.13) through the Time Machine from Carnegie Mellon University (**timemachine.cmucreatelab.org**).

Want to take your students to a museum in another state or country? Many museums offer virtual tours on their websites that allow students to examine the museum collections. Another resource, the Art Project, is a collaboration of several museums that allows online visitors to explore over a thousand pieces of art using the same technology employed in Google Street View (see Figure 1.14). A custom viewer allows visitors to zoom in on the artwork itself at incredibly high resolution. The information panel takes you to related videos and other related websites. So, even if you teach in Topeka, Kansas, you can take your students on a virtual tour of the Tate Britain in London.

FIGURE 1.13 The Internet supports sophisticated learning resources. The Time Machine from Carnegie Mellon University shows time-lapse views of many phenomenon, from building a sculpture to a tour of the human body. *(Reprinted courtesy of Carnegie Mellon University and the Visible Human Project®)*

FIGURE 1.14 The Google Art Project (**googleartproject.com**) uses a custom camera on a moving trolley to generate a high-resolution experience of art museums located in more than 40 different countries. *(Richard Bord/Getty Images)*

Computerized education in the classroom may prove to be the tool that helps teachers reach greater success, despite increasing class sizes and tightening financial constraints. The Khan Academy (**khanacademy.org**) is a terrific example of a technological tool for education. Salman Khan was an investment analyst in Boston who began to post videos to YouTube so that he could teach algebra to his young cousins in New Orleans. Today, his nonprofit Khan Academy contains over 6,500 videos, and several million students a month use the site.

A classroom teacher can also follow what is happening in the classroom by using the *dashboard*, a screen that shows which topics each student has mastered, which ones they are making progress with, and which ones have them spinning their wheels. Now a teacher can approach a student already knowing exactly what is frustrating them and can avoid the dreaded question, "Oh, what don't you understand?"

As an educator, being computer literate will help you constructively integrate computer technologies like those discussed here into lesson plans and interactions for your students.

Law Enforcement

Today, wearing out shoe leather to solve crimes is far from the only method available to you if you want to pursue a career in law enforcement. Computers are being used in police cars and crime labs to solve an increasing number of crimes. For example, facial reconstruction systems like the one shown in Figure 1.15 can turn a skull into a finished digital image of a face, allowing investigators to proceed far more quickly with identification than before.

One technique used by modern detectives to solve crimes uses the vast number of databases on the Internet. Proprietary law enforcement databases such as the National Center for the Analysis of Violent Crime database enable detectives to analyze a wealth of information for similarities between crimes in an attempt to detect patterns that may reveal serial crimes. In fact, a law enforcement specialty called computer forensics is growing in importance in order to fight modern crime. **Computer forensics** analyzes computer systems with specific techniques to gather potential legal evidence. For example, Steven Zirko was convicted for two Chicago-area murders based on computer forensics work. Computer forensics examiners trained by the FBI scoured Zirko's computer and located searches for terms like *hire a hitman*. In many cases, files, videos, and

FIGURE 1.15 Tissue-rendering programs add layers of muscles, fat, and skin to create faces that can be used to identify victims. *(Pixologicsstudio/Science Photo Library/Glow Images)*

conversations conducted using a computer can be recovered by forensics specialists and can be used as evidence of criminal activity.

Medicine

A career in medicine will connect you to new ways of using technology to better people's lives. Earlier we mentioned how biomedical chips may one day restore sight to the blind. Modern biomedical research is providing technological solutions to physical problems in other ways as well.

There has already been experimentation on implanting chips in humans as a means of verifying a person's identity. Called VeriMed, this personal identification chip is about the size of a grain of rice and is implanted under the skin. When exposed to radio waves from a scanning device, the chip transmits its serial number to the scanner. The scanner then connects to a database that contains the name, address, and medical conditions of the person in whom the chip has been implanted. In the course of a nursing career, you may be using a device like VeriMed to help keep Alzheimer's patients safe, for example.

The design and construction of prosthetic devices is another area of medicine impacted by modern technology. MIT's Biomechatronics lab has developed software that uses an array of pressure sensors to gauge the softness or stiffness of a patient's remaining tissue to create a better fit for a prosthetic to the limb. Meanwhile, 3D printing is allowing more inexpensive designs for prosthetic arms and legs, and more stylish artificial limbs as well (see Figure 1.16).

Digital medication has arrived with the Food and Drug Administration (FDA) approval of digestible microchips (see Figure 1.17). Looking like regular pills, these medications have embedded sensors that transmit information to the doctor. The sensor itself is the size of a grain of sand. As it is digested, a small voltage is generated and detected by a patch worn on the patient's skin. The patch then transmits to the physician that the pill was taken; it also monitors the patient's heart rate, respiration, and temperature.

FIGURE 1.17 Digital medications are able to report information back to physicians about how the patient is responding to the medicine. *(ImageBROKER/SuperStock)*

Science

Thanks to a partnership between the National Severe Storms Lab and the National Center for Supercomputing Applications, tornado forecasting is becoming increasingly accurate. Scientists have been able to create a model so detailed that it takes nine days for a supercomputer to generate it, even though the computer is executing four trillion operations a second. Simulations also can model the structure of solar magnetic flares, which can interfere with broadcasts on Earth. With a career in meteorology, you will be studying the data produced by these simulations, hoping to improve predictions about weather phenomena.

Other technological applications in the sciences are being used on some of the oldest sites on Earth (see Figure 1.18). For example, the Galassi Tomb, located in the ancient Italian city of Caere, was originally designed in 650 B.C. and was rich with ornamentation and jewelry. These treasures were taken to the Vatican State collection in the 1800s when

FIGURE 1.16 3D printing has become a tool for developing more inexpensive, and more stylish, prosthetic devices. *(Photographer Eliot Wright. Reprinted with permission of Thinking Robot Studios.)*

FIGURE 1.18 Archeologists use computer-aided design (CAD) systems to build virtual reconstructions of ancient sites like this one. *(O. Louis Mazzatenta/Getty Images)*

Reality is reality, right? So what is *augmentative reality*? And how is it different from *virtual reality*?

Augmentative reality (AR) is the addition of digital information directly into our reality, either to add more detail or at times to remove unwanted visual effects. How does this happen?

AR combines our normal sense of the world around us with an additional layer of digital information. The extra information can be displayed on a separate device, such as in augmented reality apps for smartphones. Displays in stores can augment your image with the clothing you're interested in, creating a virtual fitting room (see Figure 1.19). Microsoft has announced a product named the HoloLens that will let you manipulate holographic images as part of your reality (see Figure 1.20).

Meanwhile, researcher Stephen Mann at the University of Toronto is working with wearable computers that use "point of eye" (PoE) cameras as AR devices. A PoE camera is designed so that the camera is positioned directly in front of the eye itself. The ultimate PoE camera would be one that is implanted within the eye or eye socket. Mann's research group is exploring this as a way to assist partially sighted or blind people.

Instead of adding information to the reality you perceive, **virtual reality (VR)** replaces it with a

FIGURE 1.19 This high-tech fitting room uses augmented reality technology to allow shoppers to try on clothes virtually. *(Yoshikazu Tsuno/AFP/Getty Images)*

different world. Virtual reality creates an artificial environment that is immersive and interactive. VR environments can be as simple as a pair of goggles or as elaborate as entire "caves" that you walk into (see Figure 1.21). One "cave" (cave automatic

FIGURE 1.20 The Microsoft HoloLens augments your reality by adding holographic images you can manipulate. *(CALVETTI/Science Photo Library/Corbis)*

visual environment) is being used at Temple University to study balance in stroke victims.

VR is also coming to the consumer gaming market with the introduction of VR goggles, like Sony's Project Morpheus and the Rift by Oculus (see Figure 1.22). These goggles have high pixel count displays that wrap your full field of view.

So reality may be a bit less absolute than it once seemed. Whether it is being augmented with additional information or replaced by new virtual realms, technology is expanding our sense of what is real.

FIGURE 1.21 Virtual reality "caves" replace our ordinary reality with a new, immersive environment. *(Reprinted with permission of photographer Khairi Reda. University of Illinois at Chicago.)*

FIGURE 1.22 VR goggles like these wrap around your full field of view, creating a totally immersive environment. *(Edgar Su/ Reuters/Corbis)*

the tomb was discovered. Today, scientists are using 3D scanners and imaging software to re-create the experience of seeing the tomb and the artifacts together as they once were. This virtual re-creation is so lifelike that archaeologists can study the ruins on-screen instead of at the actual site. Will you be using these tools someday to make records of other decaying sites?

Psychology

Fear of speaking in public is common, but for people with autism spectrum disorders, making proper eye contact and reacting to social cues is so difficult it can severely limit their opportunities for jobs and relationships. Researchers at the MIT Media Lab have developed a system to help improve interpersonal skills for people who have autism.

MACH (My Automated Conversation CoacH) is a computer system that generates an on-screen person that can, for example, conduct a job interview or appear ready for a first date. The computerized person (see Figure 1.23) nods and smiles in response to the user's speech and movement. This is an example of **affective computing**, developing systems that can recognize and simulate human emotions. MACH users can practice as many times as they wish in a safe environment. They receive an analysis that shows how well they modulated their voices, maintained eye contact, smiled, and how often they lapsed into "umms" and "uhhhs." The software runs on an ordinary laptop, using a webcam and microphone.

While engineers work to create computers that can process data faster and faster, psychologists and computer scientists

FIGURE 1.23 My Automated Conversation CoacH (MACH) generates an on-screen interviewer you can practice with over and over. *(Cultura Limited/SuperStock)*

are also working to evolve systems toward a more complete understanding of human behavior. With a career that blends computer science and psychology, you could find yourself at the heart of developing a new kind of relationship between man and machine. ■

> Before moving on to the Chapter Review:
> 1. Watch Replay Video 1.2 ▷.
> 2. Then check your understanding of what you've learned so far.

check your understanding // review & practice

For a quick review to see what you've learned so far, answer the following questions.

multiple choice

1. Analyzing computer systems to gather legal evidence is known as the field of
   a. crowdsourcing.
   b. information technology.
   c. computer forensics.
   d. simulation theory.

2. The MACH project shows that
   a. there is a digital divide limiting access to computer systems.
   b. sports performance can be recorded and analyzed by software.
   c. there are some things computers cannot teach.
   d. computers can help people with interpersonal skills development.

3. Which of the following allows retailers to respond to consumer buying patterns?
   a. outsourcing
   b. data mining
   c. smart labels
   d. Bluetooth technology

4. Computer technology is used in the arts by
   a. integrating it into new works of performance art.
   b. creating web pages to advertise and sell art.
   c. creating multimedia museum tours.
   d. all of the above

5. IT is the abbreviation for
   a. information training.
   b. Internet training.
   c. Internet technology.
   d. information technology.

MyITLab Go to **MyITLab** to take an autograded version of the *Check Your Understanding* review and to find all media resources for the chapter.

TECHBYTES WEEKLY
Stay current with the TechBytes Weekly Newsletter.

Continue

Chapter Review

summary //

How Will You Put Technology in Action?

Learning Outcome 1.1 You will be able to discuss the impact of technology on global and national issues.

Technology on the World Stage

Objective 1.1 *Recognize how becoming proficient with technology can help you understand and participate in political issues in the world at large.*

- Technology can be the means by which you find your voice in the world and impact others in meaningful ways.
- Social media is impacting elections worldwide.
- Crisis-mapping tools are an example of technology helping in different kinds of global conflicts and disasters.

Objective 1.2 *Describe how technology affects social issues in different societies.*

- Global health care issues, like the spread of disease, require international cooperation and technological solutions.
- Environmental issues are global in nature and will require technology to address.
- The digital divide, an uneven distribution of access to computer technology, will make it difficult for us to solve global problems.

Technology and Our Society

Objective 1.3 *Describe how technology is changing our cognitive processes.*

- Web 2.0 is a set of features and functionality that allows Internet users to contribute content easily and to be easily connected to each other.
- Cognitive surplus is the combination of leisure time and access to tools to work on problems and be creative.

Objective 1.4 *Explain how technology is expanding the ways we collaborate.*

- New collaborative tools available on the Internet allow us to work together on projects with much larger groups.
- Crowdfunding is a group of people connecting through the Internet to fund projects by strangers.

Objective 1.5 *Summarize how technology has impacted how commerce is conducted.*

- Marketing is changing because most consumers now shop with Internet access on their phones and can therefore check competing prices and online review.
- The idea of ownership is changing because technology is allowing subscription services for products like cars and bikes to be available. Such collaborative consumption means that we are joining together as a group to use specific products more efficiently.

How Will Technology Improve Your Life?

Learning Outcome 1.2 You will be able to discuss personal impacts technology can have on your life and your career.

Technology at Home

Objective 1.6 *Characterize computer literacy, and list some of its benefits.*

- If you're computer literate, you understand the capabilities and limitations of computers and know how to use them wisely.
- By understanding how a computer is constructed and how its various parts function, you'll be able to get the most out of your computer.
- You'll be able to avoid hackers, viruses, and Internet headaches; protect your privacy; and separate the real risks of privacy and security from things you don't have to worry about.
- You'll also be better able to maintain, upgrade, and troubleshoot your computer; make good purchasing decisions; and incorporate the latest technologies into your existing equipment.

- Being computer literate also enables you to understand the many ethical, legal, and societal implications of technology today.

Technology and Your Career

Objective 1.7 *Characterize the impact computer literacy has on a variety of careers.*

- Computer literacy impacts the full range of careers, from arts and psychology to science and≈medicine.
- Understanding how to use software, how to use and maintain computer hardware, and how to take advantage of Internet resources will help you be a more productive and valuable employee, no matter which profession you choose.

 Be sure to check out **MyITLab** for additional materials to help you review and learn. And don't forget the Replay Videos.

key terms //

affective computing **20**	crisis-mapping tool **5**	social media **4**
augmentative reality (AR) **19**	crowdfunding **8**	software **13**
Big Data **15**	crowdsourcing **8**	spam **13**
cognitive surplus **7**	data mining **15**	virtual reality (VR) **19**
collaborative consumption **8**	digital divide **6**	Web 2.0 **7**
computer forensics **17**	information technology (IT) **15**	
computer literate **12**	quick response (QR) code **8**	

chapter quiz // assessment

For a quick review to see what you've learned, answer the following questions. Submit the quiz as requested by your instructor. If you are using **MyITLab**, the quiz is also available there.

multiple choice

1. Social media

   a. prevents two-way dialog between people.

   b. is incorporated as part of a political strategy by many politicians.

   c. cannot be immediate enough to react to quickly developing issues.

   d. only is useful for personal friendships.

2. Web 2.0 has led to a shift from just consuming content toward

   a. spending all our time on leisure activities.

   b. less sharing of the work we produce.

   c. new standards for HTML.

   d. producing content.

3. Examples of crowdfunding and crowdsourcing include

   a. Kickstarter and MobileVoice.

   b. Bing and Google.

   c. Call a Bike and Zipcar.

   d. Ushahidi and Kiva.

4. Being computer literate includes being able to

   a. avoid spam, adware, and spyware.

   b. use the web effectively.

   c. diagnose and fix hardware and software problems.

   d. all of the above

5. Computer forensics

   a. tests computers for hardware malfunction.

   b. analyzes computer systems to gather potential legal evidence.

   c. analyzes the design of a computer system.

   d. is used to create three-dimensional art.

6. Data mining is

   a. important now because it is so easy to gather enormous data sets.

   b. the study of data using algorithms to detect patterns.

   c. the translation of Big Data sets into meaningful information.

   d. all of the above

true/false

_____ **1.** The move toward access instead of ownership is a sign of collaborative consumption.

_____ **2.** The Next Einstein Initiative uses the power of supercomputing to enhance mathematical education.

_____ **3.** Virtual reality is the addition of infographics to your visual field.

_____ **4.** Web-based databases are being used to help investigators solve criminal cases.

critical thinking

1. **What Occupies Your Mind?**

   What we think about is influenced by the information fed to our mind all day long. Web 2.0 has created numerous channels for people to offer their own work for free—open source software, free music, books, and artwork. How has this affected your thinking? Have you created things to share freely with the online world? Has it changed the value you put on music, books, and art?

2. **Career and Computers**

   This chapter lists many ways in which becoming computer literate is beneficial. Think about what your life will be like once you're started in your career. What areas of computing will be most important for you to understand? How would an understanding of computer hardware and software help you in working from home, working with groups in other countries, and contributing your talents?

team time //

A Culture of Sharing

Problem

As more and more peer-to-peer music-sharing services appeared, like BitTorrent and LimeWire, many felt a culture of theft was developing. Some argued there was a mindset that property rights for intellectual works need not be respected and that people should be able to download, for free, any music, movies, or other digital content they wanted.

But there is another view of the phenomenon. Some are suggesting that the amount of constant access to other people—through texting, e-mail, blogging, and the easy exchange of digital content—has created a culture of trust and sharing. This Team Time will explore both sides of this debate as it affects three different parts of our lives—finance, travel, and consumerism.

Task

Each of three groups will select a different area to examine—finance, travel, or consumerism. The groups will find evidence to support or refute the idea that a culture of sharing is developing. The finance group will want to explore projects like Kickstarter (**kickstarter.com**) and Kiva (**kiva.org**). The travel group should examine what is happening with Couchsurfing (**couchsurfing.com**) to start their research. The team investigating consumerism will want to look at goods-exchange programs like Freecycle (**freecycle.org**).

Process

1. Divide the class into three teams.
2. Discuss the different views of a "culture of sharing." With the other members of your team, use the Internet to research up-and-coming technologies and projects that would support your position. People use social media tools to connect into groups to exchange ideas. Does that promote trust? Does easy access to digital content promote theft, or has the value of content changed? Are there other forces like the economy and the environmental state of the world that play a role in promoting a culture of sharing? What evidence can you find to support your ideas?
3. Present your group's findings to the class for debate and discussion.
4. Write a strategy paper that summarizes your position and outlines your predictions for the future. Will the pace of technology promote a change in the future from the position you are describing?

Conclusion

The future of technology is unknown, but we do know that it will impact the way our society progresses. To be part of the developments that technology will bring will take good planning and attention, no matter what area of the culture you're examining. Begin now—learn how to stay on top of technology.

Can Big Data Predict Your Grade?

Problem

As you move through your academic career, you leave an enormous swath of data: which courses you chose to register for, which ones you looked at but didn't pick, and how you did on each homework assignment, test, and project. Could this massive amount of data be analyzed to predict your grade in a course? To suggest which courses you should take next? Should those predictions be public to your instructor? To you? To financial aid officers?

Research Topics to Consider

- Course Signals
- Degree Compass, Austin Peay State University

Process

1. Divide the class into teams. Each team will select a web-based tool that allows access to information.

2. Team members should each think of a situation where a person would benefit from the type of results data mining of Big Data can bring to a campus and a situation where it might be undesirable.

3. Team members should select the most powerful and best-constructed arguments and develop a summary conclusion.

4. Team members should present their findings to the class or submit a PowerPoint presentation for review by the rest of the class, along with the summary conclusion they developed.

Conclusion

As technology becomes ever more prevalent and integrated into our lives, ethical dilemmas will present themselves to an increasing extent. Being able to understand and evaluate both sides of the argument, while responding in a personally or socially ethical manner, will be an important skill.

How Technology Is Used on the World Stage and in My Personal Life

In this activity, you'll use Microsoft Word to reflect on how technology is affecting the world as well as you, personally and professionally. Reflect on the content in Chapter 1 as you work through this exercise.

You will use the following skills as you complete this activity:

- Open and Modify a Document Template
- Apply Styles and Advanced Font Formats
- Use Format Painter
- Insert Text
- Apply Themes
- Create a Header and Footer

Instructions

1. Start Microsoft Word 2016 and open the Facet design (blank) template. Save the document as **TIA_Ch1_LastFirst**, using your own Last and First names.

2. Double-click the **Title placeholder** and type **Technology**, then double-click the **Heading placeholder** and type **Introduction**. Replace the remaining placeholder text with the following: **Political and global issues are showing that technology is accelerating change around the world and galvanizing groups of people in new ways. Technology allows us to refine how we connect with each other, and it also impacts our daily personal and professional experiences.** Press **Enter**.

3. Type **How Technology Impacts Society**, press **Enter**, and then type a few sentences that describe how technology is impacting global events such as political revolutions, health care, the environment, and the digital divide. In addition, address how businesses are using social media. Press Enter.

4. Type **How Technology Impacts Me Personally and Professionally**, press **Enter**, and then type a few sentences that describe how technology is impacting your personal life. You should address the importance of being computer literate. You should also address the kinds of technology being used in the industry of your current or desired career.

5. Click anywhere in the heading *Introduction*, then using **Format Painter**, apply the **Heading 1** format to the paragraph headers: *How Technology Impacts Society* and *How Technology Impacts Me Personally and Professionally*.

   a. Hint: Format Painter is in the Clipboard group on the Home tab.

6. Change the Document Theme style to the **Slice Theme**.

   a. Hint: Document Themes are found on the Design tab, in the Document Formatting group.

7. Select the title *Technology*, then format the font as **Small Caps**. **Center align** the title.

   a. Hint: Click the dialog box launcher in the Font group on the Home tab to access the Small caps font effects.

8. Apply the **Whisp header style** to the document. Click to add Today's date in the Date header and delete the Document title header. Add a **File Path** to the document footer. Select the footer text and change the font size to **8**. Close the Header and Footer.

   a. Hint: Headers are found on the Insert tab in the Header & Footer group. File Path is found in Document Info in the Insert group on the Header & Footer Tools Design tab.

9. Save the document and submit based on your instructor's directions.

Make This: MAKE: A Mobile App on **page 49**

All media accompanying this chapter can be found in MyITLab.

For an overview of the chapter, watch the **Preview Video**.

(Edelweiss/Fotolia, Petr Malyshev/Fotolia, Destina/Fotolia, Vizafoto/Fotolia, BillionPhotos/Fotolia, Rukanoga/Fotolia, Sebastian Kaulitzki/Shutterstock)

HOW COOL IS THIS?

Now that we are used to the **touch experience** with our devices, where do we go next? How about **no touch**! The Ring ZERO from Logbar Inc. is a wearable device that **senses the movements of the finger** on which it is worn and transmits those gestures to compatible devices (iOS and Android). You can type text, control home appliances, or make payments all by **making gestures with one finger**. The device has preprogrammed gestures, but you can also customize them (or create your own) with the **companion app**. So controlling your devices may soon only require a small wave of your finger! *(Logbar)*

Understanding Digital Components

Learning Outcome 2.1 You will be able to describe the devices that make up a computer system.

After reading Chapter 1, you can see why becoming computer literate is important. But where do you start? You've no doubt gleaned some knowledge about computers just from being a member of society. However, even if you have used a computer before, do you really understand how it works, what all its parts are, and what those parts do?

understanding your
COMPUTER

Let's start our look at computers by discussing what a computer does and how its functions make it such a useful machine.

Computers Are Data Processing Devices

Objective 2.1 *Describe the four main functions of a computer system and how they interact with data and information.*

What exactly does a computer do? Strictly defined, a **computer** is a data processing device that performs four major functions:

1. **Input:** It gathers data or allows users to enter data.
2. **Process:** It manipulates, calculates, or organizes that data into information.
3. **Output:** It displays data and information in a form suitable for the user.
4. **Storage:** It saves data and information for later use.

What's the difference between data and information? People often use the terms *data* and *information* interchangeably. Although they may mean the same thing in a simple conversation, the distinction between data and information is an important one.

In computer terms, **data** is a representation of a fact, a figure, or an idea. Data can be a number, a word, a picture, or even a recording of sound. For example, the number 7135553297 and the names Zoe and Richardson are pieces of data. Alone, these pieces of data probably mean little to you. **Information** is data that has been organized or presented in a meaningful fashion. When your computer provides you with a contact listing that indicates that Zoe Richardson can be reached at (713) 555-3297, the data becomes useful—that is, it becomes information.

How do computers interact with data and information? Computers are excellent at **processing** (manipulating, calculating, or organizing) data into information. When you first arrived on campus, you probably were directed to a place where you could get an ID card. You most likely provided a clerk with personal data that was entered into a computer. The clerk then took your picture with a digital camera (collecting more data). All of the data was then processed appropriately so that it could be printed on your ID card (see Figure 2.1). This organized output of data on your ID card is useful information.

FIGURE 2.1 Computers process data into information. *(mocker_bat/Fotolia)*

Bits and Bytes: The Language of Computers

Objective 2.2 *Define bits and bytes, and describe how they are measured, used, and processed.*

How do computers process data into information? Unlike humans, computers work exclusively with numbers (not words). To process data into information, computers need to work in a language they understand. This language, called **binary language**, consists of just two digits: 0 and 1. Everything a computer does, such as processing data, printing a report, or editing a photo, is broken down into a series of 0s and 1s. Each 0 and 1 is a **binary digit**, or **bit** for short. Eight binary digits (or bits) combine to create one **byte**. In computers, each letter of the alphabet, each number, and each special character (such as @, pronounced "at") consists of a unique combination of eight bits, or a string of eight 0s and 1s. So, for example, in binary language, the letter *K* is represented as 01001011. This is eight bits or one byte.

What else can bits and bytes be used for? Bits and bytes not only are used as the language that tells the computer what to do, they are also used to represent the *quantity* of data and information that the computer inputs and outputs. Word processing files, digital pictures, and even software are represented inside computing devices as a series of bits and bytes. These files and applications can be quite large, containing millions or billions of bytes.

To make it easier to measure the size of such files, we need units of measure larger than a byte. Kilobytes, megabytes, and gigabytes are therefore simply larger amounts of bytes. As shown in Figure 2.2, a **kilobyte (KB)** is approximately 1,000 bytes, a **megabyte (MB)** is about 1 million bytes, and a **gigabyte (GB)** is around 1 billion bytes. Today, personal computers are capable of storing **terabytes (TB)** of data (around 1 trillion bytes), and many business computers can store up to a **petabyte (PB)** (1,000 terabytes) of data. The Google search engine processes more than 1 PB of user-generated data per *hour*!

How does your computer process bits and bytes? Your computer uses hardware and software to process data into information that lets you complete tasks such as writing a letter or playing a game. **Hardware** is any part of the computer you can physically touch. However, a computer needs more than just hardware to work. **Software** is the set of computer programs that enables the hardware to perform different tasks.

There are two broad categories of software: *application software* and *system software*. **Application software** is the set of programs you use on a computer to help you carry out tasks such as writing a research paper. If you've ever typed a document, created a spreadsheet, or edited a digital photo, for example, you've used application software.

System software is the set of programs that enables your computer's hardware devices and application software to work together. The most common type of system software is the **operating system (OS)**—the program that controls how your computer system functions. It manages the hardware, such as the monitor and printer, and provides a means by which users can interact with the computer. Most likely, the computer you own or use at school runs a version of Windows as the system software. However, if you're working on an Apple computer, you're probably running OS X.

Types of Computers

Objective 2.3 *List common types of computers, and discuss their main features.*

What types of computers are popular for personal use? There are two basic designs of computers: portable and stationary. For portable computers, a number of options exist:

- A **tablet computer**, such as the iPad or Microsoft Surface, is a portable computer integrated into a flat multitouch-sensitive screen. It uses an on-screen virtual keyboard, but you can connect separate keyboards to it via Bluetooth or wires.

- A **laptop** or **notebook computer** is a portable computer that has a keyboard, monitor, and other devices integrated into a single compact case.

- An **ultrabook** is a full-featured but lightweight laptop computer designed to compete with the MacBook Air. Ultrabooks feature low-power processors and solid-state drives and try to reduce their size and weight to extend battery life without sacrificing performance.

- A **2-in-1 PC** is similar to a laptop computer, but the monitor swivels and folds flat (see Figure 2.3a). This allows it to function both as a conventional laptop and as a tablet computer using its touchscreen.

- A **Chromebook** is a special breed of laptop that uses the Google Chrome OS and is designed to be connected to the Internet at all times. Documents and apps are stored primarily in the cloud as opposed to on the local hard drive.

A **desktop computer** is intended for use at a single location, so it's stationary. Most desktop computers consist of a separate case or tower (called the **system unit**) that houses the main components of the computer plus peripheral devices. A **peripheral device** is a component, such as a monitor or keyboard, that connects to the computer. An

FIGURE 2.2

How Much Is a Byte?

NAME	NUMBER OF BYTES	RELATIVE SIZE	
Byte (B)	1 byte	One character of data (8 bits or binary digits)	
Kilobyte (KB)	1,024 bytes (2^{10} bytes)	1,024 characters or about 1 page of plain text	
Megabyte (MB)	1,048,576 bytes (2^{20} bytes)		About 4 books (200 pages, 240,000 characters)
Gigabyte (GB)	1,073,741,824 bytes (2^{30} bytes)		About 4,500 books or over twice the size of Sir Isaac Newton's library (considered very large for the time)
Terabyte (TB)	1,099,511,627,776 bytes (2^{40} bytes)	About 4.6 million books or about the number of volumes in the Rutgers University Library	
Petabyte (PB)	1,125,899,906,842,624 bytes (2^{50} bytes)		About 4.7 billion books, which would fill the Library of Congress (the United States' largest library) 140 times!
Exabyte (EB)	1,152,921,504,606,846,976 bytes (2^{60} bytes)	About 4.8 trillion books, which, if stored as they are in the Library of Congress, would occupy about 11,000 square miles or an area almost the size of the state of Maryland	
Zettabyte (ZB)	1,180,591,620,717,411,303,424 bytes (2^{70} bytes)		The library required to house the 4.9 quadrillion books equal to a ZB of data would occupy about 11.3 million square miles or an area about 1 million square miles larger than all of North America

(Ninice64/Fotolia, Georgios Kollidas/Fotolia, Daniel/Fotolia, Flavijus Piliponis/Fotolia)

FIGURE 2.3 (a) A 2-in-1 PC has a monitor that swivels (or folds) to become a touch-sensitive input device. (b) An all-in-one computer does not need a separate tower. *(Julie Jacobson/AP Images, best pixels/Shutterstock)*

all-in-one computer, such as the Apple iMac (Figure 2.3b), eliminates the need for a separate tower because these computers house the computer's processor and memory in the monitor. Many all-in-one models also incorporate touch-screen technology.

Are there other types of computers? Although you may never come into direct contact with the following types of computers, they are still very important and do a lot of work behind the scenes of daily life:

- A **mainframe** is a large, expensive computer that supports many users simultaneously. Mainframes are often used in businesses that manage large amounts of data, such as insurance companies, where many people are working at the same time on similar operations, such as claims processing. Mainframes excel at executing many computer programs at the same time.

- A **supercomputer** is a specially designed computer that can perform complex calculations extremely rapidly. Super-computers are used when complex models requiring inten-sive mathematical calculations are needed (such as weather forecasting or atomic energy research). Supercomputers are designed to execute a few programs as quickly as possible, whereas mainframes are designed to handle many pro-grams running at the same time but at a slower pace.

- An **embedded computer** is a specially designed computer chip that resides in another device, such as your car or the

electronic thermostat in your home. Embedded computers are self-contained computer devices that have their own programming and that typically don't receive input from you or interact with other systems (see Figure 2.4).

Even your smartphone is a computer. Today's **smartphones** offer many features you probably use day to day, including a wide assortment of apps, media players, high-quality cameras, and web connectivity. And just like your laptop, your smartphone has a CPU, memory, and storage.

Each part of your computer has a specific purpose that coordinates with one of the functions of the computer—input, processing, output, or storage (see Figure 2.5). Additional devices, such as WiFi adapters and routers, help a computer communicate with the Internet and other computers to facilitate the sharing of documents and other resources. Let's begin our exploration of hardware by looking at your computer's input devices. ■

FIGURE 2.4 Quadcopters and drones contain embedded computers. *(Kletr/Fotolia)*

FIGURE 2.5 Each part of the computer serves a special function.

input
DEVICES

An **input device** lets you enter data (text, images, and sounds) and instructions (user responses and commands) into your computer. Let's look at some of the most popular input devices used today.

Keyboards and Touch Screens

Objective 2.4 *Identify the main types of keyboards and touch screens.*

What is the most common way to input data and commands? A **keyboard** is an input device you use to enter typed data and commands. However, most computing devices, such as smartphones and tablets, now respond to touch. **Touch screens** are display screens that respond to commands initiated by touching them with your finger or a **stylus**—an input device that looks like a pen and that you use to tap commands or draw on a screen. Touch-screen devices use a virtual keyboard (see Figure 2.6) that displays on screen when text input is required. These keyboards show basic keyboard configurations but allow you to switch to numeric, punctuation, and other special keys.

Are all keyboards the same? Whether on-screen touch keyboards or physical keyboards, the most common keyboard layout is a standard **QWERTY keyboard**. This keyboard layout gets its name from the first six letters in the top-left row of alphabetic keys and is the standard English-language keyboard layout. The QWERTY layout was originally designed for typewriters and was meant to slow typists and prevent typewriter keys from jamming. Although the QWERTY layout is considered inefficient because it slows typing speeds, efforts to change to more efficient layouts, such as that of the Dvorak keyboard (see Figure 2.7), have not been met with much public interest.

FIGURE 2.6 Virtual keyboards are found on tablets and other touch-screen devices. *(Nathan Alliard/Glow Images)*

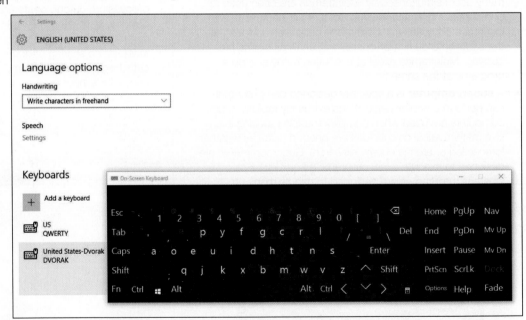

FIGURE 2.7 The Dvorak keyboard is an alternative keyboard layout that puts the most commonly used letters in the English language on "home keys"—the keys in the middle row of the keyboard. The Dvorak keyboard's design reduces the distance your fingers travel for most keystrokes, increasing typing speed. You can customize the layout of your keyboard using the Windows operating system. *(Windows 10, Microsoft Corporation)*

>*To change your keyboard layout in Windows 10, click **Settings** from the Start menu, click **Time & language**, then click **Region & language**. Select **Windows display language**, select **Options**, click **Add a keyboard**, and then select **United-States-Dvorak**.*

What alternatives are there to an onscreen touch keyboard? Touch-screen keyboards are not always convenient when a great deal of typing is required. Most computing devices can accept physical keyboards as an add-on accessory. Wired keyboards plug into a data port on the computing device. Wireless keyboards send data to the computer using a form of wireless technology that uses *radio frequency (RF)*. A radio transmitter in the keyboard sends out signals that are received either by a receiving device plugged into a port on the device or by a Bluetooth receiving device located in the device. You've probably heard of **Bluetooth technology** if you use a head-set or earpiece with your cell phone. Bluetooth is a wireless transmission standard that lets you connect devices such as smartphones, tablets, and laptops to peripheral devices such as keyboards and headsets. Often, wireless keyboards for tablets are integrated with a case to protect your tablet (see Figure 2.8a).

Flexible keyboards are a terrific alternative if you want a full-sized keyboard for your laptop or tablet. You can roll one up, fit it in your backpack, and plug it into a USB port when you need it. Another compact keyboard alternative is a *virtual keyboard* (see Figure 2.8b), which is about the size of a matchbox. They project an image of a keyboard onto any flat surface, and sensors detect the motion of your fingers as you "type." Data is transmitted to the device via Bluetooth. These keyboards work with the latest iPhones, iPads, and Android devices.

FIGURE 2.8 (a) Cases with integrated physical keyboards make tablets more typing-friendly. (b) Virtual keyboard devices project the image of a QWERTY keyboard on any surface. Sensors detect typing motions, and data is transmitted to your device via Bluetooth technology. *(Logitech, Inc.; Splash News/Hammacher Schlemmer/Newscom)*

BITS&BYTES

Distributed Computing: Putting Your Computer to Work While You Sleep

Complex scientific research, such as processing data from radio telescopes, requires vast computing power. Software has been developed to tie individual computing devices (including tablets and smartphones) into a grid to enable them to work together. This is known as **distributed** or **grid computing**. This effectively creates a cheap supercomputer that many not-for-profit research organizations use to research problems that will benefit the greater good—and your computer can help. Visit theSkyNet (**theskynet.org**) and download its software. Once installed, it allows your device to process astronomical data during the many times when your CPU is idle (or at least not working to its full potential). With theSkyNet, your computing device can help astronomers explore the heavens (see Figure 2.9).

FIGURE 2.9 Help astronomers process data by having your computer join theSkyNet. *(James Thew/Fotolia)*

Toggle keys: keys whose function changes between two options. (Example: Caps Lock key)

Internet controls

Multimedia controls

Function keys (F keys): shortcut keys you press to perform special tasks in software programs.

Numeric keypad: lets you enter numbers quickly.

Cursor control keys

Alt key: works with other keys to execute shortcuts and special tasks.

Control (Ctrl) key: used with other keys to perform shortcuts. (Example: Ctrl+B makes text bold)

Windows key: used alone, it launches the Start menu. Used with other keys, it performs shortcuts. (Example: Windows key+Tab launches Task View)

FIGURE 2.10 Keyboards have a variety of keys that help you work more efficiently. (Note that on Macs, function keys are slightly different: The Control function is the Apple key or Command key, and the Alt function is the Option key.)

How can I use my keyboard most efficiently? All keyboards have the standard set of alphabetic and numeric keys that you regularly use when typing. As shown in Figure 2.10, many keyboards for laptop and desktop computers have additional keys that perform special functions. Knowing how to use the special keys shown in Figure 2.10 will help you improve your efficiency.

Mice and Other Pointing Devices

Objective 2.5 *Describe the main types of mice and pointing devices.*

What kinds of mice are there? A **mouse** is an input device used to enter user responses and commands. The mouse type you're probably most familiar with is the **optical mouse**. An optical mouse uses an internal sensor or laser to detect the mouse's movement. The sensor sends signals to the computer, telling it where to move the pointer on the screen. Optical mice don't require a mouse pad, though you can use one to enhance the movement of the mouse on an uneven surface or to protect your work surface from being scratched.

If you have special ergonomic needs or want to customize the functionality of your mouse, there are plenty of options (see Figure 2.11). Most mice have two or three buttons that let you execute commands and open shortcut menus. (Mice for Macs sometimes have only one button.) Many customizable mice have additional programmable buttons and wheels

FIGURE 2.11 Customizable mice offer programmable buttons and adjustable fittings to meet most any need. *(kirill87/Fotolia)*

that let you quickly maneuver through web pages or games. These mice are also customizable to fit any size hand and grip style by allowing for length and width adjustments. Aside from gamers, many people use customizable mice to reduce susceptibility to repetitive strain injuries or if they suffer from physical limitations that prevent them from using standard mice.

How do wireless mice work? Wireless mice usually connect the same way that wireless keyboards do—either through Bluetooth or a receiver that plugs into a USB port. Wireless mice have receivers that often clip into the bottom of the mouse for easy storage when not in use.

Why would I want to use a mouse with a touch-screen device? If you're using a conventional keyboard with your touch-screen device, it's often easier to perform actions with a mouse rather than taking your hands off the keyboard and reaching to touch the screen. In addition, there are new kinds of mice, called *touch mice*, that are designed with touch-screen computers in mind. Unlike older mice, there are no specifically defined buttons. The top surface of a touch mouse is the button. You use one, two, or three fingers to perform touch-screen tasks such as scrolling, switching through open apps, and zooming. Touch mice also allow you to perform traditional mouse tasks, such as moving the cursor when you move the mouse.

What input devices do laptops use? Most laptops have an integrated pointing device, such as a **touch pad** (or **trackpad**)—a small, touch-sensitive area at the base of the keyboard. Mac laptops include multitouch trackpads, which don't have buttons but are controlled by various one-, two-, three-, and four-finger actions. For example, scrolling is controlled by brushing two fingers along the trackpad in any direction. Most touch pads are sensitive to taps, interpreting them as mouse clicks. Most laptops also have buttons under or near the pad to record mouse clicks.

What input devices are used with games? Game controllers such as joysticks, game pads, and steering wheels are also considered input devices because they send data to computing devices. Game controllers, which are similar to the devices used on gaming consoles such as the Xbox One and the PlayStation, are also available for use with computers. They have buttons and miniature pointing devices that provide input to the computer. Most game controllers, such as those for Rock Band and the Wii U, are wireless to provide extra mobility.

Image and Sound Input

Objective 2.6 *Explain how images and sounds are input into computing devices.*

What are popular input devices for images? Digital cameras, camcorders, and cell phones are common devices for capturing pictures and video and are all

BITS&BYTES

Keystroke Shortcuts

Did you know that you can combine certain keystrokes to take shortcuts within an application, such as Microsoft Word, or within the operating system itself? The following are a few of the most helpful Windows-based shortcuts. For more, visit **support.microsoft.com**. For a list of shortcuts for Macs, see **apple.com/support**.

TEXT FORMATTING	FILE MANAGEMENT	CUT/COPY/PASTE	WINDOWS CONTROLS
Ctrl+B applies (or removes) **bold** formatting to/from selected text.	**Ctrl+O** opens the Open dialog box.	**Ctrl+X** cuts (removes) selected text and stores it in the Clipboard.	**Windows key+Arrow key** snaps active windows to corner or side.
Ctrl+I applies (or removes) *italic* formatting to/from selected text.	**Ctrl+N** opens a new document.	**Ctrl+C** copies selected text to the Clipboard.	**Alt+Tab** switches between apps and windows using Task view.
Ctrl+U applies (or removes) underlining to/from selected text.	**Ctrl+S** saves a document.	**Ctrl+V** pastes selected text (previously cut or copied) from the Clipboard.	**Windows key+Ctrl+D** creates a new virtual desktop.
	Ctrl+P opens the Print page (backstage view) in Office 2016.		**Windows key+Ctrl+F4** closes the current virtual desktop.

Touch-screen technology was developed in 1971 and used primarily with ATMs and fast-food order displays. The technology for monitors and other displays was made popular by the iPod Touch in 2007 and is now in smartphones, tablets, and laptop and desktop monitors. But how do touch-screen monitors know where you're touching? How do they know what you want them to do?

The basic idea behind touch screens is pretty straightforward—when you place your finger or stylus on a screen, it changes the physical state of the screen and registers your touch. The location of your touch is then translated into a command. Three basic systems are used to recognize a person's touch: *resistive*, *capacitive*, and *surface acoustic wave*. All of these systems require the basic components of a touch-responsive glass panel, controller, and software driver, combined with a display and computer processor.

The *resistive system* maps the exact location of the pressure point created when a user touches the screen. The *capacitive system* (see Figure 2.12) uses the change in the electrical charge on the glass panel of the monitor, which is created by the user's touch, to generate a location. The third technology, *surface acoustic wave system*, uses two transducers (electrical devices that convert energy from one form to another) that are placed along the x and y axes of the monitor's glass plate. Reflectors, which are also placed on the glass, are used to reflect an electric signal sent from the sending transducer to the receiving transducer. The receiving transducer determines whether the signal has been disturbed by a touch event and locates the touch instantly. With all three systems, the display's software driver then translates the touch into something the operating system can understand, similar to how a mouse driver translates a mouse's movements into a click or drag.

Because the resistive system uses pressure to register a touch, it doesn't matter if the touch is created by a finger or another device. On the other hand, a capacitive system must have conductive input, so generally a finger is required. The surface acoustic wave system allows touches by any object.

The iPhone introduced another complexity to the touch-screen system—a multitouch user interface. In addition to just pressing the screen in one location, multitouch technology can process multiple simultaneous touches on the screen. For example, pinching or spreading out your thumb and finger together makes the display zoom out and in,

FIGURE 2.12 Some basic touch screens use a capacitive system to detect touches and translate them into meaningful commands that are understood by the computer's operating system.

respectively. The features of each touch, such as size, shape, and location, are also determined.

A touch-sensitive screen, like the one used with the iPhone and iPad and with many other smartphones and tablets, arranges the capacitors in a coordinate system so the circuitry can sense changes at each point along the grid (see Figure 2.13).

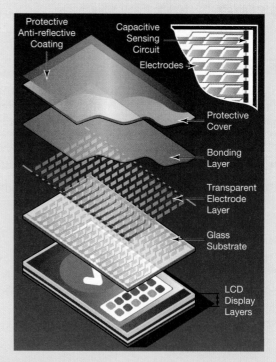

FIGURE 2.13 Multitouch screens use a coordinate-based grid to arrange the capacitors so the circuitry can detect and respond to multiple touches occurring at the same time.

Consequently, every point on the grid generates its own signal when touched and can do so even as another signal is being generated simultaneously. The signals are then relayed to the device's processor. This allows the device to determine the location and movement of simultaneous touches in multiple locations.

After detecting the position and type of touch occurring on the display, the device's processor combines this information with the information it has about the application in use and what was being done in the application when the touch occurred. The processor relays that information to the program in use, and the command is executed. All this happens seemingly instantaneously.

considered input devices. These devices can connect to your computer with a cable, transmit data wirelessly, or transfer data automatically through the Internet. **Scanners** can also input images. They work similarly to a photocopy machine; however, instead of generating the image on paper, they create a digital image, which you can then print, save, or e-mail.

How do I capture live video from my computing device? A **webcam** is a front-facing camera that attaches to a desktop computer or is built into a laptop, tablet, smartphone, or desktop monitor. Although webcams are able to capture still images, they're used mostly for capturing and transmitting live video. Videoconferencing software lets a person using a device equipped with a webcam and a microphone transmit video and audio across the Internet. Video apps such as Skype (see the Try This in Chapter 1, pages 11–12) and ooVoo make it easy to videoconference with multiple people (see Figure 2.14). With many apps, you can also exchange files, swap control of computers, and text message during calls.

How do my computing devices benefit from accepting sound input? In addition to letting others hear you in a videoconference, equipping your device to accept sound input opens up a variety of possibilities. You

can conduct audio conferences with work colleagues, chat with friends or family over the Internet, record podcasts, and even control computing devices with your voice. Inputting sound to your computer requires using a **microphone (or mic)**—a device that lets you capture sound waves (such as your voice) and transfer them to digital format on your computer. Laptops, tablets, and smartphones come with built-in microphones.

How can I use my voice to control my computing device? Voice recognition software allows you to control your computing devices by speaking into the device's microphone instead of using a keyboard or mouse. Apps like Dragon Naturally Speaking are available as stand-alone apps but voice recognition features are built into the Windows and OS X operating systems as well.

Popular extensions of voice recognition software are **intelligent personal assistants** such as Apple's Siri and Microsoft's Cortana (see Figure 2.15). These

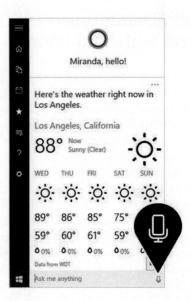

FIGURE 2.15 Just tap the microphone icon and ask Microsoft's intelligent personal assistant Cortana a question. She communicates using natural language processing techniques. *(Microsoft Cortana, Windows 10, Microsoft Corporation)*

FIGURE 2.14 Videoconferencing relies on two input devices: a *webcam* and a *microphone*. *(Rocketclips/Shutterstock)*

so-called *software agents* respond to voice commands and then use your input, access to the Internet, and location-aware services to perform various tasks, such as finding the closest pizza parlor to your present location.

What types of add-on microphones are available?
For specialized situations, built-in microphones don't always provide the best performance. You may want to consider adding other types of microphones, such as those shown in Figure 2.16, to your system for the best results. ■

(Fotolia, Joseph Branston/PC Format Magazine/Future/ Getty Images, Sumnersgraphicsinc/Fotolia, Feliks Gurevich/Shutterstock)

FIGURE 2.16

Types of Microphones

MICROPHONE TYPE	ATTRIBUTES	BEST USED FOR	MICROPHONE TYPE	ATTRIBUTES	BEST USED FOR
Close Talk	• Attached to a headset (allows for listening) • Leaves hands free	• Video conferencing • Phone calls • Speech recognition software	**Unidirectional**	• Picks up sounds from only one direction	• Recordings with one voice (podcasts)
Omnidirectional	• Picks up sounds equally well from all directions	• Conference calls in meeting rooms	**Clip-On (Lavalier)**	• Clips to clothing • Available as wireless	• Presentations requiring freedom of movement • Leaves hands free for writing on whiteboards

BITS&BYTES

Near Field Communication (NFC): Now Pay (or Get Paid) Anywhere with Your Phone

Paid for anything in a retail store with your phone lately? To accomplish this, your phone (and other devices) use a set of communication protocols called **near field communication (NFC)**. Devices equipped with NFC can communicate with each other when they are held in close proximity. When paying with your phone, NFC enables the input of payment information (your credit/debit card number) into a merchant's computer system.

But how can an artist selling his or her work at an art show in a park, for example, accept mobile payments? Now companies like Square are deploying readers (see Figure 2.17) that connect wirelessly to Apple and Android devices (like phones or tablets) and allow

customers to pay using NFC-enabled devices. Now you can sell your products and services anywhere and still accept all the latest payment technologies!

FIGURE 2.17 Portable NFC communication devices for accepting payments are now available. *(Mika Images/Alamy)*

output
DEVICES

An **output device** lets you send processed data out of your computer in the form of text, pictures (graphics), sounds (audio), or video. Let's look at some popular output devices you'll encounter at school and in the workplace.

Monitors

Objective 2.7 *Name common types of monitors, and identify important aspects of their quality.*

What are the different types of monitors? The most common output device is a **monitor** (sometimes referred to as a **display screen**), which displays text, graphics, and videos as soft copies (copies you can see only on screen). The most common type of monitor is a **liquid crystal display (LCD)**. An LCD monitor, also called a flat-panel monitor, is light and energy efficient. Some newer monitors use **light-emitting diode (LED)** technology, which is more energy efficient and may have better color accuracy and thinner panels than LCD monitors. LCD flat-panel monitors have replaced cathode ray tube (CRT) monitors. CRT monitors are considered **legacy technology**, or computing devices that use techniques, parts, and methods that are no longer popular. Although legacy technology may still be functional, it has been replaced by newer technological advances.

Organic light-emitting diode (OLED) displays use organic compounds that produce light when exposed to an electric current. Unlike LCDs and LEDs, OLEDs do not require a backlight to function and therefore draw less power and have a much thinner display, sometimes as thin as 3 mm. They are also brighter and more environmentally friendly than LCDs. Because of their lower power needs, OLED displays run longer on a single battery charge than do LEDs, which is why OLED technology is probably the technology used in your cell phone, iPod, and digital camera.

Companies like LG are now working on transparent and flexible OLED display screens (see Figure 2.18). These screens allow you to see what is behind the screen while still being able to display information on the screen. These types of screens present interesting possibilities for augmented reality. *Augmentative reality (AR)* is a view of a real-world environment whose elements are *augmented* (or supplemented) by some type of computer-generated sensory input such as video, graphics, or GPS data (see Chapter 1, pages 20–21). For instance, if you had a transparent screen on your smartphone and held it up to view street signs that were in English, you could possibly have your phone display the signs in another language. Currently, applications like this exist but require the use of a camera as well as your screen. But transparent screens will eliminate the need for the camera.

How do LCD monitors work? Monitor screens are grids made up of millions of tiny dots, called **pixels**. When

FIGURE 2.18 Because they don't need a backlight, OLED displays can be made transparent and flexible. *(Yonhap/EPA/Newscom)*

these pixels are illuminated by the light waves generated by a fluorescent panel at the back of your screen, they create the images you see on the screen or monitor. Each pixel on the newest 4K resolution TVs and monitors is actually made up of four yellow, red, blue, and green subpixels. (Older devices don't have yellow subpixels.) Some newer TVs further split the subpixels into upper and lower, which can brighten and darken independently. LCD monitors are made of two or more sheets of material filled with a liquid crystal solution (see Figure 2.19). A fluorescent panel at the back of the LCD monitor generates light waves. When electric current passes through the liquid crystal solution, the crystals move around and either block the fluorescent light or let the light shine through. This blocking or passing of light by the crystals causes images to form on the screen. The various combinations of yellow, red, blue, and green make up the components of color we see on our monitors.

What factors affect the quality of an LCD monitor? When choosing an LCD monitor, the most important factors to consider are aspect ratio and resolution. The **aspect ratio** is the width-to-height proportion of a monitor. Traditionally, aspect ratios have been 4:3, but newer monitors are available with an aspect ratio of 16:9 to accommodate HD format video. The screen **resolution**, or the clearness or sharpness of the image, reflects the number of pixels on the screen. An LCD monitor may have a native (or maximum) resolution of 1600 × 1200, meaning it contains 1600 vertical

FIGURE 2.19 A magnification of a single pixel in a conventional LCD monitor. (The newest 4K resolution TVs and monitors also have a yellow subpixel.)

columns with 1200 pixels in each column. The higher the resolution, the sharper and clearer the image will be, but generally, the resolution of an LCD monitor is dictated by the screen size and aspect ratio. Although you can change the resolution of an LCD monitor beyond its native resolution, the images will become distorted. Generally, you should buy

a monitor with the highest resolution available for the screen size (measured in inches). Figure 2.20 lists these and other factors to consider when judging the quality of an LCD monitor.

Is a bigger screen size always better? The bigger the monitor, the more you can display, and depending on what you want to display, size may matter. In general, the larger the panel, the larger number of pixels it can display. For example, a 27-inch monitor can display 2560 × 1440 pixels, whereas a 21.5-inch monitor may only be able to display 1680 × 1050 pixels. However, most new monitors have at least the 1920 × 1080 resolution required to display Blu-ray movies.

Larger screens can also allow you to view multiple documents or web pages at the same time, creating the effect of using two separate monitors side by side. However, buying two smaller monitors might be cheaper than buying one large monitor. For either option—a big screen or two separate screens—check that your computer has the appropriate video hardware to support these display devices.

What other features should I look for in an LCD monitor? Some monitors, especially those on laptop computers, come with built-in features such as speakers,

FIGURE 2.20

Factors to Consider When Shopping for a Monitor

FACTOR	POSSIBLE PROBLEMS	LOOK FOR
Aspect Ratio: Width-to-height proportion of a screen	• An odd aspect ratio may make images look distorted	• Ratios of 4:3 or 16:9 (HDTV)
Screen Resolution: Number of pixels displayed on the screen	• Low screen resolution = unclear image • High resolution on a small size monitor results in image being too small	• Highest resolution monitor is capable of displaying (make sure you are comfortable viewing that size image)
Contrast Ratio: Difference in light intensity between brightest white and darkest black a monitor can produce	• Ratio too low results in colors fading when adjusting brightness	• Ratios between 400:1 and 1,000:1
Viewing Angle: Distance in degrees from which you can move to the side of (or above or below) a monitor before the image degrades	• Angle too low means people not sitting directly in front of the monitor will see a poor image	• 150 degrees or more is preferable
Brightness: Greatest amount of light showing when the monitor is displaying pure white (measured in candelas per square meter [cd/m^2] or *nits*)	• Image will be hard to see in bright rooms if brightness level is too low	• 300 cd/m^2 or greater
Response Time: Time it takes for a pixel to change color (in milliseconds)	• High response time results in images appearing jerky	• Seek lowest possible response time if viewing live action sports

BITS&BYTES

Forget HDTV—Here Comes Ultra HD!

Now that everyone loves their HDTVs, what can manufacturers do next? Ultra HD (otherwise known as 4K) TV is the emerging standard. HDTVs feature a resolution of 1920 × 1080 pixels (height and width, respectively). Ultra HD TVs, on the other hand, boast 3840 × 2160 resolution, which provides screens with four times as many pixels as HDTV devices. More pixels generally provide a sharper picture on a large screen, so screen sizes of 50 inches and up should have a noticeable difference in picture quality.

So should you throw away your HDTV and replace it with an Ultra HD TV? Probably not yet. Ultra HD TVs

are expensive, and there is not much programming available yet in the Ultra HD format. But as more programming becomes available and prices of Ultra HD TVs fall, it may soon make sense to consider a higher resolution TV.

Or, you may just hang on and wait for 8K TVs (7680 × 4320 resolution), which may be available on the consumer market within three years. The technology to record 8K already exists—in fact, the BBC recorded much of the 2012 Summer Olympics in 8K format. Whatever happens, expect your TV picture to just keep getting better!

---

webcams, and microphones. A built-in multiformat memory card reader is convenient for displaying images directly on the monitor or for downloading pictures quickly from a camera memory card to your PC. Another nice feature to look for in a desktop LCD monitor is built-in USB ports. This feature lets you connect extra peripherals easily without reaching around the back of the PC.

How do I show output to a large group of people? A **projector** lets you project images from your computing device onto a wall or viewing screen. Projectors are commonly used in business and education settings such as conference rooms and classrooms. Many projectors are small and lightweight and some are small enough to fit in the palm of your hand. These portable projectors are ideal for businesspeople who have to make presentations at client locations. *Entertainment projectors* include stereo speakers and an array of multimedia connectors, making them a good option for use in the home to display TV programs, DVDs, digital images, or video games in a large format. If your computing device is equipped with an HDMI port, you can also choose to connect your computer directly to an HDTV using an HDMI cable. The most common HDMI connector types are shown in Figure 2.21. Full size (or type A) connectors are found on most TVs and laptops. Tablets and phones are more likely to have a mini (type C) or micro (type D) HDMI port.

Printers

Objective 2.8 *Describe various types of printers, and explain when you would use them.*

What are the different types of printers? In addition to monitors, another common output device is the **printer**, which creates hard copies (copies you can touch) of text and graphics. There are two primary categories of printers: inkjet and laser, both of which are considered nonimpact printers.

HDMI (Full Size)
TYPE A

HDMI Mini
TYPE C

HDMI Micro
TYPE D

FIGURE 2.21 Cables with the appropriate connectors are available to facilitate connection of your mobile devices to your HDTV for enhanced viewing. *(Tether Tools)*

A **nonimpact printer** such as an inkjet printer sprays ink or uses laser beams to transfer marks onto the paper. An **impact printer** has tiny hammer-like keys that strike the paper through an inked ribbon to make marks on the paper. For most users, impact printers are legacy technology.

What are the advantages of inkjet printers? An **inkjet printer** (see Figure 2.22) is the type of printer found in many homes. These printers are popular because they're affordable and produce high-quality printouts quickly and quietly. Inkjet printers work by spraying tiny drops of ink onto

 ACTIVE HELPDESK
Using Output Devices

In this Active Helpdesk, you'll play the role of a helpdesk staffer, fielding questions about different output devices.

paper and are great for printing black-and-white text as well as color images. In fact, when loaded with the right paper, higher-end inkjet printers can print images that look like professional-quality photos. One thing to consider when buying an inkjet printer is the type and cost of the ink cartridges the printer needs. Some printers use two cartridges: black and color. Others use four or more cartridges: typically, cyan, magenta, yellow, and black. The four-color printing process many inkjets use is known as **CMYK** (this acronym stands for cyan, magenta, yellow, and key, which is usually represented by black). The inks are layered onto a lighter (usually white) surface to partially or entirely mask different colors. The layering reduces the brightness of the white so this process is known as a *subtractive color model*.

Why would I want a laser printer? A **laser printer** uses laser beams and static electricity to deliver toner (similar to ink) onto the correct areas of the page (see Figure 2.23). Heat is used to fuse the toner to the page, making the image permanent. Laser printers are often used in office or classroom settings because they print faster than inkjet printers and produce higher-quality printouts. Black-and-white laser printers have also been common in homes for a decade. Over the past few years, the price of color laser printers has fallen dramatically, making them price competitive with high-end inkjet printers. Thus, color laser printers are a viable option for the home. If you print a high volume of pages, consider a laser printer. When you include

FIGURE 2.23 Laser printers print quickly and offer high-quality printouts. *(Xerox Corporation)*

the price of ink or toner in the overall cost, color laser printers can be more economical than inkjets.

What's the best way to print from portable devices such as tablets and smartphones? Wireless printers are a good option for home networks as they let several people print to the same printer from different devices and any location in the home. There are two types of wireless printers: WiFi and Bluetooth. Both WiFi and Bluetooth printers have a range of up to approximately 300 feet. WiFi, however, sends data more quickly than Bluetooth.

Wireless printers are also great for printing from portable devices. If you're using a device running Apple's iOS (such as an iPhone), AirPrint makes printing easy. AirPrint is a feature of iOS that facilitates printing to AirPrint-compatible wireless printers, and many printers produced today are AirPrint compatible.

For non-Apple mobile devices (or if your printer isn't compatible with AirPrint), you can try other solutions, such as Presto by Collobos Software and ThinPrint Cloud Printer by Cortado. Once you install one of these apps on your portable device, you can send documents to printers that are connected to PCs and Macs on your home network. It makes printing from mobile devices as simple as hitting print on your laptop.

Can I carry my printer with me? Although some inkjet printers are small enough to be considered portable, you may want to consider a printer designed for portability. These compact printers can connect to your computer, tablet, or smartphone via Bluetooth technology or through a USB port. Portable printers are often compact enough to fit in a briefcase

FIGURE 2.22 Inkjet printers are popular among home users, especially with the rise of digital photography. Many inkjet printers are optimized for printing photos from digital cameras. *(TheVectorminator/Shutterstock)*

FIGURE 2.24 Specialty printers: (a) all-in-one printer, (b) large format printer, (c) thermal printer. *(Image reprinted courtesy of Epson America, Inc.; Image reprinted courtesy of Epson America, Inc.; Vetkit/Fotolia)*

or backpack, are lightweight, and can run on batteries as well as AC power.

Are there any other types of specialty printers? Although you'll probably use laser or inkjet printers most often, you might also encounter several other types of printers (shown in Figure 2.24):

- An **all-in-one printer** combines the functions of a printer, scanner, copier, and fax into one machine. Popular for their space-saving convenience, all-in-one printers may use either inkjet or laser technology.

- A **large format printer** generates oversize images such as professional graphics, high resolution photographs, banners, posters, and infographics that require more sophisticated color detail. Some of these printers use up to 12 different inks to achieve high-quality realistic color images.

- A **thermal printer** works either by melting wax-based ink onto ordinary paper (a process called *thermal wax transfer printing*) or by burning dots onto specially coated paper (a process called *direct thermal printing*). Thermal printers are used in stores to print receipts and in airports for electronic ticketing, and many models feature wireless technology. Thermal printers are also popular for mobile printing in conjunction with smartphones and tablets.

How do I choose the best printer? Your first step is to decide what your primary printing need is. If you're planning to print color photos and graphics, an inkjet printer or color laser printer is a must, even though the cost per page will be higher. If you'll be printing mostly black-and-white text-based documents or will be sharing your printer with others, a black-and-white laser printer is best because of its speed and overall economy for volume printing. It's also important to determine whether you want just a printer or

a device that prints and scans, copies, or faxes (an all-in-one). In addition, you should decide whether you need to print from mobile devices.

Once you have narrowed down the *type* of printer you want, you can use the criteria listed in Figure 2.25 to help you determine the best model to meet your needs.

Sound Output

Objective 2.9 *Discuss options for outputting sound from your computing devices.*

What are the output devices for sound? Most computers include inexpensive **speakers**, which are the output devices for sound. These speakers are sufficient to play the standard audio clips you find on the web and usually for letting you participate in videoconferencing or phone calls over the Internet. However, if you plan to digitally edit audio files or are particular about how your music sounds, you may want a more sophisticated speaker system, such as one that includes subwoofers (special speakers that produce only low bass sounds) and surround-sound speakers. A **surround-sound system** is a set of speakers and audio processing that envelops the listener in a 360-degree field of sound. In addition, wireless speaker systems are available to help you avoid cluttering up your rooms with speaker wires.

If you work in close proximity to other employees or travel with a laptop, you may need to use headphones or earbuds to avoid distracting other people. Both devices plug into the same jack on your computing device to which speakers connect. Studies of users of portable media players have shown that hearing might be damaged by excessive volume, especially when using earbuds because they fit into the ear canals. Exercise caution when using these devices. ∎

BITS&BYTES

Does It Matter What Paper I Print On?

The quality of your printer is only part of what controls the quality of a printed image. The paper you use and the printer settings that control the amount of ink used are equally important.

- If you're printing text-only documents for personal use, using low-cost paper is fine. You also may want to consider selecting draft mode in your printer settings to conserve ink. However, if you're printing more formal documents, such as business correspondence, you may want to choose a higher-quality paper (determined by the paper's weight, whiteness, and brightness) and adjust your print setting to "normal" or "best."
- The weight of paper is measured in pounds, with 20 pounds being standard. A heavier paper may be best for projects such as brochures, but be sure to check that your printer can handle the added thickness of the paper.
- The degree of paper whiteness is a matter of personal preference. Generally, the whiter the paper, the brighter the printed color. However, for documents that are more formal, you may want to use a creamier color.
- The brightness of paper usually varies from 85 to 94. The higher the number, the brighter the paper, and the easier it is to read printed text.
- Opacity, or the "show through" of ink from one side of the paper to the other, is especially important if you're printing on both sides of the paper.

If you're printing photos, paper quality can have a big impact on your results. Photo paper is more expensive than regular paper and comes in a variety of textures ranging from matte to high gloss. For a photo-lab look, high-gloss paper is the best choice. Semigloss (often referred to as satin) is good for formal portraits, while a matte surface is often used for black-and-white photo printing.

FIGURE 2.25

Major Printer Attributes

ATTRIBUTE	CONSIDERATIONS
Speed	• Print speed is measured in *pages per minute (PPM)*. • Black-and-white documents print faster than color documents. • Laser printers often print faster than inkjets.

Resolution	• Resolution refers to a printer's image clarity.
	• Resolution is measured in *dots per inch (dpi)*.
	• Higher dpi = greater level of detail and clarity.
	• Recommended dpi:
	  • Black-and-white text: 300
	  • General purpose images: 1200
	  • Photos: 4800

Color Output	• Printers with separate cartridges for each color produce the best quality output. • Inkjet and laser color printers generally have four cartridges (black, cyan, magenta, and yellow). • Higher-quality printers have six cartridges (the four above plus light cyan and light magenta). • With separate cartridges, you only need to replace the empty one.
Cost of Consumables	• Consumables are printer cartridges and paper. • Printer cartridges can exceed the cost of some printers. • Consumer magazines such as *Consumer Reports* can help you research costs.

(Freshidea/Fotolia, Michael Nivelet/Fotolia, Thomas Amby/Fotolia, Tomislav Forgo/Fotolia)

Before moving on to Part 2:
1. **Watch Replay Video 2.1** ▷ .
2. **Then check your understanding of what you've learned so far.**

check your understanding // review & practice

For a quick review to see what you've learned so far, answer the following questions.

multiple choice

1. Which of the following is NOT one of the four major functions of a computer?

   a. input

   b. processing

   c. indexing

   d. storage

2. Which of the following can be both an input and an output device?

   a. mouse

   b. keyboard

   c. monitor

   d. laser printer

3. Which of the following display screens does not require a backlight to function?

   a. organic light-emitting diode (OLED) display

   b. liquid crystal display (LCD)

   c. light-emitting diode (LED) display

   d. cathode ray tube (CRT)

4. What type of printer sprays tiny drops of ink onto paper?

   a. inkjet

   b. impact

   c. thermal

   d. laser

5. When buying a monitor, which factor is NOT important to consider?

   a. screen resolution

   b. viewing angle

   c. color depth

   d. aspect ratio

 Go to **MyITLab** to take an autograded version of the *Check Your Understanding* review and to find all media resources for the chapter.

TECHBYTES WEEKLY

Stay current with the TechBytes Weekly Newsletter.

Continue ⟫

TRY THIS What's Inside My Computer?

Understanding what capabilities your current computer has is one of the first steps toward computer literacy. In this exercise, you'll learn how to explore the components of your Windows computer.

Step 1 To gather information about the storage devices on our computer, click **File Explorer** from the Taskbar or from the Start menu. Then in the navigation pane, click **This PC** to display information about your computer's devices. *(Windows 10, Microsoft Corporation)*

Click to launch File Explorer

Step 2 The File Explorer This PC screen displays information about internal storage devices (such as internal hard drives), optical storage devices (such as DVD drives), and portable storage devices (such as flash drives and external hard drives). To display the System screen, click the **Computer tab** on the File Explorer ribbon, and then the **System properties button**. *(Windows 10, Microsoft Corporation)*

Ribbon

Step 3 You can gather quite a bit of information from the System screen, such as:

- Version of Windows
- Type of processor
- Speed of the processor
- Amount of RAM installed
- System type (32-bit or 64-bit) *(Windows 10, Microsoft Corporation)*

Windows version

Clock speed

RAM info

Processor info

System type

Make This TOOL: App Inventor 2

MAKE: A Mobile App

Want to build your own Android app from scratch? You can, with a simple tool called **App Inventor**. To get started, have ready:

1. A computer connected to a WiFi network

2. The Chrome browser

3. A Google account

4. The MIT AI2 Companion app

5. [optional] An Android device connected to the same WiFI network

In this exercise, you'll explore the **App Inventor** tool and begin working with your first simple app. As you'll see, making your device work for you is as easy as drag and drop with **App Inventor**. *(MIT App Inventor 2, Massachusetts Institute of Technology. Creative Commons Attribution-ShareAlike 3.0 Unported License)*

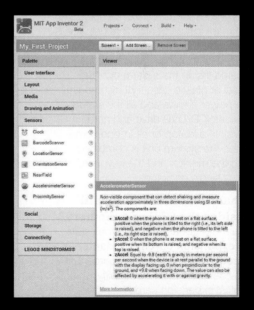

App Inventor is a programming platform used to create apps for Android devices. Using App Inventor, you can easily drag and drop components to design your App's interface and its behavior.

For the instructions for this exercise, go to MyITLab.

Processing, Storage, and Connectivity

Learning Outcome 2.2 You will be able to describe how computers process and store data and how devices connect to a computer system.

So far, we have explored the components of your computer that you use to input and output data. But where does the processing take place, and where is the data stored? And how does your computer connect with peripherals and other computers?

 processing and memory on the
MOTHERBOARD

The main processing functions of your computer take place in the CPU and memory, both of which reside on your computer's motherboard. In the following sections, we'll explore the components of the motherboard and how memory helps your computer process data.

The Motherboard and Memory

Objective 2.10 *Define motherboard and RAM.*

What exactly is a motherboard? The **motherboard** is the main circuit board that contains the central electronic components of the computer, including the computer's processor (CPU), its memory, and the many circuit boards that help the computer function (see Figure 2.26). On a desktop, the motherboard is located inside the system unit, the metal or plastic case that also houses the power source and all the storage devices (CD/DVD drive and hard drive). In a laptop or all-in-one computer, the system unit is combined with the monitor and the keyboard into a single package.

What's on the motherboard besides the CPU and memory? The motherboard also includes slots for **expansion cards (or adapter cards)**, which are circuit boards that provide additional functionality. Typical expansion cards found in the system unit are sound and video cards. A **sound card** provides a connection for the speakers and microphone, whereas a **video card** provides a connection for the monitor. Laptops and tablets have video and sound capabilities integrated into their motherboards.

High-end desktops use expansion cards to provide video and sound capabilities.

Other expansion cards provide a means for network and Internet connections. A **network interface card (NIC)**, which enables your computer to connect with other computers or to a cable modem to facilitate a high-speed Internet connection, is often integrated into the motherboard. Lastly, some expansion cards provide additional USB and Thunderbolt ports.

Memory (RAM) slots

Ports

CPU socket

Expansion slots

FIGURE 2.26 A motherboard contains the socket for the computer's processor (CPU), slots for memory (RAM) modules, ports, and slots for expansion cards. *(GIGA-BYTE Technology Co., Ltd.)*

What exactly is RAM? Random access memory (RAM) is the place in a computer where the programs and data that the computer is currently using, are stored. RAM is much faster to read from and write to than the hard drive and other forms of storage. The processor can request the RAM's contents, which can be located, opened, and delivered to the CPU for processing in a few nanoseconds (billionths of a second). If you look at a motherboard, you'll see RAM as a series of small cards (called *memory cards* or *memory modules*) plugged into slots on the motherboard.

Because the entire contents of RAM are erased when you turn off the computer, RAM is a temporary or **volatile storage** location. To save data permanently, you need to save it to your hard drive or to another permanent storage location such as a flash drive or cloud storage.

Does the motherboard contain any other kinds of memory besides RAM? In addition to RAM, the motherboard contains a form of memory called **read-only memory (ROM)**. ROM holds all the instructions the computer needs to start up when it's powered on. Unlike data stored in RAM, which is volatile storage, the instructions stored in ROM are permanent, making ROM a **nonvolatile storage** location, which means the data isn't erased when the power is turned off.

Processing

Objective 2.11 *Explain the main functions of the CPU.*

What is the CPU? The **central processing unit (CPU or processor)** is sometimes referred to as the "brains" of the computer because it controls all the functions performed by the computer's other components and processes all the commands issued to it by software instructions. Modern CPUs can perform as many as tens of billions of tasks per second without error, making them extremely powerful components.

How is processor speed measured? Processor speed is measured in units of hertz (Hz). *Hertz* is a measurement of machine cycles per second. A *machine cycle* is the process of the CPU getting the data or instructions from RAM and decoding the instructions into something the computer can understand. Once the CPU has decoded the instructions, it executes them and stores the result back in system memory. Current systems run at speeds measured in **gigahertz (GHz)** or billions of machine cycles per second. Therefore, a 3.8 GHz processor performs work at a rate of 3.8 billion machine cycles per second. It's important to realize, however, that CPU processor speed alone doesn't determine the performance of the CPU.

What else determines processor performance? Although speed is an important consideration when determining

processor performance, CPU performance is also affected by other factors. One factor is the number of *cores*, or processing paths, a processor has. Initially, processors could handle only one instruction at a time. Now, processors have been designed so that they can have two, four, or even ten different paths, allowing them to process more than one instruction at a time (see Figure 2.27). Applications such as virus protection software and the operating system, which are always running behind the scenes, can have their own processor paths, freeing up the other paths to run other applications such as a web browser, Word, or iTunes more efficiently.

Besides the number of cores, what other factors determine processing power? The "best" processor will depend on your particular needs and is not always the processor with the highest processor speed and the greatest number of cores. Intel, one of the leading manufacturers of computer processor chips, has created a pictorial rating system for CPU chips. Intel provides a website (**ark.intel.com**) that assists in comparing the performance of different models of CPUs. ∎

FIGURE 2.27 With multi-core processors, CPUs can work in parallel, processing two or more separate programs at the same time instead of switching back and forth between them.

storing data and
INFORMATION

Because RAM is volatile storage, it can't be used to store information indefinitely. To save your data and information permanently, you need to save it to a nonvolatile storage device, such as a hard drive, cloud storage location, DVD, or flash drive.

Hard Drives

Objective 2.12 *List the various types of hard drives.*

Are there different kinds of hard drives? The **hard disk drive (HDD, or hard drive)** is your computer's primary device for permanent storage of software and documents. The hard drive is a nonvolatile storage device. An **internal hard drive** resides within the system unit and usually holds all permanently stored programs and data. Today's internal hard drives (see Figure 2.28) have capacities of as much as 8 TB or more. **External hard drives** offer similar storage capacities but reside outside the system unit and connect to the computer via a port.

The most common type of hard drive has moveable parts—spinning platters and a moving arm with a read/write head—that can fail and lead to devastating disk failure. However, the **solid-state drive (SSD)** has recently become a popular option for ultrabooks and laptop storage. SSDs have no moving parts, so they're more efficient, run with no noise, emit little heat, and require little power. In addition, they're less likely to fail after being bumped or dropped.

Permanent storage devices are located in your desktop or laptop computer in a space called a **drive bay**. There are two kinds of drive bays:

1. *Internal drive bays* cannot be seen or accessed from outside the system unit. Generally, internal drive bays are reserved for internal hard drives.

2. *External drive bays* can be seen and accessed from outside the system unit. External drive bays house DVD

FIGURE 2.28 Internal hard drives (shown here open—normally, they are sealed) are a computer's primary nonvolatile storage. *(Mbongo/Fotolia)*

and Blu-ray drives, for example. On desktop computers, sometimes there are empty external drive bays that can be used to install additional drives. These extra spaces are covered by a faceplate on the front panel. Laptop computers generally do not give you the ability to add additional drives. Such expansion is done by attaching an external drive to the computer through a USB port.

Cloud Storage

Objective 2.13 *Define cloud storage, and explain how to use it.*

How can I easily access my files if I constantly switch between devices? You may find yourself using multiple devices, such as a smartphone, laptop, and a tablet, at different times during the day. Invariably, you'll find you need access to a current version of a file that is stored on a device other than the one you're using. If your devices are connected to the Internet, cloud storage provides a convenient option.

Cloud storage refers to using a service that keeps your files on the Internet (in the "cloud") rather than storing your files solely on a local device. Using a cloud storage service requires that you install software or an app on your device. A popular web-based application for storing files on the cloud is Dropbox. Dropbox supports computers running Windows, OS X, and Linux as well as many smartphones and tablets. After installing the Dropbox software on your devices, any files you save in the Dropbox folder are accessible by all your other devices via the Internet. You can also share folders in Dropbox with other Dropbox users, making it ideal for group projects.

For example, when you save a history term paper to Dropbox on your laptop, the Dropbox software also copies the paper onto a computer attached to the web. Now when you grab your smartphone and head off to class, you can access the paper created on your laptop through the Internet connection on your smartphone and make changes to it if necessary.

Dropbox storage capacity is limited to between 2 GB and 18 GB for free accounts. Other cloud storage alternatives include Microsoft OneDrive and Google Drive, each of which provide 15 GB of free space, and Apple iCloud, which offers 5 GB of free storage.

Portable and Optical Storage Options

Objective 2.14 *Describe the various portable and optical storage options.*

How can I take my files with me without relying on cloud storage? For large portable storage needs, there are portable external hard drives, which are small enough to fit into your pocket and have storage capacities of 4 TB

You've probably heard news stories about people using computers to unleash viruses or commit identity theft. You may also have read about students who were prosecuted for illegally sharing copyrighted material, such as songs and videos. These are both examples of *unethical* behavior while using a computer. However, what constitutes *ethical* behavior while using a computer?

Loosely defined, *ethics* is a system of moral principles, rules, and accepted standards of conduct (see Figure 2.29). So what are the accepted standards of conduct when using computers? The Computer Ethics Institute has developed the Ten Commandments of Computer Ethics, which is widely cited as a benchmark for companies developing computer usage and compliance policies for employees. These guidelines are applicable for schools and students, as well. The following ethical computing guidelines are based on the Computer Ethics Institute's work:

FIGURE 2.29 There are different ways to define ethics, but they all apply to a common code of behavior for groups or individuals. *(Marek/Fotolia)*

Ethical Computing Guidelines

1. Avoid causing harm to others when using computers.
2. Do not interfere with other people's efforts at accomplishing work with computers.
3. Resist the temptation to snoop in other people's computer files.
4. Do not use computers to commit theft.
5. Agree not to use computers to promote lies.
6. Do not use software (or make illegal copies for others) without paying the creator for it.
7. Avoid using other people's computer resources without appropriate authorization or proper compensation.
8. Do not claim other people's intellectual output as your own.
9. Consider the social consequences of the products of your computer labor.
10. Only use computers in ways that show consideration and respect for others.

The United States has enacted laws that support some of these guidelines, such as Guideline 6, the breaking of which would violate copyright laws, and Guideline 4, which is enforceable under numerous federal and state larceny laws. Other guidelines, however, require more subtle interpretation as to what behavior is unethical because there are no laws designed to enforce them.

Consider Guideline 7, which covers unauthorized use of resources. The school you attend probably provides computer resources for you to use for coursework. But if your school gives you access to computers and the Internet, is it ethical for you to use those resources to run an online business on the weekends? Although it might not be technically illegal, you're tying up computer resources that other students could use for their intended purpose: learning and completing coursework. (This behavior also violates Guidelines 2 and 10.)

Throughout the chapters in this book, we touch on many topics related to these guidelines. So keep them in mind as you study, and think about how they relate to the actions you take as you use computers in your life.

FIGURE 2.30 Smaller, portable external hard drives enable you to take a significant amount of data and programs on the road with you. *(Inga Nielsen/Shutterstock)*

(or larger). These devices are lightweight and enclosed in a protective case. They attach to your computer via a USB port (see Figure 2.30).

A **flash drive** (sometimes referred to as a **jump drive, USB drive,** or **thumb drive**) uses solid-state flash memory, storing information on an internal memory chip. When you plug a flash drive into your computer's USB port, it appears in the operating system as another disk drive. You can write data to it or read data from it as you would a hard drive. Because a flash drive contains no moving parts, it's quite durable. It's also tiny enough to fit in your pocket (see Figure 2.31). Despite their size, flash drives can have significant storage capacity—currently as much as 1 TB. Often, flash drives are combined with other devices such as pens or keychains for added convenience.

Wireless flash drives are available that make transferring files from portable devices easier. Although they look like normal flash drives, these wireless drives can connect to your portable devices via WiFi after installing the appropriate app. Up to eight devices can be connected to the flash drive at once, and the drive can even stream media to three devices simultaneously. So your friend could be watching a movie stored on the flash drive while you're uploading pictures from your phone.

Another convenient means of portable storage is a **flash memory card**, such as an SD card. Like the flash drive, memory cards use solid-state flash memory. Most desktops and laptops include slots for flash memory cards, but if your computer is not equipped, there are memory card readers that you can plug into a USB port. Flash memory cards let you transfer digital data between your computer and devices such as digital cameras, smartphones, tablets, video cameras, and printers. Although incredibly small—some are even smaller than the size of a postage stamp—these memory cards have capacities that exceed the capacity of a DVD. Figure 2.32 compares the storage capacities of hard drives and flash drives.

What other kinds of storage devices are available? Most desktop and all-in-one computers come

with at least one **optical drive** that can read from and maybe even write to CDs, DVDs, or Blu-ray discs. As we have moved toward streaming media services and cloud-based delivery of software, optical drives have not been included in laptops and ultrabooks to save weight and space. However, if you still have the need (or desire) to use optical drives, inexpensive portable drives that attach via USB ports are readily available.

Data is saved to optical discs as tiny pits that are burned into the disc by a high-speed laser. **Compact discs (CDs)** were initially created to store audio files. **Digital video (**or

FIGURE 2.31 Flash drives are a convenient means of portable storage and come in many different shapes and sizes. *(Ekler/ Shutterstock)*

FIGURE 2.32

Hard Drive and Flash Drive Storage Capacity

DRIVE TYPE	IMAGE	TYPICAL CAPACITY	DRIVE TYPE	IMAGE	TYPICAL CAPACITY
Solid-state drive (SSD)		1 TB or more	Flash drive		256 GB or more
External portable hard drive		4 TB or more	Flash memory card		128 GB or more
Mechanical internal hard drive		8 TB or more			

(Oleksiy Mark/Shutterstock, Julia Ivantsova/Shutterstock, D. Hurst/Alamy, Cphoto/Fotolia, ZUMA Press, Inc/Alamy)

versatile) discs (DVDs) are the same size and shape as CDs but can store up to 14 times more data than CDs.

What if you want even more storage capacity? Blu-ray is the latest incarnation of optical storage. **Blu-ray discs (BDs)**, which are similar in size and shape to CDs and DVDs, can hold as much as 50 GB of data—enough to hold approximately 4.5 hours of movies in high-definition (HD) digital format. Many desktop systems are now available with BD-ROM drives and Blu-ray burners. External BD drives are another inexpensive way to add HD storage capacity to your system. Figure 2.33 shows the storage capacities of the various optical storage media. ■

FIGURE 2.33

Optical Storage Media Capacities

MEDIUM TYPE	TYPICAL CAPACITY
Blu-ray (dual layer)	50 GB
Blu-ray	25 GB
DVD DL (dual layer)	8.5 GB
DVD	4.7 GB
CD	700 MB

 connecting peripherals to the

COMPUTER

Throughout this chapter, we have discussed peripheral devices that input, store, and output data and information. We will now look at how these types of devices are connected to computers so they can exchange data.

Computer Ports

Objective 2.15 *List the common types of ports used today.*

What is a port? A **port** is a place through which a peripheral device attaches to the computer so that data can be exchanged between it and the operating system. Although peripherals may connect to devices wirelessly, ports are still often used for connections.

What is the fastest data transfer port available on today's computing devices? Thunderbolt is the newest input/output technology on the market. It was developed by Intel using fiber optic technology and Thunderbolt 2 ports can achieve

trends in IT

Green Computing (Green IT)

"Going green" is a goal for many modern businesses. **Green computing (or green IT)** is a movement to encourage environmentally sustainable computing. The main goal is to reduce the overall carbon footprint of a company through the strategic use of computing resources and environmentally friendly computing devices. A business's *carbon footprint* is the total amount of greenhouse gases produced directly and indirectly to support the activities of the business. Carbon footprints are expressed in equivalent tons of carbon dioxide (CO_2). CO_2 is the main greenhouse gas that is contributing to global warming. Reduction of greenhouse gas emissions is critical to sustaining a healthy environment.

The main goals of green computing are

1. Reducing the use of hazardous processes or materials in the production of computing equipment
2. Promoting the use of recyclable or biodegradable materials to facilitate safe disposal of products
3. Buying products that use energy efficiently
4. Using technology to reduce employee travel

(Weerapat1003/Fotolia)

5. Reducing the use of energy and consumption of materials through shared computing resources

Sharing computing resources can make a vast difference in the consumption of resources and electricity. This is one of the reasons cloud storage is becoming so popular. Rather than having 20 individual companies each maintaining a large group of computers to hold data, savings can be achieved by having one company maintain computer resources that are able to serve the 20 other companies. However, it's not all up to businesses to practice green computing. Figure 2.34 lists a few ways you can participate:

FIGURE 2.34

Green Computing Problems and Solutions

ISSUE	ELECTRICITY	COMMUTING	USE TECHNOLOGY LONGER
Problems	• Electricity is often generated using fossil fuels, which produce greenhouse gas emissions • Devices are not energy efficient	• Cars generate greenhouse gases • Many people commute to work alone	• Items are replaced before their useful life is over • Old items are discarded instead of continuing to be used • Technology is not disposed of or recycled properly
Solutions	• Buy energy efficient computing equipment with high Energy Star ratings • Turn off computing devices when not in use • Use appropriate power management settings to use less power when operating devices	• Use technology to telecommute to your job • Use public transportation to commute, which uses energy more efficiently than cars • Use a green vehicle (bicycle, electric car) for your commute	• Only upgrade your technology when absolutely necessary • Donate your old technology to someone who will continue to use it (friends, family, charitable organization) • Only dispose of electronic devices at approved e-waste recycling facilities

(Kovalto1/Fotolia, Berc/Fotolia, Marek/Fotolia)

FIGURE 2.35 Thunderbolt ports are slim and speedy, making them popular on today's ultrabooks and laptops. *(David Paul Morris/Bloomberg/Getty Images)*

blazingly fast transfer speeds of up to 20 Gb/s (the upcoming Thunderbolt 3 protocol should double this to 40 Gb/s). **Thunderbolt ports** (see Figure 2.35) are very useful for laptops and ultrabooks because one Thunderbolt port can allow you to connect up to six different peripherals to your computer. Apple was the first computer maker to integrate the ports into their hardware although other manufacturers are now following suit.

What is the most common port on digital devices? A **universal serial bus (USB) port** is the port type most commonly used to connect input and output devices to the computer. This is mainly because of the ready availability of USB-compatible peripherals. USB ports can connect a wide variety of peripherals to computing devices, including keyboards, printers, mice, smartphones, external hard drives, flash drives, and digital cameras. The new USB 3.1 standard provides

transfer speeds of 10 Gbps and charges devices faster than previous USB ports. USB ports come in variety of standard and proprietary configurations (see Figure 2.36), plus the new Type-C connector (and port), which is expected to supplant older connections as USB 3.1 continues to roll out (see Figure 2.37).

Which ports help me connect with other computers and the Internet? Another set of ports on your computer helps you communicate with other computers. A **connectivity port** can give you access to networks and the Internet. To find a connectivity port, look for a port that resembles a standard phone jack but is slightly larger. This port is called an **Ethernet port**. Ethernet ports transfer data at speeds up to 10,000 Mbps. You can use an Ethernet port to connect your computer to either a cable modem or a network.

How do I connect monitors and multimedia devices? Other ports on the back and sides of the computer include audio and video ports. Audio ports are where you connect headphones, microphones, and speakers to the computer. Whether you're attaching a monitor to a desktop computer, or adding a second, larger display to a laptop computer, you'll use a video port. HDMI ports are now the most common video port on computing devices.

A **high-definition multimedia interface (HDMI) port** is a compact audio–video interface that allows both HD video and uncompressed digital audio to be carried on one cable. Because HDMI can transmit uncompressed audio and video, there's no need to convert the signal, which could ultimately reduce the quality of the sound or picture. All currently available monitors, DVD players, televisions, and game consoles have at least one HDMI port (see Figure 2.38).

What ports might I encounter on older computers and peripherals? The **video graphics array (VGA) port** and the **digital video interface (DVI) port** are two ports to which older LCD monitors and televisions connect (see

FIGURE 2.36 USB connectors come in a wide variety of styles. *(TaraPatta/Shutterstock)*

FIGURE 2.37 Some Apple computers now feature the new USB-C port that supports data transfer, video output, and charging all in a single port. *(EPA/Alamy)*

FIGURE 2.38 HDMI is the latest digital connector type for HD monitors, televisions, and home theater equipment. *(Feng Yu/ Shutterstock)*

FIGURE 2.40 Expansion cards fit into slots on the motherboard in a desktop computer. *(Andrew Kitching/Alamy)*

Figure 2.39). Older Apple computers feature a Mini DisplayPort for connection of video peripherals. Adapters are available for the Mini DisplayPort that allow the connection of older DVI and VGA devices.

Adding Ports: Expansion Cards and Hubs

Objective 2.16 *List the options for adding ports to your device.*

What if I don't have all the ports I need? If you're looking to add the newest ports to an older desktop computer or to expand the number of ports on it, you can install special

FIGURE 2.39 DVI (left) and VGA (right) cables are used to connect older LCD monitors and televisions to computing devices. *(Marek Kosmal/Fotolia)*

expansion cards (see Figure 2.40) into an open expansion slot on the motherboard to provide additional ports.

Another alternative is adding an expansion hub (shown in Figure 2.41). An expansion hub is a device that connects to one port, such as a USB port, to provide additional ports. It works like the multiplug extension cords used with electrical appliances. ■

FIGURE 2.41 If you don't have enough USB ports to support your USB devices, consider getting an expansion hub, which can add four or more USB ports to your system. *(Norman Chan/ Fotolia)*

 ACTIVE HELPDESK
Exploring Storage Devices and Ports

In this Active Helpdesk, you'll play the role of a helpdesk staffer, fielding questions about the computer's main storage devices and how to connect various peripheral devices to the computer.

 SOUND BYTE
Port Tour: How Do I Hook It Up?

In this Sound Byte, you'll take a tour of both a desktop system and a laptop system to compare the number and variety of available ports. You'll also learn about the different types of ports and compare their speed and expandability.

power controls and
ERGONOMICS

Conserving energy and setting up workspaces so they are comfortable for employees are goals of many businesses. However, these are also excellent goals to strive for at your house. In the next two sections, we will explore optimizing the power consumption of computing devices as well as the proper workspace setup to minimize injuries.

Power Controls

Objective 2.17 *Describe how to manage power consumption on your computing devices.*

What's the best way to turn my computer on and off? The **power supply**, which is housed inside the system unit, transforms the wall voltage to the voltages required by computer chips. Powering on your computer from a completely turned off state, such as when you start your computer in the morning, is called a **cold boot**. In Windows 10, you can turn your computer off by displaying the Start menu, selecting Power, and then choosing the Shut down option.

Should I turn off my computer every time I'm done using it? Some people say you should leave your computer on at all times. They argue that turning your computer on and off throughout the day subjects its components to stress because the heating and cooling process forces the components to expand and contract repeatedly. Other people say you should shut down your computer when you're not using it. They claim that it's not as environmentally friendly and that you'll end up wasting money on electricity from the computer running all the time.

Modern operating systems include power-management settings that allow the most power-hungry components of the system (the hard drive and monitor) to shut down after a short idle period. With the power-management options of Windows 10, for example, you only need to shut down your computer completely when you need to repair or install hardware in the system unit or move it to another location. However, if you use your computer only for a little while each day, it would be best to power it off completely after each daily use.

Can I "rest" my computer without turning it off completely? In Windows 10, the main method of power management is Sleep. When your computer enters **Sleep mode**, all of the documents, applications, and data you were using remain in RAM (memory), where they're quickly accessible when you restart your computer.

In Sleep mode, the computer enters a state of greatly reduced power consumption, which saves energy. To put your computer into Sleep mode in Windows 10, display the Start menu, select Power, then select the Sleep option. To wake up your computer, press a key or the physical power button. In a few seconds, the

computer will resume with exactly the same programs running and documents displayed as when you put it to sleep.

If you don't ever want to completely turn off your computer, you can change what happens when you press the power button or close the lid on your laptop. By accessing the Power Options System Settings window (see Figure 2.42), you can decide if you want your computer to Sleep, Hibernate, or Shut down when you press the power button. The **Hibernate** option is similar to Sleep except that your data is stored on your hard drive instead of in RAM and your computer is powered off. This uses much less battery power than Sleep and is a good choice if you won't be using your laptop for a long time and won't have the opportunity to charge it. However, Sleep is still a good option to choose if you just won't be using your computer for a short time. You may want to set your computer so it sleeps when you close the lid but hibernates when you press the power button, giving you quick access to either option.

What's the Restart option in Windows for? If you're using Windows 10, you have the option to restart the computer when you access the Power option on the Start menu (see Figure 2.43). Restarting the system while it's powered on is called a **warm boot**. You might need to perform a warm boot if the operating system or other software application stops responding or if you've installed new programs. It takes less time to perform a warm boot than to power down completely and then restart all your hardware.

Setting It All Up: Ergonomics

Objective 2.18 *Define ergonomics, and discuss the ideal physical setup for using computing devices.*

What is ergonomics? It's important that you understand not only your computer's components and how they work together but also how to set up these components safely. **Ergonomics** is the science that deals with the design and location of machines and furniture so that the people using them aren't subjected to an uncomfortable or unsafe experience. In terms of computing, ergonomics refers to how you set up your computer and other equipment to minimize your risk of injury or discomfort.

Why is ergonomics important? Studies suggest that teenagers, on average, spend 7.5 hours per day using computing devices. When you factor in other computer uses such as playing video games, there is great potential for injury. The repetitive nature of long-term computing activities can place too much stress on joints and pull at the tendons and muscles, causing repetitive stress injuries such as carpal tunnel syndrome and tendonitis. These injuries can take months or years to develop to a point where they become painful, and by the time you notice the symptoms, the damage has already taken

FIGURE 2.42 You can determine what happens when you click the power button on your computer or close the lid through the Power Options System Settings screen. *(Windows 10, Microsoft Corporation)* >*To access Power Options System Settings, from the Start Menu, select* **Settings**, *select* **System**, *select* **Power & sleep**, *click the* **Additional power settings link**, *then select* **Choose what the power button does**.

place. If you take precautionary measures now, you may prevent years of unnecessary pain later.

How can I avoid injuries when I'm working at my computer? As Figure 2.44 illustrates, it's important to arrange your monitor, chair, body, and keyboard in ways that will help you avoid injury, discomfort, and eyestrain. The following additional guidelines can help keep you comfortable and productive:

- **Position your monitor correctly.** Studies suggest it's best to place your monitor at least 25 inches from your eyes. Experts recommend that you position your monitor either at eye level or at an angle 15–20 degrees below your line of sight.
- **Purchase an adjustable chair.** Adjust the height of your chair so that your feet touch the floor (or use a footrest to get the right position). The back support needs to be adjustable so that you can position it to support your lumbar (lower back) region. You should also be able to move the seat or adjust the back so that you can sit without exerting pressure on your knees. If your chair doesn't adjust, place a pillow behind your back to provide support.
- **Assume a proper position while typing.** Improperly positioned keyboards are one of the leading causes of repetitive stress

FIGURE 2.43 The Power option on the Windows 10 Start menu presents several power options. *(Windows 10, Microsoft Corporation)* >*For a warm boot, choose* **Restart**. *To power down the computer completely, choose* **Shut down**. *To put your computer into a lower power mode, select* **Sleep**.

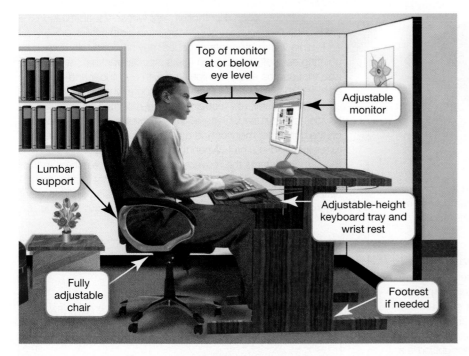

Top of monitor at or below eye level

Adjustable monitor

Lumbar support

Adjustable-height keyboard tray and wrist rest

Fully adjustable chair

Footrest if needed

FIGURE 2.44 Using proper equipment that is adjusted correctly helps prevent repetitive strain injuries while working at a computer.

- **Take breaks.** Remaining in the same position for long periods of time increases stress on your body. Shift your position in your chair and stretch your hands and fingers periodically. Likewise, staring at the screen for long periods can lead to eyestrain, so rest your eyes by periodically taking them off the screen and focusing them on an object at least 8 feet away.

- **Ensure the lighting is adequate.** Ensuring that you have proper lighting in your work area minimizes eyestrain. Eliminate sources of direct glare (light shining directly into your eyes) or reflected glare (light shining off the computer screen) and ensure there is enough light to read comfortably. If you still can't eliminate glare from your computer screen, you can buy an antiglare screen to place over your monitor.

injuries in computer users. Your wrists should be flat (not bent) with respect to the keyboard, and your forearms should be parallel to the floor. Additionally, your wrists should not be resting on the keyboard while typing. You can adjust the height of your chair or install a height-adjustable keyboard tray to ensure a proper position. Specially designed ergonomic keyboards such as the one shown in Figure 2.46 can help you achieve the proper wrist position.

Is ergonomics important when using mobile devices? Working with mobile computing devices presents interesting challenges when it comes to injury prevention. For example, many users work with laptops resting on their laps, placing the monitor outside of the optimal line of sight and thereby increasing neck strain. Figure 2.47 provides guidelines on preventing injuries when computing on the go.

So, whether you're computing at your desk or on the road, consider the ergonomics of your work environment. Doing so will help you avoid injury and discomfort.

BITS&BYTES

Save Power and Avoid Eyestrain: Use Blackle

Your computer uses less energy when it displays black as opposed to white (or other lighter colors). Also, bright colors such as white tend to increase eyestrain when viewing a computer screen (see Figure 2.45). For a quick fix, try using an alternative search engine called Blackle (**blackle.com**). Powered by Google, this customized search engine displays a predominantly black screen instead of white. Since most modern monitors don't backlight the black parts of a display, you save a little bit of energy when using this alternative search engine. Yes, it's a small amount of energy—but every little bit helps!

FIGURE 2.45 Want to save energy while reducing eyestrain? Using apps or websites that use less white and more black helps. *(Grgroup/Fotolia)*

FIGURE 2.46 Ergonomic keyboards have curved keyboards and wrist rests to help you maintain the proper hand position while typing to reduce the risk of repetitive strain injuries.
(Dmitriy Melnikov/Fotolia)

What devices are available for people with disabilities? People who have physical challenges sometimes need special devices to access computers. **Assistive** (or **adaptive**) **technology** are products, devices, equipment, or software that are used to maintain, increase, or improve the functional capabilities of individuals with disabilities. For visually impaired users and individuals who can't type with their hand, voice recognition is a common input option. For those users whose visual limitations are less severe, keyboards with larger keys are available.

People with motor control issues may have difficulty with pointing devices. To aid such users, special trackballs are available that can be easily manipulated with one finger and can be attached to almost any surface, including a wheelchair. When arm motion is severely restrained, head-mounted pointing devices can be used. Generally, these involve a camera mounted on the computer monitor and a device attached to the head (often installed in a hat). When the user moves his or her head, the camera detects the movement and moves the cursor. In this case, mouse clicks are controlled by a switch that can be manipulated by the user's hands or feet or even by using an instrument that fits into the mouth and senses the user blowing into it. ■

SOUND BYTE
Healthy Computing

In this Sound Byte, you'll see how to set up your workspace in an ergonomically correct way. You'll learn the proper location of the monitor, keyboard, and mouse, as well as ergonomic features to look for when choosing the most appropriate chair.

FIGURE 2.47

Preventing Injuries While on the Go

	SMARTPHONE REPETITIVE STRAIN INJURIES	PORTABLE MEDIA PLAYER HEARING DAMAGE	SMALL-SCREEN VISION ISSUES	LAP INJURIES	TABLET REPETITIVE STRAIN INJURIES
Malady	Repetitive strain injuries (such as DeQuervain's tendonitis) from constant typing of instant messages	Hearing loss from high-decibel sound levels in earbuds	Blurriness and dryness caused by squinting to view tiny screens on mobile devices	Burns on legs from heat generated by laptop	Pain caused from using tablets for prolonged periods in uncomfortable positions
Preventative Measures	Restrict length and frequency of messages, take breaks, and perform other motions with your thumbs and fingers during breaks to relieve tension.	Turn down volume (you should be able to hear external noises, such as people talking), use software that limits sound levels (not to exceed 60 decibels), and use external, over-ear style headphones instead of earbuds.	Blink frequently or use eye drops to maintain moisture in eyes, after 10 minutes take a break and focus on something at least 8 feet away for 5 minutes, use adequate amount of light, and increase the size of fonts.	Place a book, magazine, or laptop cooling pad between your legs and laptop.	Restrict the length of time you work at a tablet, especially typing or gaming. Use the same ergonomic position you would use for a laptop when using a tablet.

trends in IT

With the advent of the computer, many speculated that ours would become a paperless society. Instead of saving printed documents and other output as was done prior to the PC, information would be saved in a digital state: hard drives replacing filing cabinets, online photo buckets replacing photo albums and scrapbooks, and e-books replacing our favorite texts. Hard drive capacities do enable us to save more content, and online storage systems enable us to save pictures and other files to the "cloud." Additionally, e-book readers have increased in popularity. But has this push toward digital content begun to make the printer obsolete? Surprisingly, no. People still have a deep-rooted need to see, feel, mark, share, or use their digital images or information in a physical form. New technologies that push the boundaries of printing, such as printing from the cloud and 3-D printing, are being developed and refined.

Cloud Printing

To print a document from a desktop or laptop computer, you must have a printer associated with your computer. Usually, this is not a problem because at home, at school, or in the office, there is generally one printer, and all the PCs connected to it have the software and cables or wireless capabilities needed to use it. But what happens if you want to print something from your smartphone or tablet? Common solutions have been to e-mail the document to yourself or transfer the document to a web-based storage service such as Dropbox so that a printer-connected computer could access it. Another solution is Google Cloud Print, a service that lets you configure your printers so you can access them from mobile devices.

Google Cloud Print uses cloud-ready printers (see Figure 2.48) that are now available from manufacturers such as HP, Kodak, and Epson. These printers connect directly to the Internet and register themselves with Google Cloud Print without needing to be connected to a computer. Once a printer is registered with Cloud Print, printing jobs can be sent to it from mobile devices (such as tablets and smartphones) using the Internet. Conventional printers that you already own can also be registered with Cloud Print, although they require connection to the Internet through a computer.

FIGURE 2.48 Cloud-ready printers only need an Internet connection to be accessed from any mobile device.

FIGURE 2.49 3-D printing is being used to fabricate parts for all sorts of devices on demand. *(Hopsalka/Fotolia)*

3-D Printing

Printing a 3-D model of a proposed building or new prototype is common for architects and engineers. The process builds a model one layer at a time from the bottom up. The procedure begins by spreading a layer of powder on a platform. Then, depending on the technology, the printer uses nozzles similar to those in an inkjet printer to spray tiny drops of glue at specific places to solidify the powder, or the powder is solidified through a melting process. The printer repeats solidifying layers of powder until the model is built to specifications. This technology has spurred the manufacturing of a variety of consumer goods, from toys to clothing (see Figure 2.49). Shapeways (**shapeways.com**) uses 3-D printing to enable anyone to turn his or her 3-D designs into real physical models. Then, those models can be personalized, bought, or sold through Shapeways's online community.

3-D printing is being used in the medical community as well. Hearing aids are now being produced using 3-D printers and allow manufacturers to not only offer a custom fit but individual skin color matching as well (to make the devices less visible). And researchers at Wake Forest Institute for Regenerative Medicine have developed a way to use similar inkjet technologies to build heart, bone, and blood vessel tissues in the lab. They have also developed a way to "print" restorative cells directly into a soldier's wound at the site where the injury occurred, thus significantly improving the soldier's chances of survival.

Taking traditional technologies, such as inkjet printing, and applying them to solve current human struggles is a long and tedious process, but without these pioneers experimenting with different applications, society would advance a lot more slowly.

Before moving on to the Chapter Review:
1. Watch Replay Video 2.2 ▶.
2. Then check your understanding of what you've learned so far.

check your understanding // review & practice

For a quick review to see what you've learned so far, answer the following questions.

multiple choice

1. Which of the following is NOT found on a motherboard?

   a. RAM

   b. CPU

   c. sound card

   d. hard drive

2. Which of these is an example of optical storage media?

   a. DVD

   b. SSD

   c. thumb drive

   d. a flash memory card

3. Which of the following is the fastest data transfer port?

   a. HDMI

   b. VGA

   c. USB 3.1

   d. Thunderbolt

4. Which of these is considered volatile storage?

   a. SSD

   b. ROM

   c. RAM

   d. thumb drive

5. Which power control option performs a warm boot?

   a. Restart

   b. Sleep

   c. Log off

   d. Shut down

(MyITLab) Go to **MyITLab** to take an autograded version of the *Check Your Understanding* review and to find all media resources for the chapter.

TECHBYTES WEEKLY
Stay current with the TechBytes Weekly Newsletter.

Continue »»

2 Chapter Review

summary //

Understanding Digital Components

Learning Outcome 2.1 You will be able to describe the devices that make up a computer system.

Understanding Your Computer

Objective 2.1 *Describe the four main functions of a computer system and how they interact with data and information.*

- The computer's four major functions are:
(1) input: gather data or allow users to enter data;
(2) process: manipulate, calculate, or organize that data; (3) output: display data and information in a form suitable for the user; and (4) storage: save data and information for later use.
- Data is a representation of a fact or idea. The number 3 and the words *televisions* and *Sony* are pieces of data.
- Information is data that has been organized or presented in a meaningful fashion. An inventory list that indicates that 3 Sony televisions are in stock is processed information. It allows a retail clerk to answer a customer query about the availability of merchandise. Information is more powerful than raw data.

Objective 2.2 *Define bits and bytes, and describe how they are measured, used, and processed.*

- To process data into information, computers need to work in a language they understand. This language, called *binary language*, consists of two numbers: 0 and 1. Each 0 and each 1 is a binary digit or bit. Eight bits create one byte.
- In computers, each letter of the alphabet, each number, and each special character consists of a unique combination of eight bits (one byte)—a string of eight 0s and 1s.
- For describing large amounts of storage capacity, the terms *megabyte* (approximately 1 million bytes), *gigabyte* (approximately 1 billion bytes), *terabyte* (approximately 1 trillion bytes), and *petabyte* (1,000 terabytes) are used.

Objective 2.3 *List common types of computers, and discuss their main features.*

- A tablet computer is a portable computer integrated into a flat multitouch-sensitive screen.
- A laptop or notebook computer is a portable computer that has a keyboard, monitor, and other devices integrated into a single compact case.
- An ultrabook is a lightweight laptop computer featuring low-power processors and solid-state drives.
- Chromebook computers use the Google Chrome OS. Documents and apps are stored primarily in the cloud.
- Desktop computers consist of a separate case (called the system unit) that houses the main components of the computer plus peripheral devices.

Input Devices

Objective 2.4 *Identify the main types of keyboards and touch screens.*

- You use keyboards to enter typed data and commands. Most keyboards use the QWERTY layout.
- Touch screens are display screens that respond to commands initiated by a touch with a finger or a stylus.
- Wireless keyboards mainly use Bluetooth connectivity and provide alternatives to on-screen keyboards.

Objective 2.5 *Describe the main types of mice and pointing devices.*

- Mice are used to enter user responses and commands.
- Optical mice use a laser to detect mouse movement.
- Some mice can be adjusted to provide better ergonomics for users.
- Laptops have integrated pointing devices called touch pads (trackpads).

Objective 2.6 *Explain how images and sounds are input into computing devices.*

- Images are input into the computer with scanners, digital cameras, camcorders, and smartphones.
- Live video is captured with webcams and digital video recorders.
- Microphones capture sounds. There are many different types of microphones, including desktop, headset, and clip-on models.

Output Devices

Objective 2.7 *Name common types of monitors, and identify important aspects of their quality.*

- Monitors display soft copies of text, graphics, and video.
- Liquid crystal display (LCD) and light-emitting diode (LED) are the most common types of computer monitors.
- OLED displays use organic compounds to produce light and don't require a backlight, which saves energy.
- Aspect ratio, screen resolution, contrast ratio, viewing angle, brightness, and response time are key aspects to consider when choosing a monitor.

Objective 2.8 *Describe various types of printers, and explain when you would use them.*

- Printers create hard copies of text and graphics.
- There are two primary categories of printers: inkjet and laser. Laser printers usually print faster and deliver higher-quality output than inkjet printers. However, inkjet printers can be more economical for casual printing needs.
- Specialty printers are also available such as all-in-one printers, large format printers, and thermal printers.
- When choosing a printer, you should be aware of factors such as speed, resolution, color output, and cost of consumables.

Objective 2.9 *Discuss options for outputting sound from your computing devices.*

- Speakers are the output devices for sound. Most computers include basic speakers.
- More sophisticated systems include subwoofers and surround sound.
- Headphone or earbuds are useful to avoid disturbing others.

Processing, Storage, and Connectivity

Learning Outcome 2.2 You will be able to describe how computers process and store data and how devices connect to a computer system.

Processing and Memory on the Motherboard

Objective 2.10 *Define motherboard and RAM.*

- The motherboard, the main circuit board of the system, contains a computer's CPU, which coordinates the functions of all other devices on the computer.
- The motherboard also houses slots for expansion cards, which have specific functions that augment the computer's basic functions. Typical expansion cards are sound and video cards.
- RAM, the computer's volatile memory, is also located on the motherboard. RAM is where all the data and instructions are held while the computer is running.

Objective 2.11 *Explain the main functions of the CPU.*

- The CPU controls all the functions performed by the computer's other components. The CPU also processes all commands issued to it by software instructions.
- The performance of a CPU is affected by the speed of the processor (measured in GHz), the amount of cache memory, and the number of processing cores.

Storing Data and Information

Objective 2.12 *List the various types of hard drives.*

- The internal hard drive is your computer's primary device for permanent storage of software and files. The hard drive is a nonvolatile storage device, meaning it holds the data and instructions your computer needs permanently, even after the computer is turned off.

- SSD drives have no moving parts so they are more energy efficient and less susceptible to damage.
- External hard drives are essentially internal hard drives that have been made portable by enclosing them in a protective case and making them small and lightweight.

Objective 2.13 *Define cloud storage, and explain how to use it.*

- Cloud storage refers to nonvolatile storage locations that are maintained on the Internet (in the "cloud"). Examples are OneDrive, Google Drive, and Dropbox.
- Storing your data in the cloud allows you to access it from almost any computing device that is connected to the Internet.

Objective 2.14 *Describe the various portable and optical storage options.*

- Optical drives that can read from and write to CD, DVD, or Blu-ray discs are another means of permanent, portable storage. Data is saved to CDs, DVDs, and Blu-ray discs as pits that are burned into the disc by a laser.
- Flash drives are another portable means of storing data. Flash drives plug into USB ports.
- Flash memory cards let you transfer digital data between your computer and devices such as digital cameras, smartphones, video cameras, and printers.

Connecting Peripherals to the Computer

Objective 2.15 *List the common types of ports used today.*

- The fastest type of port used to connect devices to a computer is the Thunderbolt port.
- The most common type of port used to connect devices to a computer is the USB port.
- Connectivity ports, such as Ethernet ports, give you access to networks and the Internet.

- HDMI ports are the most common multimedia port. They are used to connect monitors, TVs, and gaming consoles to computing devices and handle both audio and video data.
- Audio ports are used to connect headphones, microphones, and speakers to computing devices.

Objective 2.16 *List the options for adding ports to your device.*

- Expansion cards can be plugged into the motherboard on desktop computers to add ports.
- Expansion hubs can be plugged into existing ports to provide additional ports of the same type.

Power Controls and Ergonomics

Objective 2.17 *Describe how to manage power consumption on your computing devices.*

- Turning off your computer when you won't be using it for long periods of time saves energy. In Windows 10, you can turn your computer off by accessing the Power option on the Start menu, then selecting Shut down.
- If you are not using your computer for short periods of time, selecting the Sleep option will help your computer save energy but allows it to be quickly "awakened" for use.

Objective 2.18 *Define ergonomics, and discuss the ideal physical setup for using computing devices.*

- Ergonomics refers to how you arrange your computer and equipment to minimize your risk of injury or discomfort.
- Achieving proper ergonomics includes positioning your monitor correctly, buying an adjustable chair, assuming a proper position while typing, making sure the lighting is adequate, and not looking at the screen for long periods. Other good practices include taking frequent breaks and using specially designed equipment such as ergonomic keyboards.
- Ergonomics is also important to consider when using mobile devices.

 Be sure to check out **MyITLab** for additional materials to help you review and learn. And don't forget the Replay Videos. ⟳

key terms //

chapter quiz // assessment

For a quick review to see what you've learned, answer the following questions. Submit the quiz as requested by your instructor. If you are using **MyITLab**, the quiz is also available there.

multiple choice

1. What is a gigabyte?

   a. one billion bytes

   b. one trillion bytes

   c. one billion bits

   d. one million bits

2. Which of the following is NOT an output device?

   a. touch-screen monitor

   b. optical mouse

   c. speakers

   d. laser printer

3. Monitor screens are made up of millions of tiny dots known as

   a. bytes.

   b. resolution points.

   c. pixels.

   d. bits.

4. Which of these is located on the motherboard?

   a. SSD drive

   b. RAM

   c. Hard drive

   d. DVD drive

5. Which of these is an optical storage device?

   a. flash drive

   b. SSD drive

   c. External hard drive

   d. Blu-ray drive

6. Ergonomics is an important consideration

   a. only for desktop computers.

   b. only for laptop computers.

   c. only for laptop and desktop computers, but never for mobile devices.

   d. for all computing devices.

true/false

1. Data and information are interchangeable terms.

2. Microsoft Word is a type of application software.

3. The fastest data transfer port is an HDMI port.

4. A typical CPU can complete billions of machine cycles in one second.

critical thinking

1. **Computers of the Future**

   Embedded computers keep turning up in new places. They can be found in cars, household appliances, smoke detectors, and thermostats too, enabling us to interact with even more of these "smart" devices every day. What common objects do you think might benefit from an embedded computer? What capabilities can you envision?

2. **New Display Features**

   The display screen of the future may be paper-thin, flexible, and transparent. Companies like Samsung and LG are already working on it. What uses can you envision for this new technology? What advantages and disadvantages do you foresee? Do you have any suggestions for the manufacturers to help make this successful?

Data Storage Options

Problem

You've joined a small business that's beginning to evaluate its technology setup. Because of the addition of several new sales representatives and other administrative employees, the company needs to reconsider the various ways its data is stored. You've been asked to evaluate options for on-site and off-site data storage.

Task

Split your class into teams of three and assign the following tasks:

- Member A explores the benefits and downfalls of cloud storage.
- Member B explores the benefits and downfalls of external hard drives.
- Member C explores the benefits and downfalls of portable storage devices.

Process

1. Think about what the storage needs are for the company and what information and resources you will need to tackle this project.

2. Research and then discuss the components of each method you're recommending. Are any of these options better suited for the particular needs of certain types of employees (sales representatives versus administrative staff)? Consider the types of data to be stored. Is some data confidential? How long should it be retained?

3. Consider the different types of employees in the company. Would a combination of methods be better than a single solution? If so, what kinds of employees would use which type of storage?

4. As a team, write a summary position paper. Support your recommendation for the company. Each team member should include why his or her data storage option will or will not be part of the solution.

Conclusion

There are advantages and disadvantages to any data storage option. Being aware of the pros and cons and knowing which method is best for a particular scenario or employee will help you to become a better consumer as well as a better computer user.

Green Computing

Ethical conduct is a stream of decisions you make all day long. In this exercise, you'll research and then role-play a complicated ethical situation. The role you play may or may not match your own personal beliefs, but your research and use of logic will enable you to represent whichever view is assigned. An arbitrator will watch and comment on both sides of the arguments, and together, the team will agree on an ethical solution.

Background

Green computing—conducting computing needs with the least possible amount of power and impact on the environment—is on everyone's minds. Although it's hard to argue with an environmentally conscious agenda, the pinch to our pocketbooks and the loss of some comforts sometimes make green computing difficult. Businesses, including colleges, need to consider a variety of issues and concerns before jumping into a complete green overhaul.

Research Areas to Consider

End-of-life management: e-waste and recycling

- Energy-efficient devices
- Renewable resources used in computer manufacturing
- Costs of green computing
- Government funding and incentives

Process

1. Divide the class into teams.
2. Research the areas cited above and devise a scenario in which your college is considering modifying its current technology setup to a more green information technology (IT) strategy.
3. Team members should write a summary that provides background information for their character—for example, environmentalist, college IT administrator, or arbitrator—and that details their character's behaviors to set the stage for the role-playing event. Then, team members should create an outline to use during the role-playing event.
4. Team members should arrange a mutually convenient time to meet, using a virtual meeting tool or by meeting in person.
5. Team members should present their case to the class or submit a PowerPoint presentation for review by the rest of the class, along with the summary and resolution they developed.

Conclusion

As technology becomes ever more prevalent and integrated into our lives, more and more ethical dilemmas will present themselves. Being able to understand and evaluate both sides of the argument, while responding in a personally or socially ethical manner, will be an important skill.

Technology Wish List

You are in need of a significant technology upgrade, and your parents have told you they will help you finance your purchases by loaning you the money. You will need to repay them with a modest 2.5% interest rate over two years. The only catch is that they want you to create a list of all the new devices that you need, note the cost, and provide a website for each device where they can find more information. Then, they want you to calculate how much you will need to give them each month to pay them back.

You will use the following skills as you complete this activity:

- Merge and Center
- Modify Workbook Themes
- Apply Number Formats
- Use the SUM, PMT, and COUNTA Functions

- Modify Column Widths
- Insert a Hyperlink
- Create a Formula
- Wrap Text

Instructions:

1. Open *TIA_Ch2_Start* and save as **TIA_Ch2_LastFirst**.

2. Format the title in cell A1 with the **Title Cell Style**, and format the column headers in cells A3:F3 with the **Heading 3 Cell Style**.
   a. Hint: To format cell styles, on the Home tab, in the Styles group, click **Cell Styles**.

3. **Merge and Center** cell A1 across columns A through F, and **Center align** the column headers in cells A3:F3.
   a. Hint: To Merge and Center text, on the Home tab, in the Alignment group, click **Merge & Center**.

4. Modify column widths so that Column A is **25** and Column D is **45**.
   a. Hint: To modify column widths, on the Home tab, in the Cells group, click **Format**, and then select **Column Width**.

5. In cells B4:F9, fill in the table with the Brand and Model of the six devices that you would like to purchase. The device type is filled out for you. In the *Reason* column, write a brief note as to why this device will help you. (You'll format the text so it all displays later.) Enter the cost of the device in the Cost column. Don't include tax and/or shipping.

6. Change the Workbook Theme to **Integral**.
   a. Hint: To apply the Theme, on the Page Layout tab, in the Themes group, click **Themes**.

7. In cells F4:F9, create a **Hyperlink** to a webpage that features each respective product so your grandparents can have access to more information if they need it. Ensure that each hyperlink includes the URL to the exact webpage for the device in the Address, but displays the Make/Model of the device in the worksheet.
   a. Hint: To insert a hyperlink, on the Insert tab, in the Links group, click **Hyperlink**. In the Insert Hyperlink dialog box, enter the URL in the Address: box and enter the Make/Model in the Text to display box.

8. Wrap the text in cells C4:C9, D4:D9, and F4:F9 so all text displays.
   a. Hint: To wrap text, on the Home tab, in the Alignment group, click **Wrap Text**.

9. Format the values in cells E4:E9 with the **Accounting Number format with two decimals**.

10. In cell A10, type **Subtotal**, then in cell E10, use a **SUM function** to calculate the total cost of all devices. Format the results in the **Accounting Number format with two decimals**.

11. In cell A11, type **Estimated Tax**, then in cell E11, create a formula that references the subtotal in cell E10 and multiplies it by a tax of 6%. Format the results in the **Accounting Number format with two decimals**.

12. In cell A12, type **Estimated Shipping**, then in cell E12, create a formula to calculate the shipping charge by using the **COUNTA function** to determine the number of devices being purchased and then multiplying that by a $10 shipping charge. Format the results in **Accounting Number Format with two decimals**.

13. In cell A13, type **Total Cost**, then in cell E13, use the **SUM function** to create a formula that adds up the *Subtotal*, *Estimated Tax*, and *Estimated Shipping costs*. Format the results in **Accounting Number Format with two decimals**. Format the cells A13:E13 with the **Total Cell Style**.

14. **Right align** cells A10:A13.

15. In cell D14, type **Estimated Monthly Payment**, and then in cell E14, use the **PMT function** to calculate the monthly payment owed to your parents to pay back the total purchase amount in two years at a 2.5% annual interest rate.

16. Save the workbook and submit based on your instructor's directions.

3

Using the Internet: Making the Most of the Web's Resources

Make This: MAKE: A Web-Capable App on **page 91**

All media accompanying this chapter can be found in MyITLab.

For an overview of the chapter, watch the **Preview Video.**

(Dny3d/Fotolia, Marish/Shutterstock, Gheatza/Fotolia, Maksym Yemelyanov/Fotolia, HaywireMedia/Fotolia, Totallypic/Fotolia)

HOW COOL IS THIS?

Have you ever wanted to **share your computer screen** with someone but couldn't because you didn't know how or didn't have the right software? Now you can share your computer screen **with anyone on any device via the web** with one click, hassle-free, with **Screenleap (screenleap.com)**.

All you need to do is **click a link that generates a code**, then send the code to whomever you want to share your screen with; they will be able to view your screen immediately from their web browser on their smartphone, tablet, or PC. You can share your screen publically or privately to only a select few. There is also an extension to initiate sharing directly from your Gmail account. Using this technology may help you **better communicate** with classmates or your professors when seeking or offering help. **A free account** will give you two hours of sharing time per day. So, share your screen with someone today with Screenleap! *(By studio/Fotolia)*

Working and Playing on the Web

Learning Outcome 3.1 **You will be able to explain how the Internet works and how it is used for collaboration, communication, commerce, and entertainment purposes.**

You most likely know at least a little bit about how to use the web's resources to communicate and collaborate with others, how to work with multimedia files, and how business is conducted over the web. In this section, we'll explore these and other topics. But first, let's start with a brief lesson on the history of the Internet.

the internet and how
IT WORKS

It's hard to imagine life without the Internet. The Internet is actually a network of networks that connects billions of computer users globally, but its beginnings were much more modest.

The Origin of the Internet

Objective 3.1 *Describe how the Internet got its start.*

Why was the Internet created? The concept of the **Internet**—the largest computer network in the world—was developed in the late 1950s while the United States was in the midst of the Cold War with the Soviet Union (see Figure 3.1). At that time, the U.S. Department of Defense needed a computer network that wouldn't be disrupted easily in the event of an attack.

FIGURE 3.1 How the Internet Began

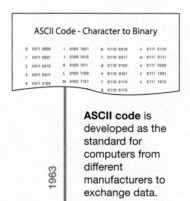

ASCII Code - Character to Binary

0	0011 0000	I	0100 1001	b	0110 0010	v	0111 0110
1	0011 0001	J	0100 1010	c	0110 0011	w	0111 0111
2	0011 0010	K	0100 1011	d	0110 0100	x	0111 1000
3	0011 0011	L	0100 1100	e	0110 0101	y	0111 1001
4	0011 0100	M	0100 1101	f	0110 0110	z	0111 1010
				g	0110 0110		

1958 The **Advanced Research Projects Agency (ARPA)** is established for the U.S. Department of Defense. This agency creates the ARPANET—the beginnings of the Internet.

1963 **ASCII code** is developed as the standard for computers from different manufacturers to exchange data.

1969 Researchers at UCLA **send the first message via a networked computer system** to researchers at Stanford University.

1964 A **new network scheme** is developed with multiple paths so if one communication path was destroyed (from a potential Soviet Union attack), the rest of the network would still be able to communicate.

(Cristi180884/Shutterstock)

At the same time, researchers for the Department of Defense were trying to get different computers to work with each other using a common communications method that all computers could use. The Internet was created to respond to these two concerns: establishing a *secure* form of communications and creating a means by which *all* computers could communicate.

Who invented the Internet? The modern Internet evolved from an early U.S. government-funded "internetworking" project called the Advanced Research Projects Agency Network (ARPANET). ARPANET began as a four-node network involving UCLA, Stanford Research Institute, the University of California at Santa Barbara, and the University of Utah in Salt Lake City. The first real communication occurred in 1969 between the computer at Stanford and the computer at UCLA. Although the system crashed after the third letter of "Login" was transmitted, it was the beginning of a revolution. Many people participated in the creation of the ARPANET, but two men, Vinton Cerf and Robert Kahn, are generally acknowledged as the "fathers of the Internet." These men earned this honor because in the 1970s, they were primarily responsible for developing the communications protocols (standards) still in use on the Internet today.

So are the web and the Internet the same thing? Because the **World Wide Web** (**WWW** or the **web**) is what we use the most, we sometimes think of the Internet and the web as being interchangeable. However, the web is only a subset of the Internet, dedicated to broadcasting HTML pages; it is the means by which we access information over the Internet. The web is based on the Hypertext Transfer Protocol (HTTP),
which is why you see an *http://* at the beginning of web addresses. What distinguishes the web from the rest of the Internet is its use of the following:

- Common communications protocols that enable computers to talk to each other and display information in compatible formats
- Special links that enable users to navigate from one place to another on the web

Who created the web? The web began in 1991. It was based on a protocol developed by Tim Berners-Lee, a physicist at the European Organization for Nuclear Research (CERN), who wanted a method for linking his research documents so that other researchers could access them. In conjunction with Robert Cailliau, Berners-Lee developed the basic architecture of the web and created the first *web browser*, software that lets you display and interact with text and other media on the web. The original browser could handle only text. Then, in 1993, the Mosaic browser, which could display graphics as well as text, was released. The once-popular Netscape Navigator browser evolved from Mosaic and heralded the beginning of the web's monumental growth.

How the Internet Works

Objective 3.2 *Explain how data travels on the Internet.*

How does the Internet work? All computers and other devices such as tablets and smartphones that are connected

Vincent Cerf and Robert develop a set of communication rules–the **TCP/IP protocol**–that allow different types of computers to communicate.

1973

Tim Berners-Lee developed and made public **HTTP protocol and the World Wide Web**. WWW is a subset of the Internet that is connected via hypertext (text containing hyperlinks to other documents and media).

1991

1972

Ray Tomlinson writes a program to send **e-mail** over the ARPANET and develops the "user@host" convention.

1978

By 1978, there were 111 Internet domains on ARPANET.

1997

By 1997, there were over 1 million Internet domains on ARPANET.

Internet Domains (1989–1997)

Domains
1,600,000
1,400,000
1,200,000
1,000,000
800,000
600,000
400,000
200,000
0

Jul-89 Dec-89 May-90 Oct-90 Mar-91 Aug-91 Jan-92 Jun-92 Nov-92 Apr-93 Sep-93 Feb-94 Jul-94 Dec-94 May-95 Oct-95 Mar-96 Aug-96 Jan-97 Jun-97

BITS&BYTES

Ever Heard of Internet2?

Although Internet2 may sound like a new and separate network meant to replace the Internet, this is not the case. Internet2 is actually a consortium of U.S. leaders in education, research, industry, and government that seeks to expand the possibilities of the existing Internet by developing new technologies and applications and then deploying them to the public. These experimental technologies require a faster and more efficient Internet, so the researchers use separate data lines that support extremely high-speed communications—up to 8.8 terabits per second (Tbps). In fact, many of the Internet's current technologies are possible because of the research done by the Internet2 consortium.

to the Internet create a network of networks. These Internet-connected devices communicate with each other in turns, just as we do when we ask a question or reply with an answer. Thus, a computer (or other device) connected to the Internet acts in one of two ways: Either it's a **client**, a computer that asks for data, or it's a **server**, a computer that receives the request and returns the data to the client. Because the Internet uses clients and servers, it's referred to as a **client/server network**.

When a client computer puts out a request for information from the server computer, the request travels along transmission lines. These transmission lines are similar to our highway

system of roads, with some roads having different speed limits. The transmission lines with the fastest speeds are referred to as **Internet backbones**.

How do computers talk to each other? Suppose you want to order something from Amazon.com. Figure 3.2 illustrates what happens when you type **www.amazon.com** into your web browser and when Amazon's home page displays on your computer monitor. As you can see, the data request from your computer (the client computer) is sent via Internet communication pathways to a server computer. The server computer (in this case, Amazon's server) processes the request and returns the requested data to your client computer via Internet communication pathways. The data reply most likely takes a different route than did the data request. The web browser on your client computer interprets the data and displays it on its monitor.

How does the data get sent to the correct computer? Each time you connect to the Internet, your computer is assigned a unique identification number. This number, called an **Internet Protocol (IP) address**, is a set of four groups of numbers separated by periods, such as 123.45.245.91, and is commonly referred to as a *dotted quad* or *dotted decimal*. IP addresses are the means by which computers connected to the Internet identify each other. Similarly, each website is assigned a unique IP address. However, because the numbers that make up IP addresses are difficult for people to remember, websites are given text versions of their IP addresses. So, Amazon's website has an IP address of 72.21.211.176 and a name of **www.amazon.com**. When you type **"www.amazon.com"** into your browser, your computer (with its unique IP address) looks for Amazon's IP address (72.21.211.176). Data is exchanged between Amazon's server computer and your computer using these unique IP addresses. ■

STEP 4: The server returns the requested data to your computer using the fastest pathway, which may be different from the one the request took.

Amazon.com's server

STEP 3: Your data flows along the backbone and on to smaller pathways until it reaches its destination, which is the server computer for Amazon's website.

HTML

STEP 5: The web browser interprets the data and displays it on your monitor.

Client

STEP 1: You enter www.amazon.com in your web browser. Your computer is the client requesting information from Amazon.com's website.

URL

STEP 2: The request is sent to the server via a system of data pathways, similar to a roadway system.

FIGURE 3.2 How the Internet's Client/Server Model Works
(Sashkin/Fotolia, peshkov/Fotolia)

collaborating and communicating
ON THE WEB

In this section, we'll explore some popular means of collaborating and communicating on the web.

Collaborating with Web 2.0 Tools

Objective 3.3 *Discuss the tools and technologies used to collaborate and communicate on the web.*

How do we collaborate and communicate on the web? Over time, our use of the web has evolved from passively browsing web pages that were created for us, to actively creating our own web content and sharing and collaborating on it with others. This new collaborative, user-created web, sometimes classified as the *social web*, in which the user is also a participant, is possible due to the advancement of **Web 2.0** technologies. Web 2.0 technologies enable us to collaborate with others through web applications such as Google Drive, to rate and recommend products or services with Yelp, to tag a friend on social networks such as Facebook, and to share a video on YouTube or a favorite image on Pinterest. These means of Web 2.0 communication are collectively called **social media** and include social networking, wikis, blogs, podcasts, and webcasts.

Social Networking

Is there more to social networking than Facebook? As you probably know, **social networking** refers to using the web to communicate and share information among your friends and others. Professional, business-oriented online networks such as LinkedIn are helpful for members seeking potential clients, business opportunities, jobs, or job candidates. Like a true business network, these sites can help you meet other professionals through the people you already know. In addition, businesses use social networking for marketing and communicating directly with their customers. For example, companies may post special deals and offers on their Facebook page or solicit responses from followers that may help with product development or future marketing campaigns.

Figure 3.3 shows various sites that are considered Web 2.0 social networking sites. As you can see, there is more to social networking than just Facebook and Twitter.

What are some dos and don'ts of social networking? When social networking sites first became popular, there was concern over privacy issues, especially for school-aged children who put personal information on their pages without considering the possibility of that information being misused by a stalker or identity thief. Although

those concerns still exist, many of the most popular social networking sites have improved their privacy policies, thereby reducing, but not eliminating, such concerns. Still, users must be cautious about the type of content they post on these sites. Consider these precautions as you use social networking sites:

- Keep your personal information personal. The year you were born, your physical address, and the routines of your life (sports games, practices, work schedules) should not be broadcast to the general public.
- Know who your friends are, and know who can see the information you post. Review your privacy settings periodically, as sites change and update their privacy practices frequently.
- Do not post information such as your favorite teacher or your first pet's name because these are often used as security questions to verify your identity.
- Use caution when posting images, and know what images others are posting of you. Although privacy settings may offer some comfort, some images may be available for viewing through search engines and may not require site registration to be seen. Online images may become public property and subject to reproduction, and you might not want some—or any—of those images to be distributed.

Many employers and colleges use social networks as a means of gaining information about potential applicants before granting an interview or extending admission or a job offer. In fact, there have been instances of people being fired from their jobs and being expelled from school for using social media, such as Facebook, Twitter, and blogs, in a questionable way. Generally, questionable content on social media includes negative discussion about the poster's job, employer, or colleagues or inappropriate content about the poster. The responsibility for your content rests with you. Even though you may have strong privacy settings, you can't control what those who you allow to see your content do with it. Therefore, treat all information posted on the web as public, and avoid posting damaging words and pictures. Bottom line: Make sure your profile, images, and site content project an image that positively and accurately represents you.

Wikis and Project Collaboration Tools

What is a wiki? Rather than needing to pass documents back and forth via e-mail and possibly losing track of which version is the most recent, wikis are a great alternative. A **wiki** is a web application that allows users to add, remove, or edit its content. Wiki content is created collaboratively by multiple users, resulting in an emergent "common" opinion rather than the opinion of an individual writer. Wikis allow all who have

(Kevin Britland/Alamy; M4OS Photos/Alamy; Anil Kumar/Alamy; Kristoffer Tripplaar/Alamy; PhotoEdit/Alamy; TP/Alamy; TP/Alamy; Web Pix/Alamy; PhotoEdit/Alamy; Shutterstock; M4OS Photos/Alamy; NetPics/Alamy)

FIGURE 3.3

Types of Social Networking Sites

	DESCRIPTION	SUGGESTED URLS
Social Exchange Networks	Allow users to connect with others, provide status updates	facebook.com twitter.com
Create Your Own Social Networks	Allow users to create their own social network around a common topic; groups can be public or private	ning.com
Business-Related Social Networks	Allow users to seek potential clients, business opportunities, jobs, or job candidates	linkedin.com
Media Sharing Networks	Allow users to share pictures and videos	youtube.com instagram.com pinterest.com
Information Sharing Networks	Allow users to share information	delicious.com wikipedia.org slideshare.net
Information Recommendations and Filtering (Bookmarking) Networks	Allow users to post their opinion of a product, service, news, or web item for others to see and use	reddit.com digg.com

access to the wiki page to post their ideas and modify the content of the current version of a single document. Wikis provide the extra benefit of users being able to access, review, and even revert to past versions at any time.

Wikipedia (**wikipedia.org**), the popular collaborative online encyclopedia, is one example of a wiki. Wiki content such as that found on Wikipedia is created collaboratively by multiple users. Because of wiki technology, Wikipedia's content can be updated continually. The Wikimedia Foundation, which hosts Wikipedia, also hosts other collaborative projects, such as Wikibooks (textbooks), Wikiversity (learning tools), and Wikisource (a document library). These wiki-type collaborative efforts apply to a variety of other useful applications. For example, wikiHow (**wikihow.com**) is an online project that uses both wikis and the collaborative process to build a large, online how-to manual.

Note that some web-based document products, such as Google Drive (**drive.google.com**), have wiki-like features to promote similar online collaboration, and specific wiki software, such as Wikispaces (**wikispaces.com**) and MediaWiki (**mediawiki.org**), is available that you can download for free.

What other web tools are used to help with project collaborations? In addition to using wikis and wiki-like documents, other tools such as videoconferencing, screen sharing, and project management tools are used to facilitate collaboration. There are full-featured business enterprise solutions, but for smaller collaborative projects, such as those you might encounter in a group project for school or in a small business environment, there are a wide variety of web-based options to choose from, many of which are free. **Project management tools** incorporate tasks and calendars so the individual components as well as the entire project can stay on schedule. Trello, for example, is a free project management

BITS&BYTES

Why Isn't Wikipedia Good to Use as a Source for a Research Paper?

The idea behind content that is managed and edited by many users, such as that found on Wikipedia and other large public wikis, is that the group will keep the content current and valid. However, because wikis are publicly editable, they can't be trusted completely. If a user adds erroneous content, the community of users can catch and correct it, but if you used Wikipedia as a source, you may have referenced erroneous content before it was corrected. To help address these concerns, Wikipedia has implemented tighter access controls, requiring users who want editing privileges to register with the site, but the risks still remain. Citizendium (**citizendium.org**), another open wiki encyclopedia, requires contributors to provide real names and sign an ethics pledge, and all postings are monitored.

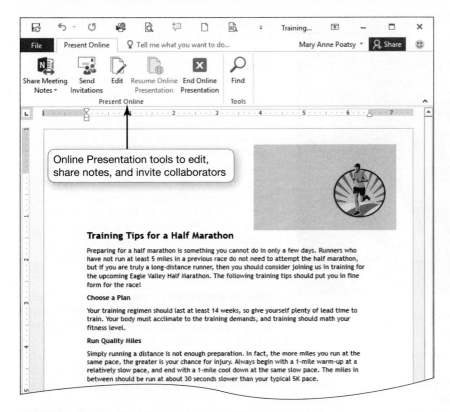

Online Presentation tools to edit, share notes, and invite collaborators

Training Tips for a Half Marathon

Preparing for a half marathon is something you cannot do in only a few days. Runners who have not run at least 5 miles in a previous race do not need to attempt the half marathon, but if you are truly a long-distance runner, then you should consider joining us in training for the upcoming Eagle Valley Half Marathon. The following training tips should put you in fine form for the race!

Choose a Plan

Your training regimen should last at least 14 weeks, so give yourself plenty of lead time to train. Your body must acclimate to the training demands, and training should math your fitness level.

Run Quality Miles

Simply running a distance is not enough preparation. In fact, the more miles you run at the same pace, the greater is your chance for injury. Always begin with a 1-mile warm-up at a relatively slow pace, and end with a 1-mile cool down at the same slow pace. The miles in between should be run at about 30 seconds slower than your typical 5K pace.

FIGURE 3.4 You can present a Word document or PowerPoint presentation to an online audience using built-in technology in Microsoft Office. *(Microsoft Word 2016, Windows 10, Microsoft Corporation; Patrimonio designs/Fotolia)*

tool that organizes projects onto boards and specific tasks onto cards. Cards can contain checklists, images, labels, discussion notes, and the like. All cards are searchable, shareable, and can have reminders.

When working with a group whose members are not in the same location, screen sharing or videoconferencing software can be helpful. Products such as Join.me and Screenleap (see the How Cool Is This? feature on page 75) offer free screen-sharing solutions. In addition, built into the latest versions of Microsoft Word and PowerPoint is the capability to present online (see Figure 3.4). When you initiate Present Online, a link is generated that you share with the desired recipients, and then anyone who uses the link can see the slide show or document while you are presenting online. Skype and Google Hangouts are also handy solutions for videoconferencing.

Blogs

Why do people write blogs? A **blog** (short for **weblog**) is a personal log or journal posted on the web. Anyone can create

SOUND BYTE
Blogging

In this Sound Byte, you'll see why blogs are one of today's most popular publishing mediums. You'll also learn how to create and publish your own blog.

a blog, and there are millions of blogs available to read, follow, and comment on. Blogs are generally written by a single author and are arranged as a listing of entries on a single page, with the most recent blog entry appearing at the top of the list. In addition, blogs are public and readers can post comments on your blog, often creating an engaging, interactive experience. Blogs have searchable and organized content, making them user friendly. They're accessible from anywhere using a web browser.

Many people use blogs as a sort of personal scrapbook. Whenever the urge strikes, they report on their daily activities. Many other blogs focus on a particular topic (see Figure 3.5). For example, the Movie Blog (**themovieblog.com**) contains reviews and opinions about movies, and Engadget (**engadget.com**) is a blog devoted to discussing technogadgets. Many corporations, such as Walmart and Best Buy, have blogs written by employees. BlogCatalog (**blogcatalog.com**) is a blog directory that can help you find blogs that fit your interests.

Are all blogs text-based? The traditional form of a blog is primarily text-based but may also include images and audio. A **video log** (**vlog** or **video blog**) is a blog that uses video as the primary content (although it can also contain text, images, and audio). Vlogs are a popular means of personal expression, and many can be found by searching YouTube (**youtube.com**).

How do I create a blog? Many websites provide the tools you need to create your own blog. Two sites that offer free blog hosting are Blogger (**blogger.com**) and WordPress (**wordpress.com**). Such tools also let you add features like pictures or subpages to your blog. You can also choose to host your blog yourself so that the URL reflects your name or the name of your business. If you choose this option, you'll need your own website and a URL so people can access it.

Are there any problems with blogs? The popularity of blogs has brought about a new problem—*spam blogs* (*splogs*)—which are artificially created blog sites filled with fake articles or stolen text (a tactic known as *blog scraping*). Splogs, which contain links to other sites associated with the splog's creator, have the intention of either increasing traffic to, or increasing search engine rankings for, these usually disreputable or useless websites. Although not really harmful, splogs are another unwanted form of content that continues to grow like weeds on the web.

Are Twitter and Tumblr considered blogs? Twitter and Tumblr are examples of *microblogs*, where users post short text with usually frequent updates. With Twitter, the posts are limited to 140 characters. Tumblr allows users to post multimedia and other content. Posts can be public or restricted to a certain audience.

FIGURE 3.5 Many online news and radio sites offer podcasts of their programs.
(DWD-Media/Alamy Stock Photo)

Podcasts and Webcasts

How can I distribute audio or video files over the Internet to a wide audience? A **podcast** is a form of digital media comprised of a series of audio or video files that are distributed over the Internet. There are podcasts for radio shows, audiobooks, magazines, and even educational programs, which you can download to any device that can play audio files. What makes podcasts different from other audio files found on the web is that podcasts deliver their content using **Really Simple Syndication (RSS)**. RSS is a format that sends the latest content of the podcast series automatically to an **aggregator** such as iTunes or Feedspot. An aggregator locates all the RSS series to which you've subscribed and automatically downloads only the new content to your computer or media player. If you have several favorite websites or podcasts, rather than checking each site for updated content, aggregators collect all the site updates in one place. These updates or changes to the content are then delivered automatically if you subscribe to the podcast, instead of you having to search for the latest content and download it manually.

Where can I find podcasts? Most online news and radio sites offer podcasts of their programs. Although many podcasts are news related, others offer entertaining and educational content. For example, you can access lessons on yoga, foreign language classes, or DIY tips. Many schools supply students with course content updates through podcasts, and instructors sometimes create podcasts of their lectures. Figure 3.6 lists some websites where you can find podcasts.

Can I create my own podcast? It's simple to create a podcast. To record the audio content all you need is a

computer with a microphone, and if you want to make a video podcast, you also need a webcam or video camera. Although high-end equipment will produce more sophisticated output, you certainly can use whatever equipment you might own. You may also need additional software to edit the audio and video content, depending on how professional you wish the podcast to be. After you've recorded and edited the podcast content, you need to export it to MP3 format. The free program Audacity (**audacity.sourceforge. net**) lets you both edit audio files and export them to MP3 format. All that's left for you is to create an RSS feed (tricky, but doable) and then upload the content to a site that hosts podcasts, such as iTunes, Podfeed, or Stitcher.

What is a webcast? A **webcast** is the (usually live) broadcast of audio or video content over the Internet. Unlike podcasts, which are prerecorded and made available for download, most webcasts are distributed in "real time," meaning that they're live or one-time events. Some webcasts are archived so they can be viewed at a later date. Webcasts are not updated automatically like podcasts.

Webcasts use continuous audio and video feeds, which let you view and download large audio and video files. Webcasts can include noninteractive content such as a simultaneous broadcast of a radio or television program, but some webcasts invite interactive responses from the viewing or listening audience. For example, ORLive (**orlive.com**) provides surgical webcasts that demonstrate the latest surgical innovations and techniques. Webcasts also are used in the corporate world to broadcast annual meetings and in the educational arena to transmit seminars.

Figure 3.7 lists the popular methods of online collaboration and communication that we've discussed.

FIGURE 3.6

Podcast Directories and Aggregators

iTunes (itunes.com)
- Software makes it easy to play, manage, and share your favorite podcasts

Podfeed (podfeed.net)
- Broad collection of podcasts

Stitcher (stitcher.com)
- Customize podcast playlists

YouTube (youtube.com)
- Good source for video blogs (vlogs)

FIGURE 3.7

Methods of Online Collaboration and Communication

SOCIAL NETWORKING

- Web 2.0 technology
- Lets you build an online network of friends
- Lets you share media content

WIKIS

- Great collaborative tool
- Content updated by many users
- Historical content kept so you can revert to past versions

PROJECT COLLABORATION

- Screen sharing
- Project management
- Videoconferencing

BLOGS

- Written by a single author
- Chronologic entries
- Searchable content
- May include images, audio, and video

PODCASTS

- Audio/video files delivered via RSS
- New RSS content collected with aggregator
- Can download and view content on portable media player

WEBCASTS

- Most often live, streamed broadcasts

E-MAIL

- Most common form of online communication
- Asynchronous (not having to be done at the same time)

INSTANT MESSAGING

- Real-time exchange
- Can be used with multiple persons simultaneously
- Video/audio chats available

(Lowe Standards/Fotolia, Michael D Brown/Shutterstock, Maglara/Shutterstock, Ayzek/Shutterstock, www.3drenderedlogos.com/Shutterstock, Batshevs/Shutterstock, Beboy/Fotolia, LiveStock/Shutterstock)

Communicating over the Web

Objective 3.4 *Summarize how e-mail and instant messaging are used to communicate over the web.*

Why do I still need e-mail? Despite the popularity of social media, **e-mail** (short for **electronic mail**)— a written message sent or received over the Internet— still remains the most widely used form of communication on the Internet. E-mail is the primary method of electronic communication worldwide because it's fast and convenient. And because it's *asynchronous*, users do not need to be communicating at the same time. They can send and respond to messages at their own convenience. E-mail is also convenient for exchanging and collaborating on documents via attachments.

How private is e-mail? Although e-mail is a more private exchange of information than public social networking sites, e-mails are not really private. Consider the following:

- Because e-mails can be printed or forwarded to others, you never know who may read your e-mail.

- Most e-mail content is not protected, so you should never use e-mail to send personal or sensitive information such as bank account or Social Security numbers. Doing so could lead to identity theft.

- Employers have access to e-mail sent from the workplace, so use caution when putting negative or controversial content in e-mail.

- Even after you've deleted a message, it doesn't really vanish. Many Internet service providers and companies archive e-mail, which can be accessed or subpoenaed in the event of a lawsuit or investigation.

What are some tips on e-mail etiquette? When you write a casual e-mail to friends, you obviously don't need to follow any specific e-mail guidelines (except to remember that your e-mail may be forwarded). But when you send e-mail for professional reasons, you should use proper e-mail etiquette. The following are a few guidelines (also see Figure 3.8):

- Be concise and to the point.
- Use the spell-checker and proofread your e-mail before sending it.

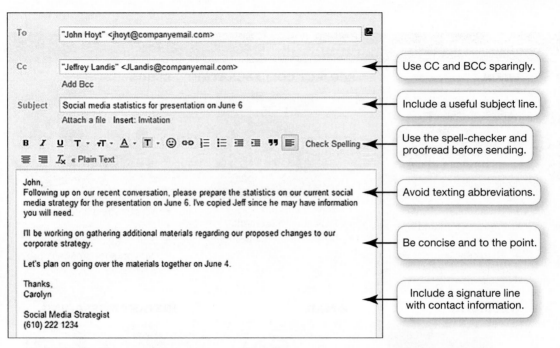

FIGURE 3.8 Using simple guidelines of e-mail etiquette can promote a professional image and make your message more effective. (*Microsoft Outlook, Windows 8.1, Microsoft Corporation*)

- Avoid using abbreviations such as *u*, *r*, *LOL*, and *BTW*.
- Include a meaningful subject line to help recipients prioritize and organize e-mails.
- Add a signature line that includes your contact information.
- Include only those people on the e-mail who truly need to receive it.

Following such guidelines maintains professionalism, increases efficiency, and might even help protect a company from lawsuits.

Are there different types of e-mail systems? There are two different types of e-mail systems:

1. **Web-based e-mail**, such as Yahoo! Mail or Gmail, is managed with your web browser and allows you to access your e-mail from the web.

2. An **e-mail client** requires a program, such as Microsoft Outlook, to be installed on your computer. When you open the program, your e-mail is downloaded to your computer.

The primary difference between the two is access. Web-based e-mail allows you to access e-mail from any Internet-connected device, but you can't use your e-mail when you're offline. With an e-mail client, you view your e-mail on the computer on which the e-mail client software has been installed, but you can then view and manage your e-mail while you're offline. Both systems can be used together for the "best of both worlds." You can have a Gmail account, for example, so that you can read your e-mail from any computer connected to the Internet, and you can also have Outlook installed on your primary computer and set up the program to display your Gmail account (see Figure 3.9).

Who uses instant messaging? Instant messaging (IM), a way of communicating in real time over the Internet, was a primary means of chatting with friends in real time. But with the proliferation of texting and social networking, instant messaging has begun to lose its attraction as a social tool. However, instant messaging still is an important means of quick and efficient communication in the business world.

Some IM systems provide mechanisms to hold conversations with more than one person, either through simultaneous individual conversations or with group chats. And some programs even let you conduct video chats using a webcam. Other advantages of using IM for business communications is that you can monitor who is allowed to contact you, and people can only communicate with you if they know your exact e-mail or IM address.

Google+ and Hangouts, Skype, and Yahoo! Messenger are proprietary IM services, meaning you can IM or chat only with those who share the same IM service and are on your contact or buddy list. Another option is to chat with those you've "friended" on Facebook through Facebook's chat option. There are also universal chat services such as Trillian and Digsby that you install on your computer and that allow you to chat with users of all popular IMs, regardless of the service they use. There are some IM services that have been developed primarily for business use such as Cisco Jabber and Oracle Beehive.

How is instant messaging different from texting? Although both IM and texting provide means to chat, there are differences. Instant messaging is synchronous: both parties need to be participating at the same time, whereas texting is asynchronous in that you do not need to immediately respond to a text once it is received. Texting uses the Short Message Service (SMS) to send short messages between mobile devices. Some texting services that use Multimedia Message Service (MMS) can include images or videos. Snapchat is a popular app that allows users to send brief videos or images. A differentiating aspect to Snapchat is that once a message is opened, the video or image is only available to be viewed for a brief amount of time and is generally not able to be saved.

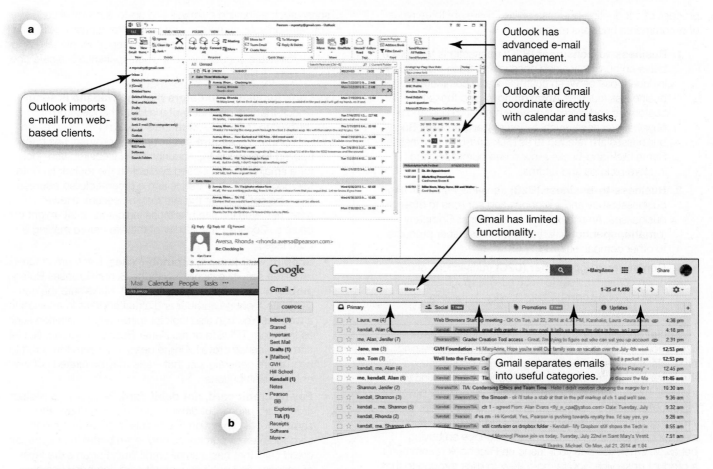

Outlook has advanced e-mail management.

Outlook and Gmail coordinate directly with calendar and tasks.

Outlook imports e-mail from web-based clients.

Gmail has limited functionality.

Gmail separates emails into useful categories.

FIGURE 3.9 (a) Client-Based and (b) Web-Based E-Mail Systems *(Microsoft Outlook, Windows 8.1, Microsoft Corporation; © 2015 Google Inc, used with permission. Google and the Google logo are registered trademarks of Google Inc.)*

Can I make phone calls over the Internet? Using apps such as Skype, FaceTime, or Google Hangouts, users can communicate using audio (voice) and video. These services use VoIP (Voice over IP) that allows calls to be transmitted over the Internet rather than over traditional phone lines or cellular networks. The advantage of VoIP is that as long as you have an Internet connection, you can make a call. In instances when Internet access is free, making long-distance or international connections with VoIP is a much more affordable option to keep in touch with friends and family far away. ■

business and entertainment
ON THE WEB

It's hard to believe that only a few years ago, many people were scared to buy things online. Today, there is little hesitation, and you can buy nearly anything on the web, including big-ticket items such as homes and cars. Similarly, the types and accessibility of multimedia on the web have become much more plentiful. In this section, we'll take a look at e-commerce and web entertainment.

Types of E-Commerce

Objective 3.5 *Describe the different types of e-commerce.*

What are the different types of e-commerce? **E-commerce**—short for **electronic commerce**—is the process of conducting business online. There are three types of e-commerce business models:

1. **Business-to-consumer (B2C)** transactions take place between businesses and consumers. Such transactions include those between customers and completely online businesses (such as **Amazon.com**) and those between customers and stores that have both an online and a physical presence, such as Target (**target.com**). Such businesses are referred to as *click-and-brick* businesses. Some click-and-bricks allow online purchases and in-store pickups and returns.

2. **Business-to-business (B2B)** transactions occur when businesses buy and sell goods and services to other businesses. An example is Omaha Paper Company (**omahapaper.com**), which distributes paper products to other companies.

3. **Consumer-to-consumer (C2C)** transactions occur when consumers sell to each other through sites such as eBay (**ebay.com**), Craigslist (**craigslist.org**), and Etsy (**etsy.com**).

Social commerce is a subset of e-commerce that uses social networks to assist in marketing and purchasing products. If you're on Facebook, you've no doubt noticed the many businesses that have Facebook pages asking you to "Like" them. Consumers are voicing their opinions on Facebook and other sites about products and services by providing ratings and reviews, and studies show that such peer recommendations have a major influence on buying behavior. When you see your friend on Facebook recommend a product or service, you're more likely to click through to that retailer and check out the product.

Other peer-influenced e-commerce trends include group-buying and individual customization. Groupon and LivingSocial are two popular deal-of-the-day group purchase websites that require a certain number of people to buy the discounted deal before the deal can go through. CafePress and Zazzle sell T-shirts and other items that are customized with your own graphic designs.

But e-commerce encompasses more than just shopping opportunities. Many people use online services to check their bank account balances, pay bills online, and check stock and mutual fund performance. Credit card companies allow you to view, schedule, and pay your credit card bill; brokerage houses allow you to conduct investment activities online.

E-Commerce Safeguards

Objective 3.6 *Summarize precautions you should take when doing business online.*

Just how safe are online transactions? When you buy something online, you may use a credit card; therefore, money is exchanged directly between your credit card company and the online merchant's bank. Because online shopping eliminates a salesclerk or other human intermediary from the transaction, it can actually be safer than traditional retail shopping.

What precautions should I take when shopping online? In addition to using some basic common computing

sense such as having a firewall and up-to-date antivirus software on your computer, and using strong passwords for all your online accounts, there are several important guidelines to follow to ensure your online shopping experience is a safe one (see Figure 3.10):

- **Look for visual indicators that the website is secure.** Check that the beginning of the URL changes from "http://" to "https://"—with the *s* standing for secure, indicating that the **secure sockets layer** protocol has been applied to manage the security of the website. Also, look for a small icon of a closed padlock in the toolbar (in both Microsoft Edge and Firefox) and a green-colored address bar—indications that the site may be secure. (However, note that even if a site has these indicators, it still might not be safe. Consider the validity of the site before making a purchase.)

- **Shop at well-known, reputable sites.** If you aren't familiar with a site, investigate it with the Better Business Bureau (**bbb.org**) or at Bizrate (**bizrate.com**). Make sure the company has a phone number and street address in addition to a website. You can also look for third-party verification such as that from TRUSTe or the Better Business Bureau. But let common sense prevail. Online deals that seem too good to be true are generally just that—and may be pirated software or illegal distributions.

- **Pay by credit card, not debit card.** Federal laws protect credit card users, but debit card users don't have the same level of protection. If possible, reserve one credit card for Internet purchases only; even better, use a prepaid credit card that has a small credit limit. For an extra layer of security, find out if your credit card company has a service that confirms your identity with an extra password or code that only you know to use when making an online transaction or that offers a one-time-use credit card number. Also, consider using a third-party payment processor such as PayPal or Apple Pay. PayPal also offers a security key that provides additional security to your PayPal account.

- **When you place an order, check the return policy, save a copy of the order, and make sure you receive a confirmation number.** Make sure you read and understand the fine print on warranties, return policies, and the retailer's privacy statements. If the site disappears overnight, this information may help you in filing a dispute or reporting a problem to a site such as the Better Business Bureau.

- **Avoid making online transactions when using public computers.** Public computers may have *spyware* installed, which are programs that track and log your keystrokes and can retrieve your private information. Similarly, unless you have specific protection on your own mobile device, avoid making wireless transactions on public hotspots.

Whether you're doing business, playing games, or communicating with friends or colleagues, the Internet makes these activities more accessible. The Internet can potentially make these experiences and activities more enriched as well, although you must take precautions for the safest of experiences.

FIGURE 3.10

Online Shopping Precautions

When shopping at home, use a firewall and antivirus software for general computer protection.

Don't shop on public WiFi networks, as they may contain spyware.

Check for visual indicators such as https:// in the URL, a closed padlock icon, and a green address bar.

Look for third-party verification from TRUSTe or the Better Business Bureau symbol.

Use a credit card, not a debit card, to protect transactions, or use a third-party payer such as PayPal or Google Wallet.

Create a strong password for all online accounts (one that includes numbers and other symbols such as @).

Deals that are too good to be true are usually just that.

Read and understand the fine print on warranties, return policies, and the retailer's privacy statements.

(Shutterstock, Roy Wylam/Alamy, Photoinnovation/Shutterstock, Newscom, Maxx-Studio/ Shutterstock, Isak55/Shutterstock, Alhovik/Shutterstock, Shutterstock)

Web Entertainment

Objective 3.7 *Describe the types of multimedia files found on the web.*

How can I use the web for entertainment? When you think of how you use the Internet for entertainment purposes, what comes to mind? Streaming audio and video, Internet radio, and social media sharing are all favorite responses. What makes all these forms of web entertainment so popular is their multimedia content. **Multimedia** is anything that involves one or more forms of media in addition to text. It includes the following:

- *Graphics* such as drawings, charts, and photos (the most basic form of multimedia)
- *Audio files* such as the clips you hear when you visit websites, MP3 files you download, podcasts and webcasts, and live broadcasts you can listen to through Internet radio
- *Video files* ranging from simple, short video clips on sites such as YouTube (**youtube.com**) to movies and television shows on sites such as Hulu (**hulu.com**)

> ### ACTIVE HELPDESK
> **Doing Business Online**
>
> In this Active Helpdesk, you'll play the role of a helpdesk staffer, fielding questions about e-commerce and e-commerce safeguards.

What is streaming media? Streaming media is multimedia (audio and video) that is continuously fed to your browser so you avoid having to wait for the entire file to download completely before listening to or watching it. Without streaming media, you wouldn't be able to watch movies on Netflix or on demand from your cable provider, listen to live audio broadcasting, or even play some online games. Internet radio also uses streaming media to present a continuous stream of audio to its listeners.

Where can I share music, pictures, and videos on the web? Social media sharing sites such as Flickr, Instagram, YouTube, and SoundCloud enable anyone to create and share multimedia. Flickr was created to store and share photos online. Although not as "social" as some other sites, Flickr enables users to tag not only their images but others' images, thus providing a strong search capability to quickly locate images with similar tags. Instagram is primarily a mobile app that allows users to take photos on their cell phones or tablets, add a caption, and then instantly upload them. SoundCloud is both a distribution platform and a music streaming service. Fledgling musicians can upload original music to share, and music enthusiasts can track and follow new and favorite artists. SoundCloud has a strong online community of followers. YouTube enables users to upload videos offering a variety of content from educational pieces to cute or funny videos. Many YouTube videos become so popular and are shared or recommended to be seen by so many that they go "viral."

BITS&BYTES

Making Safe Online Payments

When people first began making online purchases, many were not comfortable because the sites required them to give personal financial information such as credit card numbers in a web form. It was unknown who had access to that information. PayPal (**paypal.com**) resolved that issue by serving as a payment intermediary that allows anyone to pay with credit cards and bank accounts without sharing their financial information. PayPal is now a standard means of payment for many online merchants and offers buyer protection and dispute resolution services. Figure 3.11 shows how PayPal works. Similarly, for in-person retail exchanges, Apple Pay uses security features that shield your credit card information from merchants (and Apple!).

Another level of protection for securing online accounts that is becoming more popular is the use of mobile biometrics. Biometrics is the process of authenticating users by physiological or behavioral traits such as signatures, fingerprints, and even irises. Apple introduced Touch ID with a fingerprint scanner on the iPhone 5S. Many mobile apps, especially those for financial services companies, have integrated Touch ID as part of the login procedure. Touch ID systems are being built into other devices, such as Samsung smartphones, and PayPal and other companies are also incorporating the feature.

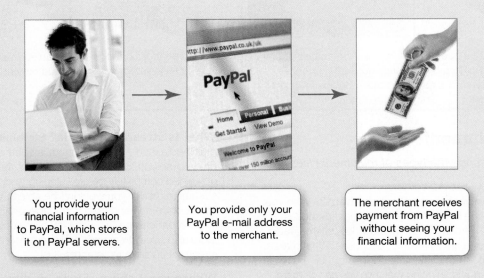

> You provide your financial information to PayPal, which stores it on PayPal servers.

> You provide only your PayPal e-mail address to the merchant.

> The merchant receives payment from PayPal without seeing your financial information.

FIGURE 3.11 How PayPal Works *(Shutterstock, AKP Photos/Alamy, Happydancing/Shutterstock)*

Is there any way to get multimedia web content to load faster? When you're on the Internet, your browser keeps track of the sites you've visited so that it can load them faster the next time you visit them. This *cache* (temporary storage place) of the text pages, images, and video files from recently visited websites can make your web surfing more efficient, but it can also slow down your hard drive. Additionally, if you don't have your cache settings configured to check for updates to the web page, your browser may not load the most recent content. To keep your system running efficiently, consider doing the following:

- Delete your temporary Internet cache every month or so, depending on your usage.

- To ensure the most recent website content is displayed, click Refresh or press the F5 key if you revisit a site in the same browsing session.
- Clear your Internet cache manually or adjust the setting in your web browser so that it clears the cache automatically every time you exit the browser. ∎

> **Before moving on to Part 2:**
> 1. **Watch Replay Video 3.1** ▷ .
> 2. **Then check your understanding of what you've learned so far.**

check your understanding // review & practice

For a quick review to see what you've learned so far, answer the following questions.

multiple choice

1. Which is NOT an event associated with the beginning of the Internet?

   a. The U.S. Department of Defense creates ARPA.

   b. TCP/IP protocol was developed that allowed different computers to communicate with each other.

   c. Amazon.com was one of the first websites on the Internet.

   d. The first e-mail program was written by Ray Tomlinson.

2. What do you need if you want to read, send, and organize e-mail from *any* computer connected to the Internet?

   a. e-mail client program

   b. e-mail server

   c. e-mail aggregator

   d. web-based e-mail account

3. Which of the following would be best for *synchronous* text-based communication?

   a. e-mail

   b. texting

   c. blogging

   d. instant messaging

4. Which technology is being used in creating a document on Google Drive?

   a. blog

   b. wiki

   c. microblog

   d. e-mail

5. Which of the following would be an example of a C2C business?

   a. BestBuy

   b. Target

   c. Etsy

   d. Google

 Go to **MyITLab** to take an autograded version of the *Check Your Understanding* review and to find all media resources for the chapter.

TECHBYTES WEEKLY
Stay current with the TechBytes Weekly Newsletter.

Continue »

Create a OneDrive Account to Store and Share Your Files in the Cloud

You probably have your favorite ways of moving your files around. Perhaps you have a USB drive or you e-mail files to yourself, or maybe you have a portable external hard drive. With any of these solutions, there can be confusion as to which is the most current version of the file if you have worked on it on multiple devices at different times. You also run the risk of losing your USB drive or deleting the e-mail attachment by mistake. These methods also make exchanging files difficult if you want to share your files or collaborate with a group.

A simpler solution is to use a web-based or cloud storage and sharing service such as OneDrive or Dropbox. OneDrive is part of Microsoft's Office Online. With 15 GB of free storage space for new users, you can store thousands of files and get to them anytime you're online.

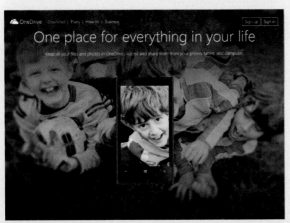

Step 1　Sign in to OneDrive: Go to **onedrive.com**. Sign in to your Microsoft account. If you don't have a Microsoft account, creating one is easy. A Microsoft account will give you access to services such as OneDrive, Xbox LIVE, and **Outlook.com**. *(Microsoft One Drive, Windows 10, Microsoft Corporation)*

Step 2　Create a Folder and Add Files: Once you're in OneDrive, you can create a folder and then begin to add files.

- To create a folder: Click **New** at the top of the page, click **Folder**, and then give your new folder a name. Click the new folder to open it.
- To add a file: Click **Upload** at the top of the page, select **Files**, then locate the file and click **Open**. To upload more than one file, press and hold **Ctrl** while you select each file. *(Microsoft One Drive, Windows 10, Microsoft Corporation)*

Step 3　Share a File or Folder: To share a file or folder, complete the following steps:

1. Right-click the file or folder that you want to share and click **Share**, or click **Share** in the top menu after selecting the desired file or folder.
2. Ensure *Invite people* is highlighted in the Share pane, then enter e-mail addresses in the To box. You can add a note if you would like.
3. Editing privileges are established by default, so if you want to restrict editing privileges, click **Recipients can edit**, then choose **Recipients can only view**.
4. If you are unsure whether the recipients have a Microsoft account, you can select **Recipients don't need a Microsoft account**.
5. Click **Share**.
6. To see what files that have been shared with you, click **Shared** in the left menu. *(Microsoft One Drive, Windows 10, Microsoft Corporation)*

Step 4 **Sync Selective Folders:** By default, all the files and folders on OneDrive are synced with the devices that have OneDrive installed. To save space on those devices with small hard drives, you can select only the folders you want to be synced. For all non-synced folders, you could still access the content from the OneDrive Online. To select specific folders to sync, complete the following steps:

1. Right-click the **OneDrive icon** from the Notification area on the taskbar.
2. Click **Settings**, then click the **Choose folders tab**.
3. Click **Choose folders**. From the dialog box, uncheck the folders you don't want to sync. Any check boxes with checks will be synced to your computer. When you're done, click **OK**. If you have OneDrive installed on several devices, you would need to repeat this process on each device, as needed. *(Microsoft One Drive, Windows 10, Microsoft Corporation)*

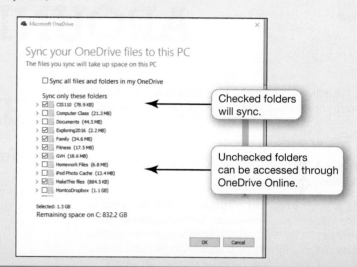

Make This ▸ TOOL: App Inventor 2

MAKE: A Web-Capable App

Want your app to be able to display a web page?

In this exercise, you'll continue your mobile app development by adding a new power to your apps: web browsing.

It's as easy as using the WebViewer component in **App Inventor**. Drag a WebViewer component onto your Designer screen, then control it with the Blocks for WebViewer. These allow you to go back, forward, to the home page, or to any specific URL. *(MIT App Inventor 2, Massachusetts Institute of Technology. Creative Commons Attribution-ShareAlike 3.0 Unported License)*

The WebViewer component allows you to control a live browser inside your mobile app.

For the instructions for this exercise, go to MyITLab.

Using the Web Effectively

Learning Outcome 3.2 **You will be able to describe the tools and techniques required to navigate and search the web.**

You no doubt know how to use the web—to buy products, send e-mail, visit Facebook, and use Google—but do you know how to use it effectively? In this section, we'll look at ways to make your online experience more enjoyable, more productive, and more efficient.

accessing and moving
AROUND THE WEB

None of the activities for which we use the web could happen without an important software application: a web browser.

Web Browsers

Objective 3.8 *Explain what web browsers are, and describe their common features.*

What is a web browser exactly? A **web browser** is a software that lets you locate, view, and navigate the web. Most browsers today are *graphical* browsers, meaning they can display pictures (graphics) in addition to text and other forms of multimedia such as sound and video. The most common browsers are displayed in Figure 3.12. Notice that a new browser, Microsoft Edge, has replaced Internet Explorer. This transition happened with the introduction of Windows 10, the latest version of Microsoft's operating system. Although Internet Explorer will still be around for businesses, individual users will only have access to Microsoft Edge. (See the Bits&Bytes box about the new features of Microsoft Edge.)

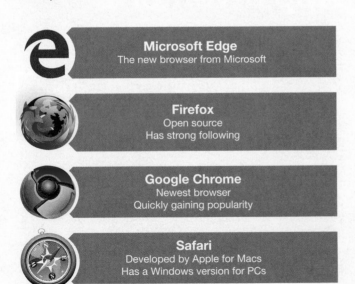

FIGURE 3.12 Common Web Browsers *(Microsoft Corporation, Lucia*

BITS&BYTES

New Browser: Microsoft Edge

When Microsoft released the latest version of its operating system, Windows 10, it said good-bye to its long-standing browser Internet Explorer and introduced Microsoft Edge, a new browser, built from scratch, intended to give users a browser that works with how they use the Internet today. In addition to the features you are most likely familiar with already, such as tabs, InPrivate Browsing, and the like, Microsoft Edge adds other features to enrich your browsing experience. For example, with Microsoft Edge, you can make "Webnotes" by annotating a web page and then share them to OneNote or Evernote or save them for later use. Microsoft Edge is also integrated with Microsoft's personal assistant Cortana, which will share web content with you based on your indicated preferences and interests. Finally, you can save online content to read later, and if the "noise" of a web page is distracting to you, you can use Reading View for a cleaner, simpler layout.

What features do web browsers offer? Most popular browsers share similar features that make the user experience more efficient (see Figure 3.13). For example, most browsers include a combined search and address bar so you can both type a website URL or search the web from the address bar. Other features include the following:

- *Tabbed browsing*: Web pages are loaded in "tabs" within the same browser window. Rather than having to switch among web pages in several open windows, you can flip between the tabs in one window. You may also save a group of tabs as a Favorites group if there are several tabs you often open at the same time.

Privacy browsing

Address/Search

Tabbed browsing

FIGURE 3.13 Tabbed and privacy browsing and an address bar that doubles as a search bar are common features in today's browsers. *(Internal Revenue Service, NASA)*

- *Pinned tabs*: You can "pin" tabs to the Start menu in Microsoft Edge or minimize and save them permanently with Google Chrome and Firefox for easier navigation of your favorite sites.
- *Tear-off tabs*: An opened tab can be dragged or moved away from its current window so it's then opened in a new window.
- *Thumbnail previews*: Another convenient navigation tool that most browsers share is providing thumbnail previews of all web pages in open tabs.
- *Tab isolation*: With this feature, tabs are independent of each other, so if one crashes, it does not affect the other tabs.
- *SmartScreen filter*: Most browsers offer built-in protection against phishing, malware, and other web-based threats.
- *Privacy browsing*: Privacy features (such as InPrivate Browsing in Microsoft Edge or Incognito in Chrome) let you browse the web without retaining a history trail, temporary Internet files, cookies, or usernames and passwords. These features are especially helpful when you use public computers at school or the public library, for example.
- *Add-ons and extensions*: *Add-ons* (also known as *extensions*) are small programs that customize and increase the functionality of the browser. Examples include Video DownloadHelper, which converts web videos like those found on YouTube to files you can save, as well as a Facebook toolbar that integrates Facebook functionality into your browser.
- *Session Restore*: Brings back all your active web pages if the browser or system shuts down unexpectedly.

 SOUND BYTE
Welcome to the Web

In this Sound Byte, you'll visit the web in a series of guided tours of useful websites. This tour serves as an introductory guide for web newcomers but is also a great resource for more experienced users.

URLs, Protocols, and Domain Names

Objective 3.9 *Explain what a URL is, and discuss its main parts.*

What do all the parts of a URL mean? You gain initial access to a particular website by typing its unique address, or **Uniform Resource Locator (URL**, pronounced "you-are-ell"), in your browser. A website is comprised of many different web pages, each of which is a separate document with its own unique URL. Like a regular street address, a URL is comprised of several parts that help identify the web document it stands for (see Figure 3.14):

- the *protocol* (set of rules) used to retrieve the document;
- the **domain name**; and
- the *path* or subdirectory.

Although every part of a URL is important information that ensures the web page you requested actually displays in your browser, you don't have to type in every part in the location or address bar of the browser. Most current browsers no longer require you to enter the http:// protocol or the "www," and most don't even require the domain if it's a .com—the browser will enter those automatically.

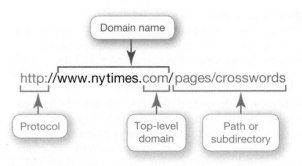

FIGURE 3.14 The Parts of a URL

FIGURE 3.15

Common Top-Level Domains and Their Authorized Users

DOMAIN NAME	WHO CAN USE IT
.biz	Businesses
.com	Originally for commercial sites, but now can be used by anyone
.edu	Degree-granting institutions
.gov	Local, state, and federal U.S. governments
.info	Information service providers
.mil	U.S. military
.net	Originally for networking organizations, but no longer restricted
.org	Organizations (often not-for-profits)

What's the protocol? You're probably most familiar with URLs that begin with *http*, which is short for **Hypertext Transfer Protocol (HTTP)**. HTTP is the protocol that allows files to be transferred from a **web server**—a computer that hosts the website you're requesting—so that you can see it on your computer. The HTTP protocol is what the web is based on.

Is HTTP the only protocol I need to use? HTTP is the most common protocol, but it's not the only one. HTTP is part of the Internet protocol suite, a group of protocols that govern how information is exchanged on a network. Another protocol in that group is the **File Transfer Protocol (FTP)**. As its name implies, FTP was originally designed to transfer files from a computer to a web server. Today, FTP is often used when you have large files to upload or download. To connect to most FTP servers, you need a user ID and password. To upload and download files from FTP sites, you can use a browser or file transfer software such as CuteFTP, Fetch, or FileZilla.

BitTorrent, like FTP, is a protocol used to transfer files, though it's not part of the Internet protocol suite. To use BitTorrent, you install a software client program. It uses a *peer-to-peer networking system* so that sharing occurs between connected computers that also have the BitTorrent client installed. BitTorrent was developed in 2001 and is popular especially among users who want to share music, movies, and games. Use caution, however, when accessing BitTorrent content. Because it is a peer-to-peer system, it's possible for copyrighted material to be shared illegally.

What's in a domain name? The domain name identifies the site's **host**, the location that maintains the computers that store the website files. For example, **www.berkeley.edu** is the domain name for the University of California at Berkeley website. The suffix in the domain name after the dot (such as "com" or "edu") is called the **top-level domain**. This suffix indicates the kind of organization to which the host belongs. Figure 3.15 lists the most frequently used top-level domains.

Each country has its own top-level domain. These are two-letter designations such as .za for South Africa and .us for the United States. A sampling of country codes is shown in Figure 3.16. Within a country-specific domain, further subdivisions can be made for regions or states. For instance, the .us domain contains subdomains for each state, using the two-letter abbreviation of the state. For example, the URL for Pennsylvania's website is **www.state.pa.us.**

What's the information after the domain name that I sometimes see? When the URL is the domain name, such as **www.nytimes.com**, you're requesting a site's home page. However, sometimes a forward slash and additional text follow the domain name, such as in **www.nytimes.com/pages/crosswords**. The information after each slash indicates a particular file or **path** (or **subdirectory**) within the website. In Figure 3.14, you would connect to the crossword page on the *New York Times* site.

Navigating the Web

Objective 3.10 *Describe tools used to navigate the web.*

What's the best way to get around in a website? As its name implies, the web is a series of interconnected paths, or links. You've no doubt moved around the web by clicking on **hyperlinks**, specially coded elements that let you jump from one web page to another within the same website or to another site altogether (see Figure 3.17). Generally, text that operates as a hyperlink appears in a different color (often blue) and is usually underlined, but sometimes images also act as hyperlinks. When you hover your cursor over a hyperlink, the cursor changes to a hand with a finger pointing upward.

FIGURE 3.16

Examples of Country Codes

COUNTRY CODE	COUNTRY
.au	Australia
.ca	Canada
.jp	Japan
.uk	United Kingdom

Note: For a full listing of country codes, refer to **iana.org/domains/root/db/**.

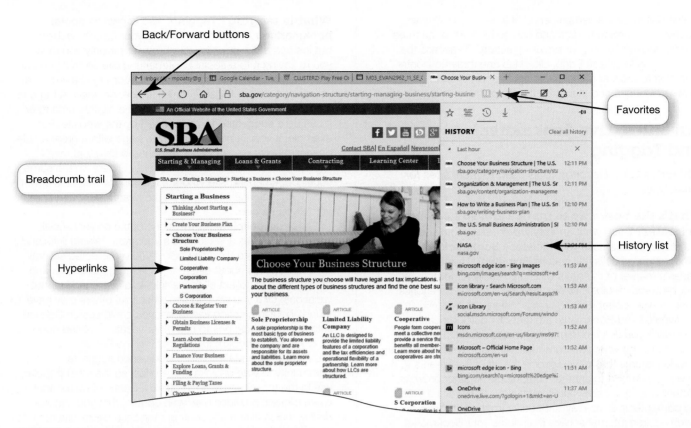

FIGURE 3.17 Navigating a Web Page *(U.S. Small Business Administration)*

What other tools can I use to navigate a website?
To move back or forward one page at a time, you can use the browser's Back and Forward buttons (see Figure 3.17).

To help navigate more quickly through a website, some sites provide a **breadcrumb trail**—a navigation aid that shows users the path they have taken to get to a web page, or where the page is located within the website. It usually appears at the top of a page. Figure 3.17 shows an example of a breadcrumb trail. "Breadcrumbs" get their name from the fairy tale "Hansel and Gretel," in which the characters drop breadcrumbs on the trail to find their way out of a forest. By clicking on earlier links in a breadcrumb trail, you can go directly to a previously visited web page without having to use the Back button to navigate back through the website.

Most browsers offer *carat browsing*, which lets you use your keyboard to grab text instead of swiping across with a mouse. To activate carat browsing, press F7 on your keyboard while you have the browser open. You might have to add an extension (Google Chrome) or enable a preference (Firefox) before you can activate the feature. Then, you can use your mouse pointer as an insertion pointer (similar to working in Word) and the arrow keys to move around. Press Shift and an arrow key to select text. Press F7 again to turn off carat browsing. This method offers more precise text selection and is very handy when you frequently copy and paste text from web pages.

The History list on your browser's toolbar is also a handy feature. The History list shows all the websites and pages

BITS&BYTES

Maintain Your Privacy While Searching the Web

Privacy is important to many people, but creating a private online experience is not always an easy task. Although you can use the privacy or incognito mode in some web browsers, these only disable your browsing history and web cache so that data generated from your searches cannot be retrieved later. DuckDuckGo (**duckduckgo.com**) is different—this search engine doesn't collect your personal browsing information to share with third parties for marketing purposes. And although most search engines sell your search term information to third parties, which then use that information to generate display ads and recommendations on pages you visit, DuckDuckGo doesn't sell your search terms to other sites. Moreover, DuckDuckGo doesn't save your search history. Using DuckDuckGo eliminates third-party sharing of your personal information.

you've visited over a certain period of time. These sites are organized according to date and can go back as far as three weeks, depending on your browsing activity. To access the History list in Microsoft Edge, click Hub (the three horizontal lines next to the star in the upper right-hand corner of the browser window) and then click the History icon.

Favorites, Live Bookmarks, and Tagging

Objective 3.11 *Describe tools used to mark sites for future use.*

What's the best way to mark a site so I can return to it later? If you want an easy way to return to a specific web page, you can use your browser's **Bookmarks** feature (Microsoft Edge calls this feature **Favorites**). This feature places a marker of the site's URL in an easily retrievable list in your browser's toolbar. To organize the sites into categories, most browsers offer tools to create folders.

Favorites and Bookmarks are great for quickly locating those sites you use most, but they're accessible to you only when you're on your own computer. Although most browsers provide features that let you export the list of bookmarks to a file you can import to another computer or another browser, another way to access your Bookmarks and Favorites from any computer is to use MyBookmarks (**mybookmarks .com**)—a free Internet service that stores your Bookmarks and Favorites online.

What are live bookmarks? Because the web is constantly changing, the site you bookmarked last week may subsequently change and add new content. Traditionally, you would notice the change only the next time you visited the site. **Live bookmarks** deliver content updates to you as soon as they become available using RSS, the same technology that updates blogs and podcasts that we described earlier in the chapter. Live bookmarks and RSS feeds are useful if you're interested in the most up-to-date news stories, sports scores, or stock prices. Firefox, Safari, and Microsoft Edge have built-in RSS readers, while Chrome requires that you add on an extension.

What is tagging? Tagging, also known as **social bookmarking**, is like bookmarking your favorite website, but instead of saving it to your browser for only you to see, you're saving it to a social bookmarking site so that you can share it with others. A social bookmark or tag is a term that you assign to a web page, digital image, or video. A tag can be something you create to describe the digital content, or it can be a suggested term provided by the website. For example, if you came across a web page with a great article on inexpensive places to go for spring break, you might tag the article with the term *vacations*. Others on the same social bookmarking site who are looking for websites about vacations may use *vacations* as the search term and find the article you tagged.

Delicious (**delicious.com**) is one of the original social bookmarking sites. Delicious lets you group related links and organize them into "bundles." So if you've collected several links to websites about different places to go to over spring break, you can collect all those links into one bundle about vacations. Or if you want to see what links others may have found about interesting vacations, you could search Delicious with the term *vacations* to see other vacation-related bundles.

Other social bookmarking sites include Reddit, StumbleUpon, and Pinterest. Reddit encourages its community to vote on links and stories, so the most popular rise to the top. StumbleUpon offers a Stumble! button that, when clicked, provides new web content that you can like or dislike, which eventually contours the Stumble results more to your interests. Unlike other social bookmarking sites, Pinterest enables you to share only images. You can post images that you find online or that you directly upload. You do not need a Pinterest account to look at other's pins and boards. ∎

ACTIVE HELPDESK
Getting Around the Web

In this Active Helpdesk, you'll play the role of a helpdesk staffer, fielding questions about web browsers, URLs, and how to use hyperlinks and other tools to get around the web.

Think about all the types of data on the web that you access manually, such as appointment times, transportation and entertainment schedules, and store locations and hours. It would seem that computers would be helpful in plugging through all this web data, but oddly, that is not the case. Web pages are designed for people to read, not for computers to manipulate. As yet, no reliable way exists for computers to process the meaning of data on a web page so that it can be used to see relationships or make decisions.

The **semantic web** (or **Web 3.0**) is an evolving extension of the web in which data is defined in such a way to make it more easily processed by computers. Right now, search engines function by recognizing keywords such as *office hours* and *dentist*, but they can't determine, for example, in which office and on what days Dr. Smith works and what his available appointment times are. By using a so-called "agent," the semantic web would enable computers to find that type of information, coordinate it with your other schedules and preferences, and then make the appointment for you.

The semantic web would also assist you in comparing products, prices, and shipping options by finding the best product option based on specified criteria and then placing the order for you. Additionally, the agent would record the financial transaction into your personal bookkeeping software and arrange for a technician to help install the software, if needed.

For the semantic web to work, businesses, services, and software would all use the same categorization structures so that similar information would share the same attributes, ensuring consistency of metadata throughout the web. The semantic web would build on this type of capability so that each website would have text and pictures (for people to read) and metadata (for computers to read) describing the information on the web (see Figure 3.18).

Although some of the semantic web's functionalities are beginning to emerge in technologies such as the digital assistants Siri, Google Now, and Cortana, the majority of its functionality and implementation are still in development. The greatest challenge is recoding all the information currently available on the web into the type of metadata that computers can recognize. The very grandeur of that task means that we will not see a fully functional semantic web until sometime in the distant future. In the meantime, we can continue to benefit from each small step toward that goal.

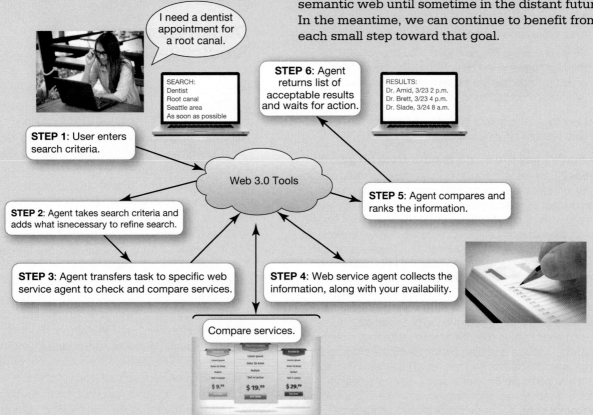

FIGURE 3.18 The Semantic Web *(jpkirakun/Fotolia, SergeyIT/Shutterstock, mileswork/Shutterstock)*

searching the web
EFFECTIVELY

You've most likely "Googled" something today, and if you did, your search is one of over five billion daily searches. Let's take a look at how to search the web effectively.

Using Search Engines

Objective 3.12 *Describe the types of tools used to search the web, and summarize strategies used to refine search results.*

How do search engines work? Google is the world's most popular **search engine**—a set of programs that searches the web for **keywords** (specific words you wish to look for or *query*) and then returns a list of the sites on which those keywords are found. Search engines have three components:

1. The first component is a program called a *spider*, which constantly collects data on the web, following links in websites and reading web pages. Spiders get their name because they crawl over the web using multiple "legs" to visit many sites simultaneously.

2. As the spider collects data, the second component of the search engine, an *indexer program*, organizes the data into a large database.

3. When you use a search engine, you interact with the third component: the *search engine software*. This software searches the indexed data, pulling out relevant information according to your search.

The resulting list appears in your web browser as a list of hits—sites that match your search.

Why don't I get the same results from all search engines? Each search engine uses a unique formula, or *algorithm*, to formulate the search and create the resulting index of related sites. In addition, search engines differ in how they rank the search results. Most search engines rank their results based on the frequency of the appearance of your queried keywords in websites as well as the location of those words in the sites. This means that sites that include the keywords in their URL or site name will most likely appear at the top of the results list. An important part of a company's marketing strategy is search engine optimization, which is designing the corporate website to ensure it ranks near the top of a search.

Search engines also differ as to which sites they search. For instance, Google and Bing search nearly the entire web, whereas specialty search engines search only sites that are relevant to a particular topic or industry. Specialty search engines exist for almost every industry or interest. DailyStocks (**dailystocks.com**) is a search engine used primarily by investors that searches for corporate information. Search Engine Watch (**searchenginewatch.com**) has a list of many specialty search engines, organized by industry.

If you can't decide which search engine is best, you may want to try a metasearch engine. **Metasearch engines**, such as Dogpile (**dogpile.com**), search other search engines rather than individual websites.

Can I use a search engine to search just for images and videos? With the increasing popularity of multimedia, search engines such as Google, Bing, and Yahoo! let you search the web for digital images and audio and video files. After putting in your search term, select Video from Google's top menu to display only the search results that are videos. You can further narrow down the video selection by using the filtering tools. Blinkx (**blinkx.com**) is a video search engine that helps you sift through all the video posted on the web.

BITS&BYTES

Digital Assistants and Predictive Search

Apple introduced Siri, the personal digital assistant for iPhones, in 2011. Using Siri's voice recognition technology, users could ask Siri for help in finding information, getting directions, creating reminders, and other everyday tasks. One year later, Google introduced Google Now, its intelligent personal assistant. In addition to offering similar digital assistant tasks that Siri offered, Google Now added predictive search capabilities: Google Now recognizes a user's repeated actions and searches and, using Google's Knowledge Graph project, offers relevant and predictive information. This might include delays in upcoming flights, news stories relevant to your interests, travel time to your next appointment, and perhaps which friend might have a birthday coming up. Most recently, with the release of Windows Phone 8.1 and Windows 10 for all Windows-based devices, Microsoft introduced Cortana. Cortana, like Google Now, has predictive search capabilities. Based on preferences that you give to Cortana when you first begin to use her, and with continued use, Cortana will offer information that is deemed relevant to you.

How can I refine my searches for better results?
You've probably searched for something on Google and gotten back a list of hits that includes thousands—even millions—of web pages that have no relevance to the topic you're interested in. Initially, Boolean operators were needed to help refine a search. **Boolean operators** are words such as *AND*, *NOT*, and *OR* that describe the relationships between keywords in a search. With the simple addition of a few words or constraints, you can narrow your search results to a more manageable and more meaningful list.

Are there other helpful search strategies? Other strategies can help refine your searches when entering your search keywords:

- **Search for a phrase.** To search for an exact phrase, place quotation marks around your keywords. The search engine will look for only those websites that contain the words in *that exact order*. For example, if you want information on the movie *The Green Hornet* and you type these words without quotation marks, your search results will contain pages that include either of the words *Green* and *Hornet*, although not necessarily in that order. Typing *"The Green Hornet"* in quotation marks guarantees that search results will include this exact phrase.

- **Search within a specific website.** To search just a specific website, you can use the search keyword, then *site*: followed by the website's URL. For example, searching with *processor site*—**www.wired.com**—returns results about processors from the **Wired.com** website. The same method works for entire classes of sites in a given top-level domain or country code.

- **Use a wild card.** The asterisk ("*") is a wild card, or placeholder, feature that is helpful when you need to search with unknown terms. Another way to think about the wild card search feature is as a "fill in the blank." For example, searching with *Congress voted * on the * bill* might bring up an article about the members of Congress who voted *no* on the *healthcare* bill or a different article about the members of Congress who voted *yes* on the *energy* bill.

How else can I customize my searches?
Many other specialty search strategies and services are available. By clicking on Search tools in Google's menu at the top of a Google

search, you can restrict search results by time, location, and even reading level (see Figure 3.19). You can also click on the Apps button in Google's main page, then click the More and Even more from Google options for all the specialized search products Google offers (see Figure 3.20):

- *Custom Search* lets you create a customized search engine to search only a selected set of sites tailored to your needs. You can add this specialized search engine to a website or blog or design it for a specific organization.

FIGURE 3.19 Using Google's Search Tools to Restrict the Time Frame, the Location, and Even the Reading Level of Your Search Results *(© 2015 Google Inc, used with permission. Google and the Google logo are registered trademarks of Google Inc.)*

Specialized Search

🔍 **Custom Search**
Create a customized search experience for your community

💡 **Patent Search**
Search the full text of US Patents

🏷️ **Google Shopping**
Search for stuff to buy

📈 **Finance**
Business info, news and interactive charts

⚛️ **Scholar**
Search scholarly papers

#️⃣ **Trends**
Explore past and present search trends

FIGURE 3.20 Google's Specialized Search Tools (© 2015 Google Inc, used with permission. Google and the Google logo are registered trademarks of Google Inc.)

- *Google Shopping* lets you search by product rather than by company. So if you're interested in buying a digital camera, Google Shopping lists cameras by popularity and provides information on the stores that carry the cameras, along with the average price.
- *Scholar* searches scholarly literature such as peer-reviewed papers, theses, and publications from academic organizations. Each search result contains bibliographic information as well.
- *Patent Search* provides access to patents from the United States Patent and Trademark Office, the European Patent Office, and the World Intellectual Property Organization.
- *Finance* gives you access to real-time stock quotes and charts as well as financial news. You can also track your portfolio holdings.
- *Trends* features trending stories in real-time, organized by category and location.

Evaluating Websites

Objective 3.13 *Describe how to evaluate a website to ensure it is appropriate to use for research purposes.*

How can I make sure a website is appropriate to use for research? When you're using the Internet for research, you shouldn't assume that everything you find is accurate and appropriate to use. The following is a list of questions to consider before you use an Internet resource; the answers to these questions will help you decide whether you should consider a website to be a good source of information:

- **Authority:** Who is the author of the article or the sponsor of the site? If the author is well known or the site is published by a reputable news source (such as *The New York Times*), then you can feel more confident using it as a source than if you are unable to locate such information. *Note*: Some sites include a page with information about the author or the site's sponsor.
- **Bias:** Is the site biased? The purpose of many websites is to sell products or services or to persuade rather than inform. These sites, though useful in some situations,

present a biased point of view. Look for sites that offer several sets of facts or consider opinions from several sources.
- **Relevance:** Is the information on the site current? Material can last a long time on the web. Some research projects (such as historical accounts) depend on older records. However, if you're writing about cutting-edge technologies, you need to look for the most recent sources. Therefore, look for a date on information to make sure it is current.
- **Audience:** For what audience is the site intended? Ensure that the content, tone, and style of the site match your needs. You probably wouldn't want to use information from a site geared toward teens if you're writing for adults, nor would you use a site that has a casual style and tone for serious research.
- **Links:** Are the links available and appropriate? Check out the links provided on the site to determine whether they're still working and appropriate for your needs. Don't assume that the links provided are the only additional sources of information. Investigate other sites on your topic, as well. You should also be able to find the same information on at least three different websites to help verify the information is accurate. ■

SOUND BYTE
Finding Information on the Web

In this Sound Byte, you'll learn how and when to use search engines and subject directories. Through guided tours, you'll learn effective search techniques, including how to use Boolean operators and metasearch engines.

ACTIVE HELPDESK
Evaluating Websites

In this Active Helpdesk, you'll play the role of a helpdesk staffer, fielding questions about how websites can be evaluated as appropriate to use for research.

trends in IT

Let's say you think that flip-flops in school colors would be a popular product. Your school's bookstore carries everything else with the school's colors and logo, but not flip-flops. You've asked your friends and several classmates, and most of them say they would buy flip-flops in the school's colors. So what do you do next? How do you move from product concept to selling a physical product?

Before the Internet, it would have been much more difficult and expensive to get your product produced and distributed. Today, however, the Internet brings the power of the global economy right to your door (see Figure 3.21). For product design and manufacturing, you can visit a site like Alibaba (**alibaba.com**), which helps entrepreneurs locate manufacturers of all sorts of products. Many manufacturers are happy to work with small business owners to custom-design products.

To sell your product, you might be able to find a retailer or you can set up a website to sell them yourself. Although there are several websites that offer great templates and tools you can use to build your own website, you might want to use a freelance professional to help by using sites such as Guru (**guru.com**) or Elance (**elance.com**). You simply create a description of the job you need done, post it on the site, and invite freelancers to bid on your job. You then contact the freelancers who look promising, review samples of their work, and decide on someone who can help you—and at a competitive price. After your website is up and running, you can place your business on social networking sites, such as Facebook, to help potential customers discover your product and spread the word about your great flip-flops. You might also want to use crowdfunding sites such as Kickstarter and Indiegogo to raise some capital to help finance your new venture.

Another hurdle is determining where you'll store your product and who will package and ship it to customers. If your parents' basement isn't large enough, you can outsource warehousing and order fulfillment to **Amazon.com**. Amazon will (for a fee) warehouse your inventory and then package and ship it when customer orders are received. Orders don't have to come through Amazon's site (although that is an option); you can provide ordering information collected on your site to Amazon, and Amazon will take care of the rest.

Although there is always a cost to starting up a business, up-front costs are much lower when you take advantage of the global marketplace and the Internet. So, take that brilliant idea you have and turn it into a business today!

FIGURE 3.21 By using the services of a few websites, you can create and distribute products, such as your own line of flip-flops. *(Pixindy/Fotolia, lucadp/Fotolia, WaD/Fotolia, Kevin Britland/Alamy, ProStockStudio/Shutterstock, Gstudio Group/Fotolia)*

using the web
ETHICALLY

As you've read in this chapter, the web offers a vast array of opportunities for business, communication, collaboration, and entertainment. It also poses some temptations for inappropriate behavior, often to seek gain at another's expense. In this section, we'll explore several ethical issues that are challenging how we use the web.

Intellectual Property and Cyberbullying

Objective 3.14 *Demonstrate an understanding of intellectual property and cyberbullying.*

What is intellectual property and what issues does it pose? Intellectual property is the result of someone's creativity and knowledge, such as music, writing, and software, which is protected by copyright law and documented by copyrights, patents, and trademarks. Anti-piracy efforts by various organizations and governments aim to protect intellectual property rights—an issue that has been an ongoing and important one, especially in the technology industry.

One of the challenges of anti-piracy efforts is the economic and trading ramifications that occur when countries refuse to enforce copyright laws. For example, countries such as China and the Philippines have been known for their high use of pirated software. Businesses and individuals in those countries and elsewhere that use illegal copies of operating and productivity software potentially gain an advantage in the international marketplace. Microsoft has taken several measures to combat illegal piracy but still hasn't managed to effectively reduce the number of pirated copies of its operating system.

The music and film industries also struggle with piracy issues. Although efforts to increase digital sales of music and film is helping, piracy challenges have placed significant pressures on existing business models for the creative arts industries, both at home and in the global marketplace. Time will tell whether copyright laws will need to be revised to adapt to the predominant digital culture, whether regulatory agencies will need to improve the methods of controlling piracy, or whether the industries themselves will need to change their business models.

What are the effects of cyberbullying? Cyberbullying involves the use of digital technologies such as the Internet, cell phones, or video to bully another (see Figure 3.22). Cyberbullying can include actions such as bombarding a victim with harassing instant messages or text messages, spreading rumors or lies on social networking sites, posting embarrassing photos or videos of a victim on the web, or infecting the victim's computer with malware, usually to spy on that person.

The effects of cyberbullying can be devastating. Infamous cases include Hannah Smith, the English girl who at 14 committed suicide after being repeatedly taunted on social

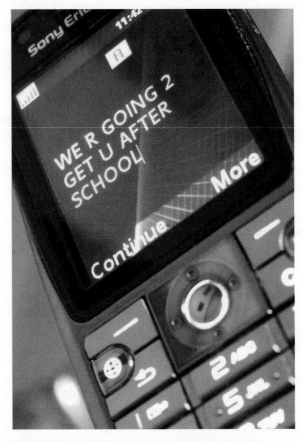

FIGURE 3.22 Cyberbullying involves the use of digital technologies both to bully and to disseminate acts of bullying. *(Rawdon Wyatt/Alamy)*

networking sites, and Tyler Clementi, a Rutgers freshman who committed suicide after his roommate showed fellow students videos of him having sex.

There is currently no federal law prohibiting cyberbullying, but a recently passed law against cyberstalking may cover this area. According to the Cyberbullying Research Center (**cyberbullying.us**), as of July 2015, all states had anti-bullying laws or policies on the books. However, only 48 state laws cover electronic harassment, and a mere 22 state laws cover cyberbullying. Many legislatures are reluctant to pass laws that instruct parents on how to raise their children because this tends to raise issues about personal freedom. Therefore, anti-cyberbullying laws tend to place the burden of detection on the schools. For instance, the Massachusetts law requires schools to provide age-appropriate education on bullying to students, to train school employees in detection and prevention of bullying, and to have plans developed for detecting and reporting bullying.

Privacy and Geolocation

Objective 3.15 *Demonstrate an understanding of the ethical issues regarding online privacy and geolocation.*

What, exactly, is privacy? The idea of privacy is often associated with hiding something (a behavior, a relationship, or a secret). However, privacy really means not being required to reveal your behavior to others. Social media sites such as Facebook are inherently about sharing information with others. Does this mean there is no such thing as personal privacy on social media sites (see Figure 3.23)?

What are the ethical issues regarding privacy online? Facebook and other social media allow you to set privacy filters on your personal information. You can choose to share information publically, share it just with your friends, or keep it totally private. Employers now routinely check social media sites to gather publically shared information on prospective employees. However, recently, many government agencies, such as police departments and some private employers, have been asking job seekers for access to their *private* Facebook information.

Although the Password Protection Act still has not been passed into law, over a dozen states, including Maryland, New Jersey, and California, have enacted similar legislation. Employers in those states are currently prohibited from asking prospective employees for passwords to social networking sites in an effort to garner information related to their gender, race, religion, age, and sexual orientation. Regardless, this information is often found in social media site profiles, and employers are finding more subtle methods, such as encouraging prospective employees to "friend" them on Facebook, which gives the company more access to a candidate's public profile. The control and privacy of information will continue to be a fine balancing act for the foreseeable future, with employers trying to gather intelligence while appeasing the concerns of privacy advocates.

FIGURE 3.24 Geolocation applications help you find cool places and businesses. But who do you want to find you? *(Cseke Timea/Fotolia)*

Leaving a trail of electronic breadcrumbs is, to a certain extent, inevitable. But cleaning up or hiding your "trail" is still important to many users, not because they're trying to hide something but because they value their basic right to privacy.

What is geolocation and what privacy risks does it pose? "Where are you?" is the burning social networking question these days, and your smartphone probably has the answer. The technology is called **geolocation** (see Figure 3.24), and most mobile devices have a GPS chip that can calculate your exact position. Starbucks, Snapchat, and Uber are just a handful of apps that have the capacity to track your location, with your permission. Why is this an issue? User location data is often shared with third-party advertising networks and even with law enforcement agencies. While you can modify or turn off the location aspects in most mobile apps, these measures cannot guarantee that data will not be shared with third parties since the location data is "leaked" in other ways. Even with app location tracking turned off, your location can be captured just when your device is turned on. This feature has been useful to pinpoint users in emergency situations, but the data, if placed in the wrong hands, or for the wrong purposes, can be a violation of your privacy. Retrospectively, historical location data can be discerned from service provider records, and additionally, WiFi hotspots can be used to track mobile devices. Moreover, other features of a smartphone, such as the camera and phone, can capture a user's geolocation data. Therefore, the privacy implications still remain. Although legislation has been initiated, no specific law has been passed to address the privacy concerns of location-tracking devices and applications. Although most mobile device users are aware of location data collection practices, they are not aware of what was being collected and how it is, and can be, used. ∎

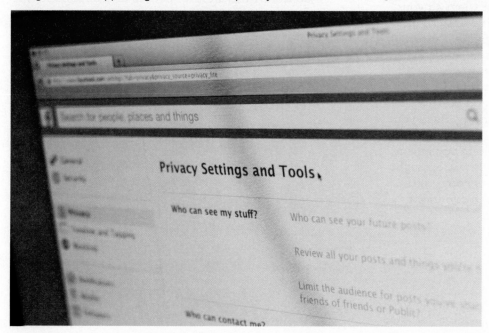

FIGURE 3.23 What information are you sharing on Facebook and with whom? *(Dolphfyn/Alamy)*

Using information from the web without receiving proper permissions is not only wrong but can also be illegal. So what can you borrow from the web and what must you seek permission to use? Consider these scenarios:

1. You copy a political cartoon into your PowerPoint presentation for your civics class.
2. For children's books that you write and later sell online, you sometimes borrow story ideas from other children's books, just changing a few characters or situations. You do not obtain permission from the originators of the story ideas you borrow.
3. You copy information from an obscure website into your research paper without documenting the source.
4. You download a song from the Internet and incorporate it into a PowerPoint presentation for a school project. Because you assume everyone knows the song, you don't credit it in your sources.

Which of the preceding scenarios represent copyright violations? Which represent plagiarism? The distinctions between these scenarios are narrow in some cases, but it's important to understand the differences.

Plagiarism occurs when you use someone else's ideas or words and represent them as your own. In today's computer society, it's easy to use information from the Internet and paste it into a Word document, change a few words, and call it your own. To avoid plagiarism, properly credit all information you obtain from the Internet by using quotation marks around all words you borrow directly, and credit your sources for any ideas you paraphrase or borrow.

Copyright violation is more serious because it, unlike plagiarism, is punishable by law. Copyright law assumes that all original work is copyrighted even if the work does not display the copyright symbol (©). Copyright violation occurs when you use another person's material for your own personal economic benefit or when you take away from the economic benefit of the originator. In most cases, citing the source is not sufficient; you need to seek and receive written permission from the copyright holder.

There are exceptions to this rule. There is no copyright on government documents, so you can download and reproduce material from any government website. Teachers and students receive special consideration that falls under a provision called *academic fair use*. As long as the material is being used for educational purposes only, limited copying and distribution is allowed.

So, do you now know which of the four scenarios above are plagiarism or copyright violations? Let's review them.

1. You are not in violation because the use of the cartoon is for educational purposes and falls under the academic fair use provision. You must still credit the source, however.
2. You are in violation of copyright laws because you are presenting others' ideas for children's stories as your own and receiving personal economic benefit from them.
3. You are guilty of plagiarism because you copied content from another source and implied it was your own work.
4. Again, because your copying is for a school project, you are not in violation of copyright laws because of the academic fair use provision. However, it's always important to document your sources.

Before moving on to the Chapter Review:
1. Watch Replay Video 3.2 ▷.
2. Then check your understanding of what you've learned so far.

check your understanding // review & practice

For a quick review to see what you've learned so far, answer the following questions.

multiple choice

1. What is the navigation aid that shows users the path they have taken to get to a web page located within a website?

   a. Favorites
   b. Breadcrumb trail
   c. Bookmarks
   d. Social bookmarks

2. Which search strategy should you use to search for a specific phrase?

   a. Use quotation marks around the phrase.
   b. Use asterisks around the phrase.
   c. Include Boolean operators in the phrase.
   d. Use a wild card around the phrase.

3. When using the Internet for research, you

   a. can assume that everything you find is accurate and appropriate.
   b. should evaluate sites for bias and relevance.
   c. can assume if there is no author listed, the site is not appropriate for research.
   d. should look for sites with many links to other resources.

4. Which of the following is not an Internet protocol?

   a. ARPANET
   b. HTTP
   c. FTP
   d. BitTorrent

5. Which type of website would StumbleUpon be classified as?

   a. Crowdfunding site
   b. Live bookmarking site
   c. Metasearch site
   d. Social bookmarking site

MyITLab   Go to **MyITLab** to take an autograded version of the *Check Your Understanding* review and to find all media resources for the chapter.

TECHBYTES WEEKLY
Stay current with the TechBytes Weekly Newsletter.

Continue ≫

3 Chapter Review

summary //

Working and Playing on the Web

Learning Outcome 3.1 **You will be able to explain how the Internet works and how it is used for collaboration, communication, commerce, and entertainment purposes.**

The Internet and How It Works

Objective 3.1 *Describe how the Internet got its start.*

- The Internet is the largest computer network in the world, connecting millions of computers.
- Government and military officials developed the early Internet as a reliable way to communicate in the event of war. Eventually, scientists and educators used the Internet to exchange research.
- Today, we use the Internet and the web (which is a part of the Internet) to shop, research, communicate, and entertain ourselves.

Objective 3.2 *Explain how data travels on the Internet.*

- A computer (or other device) connected to the Internet acts as either a client (a computer that asks for information) or a server (a computer that receives the request and returns the information to the client).
- Data travels between clients and servers along a system of communication lines or pathways. The largest and fastest of these pathways form the Internet backbone.
- To ensure that data is sent to the correct computer along the pathways, IP addresses (unique ID numbers) are assigned to all computers connected to the Internet.

Collaborating and Communicating on the Web

Objective 3.3 *Discuss the tools and technologies used to collaborate and communicate on the web.*

- Web 2.0 can be described as the social web, in which the user is also a participant. Examples of Web 2.0 technologies include social networking, blogs, wikis, podcasts, and webcasts.
- Social networking enables you to communicate and share information with friends as well as meet and connect with others.
- Blogs are journal entries posted to the web that are generally organized by a topic or area of interest and are publically available.

- Video logs are personal journals that use video as the primary content in addition to text, images, and audio.
- A wiki is a type of website that allows users to collaborate on content—adding, removing, or editing it.
- Some web tools that are useful for group collaboration online are screen sharing, project management, and videoconferencing applications.
- Podcasts are audio or video content available over the Internet. Users subscribe to receive updates to podcasts.
- Webcasts are broadcasts of audio or video content over the Internet.

Objective 3.4 *Summarize how e-mail and instant messaging are used to communicate over the web.*

- E-mail allows users to communicate electronically without the parties involved being available at the same time.
- Instant-messaging services are programs that enable you to communicate in real time with others who are online.

Business and Entertainment on the Web

Objective 3.5 *Describe the different types of e-commerce.*

- E-commerce is the business of conducting business online.
- E-commerce includes transactions between businesses (B2B), between consumers (C2C), and between businesses and consumers (B2C).

Objective 3.6 *Summarize precautions you should take when doing business online.*

- Because more business than ever before is conducted online, numerous safeguards have been put in place to ensure that transactions are protected.

Objective 3.7 *Describe the types of multimedia files found on the web.*

- Multimedia is anything that involves one or more forms of media in addition to text, such as graphics, audio, and video clips.

Using the Web Effectively

Learning Outcome 3.2 You will be able to describe the tools and techniques required to navigate and search the web.

Accessing and Moving Around the Web

Objective 3.8 *Explain what web browsers are, and describe their common features.*

- Once you're connected to the Internet, in order to locate, navigate to, and view web pages, you need software called web browser.
- The most common web browsers are Microsoft Edge, Firefox, Google Chrome, and Safari.

Objective 3.9 *Explain what a URL is, and discuss its main parts.*

- You gain access to a website by typing in its address, called a Uniform Resource Locator (URL).
- A URL is comprised of several parts, including the protocol, the domain, the top-level domain, and paths (or subdirectories).

Objective 3.10 *Describe tools used to navigate the web.*

- One unique aspect of the web is that you can jump from place to place by clicking on specially formatted pieces of text or images called hyperlinks.
- You can also use the Back and Forward buttons, History lists, and breadcrumb trails to navigate the web.

Objective 3.11: *Describe tools used to mark websites for future use.*

- Favorites, live bookmarks, and social bookmarking help you return to specific web pages without having to type in the URL and help you organize the web content that is most important to you.

Searching the Web Effectively

Objective 3.12 *Describe the types of tools used to search the web and summarize strategies used to refine search results.*

- A search engine is a set of programs that searches the web using specific keywords you wish to query and then returns a list of the websites on which those keywords are found.

- Search engines can be used to search for images, podcasts, and videos in addition to traditional text-based web content.
- Metasearch engines search other search engines.

Objective 3.13 *Describe how to evaluate a website to ensure it is appropriate to use for research purposes.*

- To evaluate whether it is appropriate to use a website as a resource, determine whether the author of the site is reputable, whether the site is intended for your particular needs, that the site content is not biased, that the information on the site is current, and that all the links on the site are available and appropriate.

Using the Web Ethically

Objective 3.14 *Demonstrate an understanding of intellectual property and cyberbullying.*

- Intellectual property is the result of someone's creativity and knowledge.
- There have been significant issues with piracy of software, music, and other online content that have placed burdens on the creative arts industries, technology industries, and regulators.
- Cyberbullying is bullying with digital technologies. It is not clear who should bear the responsibility for monitoring against cyberbullying.

Objective 3.15 *Demonstrate an understanding of the ethical issues regarding privacy and geolocation.*

- Privacy is the right to be left alone, but it is often difficult to achieve with social media.
- Apps with geolocation technology garner much information about your location. Users should be aware of why companies need to track a user's location, and what the companies will do with that location data.

MyITLab Be sure to check out **MyITLab** for additional materials to help you review and learn.

key terms //

chapter quiz // assessment

For a quick review to see what you've learned, answer the following questions. Submit the quiz as requested by your instructor. If you are using **MyITLab**, the quiz is also available there.

multiple choice

1. The Internet was created to provide
   a. a secure form of communications.
   b. a common communication means for all computers.
   c. both a and b
   d. neither a nor b

2. Which of the following describes an IP address?
   a. It is referred to as a dotted quad.
   b. It identifies any computer connecting to the Internet.
   c. It identifies a website.
   d. all of the above

3. Which of the following browsers was introduced with Windows 10?
   a. Chrome
   b. Firefox
   c. Microsoft Edge
   d. Internet Explorer

4. What web browser feature would be particularly useful when using public computers?
   a. Pinned tabs
   b. Session restore
   c. Privacy browsing
   d. all of the above

5. In the URL http://www.whitehouse.gov/blog, which part is considered the protocol?
   a. http
   b. .gov
   c. www.whitehouse.gov
   d. /blog

6. Search engines that search other search engines are called
   a. megasearch engines.
   b. betasearch engines.
   c. gigasearch engines.
   d. metasearch engines.

true/false

_____ 1. Google Docs, a part of Google Drive, uses wiki technology.

_____ 2. Webcasts are only delivered as prerecorded audio and video content.

_____ 3. The "s" in HTTPS stands for secure and indicates that the secure sockets layer protocol has been applied to the website.

_____ 4. Paraphrasing content from a website into your research paper without documenting the source is considered plagiarism.

critical thinking

1. **The Power of Google**

   Google is the largest and most popular search engine on the Internet today. Because of its size and popularity, some people claim that Google has enormous power to influence a web user's search experience solely by its website-ranking processes. What do you think about this potential power? How could it be used in negative or harmful ways?
   a. Some websites pay search engines to list them near the top of the results pages. These sponsors, therefore, get priority placement. What do you think of this policy?
   b. What effect (if any) do you think that Google has on website development? For example, do you think website developers intentionally include frequently searched words in their pages so that they will appear in more hit lists?

2. **Mobile E-Commerce Safety**

   The text lists several ways to ensure your online transactions are secure and to reduce the risk of things going awry as you shop and sell online. However, surveys indicate that many feel that shopping from a mobile device, such as a smartphone, presents additional risks. Do you agree there are additional risks when conducting e-commerce from a mobile device? Why or why not?

team time //

Collaborating with Technology

Problem

Collaborating on projects with team members is a regular part of business and academia. Many great tools are available that facilitate online collaboration, and it's important to be familiar with them. In this Team Time, each team will create a group report on a specific topic, using online collaboration tools, and compare and rate the tools and the collaboration process.

Process

Split your group into teams. To appreciate fully the benefits of online collaboration, each team should have at least five or six members. Each group will create a team report on a topic that is approved by your instructor. As part of the report, one group member should record the process the group took to create the report, including a review of the tools used and reflections on the difficulties encountered by the group.

1. Conduct a virtual meeting. Agree on an online meeting and video collaboration tool such as Skype, Google+ Hangouts, or Apple FaceTime and conduct a group chat. In this phase, outline your group project strategy and delegate work responsibilities.

2. Share documents and collaborate online. Your group must create one document that is accessible to every member at all times. Explore document-sharing sites such as Google Drive, Evernote, OneDrive, or Dropbox and collaboratively create your group document. All members are responsible for reviewing the entire document.

Conclusion

After all the team group reports have been completed and shared, discuss the following with your class: What is the benefit of using online collaboration technology to create group projects? How did collaboration technologies help or hinder the team process?

ethics project //

Plagiarism

In this exercise, you'll research and then role-play a complicated ethical situation. The role you play may or may not match your own personal beliefs, but your research and use of logic will enable you to represent whichever view is assigned. An arbitrator will watch and comment on both sides of the arguments, and together the team will agree on an ethical solution.

Problem

Plagiarism, or portraying another's work as your own, has been around for a long time and extends well beyond the classroom. For example, Nick Simmons, the son of Gene Simmons (from KISS) and a member of A&E's *Family Jewels* reality series, created a comic book series, *Incarnate*. Radical Publishing picked up the series but quickly stopped publication when Internet messages accused the author of copying from other similar series. Similarly, the Australian band Men at Work was cited for copying a melody from *Kookaburra Sits in the Old Gum Tree* for its 1980s hit *Down Under* and owes the owner years of royalties.

Research Areas to Consider

- Plagiarism violations
- Comic book series *Incarnate*
- Australian band Men at Work
- Plagiarism consequences

Process

1. Divide the class into teams. Research the areas cited above and devise a scenario in which someone has violated plagiarism rules.

2. Team members should write a summary that provides background information for their character—for example, author, publisher, or arbitrator—and that details their character's behaviors to set the stage for the role-playing event. Then team members should create an outline to use during the role-playing event.

3. Team members should arrange a mutually convenient time to meet for the exchange, using a virtual meeting tool or by meeting in person.

4. Team members should present their case to the class or submit a PowerPoint presentation for review by the rest of the class, along with the summary and resolution they developed.

Conclusion

As technology becomes ever more prevalent and integrated into our lives, more and more ethical dilemmas will present themselves. Being able to understand and evaluate both sides of an argument, while responding in a personally or socially ethical manner, will be an important skill.

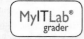
Create a Report: Conducting Research on the Web

You and a partner have been asked to write a report on alternatives to using the Google search engine, as well as how to evaluate a website for a research paper. The paper needs to cite references within the body of the text, and include a list of your works cited at the end of the report. Your partner has begun the report. You are going to modify what has been started.

You will use the following skills as you complete this activity:

- Use Find and Replace
- Format Bulleted Lists
- Insert SmartArt
- Insert a Hyperlink
- Add Sources
- Insert Citations and Bibliography

Instructions:

1. Start Word. Open *TIACh03_Start.docx* and save it as **TIACh03_LastFirst.docx**, using your last and first names.
2. Using Find and Replace, find all instances of *metasearch* and replace them with **meta-search**.
3. At the blank paragraph after the end of the second paragraph of text under *Alternative Search Engines*, insert a **Vertical Box List SmartArt graphic**. Open the text pane, if necessary. With the cursor active in the first bullet, type **Google Scholar**. (Do not include the period.) Press **Enter**, press **Tab**, and then type **Searches scholarly literature**. (Do not include the period.)

   Repeat these steps to add the following information for the next two bullets:

   Dogpile
   Meta-search engine that searches Google, Yahoo!, and Bing
   Specialty Search Engines
   Search only sites that are relevant to a topic or industry

   a. Hint: To insert a SmartArt graphic, on the Insert tab, in the Illustrations group, click **SmartArt**.
4. Change the SmartArt graphic colors to **Colorful—Accent Colors**. Move the Google Scholar box and bullet point to the bottom of the SmartArt. Change the SmartArt Style to **Intense Effect**.

   a. Hint: To change the colors, on the SmartArt Tools Design tab, in the SmartArt Styles group, click **Colors**. To move the box and bullet point, select the content, then in the Create Graphic group, click **Move Down**. To change the style, in the SmartArt Styles group, click the **More button** for Styles.
5. In the second to last sentence of the first paragraph in the *Alternative Search Engines* section, select the text **specialty search engines**. Then, create a hyperlink to the web page **bestonlineuniversities.com/2011/20-useful-specialty-search-engines-for-college-students/**.
6. At the end of the first paragraph in the *Evaluating Websites* section, immediately to the left of the period, insert a citation to a new website. Before entering information, click the check box for **Show All Bibliography Fields**. Use the following information:

   Author: **Kapoun, Jim**
   Name of Web Page: **Five criteria for evaluating web pages**
   Name of Website: **Olin & Uris Libraries, Cornell University**
   Year: **2010**
   Month: **May**
   Day: **10**
   URL: **olinuris.library.cornell.edu/ref/research/webcrit.html**.
7. In the *Evaluating Websites* section, create a bulleted list with the five points beginning with *Authority, Bias or Objectivity, Relevance, Audience,* and *Coverage*. Use a checkmark as the bullet point.
8. Press **Ctrl+End** to go to the end of the document, press **Enter** twice, and then insert a Works Cited Bibliography. Change the citation style to **APA Sixth Edition**.
9. Save the document, and then close Word.
10. Submit the document as directed.

Technology in Focus

The History of the Personal Computer

Learning Outcome 3B.1 You will be able to describe the history of personal computer hardware and software development.

Ever wonder how big the first personal computer was or how much the first laptop weighed? Computers are such an integral part of our lives that we don't often stop to think about how far they've come or where they got their start. In just over 40 years, computers have evolved from expensive, huge machines that only corporations could own to small, powerful devices that almost anyone can have. In this Technology in Focus feature, we look at the history of the personal computer.

FIGURE 1 Timeline of Early Personal Computer Development

The Altair 8800
- Only 256 bytes of memory
- No keyboard or monitor
- Switches on front used to enter data in machine code (1s and 0s)
- Lights on front indicated results of a program

1975

Commodore PET
- Featured in *Popular Science* magazine
- Popular in business settings in Europe

October 1977

1976

June 1977

Apple I

Steve Jobs and Steve Wozniak form Apple Computer

Apple II
- Featured color monitor, sound, and game paddles
- 4 KB of RAM
- Operating system stored in ROM
- Optional floppy disk to load programs (mostly games)

(B Christopher/Alamy Stock Photo, Jerry Mason/Science Source, SSPL/The Image Works, Marilyn K. Yee/Getty Images, Steve Castillo/AP Images, Science & Society Picture Library/Getty Images)

Early Personal Computers

Our journey through the history of the personal computer starts in 1975. At that time, most people weren't familiar with the mainframes and supercomputers that large corporations and the government owned. With price tags exceeding the cost of buildings, and with few (if any) practical home uses, these monster machines weren't appealing to or attainable by average Americans.

The First Personal Computer: The Altair

Objective 3B.1 *Describe the earliest personal computer ever designed.*

However, in 1975, the first personal computer, the **Altair 8800** (see Figure 1), was born. At $395 for a do-it-yourself kit or $498 for a fully assembled unit (about $2,253 in today's dollars), the price was reasonable enough that computer fanatics could finally own their own computers.

The Altair was primitive by today's standards—no keyboard, no monitor, and completely not user friendly. Despite its limitations, computer enthusiasts flocked to the machine. Many who bought it had been taught to program, but until that point,

they had access only to big, clumsy computers at their jobs. With the Altair, they could create their own programs. Within 3 months, 4,000 orders were placed for the machine.

The release of the Altair marked the start of the personal computer boom. In fact, two men whose names you might have heard were among the first Altair owners—Bill Gates and Paul Allen were so enamored by the "minicomputer" that they wrote a compiling program (a program that translates user commands into commands the computer can understand) for it. The two later convinced the Altair's developer to buy their program, marking the start of a company called Microsoft. We'll get to that story later. First, let's see what their rivals were up to.

The Apple I and II

Objective 3B.2 *Describe the distinguishing features of the Apple I and Apple II.*

Around the time the Altair was released, **Steve Wozniak**, an employee at Hewlett-Packard, was dabbling with his own computer design. **Steve Jobs**, who was working for computer game manufacturer Atari at the time, liked Wozniak's prototypes and made a few suggestions. Together, the two built a personal computer, the **Apple I**, in Wozniak's garage (see Figure 1) and formed the Apple Computer Company in 1976.

TRS-80

- Introduced by Radio Shack
- Monochrome display
- 4 KB of RAM
- Circuitry hidden under keyboard
- Wildly popular with consumers—sold 10,000 units in the first month

November 1977

IBM PC (5150)

- Marketed to businesses and consumers
- 64 KB to 256 KB of RAM
- Floppy disk drives optional
- Hard disks not supported in early models

August 1981

April 1981

- First "portable" computer
- Weighed 24.5 pounds
- 5-inch screen
- 64 kilobytes of RAM
- Two floppy disk drives
- Preinstalled with spreadsheet and word processing software

Osbourne

One year later, in 1977, the **Apple II** was born (see Figure 1). The Apple II included a color monitor, sound, and game paddles. Priced around $1,300 (about $5,245 in today's dollars), one of its biggest innovations was that the operating system was stored in read-only memory (ROM). Previously, the operating system had to be rewritten every time the computer was turned on. The friendly features of the Apple II operating system encouraged less technically oriented computer enthusiasts to write their own programs.

An instant success, the Apple II would eventually include a spreadsheet program, a word processor, and desktop publishing software. These programs gave personal computers like the Apple functions beyond gaming and special programming and led to their popularity.

Enter the Competition

Around the time Apple was experiencing success with its computers, a number of competitors entered the market. The largest among them were Commodore, Radio Shack, Osborne, and IBM. The **Commodore PET** (see Figure 1) was aimed at the business market and did well in Europe, while Radio Shack's **TRS-80** (see Figure 1) was clearly aimed at the U.S. consumer market. Just 1 month after its release in 1977, it had sold about 10,000 units.

The Osborne: The Birth of Portable Computing

Objective 3B.3 *Describe the first portable computer.*

The Osborne Company introduced the first portable computer, the **Osborne**, in 1981 (see Figure 1). Although portable, the computer weighed 24.5 pounds. It featured a minuscule 5-inch screen and carried a price tag of $1,795 (about $4,884 today). The Osborne was an overnight success, and its sales quickly reached 10,000 units per month. However, despite the computer's popularity, the Osborne Company eventually closed. Compaq bought the Osborne design and in 1983 produced its own portable computer.

IBM PCs

Objective 3B.4 *Describe the development of the IBM PC.*

Until 1980, IBM primarily made mainframe computers, which it sold to large corporations, and hadn't taken the personal computer seriously. In 1981, however, IBM released its first personal computer, the **IBM PC** (see Figure 1). Because many companies were familiar with IBM mainframes, they adopted the IBM PC. The term *PC* soon became the term used to describe all personal computers.

IBM marketed its PC through retail outlets such as Sears to reach home users, and it quickly dominated that market. In January 1983, *Time* magazine, playing on its annual person of the year issue, named the computer "1982 Machine of the Year."

Other Important Advancements

It wasn't just personal computer hardware that was changing. At the same time, advances in programming languages and operating systems and the influx of application software were leading to more useful and powerful machines.

The Importance of BASIC

Objective 3B.5 *Explain why BASIC was an important step in revolutionizing the software industry.*

The software industry began in the 1950s with programming languages such as FORTRAN, ALGOL, and COBOL. These languages were used mainly by businesses to create financial, statistical, and engineering programs. However, the 1964 introduction of **Beginners All-Purpose Symbolic Instruction Code (BASIC)** revolutionized the software industry. BASIC was a language that beginning programming students could easily learn. It thus became enormously popular—and the key language of the PC. In fact, **Bill Gates** and **Paul Allen** (see Figure 2) used BASIC to write their program for the Altair.

FIGURE 2 Bill Gates and Paul Allen are the founders of Microsoft. *(Doug Wilson/Corbis)*

As we noted earlier, this program led to the creation of Microsoft, a company that produced computer software.

The Advent of Operating Systems

Objective 3B.6 *Explain why the development of the operating system was an important step in PC development.*

Because data on the earliest personal computers was stored on audiocassettes, many programs weren't saved or reused. This meant that programs had to be rewritten whenever they were needed. In 1978, Steve Wozniak designed a 5.25-inch floppy disk drive so that programs could be saved easily and operating systems developed.

Operating systems are written to coordinate with the specific processor chip that controls the computer. At that time, Apples ran on a Motorola chip, whereas PCs (IBMs and so on) ran on an Intel chip. **Disk Operating System (DOS)**, developed by Wozniak and introduced in 1977, was the OS that controlled the first Apple computers. The **Control Program for Microcomputers (CP/M)**, developed by Gary Kildall, was the OS designed for the Intel 8080 chip (the processor for PCs).

In 1980, when IBM was entering the personal computer market, it approached Bill Gates at Microsoft to write an OS program for the IBM PC. Gates recommended that IBM investigate the CP/M OS, but IBM couldn't arrange a meeting with the founder, Gary Kildall. Microsoft reconsidered the opportunity to write an OS program and developed **MS-DOS** for IBM computers. Eventually, virtually all PCs running on the Intel chip used MS-DOS as their OS (see Figure 3). Microsoft's reign as one of the dominant players in the personal computer landscape had begun.

The Software Application Explosion: VisiCalc and Beyond

Objective 3B.7 *List early application software that was developed for the PC.*

Because the floppy disk was a convenient way to distribute software, its inclusion in personal computers set off an application software explosion. In 1978, Harvard Business School student Dan Bricklin recognized the potential for a personal computer spreadsheet program. He and his friend Bob Frankston created the program **VisiCalc**, which became an instant success. Finally, ordinary home users could see the benefit of owning a personal computer. More than 100,000 copies of VisiCalc were sold in its first year.

After VisiCalc, other electronic spreadsheet programs entered the market. **Lotus 1-2-3** came on the market in 1983, and **Microsoft Excel** entered the scene in 1985. These products became so popular that they eventually put VisiCalc out of business.

Meanwhile, word processing software was also gaining a foothold in the industry. Until then, there were separate, dedicated word processing machines; personal computers, it was believed, were for computation and data management only. However, once **WordStar**, the first word processing application, became available for personal computers in 1979, word processing became another important use for the personal computer. Competitors such as **Word for MS-DOS**

FIGURE 3 This 1983 Hewlett-Packard computer used an early version of the MS-DOS operating system as well as the Lotus 1-2-3 spreadsheet program. *(Everett Collection/SuperStock)*

(the precursor to Microsoft Word) and **WordPerfect** soon entered the market. Figure 4 lists some of the important dates in application software development.

The Graphical User Interface and the Internet Boom

Other important advancements related to personal computers came in the form of the graphical user interface and the Internet.

Xerox and Apple's Lisa and Macintosh

Objective 3B.8 *Describe the features of the Lisa and Macintosh computers and their predecessor, the Xerox Alto.*

A **graphical user interface (GUI)**, which uses icons to represent programs and actions, allowed users to interact

FIGURE 4

Application Software Development

YEAR	APPLICATION
1978	**VisiCalc:** First electronic spreadsheet application **WordStar:** First word processing application
1980	**WordPerfect:** Best DOS-based word processor, was eventually sold to Novell and later acquired by Corel
1983	**Lotus 1-2-3:** Added integrated charting, plotting, and database capabilities to spreadsheet software **Word for MS-DOS:** Introduced in the pages of *PC World* magazine on the first magazine-inserted demo disk
1985	**Excel:** One of the first spreadsheets to use a graphical user interface **PageMaker:** The first desktop publishing software

FIGURE 5 The Alto was the first computer to use a GUI, and it provided the basis for the GUI that Apple used. However, because of marketing problems, the Alto never was sold. *(Josie Lepe/MCT/Newscom)*

FIGURE 6 The Lisa was the first computer to introduce a GUI to the market. Priced too high, it never gained the popularity it deserved. *(SSPL/The Image Works)*

with the computer more easily. Until that time, users had to use complicated command- or menu-driven interfaces. Apple was the first company to take full commercial advantage of the GUI, but the GUI was not invented by a computer company.

In 1972, a few years before Apple launched its first personal computer, photocopier manufacturer **Xerox** was designing a personal computer of its own. Named the **Alto** (see Figure 5), the computer included a word processor, based on the What You See Is What You Get (WYSIWYG) principle, that incorporated a file management system with directories and folders. It also had a mouse and could connect to a network. None of the other personal computers of the time had these features. For a variety of reasons, Xerox never sold the Alto commercially. Several years later, it developed the Star Office System, which was based on the Alto. Despite its convenient features, the Star never became popular because no one was willing to pay the $17,000 asking price.

Xerox's ideas were ahead of their time, but many of the ideas present in the Alto and Star would soon catch on. In 1983, Apple introduced the **Lisa**—the first successful personal computer brought to market that used a GUI (see Figure 6). Legend has it that Jobs had seen the Alto during a visit to Xerox in 1979 and was influenced by its GUI. He therefore incorporated a similar user interface into the Lisa, providing features such as windows, drop-down menus, icons, a file system with folders and files, and a point-and-click device called a mouse. The only problem with the Lisa was its price. At $9,995 (about $24,047 in today's dollars), few buyers were willing to take the plunge.

One year later, in 1984, Apple introduced the **Macintosh**, shown in Figure 7. The Macintosh was everything the Lisa was and then some, at about a third of the cost. The Macintosh was also the first personal computer to utilize 3.5-inch floppy disks

with a hard cover, which were smaller and sturdier than the previous 5.25-inch floppies.

The Internet Boom

Objective 3B.9 *List the first successful web browsers.*

The GUI made it easier for users to work on the computer. The Internet provided another reason for people to buy computers. Now people could conduct research and communicate in a new way. In 1993, the web browser **Mosaic** was introduced. This browser allowed users to view multimedia on the web, causing Internet traffic to increase by nearly 350%.

FIGURE 7 The Macintosh became one of Apple's best-selling computers, incorporating a GUI along with other innovations such as the 3.5-inch floppy disk drive. *(Corbis)*

Meanwhile, companies discovered the Internet as a means to do business, and computer sales took off. IBM-compatible PCs became the computer system of choice when, in 1995, Microsoft introduced **Internet Explorer**, a browser that integrated web functionality into Microsoft Office applications, and **Windows 95**, the first Microsoft OS designed to be principally a GUI OS.

About one year earlier, in 1994, a team of developers launched the **Netscape** web browser, which soon became a predominant player in browser software. However, pressures from Microsoft became too strong, and in 1998, Netscape announced it would no longer charge for the product and would make the code available to the public.

Making the Personal Computer Possible: Early Computers

Billions of personal computers have been sold over the past four decades. But the computer is a compilation of parts, each of which is the result of individual inventions. Let's look at some early machines that helped to create the personal computer we know today.

The Pascalene Calculator and the Jacquard Loom

Objective 3B.10 *Discuss the features of the Pascalene calculator and the Jacquard loom that inspired modern computer elements.*

From the earliest days of humankind, we have been looking for a more systematic way to count and calculate. Thus, the evolution of counting machines led to the development of the computer we know today. The **Pascalene** was the first accurate mechanical calculator. This machine, created by the French mathematician **Blaise Pascal** in 1642, used revolutions of gears, like odometers in cars, to count by tens. The Pascalene could be used to add, subtract, multiply, and divide. The basic design of the Pascalene was so sound that it lived on in mechanical calculators for more than 300 years.

Nearly 200 years later, **Joseph Jacquard** revolutionized the fabric industry by creating a machine that automated the weaving of complex patterns. Although not a counting or calculating machine, the **Jacquard loom** (shown in Figure 8) was significant because it relied on stiff cards with punched holes to automate the weaving process. Much later, this punch-card process would be adopted as a means for computers to record and read data.

Babbage's Engines and the Hollerith Tabulating Machine

Objective 3B.11 *Discuss the contributions of Babbage's engines and the Hollerith Tabulating Machine to modern computing.*

In 1834, **Charles Babbage** designed the first automatic calculator, called the **Analytical Engine** (see Figure 9). The machine was actually based on another machine called the **Difference Engine**, which was a huge steam-powered

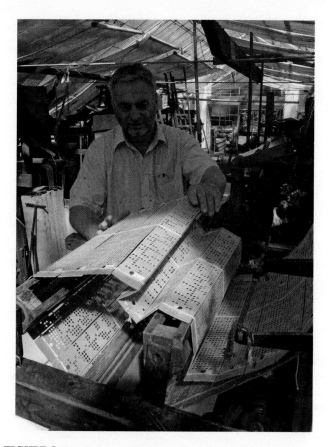

FIGURE 8 The Jacquard loom used holes punched in stiff cards to make complex designs. This technique would later be used in punch cards that controlled the input and output of data in computers. *(Janek Skarzynski/Newscom)*

mechanical calculator that Babbage designed to print astronomical tables. Although the Analytical Engine was never developed, Babbage's detailed drawings and descriptions of the machine include components similar to those found in today's computers, including the store (akin to RAM) and the mill (a central processing unit) as well as input and output devices. This invention gave Charles Babbage the title of the "father of computing."

Meanwhile, Ada Lovelace, who was the daughter of poet Lord Byron and a student of mathematics (which was unusual for women of the time), was fascinated with Babbage's engines. She translated an Italian paper on Babbage's machine and, at the request of Babbage, added her own extensive notes. Her efforts are thought to be the best description of Babbage's engines.

In 1890, **Herman Hollerith**, while working for the U.S. Census Bureau, was the first to take Jacquard's punch-card concept and apply it to computing with his **Hollerith Tabulating Machine**. Until that time, census data had been tabulated manually in a long, laborious process. Hollerith's tabulating machine automatically read data that had been punched onto small punch cards, speeding up the tabulation process. Hollerith's machine became so successful that he left

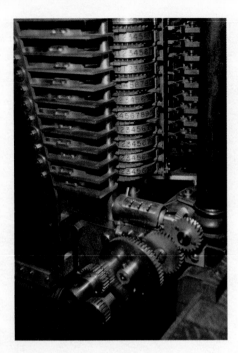

FIGURE 9 The Analytical Engine, designed by Charles Babbage, was never fully developed but included components similar to those found in today's computers. *(Chris Howes/Wild Places Photography)*

the Census Bureau in 1896 to start the Tabulating Machine Company. His company later changed its name to International Business Machines, or IBM.

The Z1, the Atanasoff–Berry Computer, and the Harvard Mark I

Objective 3B.12 *Discuss the features of the Z1, the Atansoff–Berry Computer, and the Mark I.*

German inventor **Konrad Zuse** is credited with a number of computing inventions. His first, in 1936, was a mechanical calculator called the **Z1**. The Z1 is thought to be the first computer to include certain features integral to today's systems, such as a control unit and separate memory functions.

In 1939, John Atanasoff, a professor at Iowa State University, and his student Clifford Berry built the first electrically powered digital computer, called the **Atanasoff–Berry Computer (ABC)**, shown in Figure 10. The computer was the first to use vacuum tubes, instead of the mechanical switches used in older computers, to store data. Although revolutionary at the time, the machine weighed 700 pounds, contained a mile of wire, and took about 15 seconds for each calculation. (In comparison, today's

personal computers can perform billions of calculations in 15 seconds.) Most importantly, the ABC was the first computer to use the binary system and to have memory that repowered itself upon booting. The design of the ABC would be central to that of future computers.

From the late 1930s to the early 1950s, **Howard Aiken** and **Grace Hopper** designed the Mark series of computers used by the U.S. Navy for ballistic and gunnery calculations. Aiken, an electrical engineer and physicist, designed the computer, while Hopper did the programming. The **Harvard Mark I**, finished in 1944, could add, subtract, multiply, and divide.

However, many believe Hopper's greatest contribution to computing was the invention of the **compiler**—a program that translates English-language instructions into computer language. The team was also responsible for a common computer-related expression. Hopper was the first to "debug" a computer when she removed a moth that had flown into the Harvard Mark I and had caused the computer to break down (see Figure 11). After that, problems that caused a computer not to run were called bugs.

The Turing Machine, the ENIAC, and the UNIVAC

Objective 3B.13 *Discuss the major features of the Turing Machine, the ENIAC and the UNIVAC.*

Meanwhile, in 1936, British mathematician **Alan Turing** created an abstract computer model that could perform logical operations. The **Turing Machine** was not a real

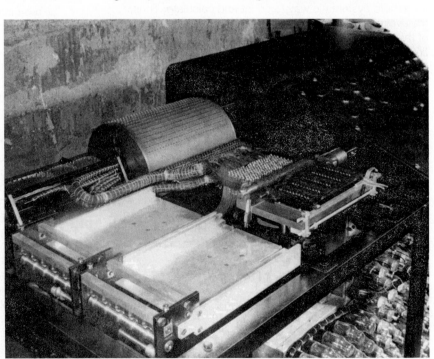

FIGURE 10 The Atanasoff–Berry Computer laid the design groundwork for many computers to come. *(Frederick News Post/AP Images)*

Actual moth pasted
into notebook

FIGURE 11 Grace Hopper coined the term *computer bug* when a moth flew into the Harvard Mark I, causing it to break down. *(Naval History & Heritage Command)*

machine but rather a hypothetical model that mathematically defined a mechanical procedure (or algorithm). Additionally, Turing's concept described a process by which the machine could read, write, or erase symbols written on squares of an infinite paper tape. This concept of an infinite tape that could be read, written to, and erased was the precursor to today's RAM.

The **Electronic Numerical Integrator and Computer (ENIAC)**, shown in Figure 12, was another U.S. government–sponsored machine developed to calculate the settings used for weapons. Created by **John W. Mauchly** and **J. Presper Eckert** at the University of Pennsylvania, it was put into operation in 1944. Although the ENIAC is generally thought of as the first successful high-speed electronic digital computer, it was big and clumsy. The ENIAC used nearly 18,000 vacuum tubes and filled approximately 1,800 square feet of floor space. Although inconvenient, the ENIAC served its purpose and remained in use until 1955.

The **Universal Automatic Computer**, or **UNIVAC**, was the first commercially successful electronic digital computer. Completed in 1951, the UNIVAC operated on magnetic tape (see Figure 13), setting it apart from its competitors, which ran on punch cards. The UNIVAC gained notoriety when, in a 1951 publicity stunt, it was used to predict the outcome of the Stevenson–Eisenhower presidential race. After analyzing only 5% of the popular vote, the UNIVAC correctly identified Dwight D. Eisenhower as the victor. After that, UNIVAC soon became a household

word. The UNIVAC and computers like it were considered **first-generation computers** and were the last to use vacuum tubes to store data.

Transistors and Beyond

Objective 3B.14 *Describe the milestones that led to each "generation" of computers.*

Only one year after the ENIAC was completed, scientists at the Bell Telephone Laboratories in New Jersey invented the

FIGURE 12 The ENIAC took up an entire room and required several people to manipulate it. *(Interfoto/Alamy Stock Photo)*

second-generation computers. Still, transistors were limited as to how small they could be made.

A few years later, in 1958, **Jack Kilby**, while working at Texas Instruments, invented the world's first **integrated circuit**—a small chip capable of containing thousands of transistors. This consolidation in design enabled computers to become smaller and lighter. The computers in this early integrated-circuit generation were considered **third-generation computers**.

Other innovations in the computer industry further refined the computer's speed, accuracy, and efficiency. However, none was as significant as the 1971 introduction by the Intel Corporation of the **microprocessor chip**—a small chip containing millions of transistors (see Figure 15). The microprocessor functions as the CPU, or brains, of the computer. Computers that use a microprocessor chip are called **fourth-generation computers**. Over time, Intel and Motorola became the leading manufacturers of microprocessors. Today, the Intel Core i7 is one of Intel's most powerful processors.

As you can see, personal computers have come a long way since the Altair and have a number of inventions and people to thank for their amazing popularity. What will the future bring? ■

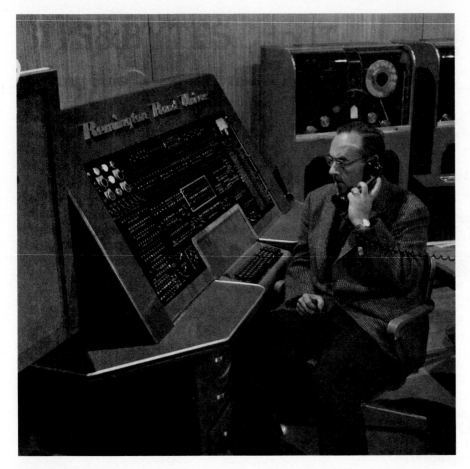

FIGURE 13 UNIVACs were the first computers to use magnetic tape for data storage. *(CBS/Landov)*

transistor—another means to store data (see Figure 14). The transistor replaced the bulky vacuum tubes of earlier computers and was smaller and more powerful than tubes. It was used in almost everything, from radios to phones. Computers that used transistors were referred to as

FIGURE 14 Transistors were one-tenth the size of vacuum tubes, faster, and produced much less heat. *(Borissos/Fotolia)*

FIGURE 15 Today's microprocessors can contain billions of transistors. *(Tudor Voinea/Shutterstock)*

check your understanding // review & practice

For a quick review of what you've learned, answer the following questions.

multiple choice

1. What was the name of the first web browser?
   a. Mosaic
   b. Internet Explorer
   c. Netscape
   d. Firefox

2. Which operating system was specifically developed for the first IBM PC?
   a. CP/M
   b. COBOL
   c. MS-DOS
   d. VisiCalc

3. Which invention replaced vacuum tubes in computers?
   a. the integrated circuit
   b. the transistor
   c. the microprocessor chip
   d. magnetic tape

4. Which computer was touted as the first personal computer?
   a. Altair
   b. Commodore PET
   c. Lisa
   d. Osborne

5. What was the importance of the Turing machine to today's computers?
   a. It described a system that was a precursor to today's notebook computer.
   b. It was the first electronic calculator and a precursor to the computer.
   c. It was the first computer to have a monitor.
   d. It described a process to read, write, and erase symbols on a tape and was the precursor to today's RAM.

6. Which computer first stored its operating system in ROM?
   a. Apple I
   b. Apple II
   c. Lisa
   d. Macintosh

7. What was the first word processing application?
   a. Word for MS-DOS
   b. WordPerfect
   c. WordStar
   d. Alto

8. Which components are a characteristic of second-generation computers?
   a. transistors
   b. vacuum tubes
   c. integrated circuits
   d. microprocessor chips

9. For what is the Atanasoft–Berry Computer best known?
   a. It was the first computer to use vacuum tubes instead of mechanical switches.
   b. It was the first computer to use the binary system.
   c. It was the first computer to incorporate a magnetic tape system.
   d. It was the first computer used as a mechanical calculator.

10. Who were the founders of Microsoft?
    a. Paul Allen and Bill Gates
    b. Steve Jobs and Steve Wozniak
    c. Steve Jobs and Bill Gates
    d. Bill Gates and Steve Wozniak

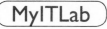 Go to **MyITLab** to take an autograded version of the *Check Your Understanding* review and to find all media resources for the chapter.

4

Application Software: Programs That Let You Work and Play

Programs That Let You Work

Learning Outcome 4.1 **You will be able to describe the basic ways to access and use software and identify the main types of productivity and business software.**

The Nuts and Bolts of Software 124

Objective 4.1 *Describe the differences between application and system software.*

Objective 4.2 *List different types of apps and software you can use on your computing devices.*

Productivity and Business Software 126

Objective 4.3 *List the types of applications included in productivity software suites, and describe their uses and features.*

Objective 4.4 *List software that individuals use to manage their finances.*

Objective 4.5 *List common types of software that large and small businesses use.*

Programs That Let You Play

Learning Outcome 4.2 **Describe the different types of multimedia and educational software available, and discuss how best to manage your software.**

Multimedia and Educational Software 140

Objective 4.6 *Describe the uses and features of digital image-editing, video-editing, and drawing software.*

Objective 4.7 *Describe the uses and features of digital audio software.*

Objective 4.8 *Describe the features of app creation software.*

Objective 4.9 *Describe common types of educational and reference software and their features.*

◀ **Sound Byte** Enhancing Photos with Image-Editing Software

🎧 **Active Helpdesk** Choosing Software

Managing Your Software 146

Objective 4.10 *Describe where to obtain the main types of software.*

Objective 4.11 *Explain how software licenses function.*

Objective 4.12 *Describe how to ensure software you purchase will work on your device.*

Objective 4.13 *Describe how to install and uninstall software.*

🎧 **Active Helpdesk** Buying and Installing Software

Make This MAKE: A More Powerful App on **page 139**

All media accompanying this chapter can be found in MyITLab.

For an overview of the chapter, watch the **Preview Video**.

(Shutterstock, Rawpixel/Shutterstock, PathDoc/Shutterstock, Timo Darco/Fotolia)

How do I use spreadsheet software? The basic element in a spreadsheet program is the *worksheet*, which is a grid consisting of columns and rows. As shown in Figure 4.5a, the columns and rows form individual boxes called *cells*. Each cell can be identified according to its column and row position. For example, a cell in column A, row 1 is referred to as cell A1. You can enter several types of data into a cell:

- *Text:* Any combination of letters, numbers, symbols, and spaces. Text is often used as labels to identify the contents of a worksheet or chart.

- *Values and Dates:* Numerical data that represents a quantity or a date/time and is often the basis for calculations.

- *Formulas:* Equations that use addition, subtraction, multiplication, and division operators, as well as values and cell references. For example, in Figure 4.5a, you would use the formula =D8-D17 to calculate net income for November.

- *Functions:* Formulas that are preprogrammed into the spreadsheet software. Functions help you with calculations ranging from the simple (such as adding groups of numbers) to the complex (such as determining monthly loan payments), without requiring you to know the exact formula. In Figure 4.5a, to calculate the total of all expenses for September, you could use the built-in addition function, which would look like this: =SUM(B10:B16).

What kinds of graphs and charts can I create with spreadsheet software? As shown in Figure 4.6, most spreadsheet applications let you create a variety of

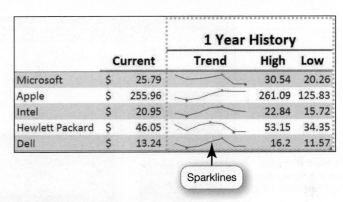

	Current	1 Year History		
		Trend	High	Low
Microsoft	$ 25.79		30.54	20.26
Apple	$ 255.96		261.09	125.83
Intel	$ 20.95		22.84	15.72
Hewlett Packard	$ 46.05		53.15	34.35
Dell	$ 13.24		16.2	11.57

Sparklines

FIGURE 4.7 Sparklines are tiny graphs that fit into a single cell. *(Windows 8.1, Microsoft Corporation)*

charts, including basic column charts, pie charts, and line charts, with or without 3-D effects. In addition to these basic charts, you can make stock charts (for investment analysis) and scatter charts (for statistical analysis) or create custom charts. A newer feature in Excel is *sparklines*—small charts that fit into a single cell and make it easy to show data trends (see Figure 4.7).

Presentation Software

How can software help with my presentations? You've no doubt sat through presentations where the speaker used **presentation software** such as Microsoft PowerPoint (see Figure 4.8) or Keynote to create a slide show. Because these applications are simple to use, you can produce high-quality presentations without a lot of training. With some of the capabilities in PowerPoint, you can embed online videos, add effects, and even trim video clips without the need for a separate video-editing program.

What are some tips to make a great presentation? Undoubtedly, you've seen at least one bad presentation. Don't make your audience suffer through another one! Here are some tips for designing good presentations:

- *Be careful with color:* Choose dark text on a light background or light text on a dark background. Avoid using clashing text and background colors.

- *Use bullets for key points:* Limit the number to four to six bulleted points per slide. Avoid full sentences and paragraphs.

- *Use images:* Images can convey a thought or illustrate a point. Make sure any text over an image can be read easily.

- *Consider font size and style:* Keep the font size large enough to read from the back of the room. Avoid script or fancy font styles. Use only one or two font styles per presentation.

- *Keep animations and/or background audio to a minimum:* They can be distracting.

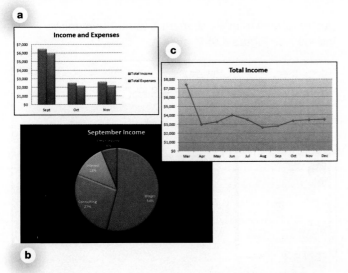

FIGURE 4.6 (a) Column charts show comparisons. (b) Pie charts show how parts contribute to the whole. (c) Line charts show trends over time.

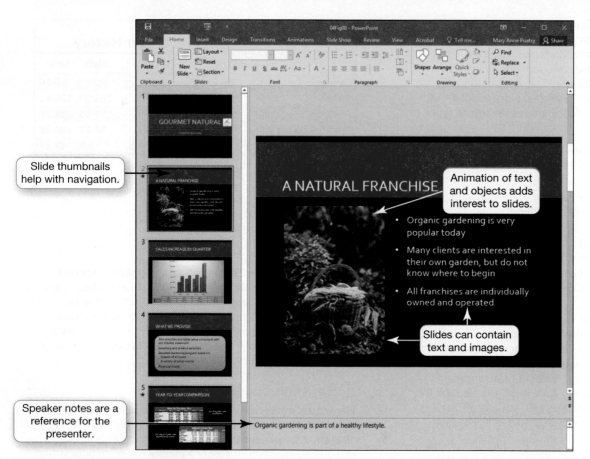

FIGURE 4.8 You can use Microsoft PowerPoint to create dynamic presentations. *(PowerPoint 2016, Windows 10, Microsoft Corporation; DIA/Fotolia)*

Slide thumbnails help with navigation.

Animation of text and objects adds interest to slides.

Slides can contain text and images.

Speaker notes are a reference for the presenter.

BITS&BYTES

Going Beyond PowerPoint

PowerPoint is generally the go-to application for creating presentation visual aids. But there are several applications that offer a compelling alternative to PowerPoint. One cool alternative is Prezi (**prezi.com**), a web-based program that uses an innovative way to produce presentations. Rather than using a set of slides, Prezi uses a large canvas in which you connect ideas. PowToon (**www.powtoon.com**) provides a library of cartoon-like characters that are easily animated to give your presentations more of a "storytelling" aspect rather than fact delivery.

Microsoft also has two new products: Sway and Office Mix. Sway is a standalone app that allows you to create presentations that are stored in the cloud and are linked to your Microsoft account. Sway facilitates importing content from a variety of sources to allow you to tell a compelling story and is designed primarily for creating web-based presentations. Office Mix is a PowerPoint add-in that gives you the power to integrate quizzes, polls, voice, video, and digital ink into your PowerPoint

presentations to make them into interactive online videos (see Figure 4.9).

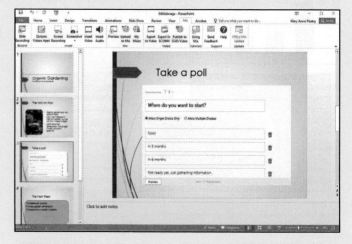

FIGURE 4.9 Office Mix adds a variety of options to enhance your PowerPoint presentations. *(PowerPoint 2016, Windows 10, Microsoft Corporation)*

FIGURE 4.10 In databases, information is organized into fields, records, and tables. *(Excel 2013, Windows 8.1, Microsoft Corporation)*

Database Software

Why is database software useful? Database software such as Oracle, MySQL, and Microsoft Access are powerful applications that let you store and organize data. As mentioned earlier, spreadsheet applications are easy to use for simple tasks such as sorting, filtering, and organizing data. However, you need to use a more robust, fully featured database application to manage larger and more complicated data that is organized in more than one table; to group, sort, and retrieve data; and to generate reports. Traditional databases are organized into *fields*, *records*, and *tables*, as shown in Figure 4.10.

How do businesses use database software? Websites like Amazon, iTunes, eBay, and Pandora all rely on databases to keep track of products, clients, invoices, and personnel information. Often, some of that information is available to a home computer user. For example, at Amazon, you can access the history of all the purchases you've ever made on the site. FedEx, UPS, and other shipping companies also let you search their online databases for tracking numbers, allowing you to get instant information on the status of your packages.

Note-Taking Software

Is there software to help me take notes? Microsoft One-Note is a popular note-taking and organizational tool you can use for research, brainstorming, and collaboration, as well as just organizing random bits of information. Using OneNote, you can organize your notes into tabbed sections (see Figure 4.11). In addition, you

can access your OneNote notes from other Microsoft Office applications. For example, if you're writing a research paper in Word, click the OneNote icon in the Word ribbon to open One-Note, where you can add your notes—perhaps a reference to a website where you found some interesting research. Later, if you open OneNote and click on that reference, it will bring you to the exact spot in the Word document where you made the reference.

You can also add audio or video recordings of lectures to OneNote, and you can search for a term across all the digital notebooks you created during the semester to find common ideas such as key points that might appear on a test. There is also a OneNote app for the iPhone and iPad.

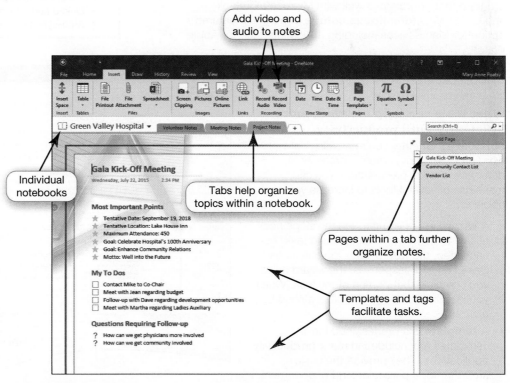

FIGURE 4.11 Microsoft OneNote is a great way to collect and organize notes and other information. The files are readily searchable and easy to share. *(One Note 2016, Windows 10, Microsoft Corporation)*

Several very good and functional free and online note-taking options are also available to help you take notes or to just jot down a quick reminder. Evernote (**evernote.com**), for example, lets you take notes via the web, your phone, or your computer and then syncs your notes between your devices. You can then share your notes with other Evernote users for easy collaboration. Figure 4.12 lists some popular alternative note-taking applications.

Personal Information Manager Software

How can software help me manage my e-mail, time, contact lists, and tasks? Most productivity suites contain some form of **personal information manager (PIM) software** to help you manage e-mail, contacts, calendars, and tasks in one place. Microsoft Outlook (see Figure 4.13) is the most widely used PIM program. If you share a network at home or at work and are using the same PIM software as others on a common network, a PIM program simplifies sharing calendars and scheduling meetings.

Many web-based e-mail clients, such as Yahoo! and Google, also include coordinating calendar and contacts similar to Microsoft Outlook. Yahoo! includes Notepad for jotting down notes and tasks. Google's calendar and contacts sync with Outlook so you can access your Outlook calendar information by logging into Google. This gives you access to your schedule anywhere you have access to a computer and an Internet connection.

There are a wide variety of other to-do lists and simple organizers that work with all your mobile and computing devices. For example, Toodledo (**toodledo.com**) is a free program that coordinates well with Microsoft Outlook, and OmniFocus (**omnifocus.com**) is a more full-featured option for Mac devices including a slick interface for Apple Watch.

Microsoft Office Productivity Software Features

What tools can help me work more efficiently with productivity software? Whether you're working on a word processing document, spreadsheet, database, or slide presentation, you can make use of several tools to increase your efficiency:

- A **wizard** walks you through the steps necessary to complete a complicated task. At each step, the wizard asks you questions. Based on your responses, the wizard helps you complete that portion of the task. When you install software, you're often guided by a wizard.

- A **template** is a predesigned form. Templates are included in many productivity applications. They provide the basic structure for a particular kind of document, spreadsheet, database, or presentation. Templates can include specific page layout designs, formatting and styles relevant

FIGURE 4.12

Beyond Microsoft OneNote: Alternative Note-Taking Applications

Evernote (evernote.com)
- Web-based
- Notes can be shared for easy collaboration
- Syncs notes between all devices

AudioNote (luminantsoftware.com)
- Synchronized note taking and audio recording
- Allows text or handwritten notes
- Highlights notes during playback

Simplenote (simplenote.com)
- Web-based, open source
- Notes organized by tags
- Mobile apps available

Notability (gingerlabs.com)
- PDF annotations
- Advanced word processing
- Linked audio recordings to notes
- Auto-sync notes between devices

E-mail inbox

Calendar items

Task reminder

FIGURE 4.13 Microsoft Outlook includes common PIM features, such as a summary of appointments, a list of tasks, and e-mail messages. *(Outlook 2016, Windows 10, Microsoft Corporation)*

BITS&BYTES

Productivity Software Tips and Tricks

Looking for tips on how to make better use of your productivity software? Some websites send subscribers periodic e-mails full of tips, tricks, and shortcuts for their favorite software programs:

- Microsoft's website includes many tips and tricks for its Office applications (**products.office.com**).
- MakeTechEasier (**maketecheasier.com**) has tidbits for a variety of applications, including Windows and Mac products, Apache OpenOffice, and cellphone applications.
- GCFLearnFree.org (**gcflearnfree.org**) offers free instructional tutorials on a variety of technology topics, including Microsoft Office applications.
- You can also find tips as videos online. To take any videos from YouTube, TED, and other websites on the road with you for future off-line reference, check out KeepVid Video Downloader (**keepvid.com**) to download videos to your computing devices.

to that particular document, and automated tasks (macros).

- A **macro** is a small program that groups a series of commands so that they will run as a single command. Macros are best used to automate a routine task or a complex series of commands that must be run frequently. For example, a

teacher may write a macro to sort the grades in her grade book in descending order and to highlight grades that add up to less than a C average. Every time she adds the results of an assignment or a test, she can set up the macro to run through this series of steps.

Personal Financial Software

Objective 4.4 *List software that individuals use to manage their finances.*

How can I use software to keep track of my finances? Financial planning software helps you manage your daily finances. Financial planning programs include electronic checkbook registers and automatic bill payment tools. With these features, you can make recurring monthly payments, such as rent or student loans, with automatically scheduled online payments. The software records all transactions, including online payments, in the checkbook register. In addition, you can assign categories to each transaction and then use these categories to create budgets and analyze your spending patterns.

Intuit's installed and web-based products, Quicken and Mint (**mint.com**), respectively, are the market leaders in financial planning software (see Figure 4.14). Both are great at tracking and analyzing your spending habits and at offering advice on how to better manage your finances. With either, you also can track your investment portfolio. With Mint, you can monitor and update your finances from any computer with a private and secure setting. You can also access Mint on a smartphone or tablet, so your information is conveniently accessible. Mint also provides access to a network of other users with whom to exchange tips and advice.

What software can I use to prepare my taxes? Tax preparation software, such as Intuit TurboTax and

FIGURE 4.14 Mint (**mint. com**) is an online financial management tool. An extensive online community provides helpful tips and discussions with other people in similar situations. *(Reprinted with permission © Intuit Inc. All rights reserved.)*

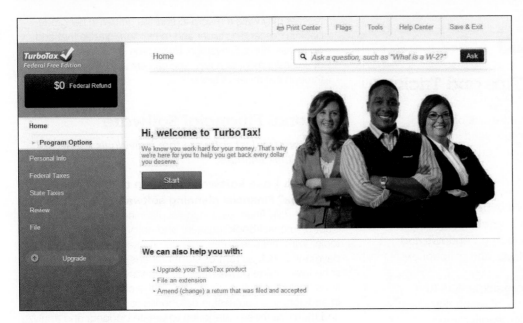

H&R Block Tax Software, lets you prepare your state and federal taxes on your own instead of hiring a professional. Both programs offer a complete set of tax forms and instructions, as well as videos that contain expert advice on how to complete each form. Each company also offers free web-based versions of federal forms and instructions. In addition, error-checking features are built into the programs to catch mistakes. TurboTax can also run a check for audit alerts, file your return electronically, and offer financial planning guidance to help you plan and manage your financial resources effectively in the following year (see Figure 4.15).

Some financial planning applications also coordinate with tax preparation software. Both Quicken and Mint, for example, integrate seamlessly with TurboTax, so you never have to go through your debit card statements and bills to find tax deductions, tax-related income, or expenses. Many banks and credit card companies also offer online services that download a detailed monthly statement into Quicken and Mint. Remember, however, that the tax code changes annually, so you must obtain an updated version of the software each year.

Business Software

Objective 4.5 *List common types of software that large and small businesses use.*

Do businesses use different kinds of software than individuals? Many businesses rely on the types of software we've discussed so far in the chapter. However, specialized software is used in many businesses, both large and small.

Small Business Software

What kinds of software are helpful for small business owners? If you have a small business or a hobby that produces income, you know the importance of keeping good records and tracking your expenses and income. **Accounting software** helps small business owners manage their finances more efficiently by providing tools for tracking accounts receivable and accounts payable. In addition, these applications offer inventory management, payroll, and billing tools. Examples of accounting applications are Intuit QuickBooks and Sage 50. Both programs include templates for invoices, statements, and financial reports so that small business owners can create common forms and reports.

If your business requires the need for newsletters, catalogs, annual reports, or other large, complicated publications, consider using **desktop publishing (DTP) software**. Although many word processing applications include some of the features that are hallmarks of desktop publishing, specialized DTP software, such as Adobe InDesign, Microsoft Publisher, and QuarkXPress, allows professionals to design books and other publications that require complex layouts.

What software do I use to create a web page? **Web authoring software** allows even the novice to design interesting and interactive web pages without knowing any HTML code. Web authoring applications often include wizards, templates, and reference materials to help novices complete most web authoring tasks. More experienced users can take advantage of these applications' advanced features to make the web content current, interactive, and interesting. Microsoft Visual Studio, Adobe InDesign, and Adobe Dreamweaver are three programs that both professionals and casual web page designers use.

Note that if you need to produce only the occasional web page, you'll find that many applications include features that let you convert your document into a web page. For example, in some Microsoft Office applications, you can choose to save a file as a web page.

FIGURE 4.16

Common Types of Large Business-Related Software

PROJECT MANAGEMENT

Creates scheduling charts to plan and track specific tasks and to coordinate resources

CUSTOMER RELATIONSHIP MANAGEMENT (CRM)

Stores sales and client contact information in one central database

ENTERPRISE RESOURCE PLANNING (ERP)

Controls many "back office" operations and processing functions such as billing, production, inventory management, and human resources management

E-COMMERCE

Facilitates website creation and hosting services, shopping cart setup, and credit card-processing services

COMPUTER-AIDED DESIGN (CAD)

Creates automated designs, technical drawings, and 3-D model visualizations for architecture, automotive, aerospace, and medical engineering industries

VERTICAL MARKET

Addresses the needs of businesses in a specific industry or market such as the real estate, banking, and automotive industries

(John T Takai/Shutterstock, Maksym Yemelyanov/Fotolia, Spiral media/Fotolia, Ivnl/Fotolia, Adimas/Fotolia, Nmedia/Shutterstock)

Software for Large and Specialized Businesses

What types of software do large businesses use? There is an application for almost every aspect of business. There are specialized programs for project management software, customer relationship management (CRM), enterprise resource planning (ERP), e-commerce, marketing and sales, finance, point of sale, security, networking, data management, and human resources, to name just a few. Figure 4.16 lists many of the common types of business-related software. Some applications are tailored to the specific needs of a particular company or industry. Software designed for a specific industry, such as property management software for real estate professionals, is called **vertical market software**.

What software is used to make 3-D models? Engineers use **computer-aided design (CAD)** programs such as Autodesk's AutoCAD to create automated designs, technical drawings, and 3-D model visualizations. Here are some cool applications of CAD software:

- Architects use CAD software to build virtual models of their plans and readily visualize all aspects of design before actual construction.
- Engineers use CAD software to design everything from factory components to bridges. The 3-D nature of these programs lets engineers rotate their models and adjust their designs if necessary, eliminating costly building errors.

- CAD software (and other 3-D modeling software) is used to generate designs for objects that will be printed using 3-D printers.
- The medical engineering community uses CAD software to create anatomically accurate solid models of the human body, developing medical implants quickly and accurately.

The list of CAD applications keeps growing as more and more industries realize the benefits CAD can bring to their product development and manufacturing processes.

What kind of software can be used for home or landscape planning? There are many software packages to help plan the layout of homes and landscapes,

FIGURE 4.17 SketchUp Make is a free, web-based 3-D modeling application that can be used for home and landscape design. *(Shutterstock)*

BITS&BYTES

Need to Work as a Team? Try These Real-Time Collaboration Tools

You're part of a group working together on a project. You need ways to keep track of project goals and achievements as well as communicate with your team members (see Figure 4.18). Consider using some of these collaboration tools:

- UberConference (**uberconference.com**) is an app that facilitates group conference calls. You can easily share your screen with others in the conference, add another person during the conference, record the conference, and mute noisy callers. You can see everyone who is on the call and even view their social networking profiles. The free version accommodates up to ten callers.
- Trello (**trello.com**) is a visually oriented app used for managing projects. Unlike traditional project management apps, it features a board filled with lists, and each list is filled with cards representing tasks to be completed. It is easy to add checklists and due dates to cards as well as upload files to them. You can easily transfer cards between lists to show progress on various aspects of a project. You can invite as many people to your board as you want. You can then assign people immediately to cards to divide up work tasks. You can easily see an overview of your entire project just by glancing at your Trello board. The free version of the app offers a very powerful feature set.
- Scribblar (**scribblar.com**) is a multiuser whiteboard with live audio chat, which is great for holding virtual brainstorm sessions.

FIGURE 4.18 A number of real-time collaboration tools can help you work together as a team. *(Cacaroot/Fotolia)*

such as the Punch! series offered by Broderbund. A simple, web-based, fairly full-featured, and free 3-D modeling application is Trimble's SketchUp Make. SketchUp Make (**sketchup.com**) lets you create a 3-D image of your dream home (see Figure 4.17). ■

Before moving on to Part 2:
1. Watch Replay Video 4.1 ⟳.
2. Then check your understanding of what you've learned so far.

check your understanding // review & practice

For a quick review to see what you've learned so far, answer the following questions.

multiple choice

1. Software that is available on demand via the Internet is called

   a. proprietary software.

   b. Software as a Service (SaaS).

   c. productivity software.

   d. open source software.

2. What type of software enables you to create dynamic slide shows?

   a. Word processing

   b. Spreadsheet

   c. Presentation

   d. Database

3. Which type of program takes advantage of automatic recalculation and what-if analysis?

   a. spreadsheet

   b. database

   c. CAD/CAM

   d. project management

4. Which of the following is true about open source software?

   a. The program code is confidential.

   b. The program can be changed and is freely distributed.

   c. The program can be freely distributed as long as the program code is not changed.

   d. The program code is subject to copyright protection.

5. What software do I use to create a web page?

   a. database

   b. spreadsheet

   c. Web authoring software

   d. both b and c

 Go to **MyITLab** to take an autograded version of the *Check Your Understanding* review and to find all media resources for the chapter.

TECHBYTES WEEKLY

Stay current with the TechBytes Weekly Newsletter.

Continue 》》

TRY THIS ▶ Citing Website Sources

You've been assigned a research paper, and your instructor requires citations and a bibliography. In the past, you might have resorted to using websites such as Son of Citation Machine (**citationmachine.net**) or EasyBib (**easybib.com**) to create your citations and generate a bibliography. But did you know there are tools built right into Microsoft Word that do the same thing?

To Add a New Citation and Source to a Document:

Step 1   Click at the end of the sentence or phrase that you want to cite.

Step 2   On the References tab, in the Citations & Bibliography group, click **Insert Citation**.

Step 3   To add the source information, click **Add New Source**.
(Word 2016, Windows 10, Microsoft Corporation)

Note: To create a citation and fill in the source information later, click **Add New Placeholder**.

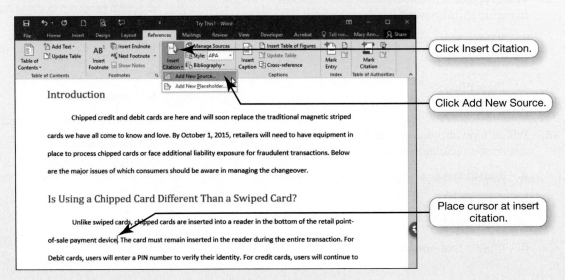

Click Insert Citation.

Click Add New Source.

Place cursor at insert citation.

Step 4   Begin to fill in the source information by clicking the arrow next to Type of Source.
(Word 2016, Windows 10, Microsoft Corporation)

Fill out the fields in the Create Source dialog box.

Step 5   The citation will appear in your document. *(Word 2016, Windows 10, Microsoft Corporation)*

The citation displays in the text.

To Create a Bibliography:

You can create a bibliography at any point after you insert one or more sources in a document. Click where you want to insert a bibliography, usually at the end of the document. Then do the following:

Step 1 On the References tab, in the Citations & Bibliography group, click **Bibliography**.

Step 2 Click a predesigned bibliography format to insert the bibliography into the document. The bibliography is automatically generated. *(Word 2016, Windows 10, Microsoft Corporation)*

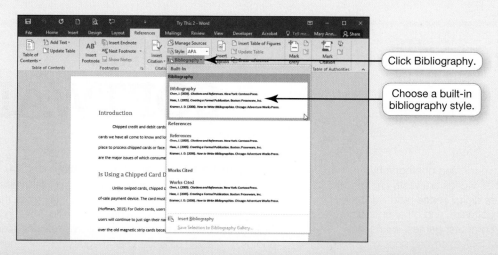

Click Bibliography.

Choose a built-in bibliography style.

Make This ▶ TOOL: App Inventor 2

MAKE: A More Powerful App

Want your app to be able to open a file from the SD card on your phone, fire up the YouTube app, or display a location in the Maps app?

In this exercise, you'll use the ActivityStarter component of App Inventor to incorporate the software already on your device into your mobile app.

It's as easy as using the Connectivity drawer of the Designer in App Inventor. Drag the ActivityStarter component onto your Designer screen, then control it with the Blocks for ActivityStarter. Your apps now have the power of all the software on your device behind them! *(MIT App Inventor 2, Massachusetts Institute of Technology. Creative Commons Attribution-ShareAlike 3.0 Unported License)*

The ActivityStarter component allows you to use the existing software on your device from within your mobile app.

For the instructions for this exercise, go to MyITLab.

Programs That Let You Play

Learning Outcome 4.2 Describe the different types of multimedia and education software available, and discuss how best to manage your software.

While many programs help you be more productive, there are also programs that entertain you with audio, video, and digital images and through games, animations, and movies. Regardless of whether the software helps you work or play, it's important to know how to work with and manage the software so that you install it correctly and use it legally. This section discusses multimedia and entertainment software, as well as how to manage any type of software.

 multimedia and educational
SOFTWARE

From movies and television to music and photography, the entertainment and education worlds are vastly digital. **Multimedia software** includes digital image- and video-editing software, digital audio software, and other specialty software required to produce computer games, animations, and movies. In this section, we look at several popular types of multimedia and education software, as shown in Figure 4.19.

Digital Image-Editing, Video-Editing, and Drawing Software

Objective 4.6 *Describe the uses and features of digital image-editing, video-editing, and drawing software.*

FIGURE 4.19 There are many varieties of multimedia and education software.

How can I edit, share, and organize digital images? One great advantage of taking digital images is that you can easily manipulate them and then share them on the web. While Facebook is a great option for sharing images, Flickr (**flickr.com**) is a website specifically designed for sharing photos. It lets you organize your images and then share them publicly with millions of users or just with your closest friends and family. Discussion boards are also available so that people can leave comments about the images.

- If you want to edit your photos before sharing, Adobe Photoshop Elements is **image-editing software** geared to the casual photographer. Image-editing software includes tools for basic modifications to digital photos such as removing red-eye; modifying contrast, sharpness, and color casts; or removing scratches or rips from scanned images of old photos. Many programs also include painting tools such as brushes, pens, and artistic media (such as paints, pastels, and oils) that let you create realistic-looking images. Some include templates so you can insert your favorite pictures into preformatted pages for digital scrapbooks or greeting cards. Google Picasa (**picasa.google.com**) is a popular application that not only lets you edit images, but also helps to organize and share your digital images (see Figure 4.20). Picasa also stores your photos on the web.

Several other online photo-sharing and photo-storing sites, such as Snapfish (**snapfish.com**) and Shutterfly (**shutterfly .com**), let you upload your digital images from your computer, create photo albums, and share them with friends and family. These sites offer printing services as well, letting you create

 SOUND BYTE
Enhancing Photos with Image-Editing Software

In this Sound Byte, you'll learn tips and tricks on how to best use image-editing software. You'll learn how to remove the red-eye from photos and to incorporate borders, frames, and other enhancements to produce professional effects.

Image-editing tools

Images placed here and arranged in collage

E-mail, print, and export tools

FIGURE 4.20 You can create collages of your favorite images using Google Picasa. (© 2015 Google Inc, used with permission. Google and the Google logo are registered trademarks of Google Inc.)

customized cards, stationery, books, and even smartphone cases with your images.

What image-editing programs might a professional use? Adobe Photoshop and Corel PaintShop Pro are fully featured image-editing applications. Gimpshop (**gimpshop.com**) is a free download that has most of the features offered by the for-pay applications, such as Photoshop and PaintShop Pro. These offer sophisticated tools for tasks like layering images and masking images (hiding parts of layers to create effects such as collages). Designers use these more sophisticated tools to create the enhanced digital images used commercially in logos, in advertisements, and on book and DVD covers.

What software do I need to edit digital videos? While it's easy to upload videos directly to YouTube or Facebook unedited, you can use **digital video-editing software** to help refine your videos. Although the most expensive products (such as Adobe Premiere Pro and Apple's Final Cut Pro) offer the widest range of special effects and tools, some moderately priced video-editing programs have enough features to keep the casual user happy. Windows Movie Moments and iMovie have intuitive drag-and-drop features that make it simple to create professional-quality movies with little or no training (see Figure 4.21).

Window used to view or edit movie clips

Video clips in clips pane

Movie clips display in clip viewer

Transition icon controls transition effects between clips.

FIGURE 4.21 Video editing programs such as Apple iMovie make it easy to create and edit movies then share them on social media. (Anthony Devlin/AP Images)

What kind of software should I use to create illustrations? Drawing software (**or illustration software**) lets you create or edit 2-D, line-based drawings. You can use it to create technical diagrams or original nonphotographic

FIGURE 4.22 Adobe Illustrator is the industry standard for creating vector art and illustrations. *(Adobe product screenshot(s) reprinted with permission from Adobe Systems Incorporated. Adobe® Illustrator® is a registered trademark of Adobe Systems Incorporated in the United States and other countries.)*

drawings, animations, and illustrations using standard tools such as pens, pencils, and paintbrushes. You also can drag geometric objects from a toolbar onto the canvas area to create images and can use paint bucket, eyedropper, and spray can tools to add color and special effects to the drawings.

Adobe Illustrator (see Figure 4.22) includes tools that let you create professional-quality creative and technical illustrations such as muscle structures in the human body. Its warping tool allows you to bend, stretch, and twist portions of your image or text. Because of its many tools and features, Illustrator is the preferred drawing software program of most graphic artists.

Digital Audio Software

Objective 4.7 *Describe the uses and features of digital audio software.*

What's the difference between all the digital audio file types on my computer? You probably have a variety of digital audio files stored on your computer, such as downloaded music files, audiobooks, or podcasts. These types of audio files have been *compressed* so they're more manageable to transfer to and from your computer and over the Internet. MP3, short for MPEG-1 Audio Layer 3, is a type of audio compression format and is the most common compressed digital format, but there are other compressed formats, such as AAC and WMA.

You may also see *uncompressed* audio files on your computer, such as WAV or AIFF files. Uncompressed files—the files found on audio CDs, for example—have not had any data removed, so the quality is a perfect representation of the audio as it was recorded. Unfortunately, the file size is much larger than that of compressed files. Compressed formats remove data such as high frequencies that the human ear does not hear in order to make the files smaller and easier to download and store. MP3 format, for example, makes it possible to transfer and play back music on smartphones and other music players. A typical CD stores between 10 and 15 songs in uncompressed format, but with files in MP3 format, the same CD can store

between 100 and 180 songs. The smaller file size not only lets you store and play music in less space, it also allows quick and easy distribution over the Internet. Ogg Vorbis (or just Ogg) is a free, open source audio compression format alternative to MP3. Some say that Ogg produces a better sound quality than MP3.

What do I use to create my own audio files? There are many digital audio applications that let you create and record your own audio files. With programs such as MAGIX Music Maker or Apple GarageBand, you can compose your own songs or soundtracks with virtual instruments, voice recorders, synthesizers, and special audio effects, and these will end up as uncompressed MIDI files. Other programs, such as Audacity and Cakewalk SONAR, let you record audio files from live sources such as musicians or the spoken word.

Can I edit audio files? Audio-editing software includes tools that make editing audio files as easy as editing text files. Software such as the open source Audacity (**audacity.source-forge.net**) and Sony Sound Forge Pro (**sonycreativesoftware.com**) lets you perform such basic editing tasks as cutting dead air space from the beginning or end of a song or clipping a portion from the middle. You can also add special sound effects, such as reverb or bass boost, and remove static or hiss from MP3 files. AudioAcrobat (**audioacrobat.com**), a web-based program, makes it easy to record and stream audio and video and hosts your audio files. These applications support recording sound files from a microphone or any source you can connect through the input line of a sound card.

 ACTIVE HELPDESK
Choosing Software

In this Active Helpdesk, you'll play the role of a helpdesk staffer, fielding questions about the different kinds of multimedia software, educational and reference software, and entertainment software.

Have you ever done any of the following?

- Posted pictures on Facebook that your friends accessed from their iPhone
- Used Dropbox or OneDrive to store your files instead of carrying around a flash drive
- Used Google Docs or Microsoft Office Online to collaborate on a team project
- Used Carbonite to back up your data online

By doing any of these activities, you have participated in cloud computing. So what exactly is cloud computing?

Cloud computing refers to storing data, files, and applications on the web and being able to access and manipulate these files and applications from any Internet-connected device. Being able to work from the cloud eliminates the need to have everything stored on your own computer's drives and lets you access your pictures, music, files, and programs from any device as long as you have access to the Internet. In addition, cloud computing makes it easier to collaborate and communicate with others, and it can cut down on administrative tasks for organizations maintaining large amounts of computer hardware and software.

There are two sides to cloud computing:

1. The *front end* is the side we see as users. It involves a web browser like Microsoft Edge, Mozilla Firefox, or Google Chrome.
2. The *back end* consists of various data centers and server farms that house the files and programs you access "on the cloud" (see Figure 4.23). These data centers and server farms are warehouses full of computers and servers, and they are being created all over the world, providing us with "cloud storage." The computers in the data centers or server farms are designed to work together, adjusting to the varying degrees of demand placed on them at any time.

Google is one of the first true explorers in the cloud, building applications such as Google Drive, Gmail, and the Chrome web browser in an effort to create a completely virtual operating environment. A fully functioning operating environment would enable users to sign in on any computer and have "their" computer setup (desktop configurations and images, programs, files, and other personalized settings) display. Additionally, cloud computing would reduce the need for all of us to have the fastest computers with the most memory and storage capabilities. Instead, we could all have simple front-end terminals with basic input and output devices because the computers on the back end will be providing all the computing muscle.

The Chromebook is Google's first attempt at a notebook where all the applications and files are stored on the web. Nothing is installed or saved to a hard drive, not even the operating system! All programs are accessed and all work is done through the web-based browser, so sending e-mail, editing photos, and working on documents are all done via web-based applications. Since the Chromebook requires an Internet connection to get

FIGURE 4.23 There are two sides to cloud computing: the side we see as users and the banks of computers and servers that house the files and programs we access. *(Diego Cervo/Fotolia, Nicotombo/Fotolia, WavebreakMediaMicro/Fotolia, Alexandr Mitiuc/Fotolia, PhotoEdit/Alamy, Digitallife/Alamy, Anatolii Babii/Alamy, PhotoEdit/Alamy)*

most tasks done, users must be near a WiFi connection or pay for a data plan.

There are some considerations with cloud computing of which you need to be aware:

- *Security and privacy:* Right now, the security of information stored on the web is built on trusting that the passwords we set and the security systems that the data centers put in place are able to keep our information away from unauthorized users. Caution is always warranted, as nothing is completely safe and private.
- *Backup:* Because even the devices in these large data centers and server farms inevitably will break down, the cloud computing systems have redundant systems to provide backup. However, for critical files that you must have, it might be a good idea not to completely rely on the cloud, but to have your own offline backup system, as well.
- *Access issues:* With cloud computing, you access your files and programs only through the Internet. If you couldn't access the Internet due to a power failure or system failure with your Internet service provider, you wouldn't be able to access your files. Storing your most critical files and programs offline will help reduce the inconvenience and loss of productivity while access to the Internet is being restored.

Before relying on cloud computing, consider the above concerns against the advantages of the convenience of having your information when and where you want it and the ability to promote better collaboration.

App Creation Software

Objective 4.8 *Describe the features of app creation software.*

How do I make my own video games? Now that video games represent an industry that generates billions in revenue each year, designing and creating video games is emerging as a desirable career opportunity. Professionally created video games involve artistic storytelling and design, as well as sophisticated programming. Major production houses such as Electronic Arts use applications not easily available to the casual home enthusiast. However, you can use the editors and game engines available for games such as EverQuest, Oblivion, and Unreal Tournament to create custom levels and characters to extend the game.

If you want to try your hand at creating your own video games, multimedia applications such as Unity, and RPG Maker VX provide the tools you need to explore game design and creation. The program GameMaker (**yoyogames.com**) is a free product that lets you build a game without any programming; you drag and drop key elements of the new game creation into place. Alice (**alice.org**) is another free environment to check out; it lets you easily create 3-D animations and simple games.

Other than games, what other apps can I develop? There are many programming environments that are approachable for beginners. MIT's App Inventor (which we use in the Make This exercises in this book) is an open source web application that makes it easy for beginners to create functional apps for Android devices (see Figure 4.24). Featuring a drag and drop interface, users can quickly begin developing powerful apps without actually knowing how to write program code.

Scratch is another MIT programming environment that facilitates the creation of interactive stories, games, and animations that you can then share with an online community. The programming interface of Scratch is somewhat similar to App Inventor. Many elementary schools use Scratch to introduce young children to the ideas behind computer programming.

Corona SDK (**coronalabs.com**) is a powerful, free programming environment that has been used to develop games and business apps. Corona comes with a large library of application programming interfaces (APIs) that can be used as building blocks to make writing computer code less time consuming (although you will actually have to learn the Lua programming language). But the Composer GUI is a visual editor for Corona, which makes it even easier to create apps without doing as much actual coding. Corona supports all major platforms including iOS, Android, and Windows Phone.

Apple also has a powerful development environment for iOS, OS X, and watchOS called Swift. Swift uses more concise code

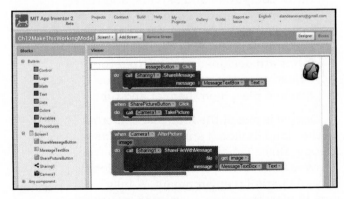

FIGURE 4.24 MIT's App Inventor is an open source web application that enables beginners to create apps. *(MIT App Inventor 2)*

than some other programming environments. It has a feature that allows you to visually see the results of each line of code as you write it. Many professional developers like using Swift because the code works side-by-side with Objective-C, which is a major programming language used in many businesses. Despite the power of the Swift environment, it is still very approachable for students.

Educational and Reference Software

Objective 4.9 *Describe common types of educational and reference software and their features.*

What fun educational and reference software should I check out? If you want to learn more about a subject, you can turn to the web for many instructional videos and documents. But sometimes, it's best to use software for more complete or detailed instructions. Educational and reference software is available to help you master, study, design, create, or plan. As shown in Figure 4.25, there are software products

that teach new skills such as typing, languages, cooking, and playing the guitar.

Students who will be taking standardized tests like the SAT often use test preparation software. In addition, many computer and online brain-training games and programs are designed to improve the health and function of your brain. Lumosity (**lumosity.com**) is one such site that has a specific "workout" program that you can play on your PC or smartphone. Brain Age (**brainage.com**) has software for the Nintendo DS and is designed for players of all ages.

What types of programs are available to train people to use software or special machines? Many programs provide tutorials for popular computer applications (you may even use one in your course provided with MyITLab). These programs use illustrated systematic instructions to guide users through unfamiliar skills in an environment that acts like the actual software, without the software actually being installed.

FIGURE 4.25

Educational and Reference Software: A Sample of What's Available

TEST PREPARATION

Designed to improve your performance on standardized tests

SIMULATION

Allows you to experience a real situation through a virtual environment

INSTRUCTIONAL

Designed to teach you almost anything from playing a musical instrument to learning a language or cooking

TRIP PLANNING

Generates maps and provides driving instructions; some incorporate hotel, restaurant, and other trip information

HOME DESIGN/ IMPROVEMENT

Provides 2-D or 3-D templates and images to let you better visualize indoor and outdoor remodeling projects and landscaping ideas

COURSE MANAGEMENT

Web-based software system that creates a virtual learning experience, including course materials, tests, and discussion boards

BRAIN TRAINING

Features games and activities to exercise your brain to improve your memory, processing speed, attention, and multitasking capabilities

GENEALOGY

Helps chart the relationships between family members through multiple generations

Some training programs, known as **simulation programs**, allow you to experience or control the software as if it were an actual event. Such simulation programs include commercial and military flight training, surgical instrument training, and machine operation training. One benefit of simulated training programs is that they safely allow you to experience potentially dangerous situations such as flying a helicopter during high winds. Consequently, users of these training programs are more likely to take risks and learn from their mistakes—something they could not afford to do in real life. Simulated training programs also help prevent costly errors. Should something go awry, the only cost of the error is restarting the simulation program.

Do I need special software to take courses online? Although some courses are run from an individually developed website, many online courses are run using **course management software** such as Blackboard, Moodle, and Canvas. In addition to traditional classroom tools such as calendars and grade books, these programs provide special areas for students and instructors to exchange ideas and information through chat rooms, discussion forums, and e-mail. In addition, collaboration tools such as whiteboards and desktop sharing facilitate virtual office hour sessions. Depending on the content and course materials, you may need a password or special plug-ins to view certain videos or demos. ∎

 # managing your
SOFTWARE

It's important to know how to pick out the best software for your computer, how to get it onto your computer correctly, and how to take it off. We discuss all of these topics next.

Getting Software

Objective 4.10 *Describe where to obtain the main types of software.*

What's the best place to get software? Software can be purchased in a variety of locations including retail stores or directly from software development companies (such as Adobe). The most common method for obtaining software today is via download from websites.

With the rise in mobile devices, **app marketplaces** (or **app stores**) have become a common place to purchase and download software (see Figure 4.26). Apps are written for specific operating systems (such as Android, iOS or Windows) and you need to purchase apps that were written for your particular computing device. Although originally developed to distribute mobile software, some app stores now also distribute

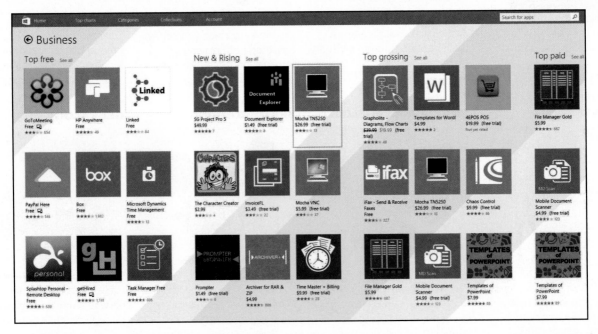

FIGURE 4.26 Depending on your operating system, head off to the correct app marketplace to look for software for your device. *(Microsoft Windows Store, Edge, Windows 10, Microsoft Corporation)*

software that can be installed on desktop or laptop computers. There are three main app stores:

- *Google Play:* Google maintains this app store to provide apps for Android devices. If you have a smartphone or tablet running the Android OS, you will get most of your apps from Google Play.
- *App Store:* Apple was the first major company with an app marketplace. The App Store was established to deliver apps that will run on iPhones, iPads, or the iPod Touch. Apple has also launched a separate Mac App Store that sells apps for their desktops and laptops running OS X.
- *Windows Store:* Microsoft launched Windows Store with the release of Windows 8. The store is designed to deliver apps that run on all Windows platforms including phones, tablets, desktops, and laptops.

BITS&BYTES

How to Open Unknown File Types

Normally, when you double-click a file to open it, the program associated with the file runs automatically. For example, when you double-click a file with a .doc or .docx extension, the file opens in Microsoft Word. However, if the file has no extension or Windows has no application associated with that file type, an Open with dialog box appears and asks what program you want to use to open the file. In other cases, a document may open with a program other than the one you wanted to use. This is because many applications can open several file types, and the program you expected the file to open in is not currently the program associated with that file type. To assign a program to a file type or to change the program to open a particular file type, follow these instructions:

1. Use the search and navigation tools in File Explorer to locate the file you want to change. (For example, you can search for all Word files by searching for *.doc or *.docx.) Right-click on the file, and then point to **Open with**.
2. A list of programs installed on your computer appears. Click the program you want to use to open this file type. If you're sure the selected program is the one that should always be used for this file type, then instead select **Keep using this app**, and make sure to check "**Always use this app to open [extension] files**," and click the default program from the list.

When you double-click that file in the future, the file will open in the program you selected.

Is discounted software for students available? If you're a student, you can sometimes buy substantially discounted software that is no different from regularly priced software. Campus computer stores and college bookstores offer discounted prices to students who possess a valid student ID. Online software suppliers such as Journey Education Marketing (**journeyed.com**) and Academic Superstore (**academicsuperstore.com**) also offer popular software to students at reduced prices. Software developers, such as Microsoft and Adobe, often offer their products to students at a discount so it's always good to check their websites before purchasing software or hardware.

Can I get software for free legally? In addition to open source software, discussed previously in this chapter, **freeware** is copyrighted software that you can use for free. Explore sites like FileHippo (**filehippo.com**) and MajorGeeks (**majorgeeks.com**) to see how many good freeware programs are available. However, while much legitimate freeware exists, some unscrupulous people use freeware to distribute viruses and malware. Be cautious when installing freeware, especially if you're unsure of the provider's legitimacy.

Can I try new software before it's released? Some software developers offer beta versions of their software free of charge. A **beta version** is an application that is still under development. By distributing free beta versions, developers hope users will report errors, or bugs, they find in their programs. Many beta versions are available for a limited trial period and are used to help developers respond to issues before they launch the software on the market.

Are there risks associated with installing beta versions, freeware, or downloading software from the Internet? By their very nature, beta products are unlikely to be bug free, so you always run the risk of something going awry with your system by installing and using beta versions. Unless you're willing to deal with potential problems, it may be best to wait until the last beta version is released—often referred to as the *gold version*. By that time, most of the serious bugs have been worked out.

As a precaution, you should be comfortable with the reliability of the source before downloading a freeware or beta version of software. If it's a reliable developer whose software you're familiar with, you can be more certain that a serious bug or virus isn't hiding in the software. Similarly, you should be sure that the software you're downloading is meant for your system and that your system has met all the necessary hardware and operating system requirements.

Before installing any software, it's always good to make sure your virus protection software is up to date. It's equally important that you back up your system as well as create a *restore point*. That way, if something does go awry, you can return your system to the way it was before you started. You can create a restore point by using Windows 10 System protection tools. To access the System protection tools, click System and Security from the Control Panel, and then click System. In the left pane, click System protection to display the System Properties dialog box. On the System Protection tab, click the Create button, type a description for the restore point (such as "Before installing [name of software]"), and click Create. You will be notified when the restore point is created.

Software Licenses

Objective 4.11 *Explain how software licenses function.*

Don't I own the software I buy? Most people don't understand that, unlike other items they purchase, the software they buy doesn't belong to them. The only thing they're actually purchasing is a license that gives them the right to use the software for their own purposes as the *only* user of that copy. The application is not theirs to lend.

A **software license**, also known as an **End User License Agreement (EULA)**, is an agreement between you, the user, and the software company (see Figure 4.27). You accept this agreement before installing the software on your machine. It's a legal contract that outlines the acceptable uses of the program and any actions that violate the agreement. Generally, the agreement states who the ultimate owner of the software is, under what circumstances copies of the software can be made, and whether the software can be installed on any other machine. Finally, the license agreement states what, if any, warranty comes with the software.

Does a license only cover one installation? Some software is purchased with a single license to cover one person's specific use. You can't share these licenses, and you can't "extend" the license to install the software on more than one of your computers. Many manufacturers are now offering licensing bundles to allow several computers in one household to be installed with a legal copy. For example, Apple offers a Family Pack Software License Agreement that permits a user to install the purchased software legally on as many as five computers in the same household, and some versions of Microsoft Office come with the ability

FIGURE 4.27 You must accept the terms of the software license before using the product. *(Windows 8.1, Microsoft Corporation)*

to install the software on multiple computers in the same household.

Businesses and educational institutions often buy multiuser licenses that allow more than one person to use the software. Some multiuser licenses are per-seat and limit the number of users overall, whereas others, called *concurrent licenses*, limit the number of users accessing the software at any given time.

BITS&BYTES

Run Versus Save When Downloading Software

When you download software from the web, often you're given the choice to run or save it (see Figure 4.28). What's the difference? When you select Run, the program is downloaded to your machine and generally stored in Temporary Internet Files. Then the file is "run," meaning that it is loaded into memory and the operating system executes (runs) it. Use the Run option when you need to use the downloaded file on a limited basis, such as a song or video that you only plan to watch once or twice. Some installation programs instead install the software on your machine in a permanent location when Run is selected.

When you select Save (or sometimes Save As) on a download, the file will be copied to your hard disk. There may be an AutoRun program associated with the file that starts the installation automatically. Otherwise, you may need to navigate to the stored location and execute (or run) the file independently. The big difference is that the saved file is not downloaded into a temporary location. Use Save when you want to keep the file for a longer period of time or when you want to control where the file or program is saved.

FIGURE 4.28 When downloading software, you have the choice to Run or Save. *(© 2015 Google Inc, used with permission. Google and the Google logo are registered trademarks of Google Inc.)*

As noted in the chapter, when you purchase software, you're purchasing a license to use it rather than purchasing the actual software. That license tells you how many times you can install the software, so it is important to read it. If you make more copies of the software than the license permits, you're participating in **software piracy** (see Figure 4.29). Historically, the most common way software has been pirated has been by borrowing installation disks from others and installing the software on other computers. Larger-scale illegal duplication and distribution by counterfeiters are quite common as well. In addition, the Internet provides various ways to copy and distribute pirated software illegally.

Is it really a big deal to copy a program or two? As reported by the Business Software Alliance, nearly half of all software used is pirated. Not only is pirating software unethical and illegal, the practice has financial impacts on all software consumers. The financial loss to the software industry is estimated to be over $62 billion. This loss decreases the amount of money available for further software research and development, while increasing the up-front costs to legitimate consumers.

To determine whether you have a pirated copy of software installed on your computer, conduct a software audit. The Business Software Alliance website (**bsa.org**) has several free third-party software audit tools that help you identify and track software installed on your computer and networks. These programs check the serial numbers of the software installed on your computer against software manufacturer databases of officially licensed copies and known fraudulent copies. Any suspicious software installations are flagged for your attention.

As of yet, there's no such thing as an official software police force, but if you're caught with pirated software, severe penalties do exist. A company or individual can pay up to $150,000 for each software title copied. In addition, you can be criminally prosecuted for copyright infringement, which carries a fine of up to $250,000, a five-year jail sentence, or both.

Efforts to stop groups involved with counterfeit software are in full force. Software manufacturers also are becoming more aggressive in programming mechanisms into software to prevent illegal installations. For instance, with many products, installation requires you to activate the serial number of your software with a database maintained by the software manufacturer. Failure to activate your serial number or attempting to activate a serial number used previously results in the software going into a "reduced functionality mode" after a certain number of uses. This usually precludes you from doing useful things like saving files created with the software.

FIGURE 4.29 Making more copies than the software license permits is pirating and is illegal. *(Igor Prole/Getty Images)*

Does open source software require a license?
As you learned earlier, anyone using open source software has access to the program's code. Therefore, open source software programs can be tweaked by another user and redistributed. A free software license, the *GNU General Public License*, is required and grants the recipients the right to modify and redistribute the software. Without such a license, the recipient would be in violation of copyright laws. This concept of redistributing modified open source software under the same terms as the original software is known as **copyleft**. Thus, all enhancements, additions, and other changes to copyleft software must also be distributed as free software.

Getting the Right Software for Your System

Objective 4.12 *Describe how to ensure software you purchase will work on your device.*

How do I ensure the software I buy will work on my computer? If you're obtaining software from an app marketplace, usually before the software is downloaded, your device is checked for compatibility with the program. If you're buying the software elsewhere, it's your responsibility to check for compatibility with your system.

Every software program has a set of **system requirements** that specify the minimum recommended standards for the operating system, processor, primary memory (random access memory, or RAM), and hard drive capacity. Sometimes there are other specifications for the video card, monitor, optical drive, and other peripherals. These requirements are printed on the software packaging or are available at the manufacturer's website. Before installing software on your computer, ensure that your system setup meets the minimum requirements as specified by the developer.

When is it worth buying a newer version? Periodically, software developers improve the functionality of their software by releasing a software upgrade. Although software developers suggest otherwise, there's no need to rush out and buy the latest version of a software program every time one is available. Depending on the software, some upgrades may not be sufficiently different from the previous version to make it cost-effective for you to buy the newest version. Unless the upgrade adds features that are important to you, you may be better off waiting to upgrade every other release. You also should consider whether you use the software frequently enough to justify an upgrade and whether your current system can handle the new system requirements of the upgraded version. In between upgrades, developers will make available *software updates* (sometimes referred to as *software patches*). Updates are usually downloaded and provide smaller enhancements to the software or fix program bugs.

If I have an older version of software and someone sends me files from a newer version, can I still open them? Software vendors recognize that people work on different versions of the same software.

Vendors, therefore, make new versions backward compatible, meaning that the new versions can recognize (open) files created with older versions. However, some software programs are not forward compatible, so these older versions are not able to recognize files created on newer versions of the same software. Files created on newer versions of software can be recognized by older versions if the correct file extension is chosen under Save As Type. For example, a .docx can be recognized by an older version of Microsoft Word if it is saved as .doc (Word 97-2003 document).

Installing and Uninstalling Software

Objective 4.13 *Describe how to install and uninstall software.*

What's the difference between a custom installation and a full installation? Before you use most software, you must permanently place it, or install it, on your system. The installation process may differ slightly depending on whether you're installing the software from a DVD, purchasing it from an app marketplace, or downloading it from the web. One of the first steps in the installation wizard asks you to decide between a full installation and a custom installation. A **full installation** (often referred to as a *typical installation*) copies all the most commonly used files and programs from the distribution disc to your computer's hard drive. By selecting **custom installation**, you can decide which features you want installed on your hard drive. Installing only the features you want saves space on your hard drive.

How do I uninstall a program? An application contains many different files—library files, help files, and other text files—in addition to the main file you use to run the program. By deleting only the main file, you're not ridding your system of all the pieces of the program. Windows 10 makes it easy to uninstall a program: On the Start menu, select All apps, then right-click the app and select Uninstall.

If my computer crashes, can I get the preinstalled software back? Although some preinstalled software is not necessary to replace if your computer crashes, other software such as the operating system is critical to reinstall. Most manufacturers use a separate partition on the hard drive to hold an image, or copy, of the preinstalled software. However, it's not always possible to reboot from the partitioned hard drive, especially when your computer crashes, so one of the first things you should do after you purchase a new computer is create a recovery drive. Generally, the manufacturer will have placed a utility on your system, or you can use the Recovery utility included in Windows to create a recovery drive. You can access the Advanced Recovery tools in Windows 10 by typing Recovery in the Cortana search box, and then selecting Recovery Control panel. When the Recovery dialog box opens, click the Create a recovery drive link. Then, to create the recovery drive, insert a blank flash drive in a USB port and follow the steps in the wizard. Once the recovery drive has been made, label the flash drive and put it away in a safe place.

BITS&BYTES

Ridding Your Computer of "Bloat"

Manufacturers often include software on new computers that you don't want or need. Called *bloatware*, this software can slow down your computer and degrade its performance. How do avoid it or get rid of it? Microsoft offers "Signature Editions" of popular PCs and tablets that are free from bloatware. However, if you purchase a computer with bloatware, you can install an application such as Should I Remove It? (**shouldiremoveit.com**), which actually helps you decide which programs you should remove. Or, if you'd rather do it yourself, consider some of these tips:

- *Uninstall preinstalled antivirus software:* If you have antivirus software on your old computer, you may be able to transfer the unexpired portion of your software license to your new computer. If this is the case, you can uninstall the preinstalled trial version on your new computer.
- *Uninstall unwanted toolbars:* Many computers come with Google, Bing, and other toolbars preinstalled. Go through Programs and Features in the Control Panel to uninstall any toolbars (or other programs) you don't want.
- *Remove manufacturer-specific software:* Some computer manufacturers install their own software. Some of these programs can be useful, but others are help features and update reminders that are also found in your operating system. You can remove any or all of these support applications and instead just check the manufacturer's website periodically for updates or new information.

How do I recover software that I installed on my device if my computer crashes? Most app marketplaces keep track of the software you have purchased and installed on your devices. So if you device crashes, you can log in to the marketplace and reinstall software you have previously purchased. We'll cover backup and recovery strategies for software in greater depth in Chapter 9.

There is an application for almost anything you want or need to do on your computer, whether it is school or work related or just for entertainment purposes. And there are a variety of types of applications, such as proprietary, open source, web-based, and freeware. Have fun exploring all the various possibilities! ■

 ACTIVE HELPDESK
Buying and Installing Software

In this Active Helpdesk, you'll play the role of a helpdesk staffer, fielding questions about how to best purchase software or to get it for free, how to install and uninstall software, and where you can go for help when you have a problem with your software.

Before moving on to the Chapter Review:
1. **Watch Replay Video 4.2** ⟳ .
2. **Then check your understanding of what you've learned so far.**

check your understanding // review & practice

For a quick review to see what you've learned so far, answer the following questions.

multiple choice

1. The minimum set of recommended standards for a program is known as the
   a. operating system.
   b. system requirements.
   c. setup guide.
   d. installation specs.

2. Which of the following is an uncompressed audio file format?
   a. AAC
   b. WAV
   c. MP3
   d. WMA

3. Which of the following is considered a benefit of using simulation programs?
   a. They allow users to experience potentially dangerous situations without risk.
   b. They help to prevent costly errors.
   c. They allow users to train on software that is not installed on their systems.
   d. all of the above

4. Which of the following is NOT necessary to do before installing beta software?
   a. creating a restore point
   b. backing up your system
   c. defragging the hard drive
   d. ensuring your virus protection software is updated

5. Which of the following is not a website for managing your digital pictures?
   a. Shutterfly
   b. Snapfish
   c. Picasa
   d. Lumosity

 Go to **MyITLab** to take an autograded version of the *Check Your Understanding* review and to find all media resources for the chapter.

TECHBYTES WEEKLY
Stay current with the TechBytes Weekly Newsletter.

 Continue

summary //

Programs That Let You Work

Learning Outcome 4.1 **You will be able to describe the basic ways to access and use software and identify the main types of productivity and business software.**

The Nuts and Bolts of Software

Objective 4.1 *Describe the differences between application and system software.*

- The term *software* refers to a set of instructions that tells the computer what to do.
- *Application software* is the software you use to do everyday tasks at home, school, and work. Microsoft Word and the Edge browser are examples of application software.
- *System software* is the software that helps run the computer and coordinates instructions between application software and the computer's hardware devices. System software includes the operating system and utility programs.

Objective 4.2 *List different types of apps and software you can use on your computing devices.*

- There are two basic types of software that you can install on your computer:
  - *Proprietary (or commercial) software* is software you buy.
  - *Open source software* is program code that is free and publicly available with few licensing and copyright restrictions. The code can be copied, distributed, or changed without the stringent copyright protections of software products you purchase.
- Software can be accessed (used) in three ways:
  - *Local apps* are installed on your computing device. They generally do not require an Internet connection to function.
  - *Mobile apps* are also installed on your device, but need to be connected to the Internet to achieve full functionality
  - *Web-based apps* are those that are hosted online by the vendor and made available to the customer over the Internet. This web-based distribution model is also referred to as Software as a Service (SaaS).

Productivity and Business Software

Objective 4.3 *List the types of applications included in productivity software suites, and describe their uses and features.*

- Productivity software programs include the following:
  - Word processing: to create and edit written documents
  - Spreadsheet: to do calculations and numerical and what-if analyses easily
  - Presentation: to create slide presentations
  - Database: to store and organize data
  - Note-taking: to take notes and easily organize and search them
  - Personal information manager (PIM): to keep you organized by putting a calendar, address book, notepad, and to-do lists within your computer

Objective 4.4 *List software that individuals use to manage their finances.*

- *Financial planning software* helps you manage your daily finances. Examples include Quicken and Mint.
- *Tax preparation software*, such as Intuit TurboTax and H&R Block Tax Software, lets you prepare your state and federal taxes on your own instead of hiring a professional.

Objective 4.5 *List common types of software that large and small businesses use.*

- *Accounting software* is used to track accounts receivable and accounts payable, manage inventory, prepare payroll, and generate customer bills.
- *Desktop publishing software (DTP)* is used for generating publications with complex layouts such as catalogs, annual reports, books, and newsletters.

- *Web authoring software* allows businesses to design interactive web pages. Examples are Adobe InDesign and Dreamweaver.
- *Customer relationship management (CRM), enterprise resource planning (ERP), and project management software* are used to manage complex processes and tasks.

- Computer-aided design (CAD) software facilitates the production of automated designs, technical drawings, and 3-D model visualizations.
- Businesses may use specialized business software (or vertical market software) that is designed for their specific industry.

Programs That Let You Play

Learning Outcome 4.2: **Describe the different types of multimedia and educational software available, and discuss how best to manage your software.**

Multimedia and Educational Software

Objective 4.6 *Describe the uses and features of digital image-editing, video-editing, and drawing software.*

- *Image-editing software* includes tools for basic modifications to digital photos such as removing red-eye; modifying contrast, sharpness, and color casts; or removing scratches or rips from scanned images of old photos.
- *Digital video-editing software* is used to apply special effects, change the sequence of scenes, or combine separate video clips into one movie.
- Drawing (or illustration) software facilitates the creation and editing of 2-D, line-based drawings. It is used for the creation of technical diagrams and original nonphotographic drawings.

Objective 4.7 *Describe the uses and features of digital audio software.*

- *Digital audio software* allows you to compose songs or soundtracks with virtual instruments, voice recorders, synthesizers, and special audio effects; record audio files from live sources such as musicians or spoken word; and edit audio files to improve sound quality.

Objective 4.8 *Describe the features of app creation software.*

- *App creation software* provides professionals and novices alike with the ability to create their own apps.
- Although used widely in game development, app creation software can be used to create many other types of apps that have business applications.

Objective 4.9 *Describe common types of educational and reference software and their features.*

- *Test preparation software* is designed to improve your performance on standardized tests.
- *Simulation software* allow you to experience or control the software as if it were an actual event. Often this allows experiencing dangerous situations safely.
- *Instructional software* is designed to teach specific skills.
- *Course management software* creates a virtual learning experience for students and houses course materials, tests, and discussion boards.
- *Brain training software* features games and activities designed to improve memory, processing speed, attention span, and multitasking.
- *Genealogy software* helps chart relationships between family members through multiple generations.

Managing Your Software

Objective 4.10 *Describe where to obtain the main types of software.*

- *App marketplaces* (or *app stores*) are the most common place to purchase and download software. The main app marketplaces are Google Play, App Store (Apple), and Windows Store.
- Although most software today is downloaded from the web, it can also be purchased at retail stores or directly from software developers.
- *Beta software* are apps that are still under development but are released to the public to gather feedback on design features and errors.

Objective 4.11 *Explain how software licenses function.*

- A *software license*, also known as an *End User License Agreement (EULA)*, is an agreement between you, the user, and the software company who owns the software.

- When you purchase software, you're actually purchasing the license to use it and therefore must abide by the terms of the licensing agreement you accept when installing the program.
- Software licenses permit installation on a specific number of devices.

Objective 4.12 *Describe how to ensure software you purchase will work on your device.*

- Before installing software on your computer, ensure that your system setup meets the *system requirements*.
- *System requirements* specify the minimum recommended standards for the operating system, processor, primary memory (RAM), and hard drive capacity.

Objective 4.13 *Describe how to install and uninstall software.*

- When installing software, you're often given the choice between a full (typical) or custom installation.
- When uninstalling software, it's best to use the uninstall feature that comes with the operating system. To uninstall an app in Windows 10, on the Start menu, select All apps, then right-click the app and select Uninstall.

 Be sure to check out **MyITLab** for additional materials to help you review and learn. And don't forget the Replay Videos ▸ .

key terms //

chapter quiz // assessment

For a quick review to see what you've learned, answer the following questions. Submit the quiz as requested by your instructor. If you are using **MyITLab**, the quiz is also available there.

multiple choice

1. Which software application would you use to calculate and manipulate numerical data?

   a. Microsoft Office Excel

   b. Apple iWork Numbers

   c. Apache OpenOffice Calc

   d. all of the above

2. PowToon and HaikuDeck are alternatives to

   a. Microsoft Word.

   b. Microsoft PowerPoint.

   c. Adobe InDesign.

   d. Apple iWork Pages.

3. Calendars, tasks, and e-mail will be found in which application?

   a. Excel   c. Outlook

   b. OneNote   d. Access

4. Which of the following describes copyleft?

   a. terms enabling redistributing proprietary software

   b. terms enabling redistributing open source software

   c. terms enabling free use of software content

   d. terms restricting free use of software content

5. When a vendor hosts software on a website and you don't need to install the software on your device, this is known as:

   a. Software as a Service.

   b. Open source software.

   c. Beta software.

   d. Freeware.

6. Which type of software is used to make 3-D models?

   a. spreadsheet   c. DTP

   b. CAD   d. simulation

true/false

_____ 1. Productivity software suites are available as web-based software.

_____ 2. A macro is a software tool that offers a step-by-step guide through complicated tasks.

_____ 3. Removing red-eye, cropping, and altering pictures with pen- and brush-like tools are features of image-editing software.

_____ 4. When you buy software, you can only use it as specified in the EULA.

critical thinking

1. **Living on the Cloud**

   Cloud computing is becoming more popular, and many users are working from the cloud and not even realizing it. Open Google Docs and Office Online and compare one of the applications in these online suites with an installed counterpart (e.g., Excel Online and Google Spreadsheets versus Excel). What similarities and differences do you find between the online applications and the installed version? Envision a time when all software is web-based and describe how being totally on the cloud might be an advantage. What disadvantages might a cloud-based environment present?

2. **App Marketplaces and Software Piracy**

   Since app marketplaces work so well with mobile devices, it is difficult to find alternate sources of software. Will this end software piracy since mobile apps are not distributed on DVDs and have to be purchased within one specified place? Should software for laptops and desktops be only distributed through app marketplaces to prevent piracy? What else might be done to combat software piracy? Explain your answers.

team time //

Software for Startups

Problem

You and your friends have decided to start Recycle Technology, a not-for-profit organization that would recycle and donate used computer equipment. In the first planning session, your group recognizes the need for certain software to help you with various parts of the business such as tracking inventory, designing notices, mapping addresses for pickup and delivery, and soliciting residents by phone or e-mail about recycling events, to name a few.

Task

Split your class into as many groups of four or five as possible. Make some groups responsible for locating free or web-based software solutions and other groups responsible for finding proprietary solutions. Another group could be responsible for finding mobile app solutions. The groups will present and compare results with each other at the end of the project.

Process

1. Identify a team leader who will coordinate the project and record and present results.

2. Each team is to identify the various kinds of software that Recycle Technology needs. Consider software that will be needed for all the various tasks required to run the organization such as communication, marketing, tracking, inventory management, and finance.

3. Create a detailed and organized list of required software applications. Depending on your team, you will specify either proprietary software or open source software.

Conclusion

Most organizations require a variety of software to accomplish different tasks. Compare your results with those of other team members. Were there applications that you didn't think about, but that other members did? How expensive is it to ensure that even the smallest company has all the software required to carry out daily activities, or can the needs be met with free, open source products?

ethics project //

Open Source Software

Ethical conduct is a stream of decisions you make all day long. In this exercise, you'll research and then role-play a complicated ethical situation. The role you play might or might not match your own personal beliefs, but your research and use of logic will enable you to represent the view assigned. An arbitrator will watch and comment on both sides of the arguments, and together, the team will agree on an ethical solution.

Topic: Proprietary Software Versus Open Source Software

Proprietary software has set restrictions on use and can be very expensive, whereas open source software is freely available for users to use as is or to change, improve, and redistribute. Open source software has become acceptable as a cost-effective alternative to proprietary software—so much so that it is reported that the increased adoption of open source software has caused a drop in revenue to the proprietary software industry. But determining which software to use involves more than just reducing the IT budget.

Research Areas to Consider

- Open source software
- Proprietary software
- Copyright licensing
- Open source development

Process

1. Divide the class into teams.
2. Research the areas cited above and devise a scenario in which someone is a proponent for open source software but is being rebuffed by someone who feels that "you get what you pay for" and is a big proponent of using proprietary software.
3. Team members should write a summary that provides background information for their character—for example: open source proponent, proprietary developer, or arbitrator—and that details their character's behaviors to set the stage for the role-playing event. Then, team members should create an outline to use during the role-playing event.
4. Team members should present their case to the class or submit a PowerPoint presentation for review by the rest of the class, along with the summary and resolution they developed.

Conclusion

As technology becomes ever more prevalent and integrated into our lives, more and more ethical dilemmas will present themselves. Being able to understand and evaluate both sides of the argument, while responding in a personally or socially ethical manner, will be an important skill.

Solve This

MyITLab® grader

Analyzing Benchmark Data

You work for a design firm that uses many of the software applications in the Adobe Creative Suite, especially Photoshop, Illustrator, and InDesign. You have been asked to evaluate whether it would be worthwhile to upgrade the software to the latest version. In addition to reviewing any new or revised features, you also want to provide an analysis on any improvements in product efficiency and performance, so you have repeated doing the same skills with the current and new data and have recorded the results. Now you just need to analyze it.

> You will use the following skills as you complete this activity:
>
> - AutoFill Data
> - Insert AVERAGE Function
> - Add Borders
> - Align and Wrap Text
> - Apply Conditional Formatting
> - Create Bar Chart

Instructions

1. Open *TIA_Ch4_Start* and save as **TIA_Ch4_LastFirst**.

2. In cell F1, type **Current Average**, and in cell J1, type **New Average**.

3. In cell F2, use the **AVERAGE function** to compute the average of range C2:E2. In cell J2, use the **AVERAGE function** to compute the average of range G2:I2.

4. Select **cell F2**, then drag the **Fill Handle** to cell F13. Select **cell J2**, then drag the **Fill Handle** to cell J13.

5. Select **range C2:J13**, then format the cell contents with **Number format with one decimal**.

6. Select **cell A2**, and **Merge and Center** across **cells A2:A5**. Then adjust the orientation of the text to **Rotate Text Up (90 degrees). Middle Align** cell contents and **Bold** text.

7. Use **Format Painter** to copy these formats to cell A6 and cell A10.

8. Select **range A2:J5**, then apply **Thick Outside Border**. Repeat with **ranges A6:J9** and **A10:J13**.

9. Select **range F1:F13**, then apply **Thick Outside Border**. Repeat with range J1:J13.

10. Select **range J2:J13**, then apply a **Conditional Format** that will format cells that are Less Than those cells in range F2:F13 with Green Fill and Dark Green Text.

    a. Hint: In the Format cells that are LESS THAN box, enter **=F2** (*not* F2). The rest of the cells in the range will update automatically.

11. Create a Clustered Bar Chart using ranges B1:B13, F1:F13, J1:J13.

    a. Hint: Hold down the **Ctrl button** as you select ranges F1:F13 and J1:J13.

12. Add the title **Benchmark Comparison: New and Current Versions of CS Software** to the Clustered Bar Chart, and add a Horizontal Axis title and type **Seconds**. Position and resize the chart so it fills range A16:J34.

13. Save the workbook and submit based on your instructor's directions.

5

System Software: The Operating System, Utility Programs, and File Management

Understanding System Software

Learning Outcome 5.1 **You will be able to explain the types and functions of an operating system and explain the steps in the boot process.**

Operating System Fundamentals 162

Objective 5.1 *Discuss the functions of the operating system.*

Objective 5.2 *Explain the different kinds of operating systems for machines, networks, and business.*

Objective 5.3 *Explain the most common operating systems for personal use.*

🔊 **Sound Byte:** Customizing Windows

What the Operating System Does 167

Objective 5.4 *Explain how the operating system provides a means for users to interact with the computer.*

Objective 5.5 *Explain how the operating system helps manage hardware such as the processor, memory, storage, and peripheral devices.*

Objective 5.6 *Explain how the operating system interacts with application software.*

Starting Your Computer 172

Objective 5.7 *Discuss the process the operating system uses to start up the computer and how errors in the boot process are handled.*

🧑 **Active Helpdesk:** Starting the Computer: The Boot Process

Using System Software

Learning Outcome 5.2 **You will be able to describe how system software is used, including managing the user interface, file management, and utility programs.**

The Windows Interface 178

Objective 5.8 *Describe the main features of the Windows interface.*

File Management 181

Objective 5.9 *Summarize how the operating system helps keep your computer organized.*

🔊 **Sound Byte:** File Management

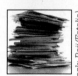

Objective 5.10 *Summarize how to view, sort, name, and manage files and folders.*

🧑 **Active Helpdesk:** Organizing Your Computer: File Management

Objective 5.11 *Summarize how file compression works.*

🔊 **Sound Byte:** File Compression

Utility Programs 189

🧑 **Active Helpdesk:** Using Utility Programs

Objective 5.12 *Outline the tools used to enhance system productivity.*

🔊 **Sound Byte:** Letting Your Computer Clean Up After Itself

Objective 5.13 *Summarize the utilities used to backup and restore files and the computer system.*

🔊 **Sound Byte:** Hard Disk Anatomy

Objective 5.14 *Describe the assistive technology utilities used to make using the computer system easier.*

Make This: MAKE: A Notification Alert on **page 177**

All media accompanying this chapter can be found in MyITLab.

For an overview of the chapter, watch the **Preview Video.**

(Dizain/Fotolia; Artender/Fotolia; Revers/Shutterstock; Windows 8.1, Microsoft Corporation; Stanislav Popov/Shutterstock; Reji/Fotolia)

HOW COOL IS THIS?

Tony Stark built the Iron Man suit using a **hologram**. Princess Leia delivered her message to Obi-Wan Kenobi as a hologram. Now, thanks to Microsoft, you might be able to use holograms in your own home. What's a hologram? Holograms are **three-dimensional photographic images** that appear to be **freestanding images**. They are created using two two-dimensional images of the same object taken from different angles and superimposed to display what appears to the brain to be one image. Microsoft is incorporating this holographic technology with **HoloLens**. HoloLens are wireless lenses that will enable you to **interact freely with holograms**. What can you do with holograms? The possibilities are still being explored, but think of how you might interact with a touch-screen device, and then remove the need to physically touch the device. Instead, you'll interact with a holographic image. It might not be long before you're using holographic technology for your next project. *(Corbis)*

Understanding System Software

As discussed in the previous chapter, your computer uses two basic types of software: application software and system software. *Application software* is the software you use to do everyday tasks at home and at work. *System software* is the set of programs that helps run the computer and coordinates instructions between application software and the computer's hardware devices. From the moment you turn on your computer to the time you shut it down, you're interacting with system software.

operating system
FUNDAMENTALS

Every computer, from the smallest laptop to the largest supercomputer, has an operating system. Even cell phones, game consoles, cars, and some appliances have operating systems. The role of the operating system is critical; a computer can't operate without it.

Operating System Basics

Objective 5.1 *Discuss the functions of the operating system.*

What does the operating system do? System software consists of two primary types of programs: the *operating system* and *utility programs*. The **operating system (OS)** is a group of programs that controls how your computer functions. The operating system has three primary functions:

- It manages the computer's hardware, including the processor, memory, and storage devices, as well as peripheral devices such as the printer.
- It provides a consistent means for application software to work with the central processing unit (CPU).
- It is responsible for the management, scheduling, and coordination of tasks.

You interact with your OS through the **user interface**—the *desktop*, *icons*, and *menus* that let you communicate with your computer.

A **utility program** is a small program that performs many of the general housekeeping tasks for your computer, such as system maintenance and file compression. A set of utility programs is bundled with each OS, but you can also buy standalone utility programs that often provide more features. We'll discuss utility programs in more detail later in the chapter.

Are all operating systems alike? You're probably familiar with Microsoft Windows, Apple OS X, and perhaps the Android operating system if it's on your phone, but many other operating systems exist. Laptops, tablet computers, and smartphones all need specific operating systems designed to take advantage of their unique characteristics. However, as devices begin

FIGURE 5.1

Common Operating Systems		
OS NAME	**DEVELOPED BY**	**AVAILABLE ON**
Windows	Microsoft	Laptops, tablets, desktops, all-in-ones, cell phones
OS X	Apple	Laptops, desktops, all-in-ones
iOS	Apple	Tablets, iPhones, iPod touches
Android	Google	Cell phones, tablets
Linux	Open source	Laptops, desktops, tablets

(Top Photo Group/Alamy, Aleksey Boldin/Alamy, David Paul Morris/Bloomberg/ Getty Images, YAY Media AS/Alamy, Tibbbb/Fotolia)

to converge in terms of functionality, and operating systems continue to become more powerful, developers such as Microsoft and Apple are making operating systems that have similar functionality (such as OS X and iOS) or single operating systems (such as Windows 10) that can run on a variety of devices. Figure 5.1 lists a number of common operating systems.

When operating systems were originally developed, they were designed for a single user performing one task at a time (that is, they were *single-user, single-task operating systems*). However, modern operating systems allow a single user to **multitask**—to perform more than one process at a time. And operating systems such as Windows and OS X provide networking capabilities as well, essentially making them *multiuser, multitasking operating systems*.

Operating systems can be categorized by the type of device in which they're installed, such as robots and specialized equipment with built-in computers, mainframes and network computers, mobile devices, and personal computers. Next, we'll look at these different types of operating systems.

Operating Systems for Machinery, Networks, and Business

Objective 5.2 *Explain the different kinds of operating systems for machines, networks, and business.*

Why do machines with built-in computers need an OS? Machinery that performs a repetitive series of specific

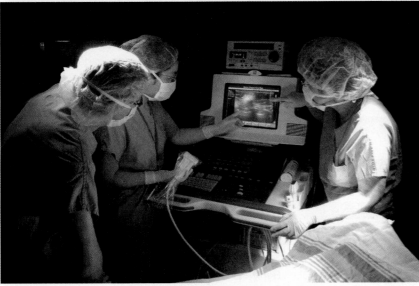

FIGURE 5.2 Devices such as TV sky cameras, cars, and medical equipment use RTOSs. *(John Pyle/Cal Sport Media/Newscom, Mark Gail/The Washington Post via Getty Images, Elfstrom/Getty Images)*

tasks in an exact amount of time requires a **real-time operating system (RTOS)**. Also referred to as *embedded systems*, RTOSs require minimal user interaction. This type of OS is a program with a specific purpose, and it must guarantee certain response times for particular computing tasks; otherwise, the machine is useless. The programs are written specifically for the needs of the devices and their functions. Therefore, there are no commercially available standard RTOS software programs. Devices that must perform regimented tasks or record precise results—such as measurement instruments found in the scientific, defense, and aerospace industries—require RTOSs. Examples include digital storage oscilloscopes and the Mars Reconnaissance Orbiter.

You also encounter RTOSs every day in devices such as fuel-injection systems in car engines, automobile "infotainment" systems, and some common appliances. RTOSs are also found in many types of robotic equipment. Television stations use robotic cameras with RTOSs that glide across a suspended cable system to record sports events from many angles (see Figure 5.2).

What kind of operating systems do networks use? A **multiuser operating system** (or **network operating system**) lets more than one user access the computer system at a time by handling and prioritizing requests from multiple users. Networks (groups of computers connected to each other so that they can communicate and share resources) need a multiuser OS because many users simultaneously access the server (the computer that manages network resources such as printing and communications). The latest versions of Windows and OS X can be considered network operating systems: They enable users to set up basic networks in their homes and small businesses.

In larger networks, a more robust network OS is installed on servers and manages all user requests. For example, on a network where users share a printer, the network OS ensures that the printer prints only one document at a time in the order the requests were made. Examples of network operating systems include Windows Server, Linux, and UNIX.

What is UNIX? UNIX is a multiuser, multitasking OS that is used as a network OS, although it can also be found on PCs. Developed in 1969 by Ken Thompson and Dennis Ritchie of AT&T's Bell Labs, the UNIX code was initially not proprietary—in other words, no company owned it. Rather, any programmer was allowed to use the code and modify it to meet his or her needs. UNIX is now a brand that belongs to the company The Open Group, but any vendor that meets the testing requirements and pays a fee can use the UNIX name. Individual vendors then modify the UNIX code to run specifically on their hardware.

What other kinds of computers require a multiuser OS? Mainframes and supercomputers also require multiuser operating systems. Mainframes routinely support hundreds or thousands of users at time, and supercomputers are often accessed by multiple people working on complex calculations. Examples of mainframe operating systems include UNIX, Linux on System z, and IBM's z/OS, whereas the vast majority of supercomputers use Linux.

Operating Systems for Personal Use

Objective 5.3 *Explain the most common operating systems for personal use.*

What kind of OS does a smartphone use? Figure 5.3 shows the market share for the most common operating systems found on smartphones. The two major players in this arena are Android and Apple with its iOS operating system. Microsoft, with its newest cross-platform operating system, is gaining market share, leaving Blackberry, once the leader in the field, and others such as Symbian to barely have an impact on the market. Today's smartphone operating systems offer personal assistants with predictive search capabilities, the ability to use a wide variety of apps, a search engine, a camera, and of course a phone, as well as texting and e-mail capabilities. Some even enable note taking on their touch-screen displays. Most smartphones support Bluetooth and WiFi as standard, and some are introducing near field communication (NFC) for wireless transfers and mobile payments.

What OS do tablets use? Popular tablet operating systems include iOS, Android, and Windows. iPads use iOS, whereas a number of different tablets (such as the Samsung Galaxy Tab and the Google Nexus) use versions of Android. The Kindle Fire also runs a customized version of Android. Until the release of Windows 8 in 2012, Microsoft didn't have a popular tablet OS, but the company is expected to have a 10% market share by 2017. Such growth was spurred on by the introduction of Windows 8, which was optimized for tablet devices like Microsoft's Surface tablet, as well as by the latest release of Windows 10.

Do gaming consoles and iPods use an OS? Gaming systems such as Microsoft's Xbox 360, the Nintendo Wii, and the Sony PlayStation, as well as personal media players such as the iPod, all require system software developed specifically for the particular device. The system software controls the physical aspects of the device (such as game controllers) as well as other application programs that come with the device. For example, the operating systems on gaming consoles control web browsing and file storage of media and photos as well as playing of DVDs and games.

What are the most popular operating systems for personal computers? Microsoft Windows, Apple OS X, and Linux (an open source OS) are the top three operating systems for personal computers. Although they share similar features, each is unique.

What's special about Windows? Microsoft **Windows** is an operating environment that incorporates a user-friendly, visual interface like the one that was first introduced with Apple's OS. Over time, improvements in Windows have

FIGURE 5.3 Popular Smartphone Operating Systems *(Data from Smartphone OS Market Share, 2015 Q2, IDC Corporate USA - available at http://www.idc.com/prodserv/smartphone-os-market-share.jsp)*

concentrated on increasing user functionality and friendliness, improving Internet capabilities, supporting home networks, and enhancing file privacy and security. Microsoft's newest OS, **Windows 10**, provides an interface optimized for touchscreen devices and is designed to run across all devices: phones, tablets, laptops, and desktops.

What's special about the Mac OS? In 1984, **Mac OS** became the first commercially available OS to incorporate the ability to interact with the computer with user-friendly point-and-click technology. With the release of the Mountain Lion version, Apple added many of the popular and innovative features loved by iOS users, such as messages, reminders, notes, and a notification center. The latest version, El Capitan, released in the fall of 2015, offers new features such as Split View (similar to Snap in Windows), touch-screen functionality, and natural language capabilities to Spotlight, OS X's search feature. OS X uses the same desktop metaphors as Windows, including icons for folders and a Trash Can (similar to a Recycle Bin) for deleted files. OS X also includes a window-based interface like the one in Windows.

OS X is based on the UNIX operating system, which is exceptionally stable and reliable. However, just as with any other OS, you still need to install updates as they become available and protect yourself from viruses, spyware, and other malicious software.

What is Linux? **Linux** is an open source OS designed for use on personal computers and as a network OS. Open source software is freely available for anyone to use or modify as he or she wishes. Linux began in 1991 as a part-time project of Finnish university student Linus Torvalds. It has since been tweaked by scores of programmers as part of the Free Software Foundation GNU Project (**gnu.org**).

Linux has a reputation as a stable OS that is not subject to crashes or failures. Because the code is open and available to anyone, Linux can be modified or updated quickly by hundreds of programmers around the world.

Where can I get Linux? Linux is available for download in various packages known as **distributions** or **distros**. Distros include the underlying Linux kernel (the code that provides Linux's basic functionality) and special modifications to the OS, and may also include additional open source software (such as OpenOffice). A good place to start researching distros is **distrowatch.com**. This site tracks Linux distros and provides helpful tips for beginners on choosing one.

Does it matter what OS is on my computer? An OS is designed to run on specific CPUs. CPUs have different designs, which can require modifying the OS software to allow it to communicate properly with each CPU. The combination of an OS and a specific processor is referred to as a computer's **platform**.

For user convenience, computers and other devices usually come with an OS already installed. Windows and Linux can run on most of the hardware being sold today. Your choice of an OS in this case is mostly a matter of price and personal preference. However, Apple equipment—computers, iPhones,

BITS&BYTES

Upgrading Your Operating System

Every couple of years or so, Apple and Windows announce plans to upgrade their operating systems. For Apple OS X users, the most recent upgrades have been delivered via a download. For Windows users, upgrades have been released on new devices and were subsequently offered for purchase to install on your current device, should you decide to do so. The decision to upgrade to the newest version of Windows depended on several factors, such as whether Microsoft would still be supporting the OS you were using, whether there were significantly different or enticing features in the new version that you wanted, whether your hardware could support the new version of the OS, or whether your application software was compatible with the new OS.

With the release of Windows 10, Microsoft is changing all of that. The company has claimed that this will be "the last version of Windows." Windows 10 was offered free of charge for the first year to anyone running Windows 7 or 8 (or 8.1). From now on, Microsoft's "Windows as a Service" model will deliver automatic OS updates, including new features, apps, and patches, as necessary, without any additional notice. That is, we shouldn't expect there to be a Windows 11, 12, or anything else. The days of deciding whether to upgrade your operating system may be over.

iPads, and iPod touches—can only work with the Apple operating system made for that device. iOS is the operating system for mobile devices, and OS X is the operating system for desktop and laptop computers.

Also, most *application software* is OS dependent. You need to make sure you get the correct version of the application software for your OS. For example, you would need Microsoft Office 2016 for Mac for Apple devices and Microsoft Office 2016 for Windows for Windows devices.

 SOUND BYTE
Customizing Windows

In this Sound Byte, you'll find out how to customize your desktop. You'll learn how to configure the desktop, set up a screen saver, change pointer options, customize the Start menu, and manage user accounts.

Can I have more than one OS on my computer?

Many people run more than one OS on their computers because different operating systems offer different features. For example, Windows and Linux both run well on Apple computers. A standard utility included in OS X called Boot Camp lets you boot into either Windows or OS X. And if you want to run both OS X and Windows at the same time, you can create "virtual drives" using virtualization software such as Parallels or VMware Fusion.

In Windows, you can create a separate section of your hard drive (called a *partition*) and install another OS on it while leaving your original Windows installation untouched. After installing the second OS, when your computer starts, you're offered a choice of which OS to use.

How do operating systems use the "cloud"? Now

that broadband Internet access and providing computer resources via the Internet (so-called cloud computing) are becoming more commonplace, operating systems have features that are tied to cloud computing. Here are a few examples:

- Windows 10 features tighter integration with the cloud. Using your *Microsoft account*, Windows 10 stores your settings and keeps track of applications you've purchased from the Windows store online. You can easily access and store files online in your *OneDrive account*. You can also log into your Windows account from any Windows-based machine and be able to see your familiar desktop and applications.
- Similarly, OS X allows you to sign in with your *Apple ID*, which provides access to Apple's *iCloud* system. iCloud

FIGURE 5.4 The Google Chrome OS has a very minimalist look.

stores your content online and automatically pushes it out to all your Apple devices.
- Google has launched the *Google Chrome OS* (see Figure 5.4), which is a web-based OS. With the Chrome OS, virtually no files are installed on your computing device. Rather, the main functionality of the OS is provided by accessing the web through a web browser. Chrome OS is only available on certain hardware from Google's manufacturing partners, and these devices are called *Chromebooks*. The Chrome OS should not be confused with the *Google Chrome browser*. The browser is application software that can run in many different operating systems. ∎

BITS&BYTES

OS Market Share Battle

So who is winning the OS market share war? It depends on the type of device. For conventional desktop and laptop computers, hands down the winner is still various versions of Windows, with 90.7% of the market (see Figure 5.5). But as of July 2015, Windows only had a 2.5% market share on mobile devices versus Android's 51%. Apple comes in second in both races with 7.6% market share of desktop operating systems and 41.5% market share of mobile operating systems.

FIGURE 5.5 Operating System Market Share *(Data from Market Share Reports, NetMarketShare - available at http://www.netmarketshare.com/)*

what the operating SYSTEM DOES

As shown in Figure 5.6, the OS is like an orchestra's conductor. It coordinates and directs the flow of data and information through the computer system. In this section, we explore the operations of the OS in detail.

The User Interface

Objective 5.4 *Explain how the operating system provides a means for users to interact with the computer.*

How does the OS control how I interact with my computer? The OS provides a user interface that lets you interact with the computer. The first personal computers used *Microsoft Disk Operating System* (*MS-DOS* or just *DOS*), which had a command-driven interface, as shown in Figure 5.7a. A **command-driven interface** is one in which you enter commands to communicate with the computer system. The DOS commands were not

always easy to understand; as a result, the interface proved to be too complicated for the average user. Therefore, PCs were used primarily in business and by professional computer operators.

The command-driven interface was later improved by incorporating a menu-driven interface, as shown in Figure 5.7b. A **menu-driven interface** is one in which you choose commands from menus displayed on the screen. Menu-driven interfaces eliminated the need for users to know every command because they could select most of the commonly used commands from a menu. However, they were still not easy enough for most people to use.

What kind of interface do operating systems use today? Current computer and mobile operating systems such as Microsoft Windows and OS X use a **graphical user interface** or **GUI** (pronounced "gooey"). Unlike command- and menu-driven interfaces, GUIs display graphics and use the point-and-click technology of the mouse and cursor (or human finger), making them much more user-friendly.

Manages computer hardware and peripherals

Provides a user interface

Provides a consistent interaction between applications and the CPU

The Operating System

Manages memory and storage

Manages the processor

(StockPhotosArt/Shutterstock; Ra2studio/Shutterstock; Ragnarock/Shutterstock; Arno van Dulmen/Shutterstock; Shcherbakov Roman/Shutterstock)

FIGURE 5.6 The OS is the orchestra conductor of your computer, coordinating its many activities and devices.

FIGURE 5.7 (a) A command-driven interface. (b) A menu-driven interface. *(Windows 8.1, Microsoft Corporation)*

Linux-based operating systems do not have a single default GUI interface. Instead, users are free to choose among many commercially available and free interfaces, such as GNOME and KDE, each of which provides a different look and feel.

Hardware Coordination

Objective 5.5 *Explain how the operating system helps manage hardware such as the processor, memory, storage, and peripheral devices.*

Why does the OS need to manage the processor? When you use your computer, you're usually asking the processor (also called the CPU) to perform several tasks at once. For example, you might be printing a Word document, chatting with your friends on Facebook, and watching a movie using the Blu-ray drive—all at the same time, or at least what appears to be at the same time. Although the CPU is powerful, it still needs the OS to arrange the execution of all these activities in a systematic way.

To do so, the OS assigns a slice of its time to each activity that requires the processor's attention. The OS must then switch among different processes billions of times a second to make it appear that everything is happening seamlessly. Otherwise, you wouldn't be able to watch a movie and print at the same time without experiencing delays in the process.

How exactly does the OS coordinate all the activities? When you create and print a document in Word while also watching a Blu-ray movie, for example, many different devices in the computer are involved, including your keyboard, mouse, Blu-ray drive, and printer. Every keystroke, every mouse click (or touch on the screen), and each signal to the printer and from the Blu-ray drive creates an action, or **event**, in the respective device (keyboard, mouse, Blu-ray drive, or printer) to which the OS responds.

Sometimes these events occur sequentially (such as when you type characters one at a time), but other events involve two or more devices working concurrently (such as the printer

printing while you type and watch a movie). Although it looks as though all the devices are working at the same time, the OS in fact switches back and forth among processes, controlling the timing of events on which the processor works.

For example, assume you're typing and want to print a document. When you tell your computer to print your document, the printer generates a unique signal called an **interrupt** that tells the OS that it's in need of immediate attention. Every device has its own type of interrupt, which is associated with an **interrupt handler**, a special numerical code that prioritizes the requests. These requests are placed in the interrupt table in the computer's primary memory (RAM). The OS processes the task assigned a higher priority before processing a task assigned a lower priority. This is called **preemptive multitasking**.

In our example, when the OS receives the interrupt from the printer, it suspends the CPU's typing activity and Blu-ray activity and puts a "memo" in a special location in RAM called a *stack*. The memo is a reminder of what the CPU was doing before it started to work on the printer request. The CPU then retrieves the printer request from the interrupt table and begins to process it. On completion of the printer request, the CPU goes back to the stack, retrieves the memo it placed about the keystroke or Blu-ray activity, and returns to that task until it is interrupted again, in a very quick and seamless fashion, as shown in Figure 5.8.

What happens if more than one document is waiting to be printed? The OS also coordinates multiple activities for peripheral devices such as printers. When the processor receives a request to send information to the printer, it first checks with the OS to ensure that the printer is not already in use. If it is, the OS puts the request in another temporary storage area in RAM, called the *buffer*. The request then waits in the buffer until the **spooler**, a program that helps coordinate all print jobs currently being sent to the printer, indicates the printer is available. If more than one print job is waiting, a line (or *queue*) is formed so that the printer can process the requests in order.

STEP 2: CPU receives an interrupt request from the printer.

STEP 1: CPU is playing a movie.

STEP 4: CPU executes printing.

STEP 6: CPU resumes playing the movie.

CPU Processing Activity

STEP 3: Memo about movie stored in stack.

Stack

STEP 5: Memo about movie retrieved from stack.

RAM

FIGURE 5.8 How Preemptive Multitasking Works

Memory and Storage Management

Why does the OS have to manage the computer's memory? As the OS coordinates the activities of the processor, it uses RAM as a temporary storage area for instructions and data the processor needs. The processor then accesses these instructions and data from RAM when it's ready to process them. The OS is, therefore, responsible for coordinating the space allocations in RAM to ensure there is enough space for all the pending instructions and data. The OS then clears the items from RAM when the processor no longer needs them.

Can my computer ever run out of RAM? RAM has limited capacity. Like most users, you will add new software and peripherals to your computer over time. Most computers sold for home use have between 4 and 16 GB of RAM. As you add and upgrade software and increase your usage of the computer system, you might find that the amount of RAM you have is no longer sufficient for your needs. If you have an older computer system with less RAM, it might be time to consider buying a new computer or adding more RAM.

What happens if my computer runs out of RAM? When there isn't enough RAM for the OS to store the required data and instructions, the OS borrows from the more spacious hard drive. This process of optimizing RAM storage by borrowing hard drive space is called **virtual memory**. As shown in Figure 5.9, when more RAM is needed, the OS swaps out from RAM the data or instructions that haven't recently been used and moves them to a temporary storage area on the hard drive called the **swap file** (or **page file**). If the data or instructions in the swap file are needed later, the OS swaps them back into active RAM and replaces them in the hard drive's swap file with less active data or instructions. This process of swapping is known as **paging**.

Can I ever run out of virtual memory? Only a portion of the hard drive is allocated to virtual memory. You can manually change this setting to increase the amount of hard drive space allocated, but eventually your computer will become sluggish as it is forced to page more often. This condition of excessive paging is called **thrashing**. The solution to this

Data and instructions not recently used.

RAM

Operating System

Data and instructions needed now.

Location of the swap file

FIGURE 5.9 Virtual memory borrows excess storage capacity from the hard drive when there isn't enough capacity in RAM. (*Arno van Dulmen/Shutterstock, Ragnarock/Shutterstock*)

problem is to increase the amount of RAM in your computer, if there is excess capacity available, so that it won't be necessary for it to send data and instructions to virtual memory. If you cannot add additional RAM to your computer, then it may be time to get a new device.

How does the OS manage storage? If it weren't for the OS, the files and applications you save to the hard drive and other storage locations would be an unorganized mess. Fortunately, the OS has a file-management system that keeps track of the name and location of each file you save and the programs you install. We'll talk more about file management later in this chapter.

Hardware and Peripheral Device Management

How does the OS manage the hardware and peripheral devices? Each device attached to your computer comes with a special program called a **device driver** that facilitates communication between the device and the OS. Because the OS must be able to communicate with every device in the computer system, the device driver translates the device's specialized commands into commands the OS can understand, and vice versa. Devices wouldn't function without the proper device drivers because the OS wouldn't know how to communicate with them.

Do I always need to install drivers? Today, most devices, such as flash drives, mice, keyboards, and digital cameras, come with the driver already installed in Windows. The devices whose drivers are included in Windows are called Plug and Play devices. **Plug and Play (PnP)** is a software and hardware standard designed to facilitate the installation of new hardware in PCs by including in the OS the drivers these devices need in order to run. Because the OS includes this software, incorporating a new device into your computer system seems automatic. PnP lets you plug a new device

FIGURE 5.10 A Windows message showing a successful driver installation the first time an external hard drive was connected to the computer. *(Windows 8.1, Microsoft Corporation)*

into your computer, turn it on, and immediately play (use) the device (see Figure 5.10).

What happens if the device is not PnP? Sometimes you may have a device that is so new the drivers aren't yet available automatically in Windows. You'll then be prompted to install or download from the Internet the driver that was provided with the device. If you obtain a device secondhand without the device driver, or if you're required to update the device driver, you can often download the necessary driver from the manufacturer's website. You can also go to websites such as DriverZone (**driverzone.com**) to locate drivers.

Can I damage my system by installing a device driver? Occasionally, when you install a driver, your system may become unstable (that is, programs may stop responding, certain actions may cause a crash, or the device or the entire system may stop working). Although this is uncommon, it can happen. Fortunately, to remedy the problem, Windows has a Roll Back Driver feature that removes a newly installed driver and replaces it with the last one that worked (see Figure 5.11).

FIGURE 5.11 The Roll Back Driver feature in Windows removes a newly installed driver and replaces it with the last one that worked. *(Windows 8.1, Microsoft Corporation)*
>To access Device Manager, right-click the **Start button** and select **Device Manager**. To display the device's property dialog box, double-click on a device. Click the **Driver tab**.

Many Mac users feel they are impervious to viruses and malware (software that can disable or interfere with the use of a computing device) because those are "just Windows problems." This means that Mac users often run their computers with only the basic protection provided by Apple in its operating system software. Are Mac users wild risk takers, or are they actually safe from hackers? As with many issues, it's a little bit of both.

Threats Are Out There

Windows users have been bombarded by malware and virus attacks for decades. When you bought your last Windows device, it invariably came with a trial version of third-party antivirus/anti-malware software. Running a Windows computer without antivirus/anti-malware software is just asking for trouble.

However, over the past several years, the attacks against Macs have also increased. Why weren't Macs attacked frequently in the past? Most malware is designed to steal sensitive information such as credit card numbers. When thieves expend the time, money, and effort to develop malware, they want to ensure that it targets the largest population of potential victims. As OS X gains market share, Mac users are becoming a larger group of potential targets. In fact, in many affluent nations, Mac ownership has reached 20% of the market. And since Macs tend to cost more than Windows machines, it can be argued that Mac users may have more disposable income than other computer buyers. And wealthy people always make attractive targets for thieves.

But Isn't OS X Just Safer Than Windows by Design?

To a certain extent, this is true. OS X does have certain design features that tend to prevent the installation and spread of malware. Apple has also designed current versions of iOS and OS X to prevent the installation of unapproved software (i.e., software not available on Apple's approved online outlets like the App Store). In addition, apps sold on the App Store are required to be designed using the access control technology known as *App Sandbox*.

When most software programs or apps are running, they have broad latitude to interact with the OS. Usually, they have all the rights that the user has over the OS. So if hackers can design an exploit that takes advantage of a security flaw in an app, they can potentially gain extensive control over the computer using the access that the user has to the OS. As noted, Apple requires all approved apps to be "sandboxed." When an app is sandboxed, the developer defines what the app needs to do in order to interact with the OS. The OS then grants only those specific rights and privileges to the app and nothing else. By doing this, it severely limits what hackers can do in an OS if they breach the security of an app. It's like being in a high-walled sandbox (or playpen) as a child. You can play within the confines of your space, but you can't make mischief outside certain limits.

So I'll Buy a Mac and Be Safe Forever, Right?

Alas, it's not that simple. Although it's more difficult to design exploits for OS X and iOS, it's not impossible. And a great deal of cybercrime relies on social engineering techniques like those used in scareware scams. *Scareware* is software designed to make it seem as if there is something wrong with your computer. The author of the scareware program then "persuades" you to buy a solution to the problem, acquiring your credit card number in the process. Scareware victims can be both Mac and PC users, so even if you own a Mac, you need to be aware of such scams and avoid falling prey to them (see Chapter 9).

The Solution: Extra Security Precautions

The current versions of OS X, iOS, and Windows all include some level of security tools and precautions. But there are a few things you should do to protect yourself:

1. **Make sure your software is set to download and install updates automatically.** As OS developers discover holes in their software's security, they provide updates to repair these problems.
2. **Use third-party antivirus/anti-malware software (even on a Mac).** Although no product will detect 100% of malware, detecting some is better than detecting none.
3. **Be aware of social engineering techniques.** Use vigilance when surfing the Internet so you don't fall prey to scams.

So, no OS is 100% safe. But if you're informed and proceed with caution, you can avoid a lot of schemes perpetrated by hackers and thieves.

Software Application Coordination

Objective 5.6 **Explain how the operating system interacts with application software.**

How does the OS help application software run on the computer? Every computer program, no matter what its type or manufacturer, needs to interact with the CPU using computer code. For programs to work with the CPU, they must contain code the CPU recognizes. Rather than having the same blocks of code for similar procedures in each program, the OS includes the blocks of code—each called an **application programming interface (API)**—that application software needs in order to interact with the CPU. Microsoft DirectX, for example, is a group of multimedia APIs built into

the Windows OS that improves graphics and sounds when you're playing games or watching videos on your PC.

What are the advantages of using APIs? To create applications that can communicate with the OS, software programmers need only refer to the API code blocks when they write an application. They don't need to include the entire code sequence. APIs not only prevent redundancies in software code, they make it easier for software developers to respond to changes in the OS. Software companies also take advantage of APIs to make applications in software suites (such as Microsoft Office) that have a similar interface and functionality. And since these applications share common APIs, data exchange is facilitated between two programs, such as inserting a chart from Excel into a Word document. ■

 starting
YOUR COMPUTER

Many things happen quickly between the time you turn on your computer and the time it's ready for you to start using it. As we discussed earlier, all data and instructions, including the OS, are stored in RAM while your computer is on. When you turn off your computer, RAM is wiped clean of all its data, including the OS. How does the computer know what to do when you turn it on if there is nothing in RAM? It runs through a special start-up process to load the OS into RAM.

The Boot Process

Objective 5.7 *Discuss the process the operating system uses to start up the computer and how errors in the boot process are handled.*

What are the steps involved in the boot process? As illustrated in Figure 5.12, the **boot process** consists of four basic steps. The term *boot*, from *bootstrap loader* (a small program used to start a larger program), alludes to the straps of leather, called *bootstraps*, that people used to use to help them pull on their boots. This is also the source of the expression "pull yourself up by your bootstraps." Let's look at each step of the boot process in detail.

Step 1: Activating BIOS
What's the first thing that happens after I turn on my computer? In the first step of the boot process, the CPU activates the **basic input/output system (BIOS)**. BIOS is a program that manages the exchange of data between the OS and all the input and output devices attached to the system. BIOS is also responsible for loading the OS into RAM from its permanent location on the hard drive. BIOS itself is stored on a read-only memory (ROM) chip on the

motherboard. Unlike data stored in RAM, data stored in ROM is permanent and is not erased when the power is turned off.

Step 2: Performing the Power-On Self-Test
How does the computer determine whether the hardware is working properly? The first job BIOS performs is to ensure that essential peripheral devices are attached and operational—a process called the **power-on self-test (POST)**. The BIOS compares the results of the POST with the various hardware configurations permanently stored in CMOS (pronounced "see-moss"). CMOS, which stands for *complementary metal-oxide semiconductor*, is a special kind of memory that uses almost no power. A small battery provides enough power so that the CMOS contents won't be lost after the computer is turned off. CMOS contains information about the system's memory, types of disk drives, and other essential input and output hardware components. If the results of the POST compare favorably with the hardware configurations stored in CMOS, the boot process continues.

Step 3: Loading the OS
How does the OS get loaded into RAM? Next, BIOS goes through a preconfigured list of devices in its search for the drive that contains the **system files**, the main files of the OS. When it is located, the OS loads into RAM from its permanent storage location on the hard drive.

Once the system files are loaded into RAM, the **kernel** (or **supervisor program**) is loaded. The kernel is the essential component of the OS. It's responsible for managing the processor and all other components of the computer system. Because it stays in RAM the entire time your computer is powered on, the kernel is said to be *memory resident*. Other,

STEP 2: Power-on self-test (POST).
- Tests components of the computer
- Compares results with configuration information in CMOS

STEP 1: CPU activates BIOS.
- Basic input/output system
- Stored permanently in ROM

CPU

ROM chip

STEP 3: Load OS to RAM.
- OS loaded from hard drive
- Kernel is *memory resident*

STEP 4: Configuration and customization settings checked and Start screen displays.

FIGURE 5.12 The Boot Process *(Arno van Dulmen/Shutterstock, Ragnarock/Shutterstock)*

less critical, parts of the OS stay on the hard drive and are copied over to RAM on an as-needed basis so that RAM is managed more efficiently. These programs are referred to as *nonresident*. Once the kernel is loaded, the OS takes over control of the computer's functions.

Step 4: Checking Further Configurations and Customizations

Is that it? Finally, the OS checks the registry for the configuration of other system components. The **registry** contains all the different configurations (settings) used by the OS and by other applications. It contains the customized settings you put into place, such as mouse speed, as well as instructions as to which programs should be loaded first.

Why do I sometimes need to enter a login name and password at the end of the boot process? The verification of your login name and password is called **authentication**. The authentication process blocks unauthorized users from entering the system. You may have your home computer set up for authentication, especially if you have multiple users accessing it. All large networked

environments, like your college, require user authentication for access.

On a Windows 10 computer, after your computer has completely booted up, you are brought to the Lock Screen where you are to log into your **Microsoft account**. Your Microsoft account is a combination of an e-mail address and a password. Because configuration settings are stored online and associated with a particular Microsoft account, it is easy for multiple people to share any Windows 10 computer and have access to their individual settings and preferences.

How do I know if the boot process is successful? The entire boot process takes only a few minutes to complete. If the entire system is checked out and loaded properly, the

 ACTIVE HELPDESK
Starting the Computer: The Boot Process

In this Active Helpdesk, you'll play the role of a helpdesk staffer, fielding questions about how the operating system helps the computer start up.

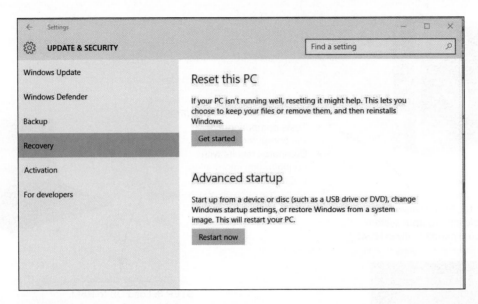

FIGURE 5.13 The recovery control in Windows 10 provides access to Reset this PC option.
(Windows 10, Microsoft Corporation)
>*To access the Recovery control, from the Start menu, click* **Settings**, *then click* **Update & security**. *On the Update & security screen, select* **Recovery**.

process completes by displaying the lock screen. After logging in, the computer system is now ready to accept your first command.

Handling Errors in the Boot Process

What should I do if my computer doesn't boot properly? Sometimes problems occur during the boot process. Here are some suggestions for solving a boot problem:

- If you've recently installed new software or hardware, try uninstalling it. (Make sure you uninstall through *Apps & features* in System Settings to remove the software.) If the problem no longer occurs when rebooting, you can reinstall the device or software.
- Try accessing the Windows Advanced Options Menu (accessible by pressing the F8 key during the boot process). If Windows detects a problem in the boot process, it will add Last Known Good Configuration to the Windows Advanced Options Menu. Every time your computer boots successfully, a configuration of the boot process is saved. When you choose to boot with the Last Known Good Configuration, the OS starts your computer by using the registry information that was saved during the last shut down.
- Try resetting your computer (in Update & Security Settings).

What happens when a PC is "reset"? Sometimes Windows does not boot properly or the system does not respond properly. You may even see messages related to "fatal exceptions." **Reset this PC** is a utility program in Windows 10 that attempts to diagnose and fix errors in your Windows system files that are causing your computer to

behave improperly (see Figure 5.13). When a PC is reset, the following occurs:

- Your data files (documents, music, videos, etc.) and personalization settings are not removed or changed.
- Apps that you have downloaded from the Windows Store are kept intact.
- Apps that you have downloaded from the Internet or installed from DVDs will be removed from your PC. Therefore, you'll need to reinstall them after the reset.

It's recommended that you back up your PC prior to resetting it as a precautionary measure. Finally, if all other attempts to fix your computer fail, try *Go back to an earlier build* to revert to a past configuration. System Recovery is covered in more detail later in this chapter.

What should I do if my keyboard or another device doesn't work after I boot my computer? Sometimes during the boot process, BIOS skips a device (such as a keyboard) or improperly identifies it. Your only indication that this problem has occurred is that the device won't respond after the system has been booted. When that happens, try restarting the computer. If the problem persists, check the OS's website for any patches (or software fixes) that may resolve the issue. If there are no patches or the problem persists, you may want to try to update the device driver or get technical assistance. ∎

> **Before moving on to Part 2:**
> 1. **Watch Replay Video 5.1** ⟳ .
> 2. **Then check your understanding of what you've learned so far.**

check your understanding // review & practice

For a quick review to see what you've learned so far, answer the following questions.

multiple choice

1. Which is NOT an example of a mobile operating system?

   a. iOS

   b. OS X

   c. Android

   d. Windows 10

2. You are most likely to find an RTOS

   a. in a robotic camera.

   b. on a supercomputer.

   c. on a mainframe.

   d. on an iPad.

3. The blocks of code that application software needs to interact with the CPU is called

   a. Automatic Programming Interface.

   b. Automatic Program Instruction.

   c. Application Programming Interface.

   d. Application Program Instruction.

4. Operating systems that have windows and icons have what type of user interface?

   a. command-driven

   b. graphical user

   c. menu-driven

   d. magnetic tape–based

5. The OS can optimize RAM storage by using

   a. thrashing.

   b. virtual memory.

   c. an interrupt handler.

   d. a spooler.

 Go to **MyITLab** to take an autograded version of the *Check Your Understanding* review and to find all media resources for the chapter.

TECHBYTES WEEKLY
Stay current with the TechBytes Weekly Newsletter.

Continue ≫

TRY THIS ▶ Using Virtual Desktops in Windows 10

Virtual desktops are a great way to organize your working space into different displays when you're multitasking between projects, job and school, or just work and entertainment. This exercise will walk you through the process of organizing your files into virtual desktops.

Step 1 Click **Task View** on the Task bar to bring up the Task View interface. This interface consists of a display area that shows large thumbnails of all the open windows running on your system. If you haven't created any virtual desktops, this is all you'll see. Task View is also a way to switch between open windows: You can make active any window by clicking on the desired thumbnail. This is similar to what you would see if you used Alt+Tab to cycle through all open **windows.** *(Windows 10, Microsoft Corporation)*

Thumbnails of all open windows

Task View

Step 2 In order to organize your open windows into specific groups, you need to create virtual desktops. To create virtual desktops, while in Task View, click **+New desktop** in the lower right corner. This adds another virtual desktop, Desktop 2. When you click **Task View** again, all your open windows display in Desktop 1, and Desktop 2 is empty. *(Windows 10, Microsoft Corporation)*

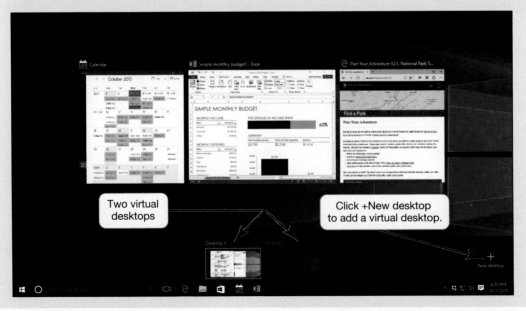

Two virtual desktops

Click +New desktop to add a virtual desktop.

Step 3   To move programs from Desktop 1 to the newly created Desktop 2, click **Task View**, then click and drag the window you want to move to Desktop 2. Alternatively, you can right-click the window you want to move, select **Move to**, and then select **Desktop 2**. While in Task View, when you hover the mouse over the desktop thumbnail, all open windows in that desktop display. *(Windows 10, Microsoft Corporation)*

> Right-click window, select Move to, and pick the desired desktop, or create a new desktop.

Step 4   To move between desktops, press the **Windows key+Tab**, or open Task View and click on the desired desktop to switch. To delete desktops, click **Task View**, point to the thumbnail of the desktop you want to delete, and then click the **(X)** that displays above the desktop thumbnail. *(Windows 10, Microsoft Corporation)*

> Drag a window directly to the desired desktop.

Make This ▷ TOOL: App Inventor 2

MAKE: A Notification Alert

Does your app need to communicate with or provide feedback to the user? With the Notifier component of **App Inventor**, you can make your program generate message boxes or ask for a response from the user.

In this exercise, you'll use the Notifier component of **App Inventor** to show a message box, post a user choice with two buttons for response, or post an alert. Your apps can now use more of the features of the Android operating system to communicate! *(MIT App Inventor 2, Massachusetts Institute of Technology. Creative Commons Attribution-ShareAlike 3.0 Unported License)*

The Notifier component allows you to communicate with alerts, message boxes, and text choice popups within your mobile app.

For the instructions for this exercise, go to MyITLab.

Learning Outcome 5.2 You will be able to describe how system software is used, including managing the user interface, file management, and utility programs.

Now that you know how system software works, let's explore how specific operating systems and their tools function.

 the windows

INTERFACE

As noted earlier, one of the functions of the operating system is to provide a *user interface* that lets you communicate with your computer. As was explained earlier, today's operating systems use a graphical user interface. We describe the Windows 10 user interface in this section, but it is very similar to the user interfaces for the OS X and Linus operating systems.

Using Windows 10

Objective 5.8 *Describe the main features of the Windows interface.*

How do I accomplish tasks in Windows 10? Starting with Windows 8, and now with Windows 10, the Windows operating system is designed to run on multiple devices: desktops, laptops, tablets, and phones, including those devices with touch screens. To enable Windows 10 to function on all types of devices and displays, there are often three different ways to accomplish tasks:

1. Using a mouse
2. Touching the screen (on touch-enabled devices)
3. Using keystrokes

Which method you use depends on the type of device you're using and, to a large extent, on your personal preferences.

What are the main features of the Windows 10 desktop? After logging into your Microsoft account by entering or confirming your e-mail address and entering a password, you're brought to the primary working area: the **desktop**. The Windows 10 desktop still has features like the **taskbar**, which displays open and favorite applications for easy access. You can

point to an icon to preview windows of open files or programs, or move your mouse over a thumbnail to preview a full-screen image. You can also right-click an icon to view a Jump List — the most recently or commonly used files or commands for that application.

Opening into the desktop is a modification from the Windows 8 experience, in which you were initially brought into the Start screen and then had to switch to the desktop. In Windows 10, you display the **Start menu** by clicking the Windows icon (or Start button) on the lower left corner of the screen or by pressing the Windows key on the keyboard. The Windows 10 Start menu provides you with access to all your applications in one convenient screen. We'll discuss personalizing the Start menu later in this section.

What are the main features of the Windows 10 Start menu? The Start menu is divided into two sections (see Figure 5.14a). The right side has the block tiles introduced with Windows 8. The tiles represent installed

FIGURE 5.14 (a) The Windows 10 Start menu provides access to your most used programs and apps. (b) Click All apps to display an alphabetical listing of all installed programs and apps.
(Windows 10, Microsoft Corporation)

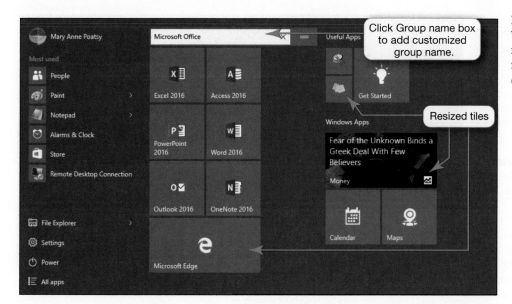

FIGURE 5.15 You can customize the Windows 10 Start menu by adding, resizing, and grouping tiles of your favorite programs and apps.
(Windows 10, Microsoft Corporation)

software and Windows apps (such as Weather, Skype, and Money). In addition to programs, tiles can represent files and folders. If there are more tiles on the Start menu than displayed, a scroll bar becomes available. The left side of the Start menu provides access to *Most used* programs as well as to File Explorer, Settings, Power, and All apps. When you click All apps, the left side changes to display a list of all the installed apps and programs on your computer (see Figure 5.14b).

How can I add programs to the Start menu? The most useful feature of the Start menu is that it lets you customize it to meet your needs (see Figure 5.15). It is easy to add, remove, resize, move, and group application tiles on the Start menu. You can choose which applications are visible on the Start menu through a process called **pinning**. Just right-click any application in the All apps list or in the Most Used list, and chose Pin to Start.

Once on the Start menu, a tile can be resized by right-clicking the tile, pointing to Resize, and then selecting the desired size. Most apps can be sized to Small, Medium, Wide, and Large, although some are limited to only Small or Medium. You can rearrange apps on the Start menu by dragging them. You can also arrange several tiles near each other to create a group. Point to the top of the group to display a name box where you can type a group name. If there is a tile on the Start menu you don't need, just right-click it (or touch and hold), and select Unpin from Start.

Because of the potential for customization, the Start menu on your computer may be different from the Start menu on your friend's computer. And because your Windows 10 settings and preferences are saved in your Microsoft account, when you log on to any Windows 10 computer, you'll see your own personal settings, preferences, and applications reflected on the Start menu.

How can I change the appearance of my Start menu and desktop? You can personalize the desktop, Start menu, and lock screen (the screen where you enter a password to resume using your computer) to suit your tastes. You'll find Personalization settings in Settings. For example, you can choose to have a picture, a slide show, or a single color display on the desktop and lock screen. You can also determine whether you'd like other information to display on the lock screen, such as the weather, time, or your e-mail or calendar. Choosing a theme sets a color and font scheme for your entire system. You can also determine which folders display on the left side of the Start menu. The default is File Explorer and Settings, but there are others to choose from, including Music, Pictures, or Documents.

How can I see more than one window on my screen at a time? Windows 7 introduced "snapping" windows: fixing open programs into place on either the left or right

BITS&BYTES

The Snipping Tool

The Snipping Tool is a Windows tool found in the Windows Accessories Folder in All apps that enables you to capture, or snip, a screen display so that you can save, annotate, or share it. You can capture screen elements as a rectangular, free-form window or as a full-screen snip. You can also draw on or annotate the screen capture, save it, or send it to others. In Windows 10, a new feature to the Snipping Tool is a delay timer so you can pause the capturing process for up to five seconds to set up screenshots of dialog boxes, menus, or other features that don't stay displayed when you initiate the Snipping Tool.

side of the screen, to easily display two apps at the same time. Windows 10 goes a bit further with more snapping options. Once you snap a window into place, thumbnails of all the other windows display. Clicking any thumbnail will snap that window into place. You can also snap windows to the corners, thus having up to four windows displayed at the same time.

How can I see open windows and quickly move between them? A new feature on the Windows 10 taskbar is Task View, which allows you to view all the tasks you're working on in one glance. For example, you might have a Word document, a web browser, and a PowerPoint presentation all open as you pull together a presentation that is required from a research paper you wrote for your business class, and a Word document and an Excel spreadsheet for a project you're working on for your job. To see all documents at once, click Task View on the taskbar.

Can I group my open programs and windows into task-specific groups? When faced with situations in which you're working with multiple documents for multiple projects, it might be easier to group the sets of documents together for each project and just switch between projects. You can do that now in Windows 10 with a feature called **virtual desktops**, which allow you to organize groups of windows into different displays (see Figure 5.16). There is no limit as to the number of desktops you can create. You can see all virtual desktops by clicking Task View. For more information on how to work with virtual desktops in Windows 10, see the Try This on pp. 176–177.

FIGURE 5.16 Virtual Desktops enable you to organize your open files into separate working spaces. *(Windows 10, Microsoft Corporation)*

Mac and Linux User Interfaces

How does the Mac user interface compare with Windows 10? Although the OS X and the Windows operating systems aren't compatible, they're extremely similar in terms of functionality. For example, as is the case with Windows, OS X programs appear in resizable windows and use menus and icons. However, instead of the Start menu, OS X features a Dock with icons on the bottom for your most popular programs (see Figure 5.17). Although Windows 10 will be deployed on all types of devices, as noted earlier, Apple runs two separate operating systems: OS X for desktops and laptops and iOS for the iPhone and iPad. However, the latest version of OS X, El Capitan, and its predecessor Yosemite, feature tight integration between OS X and portable devices running iOS. Apple wants to

FIGURE 5.17 OS X El Capitan is Apple's latest operating system for desktop and laptop computers.
(Aleksey Boldin/Alamy)

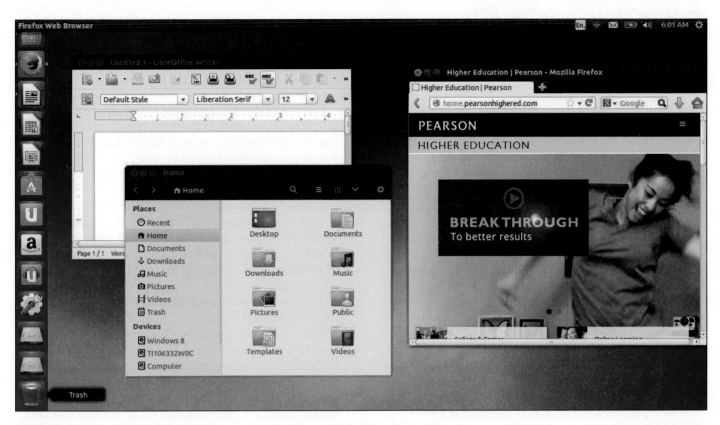

FIGURE 5.18 The Ubuntu Linux user interface resembles the Windows desktop. *(Ubuntu is a trademark of Canonical Limited and is used with the permission of Canonical Limited. Pearson is not endorsed by or affiliated with Canonical Limited or the Ubuntu project.)*

make transferring data and tasks from one device to another seamless.

Is a Linux user interface similar to OS X and Windows? Different distros of Linux feature different user interfaces. But most of them, like Ubuntu (see Figure 5.18), are based on familiar Windows and OS X paradigms, such as using icons to launch programs and having apps run in a window environment. ◼

file
MANAGEMENT

So far we've discussed how the OS manages the processor, memory, storage, and devices, and how it provides a way for applications and users to interact with the computer. An additional function of the OS is to enable **file management**, which provides an organizational structure to your computer's contents. In this section, we discuss how you can use this organizational structure to make your computer more organized and efficient.

Organizing Your Files

Objective 5.9 *Summarize how the operating system helps keep your computer organized.*

How does the OS organize files? Windows organizes the contents of your computer in a hierarchical **directory** structure composed of *drives*, *libraries*, *folders*, *subfolders*, and *files*. The hard drive, represented as the C: drive, is where

Proprietary software such as Microsoft Windows and Apple's OS X is developed by corporations and sold for profit. This means that the source code, the actual lines of instructional code that make the program work, is not accessible to the general public. Without being able to access the source code, it's difficult for a user to modify the software or see exactly how the program author constructed various parts of the OS.

Restricting access to the source code protects companies from having their programming ideas stolen, and it prevents customers from using modified versions of the software. However, in the late 1980s, computer specialists became concerned that the large software companies were controlling a large portion of market share and driving out competitors. They also felt that proprietary software was too expensive and contained too many bugs.

These people felt that software should be developed without a profit motive and distributed with its source code free for all to see. The theory was that if many computer specialists examined, improved, and changed the source code, a more full-featured, bug-free product would result. Hence, the open source movement was born, and Linux evolved as an open source operating system.

So, if an OS such as Linux is free and relatively bug-free, why does Windows, which users must pay for, have such a huge market share? One reason is that corporations and individuals have grown accustomed to one thing that proprietary software makers can provide: technical support. It's almost impossible to provide technical support for open source software because anyone can freely modify it. Similarly, corporations have been reluctant to install open source software extensively because of the cost of the internal staff of programmers that must support it.

Companies such as Red Hat, Ubuntu, and Xandros have been combating this problem. Red Hat offers a free, open source OS called Fedora (see Figure 5.19). In addition, Red Hat has modified the original Linux source code and markets a version, Red Hat Enterprise Linux, as a proprietary program. Fedora is the testing ground for what eventually goes into this proprietary program. Red Hat Enterprise Linux comes in versions for servers and desktops. Purchasers of Red Hat Enterprise Linux receive a warranty and technical support. Packaging open source software in this manner has made its use much more attractive to businesses. As a result, many web servers are hosted on computers running Linux.

FIGURE 5.19 Companies like Red Hat provide free or low-cost Linux software, such as Fedora, but technical support is often not available (or not free). *(AP Images)*

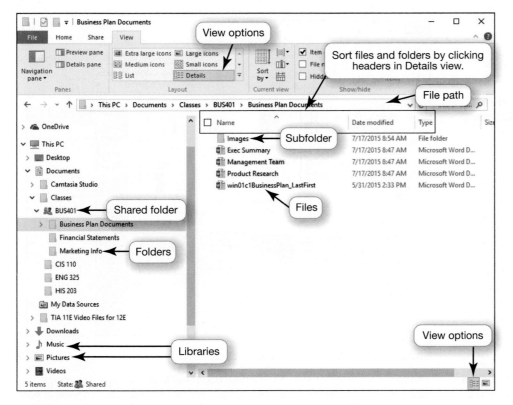

FIGURE 5.20 File Explorer lets you see the contents of your computer.
(Windows 10, Microsoft Corporation)
>*Click **File Explorer** from the Start menu or from the taskbar.*

you permanently store most of your files. Each additional storage drive, such as optical drive, flash drive, or external hard drive, is given a unique letter (*D*, *E*, *F*, and so on). The C: drive is like a large filing cabinet in which all files are stored. As such, the C: drive is the top of the filing structure of your computer and is referred to as the **root directory**. All other folders and files are organized within the root directory. There are areas in the root directory that the OS has filled with files and folders holding special OS files. The programs within these files help run the computer and generally shouldn't be accessed. Sometimes the manufacturer will store files used to reinstate your computer back to the original factory state. Those files should not be accessed unless necessary.

What exactly are files, folders, and libraries? In an OS, a **file** is a collection of program instructions or data that is stored and treated as a single unit. Files can be generated from an application such as a Word document or an Excel workbook. In addition, files can represent an entire application, a web page, a set of sounds, an image, or a video. Files can be stored on the hard drive, a flash drive, online, or on any other permanent storage medium. As the number of files you save increases, it becomes more important to keep them organized in folders and libraries. A **folder** is a collection of files.

How can I easily locate and see the contents of my computer? In Windows, **File Explorer** is the main tool for finding, viewing, and managing the

contents of your computer. It shows the location and contents of every drive, folder, and file. As illustrated in Figure 5.20, File Explorer is divided into two panes or sections:

1. The *Navigation pane* on the left shows the contents of your computer. It displays commonly accessed areas, organized by Favorites and Libraries (Documents, Music, Pictures, and Videos).

2. When you select a folder, drive, or library from the Navigation pane, the contents of that particular area are displayed in the *File list* on the right.

For those folders that have been shared with others using an online storage system such as OneDrive or Dropbox, there is a new feature in Windows 10 that displays a shared icon instead of the traditional yellow folder icon.

When you save a file for the first time, you give the file a name and designate where you want to save it. For easy reference, the OS includes libraries where files are saved unless you specify otherwise. In Windows, the default libraries are Documents for files, Music for audio files, Pictures for graphics files, and Videos for video files.

You can determine the location of a file by its **file path**. The file path starts with the drive in which the file is located and includes all folders, subfolders (if any), the file name, and the extension. For example, if you were saving a picture of Andrew Carnegie for a term paper for a U.S. History course, the file path might be C:\Documents\HIS182\Term Paper\Illustrations\ACarnegie.jpg.

As shown in Figure 5.21, "C:" is the drive on which the file is stored (in this case, the hard drive), and "Documents" is the file's primary folder. "HIS182," "Term Paper," and "Illustrations" are successive subfolders within the "Documents" main folder. Last comes the file name, "ACarnegie," separated from the file extension (in this case, "jpg") by a period. The backslash character (\), used by Windows, is referred to as a **path separator**. OS X files use a colon (:), whereas UNIX and Linux files use the forward slash (/) as the path separator.

C:\Documents\HIS182\Term Paper\Illustrations\ACarnegie.jpg

Drive | Primary folder | Subfolders | File name | Extension

FIGURE 5.21 Understanding File Paths

Working with Files and Folders

Objective 5.10 *Summarize how to view, sort, name, and manage files and folders.*

Are there different ways I can view and sort my files and folders? Clicking on the View tab in File Explorer offers you different ways to view the folders and files.

1. *Details view:* This is the most interactive view. As shown in Figure 5.20 on the previous page, files and folders are displayed in list form, and the additional file information is displayed in columns alongside the name of the file. You can sort and display the contents of the folder by any of the column headings, so you can sort the contents alphabetically by name or type or hierarchically by date last modified or file size. Right-click the column heading area to modify the display of columns.

2. *Icons view:* There are a number of icon views that display files and folders in sizes ranging from small to extra-large. In most icon views, the folders are displayed as *Live Icons*. Live Icons allow you to preview the actual contents of a specific folder without opening the folder. As shown in Figure 5.22, Large Icons view is the best view to use if your folder contains picture files because you can see a bit of the actual images peeking out of the folder. It's also good to use if your folder contains PowerPoint presentations because the title slide of the presentation will display, making it easier for you to distinguish among presentations.

You can change the views from the Layout group on the View tab, or by clicking between Details view and Large Icon view from the bottom right corner of File Explorer. The View

FIGURE 5.22 The Large Icons view is a good way to display the contents of files and folders. The Preview pane on the right lets you see the first page of your document without first opening it. *(Windows 10, Microsoft Corporation)*
>*To access Large Icons view, click the* **View tab** *in File Explorer, and then select* **Large Icons** *in the Layout group. To display the* **Preview pane**, *click Preview pane in the Panes group on the File Explorer View tab.*

🔊 SOUND BYTE
File Management

In this Sound Byte, you'll examine the features of file management and maintenance. You'll learn the various methods of creating folders, how to turn a group of unorganized files into an organized system of folders with related files, and how to maintain your file system.

BITS&BYTES

Tips for Organizing Your Files

Creating folders is the key to organizing files because folders keep related documents together. For example, you might create one folder called "Classes" to hold your class work. Inside the "Classes" folder, you could create subfolders for each of your classes (such as ENG 325 and BUS 401). Inside each of those subfolders, you could create further subfolders for each class's assignments, homework, and so on.

Grouping related files into folders makes it easier for you to identify and find files. Which would be easier—going to the BUS 401 folder to find a file or searching through the hundreds of individual files in the Documents library hoping to find the right one? Grouping files in a folder also allows you to move files more efficiently, so you can quickly transfer critical files needing frequent backup, for instance.

BITS&BYTES

Save Files in the Cloud Right from Your Apps

When you sign up for a Windows account, you automatically get free storage on OneDrive, Microsoft's cloud storage site. Taking advantage of this free storage space helps ensure that you have files available to you whenever you need them and have access to the Internet.

Fortunately, it's easy to save files to OneDrive in Windows 10. When you use the Save As command in an application, OneDrive shows up as a location (see Figure 5.23) to which you can save files. So instead of saving your research paper to your C: drive, save it to a folder on OneDrive. Other cloud services like Dropbox and Google Drive work in the same manner. Using cloud storage will ensure the availability of your files when you need them.

FIGURE 5.23 OneDrive displays as a location in which you can create folders and save files. *(Windows 10, Microsoft Corporation)*

---

tab also enables you to display a Preview pane or a Details pane. The Preview pane displays the first page of the selected document, and the Details pane displays the file or folder's properties.

Naming Files

Are there special rules I have to follow when I name files? The first part of a file, or the **file name**, is generally the name you assign to the file when you save it. For example, "bioreport" may be the name you assign a report you have completed for a biology class.

In a Windows application, an **extension** or **file type**, follows the file name and a period or dot (.). Like a last name, this

extension identifies what kind of family of files the file belongs to, or which application should be used to read the file. For example, if "bioreport" is a spreadsheet created in Microsoft Excel 2016, it has an .xlsx extension and its name is "bioreport.xlsx." You can choose to display file extensions by checking or unchecking the File name extensions box in the Show/hide group on the View tab in File Explorer.

Figure 5.24 lists some common file extensions and the types of documents they indicate.

Why is it important to know the file extension? When you save a file created in most applications running under the Windows OS, you don't need to add the extension to

FIGURE 5.24

Common File Name Extensions

EXTENSION	TYPE OF DOCUMENT	APPLICATION
.docx	Word processing document	Microsoft Word 2007 and later
.xlsx	Workbook	Microsoft Excel 2007 and later
.accdb	Database	Microsoft Access 2007 and later
.pptx	Presentation	Microsoft PowerPoint 2007 and later
.pdf	Portable Document Format	Adobe Acrobat or Adobe Reader
.rtf	Text (Rich Text Format)	Any program that can read text documents
.txt	Text	Any program that can read text documents
.htm or .html	HyperText Markup Language (HTML) for a web page	Any program that can read HTML
.jpg	Joint Photographic Experts Group (JPEG) image	Most programs capable of displaying images
.zip	Compressed file	Various file compression programs

FIGURE 5.25

File-Naming Conventions

	OS X	WINDOWS
File and folder name length	As many as 255 characters*	As many as 255 characters
Case sensitive?	Yes	No
Forbidden characters	Colon (:)	" / \ * ? <> | :
File extensions needed?	No	Yes

*Although OS X supports file names with as many as 255 characters, many applications running on OS X still support only file names with a maximum of 31 characters.

the file name; it is added automatically for you. Mac and Linux operating systems don't require file extensions. This is because the information as to the type of application the computer should use to open the file is stored inside the file itself. However, if you're using the Mac or Linux OS and will be sending files to Windows users, you should add an extension to your file name so that Windows can more easily open your files.

Have you ever been sent a file by e-mail and couldn't open it? Most likely, that was because your computer didn't have the program needed to open the file. Sometimes, similar programs that you already have installed can be used to open the file, so it's helpful to know what the file extension is. Sites such as FILExt (**filext.com**) can help you identify the source program.

Are there things I shouldn't do when naming my files? Each OS has its own naming conventions, or rules, which are listed in Figure 5.25. Beyond those conventions, it's important that you name your files so that you can easily identify them. File names can have as many as 255 characters, so don't be afraid to use as many characters as you need. A file name such as "BIO 101 Research Paper First Draft.docx" makes it very clear what that file contains.

Keep in mind, however, that all files must be uniquely identified, unless you save them in different folders or in different locations. Therefore, although files may share the same file name (such as "bioreport.docx" or "bioreport.xlsx") or share the same extension ("bioreport.xlsx" or "budget.xlsx"), no two files stored in the same folder can share *both* the same file-name and the same file extension.

Copying, Moving, and Deleting Files

How can I move and copy files? Once you've located your file with File Explorer, you can perform many other file management actions such as opening, copying, moving,

ACTIVE HELPDESK
Organizing Your Computer: File Management

In this Active Helpdesk, you'll play the role of a helpdesk staffer, fielding questions about the desktop, window features, and how the OS helps keep the computer organized.

BITS&BYTES

Use Cortana to Find Your Files

Microsoft's personal assistant, Cortana, was originally a part of Windows Phone but is now incorporated into the Windows 10 operating system deployed across all devices. In Windows 10, Cortana lives on the taskbar, to the right of the Start button. Click on the microphone icon to initiate voice-activated commands, or type your queries in the text box. You can ask Cortana to set reminders, create appointments, as well as tell you the weather or the current scores of your favorite teams. In addition, you can use Cortana to find files and folders. Cortana understands natural language, so she could respond to a query such as *Show me files relating to the fundraiser* or you could type *Fundraiser* into the Search box. Click MyStuff for Cortana to search File Explorer and OneDrive, or click Web for Cortana to offer related contents on the web.

renaming, and deleting files. You open a file by double-clicking the file from its storage location. You can copy a file to another location using the Copy command. To move a file from one location to another, use the Cut command. You can access both of these commands easily by right-clicking on a file's name, which displays a shortcut menu.

Where do deleted files go? The **Recycle Bin** is a folder on the desktop, represented by an icon that looks like a recycling bin, where files deleted from the hard drive reside until you permanently purge them from your system. Unfortunately, files deleted from other drives don't go to the Recycle Bin but are deleted from the system immediately. In addition, files stored in the cloud are not cycled through the Recycle Bin. When you delete a file from a thumb drive or a network drive, consider it gone forever!

Mac systems have something similar to the Recycle Bin, called Trash, which is represented by a wastebasket icon. To delete files on a Mac, drag the files to the Trash icon.

How do I permanently delete files from my system? Files placed in the Recycle Bin or the Trash remain in the system until they're permanently deleted. To delete files from the Recycle Bin permanently, select Empty Recycle Bin after right-clicking the desktop icon. On Macs, select Empty Trash from the Finder menu in OS X.

What happens if I need to recover a deleted file? Getting a file back after the Recycle Bin has been emptied still may be possible using one of two methods:

- File History is a Windows 10 utility that automatically backs up files and saves previous versions of files to a designated drive (such as an external hard drive). If you're using File

History, you can restore previously deleted files or even previous versions of files you've changed. (We'll discuss File History in more detail later in the chapter.)

- When the Recycle Bin is emptied, only the reference to the file is deleted permanently, so the OS has no easy way to find the file. The file data actually remains on the hard drive until it's written over by another file. You may be able to use a program such as FarStone's RestoreIT or Norton Online Backup to try to retrieve files you think you've permanently deleted. These programs reveal files that are still intact on the hard drive and help you recover them. This is how they do it on *CSI*!

File Compression

Objective 5.11 *Summarize how file compression works.*

Why would I want to compress a file? File compression makes a large file more compact, making it easier and faster for you to send large attachments by e-mail, upload them to the web, or save them onto a flash drive or other storage medium. As shown in Figure 5.26, Windows has a built-in

file compression utility that takes out redundancies in a file (zips it) to reduce the file size. You can also obtain several stand-alone freeware and shareware programs, such as WinZip (for Windows) and StuffIt (for Windows or Mac), to compress your files.

How does file compression work? Most compression programs look for repeated patterns of letters and replace these patterns with a shorter placeholder. The repeated patterns and the associated placeholder are cataloged and stored temporarily in a separate file called the *dictionary*.

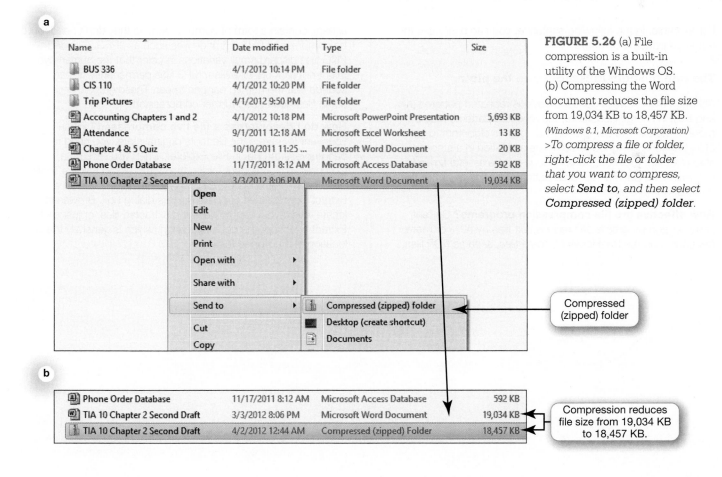

FIGURE 5.26 (a) File compression is a built-in utility of the Windows OS. (b) Compressing the Word document reduces the file size from 19,034 KB to 18,457 KB. *(Windows 8.1, Microsoft Corporation)* >*To compress a file or folder, right-click the file or folder that you want to compress, select **Send to**, and then select **Compressed (zipped) folder**.*

FIGURE 5.27 Extracting files from a zipped folder is simply done through the Extract all feature in File Explorer. *(Windows 10, Microsoft Corporation)*

For example, in the following sentence, you can easily see the repeated patterns of letters.

The rain in Spain falls mainly on the plain.

Although this example contains obvious repeated patterns (ain and the), in a large document, the repeated patterns may be more complex. The compression program's algorithm (a set of instructions designed to complete a solution in a step-by-step manner), therefore, runs through the file several times to determine the optimal repeated patterns needed to obtain the greatest compression.

How effective are file compression programs? Current compression programs can reduce text files by 50% or more, depending on the file. However, some files, such as PDF files, already contain a form of compression, so they don't need to be compressed further. Image files such as JPEG, GIF, and PNG files discard small variations in color that the human eye might not pick up. Likewise, MP3 files permanently discard sounds that the human ear can't hear. These graphic and audio files don't need further compression.

How do I decompress a file I've compressed? When you want to restore the file to its original state, you need to *decompress* the file. In File Explorer, when you click on a Compressed (or zipped) folder, the Compressed Folders Tools tab displays (see Figure 5.27). Click Extract all to open the Extract Compressed (Zipped) Folders dialog box. Browse to locate where you want to save the extracted files, or just click Extract to accept the default location (which is generally the location of the zipped folder). ■

utility

PROGRAMS

The main component of system software is the OS. However, *utility programs*—small applications that perform special functions on the computer—are also an essential part of system software. Utility programs come in three flavors:

1. Those that are included with the OS (such as System Restore)
2. Those sold as stand-alone programs (such as Norton antivirus)
3. Those offered as freeware (such as anti-malware software like Ad-Aware from Lavasoft)

Figure 5.28 lists some of the various types of utility programs available within the Windows OS as well as some alternatives available as stand-alone programs. In general, the basic utilities designed to manage and tune your computer hardware are incorporated into the OS. The stand-alone utility programs typically offer more features or an easier user interface for backup, security, diagnostic, or recovery functions. For some Windows programs, like Task Manager and Resource Monitor, no good stand-alone alternatives exist.

Windows Administrative Utilities

Objective 5.12 *Outline the tools used to enhance system productivity.*

What utilities can make my system work faster? Disk Cleanup is a Windows utility that removes unnecessary

files from your hard drive. These include files that have accumulated in the Recycle Bin as well as temporary files—files created by Windows to store data temporarily while a program is running. Windows usually deletes these temporary files when you exit the program, but sometimes it forgets to do this or doesn't have time because your system freezes or incurs a problem that prevents you from properly exiting a program.

Disk Cleanup also removes temporary Internet files (web pages stored on your hard drive for quick viewing) as well as offline web pages (pages stored on your computer so you can view them without being connected to the Internet). If not deleted periodically, these unnecessary files can slow down your computer.

How can I control which files Disk Cleanup deletes? When you run Disk Cleanup, the program scans your hard drive to determine which folders have files that can be deleted and calculates the amount of hard drive space that will be

 ACTIVE HELPDESK
Using Utility Programs

In this Active Helpdesk, you'll play the role of a helpdesk staffer, fielding questions about the utility programs included in system software and what these programs do.

FIGURE 5.28

Utility Programs Available Within Windows and as Stand-Alone Programs

WINDOWS UTILITY PROGRAM	STAND-ALONE ALTERNATIVES	WHAT IT DOES
Disk Cleanup	McAfee Total Protection	Removes unnecessary files from your hard drive
Disk Defragmenter	Norton Utilities, iDefrag	Rearranges files on your hard drive to allow for faster access of files
Task Manager and Resource Monitor	Process Explorer	Displays performance measures for processes; provides information on programs and processes running on your computer
File History, File Recovery	Acronis True Image, Norton Online Backup	Backs up important files, makes a complete mirror image of your current computer setup
System Restore	FarStone RestoreIT, Acronis True Image	Restores your system to a previous, stable state

	Total space possible to be freed
	Space freed with the selections made
	Description of folder contents

FIGURE 5.29 Using Disk Cleanup will help free space on your hard drive.
(Windows 10, Microsoft Corporation)
*>To access Disk Cleanup, click **All apps** on the Start menu, scroll to Windows Administrative Tools, click **Disk Cleanup**.*

FIGURE 5.30 You can use Task Manager to close nonresponsive programs.
(Windows 10, Microsoft Corporation)
*>To access Task Manager, click **All apps** on the Start menu, scroll to Windows System, click **Task Manager**.*

freed up by doing so. You check off which type of files you would like to delete, as shown in Figure 5.29.

How can I check on a program that's stopped running? If a program has stopped working, you can use the Windows **Task Manager** utility (see Figure 5.30) to check on the program or to exit the nonresponsive program. The Processes tab of Task Manager lists all the programs you're using and indicates their status. "Not responding" will be shown next to a program that stopped improperly. If the status section is blank (Figure 5.30), then the program is working normally. You can terminate programs that aren't responding by right-clicking the app name and selecting End Task from the shortcut menu.

How can I improve my computer's performance? After you have used your computer for a while, uploading, creating, changing, and deleting content, the hard drive becomes fragmented: parts of files get scattered (fragmented) around the hard disk making the hard disk do extra work which can slow down your computer. **Disk defragmentation** rearranges fragmented data so that related file pieces are unified. The Disk Defragmenter utility is found in the Windows Administrative Tools folder in All apps. Before you defragment your hard drive, you should first determine if the disk needs to be defragmented by selecting Analyze disk. If your disk is more than 10% fragmented, you should run the disk defragmenter utility. See the Dig Deeper, *How Disk Defragmenter Utilities Work* for more information.

> **SOUND** BYTE
> **Letting Your Computer Clean Up After Itself**
>
> In this Sound Byte, you'll learn how to use the various maintenance utilities within the OS. You'll also learn why maintenance tasks should be done on a routine basis to make your system more efficient.

How Disk Defragmenter Utilities Work

Disk defragmenting programs group together related pieces of files on the hard drive, allowing the OS to work more efficiently. To understand how disk defragmenter utilities work, you first need to understand the basics of how a hard disk drive stores files. A hard disk drive is composed of several platters, or round, thin plates of metal, covered with a special magnetic coating that records the data. The platters are about 3.5 inches in diameter and are stacked onto a spindle. There are usually two or three platters in any hard disk drive, with data stored on one or both sides. Data is recorded on hard disks in concentric circles called **tracks**. Each track is further broken down into pie-shaped wedges, each called a **sector** (see Figure 5.31). The data is further identified by **clusters**, which are the smallest segments within the sectors.

When you want to save (or write) a file, the bits that make up your file are recorded onto one or more clusters of the drive. To keep track of which clusters hold which files, the drive also stores an index of all sector numbers in a table. To save a file, the computer looks in the table for clusters that aren't already being used. It then records the file information on those clusters. When you open (or read) a file, the computer searches through the table for the clusters that hold the desired file and reads that file. Similarly, when you delete a file, you're actually not deleting the file itself but rather the reference in the table to the file.

So, how does a disk become fragmented? When only part of an older file is deleted, the deleted section of the file creates a gap in the sector of the disk where the data was originally stored. In the same way, when new information is added to an older file, there may not be space to save the new information sequentially near where the file was originally saved. In that case, the system writes the added part of the file to the next available location on the disk, and a reference is made in the table as to the location of this file fragment. Over time, as files are saved, deleted, and modified, the bits of information for various files fall out of order and the disk becomes fragmented.

Disk fragmentation is a problem because the OS isn't as efficient when a disk is fragmented. It takes longer to locate a whole file because more of the disk must be searched for the various pieces, slowing down your computer.

Defragmenting tools take the hard drive through a defragmentation process in which pieces of files scattered over the disk are placed together and arranged sequentially on it. Also, any unused portions of clusters that were too small to save data in before are grouped, increasing the available storage space on the disk. Figure 5.32 shows before and after shots of a fragmented disk that has gone through the defragmentation process.

The disk defragmentation utility in Windows 10 is set by default to automatically defragment the hard drive on a regular basis. Macs don't have a defragmentation utility built into the system. Those users who feel the need to defragment their Mac can use iDefrag, an external program from Coriolis Systems.

For more about hard disks and defragmenting, check out the Sound Byte "Hard Disk Anatomy."

FIGURE 5.31 On a hard disk platter, data is recorded onto tracks, which are further divided into sectors and clusters.

FIGURE 5.32 Defragmenting the hard drive arranges file fragments so that they are located next to each other. This makes the hard drive run more efficiently.

SOUND BYTE
Hard Disk Anatomy

In this Sound Byte, you'll watch a series of animations that show various aspects of a hard drive, including the anatomy of a hard drive, how a computer reads and writes data to a hard drive, and the fragmenting and defragmenting of a hard drive.

File and System Backup Utilities

Objective 5.13 *Summarize the utilities used to backup and restore files and the computer system.*

How can I protect my data in the event something malfunctions in my system? As noted earlier, when you use the **File History** utility, you can have Windows automatically create a duplicate of your libraries, desktop, contacts, and favorites and copy it to another storage device, such as an external hard drive (see Figure 5.33). A backup copy protects your data in the event your hard drive fails or files are accidentally erased. File History also keeps copies of different versions of your files. This means that if you need to go back to the second draft of your history term paper, even though you are now on your fifth draft, File History should allow you to recover it. File History needs to be turned on by the user and

requires an external hard drive (or network drive) that is always connected to the computer to function. You can choose to backup all folders on the C: drive, or select certain ones that you use most often or contain the most sensitive files to backup.

Windows 10 also includes recovery tools that allow you to complete backups of your entire system (system image) that you can later restore in the event of a major hard drive crash.

How can I recover my entire system? Suppose you've just installed a new software program and your computer freezes. After rebooting the computer, when you try to start the application, the system freezes once again. You uninstall the new program, but your computer continues to freeze after rebooting. What can you do now?

Windows has a utility called **System Restore** that lets you roll your system settings back to a specific date when everything was working properly. A **system restore point**, which is a snapshot of your entire system's settings, is generated prior to certain events, such as installing or updating software, or automatically once a week if no other restore points were created in that time. You also can create a restore point manually at any time.

Should problems occur, if the computer was running just fine before you installed new software or a hardware device, you could restore your computer to the settings that were in effect before the software or hardware installation (see Figure 5.34). System Restore doesn't affect your personal data files (such as Word documents or e-mail), so you won't lose changes made to these files.

OS X includes a backup utility called Time Machine that automatically backs up your files to a specified location. Apple also offers backup hardware called Time Capsules, which are hard disk drives with wireless connectivity, designed to work with Time Machine and record your backup data. Because Time Machine makes a complete image copy of your system, it can also be used to recover your system in the case of a fatal error. (For more information on backing up your files, see Chapter 9.)

Accessibility Utilities

Objective 5.14 *Describe the assistive technology utilities used to make using the computer system easier.*

What utilities are designed for users with special needs? Microsoft Windows includes an Ease of Access Center, which is a centralized location for assistive technology and tools to adjust accessibility settings. In the Ease of Access Center, which is accessible from Settings, you can find the tools to help users with disabilities, shown in Figure 5.35. The tools shown in the figure are just a sampling of the available tools. If you're not sure where to start or what settings might help, a questionnaire asks you about routine

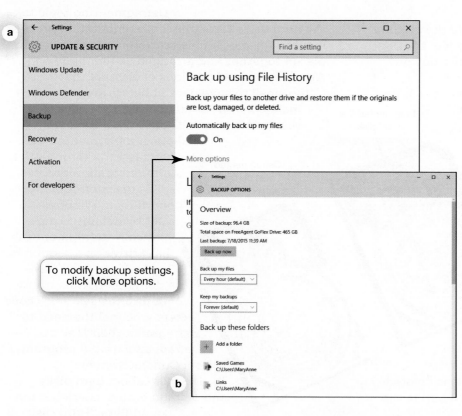

FIGURE 5.33 File History backs up files to an external hard drive. *(Windows 10, Microsoft Corporation)*

*>To turn on File History, choose **Settings**, select **Update & security**, and then select **Backup**. To modify File History and Backup settings, click **More options**.*

FIGURE 5.34 This System Restore Wizard shows restore points set manually by a user and automatically by Windows when updates were installed. Setting a restore point is good practice before installing any hardware or software. *(Windows 10, Microsoft Corporation)*

*>To access System Restore, right-click the **Start button**, choose **System**, select **System Protection**, and then click **System Restore**. The System Restore Wizard displays, with the restore points shown on the second page of the Wizard.*

tasks and provides a personalized recommendation for settings that will help you better use your computer.

Whether you use Windows, OS X, Linux, or another operating system, a fully featured OS is available to meet your needs. As long as you keep the operating system updated and regularly use the available utilities to fine-tune your system, you should experience little trouble from your OS. ■

Before moving on to the Chapter Review:
1. **Watch Replay Video 5.2** ▷ .
2. **Then check your understanding of what you've learned so far.**

FIGURE 5.35

Windows Ease of Access Tools

MAGNIFIER
- Creates a separate window that displays a magnified portion of the screen

NARRATOR
- Reads what is on screen
- Can read the contents of a window, menu options, or text you have typed

SPEECH RECOGNITION
- Allows you to dictate text and control your computer by voice

ON-SCREEN KEYBOARD
- Allows you to type with a pointing device

HIGH CONTRAST
- Color schemes invert screen colors for vision-impaired individuals

(Imagery Majestic/Fotolia, Anatoly Maslennikov/Fotolia, iqoncept/123RF, Pockgallery/Shutterstock)

*>To access Ease of Access, click **Settings**, then select **Ease of Access**.*

check your understanding // review & practice

For a quick review to see what you've learned so far, answer the following questions.

multiple choice

1. What is used to reduce the file size of a file or folder?

   a. defragmenter

   b. compression

   c. extraction

   d. shrinker

2. The process of adding a Windows 10 app to the Start menu is known as

   a. clipping.

   b. visualizing.

   c. pinning.

   d. screening.

3. The Windows app used for locating files and folders is

   a. Disk Manager.

   b. Finder.

   c. File Explorer.

   d. Library Explorer.

4. Which of the following is NOT a common file name extension?

   a. .docx

   b. .jpg

   c. .pptx

   d. .zipped

5. Which utility is used to exit out of a nonresponsive program?

   a. Task Manager

   b. Disk Cleanup

   c. System Refresh

   d. File Explorer

MyITLab   Go to **MyITLab** to take an autograded version of the *Check Your Understanding* review and to find all media resources for the chapter.

TECHBYTES WEEKLY
Stay current with the TechBytes Weekly Newsletter.

Continue »

5 Chapter Review

summary //

Understanding System Software

Learning Outcome 5.1 **You will be able to explain the types and functions of an operating system and explain the steps in the boot process.**

Operating System Fundamentals

Objective 5.1 *Discuss the functions of the operating system.*

- System software is the set of software programs that helps run the computer and coordinates instructions between application software and hardware devices. It consists of the operating system (OS) and utility programs.
- The OS controls how your computer system functions. It manages the computer's hardware, provides a means for application software to work with the CPU, and is responsible for the management, scheduling, and coordination of tasks.
- Utility programs are programs that perform general housekeeping tasks for the computer, such as system maintenance and file compression.
- Modern operating systems allow for multitasking—to perform more than one process at a time.

Objective 5.2 *Explain the different kinds of operating systems for machines, networks, and business.*

- Real-time operating systems (RTOSs) require no user intervention.
- A multiuser operating system (network operating system) provides access to a computer system by more than one user at a time.
- UNIX is a multiuser, multitasking OS that is used as a network OS, though it can be used on PCs.
- Mainframes and supercomputers are specialty computers that require mainframe operating systems.

Objective 5.3 *Explain the most common operating systems for personal use.*

- Smartphones have their own specific operating systems, which allow the user to multitask.
- Some operating systems allow interaction with touch-screen interfaces.
- Gaming consoles use operating systems developed specifically for those particular devices.

- Microsoft Windows is the most popular OS. The most recent release is Windows 10. The Mac OS, which is designed to work on Apple computers, and Linux is an open source OS based on UNIX and designed primarily for use on personal computers.
- An OS is designed to run on specific CPUs. The combination of an OS and a CPU is a computer's platform. Application software is OS dependent.
- All personal operating systems incorporate elements to share and store on the Internet.

What the Operating System Does

Objective 5.4 *Explain how the operating system provides a means for users to interact with the computer.*

- The OS provides a user interface that enables users to interact with the computer.
- Most OSs today use a graphical user interface (GUI). Common features of GUIs include windows, menus, and icons.

Objective 5.5 *Explain how the operating system helps manage hardware such as the processor, memory, storage, and peripheral devices.*

- When the OS allows you to perform more than one task at a time, it is multitasking. To provide for seamless multitasking, the OS controls the timing of the events on which the processor works.
- As the OS coordinates the activities of the processor, it uses RAM as a temporary storage area for instructions and data the processor needs. The OS coordinates the space allocations in RAM to ensure that there is enough space for the waiting instructions and data. If there isn't sufficient space in RAM for all the data and instructions, then the OS allocates the least necessary files to temporary storage on the hard drive, called *virtual memory*.

- The OS manages storage by providing a file management system that keeps track of the names and locations of files and programs.
- Programs called *device drivers* facilitate communication between devices attached to the computer and the OS.

Objective 5.6 *Explain how the operating system interacts with application software.*

- All software applications need to interact with the CPU. For programs to work with the CPU, they must contain code that the CPU recognizes.
- Rather than having the same blocks of code appear in each application, the OS includes the blocks of code to which software applications refer. These blocks of code are called *application programming interfaces* (APIs).

Starting Your Computer

Objective 5.7 *Discuss the process the operating system uses to start up the computer, and how errors in the boot process are handled.*

- When you start your computer, it runs through a special process called the *boot process*.
- The boot process consists of four basic steps: (1) The basic input/output system (BIOS) is activated when the user powers on the CPU. (2) In the POST check, the BIOS verifies that all attached devices are in place. (3) The OS is loaded into RAM. (4) Configuration and customization settings are checked.
- An authentication process occurs at the end of the boot process to ensure an authorized user is entering the system.
- Sometimes errors occur in the boot process, or otherwise. Try rebooting the computer or resetting the computer if the problem persists.

Using System Software

Learning Outcome 5.2 You will be able to describe how system software is used, including managing the user interface, file management, and utility programs.

The Windows Interface

Using Windows 10

Objective 5.8 *Describe the main features of the Windows interface.*

- In Windows 10, the Start menu provides access to your computer's apps, tools, and commonly used programs and the desktop is the main working area.
- You can customize the Start menu by pinning and resizing tiles and organizing tiles into groups.
- Virtual desktops are used to organize open programs into different working areas.

File Management

Objective 5.9 *Summarize how the operating system helps keep your computer organized.*

- Files and folders are organized in a hierarchical directory structure composed of drives, libraries, folders, subfolders, and files.
- The C: drive represents the hard drive and is where most programs and files are stored.
- File Explorer is the main tool for finding, viewing, and managing the contents of your computer.

Objective 5.10 *Summarize how to view, sort, name, and manage files and folders.*

- File Explorer helps you manage your files and folders by showing the location and contents of every drive, folder, and file on your computer.
- There are specific rules to follow when naming files.
- The Recycle Bin is the temporary storage location for deleted files from the hard drive.

Objective 5.11 *Summarize how file compression works.*

- File compression reduces the size of a file by temporarily storing components of a file and then when the file is extracted (uncompressed) the removed components are brought back into the file.

Utility Programs

Objective 5.12 *Outline the tools used to enhance system productivity.*

- Task Manager is used to exit nonresponsive programs.
- Disk Cleanup removes unnecessary files from your hard drive. If not deleted periodically, these unnecessary files can slow down your computer.

- Disk Defragmentation rearranges fragmented data so that related file pieces are unified. When a disk is fragmented, it can slow down your computer.

Objective 5.13 *Summarize the utilities used to backup and restore files and the computer system.*

- File History automatically creates a duplicate of your hard drive (or parts of your hard drive) and copies it to another storage device, such as an external hard drive. You can use File History to recover deleted or corrupted files.

- System Restore lets you roll your system settings back to a specific date (restore point) when everything was working properly.

Objective 5.14 *Describe the assistive technology utilities used to make using the computer system easier.*

- Windows Ease of Access Center includes tools that help adjust computer settings for those users with disabilities.

 Be sure to check out **MyITLab** for additional materials to help you review and learn. And don't forget the Replay Videos .

key terms //

chapter quiz // assessment

For a quick review to see what you've learned, answer the following questions. Submit the quiz as requested by your instructor. If you are using MyITLab, the quiz is also available there.

multiple choice

1. Which of the following would you not see on a Windows 10 Start menu?

    a. tiles
    c. All apps

    b. power
    d. Task View

2. When an OS processes tasks in a priority order, it is known as

    a. preemptive interrupting.

    b. interruptive multitasking.

    c. preemptive multitasking.

    d. multitasking handling.

3. An example of an open source OS is

    a. Windows.
    c. Linux.

    b. OS X.
    d. DOS.

4. Which of the following is not considered an accessibility utility?

    a. System Restore
    c. Narrator

    b. Magnifier
    d. Speech Recognition

5. Special programs that facilitate communication between a device and the OS are called

    a. APIs.

    b. device drivers.

    c. utility programs.

    d. hardware player.

6. A new feature in Windows 10 that is used to organize open windows into task-specific groups is called

    a. Program Manager.
    c. Snap Assist.

    b. Virtual Desktops.
    d. Task View.

true/false

_____ 1. Different versions of Linux are known as distros.

_____ 2. The power-on self-test (POST) ensures all peripheral devices are attached an operational.

_____ 3. System restore points can only be created by Windows automatically on a regular schedule.

_____ 4. Files deleted from a flash drive are sent to the Recycle Bin and could be recovered, if necessary.

critical thinking

1. **Protecting Embedded Systems**

    As more devices and appliances make use of RTOSs, the necessity of protecting them from hackers becomes increasingly critical. Developers are working to improve the security of the software and to safeguard communications between such devices. How concerned are you about the security of RTOSs in cars, smart homes, and wearable technology? Is enough being done to ensure the safety of these devices? What else can be done?

2. **Ease of Access**

    Windows and Mac OS X both include a number of features and utilities designed for users with special needs. Compare the offerings of each OS. Are there options offered by one OS that are not available in the other? Which OS do you think has the best selection? Can you think of any areas that have not been addressed by this assistive technology? Research software from third-party developers to see if there are other tools that would also be useful. Should these tools be included in the OS? Why or why not?

team time //

Choosing the Best OS

Problem

You're the owner of a technology consulting firm. Your current assignments include advising start-up clients on their technology requirements. The companies include a nonprofit social service organization, a small interior design firm, and a social media advertising agency. Obviously, one of the critical decisions for each company is the choice of OS.

Task

Recommend the appropriate OS for each company.

Process

1. Break up into teams that represent the three primary operating systems: Windows, Mac, or Linux.
2. As a team, research the pros and cons of your OS. What features does it have that would benefit each company? What features does it not have that each company would need? Discuss why your OS would be the appropriate (or inappropriate) choice for each company?
3. Develop a presentation that states your position with regard to your OS. Your presentation should have a recommendation and include facts to back it up.
4. As a class, decide which OS would be the best choice for each company.

Conclusion

Because the OS is the most critical piece of software in the computer system, the selection should not be taken lightly. The OS that is best for a nonprofit social service organization may not be best for an interior design firm. A social media advertising agency may have different needs altogether. It is important to make sure you consider all aspects of the work environment and the type of work being done to ensure a good fit.

ethics project //

Upgrade Your World

In this exercise, you'll research and then role-play a complicated ethical situation. The role you play may or may not match your own personal beliefs, but your research and use of logic will enable you to represent whichever view is assigned. An arbitrator will watch and comment on both sides of the arguments, and together, the team will agree on an ethical solution.

Problem

With the release of Windows 10, Microsoft began the "Upgrade your World" program, to work with 10 global nonprofit groups and 100 local nonprofits (10 in 10 countries). Microsoft has identified nine organizations around the world and will determine the 10th global nonprofit, as well as the 100 local nonprofits through crowdsourcing. Each local nonprofit will receive $50,000 cash investment plus technology from Microsoft.

Research Areas to Consider

- Windows 10 features
- Upgrade Your World Project
- The nine global Upgrade Your World nonprofits (Care, Code.org, Keep a Child Alive, Malala Fund, Pencils of Promise, Save the Children, Special Olympics, The Global Poverty Project, and The Nature Conservancy)

Process

1. Divide the class into teams. Each team member will play a different character. Each character has an individual perspective toward the decision at hand.
2. Research the areas cited above and determine a local nonprofit that you think would be deserving of an Upgrade Your World grant.
3. Team members should write a summary that provides background information for their character—for example, representative of Microsoft, nonprofit executive, local small business executive who thinks his business is worthier to receive the grant, a local community member, and arbitrator—and that details their character's behaviors to set the stage for the role-playing event. Then, team members should create an outline to use during the role-playing event.
4. Team members should determine the pros and cons of awarding the local nonprofit nominee the Upgrade Your World grant, and reach an agreeable conclusion. The team will present their case to the class or submit a PowerPoint presentation for review by the rest of the class, along with the summary and resolution they developed.

Conclusion

As deserving as most nonprofits seem to be, some may benefit more than others, and ultimately serve the community better than others, after receiving a substantial grant such as Upgrade Your World. Being able to understand and evaluate a decision, while responding in a personally or socially ethical manner, will be an important skill.

Mobile Operating Systems: Changing Market Share

Using Excel 2016, you will display the market share statistics of both mobile and desktop operating systems using line, column, and pie charts.

You will use the following skills as you complete this activity:

- Create a Line Chart
- Create and Format a Pie Chart
- Create and Format a Column Chart
- Add Shape to Chart
- Insert Sparklines

Instructions:

1. Open *TIA_Ch5_Start* and save as **TIA_Ch5_LastFirst**.

2. Create a 2-D Line chart from the range A3:F8. Modify the chart as follows:
   a. Add a title: **Change in Mobile OS Market Share 2011–2015**. *2011–2015* should be on a separate line. Change the font size of *2011–2015* to **10**.
   b. Move the chart to a separate worksheet. Rename the new worksheet **Line Chart**, and place after the Data worksheet.
   c. Filter out the *Symbian* and *Others* data so only *Android*, *iOS*, and *Windows* data displays.
   d. Add a **Line Callout 1 shape** to the chart with the line pointing where the Android and the iOS lines intersect. Add text to the callout: **2014: When Android surpassed iOS**.
      Hint: Line Callout 1 is in the Callouts section in the Insert Shape group on the Format Chart Tools tab.

3. Create a 2-D Pie chart from the ranges A3:A8 and F3:F8.

   Hint: Press the **Ctrl key** while selecting nonadjacent ranges. Modify the chart as follows:

   a. Add a title: **2015 Mobile OS Market Share**
   b. Use **Quick Layout 1** to add data % and Series data labels to each data point.
   c. Resize the chart so it fits in the range A14:H30.

4. Create a Clustered Column chart that compares just Android and iOS data for 2011–2015. Modify the chart as follows:
   a. Add a title: **Android versus iOS Market Share**
   b. Format the chart with **Style 8**.
   c. Move the chart to a separate worksheet. Rename the new worksheet **Column Chart**, and place it after the *Line Chart* worksheet.

5. On the Data worksheet, add a **Line Sparkline** to cell G4 using the data in range B4:F4. Using the **Fill Handle**, copy the Sparkline to range G5:G8. Add a **High Point** to each Sparkline.

6. Save the document and submit based on your instructor's directions.

Learning Outcome 5B.1 You will be able to define ethics, describe different types of ethical systems, and explain how personal ethics develop.

The ethical choices we make have a far-reaching impact on our lives. In this Technology in Focus feature, we examine how technology and ethics affect each other. We'll discuss several key issues related to technology and ethics, including the following:

- Social justice
- Intellectual property
- Privacy
- Property rights
- Electronic information access
- Computer abuse

We'll discuss both personal ethics as well as how our technology affects our personal ethics. Then we'll consider what your personal ethics are and how you make ethical choices.

Ethics

Let's get started by asking an important question: What is ethics?

Defining Ethics and Examining Ethical Systems

Objective 5B.1 *Define ethics, and describe the five major ethical systems.*

Ethics is the study of the general nature of morals and of the specific moral choices individuals make. Morals involve conforming to established or accepted ideas of right and wrong (as generally dictated by society) and are usually viewed as being black or white. Ethical issues often involve subtle distinctions, such as the difference between fairness and equity. Ethical principles are the guidelines you use to make decisions each day.

For example, say you stop to use a photocopier on campus. You discover a copy of the upcoming final exam for your psychology course that your teacher left behind. Do you give it back to your professor without looking at the questions? Do you share it with your friends so you can all get good grades on the final? Do you give

a copy to your friend who really needs to pass the course in order to prevent losing his or her financial aid?

Doesn't everyone have the same basic ethics? There are many systems of ethical conduct. Figure 1 lists the five major ethical systems.

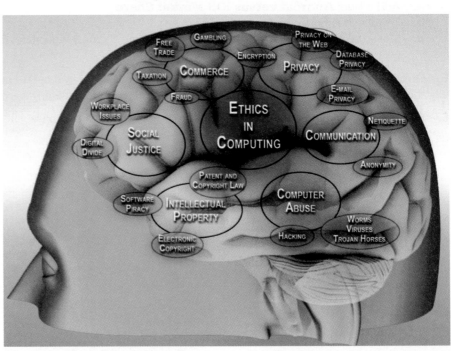

FIGURE 1

Systems of Ethics

ETHICAL SYSTEM	BASIC TENETS	EXAMPLES
Relativism	• No universal moral truth • Moral principles dictated by cultural tastes and customs	Topless bathing is prevalent in Europe but generally banned on public beaches in the United States
Divine Command Theory	• God is all-knowing and sets moral standards • Conforming to God's law is right; breaking it is wrong	Christians believe in rules such as the Ten Commandments
Utilitarianism	• Actions are judged solely by consequences • Actions that generate greater happiness are judged to be better than actions that lead to unhappiness • Individual happiness is not important—consider the greater good	Using weapons of mass destruction ends a war sooner and therefore saves lives otherwise destroyed by conventional fighting
Virtue Ethics	• Morals are internal • Strive to be a person who behaves well spontaneously	A supervisor views the person who volunteered to clean up a park as a better person than the workers who are there because of court-ordered community service
Deontology (Duty-Based)	• Focus on adherence to moral duties and rights • Morals should apply to everyone equally	Human rights (like freedom of religion) should be respected for all people because human rights should be applied universally

Aren't laws meant to guide people's ethical actions? Laws are formal, written standards designed to apply to everyone. Laws are enforced by government agencies and interpreted by the courts. However, it's impossible to pass laws that cover every possible behavior in which humans can engage. Therefore, ethics provide a general set of unwritten guidelines for people to follow.

Is unethical behavior the same as illegal behavior? Unethical behavior isn't necessarily illegal. Take the death penalty. In many U.S. states, putting convicted criminals to death for certain crimes is legal. However, many people consider it unethical to execute a human for any reason.

Not all illegal behavior is unethical, though. Civil disobedience, which is manifested by intentionally refusing to obey certain laws, is used as a form of protest to effect change. Gandhi's nonviolent resistance to the British rule of India, which led to India's establishment as an independent country, is an example of civil disobedience. Is it ever ethical for one country to control another country's people?

Note that there is also a difference between *unethical* behavior and *amoral* behavior:

- *Unethical behavior* can be defined as not conforming to a set of approved standards of behavior. For instance, using your phone to text message a test answer to your friend during an exam is unethical.
- *Amoral behavior* occurs when a person has no sense of right and wrong and no interest in the moral consequences of his or her actions, such as when a murderer shows no remorse for his or her crime.

Which system of ethics works best? There is no universal agreement on which is the best system of ethics. Most societies use a blend of different systems. Regardless of the ethical system of the society in which you live, all ethical decisions are greatly influenced by personal ethics.

Personal Ethics

Objective 5B.2: *Define personal ethics, and describe influences on the development of personal ethics.*

What are personal ethics? Every day you say and do certain things, and each time, you're making decisions. As you choose your words and actions, you're following a set of **personal ethics**—a set of formal or informal ethical principles you use to make decisions in your life. Some people have a clear, well-defined set of principles they follow. Others' ethics are inconsistent or are applied differently in different situations.

It can be challenging to adhere to your own ethical principles if the consequences of your decisions might lead to an

FIGURE 2 It would be nice if there were signposts to ethical conduct, but the issues are complex. *(iQoncept/Shutterstock)*

unhappy result. For example, to get the job of your dreams, should you say on your résumé that you've already finished your degree, even though you're still one credit short? Is this lying? Is such behavior justified in this setting? After all, you do intend to finish that last credit, and you would work really hard for this company if you were hired. If you tell the truth and state that you haven't finished college yet, you might be passed over for the position. Making this choice is an ethical decision (see Figure 2).

How do a person's ethics develop? Naturally, your family plays a major role in establishing the values you cherish in your own life, and these might include a cultural bias toward certain ethical positions (see Figure 3). Your religious affiliation is another major influence on your ethics because most religions have established codes of ethical conduct. How these sets of ethics interact with the values of the larger culture is often challenging. Issues such as abortion, the death penalty, and war often create conflict between personal ethical systems and the larger society's established legal–ethical system.

As you mature, your life experiences also affect your personal ethics. Does the behavior you see around you make sense within the ethical principles that your family, your church, or your first-grade teacher taught you? Has your experience led you to abandon some ethical rules and adopt others? Have you modified how and when you apply these laws of conduct depending on what's at stake?

Define Your Own Personal Values

Objective 5B.3: *Define your personal values that form your ethics.*

What if I'm not sure what my personal ethics are? When you have a clear idea of what values are important to you, it may be easier to handle situations in your life that demand ethical action. Follow these steps to help define a list of personal values:

1. **Describe yourself.** Write down words that describe who you are, based on how others view you. Would a friend describe you as honest, or helpful, or kind? These keywords will give you a hint as to the values and behaviors that are important to you.

2. **List the key principles you believe in.** Make a list of the key principles that influence your decisions. For example, would you be comfortable working in a lab that used animals for medical research? If not, is it because you

Family

Don't litter.

Religion

Don't tell lies.

Teachers

Don't cheat on tests or
you'll fail.

Experience

Don't speed or you'll
get a ticket.

Your ethical behavior

FIGURE 3 Many different
forces shape your personal
ethics. *(imtmphoto/Fotolia,
Jovannig/Fotolia, Michaeljung/
Fotolia, Lisa F. Young/
Shutterstock)*

value protecting any living being? How important is it to you that you never tell a lie? Or do you feel it is kind to lie in some situations? List the key ideas you believe to be important in conducting your life. Do you always behave this way, or are you flexible? Are there situations in which your answers might change (say, if the medical research was to cure cancer or the lie was to protect someone's feelings)?

3. **Identify external influences.** Where did your key principles come from—your parents? Your friends? Spiritual advisors? Television and movies? You may want to question some of your beliefs once you actually identify where they came from.

4. **Consider why.** After writing down your beliefs, think about *why* you believe them. Have you accepted them without investigation? Do they stand up in the context of your real-world experiences?

5. **Prepare a statement of values.** Distill what you have written into a short statement. By having a well-defined statement of the values you hold most important in your own life, which you can refer to in times of challenge, it will be easier for you to make ethical decisions.

Benefits to Ethical Living

Objective 5B.4: *Describe the benefits of ethical living.*

What are the benefits of ethical living? Society has established its own set of rules of conduct in the form of laws.

Ignoring or being inconsistent in following these rules can have an immediate impact. And more and more research is showing the health benefits of ethical living. When your day-to-day decisions are in conflict with your ethical principles, you often develop stress and anger.

Perhaps even happiness itself is a result of living ethically (see Figure 4). **Positive psychology** is a new focus in the field of psychology. Pioneered by Dr. Martin Seligman of the University of Pennsylvania, this field works to discover the *causes* of happiness instead of addressing the treatment of mental dysfunctions. Dr. Seligman's research has shown that by identifying your personal strengths and values and then aligning your life so that you can apply them every day, you can be happier (and suffer less depression)—an effect equivalent to that of antidepressant medication and therapy. Thus, finding a way to identify and then apply your ethics and values to your daily life can impact your health and happiness.

Personal Ethics and Your Work Life

Objective 5B.5: *Describe the interaction between a person's work life and his or her personal ethics.*

How do employers affect personal ethics? You may have a set of personal ethics that guide your behavior, but do your ethics change when you go to work? Of course, your employer expects you to follow the rules of conduct established for the business. However, this doesn't mean you need to blindly follow corporate practices that you feel are unethical or detrimental to society (see Figure 5).

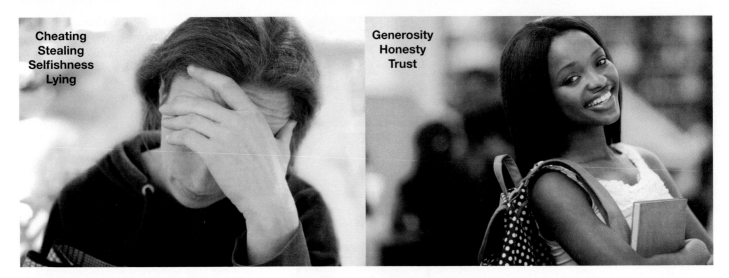

FIGURE 4 The field of positive psychology shows that living and working ethically affects your happiness. *(Holbox/Shutterstock, Michaeljung/ Shutterstock)*

Cheating
Stealing
Selfishness
Lying

Generosity
Honesty
Trust

If you spot unethical behavior at your company, what do you do? Whistle-blowers are people who report businesses to regulatory agencies for committing illegal acts, or who expose unethical (but still legal) acts committed by their employers by publicizing unethical behavior through various media outlets. The Sarbanes–Oxley Act of 2002 requires companies to provide mechanisms for employees and third parties to report complaints, including ethics violations, anonymously. In addition, many businesses are using their websites to allow whistle-blowers to report wrongdoing anonymously, replacing previously used e-mail and telephone hotline systems, which did not shield employees from being identified. With an online system, it's easier for a company to sort and classify complaints and designate them for appropriate action.

Should your employer have control over your conduct outside of the office? Do behavior, integrity, and honesty off the job relate to job performance? They might. But even if they don't, from your employer's perspective, your actions could reflect poorly on your employer. Consider the day-care employee in Texas who was fired because of a comment on Facebook before she even started her job. The management of the day-care company didn't appreciate her post about starting a new job but *hating working in a day-care center*. The day-care owners probably assumed customers wouldn't want an employee with these feelings taking care of their children. Therefore, although your ethics might dictate one mode of behavior, you need to consider how your employer might view your actions.

How does making ethical choices in a business setting differ from making personal ethical choices? Most personal ethical decisions involve few people. However, before making an ethical choice for a business, you need to consider the effect your choice will have on all of the business's stakeholders. **Stakeholders** are those people or entities who are affected by the operations of a business. Typical business stakeholders include

FIGURE 5 How should you respond if you see people in authority at work behaving unethically? *(Kritchanut/Shutterstock)*

customers, suppliers, employees, investors (shareholders), financial lenders, and society at large.

For instance, suppose you decide to cut costs in your restaurant by hiring workers "off the books" by paying them in cash. Although doing so might boost profits in the short term, the long-term impact on stakeholders can be severe. If you're caught avoiding paying payroll taxes by paying workers in cash, fines will be levied against your business, which may cause investors to lose money and may affect the company's ability to repay lenders. The negative publicity from being caught doing something illegal may cause a downturn in business, which, in turn, might force layoffs of employees or even closure of the business. Your simple decision on cutting costs isn't as simple as it may seem.

In summary, in a business environment, your behavior is guided by the ethical principles defined by the business owner or management, but you're ultimately guided by your own personal ethics.

Technology and Ethics: How One Affects the Other

Because technology moves faster than rules can be formulated to govern it, how technology is used is often left up to the individual and the guidance of his or her personal ethics. In the rest of this Technology in Focus feature, we explore situations in which ethics and technology affect each other: social justice (robotic ethics), intellectual property (3D printers), privacy (implanted data chips), property rights (ownership of outer space), electronic information access (business and free speech), and computer abuse (hacking).

Ethical considerations are never clear-cut. They're complex, and reasonable people can have different, yet equally valid, views. We present alternative viewpoints in each setting for you to consider and discuss. Figure 6 summarizes the issues we'll be discussing.

FIGURE 6

Ethics in Computing

TOPIC	ETHICAL DISCUSSION	DEBATE ISSUE
Social Justice	Should the ethics of robotic systems be programmable by individuals?	Should manufacturers, the government, or individuals set the ethical parameters of robotic systems?
Intellectual Property	Who is responsible when 3D printers are misused?	Can we impose regulations effectively on 3D printers?
Privacy	Do human-implanted data chips benefit society or violate personal privacy?	Should personal privacy be protected at all costs?
Property Rights	Should any country, company, or individual own outer space?	Should we develop laws governing ownership of outer space?
Electronic Information Access	When does big business limit free speech?	Should companies allow the Chinese government to dictate when to curtail free speech?
Computer Abuse	Is hacktivism civil disobedience or terrorism?	Is hacking a natural extension of civil disobedience or a crime?

SOCIAL JUSTICE

Who Sets the Ethics for Robots?

Summary of the Issue

The rise of the Internet of Things means that more embedded computers and robotics are being included in devices every year. Personal robots in households are not far off. But who controls the ethical constraints by which robotic machinery operates?

Automobiles now contain sophisticated robotic systems to exercise control over the vehicle and respond faster than humans can. Using radar, accident-avoidance systems can apply the brakes and even change lanes to help drivers avoid accidents. In the coming years, these systems may exercise even more control of your vehicle, such as the self-driving cars that are under development by Google.

Consider this scenario: You come up over the crest of a hill. A school bus is disabled in your lane and you're traveling too fast to brake in time to avoid hitting it. To the left is a lane of oncoming traffic. To the right is a large grove of trees. A robotic system controlling your car has three options: (1) Apply the brakes to slow the vehicle. You will hit the school bus, but at a lower speed. You will survive, but some occupants of the bus may be killed. (2) Swerve to the left into oncoming traffic to avoid hitting the school bus. You may hit another car, but the risk of loss of human life is limited to just the occupants of two vehicles. (3) Swerve to the right into the trees. Only you are at risk of being killed if your car hits a tree. So which scenario does the robotic system controlling your car choose?

At this point, automobile manufacturers program robotic devices when they build the cars. But should owners have a choice of overriding the programming in their vehicles and adjust the ethical parameters of the robotic systems? If an owner was selfless, he or she could program the car to always make decisions that resulted in less harm to others (option 3 above). Alternatively, he or she could program the car to choose option 1, which minimizes his or her chance of injury.

And what would you as a manufacturer do until laws are passed regarding robotic ethics? If you program the car to protect the driver's life at all costs and the accident described above results in children on the bus dying, you could be sued by the families of the bus occupants. On the other hand, if you program the car to minimize harm to others, you could be sued by the driver's family when the car swerves into the woods and crashes into a tree killing the driver.

Meanwhile, researchers at Harvard University are experimenting with *robot swarms* — groups of robots that are programmed to work together to perform tasks without human intervention. But what happens if something goes wrong? Say a swarm of robots is assembling a building and they malfunction, causing a section of the building to collapse and injuring several bystanders. Who is responsible? Should it be the company who manufactured the robots or the human foreman who was supposedly supervising the job site?

What is best for society as a whole? The answer is not very clear-cut but is one we will need to wrestle with in the coming years.

Questions to Think About and Research

1. Who should be responsible for controlling the ethics of robotic systems? Why?

2. If a collision avoidance system in an automobile takes control of the vehicle to avoid an accident and a death results, who is responsible—human or machine?

3. When do the benefits of robotic controls outweigh the risks of the technology taking ethical decisions out of the hands of human beings?

4. Does relying on robots to make ethical decisions make us less human?

POINT

Individuals Should Have the Right to Set Ethics for Robotic Systems They Own

Advocates of individual choice over robotic ethics feel that just as individuals are free to make choices in their own lives, these choices should be extended to robots that they own.

1. Society dictates what is legal and illegal by passing laws. As long as choices over robotic ethics don't violate laws, they should be in the hands of individual owners.

2. Individuals should have the right to set ethical parameters for their robots because they may wish to be even more selfless than society dictates (i.e., by having the robots protect other people's lives, even at the cost of their own life).

3. When devices such as automobiles don't have robotic systems, individuals make ethical decisions in times of crisis. Robotic systems should be an extension of the individual's ethical values.

COUNTERPOINT

Robotic Ethics Should Be Controlled by the Government or Manufacturers

Critics maintain that individuals cannot be trusted to make decisions on robotic ethics that will benefit society as a whole. The greater good is served by making universal ethics programming decisions at the point of manufacture.

1. If robots do not contain ethical constraints that prevent harm to human beings, human lives may be lost.

2. Robots must have ethical programming that allows them to make decisions regarding the best possible outcomes in life and death situations.

3. Allowing individuals to adjust the ethics of robotic devices exposes society to risks from careless, thoughtless, or psychotic individuals.

FIGURE 7 Who should set the ethics for robotic systems? Individuals? Manufacturers? The government? *(Magictorch/Alamy)*

3D Printing: Who Is Responsible When Things Go Awry?

Summary of the Issue

3D printing is potentially going to revolutionize the way items are manufactured. With the cost of 3D printers falling, it may soon be practical and cost effective to produce a wide variety of products at home instead of buying them from a retail outlet or a manufacturer. However, this shift will potentially cause a range of issues involving intellectual property rights and liability.

In traditional manufacturing, it is relatively easy to enforce safety laws. Consider the manufacture of bicycle safety helmets. Traditional manufacturers are held accountable for delivering safely designed products free from defects in workmanship. Products are subjected to safety testing prior to being sold to the public and must conform to legal safety guidelines. If you buy a helmet and are injured while riding your bike because of a defect in the design of or materials used in the helmet, you would sue the manufacturer for damages. Manufacturers protect their designs (intellectual property) by obtaining patents.

3D printers produce objects from design plans generated with various types of software. Anyone that is reasonably proficient with design software can generate a design for an object to be printed. However, a person could also use a 3D scanner to scan an existing object (say a helmet designed and sold by a traditional manufacturer) and use design software to create their own plan for how to print it. If the object is patented, this would be a violation of the law. But it certainly makes it easier to steal someone's intellectual property.

Design plans for objects are often shared online. Even if the same design is used, the product quality can be vastly different depending on the type of 3D printer used and the raw materials (usually plastics) selected to be used when printing.

So you buy a 3D printer and raw materials. You download a design for a bicycle helmet from the Internet. You print out a helmet on your printer and give it to your neighbor. While riding his bicycle your neighbor is injured because the design of the helmet was flawed and the materials you used to make it were substandard. Who is responsible for the injuries? The manufacturer of the printer? The owner of the printer (i.e., you)? The manufacturer of the raw materials used to make the helmet? The creator of the flawed design plans? The person who decided to produce and distribute an untested product (again, you)? The person who decided to use an untested product (i.e., your neighbor)? What if the design you used was created from a patented product? You could be sued by the company that owns the patent for illegally producing its product design.

Questions to Think About and Research

1. Should individuals be allowed to distribute (or sell) products they make at home on 3D printers, or should the output be limited to personal use?

2. What regulations should the government put in place to regulate the safety and efficacy of product designs distributed for use on 3D printers? Are there any existing laws in the United States covering 3D printing technology?

3. How can we enforce intellectual property laws against the owners of 3D printers?

POINT

Regulating 3D Printing Protects Designers and the Public

Those arguing that 3D printing must be regulated contend the following:

1. Manufacturers depend on the integrity of the protection of intellectual property to make a fair profit on their work. The general public expects products to be produced that are free from design and material defects. If governments do not regulate 3D printing materials and designs, the public is placed in unnecessary peril.

2. Because designs of existing products are easy to produce, there is an increased chance of intellectual property theft.

3. Users of 3D printers need to understand the risks, responsibilities, and liabilities of producing products on demand for their use and for resale.

COUNTERPOINT

Unregulated 3D Printing Encourages Creativity

3D printing enthusiasts who believe that 3D printing should not be regulated argue the following:

1. The existing laws on intellectual property have worked to serve the interests of manufacturers. Manufacturers can seek legal remedies for violation of designs under existing laws.

2. Heavily regulating 3D printing will stifle creativity and ingenuity in the design and production of new products.

3. Consumers should be aware of the principle of "caveat emptor" (let the buyer beware) when using untested or unproven products. People should use untested products wisely and cautiously.

FIGURE 8 Many objects can be produced by 3D printers. But who bears the responsibility when a product is defective? *(Wsf s/Shutterstock)*

PRIVACY

Human-Implanted Data Chips: Protection or Orwellian Nightmare?

Summary of the Issue

Like respect and dignity, many people perceive privacy as a basic human right. However, many of us give up quite a bit of our privacy voluntarily via the devices we carry and the apps we use. Our smartphones include GPS chips that track our location, allowing us to check in on social media to let our friends know where we are. Activity trackers such as the Fitbit and even more sophisticated wireless medical devices can monitor our health. Even our smartphones use biometric data such as fingerprints to identify their owners. So why does the thought of implanting a data chip inside the human body cause so much uproar and dissent?

Human-implantable microchips have been available in the United States since 2004, when the FDA approved the VeriChip (now PositiveID). The basic advantages of implanted chips are that they can receive and transmit information and are extremely difficult to counterfeit. An implanted chip could positively identify you when you make a retail transaction, virtually eliminating fraud. Your chip could provide instant access to your medical records when you arrive in the emergency room unconscious after a car accident. Parents (and law enforcement) could potentially use the chips to locate lost or missing children. Alzheimer's patients could be tracked down if they go missing. And law enforcement could track the movement of convicted criminals out on parole. Sounds like a utopia, doesn't it?

Not at all, say a great deal of people. In fact, the idea of having a tracking chip or information-gathering chip implanted in the body makes many people extremely uncomfortable. It seems to go even one step further than the society in George Orwell's classic novel *1984* where everyone was monitored via cameras in public and at home. Despite the benefits, people see great potential for privacy infringement and potential misuse of data. Would you want your parents (or the government) to know where you are at any time? Would someone be able to read the medical information in your chip without your permission and use it against you? In fact, there is so much resistance from the public to implants that some states such as Wisconsin, California, Georgia, and North Dakota have already enacted legislation to prohibit mandatory data chips implants in the future, even though it is not being considered now.

The debate will most likely rage on as technologies continue to be developed that will allow implanted chips to gather and provide even more data. Whether the public embraces this technology remains to be seen.

Questions to Think About and Research

1. Would you ever be willing to have a data chip implanted in your body? Why or why not?

2. What data do you think would be useful to have on an implanted chip? What precautions should be taken to ensure that the data is not misused or collected without your knowledge?

3. Are there groups of people that you feel should be required to have chips implanted in them for the public good? If yes, list the groups and explain your rationale. If no, justify your answer.

4. In which states are mandatory chip implants currently illegal? Is there any federal legislation pending regarding chip implants?

POINT

Chip Implants Would Benefit Society

Advocates for personal chip implants feel the advantages of such implants outweigh the potential loss of privacy. They argue the following:

1. Data from implants can be used responsibly given adequate laws and safeguards to prevent misuse of data.

2. The benefits gained from monitoring criminals, vulnerable adults, and children outweigh the likelihood that individuals will be harmed by a loss of privacy.

3. In the digital age, loss of a certain amount of privacy is inevitable.

COUNTERPOINT

Chip Implants Would Lead to an Erosion of Personal Privacy

Advocates of protecting privacy in the United States contend that privacy concerns should outweigh the needs of governments, individuals, or businesses to have unrestricted access to personal information. They argue the following:

1. If businesses or government entities screen personal information contained in the implants, they might misuse or lose control of the data.

2. People should be able to choose not to share sensitive information, but implants take away individual control.

3. Being monitored without your explicit consent, via a mandatory implant, violates the basic human right to privacy.

FIGURE 9 Data chip implants could provide physicians with faster access to medical records—but at what cost to our privacy? *(Juan Pablo Rada/Shutterstock)*

PROPERTY RIGHTS

Mining an Asteroid: Who Owns Outer Space?

Summary of the Issue

Development of technology hardware requires lots of rare metals. Metals are mainly obtained from Earth via mining (although some metals could potentially be recovered from seawater). Whoever owns a piece of land usually owns the mineral rights to it as well and can mine it for its wealth. But there are places beyond Earth, like asteroids and planets, which appear to contain a wealth of minerals and metals. It's pretty clear who owns real estate on Earth (except for Antarctica, which isn't owned by any sovereign nation). But who owns the moon? Or Pluto? Or the asteroids in the asteroid belt between Mars and Jupiter?

Real property (or real estate) is either land or something built on land (like a building) considered immovable. Personal property items, such as cars and smartphones, are generally moveable from place to place. For personal property, possession usually presumes ownership. (You wouldn't have your neighbor's TV in your home, would you?) Real estate property ownership is usually proven by registered title or deed to avoid possession disputes. You may want to own land but not live on it, so to prove you own it and keep squatters from claiming it, you have a legal document proving ownership. So how do you get a deed to the moon?

The major law governing ownership of extraterrestrial territory (currently ratified by all spacefaring nations) is the 1967 Outer Space Treaty (OST). This treaty was mainly the result of the Cold War space race to the moon between the United States and the Soviet Union. Neither country wanted the other claiming the moon as their territory and building missile bases on it. The OST states that "outer space, including the moon and other celestial bodies, is not subject to national appropriation by claim of sovereignty, by means of use or occupation, or by any other means." So this means that the United States was unable to claim the moon as part of U.S. territory when it became the first country to land men on the moon. However, the OST language is vague on whether territory in outer space can be claimed by private parties for commercial purposes such as mining. With current advances in technology, it may soon be economically feasible to mine planets or asteroids.

So say your company identifies an asteroid that is rich in platinum. How do you gain ownership? That is currently unclear. Space mining rights are a bit like the Wild West at this point. Small asteroids, unlike planets or moons, are movable. If you find an asteroid and tow it back to Earth's orbit for mining, is it personal property? Possession might then signify ownership. But what about mining on the moon? On Earth, mining companies like to establish ownership to mineral rights before beginning operations through deeds or licenses. But because no one technically "owns" the moon, how do you protect the rights to your lunar mine? What if another company takes over your lunar mine by force? Who do you go to for resolution of the dispute?

Questions to Think About and Research

1. The moon is defined as a "celestial body" in the OST. Does the term *celestial body* in the OST include asteroids? If not, can a country claim ownership to asteroids because they are movable?

2. What would constitute laying claim to an asteroid? Would sending a probe to an asteroid to assess mineral content and leaving a radio transponder constitute ownership? Or would the asteroid need to be occupied by people? Would towing the asteroid into Earth's orbit constitute ownership?

3. Currently, if a meteor falls from space and destroys personal property, no one is to blame. What if while mining an asteroid a chunk (now a meteor) falls to Earth and destroys a building? Who should bear the risks of parking and mining asteroids in Earth's orbit?

4. Should the OST treaty be rescinded? Should governments be allowed to claim parts of outer space as their sovereign territory? Would being able to claim territory in space head off disputes that might otherwise arise?

POINT

Outer Space Belongs to the Human Race

The advocates of sharing outer space resources feel that no one country has the right to claim them, and all mankind should benefit from exploration and exploitation. They argue the following:

1. Cost of exploration can be controlled by consortiums of nations providing funding and offsetting costs incurred before distributing excess wealth recovered.

2. Space is large and there are plenty of resources for everyone to share.

3. Once a country claimed a territory, it would only recognize the rights of its sovereign citizens to that territory and that the country would actively defend its citizens' claims from incursions by other nations. Society must avoid such unproductive conflicts over ownership of outer space territory.

COUNTERPOINT

Outer Space Can Be Claimed by Private Companies

The advocates for private ownership of outer space generally feel that those who "discover" a territory and hold it (usually by occupation of citizens and a standing army) should have claim to it and the available resources. They argue the following:

1. The high cost of outer space exploration and mining deserves to be offset by the exploitation of resources recovered. Exploration will be limited if there is no incentive for profit.

2. Laws and regulations will need to be created to create ownership records (deeds and titles) to outer space properties claimed. Mining rights need to be protected in outer space so that claims are not "jumped" by unlawful individuals.

3. Competition for limited resources spurs innovation.

FIGURE 10 Asteroids are rich in rare metals. But who owns an asteroid? *(Johan Swanepoel/Fotolia)*

ELECTRONIC INFORMATION ACCESS

Should Everyone Have Free Access to Uncensored Information?

Summary of the Issue

In the United States, we expect free and uncensored access to the Internet. However, people in other parts of the globe do not always enjoy these same freedoms. For instance, India's IT Act Rule 12 states that websites can be blocked if it is "necessary or expedient so to do in the interest of sovereignty and integrity of India, defense of India, security of the State, friendly relations with foreign states or public order or for preventing incitement to the commission of any cognizable offence relating to above." Citing this rule, India banned and blocked over 800 pornographic sites in August 2015. The ban sparked a huge debate among the populace about free speech and personal freedom. The ban was partially lifted in a few days with only sites deemed to be promoting child pornography still blocked. Blocking child pornography is obviously a laudable goal, but other countries block many different types of websites.

In early 2006, when Google launched its search engine services in China, it conceded to the Chinese government's demands that it self-censor its search engine, restricting search results for sensitive information such as the details of the Tiananmen Square protests and of human rights groups. This decision prompted much discussion, with some condemning Google's decision for putting business profits over what they saw as basic human rights (see Figure 11). Google justified its actions by stating that a company must operate within the rules of the market in which it operates and that the benefits of increased access to information for people in China "outweighed our discomfort in agreeing to censor some results." And, compared with search results from **Baidu.com**, the leading Chinese search engine, Google was not censoring all information.

However, in 2010, Google announced that it was no longer willing to censor search results and moved the site to Hong Kong, where it hoped there would be less censorship. The departure was a reaction to a sophisticated, targeted cyberattack that Google believes was done to gather information on Chinese human rights activists. At that time, Google had about a 35% market share.

Microsoft had only a 1% share of the market, so it decided to partner with **Baidu.com** to provide English-language search results for China's largest search engine. Microsoft stated it would agree to abide by Chinese censorship laws (so search terms like *freedom* and *democracy* deliver filtered results), thereby respecting the laws of the countries where it operates. However, before honoring any censor requests, Microsoft insisted that Chinese authorities made legally binding requests in writing.

So how did it all work out? As of the end of 2014, Google's market share had dropped to 12.04% in China, whereas **Baidu.com** has increased its market share to 79.45%. Microsoft's decision to keep censoring its searches appears to have paid off—at least from a monetary perspective. But is the financial result more important than the social implications of its behavior?

Questions to Think About and Research

1. Is there anything else that Google could have done that would have a major impact on China's censorship laws?

2. Has Microsoft's compliance with censorship laws furthered the Chinese government's cooperation in combating software piracy in China? Are Microsoft's financial incentives even deeper than just Internet market share?

3. Can the U.S. government compel technology companies to take a firmer stance on free speech in China and elsewhere by instituting criminal charges if U.S. companies do not take reasonable steps to protect human rights?

POINT

U.S. Companies Should Comply with Local Laws in Foreign Countries

Those in favor of Microsoft's actions to remain in China feel that if a company chooses to operate in a foreign country, it knows the local laws and should be prepared to work within those laws as it does business. They argue the following:

1. It is not the place of a company to try to change laws of foreign countries. Reform must come from within.

2. Working in China does not mean a company supports all of China's policies.

3. Microsoft's presence continues to advance the progress the Chinese government is making toward democracy. U.S. companies can ethically stay in China if they make an effort to improve human rights there. U.S. companies operating in China should agree on guidelines that respect human rights.

COUNTERPOINT

U.S. Companies Should Put What Is Right Ahead of What Is Financially Expedient

Those in favor of Google's actions believe that international corporations should begin to take a firm stance against governments that do not promote basic human rights. They argue the following:

1. China will never change unless there are financial and political incentives to do so. Google's departure helps pressure the Chinese government.

2. Google's withdrawal from China threatens the viability of many advertising resellers in China.

3. Google's decision to leave helps put pressure on China's government to play by global standards. China cannot expect to compete in the global marketplace while refusing to have a global exchange of ideas.

FIGURE 11 Is free access to content attainable in countries (such as China and India) where information availability can be restricted by law? *(Deeepblue/Shutterstock)*

COMPUTER ABUSE

Hacktivism: Civil Disobedience or Terrorism?

Summary of the Issue

Civil disobedience and the right to assemble and protest are basic liberties to which many Americans feel entitled. After all, this type of activism is part of what helped create America. Remember that little protest in 1773 that became known as the Boston Tea Party or that little document called the *Declaration of Independence*? Those are both shining examples of civil disobedience.

With the rise of e-commerce, it might be difficult to stage an event such as the Boston Tea Party. For instance, suppose you felt Amazon was treating some segment of their customers unfairly. Where would you go to protest when Amazon doesn't have any physical stores? This type of problem has given rise to acts of hacktivism.

Hacktivism (derived from *hack* and *activism*) involves using computers and computer networks in a subversive way to promote an agenda usually related to causes such as free speech, human rights, or freedom of information. Essentially, it's using computer hacking to affect some sort of social change. As computer security has grown more sophisticated, attacks today are usually carried out by groups of hackers (such as Anonymous or LulzSec) or groups of computer scientists funded by nation states for the specific purpose of hacking.

Hacktivism often takes the form of denial-of-service attacks in which websites are bombarded with requests for information until they are overwhelmed and legitimate users can't access the site. Other times, they take the form of cyberterrorism, where the objective is to embarrass or harass a company by penetrating its computer networks and stealing (and often publishing) sensitive information. Certain countries (like China) are rumored to maintain cadres of computer scientists whose main goal is to spy on other countries by hacking into their computer networks.

One of the most famous instances of hacktivism revolved around the scheduled release of the movie *The Interview* by Sony Entertainment Pictures in late 2014. With a plot revolving around two television personalities who are recruited by the CIA to assassinate leader of North Korea Kim Jong Un, the movie was controversial as soon as its preview was released and sparked protests from the North Korean government. In late November 2014, a hacktivist group penetrated Sony's computer networks and stole a tremendous amount of confidential data. It then posted four unreleased movies to pirate websites and threatened to publish additional data unless the release of *The Interview* was canceled. In addition, the group totally trashed Sony's internal networks, making them unusable. Eventually, over 38 million files of confidential data were leaked, including personal finance information and e-mails of Sony employees.

Many saw the Sony incident as an example of terrorism given the viciousness of the attack. But other attacks that change the content of websites to promote agendas might seem less harmful. Regardless of the intent of the hacktivists, hacking into computer systems is illegal in almost every part of the globe. However, civil disobedience does involve breaking the law to bring to light social injustice. So is hacking a computer network any different than tossing tea overboard in the Boston Harbor? Or is it just civil disobedience 21st-century style?

Questions to Think About and Research

1. Can you think of any instances where hacking a computer system is morally justified? For your examples, what other types of protest strategies could be used other than hacking?

2. There are federal laws that make hacking a crime. Are there instances where these laws should be ignored, such as if public opinion is overwhelmingly on the side of an issue?

3. What responsibility does the government have to combat hacktivism attacks on private companies such as Sony Pictures? Should security of digital information be a constitutional right?

POINT

Hacking Is a Natural Extension of Civil Disobedience

Proponents of hacktivism generally feel that the ends justify the means. They argue the following:

1. Society as a whole benefits when injustices are exposed.
2. Civil disobedience is an inalienable right upon which the United States was born.
3. Methods of civil disobedience need to keep pace with modern technology in order to have the greatest impact possible.

COUNTERPOINT

Hacktivism Is Illegal and Therefore Wrong

Opponents of hacktivism usually cite the fact that there are laws preventing the unauthorized penetration of computer systems. They argue the following:

1. Computer technology provides many opportunities for reaching a wide audience with a message without resorting to illegal activities such as hacking.
2. Personal data of individuals needs to be protected as a basic right of privacy.
3. Hacking into computer systems for alleged acts of "civil disobedience" are often hard to distinguish from acts of cyberterrorism.

FIGURE 12 Is hacktivism civil disobedience or terrorism? It can be difficult to tell the difference. *(Frank Peters/Shutterstock)*

Using Computers to Support Ethical Conduct

Although there are many opportunities to use computers and the Internet unethically, we can also use technology to support ethical conduct. For example, many charitable organizations use the Internet and other technology tools for fundraising. When a severe earthquake swept through Nepal in April 2015, the Red Cross and other charities received many pledges via their websites.

Google Crisis Response is a project sponsored by Google that helps disseminate information before and after a crisis to coordinate relief efforts and provide updates to the public (see Figure 13). Google Person Finder, part of Google Crisis Response, helps individuals and organizations to provide information and updates on persons missing (or located) after a disaster.

Computing devices and the Internet provide many opportunities for you to start or get involved in ethical initiatives. Consider the Empty Bowls movement that was started by students at Wichita State University. Local potters, students, and educators worked to create bowls and then guests were invited to consume a simple meal of bread and soup from them. For a donation to help local organizations feed the hungry, donors were encouraged to keep the bowls as a reminder of all the empty bowls in the world. This movement is now spreading across the United States through the website **emptybowls.net**. What can you and your fellow students do in your community?

Throughout your life, you'll encounter many ethical challenges relating to information technology. Your personal ethics—combined with the ethical guidelines your company provides and the general ethical environment of society—will guide your decisions.

For further information on ethics, check out the following websites:

- Ethics in Computing (**ethics.csc.ncsu.edu**)
- The Center for Ethics in Science and Technology (**ethicscenter.net**)
- Business Ethics: The Magazine of Corporate Responsibility (**business-ethics.com**)
- Council for Ethical Leadership at Capital University (**businessethics.org**)
- John J. Reilly Center at University of Notre Dame (**reilly.nd.edu**)

FIGURE 13 Tools provided by Google Crisis Response help disseminate information and locate lost individuals after a disaster such as the earthquake in Nepal in 2015. *(© 2015 Google Inc. All rights reserved. Google and the Google Logo are registered trademarks of Google Inc.)*

check your understanding // review & practice

For a quick review of what you've learned, answer the following questions.

multiple choice

1. Which ethical theory focuses on adherence to moral duties and rights?

   a. deontology

   b. divine command theory

   c. utilitarianism

   d. relativism

2. The ethical theory that states that deities are all-knowing and set moral truth is

   a. utilitarianism.

   b. virtue ethics.

   c. deontology.

   d. divine command theory.

3. Which ethical philosophy states that morals are internal?

   a. deontology

   b. virtue ethics

   c. relativism

   d. divine command theory

4. Which of the following statements is *false*?

   a. Individuals who have no sense of right or wrong exhibit amoral behavior.

   b. Ethical decisions are usually influenced by personal ethics.

   c. Unethical behavior is always illegal.

   d. Life experience affects an individual's personal ethics.

5. Unethical behavior is

   a. the same as illegal behavior.

   b. based on civil disobedience.

   c. different from illegal behavior.

   d. governed by specific laws passed by legislative bodies.

6. The field of psychology that theorizes that happiness results from ethical living is known as

   a. principled psychology.

   b. positive psychology.

   c. moral psychology.

   d. affirmative psychology.

7. Which system of ethics states there is no universal moral truth?

   a. utilitarianism

   b. relativism

   c. virtue ethics

   d. There is no universally agreed-on best system.

8. What should you do if you spot unethical behavior at your workplace?

   a. Nothing, as long as the behavior is legal.

   b. Report it to the police immediately.

   c. Follow company procedures for reporting unethical behavior.

   d. Start looking for a new job.

9. Which of the following actions would NOT help to identify your personal ethics?

   a. Describe yourself.

   b. Identify the influences of your work environment.

   c. Conduct a genealogic study of your extended family.

   d. Prepare a list of values that are most important to you.

10. Ethical decisions in business affect which of the following?

    a. employees

    b. business's clients and customers

    c. suppliers and financial lenders

    d. all stakeholders

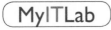 Go to **MyITLab** to take an autograded version of the *Check Your Understanding* review and to find all media resources for the chapter.

Understanding and Assessing Hardware: Evaluating Your System

Trust
Assured reliance
confidence or fai
the truth, worth
dependence on
belief in the ho

Make This: MAKE: A Location-Aware App on **page 241**

All media accompanying this chapter can be found in MyITLab.

For an overview of the chapter, watch the **Preview Video**.

(Wavebreakmedia Micro/Fotolia, Lucadp/Fotolia, Joppo/Shutterstock, Oleksiy Mark/Shutterstock, Leigh Prather/Shutterstock, Ivelin Radkov/Alamy)

HOW COOL IS THIS?

Want to create something really cool? The **Arduino microcontroller** project has fueled an abundance of DIY (do-it-yourself) electronics projects and created an energized community of do-it-yourselfers. This small **printed circuit board** is based on a microcontroller and includes everything you need: You just plug it in and begin your DIY project. The **open source hardware** is licensed under the Creative Commons license, so schematics are freely available to be changed or re-created as you wish.

The **LilyPad** variation of the Arduino, designed by MIT engineer Leah Buechley, is often used to create **wearable projects**. Conductive thread runs from the Arduino output pins to LEDs, and the finished garments are washable. The LilyPad project seen here, a glove that remotely controls a robotic hand, was designed at a hackathon in Warsaw, Poland. **Hackathons** are workshops that help people learn to design software and electronic hardware. *(epa european pressphoto agency b.v./Alamy)*

Evaluating Key Subsystems

Learning Outcome 6.1 You will be able to evaluate your computer system's hardware functioning.

It can be tough to know if your computer is the best match for your needs. New technologies emerge so quickly, and it's hard to determine whether they're expensive extras or tools you need. Do you need USB 3.1 instead of USB 3.0? Doesn't it always seem like your friend's computer is faster than yours? Maybe you could get more out of newer technologies, but should you upgrade the system you have or buy a new machine? In this chapter, you'll learn how to measure your system's performance and gauge your needs so that you end up with a system you love.

 your ideal

COMPUTING DEVICE

There never seems to be a perfect time to buy a new computer. It seems that if you can just wait a year, computers will be faster and cost less. But is this actually true?

Moore's Law

Objective 6.1 *Describe the changes in CPU performance over the past several decades.*

How quickly does computer performance improve? As it turns out, it is true that if you wait just a while, computers will be faster and cost less. In fact, a rule of thumb often cited in the computer industry called **Moore's Law** describes the pace at which central processing units (CPUs) improve. Named for Gordon Moore, the cofounder of the CPU chip manufacturer Intel, this rule predicts that the number of

transistors inside a CPU will increase so fast that CPU capacity will double about every two years. (The number of transistors on a CPU chip helps determine how fast it can process data.)

This rule of thumb has held true for over 50 years. Figure 6.1 shows a way to visualize this kind of exponential growth. If CPU capacity were put into terms of population growth, a group of 2,300 people at the start of CPU development would now be a country of over 1 billion! Moore himself has predicted that around the year 2020, CPU chips will be manufactured in a different way, thus changing or eliminating the effects of Moore's Law altogether.

In addition to the CPU becoming faster, other system components also continue to improve dramatically. For example, the capacity of memory chips such as dynamic random access memory (DRAM)—the most common form of memory found in personal computers—increases about 60% every

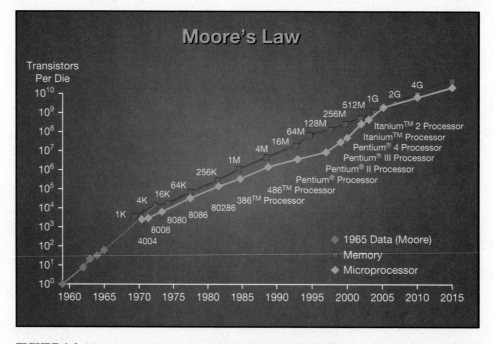

FIGURE 6.1 Moore's Law illustrates the amazing pace of growth in CPU capabilities.

FIGURE 6.2

What Kind of Technology User Are You?

Casual User
- Uses the computer primarily for Internet access
- Uses some software applications locally, like Microsoft Office
- Uses videos and software but does not create them

Power User
- Needs fast, powerful processing
- Needs fast storage and lots of it
- Creates videos and software programs

Mobile User
- Needs a lightweight device
- Needs a long battery life
- Is happy to sacrifice some capabilities for less weight

(Ilaszlo/Shutterstock, ColorBlind Images/Getty Images, Ollyy/Shutterstock)

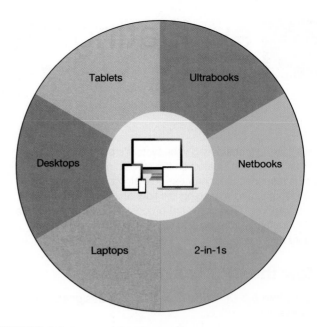

FIGURE 6.3 Range of Computing Devices

year. Meanwhile, hard drives have been growing in storage capacity by some 50% each year.

OK, things change fast. How do I know what's best for me? Consider what kind of user you are and what needs you have. For example, are you a power user who wants a machine for doing video editing and high-end gaming? Are you a more casual user, mainly using a device for word processing and Internet access? Are you on the move and need to bring your computer with you everywhere? Figure 6.2 shows a few different types of users—which type (or types) are you?

Now ask yourself, does your current computer match your needs? As we evaluate the pieces of your system, it'll become clear whether you need a few upgrades or perhaps a new machine better suited to you.

Select a Computing Device

Objective 6.2 *Compare and contrast a variety of computing devices.*

How do I pick from all the types of devices available? A huge number of choices are on the market (see Figure 6.3):

- Tablets (like the iPad or Galaxy)
- Ultrabooks (like the MacBook Air)
- Netbooks (like the Chromebook)
- 2-in-1s (which can serve as a tablet but also have a full keyboard)
- Laptops (or notebooks)
- Desktops

The main distinction among the available options is based on your need for mobility versus your need for processing power.

If you're on the move all the time and have to have the lightest solution possible, an ultrabook may be best for you. At less than three pounds, they're great on weight but don't include an optical drive for DVDs/Blu-rays or much storage space. Even lighter are tablets like the iPad, but they have less processing power and may not be able to run all the software you need.

Why would I consider buying a desktop? Desktop systems are invariably a better value than lighter, more mobile computers. You'll find you get more computing power for your dollar, and you'll have more opportunity to upgrade parts of your system later. In addition, desktops often ship with a 24-inch or larger monitor, whereas lighter computers offer screens between 10 and 17 inches.

Desktop systems are also more reliable. Because of the vibration that a laptop experiences and the added exposure to dust, water, and temperature fluctuations that portability brings, laptops often have a shorter lifespan than desktop computers. You'll have less worry over theft or loss with a desktop, too. Manufacturers do offer extended warranty plans that cover laptop computers for accidental damage and theft; however, such plans can be costly.

How long should I plan on keeping my computing device? You should be able to count on two years, and maybe even four or five years. The answer depends in part on how easy it is to upgrade your system. Take note of the maximum amount of memory you can install in your device. Also, check whether you can upgrade your device's graphics capabilities down the road.

How can I tell if my current system is good enough? We'll begin by conducting a **system evaluation**. To do this, we'll look at your computer's subsystems, see what they do, and check how they perform during your typical workday. Then we'll compare that with what is available on the market, and the path forward for you will become clearer. Even if you're not in the market for a new computer, conducting a system evaluation will help you understand what you might want down the road. ∎

evaluating the
CPU SUBSYSTEM

Let's start by considering your system's processor, or CPU. The CPU is located on the system motherboard and is responsible for processing instructions, performing calculations, and managing the flow of information through your computer. The dominant processors on the market are the Core family from Intel, featuring the i7, i5, and i3 (see Figure 6.4).

How the CPU Works

Objective 6.3 *Describe how a CPU is designed and how it operates.*

How can I find out what CPU my computer has? If you're running Windows, the System window will show you the type of CPU you have installed. For example, the computer in Figure 6.5 has an Intel i5 CPU running at 1.6 GHz. AMD is another popular manufacturer of CPUs; you may have one of its processors, such as the FX-83150 or the Phenom 2 X6X4. But more detailed information about your CPU, such as its number of cores and amount of cache memory, is not shown on this screen. Let's dive into that.

How does the CPU actually work? The CPU is composed of two units: the *control unit* and the *arithmetic logic unit (ALU)*. The control unit coordinates the activities of all the other computer components. The ALU is responsible for performing all the arithmetic calculations (addition, subtraction, multiplication, and division). It also makes logic and comparison decisions, such as comparing items to determine if one is greater than, less than, or equal to another.

FIGURE 6.4 The Intel i5 and i7 CPU chips run many of the laptop and desktop offerings on the market today. *(David Caudery/ PC Format Magazine/Getty Images)*

Every time the CPU performs a program instruction, it goes through the same series of steps:

1. It *fetches* the required piece of data or instruction from random access memory (RAM), the temporary storage location for all the data and instructions the computer needs while it's running.
2. It *decodes* the instruction into something the computer can understand.
3. It *executes* the instruction.
4. It *stores* the result to RAM before fetching the next instruction.

FIGURE 6.5 The System window identifies your computer's CPU as well as its speed. This computer has an Intel i5 running at 1.6 GHz. *(Windows 10, Microsoft Corporation)*
>*To access your system settings, right-click the **Start button**. From the menu that displays, choose **System**.*

This process is called a **machine cycle**. (We discuss the machine cycle in more detail in the Technology in Focus feature "Under the Hood."

What makes one CPU different from another?

You pay more for a computer with an Intel i7 than one with an i5 because of its increased processing power. A CPU's processing power is determined by the following:

- Its *clock speed*
- Whether it has multiple *cores*
- Its amount of *cache memory*

How does a CPU with a higher clock speed help me?

The **clock speed** of a CPU dictates how many instructions the CPU can process each second. It is measured in gigahertz (GHz), or billions of steps per second. The faster the clock speed, the more quickly the next instruction is processed. CPUs currently have clock speeds of up to 4 GHz. There is a huge difference between a computer with a 2 GHz CPU and one with a 4 GHz CPU.

Some users push their hardware to perform faster, **overclocking** their processor. Overclocking means that you run the CPU at a faster speed than the manufacturer recommends. It produces more heat, meaning a shorter lifetime for the CPU, and usually voids any warranty, but in gaming systems, you'll see this done quite often.

How does a multi-core CPU help me?

A **core** on a CPU contains the parts of the CPU required for processing. As shown in Figure 6.6a, with multiple-core technology, two or more complete processors live on the same chip, enabling the independent execution of two sets of instructions at the same time.

If you had a clone of yourself sitting next to you working, you could get twice as much done: That is the idea of multi-core processing. With multi-core processing, applications that are always running behind the scenes, such as virus protection software and your operating system (OS), can have their own dedicated processor, freeing the other processors to run other

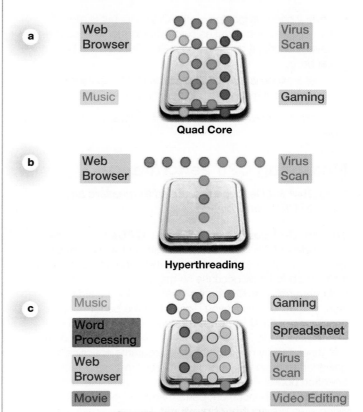

FIGURE 6.6 (a) Intel Quad Core processors have four cores that are able to run four programs simultaneously. (b) Hyperthreading allows work on two processes to happen in one core at the same time. (c) So, a four-core hyperthreaded processor can be working on eight programs at one time.

applications more efficiently. This results in faster processing and smoother multitasking.

CPUs began to execute more than one instruction at a time when **hyperthreading** was introduced in 2002. Hyperthreading provides quicker processing of information by enabling a new set of instructions to start executing *before the previous set has finished*. As shown in Figure 6.6b, hyperthreading allows two different programs to be processed at one time, but they're sharing the computing resources of the chip.

All of the Intel Core processors have multiple cores *and* hyperthreading (see Figure 6.6c). The Intel i7-990X has six cores, each one using hyperthreading, so it simulates having 12 processors!

How does more cache memory help me?

The CPU's **cache memory** is a form of RAM that gets data to the CPU for processing much faster than bringing the data in from the computer's RAM. There are three levels of cache memory, defined by their proximity to the CPU:

- *Level 1 cache* is a block of memory built on the CPU chip itself for storage of data or commands that have just been used. That gets the data to the CPU blindingly fast!

- *Level 2 cache* is located on the CPU chip but is slightly farther away and so takes somewhat longer to access than Level 1 cache. It contains more storage area than Level 1 cache.
- *Level 3 cache* is also located on the CPU chip itself but is slower to reach and larger in size than Level 2 cache.

The more expensive the CPU, the more cache memory it will have.

Measuring CPU Performance

Objective 6.4 *Describe tools used to measure and evaluate CPU performance.*

So how do I compare different CPUs? You'll often see models of the same computer with just a different CPU varying in cost by $200 or more. Is the price difference worth it? It's hard to know because so many factors influence CPU performance. Picking the best CPU for the kind of work you do is easier if you research some performance benchmarks. **CPU benchmarks** are measurements used to compare performance between processors. Benchmarks are generated by running software programs specifically designed to push the limits of CPU performance. Articles are often published comparing CPUs, or complete systems, based on their benchmark performance. Investigate a few, using sites like **cpubenchmark.net**, before you select the chip that's best for you.

How can I tell whether my current CPU is meeting my needs? One way to determine whether your CPU is right for you is to watch how busy it is as you work. You can do this by checking out your **CPU usage**—the percentage of time your CPU is working.

Your computer's OS has utilities that measure CPU usage. These are incredibly useful, both for considering whether you should upgrade and for investigating if your computer's performance suddenly seems to drop off for no apparent reason.

On Windows systems, the Task Manager utility lets you access this data (see Figure 6.7). The **CPU usage graph** records your CPU usage for the past minute. (Note that if you have multiple cores and hyperthreading, you'll see only one physical processor listed, but it will show that you have several virtual processors.) Of course, there will be periodic peaks of high CPU usage, but if your CPU usage levels are greater than 90% during most of your work session, a faster CPU will contribute a great deal to your system's performance.

To walk through using the Task Manager, check out the Try This on pages 240–241 and watch the "Using Windows to Evaluate CPU Performance" Sound Byte. Mac OS X has a similar utility named Activity Monitor, which is located in the Utilities folder in the Applications subfolder.

How often do I have to be watching the CPU load? Keep in mind that the workload your CPU experiences depends on how many programs are running at one time.

FIGURE 6.7 The Performance tab of the Windows Task Manager utility shows you how busy your CPU is. *(Windows 8.1, Microsoft Corporation)*
*>To access the Performance tab, right-click the **Start button**. From the menu, select **Task Manager**, and then click the **Performance tab**.*

Even though the CPU may meet the specs for each program separately, how you use your machine during a typical day may tax the CPU. If you're having slow response times or decide to measure CPU performance as a check, open the Task Manager and leave it open for a full day. Check in at points when you have a lot of open windows and when you have a lot of networking or disk-usage demand.

So a better CPU means a better-performing system? Your CPU affects only the *processing* portion of the system performance, not how quickly data can move to or from the CPU. Your system's *overall* performance depends on many factors, including the amount of RAM installed as well as hard drive speed. Your selection of CPU may not offer significant improvements to your system's performance if there is a bottleneck in processing because of insufficient RAM or hard drive performance, so you need to make sure the system is designed in a balanced way. Figure 6.9 lists factors to consider as you decide which specific CPU is right for you. ■

BITS&BYTES

Tower Design

We talked about using liquid to keep the CPU cool (see Figure 6.8). There is another approach as well: changing the shape of the case that holds the computer parts. One innovative approach is Apple's Mac Pro. A 10-inch cylinder is built around a triangular collection of printed circuit boards to allow constant air flow from bottom to top, cooling all the computer components with a single fan.

FIGURE 6.8 Keeping the processor cool is an important aspect of tower design. *(Gazlast/Shutterstock)*

- Power users: Clock speed is very important; consider whether overclocking is worth sacrificing CPU longevity
- Casual/Mobile users: Clock speed is not as important

- Power users: Get as many cores as possible
- Casual users: Fewer cores is acceptable
- Mobile users: Low power draw is more critical than number of cores

Clock Speed

Multiple Cores

CPU

Cache Memory

CPU Benchmarks

- Power users: Paying for more cache memory is a good investment
- Casual/Mobile users: Save your money

- Use benchmarks to get an exact measure of the difference between two CPUs

FIGURE 6.9 Evaluating the CPU

evaluating the

MEMORY SUBSYSTEM

Let's now take a peek at the memory subsystem of your computer. The memory subsystem can have a terrific impact on your system's processing speed if it is well matched to the power of your CPU. In this section, we'll look at how to measure that and how to upgrade if you need to.

Random Access Memory

Objective 6.5 *Discuss how RAM is used in a computer system.*

What is RAM? Random access memory (RAM) is your computer's temporary storage space. It really is the computer's short-term memory. When the computer is running, the RAM remembers everything that the computer needs in order to process data, such as data that has been entered and software instructions. But when the power is off, the data stored in RAM disappears. So RAM is an example of **volatile storage**. This is why systems always include both RAM and **nonvolatile storage** devices for permanent storage of instructions and data. Read-only memory (ROM), for example, holds the critical startup instructions. Hard drives provide the largest nonvolatile storage capacity in the computer system.

Why not use a hard drive to store the data and instructions? It's about one million times faster for the CPU

to retrieve a piece of data from RAM than from a mechanical hard drive. The time it takes the CPU to grab data from RAM is measured in nanoseconds (billionths of seconds), whereas pulling data from a fast mechanical hard drive takes an average of 10 milliseconds (ms), or thousandths of seconds.

Figure 6.10 shows the various types of memory and storage distributed throughout your system: memory that is actually part of the CPU (such as CPU registers and cache), RAM, virtual memory, optical drives, solid state drives (SSDs), and mechanical hard drives. Each of these has its own tradeoff of speed versus price. Because the fastest memory is so much more expensive, systems are designed with much less of it. This principle is influential in the design of a balanced computer system and can have a tremendous impact on system performance.

Are there different types of RAM? Yes, but in most current systems, the type of RAM used is double data rate 3 (DDR3) memory modules, available in several different speeds (1066 MHz, 1333 MHz, and 1600 MHz). The higher the speed, the better the performance. High-performance systems use DDR4 memory, and high-performance video graphics cards often use DDR5 memory, which has an even faster data transfer rate,

RAM appears in the system on **memory modules** (or **memory cards**), small circuit boards that hold a series of

FIGURE 6.10 A computer system's memory has many different levels, ranging from the small amounts in the CPU to the much slower but more plentiful storage of a mechanical hard drive.

FIGURE 6.11 A DIMM memory module holds a series of RAM chips and is wrapped with an aluminum heatsink plate to pull away heat. *(Scanrail/123RF)*

RAM chips and fit into special slots on the motherboard. Most memory modules in today's systems are packaged as a *dual inline memory module (DIMM)*, a small circuit board that holds several memory chips (see Figure 6.11).

How can I tell how much RAM is installed in my computer? The amount of RAM actually sitting on memory modules in your computer is your computer's **physical memory**. The easiest way to see how much RAM you have is to look in the System window. (On a Mac, choose the Apple menu and then About This Mac.) This is the same window you looked in to determine your system's CPU type and speed, and is shown in Figure 6.5. RAM capacity is measured in gigabytes (GB), and most machines sold today have at least 4 GB of RAM.

How can I tell how my RAM is being used? To see exactly how your RAM is being used, open the Resource Monitor and click on the Memory tab (see Figure 6.12). The Resource Monitor gives additional details on CPU, disk,

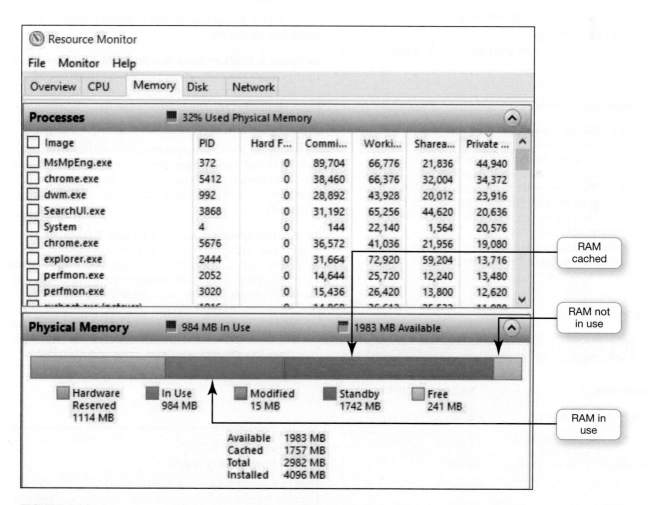

FIGURE 6.12 The Resource Monitor's Memory tab shows a detailed breakdown of how the computer is using memory. *(Windows 10, Microsoft Corporation)*

*>To access the Resource Monitor, from the Start menu, select **All apps**, click **Windows Administrative**, click **Resource Monitor**, and then click the **Memory tab**.*

network, and memory usage inside your system, and you can use it to see how you're using all the RAM you paid for.

Windows uses a memory-management technique known as **SuperFetch**. SuperFetch monitors the applications you use the most and preloads them into your system memory so that they'll be ready to be used when you want them. For example, if you have Microsoft Word running, Windows stores as much of the information related to Word in RAM as it can, which speeds up how fast your application responds. This is because pulling information from RAM is much faster than pulling it from the hard drive. You can watch this process at work using the Resource Monitor. Figure 6.12 shows how the 4 GB of installed RAM is being used:

- 1.1 GB is reserved to run the hardware systems
- 0.98 GB is running programs
- 1.7 GB is holding cached data and files ready for quick access
- 0.2 GB is currently unused

This is a system that would benefit from additional memory.

How much RAM do I need? At a minimum, your system needs enough RAM to run the OS. Running the 64-bit version of Windows 10 requires a minimum of 2 GB of RAM. However, because you run more applications at one time than just the OS, you'll want to have more RAM than just what's needed for the OS. For example, Figure 6.13 shows how much RAM is recommended for the OS, a web browser, and some software.

It's a good idea to have more than the minimum amount of RAM you need now so you can use more programs in the

future. Remember, too, that "required" means these are the *minimum values* recommended by manufacturers; having more RAM often helps programs run more efficiently. As noted above, new systems today ship with at least 4 GB of RAM. High-end systems can come with 24 GB of RAM. The rule of thumb: When buying a new computer, buy as much RAM as you can afford.

Adding RAM

Objective 6.6: *Evaluate whether adding RAM to a system is desirable.*

Is there a limit to how much RAM I can add to my computer? The motherboard is designed with a specific number of slots into which the memory cards fit, and each slot has a limit on the amount of RAM it can hold. To determine your specific system limits, check the system manufacturer's website.

In addition, the OS running on your machine imposes its own RAM limit. For example, the maximum amount of RAM for the 32-bit version of Windows 10 is 4 GB, whereas the maximum memory limit using the 64-bit version of Windows 10 Pro is 512 GB.

Is it difficult or expensive to add RAM? Adding RAM is fairly easy (see Figure 6.14). Be sure that you purchase a memory module that's compatible with your computer. Also be sure to follow the installation instructions that come with the RAM module. Typically, you simply line up the notches and gently push the memory module in place.

RAM is a relatively inexpensive system upgrade. The cost of RAM does fluctuate in the marketplace as much as 400% over time, though, so if you're considering adding RAM, you should watch the prices of memory in online and print advertisements. ∎

FIGURE 6.13

Sample RAM Allocation	
APPLICATION	**RAM RECOMMENDED**
Windows 10 (high resolution)	2 GB
Microsoft Office Professional 2016	2 GB
Microsoft Edge	1 GB
iTunes 12	2 GB
Adobe Photoshop Elements 13	2 GB
Total RAM recommended to run all programs simultaneously	**9 GB**

FIGURE 6.14 Adding RAM to a computer is quite simple and relatively inexpensive. On a laptop, you often gain access through a panel on the bottom. *(Editorial Image, LLC/Alamy)*

 # evaluating the
STORAGE SUBSYSTEM

Remember, there are two ways data is stored on your computer: temporary storage and permanent storage. RAM is a form of temporary (or volatile) storage. The information residing in RAM is not stored permanently. It's critical to have the means to store data and software applications permanently, which we discuss in this section.

Types of Storage Drives

Objective 6.7 *Classify and describe the major types of nonvolatile storage drives.*

Permanent storage options include internal hard drives, SSDs, optical drives, and external hard drives. When you turn off your computer, the data that has been written to these devices will be available the next time the machine is powered on. These devices therefore provide *nonvolatile* storage.

Mechanical Hard Drives

What makes the hard drive such a popular storage device? With storage capacities exceeding 4 terabytes (TB), a mechanical **hard drive** has the largest capacity of any storage device. And because it offers the most storage per dollar, the hard drive is also a more economical device than other options.

Today, most desktop system units are designed to support more than one internal hard drive. The Apple Mac Pro

has room for four hard drives, and the Thermaltake Level 10 can support six hard drives. Each one simply slides into place when you want to add more storage.

How is data stored on a hard drive? A hard drive is composed of several coated, round, thin plates of metal stacked on a spindle. Each plate is called a **platter**. When data is saved to a hard drive platter, a pattern of magnetized spots is created on the iron oxide coating of each platter. When the spots are aligned in one direction, they represent a *1*; when they're aligned in the other direction, they represent a *0*. These *0*s and *1*s are *bits* (or *binary digits*) and are the smallest pieces of data that computers can understand. When data stored on the hard drive platter is retrieved (or read), your computer translates these patterns of magnetized spots into the data you have saved.

How quickly does a hard drive find information? The hard drive's **access time**, the time it takes a storage device to locate its stored data and make it available for processing, is faster than optical drives. Mechanical hard drive access times are measured in milliseconds (ms). For large-capacity drives, access times of approximately 12 to 13 milliseconds are typical. For comparison, a DVD drive can take over 150 milliseconds to access data.

Solid State Drives

Do mechanical hard drives have the fastest access times? A **solid state drive (SSD)** uses electronic memory and has no mechanical motors or moving parts. Having no mechanical motors allows SSDs to offer incredibly fast access times, reaching data in only a tenth of a millisecond (0.1 ms). That's about 100 times faster than mechanical hard drives. SSDs also have a great advantage when booting up because a mechanical hard drive has to wait for motors to bring the plates up to the final rotation speed. The start-up time of SSDs is so fast, in fact, that most desktop and laptop systems offer an option to use at least one SSD. This "system drive" may only be 20 GB large, but it holds the operating system and means the wake-up time for the system will be very fast. In addition, SSDs run with no noise, generate very little heat, and require very little power, making them a popular option in ultrabooks.

Storage capacities for SSDs now range up to 4 TB, but such a large SSD is very expensive. Systems now often offer an SSD of 128 GB or 256 GB and then a mechanical hard drive, or two, to provide TBs of inexpensive slower storage space.

Solid State Hybrid Drives

Another new storage option is the **solid state hybrid drive (SSHD)**. An SSHD drive is a combination of both a mechanical hard drive and an SSD into a single device (see Figure 6.15). SSHD drives offer a very small amount of SSD storage space, perhaps 8 GB. If it is enough to store the operating system however, it can have a huge impact on the system boot time.

Optical Drives

How do optical drives work? Optical drives are disc drives that use a laser to store and read data. Data is saved to a compact disc (CD), digital video disc (DVD), or Blu-ray disc (BD) (collectively called **optical media**) within established tracks and sectors, just like on a hard drive. But optical discs store data as tiny pits that are burned into the disc by a high-speed laser. These pits are extremely small, less than 1 micron (a millionth of a meter).

Data is read from a disc by a laser beam, with the pits and nonpits (called *lands*) translating into the *1*s and *0*s of the binary code that computers understand. CDs and DVDs use a red laser to read and write data. Blu-ray discs get their name because they are read with a blue laser light, which has a shorter wavelength and can focus more tightly and pack more information on a disc. Blu-ray drives are the fastest optical devices and deliver the high-definition quality video that larger displays and monitors demand.

FIGURE 6.15 The SSHD drive is a single unit that contains both an SSD and a mechanical hard drive. *(Zern Liew/Shutterstock)*

Should I bother having an optical disc drive? Traditionally, optical media delivered music and movies, but these are now available through streaming services. Likewise, in the past, software was often installed from a DVD, but now you can buy almost all software through an online download. Therefore, many lightweight systems have stopped including optical drives. For example, ultrabooks are so thin and lightweight they often leave out an optical drive but may include a slot for an SD memory card to allow you to transfer files. You can buy external optical drives, but if you have a need for optical drives, you're probably better off purchasing a laptop computer with an optical drive.

DIG DEEPER How Hard Drives Work

The thin metal platters that make up a mechanical hard drive are covered with a special magnetic coating that enables the data to be recorded onto one or both sides of the platter. Hard drive manufacturers prepare the disks to hold data through a process called *low-level formatting*. In this process, concentric circles, each called a **track**, and pie-shaped wedges, each called a **sector**, are created in the magnetized surface of each platter, setting up a gridlike pattern that identifies file locations on the hard drive. A separate process called *high-level formatting* establishes the catalog that the computer uses to keep track of where each file is located on the hard drive. More detail on this process is presented in the Dig Deeper feature "How Disk Defragmenter Utilities Work" in Chapter 5.

Hard drive platters spin at a high rate of speed, some as fast as 15,000 revolutions per minute (rpm). Sitting between the platters are special "arms" that contain read/write heads (see Figure 6.16).

A **read/write head** moves from the outer edge of the spinning platter to the center, as frequently as 50 times per second, to retrieve (read) and record (write) the magnetic data to and from the hard drive platter. As noted earlier, the average total time it takes for the read/write head to locate the data on the platter and return it to the CPU for processing is called its *access time*. A new hard drive should have an average access time of approximately 12 ms.

Access time is mostly the sum of two factors—seek time and latency:

1. The time it takes for the read/write heads to move over the surface of the disk, moving to the correct track, is called the **seek time**. (Sometimes people incorrectly refer to this as access time.)
2. Once the read/write head locates the correct track, it may need to wait for the correct sector to spin to the read/write head. This waiting time is called **latency** (or **rotational delay**).

The faster the platters spin (or the faster the rpm), the less time you'll have to wait for your data to be accessed. Currently, most hard drives for home systems spin at 7,200 rpm.

The read/write heads don't touch the platters of the hard drive; rather, they float above them on a thin cushion of air at a height of 0.5 microinches. As a matter of comparison, a human hair is 2,000 microinches thick and a particle of dust is larger than a human hair. Therefore, it's critical to keep your hard drive free from all dust and dirt because even the smallest particle could find its way

between the read/write head and the disk platter, causing a **head crash**—a stoppage of the hard drive that often results in data loss.

SSDs free you from worry about head crashes at all. The memory inside an SSD is constructed with electronic transistors, meaning there are no platters, no motors, and no read/write arms. Instead, a series of cells are constructed in the silicon wafers. If high voltage is applied, electrons move in and you have one state. Reverse the voltage and the electrons flow in another direction, marking the cell as storing a different value. The limiting factor for an SSD's lifespan is how many times data can be written to a cell. But the current generation of SSDs is proving to have very strong performance over time. Intel, one manufacturer of SSDs, says its drives will last five years when being written to heavily (20 GB per day).

However, the high cost of SSD drives means they can only provide smaller amounts of storage. One compromise solution is the *SSHD*, a single drive that has both a small (perhaps 8 GB) SSD as well as a high-capacity mechanical hard drive. The faster SSD space can be used to store the operating system so that boot-up times are greatly reduced. These drives will continue to be popular as a cost-effective combination of nonvolatile storage.

Capacities for mechanical hard drives can exceed 4,000 GB (4 TB) and SSD drives are now storing 1 TB. Increasing the amount of data stored in mechanical drives is achieved either by adding more platters or by increasing the amount of data stored on each platter. SSD capacities continue to increase as the density of transistors on silicon wafers increases. Modern technology continues to increase the quantities of data that can be stored in small places.

FIGURE 6.16 A mechanical hard drive is a stack of platters enclosed in a sealed case. Special arms fit between each platter. The read/write heads at the end of each arm read data from and save data to the platters. *(Skaljac/Shutterstock)*

Storage Needs

Objective 6.8 *Evaluate the amount and type of storage needed for a system.*

How do I know how much storage capacity I have? Typically, hard drive capacity is measured in gigabytes (GB) or terabytes (1 TB = 1,000 GB). Accessing This PC from File Explorer will display the hard drives, their capacity, and usage information, as shown in Figure 6.17. To get a slightly more detailed view, select a drive and then right-click and choose Properties.

How much storage do I need? You need enough space to store the following:

- The OS
- The software applications you use, such as Microsoft Office, music players, and games
- Your data files
- Your digital music library, photos, videos of television shows and movies, and so on

Figure 6.18 shows an example of storage calculation. If you plan to have a system backup on the same drive, be sure to budget for that room as well. However, note that if you're going to store your data files only online instead of on your computer, you may not need much hard drive space. For example, if you stream all the movies you watch from Netflix, keep all your data files in Microsoft OneDrive, and use online software like Google Docs to edit, you may need very little hard drive space. Most ultrabooks like the Dell XPS 13 or the Apple MacBook Air are configured with 128-GB drives. In fact, many Chromebooks have only a 16-GB drive.

Also note that you don't need to meet all your storage needs with an internal hard drive. You can also add an external hard drive to your system, many of which use a USB port to connect. If you're looking to buy an external

FIGURE 6.17 In Windows, the free and used capacity of each device in the computer system is shown in the Computer window. The General tab of the Properties dialog box gives you more detailed information. *(Windows 10, Microsoft Corporation)* >*To view hard drive capacity, launch File Explorer, and then click* **This PC**. *To view the pie chart, right-click the* **C drive**, *and select* **Properties**.

hard drive, the USB 3.0 standard is about 10 times faster than USB 2.0, so if your system supports USB 3.0, that's the better choice.

Is it better to have one huge drive or several smaller drives? It depends on what's important to you: speed or security. If you purchase two smaller drives, you can combine them using RAID technology. A **redundant array of independent disks (RAID)** is a set of strategies for using more than one drive in a system (see Figure 6.19). RAID 0 and RAID 1 are the most popular options for consumer machines.

FIGURE 6.18

Sample Hard Drive Space Requirements

APPLICATION/DATA	HARD DRIVE SPACE REQUIRED	HEAVY CLOUD STORAGE USER
Windows 10	20 GB	20 GB
Microsoft Office 2016 Professional	3.5 GB	3.5 GB
Adobe Photoshop Elements 13	4 GB	4 GB
Adobe Premiere Pro CC	10 GB	10 GB
Video library of movies	80 GB (about 40 HD movies)	Streamed through online services
Music library	50 GB (about 7,000 songs)	Stored in cloud (iCloud or Amazon Cloud Drive)
Photographs	5 GB	Stored in iCloud or Dropbox
Total storage in use	**172.5 GB**	**37.5 GB**
Full backup	172.5 GB	Stored in cloud using Carbonite
Total required	**345 GB**	**37.5 GB**

- When you run two hard drives in **RAID 0**, the time it takes to write a file is cut in half. If disk performance is very important—for example, when you're doing video editing or sound recording—using two files in RAID 0 could be important. RAID 0 is faster because every time data is written to a hard drive, it's spread across the two physical drives (see Figure 6.19a). The write begins on the first drive, and while the system is waiting for that write to be completed, the system jumps ahead and begins to write the next block of data to the second drive. This makes writing information to disk almost twice as fast as using just one hard drive. The downside is that if either of these disks fail, you lose all your data because part of each file is on each drive. So RAID 0 is for those most concerned with performance.
- If you're really paranoid about losing data, you should consider having two drives in RAID 1. In a **RAID 1** configuration, all the data written to one drive is instantly perfectly mirrored and written to a second drive (see Figure 6.19b). This provides you with a perfect, instant-by-instant backup of all your work. It also means that if you buy two 1-TB drives, you only have room to store 1 TB of data because the second 1-TB drive is being used as the "mirror."

BITS&BYTES

How Much Storage to Buy?

No matter what kind of device you purchase, you'll have to decide how much storage you're willing to pay for. Does your Nexus 7 tablet need 16 GB? 32 GB? Should the SSD drive in your ultrabook be 128 GB? 256 GB? 512 GB? When you make your decision, keep in mind two factors:

1. Check whether you can add storage later using an SD card. If you can use a few SD cards to store music or photos, that will be a cheaper option.
2. Check how much usable storage is available in the device. For example, a 128-GB drive might offer less than 90 GB of available storage space after the operating system, the manufacturer software, and backup storage space are accounted for.

FIGURE 6.19 (a) A RAID 0 configuration speeds up file read/write time. (b) A RAID 1 configuration gives you an instant backup. *(Sergey Nivens/Fotolia)*

FIGURE 6.20

Evaluating Storage

- How much storage space do you need?
- Do you need a RAID 0 configuration for better performance?
- Do you want a RAID 1 configuration for immediate constant backup?

- Do you want very fast start-up of the system at boot-up and from sleep mode?
- Are you okay having a second hard disk drive for larger storage space?

Mechanical Hard Drive

Solid-State Drive

Optical Drive

Storage

Solid-State Hybrid Drive

- Do you need to read or produce DVD/CDs?
- Do you need to read Blu-ray discs?
- Do you need to produce Blu-ray discs?

- Do you want the speed advantage at boot-up of an SSD, the large storage capacity of a hard drive, and only one drive?

(Maxim_Kazmin/Fotolia)

RAID 0 and RAID 1 configurations are available on many desktop systems and are even beginning to appear on laptop computers.

So how do my storage devices measure up?
Figure 6.20 summarizes the factors you should consider in evaluating your storage subsystem. ■

Before moving on to Part 2:
1. Watch Replay Video 6.1 ⊙ .
2. Then check your understanding of what you've learned so far.

check your understanding // review & practice

For a quick review to see what you've learned so far, answer the following questions.

multiple choice

1. Which statement about ultrabook computers is *false*?

   a. Ultrabooks have the fastest optical drives.

   b. Ultrabooks are equipped with SSD drives for fast start-up.

   c. Ultrabooks typically weigh less than 3 pounds.

   d. Ultrabooks are available for either Windows or the OS X operating systems.

2. SSDs are classified as what type of storage?

   a. volatile

   b. nonvolatile

   c. video

   d. cache

3. When would you want to consider RAID 1 technology?

   a. when you need the fastest solution for writing data

   b. when you need an instant backup of your work

   c. if you think that SSDs are too expensive

   d. when you only want to have one hard disk drive

4. The limit to how much RAM you can add to your system

   a. depends on the design of the motherboard.

   b. depends on the operating system running on your system.

   c. depends on the amount of memory each memory card slot supports.

   d. all of the above

5. SuperFetch

   a. is a feature of Windows that supports optimal memory management.

   b. makes the boot-up time for the system very quick.

   c. is a video optimization that downloads high definition video faster.

   d. is a tool that defragments the hard drive to increase performance.

MyITLab   Go to **MyITLab** to take an autograded version of the *Check Your Understanding* review and to find all media resources for the chapter.

TECHBYTES WEEKLY

Stay current with the TechBytes Weekly Newsletter.

Continue

TRY THIS

Measure Your System Performance

Using the Windows Task Manager and the Resource Monitor can provide you with a lot of useful information about your computer system. Let's make sure you can use these Windows tools to keep an eye on your system performance.

Step 1 Hold the **Windows key** and press **X**. From the pop-up menu, select **Task Manager**. Click **More Details**, and then click the **Processes tab**.

(Windows 10, Microsoft Corporation)

Step 2 If you leave this window open while you work, you can pop in and check the history of how your CPU, disk, memory, and network are performing. Let's start by clicking on the **Performance tab**, and then looking at CPU utilization.

This computer is only occasionally going over 30%, so the system isn't limited by CPU performance.

(Windows 10, Microsoft Corporation)

Step 3 Clicking on **Memory** in the left panel shows that we have 4 GB of DDR3 memory installed in this computer.

Notice that memory usage is consistent at about 2 GB. We have memory available so this system isn't limited by memory capacity with its current workload.

(Windows 10, Microsoft Corporation)

Step 4 Clicking on **Disk** in the left panel shows that here we have one disk drive, a 128-GB internal SSD hard drive. The lower graph shows the history of data moving back and forth to the disk, the disk transfer rate. The larger upper graph shows how active the disk is—what percentage of time it is reading and writing. This system was doing a large file download so the disk usage is 100%. If that is consistently high, upgrading to a faster, larger disk will have a big performance impact. *(Windows 10, Microsoft Corporation)*

Make This > Tool: App Inventor 2

MAKE: A Location-Aware App

Your smartphone comes equipped with a number of built-in sensors that can, for example, read accelerations (to tell if your phone is shaking), location (using GPS satellites), and even atmospheric pressure. App Inventor can work with sensor data and supports a wide set of sensors used in the Lego Mindstorms kits to recognize color or respond to touch and sound.

In this exercise, you'll use the LocationSensor component in App Inventor to combine information about your environment into your apps. *(MIT App Inventor 2)*

The LocationSensor component allows you to work with live GPS data within your mobile app.

For the instructions for this exercise, go to MyITLab.

Evaluating Other Subsystems and Making a Decision

Learning Outcome 6.2 **You will be able to evaluate your system's reliability and decide whether to purchase a new system or upgrade an existing one.**

The audio and video subsystems of your computer affect much of your enjoyment of the machine. Let's evaluate those subsystems and consider what state-of-the-art audio/video would add to your computing experience. Then let's consider how to make sure your system is reliable—nothing interferes with enjoying technology like a misbehaving computer!

 evaluating the
MEDIA SUBSYSTEMS

Enjoying interactive media through your computer demands both good video processing hardware and good audio processing hardware. Video quality depends on two components: your video card and your monitor. If you're considering using your computer to display complex graphics, edit high-definition videos, or play graphics-rich games with a lot of fast action, you may want to consider upgrading your video subsystem. Let's start our look at the media subsystems by examining video cards.

Video Cards

Objective 6.9 *Describe the features of video cards.*

What exactly is a video card? A **video card** (or **video adapter**) is an expansion card that's installed inside the system unit to translate binary data into the images you view on your monitor. Modern video cards like the ones shown in Figure 6.21 let you connect video equipment using a number of different ports:

- *DVI ports* for digital LCD monitors
- *HDMI ports* for high-definition TVs, Blu-ray players, or gaming consoles
- *DisplayPort* for digital monitors or projectors

How much memory does my video card need? All video systems include their own RAM, called **video memory**. Several standards of video memory are available, including graphics double data rate 3 (GDDR3) memory and the newer **graphics double data rate 5 (GDDR5)** memory.

The amount of video memory on your video card makes a big impact on the resolution the system can support and on how smoothly and quickly it can render video. Most new laptop computers come with video cards equipped with a minimum of 1 GB of video memory. For the serious gamer, 2 GB or more is essential, and cards with 8 GB are available. These high-end video cards allow games to generate smoother animations and more sophisticated shading and texture.

FIGURE 6.21 Video cards require their own fan for cooling. They support multiple monitors with multiple styles of ports like HDMI, DVI, and DisplayPort. *(YamabikaY/Shutterstock)*

How can I tell how much memory my video card has? You'll find information about your system's video card in the Advanced Display Settings of the Screen Resolution window. To get to the Screen Resolution window, right-click on your desktop and select Display settings. In the Screen Resolution window, click the Advanced display settings link and then click the Display Adapter Properties link. A dialog box will appear that shows you the type of video card installed in your system, as well as its memory capacity.

How does the CPU handle intensive video calculations? Because displaying graphics demands a lot of computational work from the CPU, video cards come with their own **graphics processing unit (GPU)**. The GPU is a separate processing chip specialized to handle 3-D graphics and image and video processing with incredible efficiency and speed. When the CPU is asked to process graphics, it redirects those tasks to the GPU, significantly speeding up graphics processing. Figure 6.22 shows how the CPU can run much more efficiently when a GPU does all the graphics computations.

FIGURE 6.22 The GPU is specialized to handle processing of photos, videos, and video game images. It frees up the CPU to work on other system demands.

In addition, special lighting effects can be achieved with a modern GPU. Designers can change the type of light, the texture, and the color of objects based on complex interactions. Some GPU designs incorporate dedicated hardware to allow high-definition movies to be decoded or special physics engines to model water, gravity, and rigid body movements.

Why do some people use more than one video card in the same system? For users who are primarily doing text-based work, one video card is certainly enough. Computer gamers and users of high-end visualization software, however, often take advantage of the ability to install more than one video card at a time. Two or even three video cards can be used in one system.

The two major video chip set manufacturers, Nvidia and AMD, have each developed their own standards supporting the combining of multiple video cards. For Nvidia, this standard is named SLI; for AMD, it is called CrossFire X. When the system is running at very high video resolutions, such as 1920 × 1200 or higher, multiple video cards working together provide the ultimate in performance. If you're buying a new system and might be interested in employing multiple video cards, be sure to check whether the motherboard supports SLI or CrossFire X.

Can I run a few monitors from one video card? Working with multiple monitors is useful if you often have more than one application running at a time (see Figure 6.23) or even if you just want to expand your gaming experience. Some video cards can support up to six monitors from a single card. The AMD Radeon graphics cards, for example, let you merge all six monitors to work as one screen or to combine them into any subset—for example, displaying a movie on two combined screens, Excel on one monitor, Word on another, and a browser spread across the final two.

Can I have a 3-D experience from a computer monitor? 3-D panels are available for desktop monitors and for some laptops. Using the 3-D wireless vision glasses included with the panels, the glasses make existing games or 3-D movies display in stereoscopic 3-D.

FIGURE 6.23 AMD Radeon technology supports six monitors, which can be combined in any way. *(Satopon/Fotolia)*

trends in IT

USB 3.1 and USB-C

When the USB standard was introduced, a number of different ports began to fade from use. With USB, one port could be used to connect a keyboard, a mouse, a flash drive, an external hard drive, and a camera. For sure, USB seemed to be the perfect standard.

But as the need for larger file transfers grew with larger HD video files and higher-resolution image files, the USB standard needed to keep improving to offer faster data transfer rates. The USB connector also needed to be redesigned to different sizes so it could be used in phones, cameras, and thinner ultrabooks. This resulted in a collection of USB 1.0, 2.0, and 3.0 devices along with USB 1.0 and 2.0 ports, blue USB 3.0 ports, tiny mini USB ports, and even tinier micro USB ports. And of course, each connector was oriented in a certain way so we found ourselves spinning the cable around to try to find the right orientation to actually fit the connector into the port.

The USB standard faced competition as well, with the Thunderbolt technology appearing on Apple products. Thunderbolt supports fast transfer rates of 10 Gb/s, zooming past the limit of the USB 3.0, which is 4.8 Gb/s. How fast is that? Intel, the company that developed the technology, claims that Thunderbolt can transfer a full-length HD movie in under 30 seconds, or copy in just 10 minutes a library of music that would take a solid year to play through.

USB-C KEY ASPECTS

ENTIRELY NEW DESIGN
Made for Emerging Product Designs

SUPPORTS SCALABLE POWER CHARGING

FUTURE SCALABILITY
Designed to Establish Future USB Needs

USABILITY ENHANCEMENTS
Reversible Plug Orientation and Cable Direction

NEW SMALLER SIZE

FIGURE 6.24 USB-C brings a reversible, durable plug capable of charging with 100 W of power. *(Crystal Eye Studio/Shutterstock)*

Intel used fiber optics—the transmission of digital data through pure glass cable as thin as human hair—to develop Thunderbolt. And Thunderbolt supplies much more power to devices than the USB 3.0 standard allows. It also has a very slim connector design, allowing laptop designers to make their systems even thinner. And Thunderbolt can be used to connect displays!

But now here comes the most recent release of the USB standard, USB 3.1. It addresses all of these issues. The USB 3.1 speed limit matches the 10 Gb/s of Thunderbolt, making it twice as fast as USB 3.0. It also can transfer up to 100 watts of power, compared to just 10 watts for USB 3.0. This means a USB 3.1 port could be used to replace even the power charging port of a laptop. If the USB 3.1 standard is implemented using a USB-C connector, then we have the best of all worlds. The USB-C connector, shown in Figure 6.24, is thin, small, and reversible, so the connector will slide into the port in either up or down orientation.

What will this mean to laptop designers? Apple redesigned its popular MacBook laptop with a radical port layout: a single USB 3.1 C port. The Google Pixel computer still has two of the familiar USB 3.0 ports, but it has added a USB 3.1 C port to each side of the machine (see Figure 6.25). Look for a USB 3.1 C port on your next phone, camera, and laptop!

FIGURE 6.25 The Google Pixel computer has one USB-C port on each side but also includes two USB 3.0 jacks. *(Jeff Chiu/AP Images)*

BITS&BYTES

Wall of Monitors

You may have an old monitor and be working with two monitors side by side, or even a "video wall" of four or more monitors. What if you want to play a video and spread it across all the monitors? The free program VLC will do that for you. Run VLC and load the video. Then select Tools->Effects and Filters->Video Effects->Vout/ Overlay tab, and then check Wall. Set the number of columns and rows, and your video will fill up your monitors!

How do I know if I'm putting too much demand on my video card? If your monitor takes a while to refresh when you're editing photos or playing a graphics-rich game, then the video card could be short on memory or the GPU is being taxed beyond its capacity. You can evaluate this precisely using the software that came with your card. For example, AMD Overdrive software monitors the GPU usage level, the current temperature, and the fan speed.

Review the considerations listed in Figure 6.26 to see if it might be time to upgrade your video card. On a desktop computer, replacing a video card is fairly simple: Just insert the new video card in the correct expansion slot on the motherboard. The video card in a laptop is more difficult to upgrade because the display and keyboard usually have to be removed to replace the video card. Note that some very basic laptop systems have video adapters integrated into the motherboard, so these video cards can't be upgraded.

Sound Cards

Objective 6.10 *Describe the features of sound cards.*

What does the sound card do? For many users, a computer's preinstalled speakers and sound card are adequate. However, if you often use your computer to play games, music, and video, you may want to upgrade your speakers or your sound card. Like a video card, a **sound card** is an expansion card that attaches to the motherboard inside your system unit. A sound card enables the computer to drive the speaker system. Most desktop systems have a separate sound card, although low-end computers often have integrated the job of managing sound onto the motherboard itself.

What does a basic sound card do for me? Many computers ship with a **3-D sound card**. 3-D sound technology is better at convincing the human ear that sound is omnidirectional, meaning that you can't tell from which direction the sound is coming. This tends to produce a fuller,

FIGURE 6.26

Evaluating the Video Card

- How much total **memory** is on the card?
- How many **monitors** can it support?
- Does it have the **ports** you need?
- Is the **GPU** fast enough?
- Video

richer sound than stereo sound. However, 3-D sound is not surround sound.

What is surround sound, then? Surround sound is a type of audio processing that makes the listener experience sound as if it were coming from all directions by using multiple speakers. The current surround-sound standard is from Dolby. There are many formats available, including Dolby Digital EX and Dolby Digital Plus for high-definition audio. Dolby TrueHD is the newest standard. It features high-definition and lossless technology, which means that no information is lost in the compression process.

To create surround sound, another standard, Dolby Digital 7.1, takes digital sound from a medium (such as a Blu-ray disc) and reproduces it in eight channels. Seven channels cover the listening field with placement to the left front, right front, left rear, right rear, and center of the audio stage, as well as two extra speakers to the side, as shown in Figure 6.27. The eighth channel holds extremely low-frequency (LFE) sound data and is sent to a subwoofer, which can be placed anywhere in the room.

The name 7.1 surround indicates that there are seven speakers reproducing the full audio spectrum and one speaker handling just lower frequency bass sounds. There is also a 5.1 surround-sound standard, which has a total of six speakers—one subwoofer, a center speaker, and four speakers for right/left in the front and the back. If you have a larger space or want precise location of sounds, use the newer 7.1 system.

To set up surround-sound on your computer, you need two things:

1. A set of surround-sound speakers and, for the greatest surround-sound experience,

2. A sound card that is Dolby Digital compatible

Evaluating the Media Subsystems   **245**

FIGURE 6.27 Dolby Digital 7.1 surround sound gives you a better quality audio output. *(Dolby Laboratories, Inc.)*

FIGURE 6.28 Sample Home Recording Studio Setup *(Fotolia, Aleksangel/Fotolia, Maksym Yemelyanov/Fotolia, Sashkin/Fotolia, Mariusz Blach/Fotolia, AbsentAnna/Fotolia, Nakov/Fotolia)*

Does it matter what kind of speakers my laptop has? The limited size for speakers in a laptop and the added weight of circuitry to drive them means most people use headphones or ear buds for great audio instead of speakers. However, some laptops have built-in higher-quality speakers, like the Alienware line featuring Klipsch speakers and the HP series offering Beats speakers.

What setup do I need if I want to use my computer for recording my band? You can connect MIDI instruments, high-quality microphones, and recording equipment to your computer through an **audio MIDI interface** box. MIDI is an electronics standard that allows different kinds of electronic instruments to communicate with each other and with computers. The audio interface box attaches to your computer through a USB port and adds jacks for connecting guitars and microphones. You can edit and mix tracks through many different software packages, like Ableton Live or GarageBand. Figure 6.28 shows a simple home recording studio setup.

Figure 6.29 lists the factors to consider when deciding whether your audio subsystem meets your needs. ∎

FIGURE 6.29

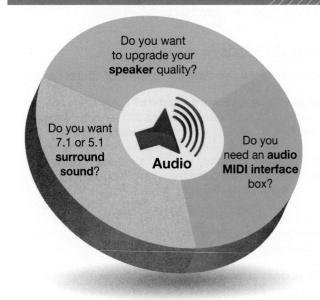

Evaluating the Audio Subsystem

Do you want to upgrade your **speaker** quality?

Do you want 7.1 or 5.1 **surround sound**?

Do you need an **audio MIDI interface** box?

Audio

ACTIVE HELPDESK
Evaluating Computer System Components

In this Active Helpdesk, you'll play the role of a helpdesk staffer, fielding questions about the computer's storage, video, and audio devices and how to evaluate whether they match your needs as well as how to improve the reliability of your system.

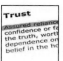

evaluating system reliability
AND MOVING ON

Many computer users decide to buy a new system because they're experiencing problems such as slow performance, freezes, and crashes. Over time, even normal use can cause your computer to build up excess files and to become internally disorganized. This excess, clutter, and disorganization can lead to deteriorating performance or system failure. If you think your system is unreliable, see if the problem is one you can fix before you buy a new machine. Proper upkeep and maintenance also may postpone an expensive system upgrade or replacement.

Maintaining System Reliability

Objective 6.11 *Describe steps you can take to optimize your system's reliability.*

What can I do to ensure my system stays reliable? Here are several procedures you can follow to ensure your system performs reliably (see also Figure 6.30):

- **Install a reliable antivirus package.** Make sure it's set to update itself automatically and to run a full system scan frequently.

- **Run spyware and adware removal programs.** These often detect and remove different pests and should be used in addition to your regular antivirus package.

- **Clear out unnecessary files.** Temporary Internet files can accumulate quickly on your hard drive, taking up unnecessary space. Running the Disk Cleanup utility is a quick and easy way to ensure your temporary Internet files don't take up precious hard drive space. Likewise, you should delete any unnecessary files from your hard drive regularly because they can make your hard drive run more slowly.

- **Run the Disk Defragmenter utility on your hard drive.** When your hard drive becomes fragmented, its storage capacity is negatively affected. When you defragment (defrag) your hard drive, files are reorganized, making the hard drive work more efficiently. But remember that this only makes sense for mechanical drives. With no motors, there is no need to defrag an SSD drive.

- **Automate the key utilities.** The utilities that need to be run more than once, like Disk Cleanup, Disk Defragmenter, and the antivirus, adware, and spyware programs, can be configured to run automatically at any time interval you want. You can use Windows Task Scheduler or third-party programs like Norton Security Suite to set up a sequence of programs to run one after the other every evening while you sleep, so you can wake up each day to a reliable, secure system.

What can I do when my system crashes? Computer systems are complex. It's not unusual to have your system stop responding occasionally. If rebooting the computer doesn't help, you'll need to begin troubleshooting:

1. **If your system isn't responding, try a System Restore.** Windows automatically creates restore points before any major change to the system takes place, such as when you install a new program or change a device driver. You can also click on System and Security and manually create a restore point at any time. You can then select any restore point and bring your system back to the state it was in at that point. Click on Settings and then select Update & Security then Recovery to learn more about System Restore.

FIGURE 6.30

Utilities to Keep Your System Reliable

TO AVOID THIS PROBLEM	USE THIS TOOL	FOR MORE INFO
Your hard drive is running low on space, making it run slowly	Disk Cleanup utility	Chapter 5
Your system is slowing down; browsers or other programs are behaving strangely	Antivirus softwareSpyware and adware removal software	Chapter 9
Files are spread across many spots on the hard drive, making the hard drive run slowly	Disk Defragmenter utility	Chapter 5
System not responding	Windows Refresh	Chapter 5

FIGURE 6.31 Mac's Time Machine keeps copies of files, folders, and libraries and can restore your system back to a previous point in time. *(Screen shot(s) reprinted with permission from Apple, Inc.)*

For Mac systems, the Mac OS X Time Machine, shown in Figure 6.31, provides automatic backup and enables you to look through and restore (if necessary) files, folders, libraries, or the entire system.

2. **If a System Restore wasn't enough to fix the problem, consider a Windows Refresh on your system.** This Windows utility removes all the changes you've made to the system and brings it back to the state it came to you from the factory. It removes all the applications from third-party vendors, but it won't remove personal files like your music, documents, or videos.

3. **Check that you have enough RAM.** You learned how to do this in the "Evaluating the Memory Subsystem" section earlier in this chapter. Systems with insufficient RAM often crash.

4. **If you see an error code in Windows, visit the Microsoft Knowledge Base (support.microsoft.com).** This online resource helps users resolve problems with Microsoft products. For example, it can help you determine what an error code indicates and how you may be able to solve the problem.

5. **Search Google.** If you don't find a satisfactory answer in the Knowledge Base, try copying the entire error message into Google and searching the larger community for solutions.

Can my software affect system reliability? Having the latest version of software makes your system much more reliable. You should upgrade or update your OS, browser software, and application software as often as new patches (or updates) are reported for resolving errors. Sometimes these errors are performance related; sometimes they're potential system security breaches.

If you're having a software problem that can be replicated, use the Steps Recorder to capture the exact steps that lead to it. In Windows, type "ste" in the search box and select the Steps Recorder desk app. Now run the Steps Recorder and go through the exact actions that create the problem you're having. At any particular step, you can click the Add Comment button and add a comment about any part of the screen. The Steps Recorder then produces a documented report, complete with images of your screen and descriptions of each mouse movement you made. You can then e-mail this report to customer support to help technicians resolve the problem.

How do I know whether updates are available for my software? You can configure Windows so that it automatically checks for, downloads, and installs any available updates for itself, the Microsoft Edge browser, and other Microsoft applications such as Microsoft Office. Type "update" in the Windows search bar and select Check for updates in System Settings. Click Advanced options and customize your update strategy.

Many other applications now also include the ability to check for updates. Check under the Help menu of the product, and you'll often find a Check for Updates command.

What if none of this helps? Is buying a new system my only option? If your system is still unreliable after these changes, consider upgrading your OS to the latest version. There are often substantial increases in reliability with a major release of a new OS. However, upgrading the OS may require hardware upgrades such as additional RAM, an updated graphics processor, and even a larger hard drive. The Windows 10 installer automatically checks for any incompatibilities, but the upgrade from Windows 8.1 to Windows 10 has very few changes in hardware requirements.

So is it time to buy a new computer? Now that you've evaluated your computer system, you need to shift to questions of *value*. How close does your system come to meeting your needs? How much would it cost to upgrade your current system to match what you'd ideally like your computer to do, not only today but also a few years from now? How much would it cost to purchase a new system that meets these specifications?

To know whether upgrading or buying a new system would have better value for you, you need to price both scenarios. Conduct a thorough system evaluation (Figure 6.32) to gather the data to help you decide. Purchasing a new system is an important investment of your resources, and you want to make a well-reasoned, well-supported decision.

Getting Rid of Your Old Computer

Objective 6.12 *Discuss how to recycle, donate, or dispose of an older computer.*

What should I do with my old computer? If the result of your system evaluation is that you need a new computer, you are probably thinking with excitement of your next new system. But what can you do with your old machine? You have options. Before you get rid of your computer, be sure to consider what benefit you might obtain by having two systems. Would you have a use for the older system? Would you be able to donate it?

Also, before you decide to throw it away, consider the environmental impact (Figure 6.33). Mercury in LCD screens, cadmium in batteries and circuit boards, and flame retardants in plastic housings all are toxic. An alarming, emerging trend is that discarded machines are beginning to create an e-waste crisis.

FIGURE 6.32

Key Items in System Evaluation

CPU

- What is your CPU usage level?

RAM

- Do you have at least 4 GB?

Storage

- Do you need an SSD drive for fast start-up?
- Do you have a fast-access mechanical drive for large storage space?
- Do you need RAID 0 or RAID 1 storage drives for extra-fast performance or mirroring?

Video

- Do you have enough graphics memory?
- Is your GPU powerful enough?
- Do you have HDMI ports?
- How many monitors do you need to run simultaneously?

Audio

- Do you have 7.1 or 5.1 surround sound?

(Oleksandr Delyk/Fotolia, Hugh Threlfall/Alamy, Nikkytok/Shutterstock, Valdis torms/Fotolia)

So how can I recycle my old computer? Instead of throwing your computer away, you may be able to donate it to a nonprofit organization. Here are a few ways to do this:

- Many manufacturers, such as Dell, offer recycling programs and have formed alliances with nonprofit organizations to help distribute your old technology to those who need it.

- Sites like Computers with Causes (**computerswithcauses .org**) organize donations of both working and nonworking computers, printers, and mice.
- You can also take your computer to an authorized computer-recycling center in your area. The Telecommunications Industry Association provides an e-cycling information site you can use to find a local e-cycling center (**ecyclingcentral.com**).

For companies that need to retire large quantities of computers, the risk of creating an environmental hazard is serious. Firms like GigaBiter (**gigabiter.com**) offer a solution. GigaBiter eliminates security and environmental risks associated with electronic destruction by first delaminating the hard drive and then breaking down the computer e-waste into recyclable products. The result of the final step is a sand-like substance that is 100% recyclable.

Can I donate a computer safely, without worrying about my personal data? Before donating or recycling a computer, make sure you carefully remove all data from your hard drive. Built into Windows is an option to help with this. In the Windows search bar, type Reset and select Reset this PC from System settings. Under Recovery you will have the option to keep or remove your files and then reinstall Windows.

Becoming a victim of identity theft is a serious risk. Credit card numbers, bank information, Social Security numbers, tax records, passwords, and personal identification numbers (PINs) are just some of the types of sensitive information that we casually record to our computers' hard drives. Just deleting files that contain proprietary personal information is not protection enough. Likewise, reformatting or erasing your hard drive does not totally remove data, as was proved by two MIT graduate students. They bought more than 150 used hard drives from various sources. Although some of the hard drives had been reformatted or damaged so that the data was supposedly nonrecoverable, the two students were able to retrieve medical records, financial information, pornography, personal e-mails, and more than 5,000 credit card numbers!

FIGURE 6.33 An electronics garbage dump can cause environmental concerns like the leaching of lead and mercury into the ground.
(Ton Koene/AGE Fotostock)

The open source software movement has flourished over the past decade. In response to increasing prices and the limitations placed on commercially available software, programmers began to donate time to design, develop, and support software systems. These products, like Gimp (a photo-editing tool), were then made freely available.

In the world of hardware, a similar but different approach called the open source hardware movement has flourished. Because hardware projects require materials and tools to assemble, products distributed as open source are not free in terms of cost, but they are free from any restrictions on how you modify them. Inexpensive hardware devices now span the range from the Digispark, a $9 microcontroller the size of a quarter, to the $40 Raspberry Pi, a full Linux-based computer the size of a credit card. Sample open source hardware projects include video game systems, 3-D printers, and even do-it-yourself medical devices.

Is open hardware good for the world? Does it undermine the intellectual property of others who want to create hardware resources and sell them for a profit? What is the impact on developing countries if they have immediate access to hardware designs instead of being required to purchase these items from a for-profit company? Follow the future of open source hardware by keeping an eye on ezines like Make (**makezine .com**), developer and supplier sites like Adafruit (**adafruit.com**), and tutorial headquarters like Instructables (**instructables.com**).

The U.S. Department of Defense suggests a seven-layer overwrite for a "secure erase." This means that you fill your hard drive seven times over with a random series of *1*s and *0*s. Fortunately, several programs exist for doing this. For PCs running Windows, look for utility programs like File Shredder or Eraser. Wipe is available for Linux, and ShredIt X can be used for Mac OS X. These programs provide secure hard drive erasures, either of specific files on your hard drive or of the entire hard drive. ∎

Before moving on to the Chapter Review:
1. Watch Replay Video 6.2 ↻ .
2. Then check your understanding of what you've learned so far.

check your understanding // review & practice

For a quick review to see what you've learned so far, answer the following questions.

multiple choice

1. Dolby Digital 7.1 creates
   a. ultra-sharp high-definition video.
   b. a digital signal from an audio input.
   c. 8-channel surround sound.
   d. 7-channel surround sound.

2. Which is NOT a type of video port?
   a. HDMI
   b. USB 3.1
   c. USB 3.0
   d. DisplayPort

3. When a computer is no longer useful, it can be
   a. securely donated.
   b. recycled.
   c. turned into a sand-like substance.
   d. all of the above

4. To improve video performance, modern computers have a _____ in addition to the CPU.
   a. GPU
   b. VPU
   c. DPU
   d. APU

5. An emerging standard named _____ uses a reversible connector named _____.
   a. USB 3.0 / USB 2.0
   b. USB 3.1 / HDMI
   c. Thunderbolt / DisplayPort
   d. USB 3.1 / USB-C

 Go to **MyITLab** to take an autograded version of the *Check Your Understanding* review and to find all media resources for the chapter.

TECHBYTES WEEKLY
Stay current with the TechBytes Weekly Newsletter.

Continue ⟫

6 Chapter Review

summary //

Evaluating Key Subsystems

Learning Outcome 6.1 **You will be able to evaluate your computer system's hardware functioning.**

Your Ideal Computing Device

Objective 6.1 *Describe the changes in CPU performance over the past several decades.*

- Moore's Law describes the pace at which CPUs improve by holding more transistors. This rule predicts that the number of transistors inside a CPU will double about every two years.

Objective 6.2 *Compare and contrast a variety of computing devices.*

- A huge number of computing choices are on the market, including tablets, ultrabooks, netbooks, 2-in-1s, laptops, and desktops.
- The kind of technology user you are will determine what kind of device you need.

Evaluating the CPU Subsystem

Objective 6.3 *Describe the structure and critical qualities of a CPU.*

- The CPU is composed of two units: the *control unit* and the *arithmetic logic unit (ALU)*. The control unit coordinates the activities of all the other computer components. The ALU is responsible for performing all the arithmetic calculations (addition, subtraction, multiplication, and division). Every time the CPU performs a program instruction, it goes through the same series of steps (a machine cycle): fetch, decode, execute, and store.
- The clock speed of a CPU dictates how many instructions the CPU can process each second.
- A core contains the parts of the CPU required for processing. Modern CPUs have multiple cores.
- Hyperthreading allows two sets of instructions to be run by a single CPU core.
- The CPU's cache memory is a form of RAM that is part of the CPU chip itself so retrieving data is much faster than bringing the data in from the computer's RAM.

Objective 6.4 *Describe tools used to measure and evaluate CPU performance.*

- CPU benchmarks are measurements used to compare performance between processors.
- CPU usage is the percentage of time the CPU is busy doing work.
- On Windows systems, the Task Manager utility lets you access this data.

Evaluating the Memory Subsystem

Objective 6.5 *Discuss how RAM is used in a computer system.*

- Random access memory (RAM) is your computer's temporary storage space. RAM is an example of volatile storage. RAM appears in the system on memory modules. There are several types of RAM, including DDR3 and DDR5.
- Physical memory is the amount of RAM installed in the system.
- The Resource Monitor shows how much memory is in use at any time.

Objective 6.6 *Evaluate whether adding RAM to a system is desirable.*

- Adding RAM is simple to do and relatively inexpensive. However, there is a limit to how much RAM can be installed in a device.

Evaluating the Storage Subsystem

Objective 6.7 *Classify and describe the major types of nonvolatile storage drives.*

- Major types of nonvolatile storage include mechanical hard drives, SSDs, SSHDs, and optical drives.
- Mechanical hard drives are the least expensive and the slowest to access information.
- SSD drives are electronic so they have no moving parts, produce no heat, and are many times faster

than hard drives. However, they are much more expensive.

- An SSHD drive is a combination of both a mechanical hard drive and an SSD into a single device.
- Optical drives, like Blu-ray and DVDs, use a laser to read pits and bumps on plastic discs.

Objective 6.8 *Evaluate the amount and type of storage needed for a system.*

- Your storage needs will depend on the number and types of programs and data you use.
- It may be better to have several drives connected, either in RAID 0 for more speed or in RAID 1 for instantaneous backup protection.

Evaluating Other Subsystems and Making a Decision

Learning Outcome 6.2 **You will be able to evaluate your system's reliability and decide whether to purchase a new system or upgrade an existing one.**

Evaluating the Media Subsystems

Objective 6.9 *Describe the features of video cards.*

- A video card translates binary data into images that are displayed on a monitor.
- A video card has specialized video memory that is very fast. Some systems have multiple video cards for even greater performance.
- A video card has a graphics processing unit (GPU), which helps the CPU by handling the graphics workload.
- One video card can support multiple monitors.

Objective 6.10 *Describe the features of sound cards.*

- A sound card can support 3-D sound as well as surround sound like Dolby 7.1.
- Dolby 7.1 surround sound has one speaker for low frequency tones and seven additional speakers for a full, immersive experience.
- An audio MIDI interface unit allows you to connect musical instruments, microphones, and head-phones to your computer.

Evaluating System Reliability and Moving On

Objective 6.11 *Describe steps you can take to optimize your system's reliability.*

- There are many regular maintenance steps you should take to keep your system reliable. They include using an antivirus program, adware removal software, clearing out unnecessary files, and running a disk defragmenter.

Objective 6.12 *Discuss how to recycle, donate, or dispose of an older computer.*

- A used computer can be recycled through several manufacturers or through nonprofit organizations.
- To safely recycle or donate a computer, you must first remove all applications and personal data. There are options in Windows to help with this.

(MyITLab) Be sure to check out **MyITLab** for additional materials to help you review and learn. And don't forget the Replay Videos ▶ .

key terms //

chapter quiz // assessment

For a quick review to see what you've learned, answer the following questions. Submit the quiz as requested by your instructor. If you are using **MyITLab**, the quiz is also available there.

multiple choice

1. Moore's law refers to the
   a. amount of memory on a memory chip.
   b. overall system processing capability.
   c. number of transistors inside a CPU chip.
   d. speed of DRAM.

2. Which of the following is true?
   a. RAM is where the CPU is located.
   b. Intel is the only manufacturer of CPUs.
   c. The CPU contains the ALU.
   d. The Windows System Properties window tells you how much memory you should buy.

3. Computers are designed with
   a. volatile memory.
   b. nonvolatile memory.
   c. both volatile and nonvolatile memory.
   d. neither volatile nor nonvolatile memory.

4. A good way to assess your CPU usage is to
   a. feel the temperature of the CPU with your hand.
   b. listen for the sound of a spinning hard disk drive.
   c. check the number reported by the system defrag utility.
   d. check the Performance tab of the Task Manager.

5. The video memory in a modern video card is
   a. mechanical.
   b. several gigabytes of GDDR5.
   c. related to the size of the SSD drive.
   d. set by the CPU speed.

6. Windows creates "restore points" so that you can
   a. extend your warranty.
   b. add additional hard disk storage space.
   c. return your system to the way it was before you installed new software.
   d. protect your system from viruses.

true/false

_____ **1.** RAID 1 cuts the time it takes to write a file to disk in half.

_____ **2.** SuperFetch is a memory-management technique that pulls info from your hard drive into SSD.

_____ **3.** In Windows, if you experience unreliable behavior, try a System Restore before doing a Windows Refresh.

_____ **4.** External hard drives are constructed from GDDR5 memory.

critical thinking

1. **Measure Up**

   Briefly describe the way you would evaluate whether the CPU, memory, and storage of your system was meeting your needs. What tools would you need? What operating system programs help you evaluate performance?

2. **A Green Machine**

   Review the impacts on the environment of your computer during its entire lifecycle. How do the production, transportation, and use of the computer affect the increase of greenhouse gas emissions? How does the selection of materials and packaging impact the environment? What restricted substances (like lead, mercury, cadmium, and PVC) are found in your machine? Could substitute materials be used? How would the ultimate "green machine" be designed?

team time //

Many Different Devices for Many Different Needs

Problem

Even within one discipline, there are needs for a variety of types of computing solutions. Consider the Communications Department in a large university. There are some groups involved in video production, some groups producing digital music, and some groups creating scripts.

Process

1. Split the class into teams. Select one segment of the Communications Department that your team will represent: video production, digital music, or scripting. The video production team requires its labs to be able to support the recording, editing, and final production and distribution of digital video. The digital music group wants to establish a recording studio (after the model of the Drexel University recording label, Mad Dragon Records, at **maddragonmusic.com**). The scripting group needs to support a collaborative community of writers and voice-over actors.

2. Analyze the computing needs of that segment, with particular focus on how it needs to outfit its computer labs.

3. Price the systems you would recommend and explain how they will be used. What decisions have you made in order to guarantee they will still be useful in three years?

4. Write a report that summarizes your findings. Document the resources you used and generate as much enthusiasm as you can for your recommendations.

Conclusion

Being able to evaluate a computer system and match it to the current needs of its users is an important skill.

ethics project //

Benchmarking

In this exercise, you'll research and then role-play a complicated ethical situation. The role you play might not match your own personal beliefs; regardless, your research and use of logic will enable you to represent the view assigned. An arbitrator will watch and comment on both sides of the arguments, and together, the team will agree on an ethical solution.

Problem

We've seen that for complex systems like computers, performance often is determined by using benchmarks, software suites that test a full area of performance. The results of these tests become a major force in marketing and selling the product.

There have been a number of claims of unethical conduct in the area of benchmarking. Companies have been accused of using out-of-date testing software to skew their results. Some companies have manipulated the settings on the machine to artificially raise their score (for example, turning off the display before testing for battery life). Some companies make sure the systems sent out to magazines and other evaluators have better-performing components than you might get off the shelf. Where is the line between gaining a competitive edge and lying when it comes to hardware assessment?

Research Areas to Consider

- SysMark 2002
- BAPCo
- MobileMark
- 2009 Nobel Prize for Physics

Process

1. Divide the class into teams. Research the areas cited above from the perspective of either an Intel engineer working on a new CPU, an engineer working on a competing CPU, or a benchmark designer.

2. Team members should write a summary that provides documentation for the positions their character takes around the issue of equitable testing of hardware. Then, team members should create an outline to use during the role-playing event.

3. Team members should present their case to the class or submit a PowerPoint presentation for review, along with the summary they developed.

Conclusion

As technology becomes ever more prevalent and integrated into our lives, more and more ethical dilemmas will present themselves. Being able to understand and evaluate both sides of the argument, while responding in a personally or socially ethical manner, will be an important skill.

Laptop Alternatives

You are in need of a new laptop that is lightweight, but that has enough power to edit the videos you produce for your YouTube channel. You have asked a few of your friends for some suggestions. One friend put together a list of possible computers in an Excel workbook; the other friend created a list as a text file. You will import the text file into the Excel 2016 table, sort the data, then filter the data to display only those computers you are interested in. Using Excel 2016, you will use tables to sort, filter, and display data.

You will use the following skills as you complete this activity:

- Import Data from Text File
- Format as Table
- Sort Data
- Apply Filters
- Change Cell Fill Color

Instructions:

1. Open *TIA_Ch6_Start* and save as **TIA_Ch6_ LastFirst**.

2. Select **cell A30**, then import the text file, *TIA_Ch6_TableText*, accepting all defaults.

   a. Hint: To Import a text file, on the Data tab, in the Get External Data group, click **From Text**. You will end up with 40 rows of data.

3. Format range A1:M41 as a table, with **Table Style Medium 13**. Select **Yes** when asked to convert the selection to a table and remove all external connections.

   a. Hint: To format a range as a table, on the Home tab, in the Styles group, select **Format as Table**, then select the desired style.

4. Sort the data by **Style (A to Z)**, then by **Processor Speed (Largest to Smallest)**, then by **RAM (Largest to Smallest)**.

   a. Hint: To Sort data with multiple levels, on the Data tab, in the Sort & Filter group, click **Sort**, then click **Add level**. Select the desired column in each sort drop down list. Make sure *My data has headers* checkbox is selected.

5. Filter the data to display Ultrabooks with Intel Core i5 processors and Solid-State Drives (SSDs).

   a. Hint: To Filter data, ensure Filter is selected on the Data tab, in the Sort & Filter group. Then click the arrow for each column to be filtered, and then add or delete checkmarks for the desired category.

6. Copy the header row and four rows that display after all filters have been applied. Open a new worksheet, and paste the copied data in cell A1. Rename the new worksheet **Choices**. Click the **Data worksheet**, and press **Esc** to clear the selection.

7. Click the **Choices worksheet**, change the width of columns C, G, H, I, J, K, L to **9**, and change the width of columns D, E, G, and M to **12**. Select **cells A1:M1** and **Wrap Text**.

   a. Hint: To change the width of non-adjacent columns, select the first column heading, then hold down the **Ctrl button** while selecting the remaining column headings. Click **Format** in the Cells group, and then select **Column Width**.

8. Select **cells A3:M3**, and change the Fill Color to **Yellow**.

9. In cell A8, type **The HP Ultrabook is my choice as it has the most RAM, greatest storage capacity, and the best wireless standard of the four choices.**

10. Save the workbook and submit based on your instructor's directions.

7 Networking: Connecting Computing Devices

How Networks Function

Learning Outcome 7.1 **You will be able to explain the basics of networking, including the components needed to create networks, and describe the different ways you can connect networks to the Internet.**

Networking Fundamentals   260

Objective 7.1 *Explain what a network is and the pros and cons of having one.*

👤 **Active Helpdesk:** Understanding Networking

Network Architectures   262

Objective 7.2 *Discuss how networks are defined by distance.*

Objective 7.3 *Discuss how networks are classified by levels of administration.*

Objective 7.4 *Describe the Ethernet protocols for wired and wireless networks.*

Network Components   265

Objective 7.5 *Describe the types of transmission media used in networks.*

Objective 7.6 *Describe the basic devices necessary for networks.*

Objective 7.7 *Describe the type of software necessary for networks.*

Connecting to the Internet   269

Objective 7.8 *Compare and contrast the broadband options available to access the Internet.*

🔊 **Sound Byte:** Connecting to the Internet

Objective 7.9 *Explain how to access the Internet wirelessly.*

👤 **Active Helpdesk:** Connecting to the Internet

Objective 7.10 *Summarize the pros and cons of dial-up connections.*

Your Home Network

Learning Outcome 7.2 **You will be able to describe what you need to install and configure a home network and how to manage and secure a wireless network.**

Installing and Configuring Home Networks   276

Objective 7.11 *Explain steps you should take before creating a home network.*

Objective 7.12 *Describe what you need in order to connect devices to a network.*

🔊 **Sound Byte:** Installing a Home Computer Network

Objective 7.13 *Describe specialized devices you can add to a home network.*

Objective 7.14 *Summarize how to configure home network software.*

Managing and Securing Wireless Networks   285

Objective 7.15 *Describe the potential problems with wireless networks and how to avoid them.*

Objective 7.16 *Describe how to secure a wireless home network.*

🔊 **Sound Byte:** Securing Wireless Networks

Make This: MAKE: Networked Devices on **page 275**

All media accompanying this chapter can be found in MyITLab.

For an overview of the chapter, watch the **Preview Video**.

(Sergey Nivens/Fotolia, Nicotombo/Fotolia, AKS/Fotolia, Vlad Kochelaevskiy/123RF, Hywards/Fotolia, Mipan/Fotolia)

HOW COOL IS THIS?

Many of us have multiple wireless devices but often **no access to WiFi**, or we're too near the limit on our mobile device data plan to do what we want without costing a small fortune. Now, using **Karma WiFi**, you can travel with your own **personal hotspot**, and you can share the connection while **earning more data** as you do. All you need to do is buy a Karma device and set up an account. You get 1 GB of data, which is enough to watch a two-hour movie or listen to eight hours of music. When you've used that up, you can purchase more—no subscription needed. And you can stretch how often you need to buy more data by **sharing your connection**. As others connect to your Karma hotspot, you each earn a free 100 MB. You only share the connection—not your data—so the more you share, the more free bandwidth you accumulate. The benefits of social networking have

How Networks Function

Learning Outcome 7.1 You will be able to explain the basics of networking, including the components needed to create networks, and describe the different ways you can connect networks to the Internet.

You access wired and wireless networks all the time—when you use an ATM, print out a document, or use the Internet (the world's largest network). It's important to understand the fundamentals of networking, such as how networks are set up, what devices are necessary to establish a network, and how you can access a network so that you can share, collaborate, and exchange information among your friends, family, and colleagues.

 networking
FUNDAMENTALS

Many of today's homes have more than one computing device capable of connecting to the Internet. A typical family engages in many activities that involve sharing and accessing files over and from the Internet and using a variety of Internet-connected devices (see Figure 7.1). What makes all this technology transfer and sharing possible? A computer network!

Understanding Networks

Objective 7.1 *Explain what a network is and the pros and cons of having one.*

What exactly is a network? A computer **network** is simply two or more computers that are connected via software

and hardware so they can communicate with each other. Each device connected to a network is referred to as a **node**. A node can be a computer, a peripheral such as a printer or a game console, or a network device such as a router (see Figure 7.2).

What are the benefits of networks? There are several benefits to having computers networked:

- **Sharing an Internet connection:** A network lets you share the high-speed Internet connection coming into your home.

- **Sharing printers and other peripherals:** Networks let you share printers and other peripheral devices. For

Jackie watches a video she took while on vacation.

Andy plays PlayStation online and uploads a video he made for school.

Mom watches a lecture from her online course while she prepares a snack.

Dad watches a streaming movie and checks fantasy football scores on his iPad.

Andrea takes pictures of her dog and uploads them directly to Facebook.

FIGURE 7.1 With a home network, all family members can connect their computing devices whenever and wherever they want.

FIGURE 7.2 File Explorer shows computers, media, and other devices (such as set-top boxes) that are networked for sharing. *(Windows 10, Microsoft Corporation)*

example, say you have a laptop that isn't connected to a printer. To print a document from your laptop without a network, you would need to transfer the file using a flash drive or other device to another computer that's connected to the printer or carry your laptop to the printer and connect your laptop to it. With a network, you can print directly from your device even if it's not physically connected to the printer.

- **Sharing files:** You can share files between networked computers without having to use portable storage devices such as flash drives to transfer the files. In addition, you can set sharing options in Windows or OS X that let the user of each computer on the network access files stored on any other computer on the network.
- **Common communications:** Computers running different operating systems can communicate on the same network.

Are there disadvantages to setting up networks?

Fortunately, after most home networks have been set up, there isn't much else that needs to be done to maintain or administer the network; therefore, the benefits of using a home network outweigh the disadvantages. However, large networks involve an initial purchase of equipment to set them up. They also need to be administered, which can be costly and time consuming. **Network administration** involves tasks such as:

- Installing new computers and devices,
- Monitoring the network to ensure it is performing efficiently,
- Updating and installing new software on the network, and
- Configuring, or setting up, proper security for a network.

How fast does data move through networks? Data transfer rate (also called **bandwidth**) is the maximum speed at which data can be transmitted between two nodes on a network. **Throughput** is the actual speed of data transfer that is achieved. Throughput is always less than or equal to the data transfer rate. Data transfer rate and throughput are usually measured in *megabits per second (Mbps)*. A megabit is one million bits. One of the main factors that determines how fast data moves is the type of network, which we'll discuss later in this chapter. ■

 ACTIVE HELPDESK
Understanding Networking

In this Active Helpdesk, you'll play the role of a helpdesk staffer, fielding questions about home networks—their advantages, their main components, and the most common types—as well as about wireless networks and how they are created.

network
ARCHITECTURES

The network you have in your home differs greatly in terms of its size, structure, and cost from the one on your college campus. This difference is based in part on how the networks are designed or configured. Networks are classified according to:

- The distance between nodes
- The way in which the network is managed (or administered)
- The set of rules (or *protocol*) used to exchange data between network nodes

In this section, we'll look at these network classifications.

Network Architectures Defined by Distance

Objective 7.2 *Discuss how networks are defined by distance.*

How does the distance between nodes define a network? The distance between nodes on a network is one type of **network architecture** or network design. Networks can range from the smallest network of just one person with multiple connected devices to the largest network that spans between cities and even the world. The following are common types of networks (see Figure 7.3):

- A **personal area network (PAN)** is a network used for communication among devices close to one person, such as smartphones and tablets using wireless technologies such as Bluetooth and WiFi.
- A **local area network (LAN)** is a network in which the nodes are located within a small geographic area. Examples include a network in a computer lab at school or at a fast-food restaurant.
- A **home area network (HAN)** is a specific type of LAN located in a home. HANs are used to connect all of a home's digital devices, such as computers, peripherals, phones, gaming devices, digital video recorders (DVRs), and televisions.
- A **metropolitan area network (MAN)** is a large network designed to provide access to a specific geographic area, such as an entire city. Many U.S. cities are now deploying MANs to provide Internet access to residents and tourists. Some MANs employ WiMAX wireless technology that extends local WiFi networks across greater distances.
- A **wide area network (WAN)** spans a large physical distance. The Internet is the largest WAN, covering the globe. A WAN is also a networked collection of LANs. If a school has multiple campuses located in different towns, each with its own LAN, connecting the LANs of each campus by telecommunications lines allows the users of the LANs to communicate. All the connected LANs would be described as a single WAN.

FIGURE 7.3 Networks can be classified by the distance between their nodes.
(SiuWing/Shutterstock)

Network Architectures Defined by Levels of Administration

Objective 7.3 *Discuss how networks are classified by levels of administration.*

How does the level of administration define a network? A network can be administered, or managed, in two main ways—centrally or locally (see Figure 7.4):

• *Central administration*: In a centrally administered network, tasks performed from one computer can affect the other computers on the network. A **client/server network** is an example. In a client/server network, a *client* is a computer on which users accomplish tasks and make requests, whereas the *server* is the computer that provides information or resources to the client computers as well as central administration for network functions such as printing. Most

networks that have 10 or more nodes are client/server networks.

• *Local administration*: In a locally administered network, the configuration and maintenance of the network must be performed on each individual computer attached to the network. A **peer-to-peer (P2P) network** is an example. In a P2P network, each node connected on the network can communicate directly with every other node on the network. Thus, all nodes on this type of network are peers (equals). When printing, for example, a computer on a P2P network doesn't have to go through the computer that's connected to the printer. Instead, it can communicate directly with the printer. Because they're simple to set up, cost less than client/server networks, and are easier to configure and maintain, P2P networks are the most common type of home network. Very small schools and offices may also use P2P networks.

| Client/Server Network | Peer-to-Peer (P2P) Network |

Server

Client

Client

Client

Peer (node)

Peer (node)

Peer (node)

Peer (node)

Peer (node)

FIGURE 7.4 Client/Server and P2P Networks *(Oleksiy Mark/Fotolia, Oleksiy Mark/Fotolia, Sashkin/Fotolia, Maksym Dykha/Fotolia, Oleksiy Mark/Fotolia, Tuulijumala/Fotolia)*

BITS&BYTES

The Rise of Wearable Technology

Wearable technology is, as its name indicates, technology incorporated into things you wear. The devices become a part of your personal area network as they transfer data via Bluetooth to a mobile app or your computer. Popular wearable devices include fitness trackers, such as those from Jawbone and Fitbit, and interactive digital fabrics such as Athos Gear, which have built-in sensors that monitor specific activity as well as your heart rate while you're working out. In addition to health and fitness monitoring, smartwatches such as Apple's iWatch let you connect to your e-mail and calendar, among other personal productivity tools (see Figure 7.5). The medical industry is also implementing wearable devices, such as those to monitor cardiac patients for heart rate and blood pressure. Nearly 50% of American adults already own some form of a wearable device, and the trend is increasing at a remarkable rate. Do you have any wearable technology as a part of your PAN?

FIGURE 7.5 Smartwatches are a form of wearable technology that can monitor your activity and let you connect to personal productivity tools like your e-mail and calendar. *(Guido Mieth/Taxi/Getty Images)*

Ethernet Protocols

Objective 7.4 *Describe the Ethernet protocols for wired and wireless networks.*

What network standard is used in my home network? The vast majority of home and corporate networks are Ethernet networks. An **Ethernet network** is so named because it uses the Ethernet protocol as the means (or standard) by which the nodes on the network communicate.

The Ethernet protocol was developed by the Institute of Electrical and Electronics Engineers (IEEE), which develops many standard specifications for electronic data transmission that are adopted throughout the world. Establishing standards for networking is important so that devices from different manufacturers will work well together.

There are different standards for wired and wireless networks. The standard for wired Ethernet networks is 802.3, also known as **gigabit Ethernet**. The standard for wireless Ethernet networks, also known as **wireless fidelity (WiFi)**, is 802.11. The current version of wireless Ethernet is 802.11ac. Previous versions included 802.11n, 802.11g, 802.11b, and 802.11a.

How is the 802.11ac version different from the previous versions? The newer wireless Ethernet standard, 802.11ac, is faster and has a better signal range than the 802.11n standard. The 802.11n standard, often referred to as *dual band*, operates at either a 2.4 GHz or a 5 GHz frequency. Prior standards operated only at the 2.4 GHz frequency that many other wireless devices (such as wireless landline phones) run on. The 802.11ac standard operates at a 5 GHz frequency. This means the 802.11ac standard is more resistant to signal interference from other wireless devices in the home.

Are there emerging standards? 802.11ad, also known as WiGig, is an upcoming wireless option. WiGig is expected to deliver speeds up to 7 gigabits per second (Gbps) at 60 GHz frequencies but for short distances. It's anticipated that 802.11ac and 802.11ad will work in tandem: 802.11ad providing very fast transmission speeds for a room-sized area—perfect for delivering streaming media or quick data transfers between devices—and 802.11ac for all other wireless transmissions. Two other standards, 802.11af (Super WiFi or White-Fi) and 802.11ah (Low Power WiFi), are being developed to help accommodate the anticipated continued dependence on wireless devices.

Will devices using older WiFi standards still work on a newer network? Devices using older standards, such as 802.11n, will still work with newer 802.11ac networks, but they'll operate with slower data transfer rates and may run into some frequency interference. The ability of current devices to use earlier standards in addition to the current standard is known as **backward compatibility**.

Are there different standards for wired Ethernet? Just as there are different WiFi standards, there are different wired Ethernet standards. The most commonly used wired Ethernet standard for home networks is the gigabit Ethernet standard. A data transfer rate of up to 1 Gbps is possible using this standard. Computers generally ship with gigabit Ethernet cards installed in them.

For even faster data transfer speeds, 10, 40, and even 100 gigabit Ethernet is available, providing maximum data transfer rates of 10, 40, and 100 Gbps, respectively. However, these networks are not currently meant for home use. The 10 and 40 gigabit Ethernet (GbE) are intended for businesses, whereas 100 GbE is used for the major transmission lines of the Internet known as the *Internet backbone*. Cable Internet provider Comcast has begun to test trial markets of 10 gigabit Ethernet for home use. As promising as this may sound, the monthly charge is estimated to be $300, putting it out of reach for many home users. ∎

network
COMPONENTS

To function, all networks must include:

- A means of connecting the nodes on the network (cables or wireless technology)
- Special hardware devices that allow the nodes to communicate with each other and to send data
- Software that allows the network to run (see Figure 7.6)

Transmission Media

Objective 7.5 *Describe the types of transmission media used in networks.*

How do nodes connect to each other? All network nodes are connected to each other and to the network by transmission media. **Transmission media** can be either wired or wireless; they establish a communications channel between the nodes on a network. The media used depend on the requirements of a network and its users.

What transmission media is used on a wired network? Wired networks use various types of cable (wire) to connect nodes (see Figure 7.7). The type of network and the distance between nodes determines the type of cable used:

- **Twisted-pair cable** is made up of copper wires that are twisted around each other and surrounded by a plastic jacket. Normal telephone cable is a type of twisted-pair cable, although phone cable won't work for connecting a LAN or HAN. A slightly different type of twisted-pair cable, called **unshielded twisted-pair (UTP) cable**, is used for networks. UTP is composed of four pairs of wires twisted around each other to reduce electrical interference.
- **Coaxial cable** consists of a single copper wire surrounded by layers of plastic. If you have cable TV, the cable running into your TV or cable box is most likely coaxial cable.
- **Fiber-optic cable** is made up of plastic or glass fibers that transmit data at extremely fast speeds.

What type of cable is used in most wired home networks? The most popular transmission media option for wired Ethernet networks is UTP cable. You can buy UTP cable in varying lengths with Ethernet connectors (called RJ-45

FIGURE 7.6 Network Components *(Ifong/Shutterstock; Sergii Korolko/ Shutterstock; Image reprinted courtesy of Epson America, Inc.; Adrian Lyon/ Alamy; Epsicons/Shutterstock; Norman Chan/Shutterstock)*

FIGURE 7.7

Wired Transmission Media

Twisted-pair cable   **Coaxial cable**   **Fiber-optic cable**

(Deepspacedave/Shutterstock, Zwola Fasola/
Shutterstock, Zentilia/Shutterstock)

connectors) already attached. Ethernet connectors resemble standard phone connectors (called RJ-11 connectors) but are slightly larger and have contacts for eight wires (four pairs) instead of four wires.

Do all wired Ethernet networks use the same kind of UTP cable? The three main types of UTP cable you would consider using in wired Ethernet home networks and their data transfer rates are as follows (also see Figure 7.8):

1. *Cat 5E*: Although Cat 5E cable is the cheapest of the three types and is sufficient for many home networking tasks, it was designed for 100 Mbps–wired Ethernet networks that were popular before gigabit Ethernet networks became the standard. Therefore, you should probably not install Cat 5E cable, even though it's still available in stores.

2. *Cat 6*: Because **Cat 6 cable** is designed to achieve data transfer rates that support a gigabit Ethernet network, it's probably the best choice for home networking cable, though it's more expensive and more difficult to work with than Cat 5E cable.

3. *Cat 6a*: Cat 6a cable is designed for ultrafast Ethernet networks that run at speeds as fast as 10 Gbps. Installing a 10 gigabit Ethernet network in the home is probably unnecessary because today's home applications (even gaming and streaming media) don't require this rate of data transfer.

What transmission media is used to connect nodes on a wireless network? As noted earlier, *WiFi* is a standard for wireless transmissions using radio waves to connect computing devices to wireless networks and the Internet. With so many portable devices being connected to networks, a network with wireless connectivity is used in businesses as well as in most homes. However, note that wireless networks generally have decreased throughput compared with that of wired networks.

Why are wireless networks slower than wired networks? The following are some common reasons why wireless signals may have decreased throughput:

- Wireless signals are more susceptible to interference from magnetic and electrical sources.
- Other wireless networks (such as your neighbor's network) can interfere with the signals on your network.
  - Certain building materials (such as concrete and cinderblock) and metal (such as a refrigerator) can decrease throughput.
  - Throughput varies depending on the distance between your networking equipment.
  - Wireless networks usually use specially coded signals to protect their data, whereas wired connections don't protect their signals. This process of coding signals can slightly decrease throughput, although once coded, data travels at usual speeds.

FIGURE 7.8 The three main UTP cable types used in home networks have different data transfer rates *(Emran/Shutterstock)*

Can I have both wired and wireless nodes on the same network? One network can support nodes with both wireless and wired connections. Most people use wireless connections for portable devices such as laptops. However, many of the devices connected to a network, such as printers and TVs, usually stay in one location. Although these devices probably feature wireless connectivity, hooking them up to wired connections lets you take advantage of the faster throughput achieved by wired connectivity. In situations where you want to achieve the highest possible throughput on your portable device, you may want to use a wired connection temporarily.

Basic Network Hardware

Objective 7.6 *Describe the basic devices necessary for networks.*

What hardware is needed for different nodes on the network to communicate? For the different nodes on a network to communicate with each other and access the network, each node needs a **network adapter**. All desktop and laptop computers as well as smartphones, tablets, and many peripherals sold today contain network adapters installed *inside* the device. This type of integrated network adapter is referred to as a **network interface card (NIC)**. Different NICs are designed to use different types of transmission media. Most NICs included in computing devices today are built to use wireless media, but many can use wired media as well.

What equipment do I need in order to connect to broadband? A broadband Internet connection requires a **modem**. A modem connects your network to the Internet. Depending on the type of broadband service you have, you'll have either a cable modem or a DSL modem. Often, your Internet service provider will rent the appropriate modem to you or specify what type of modem you have

to buy to work properly with the Internet service provider's technology.

What hardware is necessary to share data through a network? Data is sent through a network in bundles called **packets**. For computers to communicate, these packets of data must be able to flow between network nodes. **Network navigation devices**, such as a router or a switch, facilitate and control the flow of data through a network:

- A **router** transfers packets of data between two or more networks. On a home network, you need a router to transfer data between your home network and the Internet, which is considered a separate network. To add WiFi to your home network, you need a router that features wireless capabilities.

- A **switch** acts like a traffic signal on a network (see Figure 7.9). All routers sold for home use have integrated switches. Switches receive data packets and send them to their intended nodes on the same network (not between different networks). During the transmission process, data packets can suffer collisions; subsequently, the data in them is damaged or lost and the network doesn't function efficiently. The switch keeps track of the data packets and, in conjunction with NICs, helps the data packets find their destinations without running into each other. The switch also keeps track of all the nodes on the network and sends the data packets directly to the node for which they're headed. This keeps the network running efficiently.

Where should you place the router on your network? Most modems today have integrated routers, so only one device is needed (see Figure 7.10). The modem/router

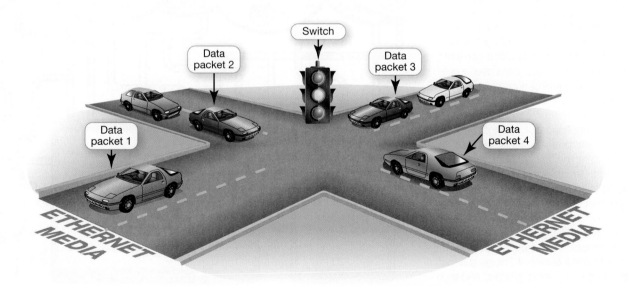

FIGURE 7.9 A simplified explanation of the function of switches is that, together with NICs, they act like traffic signals or traffic cops. They enforce the rules of the data road on an Ethernet network and help prevent data packets from crashing into each other

FIGURE 7.10 A Small Network with a Wired/Wireless Modem/Router Attached *(Beboy/Shutterstock, Laurentiu Iordache/Fotolia, Iko/Shutterstock, Sergey Peterman/Shutterstock, Oleksiy Maksymenko/Alamy)*

should connect directly to the Ethernet cable, and all computer devices—such as laptops, tablets, smartphones, HDTVs, gaming consoles, and printers—are connected to the modem/router via a wired or wireless connection.

Besides computers, what can be connected to a network? The short answer: almost anything. Have you ever heard of the **Internet of Things (IoT)**? It's not a new concept—it has been around since the new millennium. The IoT is defined as the interconnection of uniquely identifiable embedded computing devices that transfer data over a network without requiring human-to-human or human-to-computer interaction (see Figure 7.11). "Things" can be anything— machines, appliances, buildings, vehicles, even animals, people, plants, and soil. In addition to all the "smart" TVs, refrigerators, and thermostats we hear so much about, a thing can be a heart monitor implant that can warn of an oncoming problem or a device in an automobile that monitors driving behaviors so insurance companies can better assess risk. Ultimately, the Internet of Things is about connecting companies, people, and technology in real time via an extension of the Internet into the physical world. By the year 2020, there will be an estimated 50 billion connected devices.

Network Software

Objective 7.7 *Describe the type of software necessary for networks.*

What network software do home networks require? Because home networks are P2P networks, they need operating system software that supports P2P networking. Windows, OS X, and Linux all support P2P networking. You can connect computers running any of these operating systems to the same home network.

Is the same network software used in client/server networks?

As opposed to P2P networks, the nodes on a client/server network don't communicate directly with each other; rather, they communicate through a centralized server. Communicating through a server is more efficient in a network with a large number of nodes, but it requires more complex software than is necessary for P2P networks. Therefore, the servers on client/server networks have specialized **network operating system (NOS)** software installed. This software handles requests for information, Internet access, and the use of peripherals for the rest of the network nodes. Examples of NOS software include Windows Server and SUSE Linux Enterprise Server. ■

FIGURE 7.11 The Internet of Things has resulted in devices—like smoke detectors, dishwashers, and pacemakers—using the Internet more than people do. *(Fotographic1980/ Shutterstock)*

We interact with the Internet of Things (IoT)—knowingly and sometimes unknowingly—on a daily basis in both our professional and personal lives. As we become more connected to the Internet through our vast array of devices, we also become part of the information infrastructure, each of us essentially acting as nodes on the Internet of Things. Although the interconnectivity of the IoT brings with it many benefits, it also poses ethical concerns, including those related to privacy and equal access.

Let's consider privacy issues. As we use our Internet-connected devices, we generate huge amounts of data. Many organizations are acquiring and using that data to help with decision-making, resource allocation, and operations. Although we may be used to having Internet advertisers take our search data and send us targeted advertising, how would you feel about companies using information gleaned from an IoT-connected device? For example, say you wear a fitness tracker, such as a Fitbit or iWatch. The sensors in these activity monitors are connected wirelessly to smartphones and to the Internet to enable users to track their workout activities. How would you feel if the data collected by your Fitbit or iWatch was then shared by your mobile phone carrier with a third-party marketer? How would you feel if you received text messages while you were in a restaurant or grocery store offering discounts or coupons for low-calorie offerings from those third-party marketers, simply because your behavior implied that weight loss is one of your goals? Although some might welcome these opportunities, others might consider the offerings an invasion of their privacy.

The Internet of Things also adds to the ethical dilemma of the digital divide—the technological gap between those who can and cannot afford to own these devices. At the very core of the dilemma is the ability for users to access the Internet at all. Significant work has been done to provide developing countries with access to the Internet. But now, the IoT adds new considerations, not only discriminating against certain groups of people that do not have access to the Internet but also those who cannot afford IoT devices. There have been discussions about providing free nationwide wireless Internet access to bridge this gap, but the creation and delivery of that type of service is complicated and fraught with political and corporate debate, preventing any type of public access anytime soon.

As the Internet of Things continues to grow, we will continue to be faced with not only these issues but certainly others as well. Can you think of other ethical issues the Internet of Things might create?

connecting
TO THE INTERNET

One of the main reasons for setting up a network is to share an Internet connection. Broadband is the preferred way to access the Internet, but in some situations, cellular or dial-up access may be necessary.

Wired Broadband Internet Connections

Objective 7.8 *Compare and contrast the broadband options available to access the Internet.*

What exactly is broadband Internet access? Broadband, often referred to as high-speed Internet, refers to a type of connection that offers a means to connect to the Internet with faster throughput. Broadband has a data transmission rate that ranges from 1 to 500 Mbps. This high rate of access is in contrast to dial-up Internet access, which has a maximum transmission speed of 56 Kbps (kilobits per second). Some businesses and large organizations have a dedicated connection to the Internet, but other businesses and homeowners purchase Internet access from **Internet service providers (ISPs)**. ISPs may

FIGURE 7.12

Comparing Common Wired Broadband Internet Connection Options

BROADBAND TYPE	TRANSMISSION MEDIUM	SPEED CONSIDERATIONS	AVERAGE AND MAXIMUM DOWNLOAD SPEEDS
Cable	Coaxial cable, similar to cable TV wire	Cable connections are shared, so speed can drop during high-usage periods	Average speed of 10 Mbps, with maximum of 30 Mbps
DSL (Digital Subscriber Line)	Copper wire phone line	Speed drops as distance from the main signal source increases	Average speed of 3.7 Mbps, with maximum of 15 Mbps
Fiber-Optic	Strands of optically pure glass or plastic	Transmits data via light signals, which do not degrade over long distances	Average speed of 50 Mbps, with maximum of 500 Mbps

be specialized providers, like Juno, or companies like Comcast that provide additional services, such as phone and cable TV.

What types of broadband are available? As shown in Figure 7.12, the standard wired broadband technologies in most areas are *cable*, *DSL* (*digital subscriber line*), and *fiber-optic service*. *Satellite broadband* is used mostly in rural or mountain areas where DSL, cable, or fiber-optic service is unavailable or very costly.

There are also wireless broadband options. *Mobile broadband* is offered through many cell-phone service providers through 3G and 4G networks. *Wireless Internet* is also available via WiFi radio waves. We'll discuss these options later in the chapter.

How does cable Internet work? Cable Internet is a broadband service that transmits data over the coaxial cables that also transmit cable television signals; however, cable TV and cable Internet are separate services. Cable TV is a one-way service in which the cable company feeds programming signals to your television. To bring two-way Internet connections to homes, cable companies had to upgrade their networks with two-way data-transmission capabilities.

How does DSL work? DSL (digital subscriber line) uses twisted-pair cable, the same as that used for regular telephones, to connect your computer to the Internet. The bandwidth of the wires is split into three sections, like a three-lane highway. One lane is used to carry voice data. DSL uses the remaining two lanes to send and receive data separately at much higher frequencies than voice data. Although DSL uses a standard phone line, having a traditional phone line in your house doesn't mean you have access to

DSL service. Your local phone company must have special DSL technology to offer you the service.

How does fiber-optic service work? Fiber-optic service uses fiber-optic lines, which are strands of optically pure glass or plastic that are as thin as a human hair. They're arranged in bundles called *optical cables* and transmit data via light signals over long distances. Because light travels so quickly, this technology can transmit an enormous amount of data at superfast speeds. When the data reaches your house, it's converted to electrical pulses that transmit digital signals your computer can "read." Note that fiber-optic cable is not usually run *inside* the home. On a fiber-optic network, twisted-pair or coaxial cable is still used inside the home to transport the network signals.

How does satellite Internet work? To take advantage of **satellite Internet**, you need a satellite dish which is placed outside your home and connected to your computer with coaxial cable, the same type of cable used for cable TV. Data from your computer is transmitted between your personal satellite dish and the satellite company's receiving satellite dish by a satellite that sits in geosynchronous orbit thousands of miles above the Earth (see Figure 7.13).

How do I choose which broadband connection option is best for me? Depending on where you live, you might not have a choice of the broadband connection available. Check with your local cable TV provider, phone company, and satellite TV provider(s) to determine what broadband options are available and what the transfer rates are in your area.

Often, the most difficult decision is choosing between high-speed plans offered by the same company. For instance, at the time of printing, Verizon offered several fiber-optic plans that featured download speeds from 25 to 500 Mbps. Although 25 Mbps is fine for everyday browsing, e-mail, and shopping, it may not be fast enough for streaming HD movies or satisfying the needs of multiple devices on the Internet at the same time. Finally, you may also need to consider what other services you want bundled into your payment, such as phone or TV. Consulting with friends and neighbors about the plan they have and whether it's meeting their needs can help you decide on the right plan for you.

SOUND BYTE
Connecting to the Internet

In this Sound Byte, you'll learn the basics of connecting to the Internet from home, including useful information on the various types of Internet connections and selecting the right ISP.

FIGURE 7.13 Internet data is transmitted between your personal satellite dish and the satellite company's receiving satellite dish by a satellite that sits in geosynchronous orbit thousands of miles above Earth. *(Rendeeplumia/Fotolia)*

Wireless Internet Access

Objective 7.9 *Explain how to access the Internet wirelessly.*

How can I access the Internet wirelessly at home? To access the Internet wirelessly at home without relying on your cellular network, you need to establish WiFi on your home network by using a router that features wireless capabilities. You also need the right equipment on your mobile device. Virtually all laptops, smartphones, game systems, and personal media players sold today are WiFi enabled and come with wireless capability built in.

How can I access WiFi when I'm away from home? When you're away from home, you need to find a WiFi hotspot. Many public places, such as libraries, hotels, airports, and fast-food and coffee shops, offer WiFi access. Most locations are free, though a few still charge or require a special password to access the connection. Websites like Wi-Fi-FreeSpot (**wififreespot.com**) or apps such as WiFiGet help you locate a free hotspot wherever you're planning to go. When you have to buy WiFi access, you can pay for a single session or a monthly membership through services such as Boingo (**boingo.com**). Boingo has over 1 million hotspots worldwide, including airports, hotels, and restaurants. Even wireless in-flight Internet service is available. Gogo (**gogoair.com**) is a wireless broadband network that provides coverage on participating airlines across the continental United States.

How can I access the Internet when WiFi isn't available? When you're not in a WiFi hotspot but still need to access the Internet, you may want to consider mobile broadband. **Mobile broadband** connects you to the Internet through the same cellular network that cell phones use to get 3G or 4G Internet access.

3G and 4G can be thought of as "WiFi everywhere" in that they provide Internet access to your mobile devices in the same way they provide voice service to your mobile phone. *3G* and *4G* refer to the third and fourth generations, respectively, of cell-phone networks. **4G** is the latest service standard and offers the fastest data-access speeds over cell-phone networks. To utilize the 3G or 4G capabilities of a mobile device, you need to sign up for an access plan with a mobile data provider such as Verizon or AT&T.

BITS&BYTES

Net Neutrality

If you posted a blog on the Internet or created a new web-based business, it would have the same opportunity of being accessed as a new on-demand movie from Verizon or an online sale at Target. This is because data on the Internet is treated equally. There has been no differentiation by the type of user, the content that is being uploaded, or by the mode of communication. This is the concept of *net neutrality*.

However, big Internet service providers, such as Comcast, Verizon, and Time Warner Cable, would like to change that. In their perfect world, the Internet would be transformed into a tiered structure in which large users that "hog" the Internet, such as Netflix, Google, and Facebook, would have to pay for priority and faster access, whereas smaller users, for whom paying for priority access would be difficult or impossible, would have less priority and slower access. The Internet service providers claim that this type of tiered priority system would promote competition and innovation. Companies like Netflix and Google claim that having to pay for faster access would put small start-ups at a disadvantage and ultimately stifle innovation. In February 2015, the U.S. Federal Communications Commission (FCC) voted in favor of maintaining net neutrality, keeping the Internet open and free—at least for now.

How does mobile broadband Internet compare with wired Internet access? 3G performs similarly to a standard DSL connection (roughly 3 Mbps). According to the standards set for 4G, the data transfer rate you would get while in a moving vehicle is approximately 100 Mbps; from a fixed location, you can expect up to a 1 Gbps data transfer rate. Some of the early 4G systems released in the market support less than the required 1 Gbps rate and are not fully compliant with the 4G standards and so are being tagged as 4G LTE. They are still faster than 3G, however.

How can I get 3G/4G service if my device doesn't have the right equipment? Many devices, such as the iPad, Kindle Fire, Chromebook, and some laptops, are available with built-in 3G or 4G capabilities. If your device doesn't have built-in 3G or 4G equipment, you can connect to the Internet using a **mobile hotspot**. Mobile hotspots let you connect more than one device to the Internet but require access to a data plan. Although you can buy a separate mobile hotspot device, most smartphones have built-in functionality, enabling you to turn your smartphone into a mobile hotspot (see Figure 7.14). If you have several mobile devices that need wireless Internet access, this may be the most economical and functional way to

FIGURE 7.14 You can turn your smartphone into a mobile hotspot. On an iPhone, the feature is in Settings. *(Screen shot(s) reprinted with permission from Apple, Inc.)*

 ACTIVE HELPDESK
Connecting to the Internet

In this Active Helpdesk, you'll play the role of a helpdesk staffer fielding questions about various options for connecting to the Internet.

access the Internet while on the road when you can't access free WiFi.

Dial-Up Connections

Objective 7.10 *Summarize the pros and cons of dial-up connections.*

Why would I ever want to consider a dial-up connection to the Internet? Although about 90% of Internet users in the United States use high-speed Internet connections such as DSL, cable, or fiber-optic, there are still some areas (usually rural) where broadband service isn't available. A dial-up connection needs only a standard phone line and a modem to access the Internet. Therefore, some people choose to use a dial-up connection when there's no high-speed service in their area. Additionally, a dial-up connection is the least costly way to connect to the Internet, so for those who don't use the Internet frequently, the extra cost of broadband may be unnecessary.

What are the disadvantages of dial-up? The major downside to dial-up is speed. Dial-up modems transfer data about 600 times slower than a fiber-optic broadband connection. Also, dial-up uses a traditional phone line to connect to the Internet; therefore, unless you have a separate phone line just for your dial-up connection, when you're using dial-up, you tie up your phone line. ■

Before moving on to Part 2:
1. **Watch Replay Video 7.1** ↻ .
2. **Then check your understanding of what you've learned so far.**

check your understanding // review & practice

For a quick review to see what you've learned so far, answer the following questions.

multiple choice

1. An emerging standard of wireless Ethernet, also known as 802.11ad, is
   a. WiGig.
   b. Low Power WiFi.
   c. White-Fi.
   d. Super WiFi.

2. The type of network used for communication among a laptop and smartphone using Bluetooth is a
   a. WAN.
   b. PAN.
   c. LAN.
   d. MAN.

3. The fastest broadband Internet service is usually
   a. fiber-optic.
   b. DSL.
   c. cable.
   d. satellite.

4. Which of the following allows you to connect to the Internet wirelessly?
   a. WiFi
   b. 4G LTE
   c. mobile hotspot
   d. all of the above

5. The device used to connect a network to the Internet is called a
   a. gateway.
   b. switch.
   c. modem.
   d. router.

(MyITLab) Go to **MyITLab** to take an autograded version of the *Check Your Understanding* review and to find all media resources for the chapter.

TECHBYTES WEEKLY
Stay current with the TechBytes Weekly Newsletter.

Continue 》》

TRY THIS

Testing Your Internet Connection Speed

Your ISP may have promised you certain downloading and uploading data speeds. How can you tell if you're getting what was promised? Numerous sites on the Internet, such as SpeedOf.Me and speedtest.net, test the speed of your Internet connection. You can see how your results compare with others, as well as determine whether you're getting the results promised by your ISP.

Step 1 Type **SpeedOf.Me** in any browser. SpeedOf.Me is an HTML5 Internet speed test, so it will work on PCs, Macs, and Android devices. *(SpeedOf.Me)*

Type SpeedOf.Me in your browser and click Start Test.

Step 2 SpeedOf.Me tests upload and download speeds using sample files of varying sizes, starting with a 128 KB sample until it reaches a sample size that takes more than 8 seconds to upload or download (with the largest possible sample size being 128 MB). The results are based on the last sample file. As the test runs, graphics illustrate the process, with the final results displaying when the test is finished. *(SpeedOf.Me)*

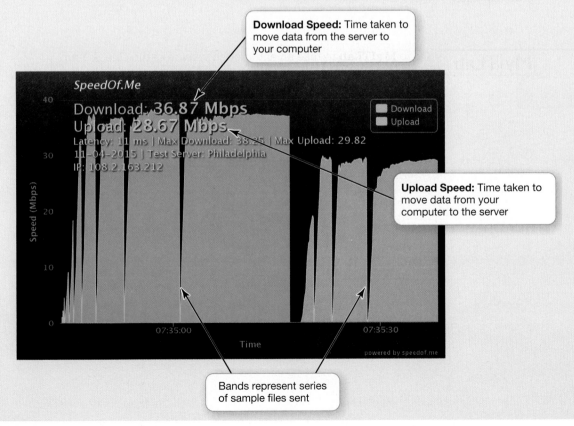

Download Speed: Time taken to move data from the server to your computer

Upload Speed: Time taken to move data from your computer to the server

Bands represent series of sample files sent

Step 3 A history chart displays at the bottom of the screen, showing the results of any tests you have run on that particular device over time. If you want to share your results, you can use the Share button to post them to your favorite social media site or by e-mail.

(SpeedOf.Me)

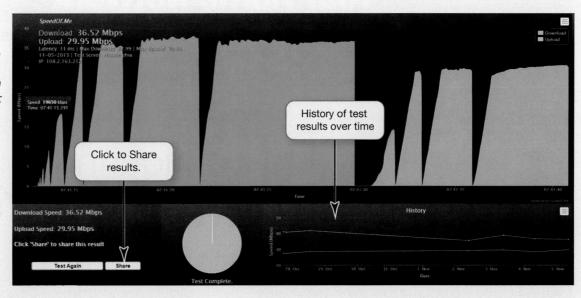

History of test results over time

Click to Share results.

Make This ➤ TOOL: Ping and Telnet

MAKE: Networked Devices

One of the nice features of programming in **App Inventor** is that you can instantly see changes on your target device as you work. The two devices connect using WiFi. But what is going on behind the scenes to allow this?

In this exercise, you'll explore how the AI Companion software works with the AI program to connect your systems. You'll see how useful networking utilities like Ping and Telnet are to investigate how network firewalls are set up.

The App Inventor Companion app and program communicate across WiFi to make your programming easier.

For the instructions for this exercise, go to MyITLab.

Learning Outcome 7.2 You will be able to describe what you need to install and configure a home network and how to manage and secure a wireless network.

You know what a network is and the advantages of having one. In this section, we look at installing or updating a home network and keeping it safe.

installing and configuring
HOME NETWORKS

Now that you understand the basic components of a network and your Internet connection options, you're ready to install a network in your home. If you already have a network in your home, it's useful to examine your network settings and configuration to make sure they're still meeting your needs, especially if you've added new devices.

Only a few years ago, most home networks included just a few computers and a printer. However, a network that can manage those devices is often very different from one that can support the smartphones, gaming consoles, tablets, and smart TVs many homes have added to their networks since. If you're using any of these additional devices and you haven't updated your network equipment or setup in a while, it may be time to do so.

Planning Your Home Network

Objective 7.11 *Explain steps you should take before creating a home network.*

Where do I start? One of the first things you should do to evaluate your network is list all the devices you're using. Consider not only the obvious devices such as computers, laptops, tablets, and printers, but also include smartphones, DVR boxes, smart TVs, wireless stereo equipment, and any other appliance that connects to the Internet wirelessly. You might be surprised at how many devices you list. Then include any devices you think you may add in the near future. Once you have a complete list, determine whether your network is sufficiently up to date to support all your devices.

What wireless Ethernet standard should my network be using? For a home network to run most efficiently and to provide the fastest experience, it's best that all network nodes—computers, network adapters (NICs), routers, and so on—use the latest Ethernet standard. Devices that support the 802.11n standard have been around for a while, so if you've bought a laptop or other portable device in the past few years, it most likely has an 802.11n NIC. Your router may also be supporting the 802.11n standard.

However, many newer devices support the 802.11ac standard. If you have the fastest 802.11ac NIC in your laptop but the router is the slower 802.11n standard, then data will be sent at the speeds supported by the lower standard. If you haven't updated your router in a while, you may want to consider getting an 802.11ac router (see Figure 7.15) to get the fastest connection speeds.

Additionally, the newer standard gives your wireless signal more range, so if you feel that some of your devices aren't connecting properly to the Internet from certain parts of your home, you may want to upgrade to the newer standard.

How can I tell what wireless standard my router supports? You may be able to tell whether your router is supporting the faster 802.11ac standard just by looking at it. Many routers have the wireless standard indicated on the device. If you're still not sure, you can search for more information on your router by entering the model number into a search engine. If your router is provided by your ISP and it's an older standard, you should consider having your ISP provide you with a new router.

FIGURE 7.15 802.11ac wireless routers offer the fastest connection speeds and a greater wireless signal range. *(Photo courtesy of Linksys)*

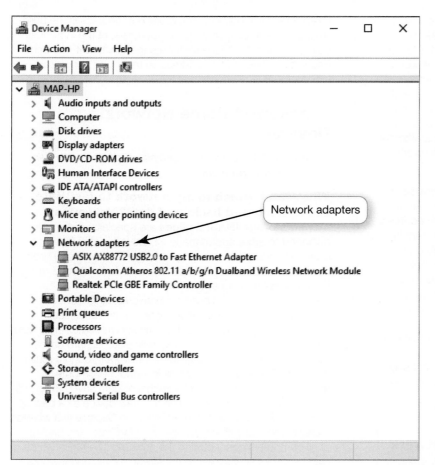

FIGURE 7.16 The Windows Device Manager shows the wireless and wired network adapters installed on a computer. *(Windows 10, Microsoft Corporation)*
>*To access the Device Manager, click* **Settings** *from the Start menu, click* **Devices**, *and then select* **Device manager** *at the bottom of the screen.*

How can I tell what network adapters are installed in my computer? To see which network adapters are installed in your Windows computer, use the Device Manager utility (see Figure 7.16), which lists all the adapters. If you can't tell which wireless standard the adapter supports from the list, search the Internet for information on your specific adapter to determine its capability. The Device Manager can also alert you if there's a problem with the adapter.

Connecting Devices to a Network

Objective 7.12 *Describe what you need in order to connect devices to a network.*

How can I directly connect multiple devices to my router? Most home routers have three or four Ethernet ports on the back to support wired connections. This is usually sufficient for the general house that has at least one computer, maybe a printer, and perhaps some entertainment devices that are connected directly to the router.

Occasionally, you also may want to connect a laptop with a wired connection to increase the bandwidth. If you need

additional ports for plugging in wired connections to your network, you can buy a stand-alone switch and plug it into one of the ports on your router (see Figure 7.17). This will give you additional ports for making wired connections. However, don't mistakenly buy another router with an embedded switch and try adding that to your network. The two routers will cause conflicts as they fight for control over network navigation.

How many wireless devices can connect to a router in a home network? Most home wireless routers can support up to 253 wireless connections at the same time, although most home networks have far fewer. Regardless of how many devices your home network has, they all share bandwidth when they're connected to a router. Therefore, the more devices actively transmitting data that you connect to a single router, the smaller the portion of the router's bandwidth each device receives.

To look at this another way, say you have a pizza that represents your router's bandwidth. You can cut the pizza into six or eight pieces (that is, you can connect either six or eight devices to the network). If you cut the pizza into eight pieces, each person who gets a slice receives a smaller portion than if you had cut the pizza into six pieces. Similarly, when you connect eight devices to the network, each device has less bandwidth than it would if only six devices were connected to the network.

Are wireless routers for Windows and OS X networks different? All routers that support the 802.11n standard and the newer 802.11ac standard should work with computers running the more recent versions of Windows or OS X. However, Apple has designed routers

Router

Switch

FIGURE 7.17 You can add ports to your network by connecting a switch to your router. *(Alarich/Shutterstock, Lexan/ Shutterstock)*

that are optimized for working with Apple computers. So if you're connecting Apple computers to your network, you may want to use the Apple AirPort Extreme router for larger home networks or the AirPort Express for smaller networks. Windows devices can also connect to an AirPort router, so it's a great choice for households with both Apples and PCs. The AirPort Extreme uses the newest 802.11ac technology for the fastest data transfers. In addition, it offers the option of creating a guest network, which can use a different password or no password at all, keeping all your networked devices and files secure.

How do I know what's connected to my router?

To determine what's connected to your router, you need to log in to an account associated with your router's IP address. You can find your router's IP address on the router manufacturer's website. Once you know it, type it into a web browser. You may need to enter a user name and password, but eventually you'll get to a configuration page that lists what wired and wireless devices are in your network. You may be surprised at all the various devices associated with your network.

Figure 7.18 shows a router network listing with wired (desktop computer) and wireless (DVR, laptop, iPhone, and iPad) devices connected in a home network. You'll notice that each device also has an IP address. You can think of your network

FIGURE 7.18 Wired and wireless connections can use the same router. *(Mary Anne Poatsy)*

as an apartment building. The router's IP address is the building's street address, while the IP addresses of the individual devices connected to the router are the apartment numbers. Each device needs an IP address so the router knows to which device to send information.

Specialized Home Networking Devices

Objective 7.13 *Describe specialized devices you can add to a home network.*

What can I attach to my network to facilitate file sharing and backup of data? Network-attached storage (NAS) devices

are specialized devices designed to store and manage all network data. Although data can always be stored on individual hard drives in computers on a network, NAS devices provide for centralized data storage and access.

Popular for years on business networks, NAS devices are now being widely marketed for home networks (see Figure 7.19). You can think of them as specialized external hard drives (many of them actually resemble external hard drives). NAS devices connect directly to the network through a router or switch. Specialized software is installed on computers attached to the network to ensure that all data saved to an individual computer is also stored on the NAS device as a backup.

For Apple computers, the AirPort Time Capsule is a wireless router combined with a hard drive that facilitates the backup of all computers connected to the network. The AirPort Time Capsule looks very similar to the AirPort router, and it works in conjunction with the Time Machine backup feature of OS X. If you buy an AirPort Time Capsule, you won't need to buy an AirPort router (or other router) because the AirPort Time Capsule also fulfills this function on your network. When the AirPort Time Capsule is installed on your network, Macs connected to the network will ask the user if they want to use the AirPort Time Capsule as their source for Time Machine backups. The AirPort Time Capsule is another type of NAS device.

FIGURE 7.19 A network-attached storage device provides centralized data storage and access. *(Alamy)*

BITS&BYTES

Mesh Networks: An Emerging Alternative

Have you ever heard of a *mesh network*? This emerging technology uses small radio transmitters instead of wireless routers as its network nodes. What is so great about mesh networks is that only one node needs to physically connect to a network connection, and then all other nodes can share wirelessly with each other. This connection sharing between nodes can extend almost endlessly, since one wired node can share its Internet connection wirelessly with other nearby nodes, and then those nodes can share their connection wirelessly with nodes closest to them—thus creating a "mesh" of connectivity. The truly wireless aspect of mesh networks poses several advantages to the wireless networks that are in place today: they are easier to install because fewer wires need to be run; they can accommodate more nodes; and they enable wireless networks to be created in outdoor and unstructured venues.

In developing nations as well as in some areas in the United States, mesh networks have helped provide access to the Internet in a more timely and inexpensive manner than waiting for the physical connections to be established. Mesh networks can also help promote cellular communications during times of disasters when traditional communications are halted. And if you have an Android mobile phone, you can participate in the Serval Mesh, which allows users to send and receive information without depending on established cellular networks.

Besides external hard drives, are there other NAS devices I could use on my network? A more sophisticated type of NAS device is a home network server. **Home network servers** are specialized devices designed to store files, share files across the network, and back up files on computers connected to the network. All computers connected to the network can access the server.

Home network servers often look like oversized external hard drives. They are configured with operating systems like Windows Server and connect directly as a node on your network. Home servers have more sophisticated functionality than NAS devices and often handle the following tasks:

- Automatically back up all computers connected to the network
- Act as a repository for files to be shared across the network
- Function as an access gateway to allow any computer on the network to be accessed from a remote location via the Internet (see Figure 7.20)

Note that even though these devices are servers, they don't convert a home P2P network into a client/server network because these servers don't perform all the functions performed on client/server networks. Also note that you can access the media stored on your Windows Server computer through your Xbox One as long as the Xbox is also connected to your home network.

What kinds of digital entertainment devices can connect directly to the network? A **network-ready device** (or Internet-ready device) can be connected directly to a network, either through a wired or wireless connection. Most game consoles, Blu-ray players, and DVRs, as well as many televisions (smart TVs) and home theater systems, are network ready. A device that is not network ready requires that the device be connected directly to another computer via a cable on the network.

Why should I connect digital entertainment devices to my network? One reason for connecting entertainment devices to your network is to access and share digital content between devices on your network. Connecting these devices to your network also connects them to the Internet so you can access a lot of entertainment content, including movies, videos, and music available online.

You can also use gaming devices to play multiplayer games with players in the next room or all over the world. The content you access is either downloaded or streamed to your devices. Newer smart TVs and other smart devices (such as Blu-ray players, game consoles, and home theater systems) are continually adding apps and video services so that you can play games, view on-demand and online videos, listen to Internet radio, and access social networking sites (see Figure 7.21). Some smart devices also feature an integrated web browser that lets you access the web directly, without the use of apps.

What if I don't have a smart TV? You can get the same services on your existing television by using a Blu-ray player that features integrated wireless connectivity to receive streaming media from various ISPs. For best video viewing, look for a Blu-ray player that has high-definition resolution and the capability to display 3D video. Some set-top boxes also provide the same types of connectivity as a Blu-ray player. Alternatively, you can use devices such as Apple TV or Google Chromecast that enable you to send Internet-based media to your traditional TV.

FIGURE 7.20 Home network servers are often configured with software such as Windows Server. *(Windows 8.1, Microsoft Corporation)*

Why should I connect my gaming consoles to my home network? Current gaming systems, like the PlayStation 4 (PS4), can function as a total entertainment platform when connected to the Internet through your network. The PS4 has a built-in Blu-ray drive and can play Blu-ray discs, DVDs, and music files. You can download movies, games, and videos from the Internet directly to the PS4. You can also use it to share media across your network and to import photos or video from cameras and phones.

If you have a PS Vita, you can use an application called Remote Play (see Figure 7.22) to access features of your PS4 from your Vita. You can use the Vita to turn your PS4 on and off; access photos, music, and video files; play games; and browse the Internet. Media is transmitted from your PS4 and displayed on the Vita screen.

How can I use my home network to enhance my home security? Monitoring cameras, both for indoor and outdoor use, are now available for the home that feature wireless connectivity so you can keep track of your home while you're away. You can connect these cameras to your network and monitor them in real time through software and portable devices such as an iPhone or Android phone (see Figure 7.23).

The software can be configured to alert you via e-mail or text message when the cameras detect movement, such as a vehicle entering your driveway. Some systems also allow you to receive alerts when there is a lack of movement. This can be useful for monitoring an aging relative or for monitoring the arrival of children coming home from school.

As time goes on, many more types of entertainment devices and home gadgets will be connected to be part of your smart home.

FIGURE 7.21 Smart TVs have their own apps and let you directly access the web. *(Robert Daly/Getty Images)*

FIGURE 7.22 The Remote Play feature of the PS Vita lets you access PS4 features directly from your Vita. *(Kyodo/AP Images)*

FIGURE 7.23 Many security systems can help you monitor your home's security from your mobile devices. *(Denys Prykhodov/Fotolia)*

Configuring Software for Your Home Network

Objective 7.14 *Summarize how to configure home network software.*

How do I set up a Windows home network for the first time? In Windows, the process of setting up a network is fairly automated, especially if you're using the same version of Windows on all your computers. The Windows examples in

this section assume all computers are running Windows 10. Before configuring the computers to the network, do the following:

1. Make sure there are network adapters on each node.
2. For any wired connections, plug all the cables into the router, nodes, and so on.
3. Make sure your broadband modem is connected to your router and that the modem is connected to the Internet.
4. Turn on your equipment in the following order (allowing the modem and the router about one minute each to power up) and configure:
   a. Your broadband modem
   b. Your router
   c. All computers and peripherals (printers, scanners, and so on)

You can add other devices, such as TVs, Blu-ray players, and gaming consoles, to the network after you configure the computers.

After you've completed the previous steps, launch the Windows network setup wizards from the Network and Sharing Center, which you access via the Network & Internet group in Settings (see Figure 7.24):

- If your computer has a wired connection to the network, you should automatically be connected. You should give the network the same secured name you give to your router (see the *Troubleshooting Wireless Network Problems* section in this chapter).

- If you're connecting wirelessly, ensure that your WiFi is turned on by selecting Wi-Fi in the Network & Internet group in Settings. Then, from the Notification area on the taskbar, click Internet access. A panel opens, displaying the wired and wireless connection options. You will need to enter your security passphrase to connect to your wireless network initially.

How do I share files with other computers on my network? For ease of file and peripheral sharing, Windows has the *HomeGroup* feature. The HomeGroup is a software device that makes it easier to allow computers on a Windows network to share peripherals and information. To create a homegroup after connecting your first Windows computer to your network, complete the steps outlined in Figure 7.25.

What if I don't have the same version of Windows on all my computers? Computers with various versions of Windows can coexist on the same network. Always set up the computers running the newest version of Windows first. Then consult the Microsoft website for guidance on how to configure computers with previous versions of Windows.

How do I connect a mobile device to a wireless network? Connecting a mobile device, regardless of its operating system, to a wireless network is an easy process

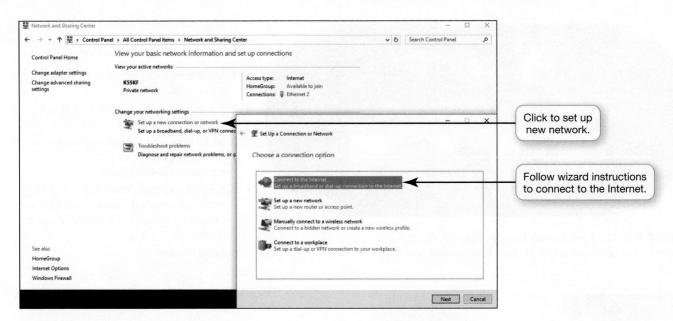

FIGURE 7.24 Connecting a Windows 10 computer to a network for the first time is fairly automated.
(Windows 10, Microsoft Corporation)

these days. When you boot up your device, your device will display a list of available networks that the NIC in your device detects. On Macs, the list pops up in the network login screen. On Windows devices, you can click on the Internet access icon in the system tray to display available networks. If there is a padlock icon next to the network name, this means that the network is secure and will require a password. Enter the password for the network in the password box, and click the Join button. For unsecure networks, you don't need a password. Checking the "Remember this network" check box will make any network a preferred network, enabling the computer to connect to the network automatically when that network is available. You can have multiple preferred networks, such as your home, school, work, and local coffee shop networks. ▪

BITS&BYTES

Analyzing Network Problems

If you have areas in your home where you have little or no WiFi coverage, try using a WiFi analyzer to gather information before embarking on ways to improve your coverage. There are free apps such as WiFi Analyzer (Android) or Wi-Fi Inspector (Windows) that provide signal strength and other details that will be helpful in remedying the problem.

FIGURE 7.25

Creating a HomeGroup in Windows

Step 1: Open Network & Internet from Settings, then click Home-Group. In the HomeGroup dialog box, click Create a homegroup.

Step 2: Choose the sharing options for computers that belong to the homegroup. You can choose to share pictures, music, videos, documents, and printers and other devices with other Windows computers that belong to the homegroup. Although these are global settings for every computer in the homegroup, you can change these settings on individual computers if you wish.

Step 3: Windows generates a password. All other computers added to the network will need this password to join the homegroup. Once you've created the homegroup on the first computer, it will belong to that homegroup. You can then begin connecting other Windows computers to the network and join them to the homegroup you created.

(Windows 10, Microsoft Corporation)

Although once thought of as a futuristic way of life, the automated home depicted in the Jetsons TV show and science fiction movies is emerging and may soon become the new normal (see Figure 7.26). The concept of a **smart home**—where devices and appliances are automated or controlled by apps installed on your smartphone or tablet—is in full play today, thanks (in part) to the power and availability of strong wireless networks and other forms of connectivity.

How do smart homes work? With smart home automation, you can dictate how and when a device should engage or respond. For some devices and appliances, all you need to do is set a schedule and the rest is automated. Other devices and appliances work using some type of sensor and react to changes in their surrounding environment, such as motion, light, or temperature. For example, some smart home thermostats learn your habits (such as waking and sleeping patterns) and heating and cooling preferences over time and create automatic settings. Some smart home draperies and blinds open and close in reaction to the timing of sunrise and sunset using geolocation settings.

Smart home automation can also alert you to unpredictable events such as water leaks and unexpected visitors to your home. But smart home technology isn't only about security and efficiency. It's also used to help control your entertainment devices as well. Altogether, smart home devices are intended to provide convenience, control, money savings, and an overall smarter home.

At the heart of many smart homes are hubs that are used to control a variety of devices from different manufacturers. A good hub, like a UN translator, receives the different wireless signals from smart devices and then translates those into one WiFi signal that your router can understand. In addition, the hub consolidates the controls required by each device and provides one single app for you to interact with, thus simplifying your experience. Other hubs, such as the Belkin WeMo, have smaller ambitions. Plug a device (e.g., a lamp or coffee maker) into the WeMo and you can control it from your phone or tablet. An alternative to a hub is getting a single home automation platform such as those offered by Google, Microsoft, Lowe's, and AT&T.

If you're really into controlling things yourself, you can use the IFTTT (If This Then That) app (**IFTTT.com**). All you need is the right device (such as a WeMo motion detector, Nest thermostat, or Philips lightbulb) and you can create your own Do Recipe, such as setting the temperature of your home at the press of a button on your phone.

Although smart homes offer numerous benefits, as of yet, no single standard has been adopted for home automation. Some devices work on WiFi, others work on Bluetooth. Some smart devices interact with apps on mobile devices, whereas others interact with each other directly. There have been some attempts at single platforms, such as Google's Android@ Home platform and Microsoft's Home 2.0 program, but neither of these programs, nor anything else, has yet to take off. Also, while costs have come down significantly on many smart home devices, the overall cost is not completely affordable to most, especially as a complete smart home solution.

Still, the smart home technology industry is estimated to increase to $44 billion by 2017. Most likely the smart home is here to stay.

FIGURE 7.26 You can remotely monitor your home with smart home technology. *(A-image/Shutterstock)*

managing and securing
WIRELESS NETWORKS

All networks require some maintenance and management, but there are some situations that are particular to wireless networks. In addition, wireless networks require additional security measures. In this section, we'll look at how to troubleshoot typical wireless network problems and how to protect wireless networks from common security threats.

Troubleshooting Wireless Network Problems

Objective 7.15 *Describe the potential problems with wireless networks and how to avoid them.*

What types of problems can I run into when installing wireless networks? The maximum range of 802.11n or 802.11ac wireless devices is about 350 feet. But as you go farther away from your router, the throughput you achieve decreases. Obstacles between wireless nodes also decrease throughput. Walls, floors, and large metal objects (such as refrigerators) are the most common sources of interference with wireless signals.

What if a node on the network seems slow? Repositioning the node within the same room (sometimes even just a few inches from the original position) can affect communication between nodes. If this doesn't work, move the device closer to the router or to another room in your house. If these solutions don't work, consider upgrading to an ac router or adding a wireless range extender to your network.

What's a wireless range extender? A **wireless range extender** is a device that amplifies your wireless signal to extend to parts of your home that are experiencing poor connectivity. For example, as shown in Figure 7.27, Laptop C on the back porch can't connect to the wireless network, even though Computer B in the den can. By placing a range extender in the den, where there is still good connectivity to the wireless network, the wireless signal is amplified and beamed farther out to the back porch. This allows Laptop C to make a good connection to the network.

Securing Wireless Networks

Objective 7.16 *Describe how to secure a wireless home network.*

Why is a wireless network more vulnerable than a wired network? All computers that connect to the Internet, whether or not they're on a network, need to be secured from intruders. This is usually accomplished by using a firewall, which is a hardware or software solution that helps shield your network from prying eyes. (We discuss firewalls at length in Chapter 9.) Wireless networks present special vulnerabilities; therefore, you should take additional steps to keep your wireless network safe.

With a wired network, it's fairly easy to tell if a hacker, someone who breaks into computer systems to create mischief or steal information, is using your network. However, the newer wireless 802.11 networks have wide ranges that may

| Bedroom | Den | Back Porch |

Wireless router

Wireless range extender

Computer A with wireless network adapter

Computer B with wireless range extender

Laptop C with wireless network adapter

FIGURE 7.27 Because a wireless range extender is installed in the den, Laptop C on the back porch can now connect to the wireless network.

extend outside your house. This makes it possible for a hacker to access your network without your knowledge.

Also, in some areas where residences are close together, wireless signals can reach a neighbor's residence. Most wireless network adapters are set up to access the strongest wireless network signal detected. **Piggybacking** is connecting to a wireless network without the permission of the owner. This practice is illegal in many jurisdictions but often happens inadvertently between neighbors.

Why should I be worried about someone logging onto my wireless network without my permission? If your neighbor is using your network connection, his or her usage could be slowing down your connection speed. Some neighbors might even be computer savvy enough to penetrate your unprotected wireless network and steal personal information, just as any other hacker would. And any cyberattack or illegal behavior a hacker initiates from your wireless network could get you in trouble with the authorities.

How is my wireless network vulnerable? Packets of information on a wireless network are broadcast through the airwaves. Savvy hackers can intercept and decode information from your transmissions that may allow them to bypass standard protections, such as a firewall, that you have set up on your network. Therefore, to secure a wireless network, take the additional precautions described in the Sound Byte "Securing Wireless Networks" and summarized as follows:

1. **Change your network name (SSID).** Each wireless network has its own name to identify it, known as the **service set identifier (SSID)**. Unless you change this name when you set up your router, the router uses a default network name that all routers from that manufacturer use (such as "Wireless" or "Netgear"). Hackers know the default names and access codes for routers. If you haven't changed the SSID, it's advertising the fact that you probably haven't changed any of the other default settings for your router either.

2. **Disable SSID broadcast.** Most routers are set up to broadcast their SSIDs so that other wireless devices can find them. If your router supports disabling SSID broadcasting, turn it off. This makes it more difficult for a hacker to detect your network and nearly impossible for a neighbor to inadvertently connect to your network.

3. **Change the default password on your router.** Routers have default user names and passwords. Hackers can use these to access your router and break into your network. Change the password on your router to something hard to guess. Use at least twelve characters that are a combination of letters, symbols, and numbers.

4. **Turn on security protocols.** Most routers ship with security protocols such as Wired Equivalent Privacy (WEP) or Wi-Fi Protected Access (WPA). Both use encryption (a method of translating your data into code) to protect data in your wireless transmissions. WPA is a much stronger protocol than WEP, so enable WPA if you have it; enable WEP if you don't.

5. **Create a passphrase.** When you enable these protocols, you're forced to create a security encryption key (passphrase). When you attempt to connect a node to a security-enabled network for the first time, you're required to enter the security key. The security key or passphrase (see Figure 7.28) is the code that computers on your network need to decrypt (decode) data transmissions. Without this key, it's extremely difficult, if not impossible, to decrypt the data transmissions from your network. The Windows 10 Networks panel shows all wireless networks within range. Moving your cursor over the network name will reveal details about the network such as whether it's a secured network. Clicking on a network name allows you to connect to it or prompts you for more information such as the SSID name and security key.

6. **Implement media access control.** Each network adapter on your network has a unique number (like a serial number) assigned to it by the manufacturer. This is called a media access control (MAC) address, and it's a number printed right on the network adapter. Many routers allow you to restrict access to the network to only certain MAC addresses. This helps ensure that only authorized devices can connect to your network.

7. **Limit your signal range.** Many routers allow you to adjust the transmitting power to low, medium, or high. Cutting down the power to low or medium could prevent your signal from reaching too far away from your home, making it tougher for interlopers to poach your signal.

8. **Apply firmware upgrades.** Your router has read-only memory that has software written to it. This software is known as **firmware**. As bugs are found in the firmware (which hackers might exploit), manufacturers issue patches, just as the makers of operating system software do. Periodically check the manufacturer's website and apply any necessary upgrades to your firmware.

If you follow these steps, you'll greatly improve the security of your wireless network. In Chapter 9, we'll explore many other ways to keep your computer safe from malicious individuals on the Internet and ensure that your digital information is secure. ■

SOUND BYTE
Securing Wireless Networks

In this Sound Byte, you'll learn some simple steps to secure your wireless network against intruders.

Before moving on to the Chapter Review:
1. **Watch Replay Video 7.2** .
2. **Then check your understanding of what you've learned so far.**

FIGURE 7.28 By accessing your router, you can configure the security protocols available on your router and change the SSID.

(Firefox logo® is a registered trademark of the Mozilla Foundation)

check your understanding // review & practice

For a quick review to see what you've learned so far, answer the following questions.

multiple choice

1. What would you use to see what network adapters are installed in your Windows computer?

   a. Device Manager utility

   b. Programs and Utilities manager

   c. Ethernet Manager utility

   d. Home Network manager

2. What device would you use to amplify your wireless signal?

   a. dual-band N router

   b. network extender device

   c. network access switch

   d. wireless range extender

3. Why would you want to disable SSID broadcast?

   a. to make it more difficult for hackers to detect your network

   b. to make it difficult for a neighbor to connect to your network

   c. both A and B

   d. neither A or B

4. To share files between computers on a Windows home network, you must

   a. enable groupsharing.

   b. create a homegroup.

   c. enable Windows sharing.

   d. none of the above

5. How can you tell what wireless devices are connected to your router?

   a. Look at the router itself.

   b. Look at the device's wireless settings.

   c. Log in to the router's IP address and check the configuration page.

   d. all of the above

 Go to **MyITLab** to take an autograded version of the *Check Your Understanding* review and to find all media resources for the chapter.

TECHBYTES WEEKLY
Stay current with the TechBytes Weekly Newsletter.

Continue

7 Chapter Review

summary //

How Networks Function

Learning Outcome 7.1 **You will be able to explain the basics of networking, including components needed to create a network, and describe the different ways a network can connect to the Internet.**

Networking Fundamentals

Objective 7.1 *Explain what a network is and the pros and cons of networks.*

- A computer network is simply two or more computers that are connected using software and hardware so they can communicate.
- Advantages of networks include allowing users to share an Internet connection, share printers and other peripheral devices, share files, and communicate with computers regardless of their operating system.
- Disadvantages for larger networks are that they require administration and that they may require costly equipment.

Network Architectures

Objective 7.2 *Discuss how networks are defined by distance.*

- Networks can be defined by the distance between nodes:
- A personal area network (PAN) is used for communication among personal mobile devices using Bluetooth or WiFi wireless technologies.
- A local area network (LAN) connects nodes that are located in a small geographic area.
- A home area network (HAN) is a specific type of LAN located in a home.
- A metropolitan area network (MAN) is a large network in a specific geographic area.
- A wide area network (WAN) spans a large physical distance.

Objective 7.3 *Discuss how networks are classified by levels of administration.*

- *Central*: A client/server network contains two types of computers: a client computer on which users perform specific tasks and a server computer that provides resources to the clients and central control for the network. Most networks that have 10 or more nodes are client/server networks.

- *Local*: Peer-to-peer (P2P) networks enable each node connected to the network to communicate directly with every other node. Most home networks are P2P networks.

Objective 7.4 *Describe the Ethernet protocols for wired and wireless networks.*

- Ethernet networks are the most common networks used in home networking.
- Most Ethernet networks use a combination of wired and wireless connections, depending on the data throughput required. Wired connections usually achieve higher throughput than wireless connections.
- Wired Ethernet home networks use the gigabit Ethernet standard.
- Wireless Ethernet networks are identified by a protocol standard: 802.11a/b/g/n/ac. 802.11ac is the newest standard. WiGig (802.11ad) is a new wireless link between devices. WiGig is similar to but faster than Bluetooth.

Network Components

Objective 7.5 *Describe the types of transmission media used in networks.*

- Wired networks use various types of cable to connect nodes, including twisted-pair cable, coaxial cable, and fiber-optic cable. The type of network and the distance between the nodes determines the type of cable used.
- Wireless networks use radio waves.

Objective 7.6 *Describe the basic devices necessary for networks.*

- All devices must have a network adapter. All devices sold today contain an integrated network interface card.
- Network navigation devices, such as routers and switches, are necessary for computers to communicate in a network.

Objective 7.7 *Describe the type of software necessary for networks.*

- Home networks need operating system software that supports peer-to-peer networking. Windows, OS X, and Linux all support P2P networking.
- Servers on client/server networks use network operating systems (NOS).

Connecting to the Internet

Objective 7.8 *Summarize the broadband options available to access the Internet.*

- Broadband connections include the following types:
- Cable transmits data over coaxial cable, which is also used for cable television.
- DSL uses twisted-pair wire, similar to that used for telephones.

- Fiber-optic cable uses glass or plastic strands to transmit data via light signals.
- Satellite is a connection option for those who do not have access to faster broadband technologies. Data is transmitted between a satellite dish and a satellite that is in a geosynchronous orbit.

Objective 7.9 *Summarize how to access the Internet wirelessly.*

- WiFi allows users to connect to the Internet wirelessly but is not as fast as a wired connection.
- Mobile broadband is a 3G or 4G service delivered by cell-phone networks.

Objective 7.10 *Summarize the pros and cons of dial-up connections.*

- Dial-up is the cheapest means of accessing the Internet, but it is also the slowest.

Your Home Network

Learning Outcome 7.2 You will be able to describe what is necessary to install and configure a home network, and how to manage and secure a wireless network.

Installing and Configuring Home Networks

Objective 7.11 *Explain what should be considered before creating a home network.*

- Most home network routers should support both wireless and wired access to the Internet.
- For a home network to run efficiently, all nodes such as NICs and routers should use the same Ethernet standard.
- The Device Manager utility in Windows lists all adapters installed on your computer.

Objective 7.12 *Describe what is necessary to connect devices to a network.*

- All devices are connected to your router, either wirelessly or with a wired connection. Wired connections deliver better throughput than wireless.
- To add additional ports to your network, you can connect a switch to your router.

Objective 7.13 *Describe some specialized devices that can be added to a home network.*

- Network-attached storage (NAS) devices let you store and share data files such as movies and music, as well as provide a central place for file backups.

- Home network servers can be used instead of an NAS device if your needs require more sophisticated functionality than NAS devices.
- Devices such as gaming consoles each have their own setup procedures for connecting to wireless networks but usually require the same information as that needed for connecting a computer to a secured wireless network.

Objective 7.14 *Summarize how to configure home network software.*

- The latest versions of Windows make it easy to set up wired and wireless networks.

Managing and Securing Wireless Networks

Objective 7.15 *Describe the potential problems with wireless networks and means to avoid them.*

- You may not get the throughput you need through a wireless connection. Therefore, you may need to consider a wired connection for certain devices.
- Distance from the router, as well as walls, floors, and large metal objects between a device and the router, can interfere with wireless connectivity.

- To solve connectivity problems, dual-band N routers allow for simultaneous support for devices running on both the 2.4 and 5 GHz frequency bands for 802.11n and earlier standards. Wireless range extenders can amplify signals to improve connectivity in areas of poor signal strength.

Objective 7.16 *Describe how to secure wireless home networks.*

- Wireless networks are even more susceptible to hacking than wired networks because the signals of most wireless networks extend beyond the walls of your home.

- Neighbors may unintentionally (or intentionally) connect to the Internet through your wireless connection, and hackers may try to access it.
- To prevent unwanted intrusions into your network, you should change the default password on your router to make it tougher for hackers to gain access, use a hard-to-guess SSID (network name), disable SSID broadcasting to make it harder for outsiders to detect your network, enable security protocols such as WPA or WEP, create a network passphrase, implement media access control, limit your signal range, and apply firmware upgrades.

 Be sure to check out **MyITLab** for additional materials to help you review and learn. And don't forget the Replay Videos ↻ .

key terms //

chapter quiz // assessment

For a quick review to see what you've learned, answer the following questions. Submit the quiz as requested by your instructor. If you are using MyITLab, the quiz is also available there.

multiple choice

1. Which of the following would NOT be a benefit of networking computers?

   a. sharing an Internet connection

   b. sharing printers and other peripherals

   c. sharing software licenses

   d. sharing files

2. Bethany is in her home, watching a video she took on vacation, while her brother is playing FIFA Soccer on his Xbox, and her dad is checking stock quotes on his iPad. What kind of network does this family have?

   a. P2P network   c. both a and b

   b. Client/server network   d. neither a and b

3. What two devices are often combined into one device in a small network to connect the home network to the Internet and to share the connection between devices on the network?

   a. router hub and switch   c. modem and router

   b. switch and router   d. modem and switch

4. Which of the following is used to access the Internet when WiFi is not available?

   a. mobile hotspot   c. 3G Internet access

   b. 4G LTE Internet access   d. all of the above

5. Which of the following should you NOT do to secure a wireless network?

   a. Implement media access control.

   b. Keep the default network name and router password.

   c. Create a security encryption passphrase.

   d. Disable SSID broadcasting.

6. Which of the following might cause interference or poor connectivity between nodes on a wireless network?

   a. concrete walls

   b. nodes that are too far apart

   c. some appliances

   d. all of the above

true/false

_____ 1. 802.11ac is the current wireless Ethernet standard.

_____ 2. 4G is the latest WiFi standard.

_____ 3. Actual data throughput is usually higher on wireless networks than on wired networks.

_____ 4. Data is sent through the network in bundles called packages.

critical thinking

1. **Using Online Storage**

   Sneakernet is jargon for physically transporting files from one location to another, as in using a flash drive. Think about the advantages and disadvantages of using flash drives versus online storage systems, such as Dropbox, Google Drive, and OneDrive. Defend your preferred method of storing and sharing files.

2. **Internet of Things**

   Think about the term "Internet of Things" in which things (objects, animals, and people) are connected to the Internet and can automatically transfer data over a network. Our society is already filled with many examples of "smart nodes"—such as cars, appliances, and entertainment devices—that are connected to the Internet. What are the advantages and disadvantages of developing a more robust Internet of Things and continuing to add more smart nodes?

Providing Wireless Internet Access to the Needy

Problem

Not everyone can afford wireless Internet access, and this can put families, especially ones with school-aged children, at a disadvantage.

Task

You're volunteering for a charity that wants to install wireless networks in the homes of needy families. The project is funded by charitable grants with the objective of providing basic broadband Internet access and networking capabilities at no cost to the recipients.

Process

Break the class into three teams. Each team will be responsible for investigating one of the following issues:

1. **Internet service providers:** Research ISPs that serve the town where your school is located. Compare maximum upload and download speeds as well as costs. Be sure to consider the cost of the modems—whether they're purchased or rented. Select what your group considers the best deal.

2. **Networking equipment and network-ready peripherals:** Each home needs to be provided with an 802.11ac-capable wireless router and a network-ready all-in-one printer. Research three options for these devices, considering price as well as functionality.

3. **Security:** Work in conjunction with the group researching routers to determine the best router to purchase since it needs to support a security protocol such as WPA. Consider other types of protection needed, such as antivirus software and firewalls.

Present your findings to your class and come to a consensus about the solution you would propose for the charity.

Conclusion

Providing technology to underserved populations on a cost-effective basis will go a long way toward closing the digital divide.

Firing Employees for Expressing Views on Social Media Sites

In this exercise, you'll research and then role-play a complicated ethical situation. The role you play may or may not match your own personal beliefs; regardless, your research and use of logic will enable you to represent the view assigned. An arbitrator will watch and comment on both sides of the arguments, and together the team will agree on an ethical solution.

Problem

Employers often are intolerant of employees who express negative opinions or expose inside information about their employers on social media sites. Given that most jurisdictions in the United States use the doctrine of employment at will (employees can be fired at any time for any reason), many employers are quick to discipline or terminate employees who express opinions with which the company disagrees. When such cases come to court, the courts often find in favor of the employers.

Research Areas to Consider

- Ellen Simonetti and Delta Airlines
- Fired for blogging about work
- Free speech
- Joyce Park or Michael Tunison

Process

1. Divide the class into teams. Research the areas above and devise a scenario in which someone has complained about an employee blogging about an issue such as cleanliness at a food manufacturing facility.

2. Team members should write a summary that provides background information for their character—for example, employee, human resources manager, or arbitrator—and that details their character's behaviors to set the stage for the role-playing event. Then, team members should create an outline to use during the role-playing event.

3. Team members should present their case to the class or submit a PowerPoint presentation for review, along with the summary and resolution they developed.

Conclusion

As technology becomes ever more prevalent and integrated into our lives, more and more ethical dilemmas will present themselves. Being able to understand and evaluate both sides of the argument, while responding in a personally or socially ethical manner, will be an important skill.

Home Networking Guide

You write a newsletter, **The Everyday Technologist**, which specializes in technology tips and tricks for the casual everyday technology user. Your current newsletter is a guide to home networks. The basic document has been created, and now using Word 2016 you need to add formatting and images to make the guide more visually appealing.

You will use the following skills as you complete this activity:

- Apply Text Effects
- Insert WordArt
- Insert Columns
- Insert Section Breaks
- Insert Column Break
- Insert Images
- Apply Text Wrapping
- Use Custom Margins

Instructions:

1. Open *TIA_Ch7_Start.docx* and save as **TIA_Ch7_LastFirst.docx**.

2. Select the title **Home Networking Guide**, and convert the text to a WordArt Object using **Gradient Fill—Blue, Accent 1, Reflection**.

3. With the WordArt object still selected, click **Layout Options**, and select **Top and Bottom**. Then, click **See more…** at the bottom of the Layout Options window, and in the Layout dialog box, in the *Horizontal* section, select the **Alignment option**, and then choose **Centered** from the dropdown box.

4. Apply the **Fill—Orange, Accent 2, Outline—Accent 2 Text Effect** to the three headings: *Hardware*, *Wireless versus Wired*, and *Powerline Adapters*. Increase the font size of each heading to 18.

5. Create custom margins so all margins are 0.7".

6. Position the cursor before the heading *Hardware*. Insert a **Section Break (Continuous)**, and then apply **Two Column** formatting.

7. Place the cursor at the end of the second bullet point paragraph in the *Hardware* section. Insert the image TIA_Ch7_Modem Router. Change the Layout Option of the image to **Square**. Resize the image so the height is **0.9"** and the width is **1.2"**, and then move the image so that the two top lines of the Router paragraph display above the image, and the left side of the image is flush with the left margin.

8. Place the cursor at the beginning of the Powerline Adapters paragraph. Insert the image TIA_Ch7_Powerline. Change the Layout Option to **Tight**. Change the height of the image to **1"**, and then move the image so the right side is flush with the right margin of the document and centered vertically in the Powerline Adapter paragraph.

9. Place the cursor at the beginning of *Current Wireless (Wi-Fi) Standards*. Insert a column break. Format the text with bold and italics.

10. Save and submit for grading.

Technology in Focus

Under the Hood

Learning Outcome 7B.1 You will be able to list the various number systems used in computers, explain how binary numbers are represented in computing devices, describe the basic steps in the CPU machine cycle, and explain technologies that make CPUs work faster.

Some people are drawn to understanding things in detail; others are happy just to have things work. If you use a computer, you may not have been tempted to "look under the hood." However, if you can understand the hardware inside a computer, you'll have some real advantages:

- You won't have to pay a technician to fix or upgrade your computer. You'll be able to fine-tune it yourself, and you'll be able to make your investment in your computer last longer.
- You'll be able to evaluate new advances in technology. For example, what's the impact of a new type of memory or a new processor?
- If you're a programmer, you'll be able to write more efficient and faster programs.

(Supergenijalac/Shutterstock)

And if you're preparing for a career in information technology, understanding computer hardware is critical for you. In this Technology in Focus feature, we'll build on what you've learned about computer hardware in other chapters and go "under the hood" to look at the components of your system unit in more detail. Let's begin by looking at the building blocks of computers: switches.

Switches and Number Systems

How does a computer process the data you input? A computer system can be viewed as an enormous collection of on/off switches. These simple on/off switches are combined in different ways to perform addition and subtraction and to move data around the system.

Electrical Switches

Objective 7B.1 *Describe the different types of technologies that have been used as representations of the binary language in computing devices.*

To process data into information, computers need to work in a language they understand. Computers understand only two states of existence: on and off. Inside a computer, these two possibilities, or states, are defined using the two numbers *1* and *0*; the language represented by these numbers is called **binary language** because just two numbers are used. Everything a computer does, such as processing data or printing a report, is broken down into a series of *0*s and *1*s. **Electrical switches** are the devices inside the computer that are flipped between the two states of *1* and *0*, signifying ON and OFF.

You use various forms of switches every day. The light switch in your kitchen is either ON, allowing current to flow to the light

bulb, or OFF. Another switch you use each day is a water faucet. As shown in Figure 1, shutting off the faucet so that no water flows could represent the value 0, whereas turning it on could represent the value 1.

Computers are built from a huge collection of electrical switches. The history of computers is really a story about creating smaller and faster sets of electrical switches so that more data can be stored and manipulated quickly.

FIGURE 1 Water faucets can be used to illustrate binary switches.

FIGURE 2 Early computers were constructed using vacuum tubes (see photo inset). The difference in size achieved by moving from tubes to transistors allowed computers to become desktop devices instead of room-sized machines. *(Corbis)*

Vacuum Tubes

The earliest generation of electronic computers used **vacuum tubes** as switches. Vacuum tubes act as switches by allowing or blocking the flow of electrical current. The problem with vacuum tubes is that they take up a lot of space, as shown in Figure 2. The first high-speed digital computer, the Electronic Numerical Integrator and Computer (ENIAC), was deployed in 1945. It used nearly 18,000 vacuum tubes as switches and was about half the size of a basketball court! In addition to being large, the vacuum tubes produced a lot of heat and burned out frequently.

Since the introduction of ENIAC's vacuum tubes, two major revolutions have occurred in the design of switches, and consequently computers, to make them smaller and faster:

1. The invention of the *transistor*
2. The fabrication of *integrated circuits*

Transistors

Transistors are electrical switches built out of layers of a special type of material called a **semiconductor**. A semiconductor is any material that can be controlled either to conduct electricity or to act as an insulator (to prohibit electricity from passing through). Silicon, which is found in common sand, is the semiconductor material used to make transistors (see Figure 3).

By itself, silicon doesn't conduct electricity particularly well, but if specific chemicals are added in a controlled way to the silicon, it begins to behave like a switch. The silicon allows electrical current to flow easily when a certain voltage is applied; otherwise, it prevents electrical current from flowing, thus behaving as an on/off switch. This kind of behavior is exactly what's needed to store digital information—the 0s (off) and 1s (on) of binary language.

The first transistors were much smaller than vacuum tubes, produced little heat, and could quickly be switched from on to off, thereby allowing or blocking electrical current. They also were less expensive than vacuum tubes.

It wasn't long, however, before transistors reached their limits. Continuing advances in technology began to require more transistors than circuit boards could reasonably handle. Something was needed to pack more transistor capacity into a smaller space. Thus, integrated circuits, the next technical revolution in switches, were developed.

Integrated Circuits

Integrated circuits (or **chips**) are tiny regions of semiconductor material that support a huge number of transistors (see Figure 4). Most integrated circuits are no more than a quarter inch in size yet can hold billions of transistors.

This advancement has enabled computer designers to create small yet powerful **microprocessors**, which are the chips that contain a central processing unit (CPU). The Intel 4004, the first complete microprocessor to be located on a single integrated circuit, was released in 1971, marking the beginning of the true miniaturization of computers. The Intel 4004 contained slightly more than 2,300 transistors. Today, more than two billion transistors can be manufactured in a space as tiny as the nail of your little finger!

Number Systems

Objective 7B.2 *List and explain the various number systems that are used in computing devices.*

FIGURE 3 This silicon wafer has the transistor circuitry for hundreds of devices etched on it. *(Justin Sullivan/Getty Images)*

FIGURE 4 An integrated circuit is packaged in a small case but holds billions of transistors. *(Edelweiss/Fotolia)*

How can simple switches be organized so that they let you use a computer to pay your bills online or write an essay? How can a set of switches describe a number or a word or give a computer the command to perform addition? Recall that to manipulate the on/off switches, the computer works in binary language, which uses only two digits, 0 and 1. Let's look at how number systems work so that we can begin to understand this more deeply.

The Base-10 Number System

A **number system** is an organized plan for representing a number. Although you may not realize it, you're already familiar with one number system. The **base-10 number system**, also known as **decimal notation**, is the system you use to represent all of the numeric values you use each day. It's called base 10 because it uses 10 digits—0 through 9—to represent any value.

To represent a number in base 10, you break the number down into groups of ones, tens, hundreds, thousands, and so on. Each digit has a place value depending on where it appears in the number. For example, using base 10, in the whole number 6,954 there are 6 sets of thousands, 9 sets of hundreds, 5 sets of tens, and 4 sets of ones. Working from right to left, each place in a number represents an increasing power of 10, as follows:

$$6,954 = (6 * 1,000) + (9 * 100) + (5 * 10) + (4 * 1)$$
$$= (6 * 10^3) + (9 * 10^2) + (5 * 10^1) + (4 * 10^0)$$

Note that in this equation, the final digit 4 is represented as $4 * 10^0$ because any number raised to the zero power is equal to 1.

The Base-2 (or Binary) Number System

Anthropologists theorize that humans developed a base-10 number system because we have 10 fingers. However, computer systems are not well suited to thinking about numbers in groups of 10. Instead, computers describe a number in powers of 2 because each switch can be in one of two positions: on or off. This numbering system is referred to as the **binary number system** (see Figure 5).

The binary number system is also referred to as the **base-2 number system**. Even with just two digits, the binary number system can still represent all the values that a base-10 number system can. Instead of breaking the number down into sets of ones, tens, hundreds, and thousands, as is done in base-10 notation, the binary number system describes a number as the sum of powers of 2—ones, twos, fours, eights, and sixteens. Binary numbers are used to represent every piece of data stored in a computer: all of the numbers, all of the letters, and all of the instructions that the computer uses to execute work.

Representing Integers. In the base-10 number system, a whole number is represented as the sum of *1*s, *10*s, *100*s, and *1,000*s—that is, sums of powers of 10. The binary system works in the same way, but describes a value as the sum of groups of *1*s, *2*s, *4*s, *8*s, *16*s, *32*s, *64*s, and so on—that is, powers of 2: 1, 2, 4, 8, 16, 32, 64, and so on.

Let's look at the number 67. In base 10, the number 67 would be six sets of *10*s and seven sets of *1*s, as follows:

Base 10: 67 = (6 * 10^1) + (7 * 10^0)

One way to figure out how 67 is represented in base 2 is to find the largest possible power of 2 that could be in the number 67. Two to the eighth power is 256, and there are no groups of 256 in the number 67. Two to the seventh power is 128, but that is bigger than 67. Two to the sixth power is 64, and there is a group of 64 inside a group of 67.

67 has	1	**group of**	64	**That leaves 3 and**
3 has	0	**groups of**	32	
	0	**groups of**	16	
	0	**groups of**	8	
	0	**groups of**	4	
	1	**group of**	2	**That leaves 1 and**
1 has	1	**group of**	1	**Now nothing is left**

FIGURE 5 Computer humor—binary has only two digits: 0 and 1! *(S Harris/Cartoonstock)*

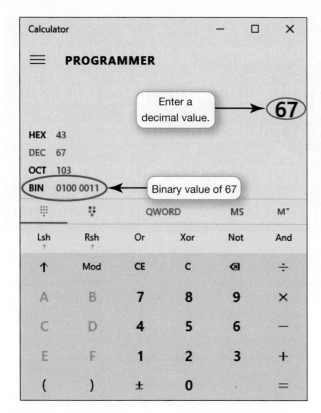

FIGURE 6 The Windows Calculator in Programmer mode instantly converts values from decimal to binary. *(Windows 10, Microsoft Corporation)*

So, the binary number for 67 is written as 1000011 in base 2:

$$
\begin{aligned}
\text{Base 2: } 67 &= 64 + 0 + 0 + 0 + 0 + 2 + 1 \\
&= (1 * 2^6) + (0 * 2^5) + (0 * 2^4) + (0 * 2^3) + \\
&\quad (0 * 2^2) + (1 * 2^1) + (1 * 2^0) \\
&= (1000011)_{\text{base 2}}
\end{aligned}
$$

It's easier to have a calculator do this for you! Some calculators have a button labeled DEC (for decimal) and another labeled BIN (for binary). Using Windows 10, you can access the Scientific Calculator that supports conversion between decimal (base 10) and binary (base 2) by entering *calculator* in the Cortana search box. From the search results, choose the Calculator app. You can enter your calculation in decimal and instantly see the binary representation in 64 bits, as shown in Figure 6.

Hexadecimal Notation. A large integer value becomes a very long string of *1*s and *0*s in binary! For convenience,

SOUND BYTE

Where Does Binary Show Up?

In this Sound Byte, you'll learn how to use tools to work with binary, decimal, and hexadecimal numbers. (These tools come with the Windows operating system.) You'll also learn where you might see binary and hexadecimal values when you use a computer.

programmers often use **hexadecimal notation** to make these expressions easier to use. Hexadecimal is a base-16 number system, meaning it uses 16 digits to represent numbers instead of the 10 digits used in base 10 or the 2 digits used in base 2. The 16 digits it uses are the 10 numeric digits, 0 to 9, plus six extra symbols: A, B, C, D, E, and F. Each of the letters A through F corresponds to a numeric value, so that A equals 10, B equals 11, and so on (see Figure 7). Therefore, the value 67 in decimal notation is 1000011 in binary or 43 in hexadecimal notation. It is much easier for computer scientists to use the 2-digit 43 than the 7-digit string 1000011. The Windows Calculator in Programmer view also can perform conversions to hexadecimal notation. (You can watch a video that shows you how to perform conversions between bases using the Windows Calculator in the Sound Byte "Where Does Binary Show Up?")

Representing Characters: ASCII. We've just been converting integers from base 10, which *we* understand, to base 2 (binary state), which the computer understands. Similarly, we need a system that converts letters and other symbols that *we* understand to a binary state the computer understands. To provide a consistent means for representing letters and other characters, certain codes dictate how to represent characters in binary format. Most of today's personal computers use the American National Standards Institute (ANSI, pronounced "AN-see") standard code, called the **American Standard Code for Information Interchange** (ASCII, pronounced "AS-key"), to represent each letter or character as an 8-bit (or 1-byte) binary code.

FIGURE 7

Sample Hexadecimal Values		
DECIMAL NUMBER	**BINARY VALUE**	**HEXADECIMAL VALUE**
00	0000	00
01	0001	01
02	0010	02
03	0011	03
04	0100	04
05	0101	05
06	0110	06
07	0111	07
08	1000	08
09	1001	09
10	1010	A
11	1011	B
12	1100	C
13	1101	D
14	1110	E
15	1111	F

Each binary digit is called a **bit** for short. Eight binary digits (or bits) combine to create one **byte**. We've been converting base-10 numbers to a binary format. In such cases, the binary format has no standard length. For example, the binary format for the number *2* is two digits (10), whereas the binary format for the number *10* is four digits (1010). Although binary numbers can have more or fewer than 8 bits, each single alphabetic or special character is 1 byte (or 8 bits) of data and consists of a unique combination of a total of eight *0*s and *1*s.

The ASCII code represents the 26 uppercase letters and 26 lowercase letters used in the English language, along with many punctuation symbols and other special characters, using 8 bits. Figure 8 shows several examples of the ASCII code representation of printable letters and characters.

Representing Characters: Unicode. Because it represents letters and characters using only 8 bits, the ASCII code can assign only 256 (or 2^8) different codes for unique characters and letters. Although this is enough to represent English and many other characters found in the world's languages, ASCII code can't represent all languages and symbols, because some languages require more than 256 characters and letters. Thus, a new encoding scheme, called **Unicode**, was created. By using 16 bits instead of the 8 bits used in ASCII, Unicode can represent nearly 1,115,000 code points and currently assigns more than 96,000 unique character symbols (see Figure 9).

The first 128 characters of Unicode are identical to ASCII, but because of its depth, Unicode is also able to represent the alphabets of all modern and historic languages and notational systems, including such languages and writing systems as Tibetan, Tagalog, and Canadian Aboriginal syllabics. As we continue to become a more global society, it's anticipated that Unicode will replace ASCII as the standard character formatting code.

Representing Decimal Numbers. The binary number system can also represent a decimal number. How can a string of *1*s and *0*s capture the information in a value such as 99.368? Because every computer must store such numbers

FIGURE 9 The written languages of the world require thousands of different characters. The Unicode Code Chart (**unicode.org/charts**) shows how Unicode provides a system allowing digital representation of over 1,100,000 unique characters. *(Vito Arcomano/Alamy)*

in the same way, the Institute of Electrical and Electronics Engineers (IEEE) has established a standard called the *floating-point standard* that describes how numbers with fractional parts should be represented in the binary number system. Using a 32-bit system, we can represent an incredibly wide range of numbers.

The method dictated by the IEEE standard works the same for any number with a decimal point, such as the number –0.75. The first digit, or bit (the sign bit), is used to indicate whether the number is positive or negative. The next 8 bits store the magnitude of the number, indicating whether the number is in the hundreds or millions, for example. The standard says to use the next 23 bits to store the value of the number.

Interpretation. *All* data inside the computer is stored as bits:

- **Positive and negative integers** can be stored using signed integer notation, with the first bit (the sign bit) indicating the sign and the rest of the bits indicating the value of the number.

- **Decimal** numbers are stored according to the IEEE floating-point standard.

- **Letters and symbols** are stored according to the ASCII code or Unicode.

These number systems and codes exist so that computers can store different types of information in their on/off switches. No matter what kind of data you input in a computer—a color, a musical note, or a street address—that data will be stored as a pattern of *1*s and *0*s. The important lesson is that the interpretation of *0*s and *1*s is what matters. The same binary pattern could represent a positive number, a negative number, a fraction, or a letter.

How does the computer know which interpretation to use for the *1*s and *0*s? When your mind processes language, it takes the sounds you hear and uses the rules of English, along

FIGURE 8

ASCII Standard Code for a Sample of Letters and Characters

ASCII CODE	REPRESENTS THIS SYMBOL	ASCII CODE	REPRESENTS THIS SYMBOL
01000001	A	01100001	a
01000010	B	01100010	b
01000011	C	01100011	c
01011010	Z	00100011	#
00100001	!	00100100	$
00100010	"	00100101	%

Note: For the full ASCII table, see **ascii-code.com**.
(Courtesy of the American National Standards Institute)

with other clues, to build an interpretation of the sound as a word. If you're in New York City and hear someone shout, "Hey, Lori!" you expect that someone is saying hello to a friend. If you're in London and hear the same sound—"Hey! Lorry!"—you jump out of the way because a truck is coming at you! You knew which interpretation to apply to the sound because you had some other information—the fact that you were in England.

Likewise, the CPU is designed to understand a specific language or set of instructions. Certain instructions tell the CPU to expect a negative number next or to interpret the following bit pattern as a character. Because of this extra information, the CPU always knows which interpretation to use for a series of bits.

How the CPU Works

Let's now take a more detailed look at how the CPU works to accomplish the many tasks for which it is responsible.

The Machine Cycle

Objective 7B.3: *Describe the basic steps in the CPU machine cycle.*

Any program you run on your computer is actually a long series of binary code describing a specific set of commands the CPU must perform. These commands may be coming from a user's actions or may be instructions fed from a program while it executes. Each CPU is somewhat different in the exact steps it follows to perform its tasks, but all CPUs must perform a series of similar general steps. These steps, also illustrated in Figure 10, are referred to as a CPU **machine cycle** (or **processing cycle**):

1. **Fetch:** When any program begins to run, the *1*s and *0*s that make up the program's binary code must be "fetched" from their temporary storage location in random access memory (RAM) and moved to the CPU before they can be executed.

2. **Decode:** Once the program's binary code is in the CPU, it is decoded into commands the CPU understands.

3. **Execute:** Next, the CPU actually performs the work described in the commands. Specialized hardware on the CPU performs addition, subtraction, multiplication, division, and other mathematical and logical operations.

4. **Store:** The result is stored in one of the **registers**, special memory storage areas built into the CPU, which are the most expensive, fastest memory in your computer. The CPU is then ready to fetch the next set of bits encoding the next instruction.

No matter what program you're running and no matter how many programs you're using at one time, the CPU performs these four steps over and over at incredibly high speeds. Shortly, we'll look at each stage in more detail. But first, let's examine components that help the CPU perform its tasks.

The Control Unit and the System Clock

Objective 7B.4: *Describe how the control unit and the system clock function.*

The CPU, like any part of the computer system, is designed from a collection of switches. How can the simple on/off switches of the CPU "remember" the fetch-decode-execute-store sequence of the machine cycle?

The **control unit** of the CPU manages the switches inside the CPU. It is programmed by CPU designers to remember the sequence of processing stages for that CPU and how each switch in the CPU should be set (i.e., on or off) for each stage. With each beat of the system clock, the control unit moves each switch to the correct on or off setting and then performs the work of that stage.

To move from one stage of the machine cycle to the next, the motherboard uses a built-in **system clock**. This internal clock is actually a special crystal that acts like a metronome,

FIGURE 10 The CPU Machine Cycle

keeping a steady beat and controlling when the CPU moves to the next stage of processing.

These steady beats or "ticks" of the system clock, known as the **clock cycle**, set the pace by which the computer moves from process to process. The pace, known as **clock speed**, is measured in hertz (Hz), which describes how many times something happens per second. Today's system clocks are measured in gigahertz (GHz) or a billion clock ticks per second. Therefore, in a 3 GHz system, there are 3 billion clock ticks each second.

Machine Cycle Stages

Objective 7B.5: *Describe what happens in each stage of the CPU machine cycle.*

Let's now look at each of the stages in the machine cycle in a bit more depth.

(Steve Young/Fotolia LLC)

Stage 1: The Fetch Stage

The data and program instructions the CPU needs are stored in different areas in the computer system. Data and program instructions move between these areas as they're needed by the CPU for processing. Programs are permanently stored on the hard drive because it offers nonvolatile storage. However, when you launch a program, it—or sometimes only its essential parts—is transferred from the hard drive into RAM.

The program moves to RAM because the CPU can access the data and program instructions stored in RAM more than one million times faster than if they're left on the hard drive. In part, this is because RAM is much closer to the CPU than the hard drive is. Another reason for the delay in transmission of data and program instructions from the hard drive to the CPU is the relatively slow speed of mechanical hard drives. The read/write heads have to sweep over the spinning platters, which takes time. Even nonmechanical SSD hard drives have slower access speeds than RAM. RAM is a type of memory that gives very fast direct access to data.

As specific instructions from the program are needed, they're moved from RAM into registers (the special storage areas located on the CPU itself), where they wait to be executed.

The CPU's storage area isn't big enough to hold everything it needs to process at the same time. If enough memory were located on the CPU chip itself, an entire program could be copied to the CPU from RAM before it was executed. This

would add to the computer's speed and efficiency because there would be no delay while the CPU stopped processing operations to fetch instructions from RAM to the CPU. However, including so much memory on a CPU chip would make these chips extremely expensive. In addition, CPU design is so complex that only a limited amount of storage space is available on the CPU itself.

Cache Memory. The CPU doesn't actually need to fetch every instruction from RAM each time it goes through a cycle. Another layer of storage, called **cache memory**, has even faster access to the CPU than RAM. Cache memory consists of small blocks of memory located directly on and next to the CPU chip. These memory blocks are holding places for recently or frequently used instructions or data that the CPU needs the most. When these instructions or data are stored in cache memory, the CPU can retrieve them more quickly than if it had to access them in RAM.

Modern CPU designs include several types of cache memory:

- **Level 1 cache:** If the next instruction to be fetched isn't already located in a CPU register, instead of looking directly to RAM to find it, the CPU first searches Level 1 cache. **Level 1 cache** is a block of memory built onto the CPU chip to store data or commands that have just been used.

- **Level 2 cache:** If the command is not located in Level 1 cache, the CPU searches Level 2 cache. Depending on the design of the CPU, **Level 2 cache** is either located on the CPU chip but slightly farther away from the CPU than Level 1, or is located on a separate chip next to the CPU and therefore takes somewhat longer to access. Level 2 cache contains more storage area than Level 1 cache. For the Intel Core i7, for example, Level 1 cache is 64 kilobytes (KB) and Level 2 cache is 1 megabyte (MB).

  Only if the CPU doesn't find the next instruction to be fetched in either Level 1 or Level 2 cache will it make the long journey to RAM to access it.

- **Level 3 cache:** The current direction of processor design is toward increasingly large multilevel CPU cache structures. Today, CPUs such as Intel's Core i7 processors have an additional third level of cache memory storage called **Level 3 cache**. On computers with Level 3 cache, the CPU checks this area for instructions and data after it looks in Level 1 and Level 2 cache but before it makes the longer trip to RAM (see Figure 11). Level 3 cache holds between 2 and 12 MB of data. With 12 MB of Level 3 cache, there is storage for some entire programs to be transferred to the CPU for execution.

As an end user of computer programs, you do nothing special to use cache memory. The advantage of having more cache memory is that you'll experience better performance because the CPU won't have to make the longer trip to RAM to get data and instructions as often. Unfortunately, because it's built into the CPU chip or motherboard, you can't upgrade cache; it's part of the original design of the CPU. Therefore, as with RAM, when buying a computer, it's important to consider the one with the most cache memory, everything else being equal.

(Andrea Danti/Fotolia)

Stage 2: The Decode Stage

The main goal of the decode stage is for the CPU's control unit to translate (or **decode**) the program's instructions into commands the CPU can understand. The collection of commands that a specific CPU can execute is called the **instruction set** for that system. Each CPU has its own unique instruction set. For example, the AMD FX 8350 eight-core processor in a Gamer Mage system has a different instruction set than the fourth-generation Intel Core i5 used in a Dell Inspiron notebook. The control unit interprets the code's bits according to the instruction set the CPU designers laid out for that particular CPU. The control unit then knows how to set up all the switches on the CPU so that the proper operation will occur.

Because humans are the ones who write the initial instructions, all the commands in an instruction set are written in a language called **assembly language**, which is easier for humans to work with than binary language. Many CPUs have similar assembly commands in their instruction sets, including the following commands:

CPU INSTRUCTION	FUNCTION
ADD	Add
SUB	Subtract
MUL	Multiply
DIV	Divide
MOVE	Move data to RAM
STORE	Move data to a CPU register
EQU	Check if equal

CPUs differ in the choice of additional assembly language commands selected for the instruction set. Each CPU design team works to develop an instruction set that is both powerful and speedy.

However, because the CPU knows and recognizes only patterns of 0s and 1s, it can't understand assembly language directly, so these human-readable instructions are translated into binary code. The control unit uses these long strings

FIGURE 11 The CPU has multiple stages of internal memory, which is just a part of the overall hierarchy of a computer's memory storage.

BITS&BYTES

Using a Little Hideaway

Taking data you think you'll be using soon and storing it nearby is a simple but powerful idea. This strategy shows up in places in your computer system other than cache memory. For example, when you're browsing web pages, it takes longer to download images than text. Your browser software automatically stores images on your hard drive so that you don't have to download them again if you want to go back and view a page you've already visited. Although this cache of files is not related to the cache storage space designed into the CPU chip, the idea is the same. The word cache is derived from the French word *cacher*, which means "to hide." A little bit of memory space used as a hideaway can give performance a big boost.

of binary code called **machine language** to set up the hardware in the CPU for the rest of the operations it needs to perform. Machine language is a binary code for computer instructions, much like the ASCII code is a binary code for letters and characters. Similar to each letter or character having its own unique combination of 0s and 1s assigned to it, a CPU has a table of codes consisting of combinations of 0s and 1s for each of its commands. If the CPU sees a particular pattern of bits arrive, it knows the work it must do. Figure 12 shows a few commands in both assembly language and machine language.

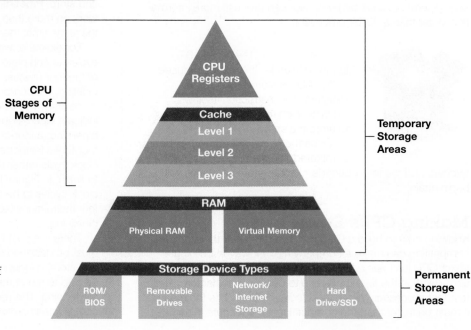

FIGURE 12

Representations of Sample CPU Commands

HUMAN LANGUAGE FOR COMMAND	CPU COMMAND IN ASSEMBLY LANGUAGE (LANGUAGE USED BY PROGRAMMERS)	CPU COMMAND IN MACHINE LANGUAGE (LANGUAGE USED IN THE CPU'S INSTRUCTION SET)
Add	ADD	1110 1010
Subtract	SUB	0001 0101
Multiply	MUL	1111 0000
Divide	DIV	0000 1111

(Taras Livyy/Fotolia)

Stage 3: The Execute Stage

The **arithmetic logic unit (ALU)** is the part of the CPU designed to perform mathematical operations such as addition, subtraction, multiplication, and division and to test the comparison of values such as *greater than*, *less than*, and *equal to*. For example, in calculating an average, the ALU is where the addition and division operations would take place.

The ALU also performs logical OR, AND, and NOT operations. For example, in determining whether a student can graduate, the ALU would need to ascertain whether the student had taken all required courses AND obtained a passing grade in each of them. The ALU is specially designed to execute such calculations flawlessly and with incredible speed.

The ALU is fed data from the CPU's registers. The amount of data a CPU can process at a time is based in part on the amount of data each register can hold. The number of bits a computer can work with at a time is referred to as its **word size**. Therefore, a 64-bit processor can process more information faster than a 32-bit processor.

(John Takai/Fotolia)

Stage 4: The Store Stage

In the final stage, the result produced by the ALU is stored back in the registers. The instruction itself will explain which register should be used to store the answer.

Once the entire instruction has been completed, the next instruction will be fetched, and the fetch-decode-execute-store sequence will begin again.

Making CPUs Even Faster

Knowing how to build a CPU that can run faster than the competition can make a company rich. However, building a faster CPU isn't easy. A new product launch must take into consideration the time it will take to design, manufacture, and test that processor. When the processor finally hits the market, it must be faster than the competition if the manufacturer

hopes to make a profit. To create a CPU that will be released 36 months from now, it must be built to perform at least twice as fast as anything currently available.

Processor manufacturers can increase CPU performance in many different ways:

- Using *pipelining*
- Designing the CPU's instruction set so that it contains *specialized instructions for handling multimedia and graphics*
- Including *multiple independent processing paths* inside the CPU

Let's explore each of these methods in more detail.

Pipelining

Objective 7B.6: *Explain why pipelining makes CPUs work faster.*

As an instruction is processed, the CPU runs sequentially through the four stages of processing: fetch, decode, execute, and store. **Pipelining** is a technique that allows the CPU to work on more than one instruction (or stage of processing) at the same time, thereby boosting CPU performance.

For example, without pipelining, it may take four clock cycles to complete one instruction (one clock cycle for each of the four processing stages). However, with a four-stage pipeline, the computer can process four instructions at the same time. The ticks of the system clock (the clock cycle) indicate when all instructions move to the next process. Using pipelining, a four-stage processor can potentially run up to four times faster because some instruction is finishing every clock cycle rather than waiting four cycles for each instruction to finish. In Figure 13a, a non-pipelined instruction takes four clock cycles to be completed, whereas in Figure 13b, the four instructions have been completed in the same time using pipelining.

There is a cost to pipelining a CPU, however. The CPU must be designed so that each stage (fetch, decode, execute, and store) is independent. This means that each stage must be able to run at the same time that the other three stages are running. This requires more transistors and a more complicated hardware design.

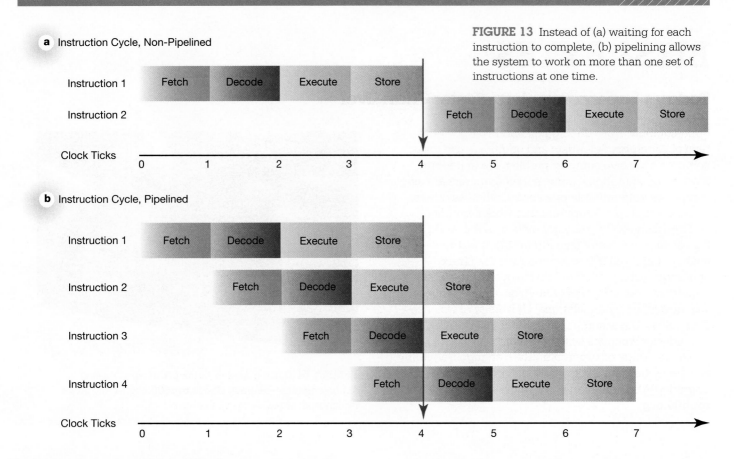

FIGURE 13 Instead of (a) waiting for each instruction to complete, (b) pipelining allows the system to work on more than one set of instructions at one time.

BITS&BYTES

Forget CPUs: SoC Is the Future for Mobile Devices!

Since consumers are demanding more powerful mobile devices such as wearables (smart watches), smartphones, and tablets, the pressure is on for chip designers to create smaller chips. But the chips also need to be more powerful than the previous generation and consume less power to keep up with software and communication demands.

Intel and other chip manufacturers have risen to the challenge by migrating away from CPUs and introducing SoC (system on a chip) architecture. While CPU architecture requires additional chips to support the CPU, SoC integrates all the computer circuitry into a single chip. This is essential for making the "brains" of small computing devices such as tablets, smartphones, and wearable technology.

The Quark line of SoCs from Intel is quite popular. While not as powerful as some previous chips like the Atom processor, Quark chips consume much less power. Low power consumption is essential for extending battery life for mobile and wearable devices. Thanks to SoC design, the future is getting smaller every year!

Specialized Multimedia Instructions

Objective 7B.7: *Explain how specialized multimedia instructions make CPUs work faster.*

Each design team that develops a new CPU tries to imagine what users' greatest needs will be in four or five years. Currently, several processors on the market reflect this consideration by incorporating specialized multimedia instructions into the basic instruction set.

Hardware engineers have redesigned the chip so that the instruction set contains new commands customized to speed up the work needed for video and audio processing. For example, Intel has integrated into its second-generation Core processor the Advanced Encryption Standard (AES) instruction set. These seven new instructions work to allow the CPU to deliver faster data protection.

Multiple Processing Efforts

Objective 7B.8: *Define parallel processing, and explain how computers function with multiple CPU cores.*

Many high-end server systems use a set of completely separate CPU chips on one motherboard. These server systems can later be scaled so that they can accommodate large numbers of processors with multiple cores, like the Tianhe-2 supercomputer, which uses Intel Xeon Ivy Bridge and Phi processors to provide 3,120,000 computing cores of power!

In personal computers, Intel uses *multi-core processing* in its Core processor line of chips. Chips with quad-core

BITS&BYTES

Today's Supercomputers: Faster Than Ever

Supercomputers are the biggest and most powerful type of computer. Scientists and engineers use these computers to solve complex problems or to perform massive computations. Some supercomputers are single computers with multiple processors, whereas others consist of multiple computers that work together.

The Tianhe-2 was recently ranked as the world's fastest supercomputer (see Figure 14). It features a whopping 3,120,000 cores and runs the Linux operating system. Tianhe-2 is deployed at the National Supercomputer Center in Guangzho, China. Since it was developed by the National University of Defense Technology, the assumption is that it will be used primarily for weapons system research.

The rankings of supercomputers change frequently as new models are deployed or older models are upgraded. You can keep up with the rankings at **top500.org**.

FIGURE 14 The Tianhe-2 in China is the world's faster supercomputer—for now! Check **top500.org** for the latest rankings. *(Long Hongtao/Xinhua Press/Corbis)*

processing capabilities have four separate parallel processing paths inside them, so they're almost as fast as four separate CPUs. It's not quite four times as fast because the system must do some extra work to decide which processor will work on which part of the problem and to recombine the results each CPU produces.

Six-core processors, like the Intel i7 Extreme Edition, and even eight-core CPUs (like the AMD FX) are available as well, executing six (or eight) separate processing paths. Multi-processor systems are often used when intensive computational problems need to be solved in such areas as computer simulations, video production, and graphics processing.

Certain types of problems are well suited to a parallel-processing environment. In **parallel processing**, there is a large network of computers, with each computer working on a portion of the same problem simultaneously. To be a good candidate for parallel processing, a problem must be able to be divided into a set of tasks that can be run simultaneously. For example, a problem where millions of faces are being compared with a target image for recognition is easily adapted to a parallel setting. The target face can be compared with many hundreds of faces at the same time. But if the next step of an algorithm can be started only after the results of the previous step have been computed, parallel processing will present no advantages.

In the future, you can expect CPUs to continue to get smaller and faster and to consume less power. This fits with the current demands of consumers for more powerful portable computing devices.

At the most basic level of binary *1*s and *0*s, computers are systems of switches that can accomplish impressive tasks. By understanding the hardware components that make up your computer system, you can use your system more effectively and make better buying decisions.

BITS&BYTES

CPU Wars

The ARM processor, which is used in wearables, tablets, and smartphones, was a CPU contender that challenged Intel for supremacy in the market. Microsoft even released a version of Windows specifically for the ARM processor, since it consumes less power and is cheaper than Intel processors. However, Intel responded recently by launching its line of Quark processors, which are even smaller and more powerful than ARM processors. Competition between these two processors has driven down the costs of mobile devices while increasing battery life. And expect new processors to be launched in coming years that are smaller and faster than the Quarks or the ARMs.

check your understanding // review & practice

For a quick review of what you've learned, answer the following questions.

multiple choice

1. Which part of the CPU is specifically designed to perform mathematical operations?
   a. fetch module
   b. ALU
   c. registers
   d. cache memory

2. What is another name for the base-2 number system?
   a. decimal notation
   b. binary number system
   c. hexadecimal notation
   d. integer system

3. Which encoding scheme can represent the alphabets of all modern and historic languages?
   a. base-2 number system
   b. Unicode
   c. ASCII
   d. scientific

4. A multi-core processor like the Intel i7 is
   a. one physical chip.
   b. several chips joined together on the motherboard.
   c. two separate cards installed in your system.
   d. a software setting you can use to speed up CPU processing.

5. To regulate the internal timing of a computer system, the motherboard uses
   a. a system clock.
   b. software simulation.
   c. RAM.
   d. a register.

6. Special areas of memory storage built into the CPU are known as
   a. switches.
   b. semiconductors.
   c. registers.
   d. DIMMs.

7. Which is the correct set and order of steps in the machine cycle?
   a. execute, store, fetch, decode
   b. store, fetch, execute, decode
   c. execute first instruction, execute second instruction, execute third instruction
   d. fetch, decode, execute, store

8. All data inside the computer is stored as
   a. words.
   b. numbers.
   c. signature patterns.
   d. cache memory.

9. Which statement about pipelining is TRUE?
   a. Pipelining does not boost CPU performance.
   b. Pipeline design is only used in computers in conjunction with parallel processing.
   c. Pipelining allows a less complicated hardware design.
   d. Pipelining allows the computer to process multiple instructions simultaneously.

10. The _____ is small blocks of memory located directly on and next to the CPU chip.
    a. ALU
    b. cache
    c. RAM
    d. buffer

 Go to **MyITLab** to take an autograded version of the *Check Your Understanding* review and to find all media resources for the chapter.

8

Digital Devices and Media: Managing a Digital Lifestyle

Mobile Devices

Learning Outcome 8.1 **You will be able to discuss the nature of digital signals and how mobile computing devices are designed and operated.**

Digital Basics   310

Objective 8.1 *Describe how digital convergence has evolved.*

Objective 8.2 *Explain the differences between digital and analog signals.*

The Power of Smartphones   313

Objective 8.3 *Describe the technologies used to communicate across cellular networks.*

◖▌ **Sound Byte:** Smartphones Are Really Smart

Objective 8.4 *Explain how to effectively use cellular devices and mobile Internet access and how to keep your devices secure.*

🔲 **Active Helpdesk:** Keeping Your Data on Hand

◖▌ **Sound Byte:** Connecting with Bluetooth

🔲 **Active Helpdesk:** Working with Smartphones

Mobile Computing   321

Objective 8.5 *Demonstrate an understanding of the range of different mobile computing devices.*

Objective 8.6 *Describe how to evaluate which mobile device is appropriate for a specific user.*

The Impact of Digital Information

Learning Outcome 8.2 **You will be able to describe how digital technology is used to produce and distribute digital texts, music, and video.**

Digital Publishing   326

Objective 8.7 *Describe e-readers, and discuss the different types of e-readers that are available.*

Objective 8.8 *Explain how to purchase, borrow, and publish e-texts.*

Digital Music   328

Objective 8.9 *Describe how digital music is created and stored.*

Objective 8.10 *Summarize how to stream and publish digital music.*

Digital Media   333

Objective 8.11 *Explain how best to create, print, and share digital photographs.*

Objective 8.12 *Describe how to create, edit, and distribute digital video.*

Make This:▶ MAKE: A Video-Playing App on **page 325**

All media accompanying this chapter can be found in MyITLab.

For an overview of the chapter, watch the **Preview Video.** ▶

(Kuroji/Fotolia, Oleksiy Mark/Fotolia, Frankie Angel/Alamy, Tetra Images/Getty Images, Future Music Magazine/Getty Images, Ralph Lee Hopkins/Corbis)

HOW COOL IS THIS?

Ever heard of CLIP? If not, you soon will, as it is maturing into a technology that is set to launch a **hardware revolution**. First-generation 3D printing consisted of "extruded plastic printing"—melting plastic down and then layering it with a very fine nozzle. **Continuous Liquid Interface Production (CLIP) 3D printers** go beyond extruded plastic using a **new, more accurate technique**. The printer's laser draws on the surface of a **pool of liquid plastic** resin. The small spots where the laser hits harden. Layer by layer, a specific shape can be formed. The accuracy and resolution of this approach far exceeds earlier 3D printers, and **different colors, transparencies**, and **flexibility** can be incorporated to create much more sophisticated printable parts. Visit sites like **Thingiverse (thingiverse.com)** to see the growing collection of objects you can print out at home. *(Leonello Calvetti/Science Photo Library/Corbis)*

Mobile Devices

Learning Outcome 8.1 You will be able to discuss the nature of digital signals and how mobile computing devices are designed and operated.

For many of us, our phone is our lifeline to the world, and if not our phone, then our laptop or tablet. We live in a digital world, and our devices have evolved to let us communicate anywhere we go, 24/7. In this section, we'll check out a number of mobile devices and their features and examine the nature of digital signals.

digital
BASICS

How did we end up in a world in which we are all tethered to our phones and able to communicate with each other whenever and almost wherever we want? Part of the story relates to the concept of *digital convergence*, as we'll explore in this section.

Digital Convergence

Objective 8.1 *Describe how digital convergence has evolved.*

What is digital convergence? Digital convergence refers to our ability to use a single device to meet all of our media, Internet, entertainment, and telephone needs. This digital convergence is exemplified in the range of devices now on the market. For example, you see digital convergence in the evolution of smartphones, which now

let you do just about anything a computer can do. The push to digital convergence can also be seen in the migration of digital devices into environments like the cabin of your car. The Tesla S features a 17-inch touch-screen display, shown in Figure 8.1a, that controls all of the electronics systems of the car, providing Internet access, mobile communications, and navigation features, including sensors that detect vehicles in your blind spot.

Even some refrigerators, like the one shown in Figure 8.1b, now include LCD touch-screen displays and network adapters so that they can display recipes from websites as well as place a call to the service center and schedule their own repair visit for you. This trend toward devices being able to be part of the Internet is named the Internet of Things (IoT). Estimates say over 50 billion devices will be on the Internet by 2020.

a

b

FIGURE 8.1 (a) Auto electronics have now converged with tablet technology. The Tesla S features a 17-inch touch-screen display. (b) Some refrigerators are now equipped with touch screens that connect to the Internet. *(Bloomberg/Getty Images, Steve Marcus/Landov)*

In fact, devices are beginning to converge so much that an organization has been created to standardize them. The Digital Living Network Alliance (**dlna.org**) is an organization working to standardize different kinds of appliances and network devices used in our homes. As our appliances, cars, and homes become designed to communicate over a common network, how we manage our media, control our living spaces, and communicate with our families will continue to change.

How have mobile devices converged? As more and more computing power is available in mobile processors, mobile devices have evolved to be able to do multiple tasks. Smartphones, tablets, and 2-in-1s have significant overlap in the tasks they can perform, so learning the differences will be important in finding the device that's just right for you. Let's start by taking a look at the foundation for all these devices: digital signals.

Digital vs. Analog

Objective 8.2 *Explain the differences between digital and analog signals.*

What does it mean to be "digital" and what advantages does it bring us? Today, no matter what you're interested in—music, movies, television, books, stock prices—digital information is the key. All forms of entertainment have migrated to the digital domain (see Figure 8.2).

FIGURE 8.2

Analog versus Digital Entertainment		
	ANALOG	**DIGITAL**
Publishing	Magazines, books	E-books, e-zines
Music	Vinyl record albums and cassette tapes	CDs, MP3 files, and streaming music stations
Photography	35-mm single-lens reflex (SLR) cameras Photos stored on film	Digital cameras, including digital SLRs Photos stored as digital files
Video	8-mm, VHS, and Hi8 camcorders Film stored on tapes	HD digital video (DV) cameras Film stored as digital files; distributed on DVD and Blu-ray discs and streamed
Radio	AM/FM radio	HD Radio, SiriusXM satellite radio
Television	Analog TV broadcast	High-definition digital television (HDTV)

Phone systems and TV signals are now digital streams of data. MP3 files encode digital forms of music, and cameras and video equipment are all digital. In Hollywood, feature films are shot entirely with digital equipment. Movie theaters receive a hard drive storing a copy of a new release to show using digital projection equipment. Satellite radio systems such as SiriusXM and HD Radio are broadcast in digital formats.

How is digital different from analog? Any kind of information can be digitized (measured and converted to a stream of numeric values). Consider sound. It's carried to your ears by sound waves, which are actually patterns of pressure changes in the air. Images are our interpretation of the changing intensity of light waves around us. These sound and light waves are called **analog** waves or continuous waves. They illustrate the loudness of a sound or the brightness of the colors in an image at a given moment in time. They're continuous signals because you would never have to lift your pencil off the page to draw them; they are just long, continuous lines.

First-generation recording devices such as vinyl records and analog television broadcasts were designed to reproduce these sound and light waves. A needle in the groove of a vinyl record vibrates in the same pattern as the original sound wave. Analog television signals are actually waves that tell an analog TV how to display the same color and brightness as is seen in the production studio.

However, it's difficult to describe a wave, even mathematically. The simplest sounds, such as that of middle C on a piano, have the simplest shapes, like the one shown in Figure 8.3a. However, something like the word *hello* generates a highly complex pattern, like the one shown in Figure 8.3b.

What advantages do digital formats have over analog ones? Digital formats describe signals as long strings of numbers. This digital representation gives us a simple way to describe sound and light waves exactly so that sounds and images can be reproduced perfectly any time they're wanted. In addition, we already have easy ways to distribute digital information, such as streaming movies or attaching files to a Facebook message. Digital information can be reproduced exactly and distributed easily. Both these reasons give digital huge advantages over an analog format.

How can a sequence of numbers express complicated analog shapes? The answer is provided by something called *analog-to-digital conversion*. In analog-to-digital conversion, the incoming analog signal is measured many times each second. The strength of the signal at each measurement is recorded as a simple number. The series of numbers produced by the analog-to-digital conversion process gives us the digital form of the wave. Figure 8.4 shows analog and digital versions of the same wave. In Figure 8.4a, you see the original, continuous analog wave. You could draw that wave without lifting your pencil from the page. In Figure 8.4b, the wave has been digitized and is no longer a single line; instead, it is represented as a series of points or numbers.

How has the change from analog to digital technologies affected our lifestyles? When the market for communication devices for entertainment

FIGURE 8.3 (a) An analog wave showing the simple, pure sound of a piano playing middle C. (b) The complex wave produced when a person says "Hello." *(Windows 8.1, Microsoft Corporation)*

media—like photos, music, and video—switched to a digital standard, we began to have products with new and useful capabilities. Small devices can now hold huge collections of a variety of types of information. We can interact with our information any time we like in ways that, prior to the conversion to digital media, had been too expensive or too difficult to learn. The implications of the shift to digital media are continually evolving. ■

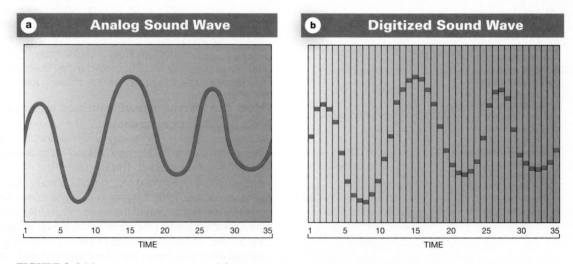

FIGURE 8.4 (a) A simple analog wave. (b) A digitized version of the same wave. *(Sony Creative Software, Inc.)*

the power of
SMARTPHONES

Communication has changed radically in the digital age. Chapter 3 discussed the use of wikis, blogs, and other web-based tools for connecting people and their ideas. All of these software applications are dependent on digital information.

Hardware devices that support communication have also evolved because of digital technologies. In this section, we'll examine how digital networks and devices are meeting out modern communication needs.

Cellular Technology

Objective 8.3 *Describe the technologies used to communicate across cellular networks.*

What makes a smartphone a smartphone?
Telephony, the use of equipment to provide voice communications over a distance, has shifted from an analog science to a digital one. Smartphones like the iPhone and the Samsung Galaxy illustrate the true power of digital convergence (see Figure 8.5). They incorporate a range of features that used to be available only in separate, dedicated devices:

- Internet access
- Personal information management (PIM) features
- Voice recording features
- The ability to play and organize music files
- GPS services
- Digital image and video capture
- Computing power to run programs like word processors and video-editing software

Isn't every phone a smartphone now?
All phones that use mobile, cellular technology can be called **cellular (cell) phones**. Although many cell phones on the market are considered smartphones, less powerful cell phones are available. Called **feature phones**, these inexpensive phones have modest processors, simpler interfaces, and often no touch screen. As more features are integrated into every cell phone product, though, it becomes difficult to distinguish a smartphone from a feature phone. Most providers, like AT&T or Verizon, label a smartphone as one that has sufficient power so that you can use Internet features easily. You often have to purchase a data plan with a smartphone. We'll use the term *cell phone* to refer to all cellular phones and *smartphones* to refer to the more powerful type of cell phone that can run more complex applications.

Are smartphones computers? All
cell phones—smartphones and feature phones—have the same components as any computer: a processor (central processing unit, or CPU), memory, and input and output

devices, as shown in Figure 8.6. Cell phones require their own operating system (OS) software and have their own application software. So, in effect, all cell phones are computers.

Smartphones use a CPU and an interface so powerful that they can take on many of the same tasks as much more expensive computers: videoconferencing, recording and editing high-definition (HD) video, and broadcasting live-streaming video.

What kind of processor is inside a smartphone?
Popular processors for smartphones include the Qualcomm Snapdragon and the Apple A8. These use a multi-core design, which used to be reserved for high-end desktop systems. The processor in a cell phone is responsible for a great number of tasks. The processor coordinates sending all of the data among the other electronic components inside the phone. It also runs the cell phone's OS, which provides a user interface

FIGURE 8.5 A single device like a smartphone can play the role of many separate devices, illustrating the concept of digital convergence. *(Fsketch/Fotolia, Maxx-Studio/Shutterstock, MrGarry/Shutterstock, Frank Peters/Shutterstock, You can more/Shutterstock, Gielmichal/Shutterstock, Bartosz Zakrzewski/Shutterstock)*

LED display
CPU
Memory
Camera module
Audio interface
Touch-screen controller
Battery

FIGURE 8.6 Inside your smartphone, you'll find a CPU; a memory chip; input devices such as a microphone, a camera, and a touch screen; and output devices such as a display screen. *(Image courtesy of iFixit)*

so that you can change phone settings, store information, play games, and so on. It must do all of this work while consuming as little power as possible so the energy of one battery charge can last all day.

Is there a standard OS for smartphones? There is not one standard. Two operating systems account for most all smartphones. Most smartphones use the Android OS, while Apple's iPhone uses iOS, a version of the OS X operating system that is used in Apple's computers. In addition to these two operating systems, Microsoft offers Windows for mobile phones, but this OS still has a very small market share. Operating systems such as these are required to translate the user's commands into instructions for the processor. Figure 8.7 illustrates the user interfaces featured among these three smartphone operating systems.

What does the memory inside a smartphone do? Your phone's memory stores all of the phone's information and programs. The OS is stored in read-only memory (ROM), the phone's permanent memory, because the phone would be useless without that key piece of software. Other phone data, such as ring tones and contact lists, is stored in separate internal memory chips.

Many smartphones let you add additional memory through micro SD flash cards (see Figure 8.8). Micro SD cards are easy to install inside a phone, and some models have external slots for an SD card. Not all smartphones allow memory upgrades in this way, however. For example, iPhones don't allow you to add memory.

What input and output devices do smartphones use? The primary input devices for a smartphone are its microphone and touch screen. Software-based keyboards can support dozens of languages and different character sets

FIGURE 8.7

Mobile Operating Systems

OPERATING SYSTEM	MANUFACTURER	USER INTERFACE
Android	Used by HTC, Samsung	
iOS	Apple	
Windows 10	Microsoft	

(Neil Godwin/T3 Magazine/Getty Images, Richard Sharrocks/Alamy Stock Photo, Robert Galbraith/ Reuters/Corbis)

 SOUND BYTE
Smartphones Are Really Smart
In this Sound Byte, you'll learn how to use a smartphone as a powerful tool to communicate, calculate, and organize your workload.

FIGURE 8.8 Micro SD flash cards add memory to some phones. *(123RF)*

(see Figure 8.9). The digital cameras in smartphones are also input devices, capturing images and video.

Cell phone output devices include a speaker and a display. Higher-end models include full-color, high-resolution OLED (organic light-emitting diode) screens. OLED displays create very bright, sharp images and draw less power than the LCD (liquid crystal display) screens found on some lower-end smartphones.

What smartphone software is available? A smartphone OS comes with a standard collection of software, such as a to-do list, contact manager, and calendar. Of course, you can also buy additional apps at web-based software stores like the App Store for the Apple iPhone and the Google Play Store for Android devices (see Figure 8.10). Each store has over 1.5 million different apps available for download.

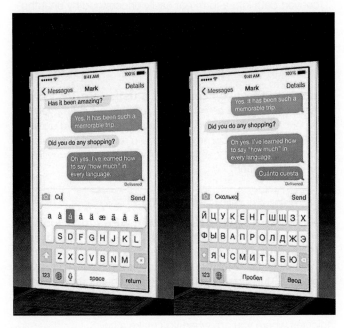

FIGURE 8.9 Software-based keyboards can easily support languages with unique character sets. *(Screen shot(s) reprinted with permission from Apple, Inc.)*

FIGURE 8.10 Google Play, the Windows Store, and Apple's App Store are some of the many online stores delivering software for mobile devices. *(Anatolii Babii/Alamy Stock Photo, Kevin Britland/Alamy, Anatolii Babii/Alamy)*

Cellular Networks

What's "cellular" about a cell phone? As noted earlier, the term *cell phone* is short for *cellular phone*. A set of connected "cells" makes up a cellular network. Each cell is a geographic area centered on a **base transceiver station**, which is a large communications tower with antennas, amplifiers, receivers, and transmitters. When you place a call on a cell phone, a base station picks up the request for service. The station then passes the request to a central location called a **mobile switching center**. The reverse process occurs when you receive an incoming call. A telecommunications company builds its network by constructing a series of cells that overlap in an attempt to guarantee that its cell phone customers have coverage no matter where they are.

As you move during your phone call, the mobile switching center monitors the strength of the signal between your cell phone and the closest base station. When the signal is no longer strong enough between your cell phone and the base station, the mobile switching center orders the next base station to take charge of your call. When your cell phone "drops out," it may be because the distance between base stations is too great to provide an adequate signal.

How do cell phones use digital signals? When you speak into a cell phone, a series of digital processing steps occur:

1. Sound enters the microphone as a sound wave. Because these sound waves need to be *digitized* (that is, converted into a sequence of *1*s and *0*s that the cell phone's processor can understand), an **analog-to-digital converter chip** converts your voice's sound waves into digital signals.

2. Next, the digital data must be *compressed*, or squeezed, into the smallest possible space so that it will transmit more quickly to another phone. The processor can't perform the mathematical operations required at this stage quickly enough, so there's a specialized chip called the **digital signal processor** included in the cell phone that handles the compression work.

3. Finally, the digital data is *transmitted* as a radio wave through the cellular network to the destination phone.

When you receive an incoming call, the digital signal processor decompresses the incoming message. An amplifier boosts the signal to make it loud enough, and it is then passed on to the speaker.

VoIP

Is the cellular network the only way to place phone calls? Cell phone service is still not 100% reliable, and dropped calls and poor reception are a problem in some areas. As an alternative, a fully digital phone service called **Voice over Internet Protocol (VoIP)** is available.

How is VoIP different from regular telephone service? VoIP is a form of voice-based Internet communication that turns a standard Internet connection into a means to place phone calls, including long-distance calls (see Figure 8.11). Traditional telephone communications use analog voice data and telephone connections. In contrast, VoIP uses

FIGURE 8.11 VoIP technology lets your computing device behave like a phone or video phone, using the Internet instead of the telephone system to transmit data. *(David Malan/Getty Images)*

technology similar to that used in e-mail to transmit your voice data digitally over the Internet.

Who are some VoIP providers? Skype is one very well-known provider. Creating a VoIP account with Skype (**skype.com**) is simple (see the Try This in Chapter 1). Skype requires that both callers and receivers have the company's free software installed on their device (computer, tablet, or phone). With Skype you can place a phone call, make an HD-video call, and even share screens between users. Calls to other Skype users are free, and you can place low-cost calls to non-Skype users. Major ISPs, like Comcast and Verizon, also provide VoIP phone services as an option you can package with your Internet or cable television plan.

What do I need to use VoIP? VoIP calls can be placed from anywhere you have Internet access. Any Android or iOS phone or tablet can also be used as a VoIP device. There are also stand-alone VoIP phones sold, sometimes called *IP phones*.

What are the advantages and disadvantages of VoIP? For people who make many long-distance phone calls, the advantage of VoIP is that it's free or low cost. Portability is another advantage: as long as you're connected to the Internet, you can sign on to your VoIP service and make your call.

Although VoIP is affordable and convenient, it does have drawbacks:

- Some people regard sound quality and reliability issues as VoIP's primary disadvantages.
- Another drawback when using VoIP at home is the loss of service if power is interrupted.
- Another issue with VoIP is security risks. Having a hacker break in to a VoIP system to make unauthorized calls is a serious but avoidable problem. Encryption services that convert data into a form not easily understood by unauthorized people are being deployed to help protect calls made over the Internet.

VoIP continues to enjoy explosive growth, and the technology will continue to improve.

What new features come with using VoIP? If you set up a VoIP service as your home telephone system, you can have your telephone messages automatically bundled up as e-mails and sent to your account. If you're watching television and a call comes in, it can be displayed on the screen with caller ID information.

Smartphone GPS

Does my smartphone contain a GPS chip? Today every cell phone and smartphone has to include a GPS chip. The Federal Communications Commission (FCC) mandated this to enable the complete rollout of the Enhanced 911 (E911) program. E911 automatically gives dispatchers precise location information for any 911 call. It also means your phone records may include this precise tracking information, which indicates where you are when you make a call.

How does GPS work? Built and operated by the U.S. Department of Defense, the **global positioning system (GPS)**

FIGURE 8.12 GPS computes your location anywhere on Earth from a system of orbiting satellites. *(BlackJack3D/Getty Images)*

is a network of 21 satellites (plus 3 working spares) that constantly orbits Earth. GPS devices use an antenna to pick up the signals from these satellites and use special software to transform those signals into latitude and longitude. Using the information obtained from the satellites, GPS devices determine geographical location anywhere on the planet to within 3 feet (see Figure 8.12). The exact accuracy depends on such things as atmospheric conditions and interference from obstacles like mountains or buildings.

Can someone track me using the GPS chip in my phone? Cell phone providers offer plans (for a monthly fee) that allow you to track where a phone is at any given time. For example, AT&T's Family Map service lets parents track all the phones on their family plan in real time. Locations of all phones are displayed over the web on a map or to an app for your phone, or the service will send an automatic text message alert with the phones' locations at a specific time each day. So a parent could have a text or e-mail sent with his or her daughter's phone location each day at 3 p.m. to be sure she made it home from school. The person being tracked can't turn off the service. This same kind of feature allows you to locate a lost phone.

Using Smartphones and Keeping Them Secure

Objective 8.4 *Explain how to effectively use cellular devices and mobile Internet access and how to keep your devices secure.*

What's the best way to synchronize data between my phone and computer? The process of updating your data so your to-do lists, schedules, and other files on your cell phone and computer are the same is called **synchronizing**, or **syncing**. There are two main ways to transfer information between your phone and computer:

1. *Wired*: Use a micro SD card or a USB cable to directly transfer data.
2. *Wireless*: Use a wireless connection to transfer data.

How does a wired transfer of data work? Almost all phones are designed to support USB. Some have a mini-USB connector, while other models require a special cable to connect the phone to a standard USB port. Once connected using a USB data cable, your phone will appear on your computer like an additional flash drive. Depending on your mobile operating system, you can then drag and drop files to the phone or software will pop up that lets you manage your phone's content. You can also charge your phone through the USB cable.

If your phone supports a high-density micro SD card, you can easily remove the card and slip it directly into a flash card reader in your computer.

How do I transfer information to and from my phone wirelessly? The easiest way is to use a wireless connection to a cloud service. A number of web services are now available to synchronize your e-mail, files, contacts, and calendars instantly and wirelessly. Both Apple and Google provide backup features in their operating systems that wirelessly syncs folders of data and photos from your mobile device to your home computer automatically (see Figure 8.13).

Cloud Service

FIGURE 8.13 A cloud service lets you keep the information on your phone instantly in sync with your other computing devices. *(Siuwing/123RF)*

ACTIVE HELPDESK
Keeping Your Data on Hand
In this Active Helpdesk, you'll play the role of a helpdesk staffer assisting people with management of their cloud storage accounts.

SOUND BYTE
Connecting with Bluetooth
In this Sound Byte, you'll learn what freedoms Bluetooth affords you and how to use Bluetooth devices.

These web services follow the model of cloud computing, where Internet-based services and resources are distributed to users instead of being installed as an application on the user's computer. Apple's iOS has cloud support integrated into applications like Calendar, iTunes, PhotoStream, Contacts, and Mail. A photo taken on your iPhone will automatically be transferred to your iPad and your home Windows or Mac computer, for example. Android Backup service does the same thing for Android devices.

There are other providers of wireless synchronization for mobile devices. The cloud storage service Dropbox provides support to allow your photos to be automatically transferred to cloud storage and removed from your phone, keeping more free space on your phone. Even the Amazon Kindle uses wireless synchronization so that if you read a bit further in your e-book on your phone, when you get to your office, the Kindle software on your PC will have automatically updated to bookmark the new page you're on.

Another way devices wirelessly transfer data is using Bluetooth. Most smartphones on the market today are Bluetooth-enabled, meaning they include a small Bluetooth chip that allows them to transfer data wirelessly to any other Bluetooth-enabled device. **Bluetooth** technology uses radio waves to transmit data signals over distances up to approximately 300 feet (for Bluetooth 4). Bluetooth 4 devices are the newest on the market and are almost twice as fast as Bluetooth 3 devices. New cars offer Bluetooth-enabled entertainment systems. As you sit down in the driver's seat, your phone sends all of its contact list, recent call list, and other data to the system so you can easily make hands-free calls.

Text Messaging
What does SMS stand for? Short message service (SMS)—often just called *text messaging*—is a technology that lets you send short text messages (up to 160 characters) over cellular networks. You can send SMS messages to other mobile devices or to any e-mail address.

Companies now support texting in many ways—for example, your bank may allow you to text commands to request account balances or details about your last transaction and the bank will text the requested information back to you.

How does SMS work? SMS uses the cell phone network to transmit messages. When you send an SMS message, an SMS calling center receives the message and delivers it to the appropriate mobile device using something called *store-and-forward* technology. This technology allows users to send SMS messages to any other SMS device in the world.

Is the same technology used to send and receive photos and videos? SMS technology lets you send only text messages. However, an extension of SMS called **multimedia message service (MMS)** lets you send messages that include text, sound, images, and video clips to other phones or e-mail addresses. MMS messages actually arrive as a series of messages; you view the text, then the image, then the sound, and so on. You can then choose to save just one part of the message (such as the image), all of it, or none of it. MMS users can subscribe to financial, sports, and weather services that will "push" information to them, sending it automatically to their phones in MMS format.

Mobile Internet
What's the best way to connect my smartphone to the Internet? There are two ways smartphones (and most mobile devices) can connect to the Internet:

1. Using a WiFi network
2. Using the cellular phone system (a 3G or 4G connection)

BITS&BYTES

Texting for Change

Can texting impact social change? Texting is now being used to address serious social issues because it is the choice communication mode of people aged 14 to 30. Studies show that texts reach the teenage population at 11 times the effectiveness of e-mail. The average number of monthly texts a teenager sends and receives is over 3,500 a month. This holds true across a wide range of socioeconomic categories.

Crisis texting hotlines are opening to reach and respond to the violence, rape, and bullying that young people experience. The site DoSomething.org (**dosomething.org**) opened a Crisis Text Line to organize their response to crisis text messages they were receiving. In addition, police around the country are establishing anonymous texting tip lines to take advantage of the prevalence of texting.

A major advantage of WiFi is that it does not add to your data plan usage. However, there may not always be a WiFi signal available where you are. Cellular networks are much more widely available, whether you're in your car or just walking down the street.

For devices like tablets, manufacturers will offer one model that can only connect to the Internet using WiFi and another model that costs more but can connect with either WiFi or cellular 3G/4G.

Who sells cellular Internet service for my smartphone? Just as you have an Internet service provider (ISP) for Internet access for your desktop or laptop computer, you must have a **wireless Internet service provider** (or **wireless ISP**) to connect your smartphone to the Internet. Phone companies (such as T-Mobile, Verizon, and AT&T) double as wireless ISPs. Most wireless ISPs also offer free login to their network of WiFi hotspots if you're a cellular customer.

How do I purchase Internet time? Providers measure your Internet usage not according to how much time you're on the Internet but according to how much data you download and upload. An Internet connectivity plan is known as a **data plan**. You pay one monthly price and are allowed data transfers up to some fixed limit per month, such as 2 GB or 5 GB. If you exceed your data limit in a month, the fee for the extra data usage is usually very expensive.

Understanding your data usage is complicated. A cellular data plan is for Internet data transfer, not texting. Providers require a separate texting plan. Note that all the data transfer you do using WiFi (instead of the 3G/4G network) does not count as part of your data plan usage.

How big a data plan do I need to buy? Before subscribing to a data plan, you should assess your needs. When you are out of reach of a WiFi network, how often do you:

- download apps, stream music, or play online games?
- watch streaming video?
- download files attached to e-mails or from your company website?

Begin by estimating how much data you transfer up and down from the Internet each month. To do so, you can use an online estimator supplied by your provider like the one shown in Figure 8.14.

The Android OS allows you to see a graph of your data usage and set alarms at specific levels. iOS keeps track of your cellular data usage too. You should reset this feature manually each month so you know how much data transfer you have left. Apps are available for any smartphone to keep track of data usage for you.

Be sure you select a data plan that provides adequate service at a good price. There are plans that allow a group of people to share data and pull from a single pool. Some plans

FIGURE 8.14 Online tools can help you estimate your monthly data usage.

(All Vectors/Fotolia, Vladvm50Fotolia, Edisainer/Fotolia, Kreizihorse/Fotolia, Jozefmicic/Fotolia)

transfer unused data over to the next month; some do not. Shop carefully.

At what speed is digital information transferred to my smartphone? Although broadband speeds of 80 megabits per second (Mbps) are achievable at home using a cable or fiber-optic connection, your smartphone will connect at a much lower speed. The exact speed will depend on which technology you're using: WiFi, 3G cellular, or 4G cellular (see Figure 8.15).

FIGURE 8.15 The range of speeds you achieve when connecting to the Internet with your smartphone or mobile device depends on the type of connection.

We discussed WiFi networks in depth in Chapter 7. These networks typically run at speeds of 4 to 5 Mbps. Currently, there are two cellular data-transfer standards:

1. *3G*: 3G brought mobile device data-transfer rates as high as 3.8 Mbps (or more, under ideal conditions). 3G is more reliable than WiFi and is less susceptible to interference. 3G blankets most major urban areas with connectivity.

2. *4G*: 4G networks are now rolling out across the United States. The promise of 4G is incredible: mobile connection speeds of up to 100 Mbps! Currently, most providers can't deliver true 4G speeds; their 4G networks deliver speeds of 6 Mbps to 13 Mbps. These options, often named "4G LTE," are faster than 3G but don't meet the rate required to be true 4G, so they're referred to as "near 4G" networks. The expansion of 4G will usher in a new generation of mobile devices.

How do I set my phone to use a WiFi connection? It will be slightly different for each mobile OS, but in general, you turn on the setting that allows your phone to look for a network. If a network is found, the phone will try to log in. If the network has security protection, you'll be prompted for a password before joining. Most smartphones then display a special icon to show that you're using a WiFi connection instead of a 3G/4G signal.

Some people choose to leave their phone in the mode where it's looking for a WiFi network so it will always use a WiFi signal if it is available, saving them on data plan usage.

BITS&BYTES

Want to Read That Voicemail?

Consider using Google Voice. Google Voice automatically transcribes your voice messages to text so if you're someplace noisy, you can still check in on that last call. The transcription also makes it easy to search for information left in a voice message. If you want, the transcribed calls can be e-mailed to you and you can text back a response right from the e-mail. You can sign up for a free Google Voice phone number at **google.com/voice**.

This does use more battery life, though, so turn off WiFi detection if you're trying to extend your battery.

Can I use my 3G/4G signal to create a WiFi hotspot for my other devices? This approach, called **tethering**, enables you to use your phone's cellular network to create a wireless network that you can share with your computer or other device to access the Internet. Both Android and iOS allow you to create this kind of "personal hotspot" on devices running their operating systems. You simply give your network a name (an SSID) and a password, and any of your other devices can connect to the Internet through the phone's 3G/4G network signal. Check with your provider, though, because they may charge an extra fee for tethering.

Smartphone Security

Can I get a virus on my smartphone? Viruses can indeed infect smartphones. Over half of users say they send confidential e-mails using their phones, and one-third of users access bank account or credit card information on their phones, so smartphones are the next most likely realm of attack by cybercriminals. Although viruses plaguing smartphones have not yet reached the volume of viruses attacking PC operating systems, with the proliferation of mobile devices, virus attacks are expected to increase.

How do I protect my phone then? Kaspersky and McAfee are among the leading companies currently providing antivirus software for mobile devices. Products are designed for specific operating systems; for example, Kaspersky Mobile Security has versions for Android phones and tablets and Windows phones. Often, businesses will have their information technology department install and configure an antivirus solution like this for all the phones used in the organization.

If no antivirus program is available for your phone's OS, the best precautions are commonsense ones. Check the phone manufacturer's website frequently to see whether your smartphone needs any software upgrades that could patch security holes. In addition, remember that you shouldn't download ring tones, games, or other software from unfamiliar websites.

How do I keep my phone number private? If you're concerned about widely distributing your phone number and potentially inviting lots of unwanted calls, consider using a virtual phone number. A virtual phone number is a phone number you create that can be assigned to ring on existing phone numbers. Companies such as Telusion (**tossabledigits.com**) will sell you a virtual number. Then, when you're filling out a registration form for some web service, you can input your virtual phone number in the web form instead of giving out your actual number. When you set up the virtual account, you can restrict the hours that you will receive calls from that number, and if you're receiving many unwanted calls, you can disable the virtual number without affecting your cell phone or smartphone service. ∎

mobile
COMPUTING

The best way to navigate all the mobile devices on the market is to be aware of the boundaries between types of devices.

Variety of Devices

Objective 8.5 *Demonstrate an understanding of the range of different mobile computing devices.*

How do different styles of computing devices work to meet your needs? In this section, we'll look at what changes when you move from one type of device to another.

Tablets

How do tablets compare with smartphones? *Tablets* are very light, portable devices. The top-selling tablets include the Apple iPad and the Samsung Galaxy, but there are over 75 tablets on the market. The main difference between any tablet and a smartphone is screen size. Whereas smartphones usually have displays that are less than 5 inches, tablets come with screen sizes between 7 and 10 inches. But manufacturers are beginning to make even larger phones, offering a "phablet" model of phone, with screen sizes almost 6 inches. The larger screen allows for a larger virtual keyboard and higher resolution.

In most other regards, smartphones and tablets are similar. They have the following features:

- Similar operating systems: Whether iOS or Android, common operating systems operate on smartphones and tablets.
- Similar processors: The processing power of smartphones and tablets is often the same.
- Touch-screen interfaces: Smartphones and tablets are both equipped with touch-screen interfaces.
- Long battery life: Most tablets and smartphones run at least 10 hours on a single charge.
- Similar software applications: Most apps available for one device are available for the other.
- Similar Internet connectivity: Both can offer 3G/4G as well as WiFi connectivity.
- Bluetooth: Both can be connected over Bluetooth to printers, keyboards, and other peripherals.

Can tablets function as a communication device? Although tablets are currently not able to make cell phone calls, they can easily place audio or video phone calls if connected to a WiFi network. A VoIP application like Skype is required for that. There are also apps available that allow tablets to handle texting. HeyWire, for example, supports free national and international texting from a range of devices, including tablets as well as phones.

2-in-1s

What is a 2-in-1 device? The *2-in-1* is a device that combines the features of a tablet along with a physical keyboard

FIGURE 8.16 The Microsoft Surface is an example of a 2-in-1 type of device: a touch-screen tablet and a detachable keyboard merged into one unit. *(Stan honda/Getty Images)*

into a single device (see Figure 8.16). This hybrid laptop tries to serve both as a laptop and as a tablet. On some models, such as Microsoft Surface devices, the touch screen is detachable from the keyboard so it can be carried and used as an independent tablet. On others, such as the Lenova Yoga, there is a hinge so that the keyboard can be folded behind the screen.

Why would I want a 2-in-1 instead of a tablet? Although more expensive than a tablet, 2-in-1s have a more powerful CPU so they can actually function as a laptop and run the same software applications. This is also because whereas a tablet runs a mobile OS, like Android or iOS, a 2-in-1 uses a full traditional OS, like Windows 10. In addition, a 2-in-1 has a physical keyboard. 2-in-1s weigh 2 pounds or less and are less expensive than an ultrabook laptop, so they are a good option if you're looking for value. Many people find a single 2-in-1 can replace the need to carry both a tablet and a laptop.

Why wouldn't I want a 2-in-1? The processing power and memory on some 2-in-1s makes it difficult to run software that does a lot of computation. 2-in-1s also have smaller screens than laptops (usually 10 inches or less). The responsiveness of the keyboard may not work for your needs, so be sure to try one out before making a purchase.

Ultrabooks

How are ultrabooks different from laptops? *Ultrabooks* are a newer category of full-featured computers that focus on offering a very thin, lightweight computing solution. Ultrabooks don't offer optical drives, for example, allowing a very thin profile. Some do not even offer traditional USB ports, instead using the more compact USB-C connector so that they are only about 13 mm at the thickest point. Most

FIGURE 8.17

Comparing Devices

FEATURE	TABLET	ULTRABOOK	2-IN-1
Operating System	Mobile OS (iOS, Android, Windows)	Traditional OS (Windows or OS X)	Traditional OS
Interface	Touch screen	Some have non-touch screens; have full-size keyboards	Touch screen; detachable full-size keyboard
Screen Size	7 to 10 inches	13 to 15 inches	10 to 14 inches
Processing Power	Mobile processor	Full quad-core Intel i5	Full quad-core i5, i7
Storage	Up to 128 GB	128 to 500 GB	Up to 128GB
Software	Specialized applications custom designed for touch interface	Standard versions of software for desktop environments (Microsoft Office, etc.)	Standard versions of desktop software

ultrabooks offer SSD drives and so have very fast response times on boot up and restoring from hibernation. They weigh in at under 3 pounds even though they feature the same operating systems and CPUs as heavier, larger laptops. They also include full-size keyboards and 13- to 15-inch screens. Examples include the Apple Macbook Air and the Asus Zenbook.

How are ultrabooks different from tablets and laptops?
Whereas tablets share a lot in common with smartphones, ultrabooks are lightweight laptops. They are good choices when you want to run a traditional OS and need a lot of computing power. Compared to a traditional laptop, ultrabooks are lighter and more inexpensive. If you are looking for the savings of having just one device, a 2-in-1 supports portability because of the removable keyboard but still uses a touch screen and a traditional OS. Figure 8.17 summarizes how all these devices compare.

Selecting a Device

Objective 8.6 *Describe how to evaluate which mobile device is appropriate for a specific user.*

With all these choices, how do I know which device is best for me? The number of devices has grown so much that you will have a lot to consider. Use these guidelines to determine what particular device best fits your personal needs. Consider the following:

- **Power:** How much computational power do you need?
- **Screen size and resolution:** These cannot be changed later so make sure the quality and size of screen will fit your needs for the years you will keep the device.
- **Style of keyboard:** Do you want a touch-based interface? Is a physical keyboard important, or is a software keyboard sufficient? Does the feel of the keyboard work for you?
- **Battery life:** Some devices can operate for 15 hours continuously, others less than 5. Investigate whether the battery can be upgraded and how much weight that would add.
- **Weight:** Does an additional 2 pounds matter? Remember to include the weight of any charging brick you would need to carry when you travel as you consider the tradeoff in price for a lighter device.
- **Number of devices:** Is this your only computing device? As technology prices fall, you may be able to have more than one device. You might find an affordable solution that includes both a very mobile device and a second more powerful one.

Figure 8.18 summarizes several different mobile device categories. ■

Laptop
* 5 to 8 lbs
* Traditional OS

Ultrabook
* Less than 3 lbs
* Traditional OS

2-in-1
• 1 to 3 lbs
• Traditional OS

Tablet
• Less than 2 lbs
• Mobile OS

Smartphone
• 0.25 lbs
• Mobile OS

Before moving on to Part 2:
1. Watch Replay Video 8.1 ▷.
2. Then check your understanding of what you've learned so far.

FIGURE 8.18 A full spectrum of mobile devices is available.
(Peter Dazeley/Getty Images, Bloomberg/Getty Images, Ethan Miller/Getty Images, Josep Lago/Getty Images, Sean Gallup/Getty Images)

check your understanding // review & practice

For a quick review to see what you've learned so far, answer the following questions.

multiple choice

1. The operating system on your cell phone

   a. can be changed from iOS to Android.

   b. is a version of Android if you are using an iPhone.

   c. is stored on the SD card in the phone.

   d. none of the above

2. VoIP is a phone service that

   a. requires a fiber-optic connection.

   b. works over an Internet connection.

   c. is only available for calls within the United States.

   d. has extremely high quality but is very expensive.

3. Which service allows you to use your cell phone or smartphone to send messages that contain images?

   a. MMS

   b. ISP

   c. SMS

   d. MiFi

4. Analog waves are still important because

   a. they have a better shape than digital waveforms.

   b. physical processes like sound waves are analog.

   c. digital waveforms cannot be created from things like vinyl recordings

   d. they are produced by analog to digital conversion.

5. The GPS positioning system is

   a. a system of 21 satellites in orbit.

   b. usable by every smartphone.

   c. can track a phone's location in real time.

   d. all of the above

 Go to **MyITLab** to take an autograded version of the *Check Your Understanding* review and to find all media resources for the chapter.

TECHBYTES WEEKLY

Stay current with the TechBytes Weekly Newsletter.

Continue 》》

TRY THIS

Creating and Publishing a Movie

You've just taken some fantastic video and photos on a trip to the zoo, and you'd like to organize the media and put it on your Facebook page. What should you do? Try Movie Maker!

Before You Start

a. Before starting, make sure you have several video clips and photos available. If you don't have any of your own, you can use the sample photos and video clips provided with Windows.

b. Movie Maker is part of the Windows Essentials package that is an add-on to Windows (this means it does not come preinstalled in Windows). To install Movie Maker, go to Microsoft's Windows Essentials website (**windows.microsoft.com/en-US/ windows-live/essentials**) and click the **Download now link**. Once installed, type **Movie Maker** in the search bar to launch.

Step 1   The first step is to import your video clips and photos to Movie Maker. On the Home tab, click the **Add Videos and Photos icon**.

Step 2   In the dialog box that appears, browse to where your media files are saved, select the files you wish to import, and then click the **Open button**. The files you've added will appear in the Media window. *(Windows 8.1, Microsoft Corporation)*

Step 3   In your movie, the video clips and pictures will display in the order shown in the media window (timeline). Click and drag your media to the spot in the timeline where you want it to appear.

Step 4   On the Home tab, click the **Add music icon** and browse to a location on your storage device where you have music files. Select the music file you wish to add as a soundtrack for your movie, and then click the **Open button**. *(Microsoft Corporation)*

Step 5 AutoMovie themes will add transitions between clips and title or credit slides based on predesigned templates. Just click one of the available themes in the AutoMovie themes group on the Home tab to apply that theme to your movie.

Step 6 Alternatively, you can manually add a title slide or credit slides by clicking on the appropriate icons on the Home tab. Just click on the slide in the preview window to enter a title for your slide.

Step 7 To preview your movie, click the **Play button** under the Preview window. When you're satisfied with your movie, go to the Home tab and click the **Save movie icon** to save it. *(Microsoft Corporation)*

Step 8 To publish your movie on Facebook, go to the Home tab, and click the **Facebook icon** in the Share group. Select a resolution for your movie, and log on to Facebook (if necessary). Movie Maker will add your movie to your Facebook page.

Click to add title.

Click to add credit screens.

Click to apply AutoMovie theme.

Music track

Click to preview movie.

Make This ▸ TOOL: AI VideoPlayer

MAKE: A Video-Playing App

Do you want to run video clips inside your app?

In this exercise, you'll continue your mobile app development by using the Video Player component in **App Inventor** to run video clips inside your app. Using the component, you can play clips stored on your device, clips that you've recorded with the built-in camera, or clips on the Internet.

The Video Player has controls to pause, play, and fast forward or rewind and lets you manipulate the size of the video screen as well as the volume. So decide how you will make your applications more media-intensive using the Video Player component in App Inventor! *(MIT App Inventor 2, Massachusetts Institute of Technology. Creative Commons Attribution-ShareAlike 3.0 Unported License)*

The Video Player component allows you to display video inside your app.

For the instructions for this exercise, go to MyITLab.

The Impact of Digital Information

Learning Outcome 8.2 **You will be able to describe how digital technology is used to produce and distribute digital texts, music, and video.**

Do you realize how many revolutionary changes are happening in all kinds of media as we continue to use digital formats? The entertainment industry has become an all-digital field. The publishing industry, the music recording industry, photography, and film production have all seen radical changes in how content is created and how it is distributed to an audience. Let's look at how digital technology has changed these pursuits.

 ## digital
PUBLISHING

The publishing industry is migrating to digital materials. How does this impact the books you purchase, write, and read?

E-Readers

Objective 8.7 *Describe e-readers, and discuss the different types of e-readers that are available.*

Are printed books dead? Electronic text (e-text) is textual information captured digitally so that it can be stored, manipulated, and transmitted by electronic devices. With the increasing usage of e-text, the market for printed materials is changing dramatically. In fact, Amazon now sells more Kindle e-books than printed books each year. Several authors, such as Stieg Larsson and James Patterson, have each sold over one million e-books.

What electronic devices are trying to replace books? E-readers (see Figure 8.19) are devices that can display e-text and have supporting tools, like note taking, bookmarks, and integrated dictionaries. They are selling at a brisk pace with a dizzying range of offerings in the market, including the Amazon Kindle and Fire and the Barnes and Noble NOOK.

Tablets are also helping to popularize the digitized e-book and electronic versions of major magazines and newspapers. In the U.S. book market, e-books seem to be settling in at between 20% to 30% of total book sales.

What features make e-readers popular? One big allure of digital publishing is distribution. Ease of access to digital books is very attractive. Even a 1,000-page book can be delivered to your e-reader in under a minute. An incredible array of titles is available—over two million books are available in the Amazon Kindle store alone. In addition, there are millions of texts without copyright that are available for free.

The basic features of e-readers offer many advantages over paper books:

- Integrated dictionaries pull up a definition just by your highlighting a word. The Kindle, for example, comes with nine different foreign language dictionaries—a help in reading foreign works.

FIGURE 8.19 E-readers are popularizing the digital e-book.
(Kristoffer Tripplaar/Alamy)

- Note taking and highlighting are supported, and you can search the text for your own notes or for specific terms. You can also easily share the notes you make on the book with others.
- URL links or links to a glossary are often live in the book.
- Bookmarks are immediately pushed through cloud technology so you can read on one device and pick up with the most current bookmark on another device.

Do I need a dedicated device just for reading e-texts? There are free software download versions of the Kindle and the NOOK that run on either PC or Apple computers. You can also download certain texts that have no copyrights and read them directly on a computer either as a PDF file or by using browser add-ons like MagicScroll.

a   **b**

FIGURE 8.20 The two main technologies for e-text display are (a) E Ink grayscale displays, like on the Amazon Kindle, and (b) high-resolution backlit color screens, like on the Amazon Fire. *(David McNew/Getty Images, Oleksiy Maksymenko Photography/Alamy)*

How is digital text displayed? There are two popular technologies used for representing digital text:

1. *Electronic ink*: **Electronic ink (E ink)** is a very crisp, sharp grayscale representation of text. The "page" is composed of millions of microcapsules with white and black particles in a clear fluid. Electronic signals can make each spot appear either white or black. E ink devices reflect the light that shines on the page, like ordinary paper. E ink gives great contrast and is much easier to read in direct sunlight because there is no glare. High-end e-readers now also offer a built-in front light so that you can read in any light. Examples of devices using E ink include the Amazon Kindle Paperwhite (see Figure 8.20a) and the Barnes and Noble NOOK.

2. *Backlit monitors*: Another option for presenting e-text is the high-resolution backlit monitors seen in readers like the iPad or the Amazon Fire (see Figure 8.20b). These screens illuminate themselves instead of depending on room lighting conditions. They display color materials, like magazines, with great clarity and full color. The glass does reflect glare, though, which makes them hard to use in bright, direct sunlight. Some people experience more fatigue when reading from a backlit device than when using E Ink. Also note that E Ink readers have a battery life of a month or two on a charge, whereas high-resolution color readers hold a charge for 8 to 10 hours. Be sure to try both under a variety of conditions before you make a purchasing decision.

What kinds of file formats are used in electronic publishing? Digital formats for publishing vary. Amazon uses a proprietary format (.azw extension), so books purchased for a

Kindle are not transportable to a non-Kindle device. An open format also exists, ePub. Some e-readers support the ePub file format. There is an ePub reader plugin available for the browser Firefox and several stand-alone software ePub readers like Stanza.

Using e-Texts

Objective 8.8 *Explain how to purchase, borrow, and publish e-texts.*

Where do I buy e-books? There are a number of vendors associated with e-reader devices:

- Amazon sells the Kindle device, and it connects directly to the Amazon Kindle store.
- The Barnes and Noble NOOK device works with the Barnes and Noble e-bookstore.
- There are many publishers selling e-books online that can be read on any kind of device.
- Textbooks can be purchased in e-book format directly from the publisher; for example, the technology publisher O'Reilly has an online e-bookstore. Another option is a company like CourseSmart, which offers a year-long subscription to a digital text that times out and disappears from your device after your subscription is up.

What if I just want to borrow a book from a library? Libraries are now including e-book and audio book lending as part of their mission (see Figure 8.21). There is

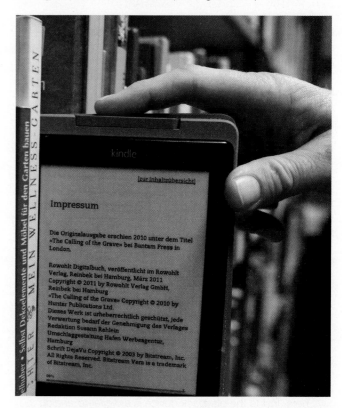

FIGURE 8.21 E-books and audio books can be borrowed for free at most public libraries. *(Alex Ehlers/dpa/picture-alliance/Newscom)*

never a late fee; the book just times out and disappears from your device when the borrowing period expires. Products like the Overdrive Media Console (**overdrive.com**) let you search to find which area library has the book you want. When you log in to the library website, you can download a text any time of day or night. Libraries have a specific number of copies of each e-book title available, so you may be added to a waiting list if all the copies are checked out, just like with paper books. However, there is a lot of friction between publishers and libraries on how to handle the impact of lending electronically. It's so convenient that some publishers are refusing to allow their e-books to be distributed through libraries.

Can I borrow an e-book from a friend? Lending of e-books is now becoming a popular feature of e-reader systems. Both the NOOK and the Amazon Kindle support lending books for up to two weeks.

Where can I find free e-books? A great source of free reading is Project Gutenberg (**gutenberg.org**). This repository site is a collection of over 49,000 free books in ePub, Kindle, and PDF formats. It contains books that are free in the United States because their copyrights have expired. The catalog includes many classic titles like *War and Peace* by Leo Tolstoy or mystery novels by Agatha Christie.

How can I publish my own works? Self-publishing is much easier in the age of digital texts. There are many options available:

- Self-publish into the *Amazon Kindle Store* in a matter of minutes and earn up to a 70% royalty on sales.
- Use a company like *Smashwords* (**smashwords.com**). It accepts a Microsoft Word document from you and then makes your book available through a number of vendors like the Apple iBooks store and the Barnes & Noble e-store. Your book can also be distributed as an app to mobile marketplaces like Google Play or the Apple App Store.
- Use a site like *Lulu* (**lulu.com**) to do social marketing for your book so that you can promote it. In addition, it offers services from editors, designers, and marketers. ▪

digital
MUSIC

Digital music has upended the recording industry, with new models of distributing music, new streaming services, and issues of copyright protection. In this section, we'll look at the mechanics of creating and distributing digital music.

Creating and Storing Digital Music

Objective 8.9 *Describe how digital music is created and stored.*

How is digital music created? In order to record digital music, the sound waves created by instruments need to be turned into a string of digital information. Figure 8.23 shows the process of digitally recording a song:

1. Playing music creates analog waves.
2. A microphone feeds the sound waves into a chip called an *analog-to-digital converter (ADC)* inside the recording device.
3. The ADC digitizes the waves into a series of numbers.
4. This series of numbers can be saved in a file then recorded onto digital media or sent electronically.
5. On the receiving end, a playback device such as a mobile device or a DVD player is fed that same series of numbers. Inside the playback device is a *digital-to-analog converter (DAC)*, a chip that converts the digital numbers to a continuous analog wave.

6. That analog wave tells the receiver how to move the speaker cones to reproduce the original waves, resulting in the same sound as the original.

More precisely, the digital wave will be *close* to exact. How accurate it is, or how close the digitized wave is in shape to the original analog wave, depends on the sampling rate of the ADC. The **sampling rate** specifies the number of times the analog wave is measured each second. The higher the sampling rate, the more accurately the original wave can be recreated. The improved sound quality higher sampling can afford also depends on the quality of the output device and speakers, of course. However, higher sampling rates also produce much more data and therefore result in bigger files. For example, sound waves on CDs are sampled at a rate of approximately 44,000 times a second. This produces a huge list of numbers for even a single minute of a song.

What file types store digital music? You're no doubt familiar with the MP3 file format used to store digital music, but many others exist, such as AAC and WMA. If you buy a song from the iTunes Store, for example, you receive an AAC-format file. There are also many formats, such as DivX, MPEG-4 (which usually has an .mp4 extension), WMV, and XviD, which hold both video and audio information. All file formats compete on sound and video quality and *compression*, which relates to how small the file can be and still provide high-quality playback. Be sure to check what kind of files your audio device understands before you store music on it.

trends in IT

Your mobile device performs many tasks, and now, thanks to near field communication (NFC) technology, it can absorb yet another function: the integration of your wallet into your phone. How? NFC technology allows a device with an NFC chip (such as a smartphone) to communicate with another NFC device (such as a checkout machine) with a single touch. In fact, with NFC, you can forget your wallet: Financial transactions can be processed just by bringing the devices within an inch of each other.

Because NFC has such a short range (up to 1.5 inches), it is being used for secure credit card transactions. Simply tap their phone near an NFC checkout device and have it automatically transmit the proper loyalty card information, select and process any coupon offers, and pay all at once (see Figure 8.22).

In countries like Japan, Spain, and Germany, NFC ticketing programs are also in place. The Deutsche Bahn rail system allows users to tap their phones to an NFC tag when they get on the train and to another on departing. The fare is automatically calculated and billed to their credit card monthly. Marketing agencies are also using NFC. An NFC chip can be stored inside a poster, for example. When a passerby touches his or her phone to a specific spot, a coupon or a website address can be transmitted.

You can experiment with this using App Inventor. In the Designer view, under the Palette you will find a category called Sensors. Inside is a Near Field component. In the Blocks view, select the Near Field component and you will see tiles that let you read and write messages to Near Field tags. You can purchase Near Field tags to program yourself at many stores, even places like Bed, Bath, and Beyond!

NFC can handle identification verification as well. The swipe cards that verify your identity for entry into secure areas can be replaced using NFC to exchange stored virtual credentials. The same technology can be used to open door locks or any system where a user name and password are used. So, opening a cabinet or logging into a computer can all be managed with a tap of your NFC-enabled phone.

Several mobile applications, such as Apple Pay and Google Wallet, are available for NFC sales transactions. These programs conduct NFC transactions as well as collect your loyalty cards, gift cards, receipts, boarding passes, tickets, and keys within your phone. Currently not all service providers will enable the NFC chip on your smartphone, however, so check before you buy a new phone.

Imagine a time soon when you're out to dinner with friends and need to split the bill. Your NFC phone is already linked to your credit card, and you simply tap your friend's phone to transfer him his share of the bill. Some are predicting the worldwide NFC market will grow to be worth $50 billion over the next few years, making this a trend to watch.

FIGURE 8.22 NFC-equipped phones and watches are shifting how we handle financial transactions and identify ourselves. *(AP Images, Bloomberg/Getty Images)*

The process of users transferring files between computers is referred to as **peer-to-peer (P2P) sharing**. Any kind of file can be made available to share with others. Often media files, songs, and movies are made easily obtainable on P2P sites. These sites don't have a central computer acting to index all this information. Instead, they operate in a true P2P sharing environment in which computers connect directly to other computers, as seen in Figure 8.26. This makes them a prime source of unwanted viruses and spyware.

Some blame peer-to-peer networks for the growth of piracy on the Internet. As more sites have made it easier to illegally download music using P2P networks, music sales have dropped significantly. The recording industry is still trying to counter losing these sales. The heavy amount of traffic on P2P sites also played into the debate on Internet neutrality. Internet

service providers like Comcast were choosing to throttle, or limit, the speed of data transfer for P2P file exchanges. Users complained this was an illegal use of a public resource and all data should be treated equally by such Internet service providers.

P2P networks defend their legality in that they do not run a central server but only facilitate connections between users. Therefore, they have no control over what the users choose to trade. There are legitimate uses of these new avenues of distribution. For example *BitTorrent (BT) Bundles* are packages of free audio, video, and print content provided for download by a musician through BitTorrent. You can unlock additional content by paying or supplying your e-mail address. Tracks that are easy to remix are provided so fans can create and share their own extensions to the work.

FIGURE 8.26 Peer-to-peer (P2P) networks do not have a central computer distributing information but instead send information between each member. *(SO47/Fotolia)*

BITS&BYTES

Need Money for Your Band? Try Indiegogo

What if your band has already built up a fan base but just needs to have the up-front money to go into the studio to record? Indiegogo (**indiegogo.com**) is a crowd-funding website specializing in creative projects and causes. Musicians have a platform to go to their fan base and raise money before a recording session or a tour, or even when tragedy strikes. When cellist Mike Block had a serious accident, he used Indiegogo to raise money to pay off his medical bills. Mike offered copies of an upcoming album or personal lessons as rewards to funders. He raised over $48,000 using Indiegogo and was able to repay years of accumulated medical expenses.

run on certain devices or a movie can only be viewed a certain number of times. A DRM-free song can be placed on as many computers or players as you wish. These song files can be moved freely from system to system.

Will streaming music services eliminate radio stations? The Internet allows artists to release new songs to their fans immediately (on sites such as Facebook) and without relying on radio airtime. This opens up new channels for artists to reach an audience and changes the amount of power radio stations have in the promotion of music. Many radio stations have increased listenership by making their stations available through Internet sites and by broadcasting in high-definition quality.

What if I want to publicize my band's music? Digital music has made distributing your own recordings very simple. You can make your own creations available using sites like SoundCloud (**soundcloud.com**) and ReverbNation (**reverbnation.com**). You can quickly create a web page for your band, post your songs, and start building a fan base through Facebook. ReverbNation will send you reports detailing who's listening to your music and what they're saying about it. ReverbNation is also a way to connect with independent recording labels and to find places that want to book your band. ■

digital MEDIA

Photography and video have also moved to fully digital formats, impacting the movie industry and creating new styles of visual performance.

Digital Photography

Objective 8.11 *Explain how best to create, print, and share digital photographs.*

What is analog photography? Before digital cameras hit the market, most people used some form of 35-mm single-lens reflex (SLR) camera. When you take a picture using a traditional SLR camera, a shutter opens, creating an aperture (a small window in the camera) that allows light to hit the 35-mm film inside. Chemicals coating the film react when exposed to light. Later, additional chemicals develop the image on the film, and the image is printed on special light-sensitive paper. A variety of lenses and processing techniques, special equipment, and filters are needed to create printed photos taken with traditional SLR cameras.

What's different about digital photography? Digital cameras do not use film. Instead, they capture images on electronic sensors called *charge-coupled device (CCD) arrays* and then convert those images to digital data, long series of numbers that represent the color and brightness of millions of points in the image. Unlike traditional cameras, digital cameras allow you to see your images the instant you shoot them. Most camera models can now record digital video as well as digital photos.

How do I select a digital camera? The first question to answer is whether you want a compact "point-and-shoot" camera or a more expensive digital SLR. If you decide you want a digital SLR, you have a number of options. Some

FIGURE 8.27 Digital SLR cameras can accommodate a range of separate auto-focus lenses. *(B@rmaley/Fotolia)*

digital SLRs let you switch among different lenses, as shown in Figure 8.27, and offer features important to serious amateur and professional photographers. Although having such flexibility in selection of lenses is a great advantage, most of these cameras are also larger, heavier, and use more battery power than the fixed-lens models. Think about how you'll be using your camera and decide which model will serve you best in the long run. One great resource to use is Digital Photography Review (**dpreview.com**), a site that compares cameras and provides feedback from owners.

What determines the image quality of a digital camera? The overall image quality is determined by many factors:

* Quality of the lenses used
* Image sensor size
* File format and compression used
* Color management software included
* Camera's **resolution**, or the number of data points it records for each image captured

A digital camera's resolution is measured in megapixels (MP). The word *pixel* is short for *picture element*, which is a single dot in a digital image. Point-and-shoot models typically offer resolutions from 12 to 20 MP. Professional digital SLR cameras, such as the Nikon D800, can take photos at resolutions as high as 36 MP.

If you're interested in making only 5" × 7" or 8" × 10" prints, a lower-resolution camera is fine. However, low-resolution images become grainy and pixelated when pushed to larger size. For example, if you tried to print an 11" × 14" enlargement from an 8 MP image taken using your smartphone's camera, the image would look grainy; you would see individual dots of color instead of a clear, sharp image. The 16 to 24 MP

BITS&BYTES

Photo Edit on Your Phone

Digital photos can be edited right on your phone using powerful apps like Snapseed or Photogene. These apps allow you to change the color of an object in the image, to correct brightness and adjust perspective to align your tilted shots, as well as to apply a wide range of filter effects like adding lens blur or light leaks and scratches. Try adding a creative twist to your next photo before you post it.

cameras on the market now have plenty of resolution to guarantee sharp, detailed images even with enlargements as big as 11" × 14".

But the size of the image sensor that actually captures the light is also very critical. Larger sensors demand larger cameras and larger lenses. Professional digital cameras use a full-frame sensor, the size of a 35-mm negative. Smartphones need to use a very compact sensor (typically about 4.5 mm) and pair that with a wider angle lens to be able to capture the full scene.

What file formats are used for digital images? To fit more photos on the same size flash memory card, digital cameras let you choose from several different file types in order to compress the image data into less memory space. When you choose to compress your images, you'll lose some of the detail, but in return you'll be able to fit more images on your flash card. The most common file types supported by digital cameras are raw uncompressed data (RAW) and Joint Photographic Experts Group (JPEG):

- *RAW files* have different formats and extensions depending on the manufacturer of a particular camera. The RAW file records all of the original image information, so it's larger than a compressed JPEG file.
- *JPEG files* can be compressed just a bit, keeping most of the details, or compressed a great deal, losing some detail. Most cameras let you select from a few different JPEG compression levels.

Often, cameras also support a very low-resolution storage option that provides images that aren't useful for printing but are so small that they're easy to e-mail. Even people who have slow Internet connections are able to quickly download and view such images on screen.

Why not just use the camera on my smartphone? The cameras on smartphones are improving in resolution, but they often employ smaller image sensors and inferior lenses compared to stand-alone cameras. In addition, many features that photographers rely on often aren't available in smartphone cameras, such as different types of autofocus and image stabilization algorithms.

What's the best way to transfer my photos to my computer? Some camera models support wireless network connections so that you can transfer the images without the fuss of connecting any cables. If that is not available, you can connect the camera through a USB port to copy the image files to your computer. Another option is to transfer the flash card from your camera directly to a built-in memory card reader on your computer.

Can I make my old photos digital? You can use a scanner to turn your hand-drawn sketches or old photos into digital files. Most scanner software lets you store the converted images as TIFF files or in compressed form as JPEG files. Some scanners include hardware that lets you scan film negatives or slides as well, or even insert a stack of photos to be scanned in sequence.

Scanner quality is measured by its resolution, which is given in dots per inch (dpi). Most modern scanners can digitize a

document at resolutions as high as 9600 × 9600 dpi in either color or grayscale mode. Scanners also typically support optical character recognition (OCR). OCR software converts pages of handwritten or typed text into electronic files. You can then open and edit these converted documents with word processing programs such as Microsoft Word.

How can I share my digital photos? You've probably shared a number of photos on Facebook or Instagram already. Other options include creating online albums at sites such as Picasa, which let you share your photos without having to print them. You can also design electronic scrapbooks on a number of digital scrapbooking sites such as **cottagearts.net**.

Of course, you can carry and display your photos on your tablet and smartphone. You can also connect your device wirelessly to your TV and deliver slide shows of your photos, complete with musical soundtracks you've selected. If you have networked your home, a TV connected to your network can display all the photos and videos stored on any computer on your network.

What are the best options for printing digital photos? If you want to print photos, you have two main options:

1. **Use a photo printer:** The most popular and inexpensive ones are inkjet printers. Some inkjet printers can print high-quality color photos, although they vary in speed, quality, and features. Dye-sublimation printers are another option. If you're interested in a printer to use for printing only photos, a dye-sublimation printer is a good choice. However, some models print only specific sizes, such as 4" × 6" prints, so be sure the printer you buy will fit your long-term needs.

2. **Use a photo-printing service:** Most photo-printing labs, including the film-processing departments at stores such as Target, offer digital printing services. The paper and ink used at these labs are higher quality than what is available for home use and produce heavier, glossier prints that won't fade. You can send your digital photos directly to local merchants such as CVS and Walgreens for printing using Windows Photo Gallery. Online services, such as Flickr (**flickr.com**) and Shutterfly (**shutterfly.com**), store your images and allow you to create hard-copy prints, albums, mugs, T-shirts, or calendars.

Digital Video

Objective 8.12 *Describe how to create, edit, and distribute digital video.*

What devices, sites, and other sources provide digital video content? Digital video surrounds us:

- Television is broadcast in digitally formatted signals.
- The Internet delivers a huge amount of digital video through YouTube, communities like Vimeo (**vimeo.com**), and webcasting sites like Ustream (**ustream.tv**).
- Many pay services are available to deliver digital video to you. These include on-demand streaming from cable providers, iTunes, Netflix, and Amazon.

- And, of course, you can create your own digital video. Although you can buy dedicated digital camcorders to record digital video, many smartphones now record HD video. Webcams also work as inexpensive devices for creating digital video.

How do I record my own digital video? Video equipment for home use stores information in a digital video format. They store hours of video on built-in hard drives or flash cards. You can easily transfer video files to your computer and, using video-editing software, edit the video at home. You can write your final product to an optical disc or upload it to a web-based video channel.

What if I decide to add special effects and a sound track? Video-editing software such as Adobe Premiere presents a storyboard or timeline with which you can manipulate your video file, as shown in Figure 8.28. You can review your clips frame by frame or trim them at any point. You can add titles, audio tracks, and animations; order each segment on the timeline in whichever sequence you like; and correct segments for color balance, brightness, or contrast. Examine online tutorial resources such as Izzy Video podcasts (**izzyvideo.com**) to learn how to make the most impact with the editing and effects you apply to your raw video footage.

What kinds of files will I end up with? Once you're done editing your video file, you can save or export it in a variety of formats. Figure 8.29 shows some of the popular video file formats in use today, along with the file extensions they use.

Your choice of file format for your finished video will depend on what you want to do with the video. For example, the QuickTime streaming file format is a great choice if your file is really large and you plan to post it on the web. The Microsoft AVI format is a good choice if you're sending your file to a wide range of users because it's the standard video format for Windows Media Player.

FIGURE 8.28 Adobe Premiere allows you to build a movie from video clips and to add sound tracks and special effects. *(Rebecca Sapp/Getty Images)*

Different compression algorithms will have different results on your particular video. Try several to see which one does a better job of compressing your particular file. A **codec** (*compression/decompression*) is a rule, implemented in either software or hardware, that squeezes the same audio and video information into less space. Some information will be lost using compression, and there are several different codecs to choose from, each claiming better performance than its competitors. Commonly used codecs include MPEG-4, H.264, and DivX. There's no one codec that's always superior—a codec that works well for a simple interview may not do a good job compressing a live-action scene.

What if I want to produce a DVD with a full menu-driven system? You can use special authoring software such as Pinnacle Studio HD or Adobe Encore. These DVD/Blu-ray software packages often include preset selections for producing video for specific mobile devices.

FIGURE 8.29

Typical File Formats for Digital Video

FORMAT	FILE EXTENSION	NOTES
QuickTime	.qt .mov	You can download the QuickTime player without charge from **apple.com/quicktime**. The Pro version allows you to build your own QuickTime files.
Moving Picture Experts Group (MPEG)	.mpg .mpeg .mp4	The MPEG-4 video standard was adopted internationally in 2000; it's recognized by most video player software.
Windows Media Video	.wmv	This is a Microsoft file format recognized by Windows Media Player (included with the Windows OS).
Microsoft Video for Windows	.avi	This is a Microsoft file format recognized by Windows Media Player (included with the Windows OS).

BITS&BYTES

Fly-By Drone Video

Thanks to recent technological advancements, aerial video is easier than ever to capture. Quadcoptors, flying remote-controlled devices with four propellers and equipped with digital video cameras, are very popular. They transmit video back to a phone or tablet so the pilot sees exactly what the flying device is seeing. There is also a huge do-it-yourself community dedicated to making the hardware and software needed by quadcoptors. Visit **dronecode.org** and **ardupilot.com** for inspiration—and lots of free code!

(Robyn Beck/Getty Images)

FIGURE 8.30 Compact cameras like the GoPro are small enough to make them part of any activity. *(Cyrus McCrimmon/ Getty Images)*

These programs can also create final discs that have animated menu systems and easy navigation controls, allowing the viewer to move quickly from one movie or scene to another. Home DVD and Blu-ray players, as well as gaming systems such as PlayStation and Xbox, can read these discs.

What's the quickest way to get my video out to viewers? The quickest way to get your video content out is to broadcast. Webcasting, or broadcasting your video live to an audience, is an option that has become simple to do. Use either your phone or a compact camera like a GoPro (see Figure 8.30), and sites like **ustream.tv** will let you quickly set up to webcast your video as it is captured to a live Internet audience. You can also display an interactive chat next to the video feed. Both the chat and the video are captured and archived for viewers who missed the live broadcast. Most smartphones record video at a quality good enough to directly webcast from your phone, and most laptops have an integrated webcam.

You may want to take time and produce a more polished video. When you have it just right, you can upload it to video-sharing sites like YouTube or Vimeo.

Of course, it's illegal for you to upload videos you don't own. You also can't take a piece of a copyrighted video and post it publicly. The Ethics in IT section in this chapter presents several legal and ethical situations that are important for you to be aware of as a content creator in the digital age.

How is HD different from "plain" digital? *HD* stands for **high definition**. It is a standard of digital television signal that guarantees a specific level of resolution and a specific *aspect ratio*, which is the rectangular shape of the image. A 1080 HDTV displays 1,920 vertical lines and 1,080 horizontal lines of video on the screen, which is over six times as many pixels as a standard definition TV. The aspect ratio used is 16:9, which makes the screen wider, giving it the same proportions as the rectangular shape of a movie theater screen (see Figure 8.31). This allows televisions to play movies in the widescreen format for which they were created, instead of "letterboxing" the film with black bars on the top and the bottom of the screen.

What types of connectivity are provided on modern TV sets? A typical HDTV set has multiple HDMI connectors, allowing game consoles, Blu-ray players, and cable boxes to be connected and to produce the highest-quality output. HDMI is a single cable that carries all of the video and all of the audio information.

Many TV sets have a built-in SD card reader. This allows users to display slide shows of photographs captured by their digital cameras. A PC VGA port is also included on most sets to allow you to feed your computer's output video signal directly to the television. There are ways to connect wirelessly from your mobile or computer device to your TV as well. Apple TV and Google's Chromecast let you view content from your device on the big screen without connecting cables.

Standard television

a

HDTV

b

Extra image area

Letterbox

c

FIGURE 8.31 (a) Standard-definition TV has a more "square" aspect ratio, whereas (b) HDTV matches the 16:9 ratio used in the motion picture industry without resorting to (c) letterboxing. *(Pichugin Dmitry/Shutterstock)*

What are the advantages to watching digital video on my TV? Other information services can be integrated with the broadcast; so, for example, if a telephone call came through during the show, a pop-up could appear identifying the caller. Additional content can be delivered in real time with the broadcast, explaining the background of characters or pulling up behind-the-scenes info. In the future, there will be more interactivity integrated so you can participate in live polls or chats on screen as the show is broadcast.

Can I record the digital video that comes over my TV? There are a variety of digital video recorders (DVRs) available that record in HD. Models like TiVo even recommend new shows you might like based on what you've been watching. You can also install personal video recording (PVR) software on your computer. Programs like Kodi (**kodi.tv**), an open source software media center, let you use your computer to view the schedule program guide, select shows to record (without commercials), and then watch them from anywhere you have Internet access.

FIGURE 8.32 Slingbox can send your digital television content to your tablet, notebook, or smartphone, wherever you may be. *(Newscom)*

Can I get digital video to watch on my portable device? Many DVR units, like TiVo, support software that lets you transfer recorded shows to files on your PC and format them for viewing on a mobile device. There are also devices like Slingbox that take the video from your TV and broadcast it to you over the Internet. With Slingbox, you can be in another room, or another country, and control and watch your home TV on your notebook or your smartphone (see Figure 8.32).

You just returned from your trip to the Grand Canyon, and your friends are raving about the photos you took. You decide to put them on Flickr so others can see them. You also think that someone might see your photos and want to use them in a commercial publication such as a magazine. Because you own the copyright to your photos, you control how they can be used—and you want to protect your rights. You add a disclaimer to Flickr indicating that all rights are reserved on your photos. Anyone who wants to use them will need to contact you and request permission.

All of a sudden, you're bombarded by requests for permission to use your photos. A high school student in Illinois wants to feature one on her travel blog. A church in Georgia wants to use a photo for its newsletter. An ad agency in Seattle wants to modify your sunrise photo and use it in an ad. How are you going to manage all these permission requests?

Copyleft, a play on the word *copyright*, is designed for this situation. *Copyleft* is a term for various licensing plans that enable copyright holders to grant certain rights to the work while retaining other rights. Creative Commons (**creativecommons.org**), a nonprofit organization, has developed various licenses you can use based on the rights you wish to grant. Simply decide which type of license best fits your goals for the work, and Creative Commons provides you with HTML you can use to add the specific licensing information to your site.

The advantage to using Creative Commons licenses is that people won't constantly send you permission requests to use your work. The licenses explain how your work can be used. Also, many advocates of copyleft policies feel that creativity is encouraged when people are free to modify other people's work instead of worrying about infringing on copyright.

Opponents of Creative Commons licenses complain that the licenses have affected their livelihoods. If millions of images are out on Flickr with Creative Commons licenses that permit free commercial use, professional photographers might have a tougher time selling their work. Furthermore, Creative Commons licenses are irrevocable. If you make a mistake and select the wrong license for your work, or you later find out a work is valuable and you've already selected a license that allows commercial use, you're out of luck.

Each of us needs to carefully consider the value of our intellectual property and decide how best to conduct our digital livelihood. Understanding the meaning of copyright, and copyleft, is both important so that you respect the rights of others and so that you can simplify your life in granting permission rights to the works you create.

Before moving on to Chapter Review:
1. **Watch Replay Video 8.2** ▷ .
2. **Then check your understanding of what you've learned so far.**

check your understanding // review & practice

For a quick review to see what you've learned so far, answer the following questions.

multiple choice

1. Copyleft is a policy

   a. that protects you from having others use your work.

   b. to legalize unlimited copying of digital music.

   c. is a term for a set of licensing plans.

   d. all of the above

2. An audio interface unit can

   a. connect a computer to musical instruments and microphones.

   b. provide Dolby surround sound.

   c. create electronic drum sounds.

   d. convert between different audio file formats.

3. P2P is an acronym for

   a. packet-to-packet networking.

   b. peer-to-peer sharing.

   c. person-to-person texting.

   d. power-to-people delivery.

4. An analog signal is different from a digital signal because it

   a. is continuous.

   b. has only specific discrete values.

   c. is easier to duplicate.

   d. is easier to transmit.

5. The open format for publishing of e-books that is optimized for mobile devices is

   a. ePub.

   b. raw.

   c. azw.

   d. pdf.

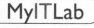 Go to **MyITLab** to take an autograded version of the *Check Your Understanding* review and to find all media resources for the chapter.

TECHBYTES WEEKLY
Stay current with the TechBytes Weekly Newsletter.

Continue ≫

8 Chapter Review

summary //

Mobile Devices

Learning Outcome 8.1 **You will be able to discuss the nature of digital signals and how mobile computing devices are designed and operated.**

Digital Basics

Objective 8.1 *Describe how digital convergence has evolved.*

- Digital convergence has brought us single devices with the capabilities that used to require four or five separate tools. With more computing power in a mobile processor, a single device can perform a wider range of tasks.

Objective 8.2 *Explain the differences between digital and analog signals.*

- Digital media is based on a series of numeric data, that is, number values that were measured from the original analog waveform. As a string of numbers, a digital photo or video file can be easily processed by modern computers.

The Power of Smartphones

Objective 8.3 *Describe the technologies used to communicate across cellular networks.*

- Like a traditional computer, a smartphone has a central processor, memory, and an OS. These components work in the same way as in a computer to process information and support communications, software applications, and other services.
- A base transceiver station defines a geographic area as a cell for mobile communications. A mobile switching center links transceiver stations together to complete your mobile call.
- Electronics like analog-to-digital converters and digital signal processors are used to allow cell phones to work with digital signals.

Objective 8.4 *Explain how to effectively use mobile Internet access and how to keep your device secure.*

- Information can be synched between devices using either wired or wireless solutions. A wired sync requires either a micro SD card or a USB cable to connect the device directly to the computer. A wireless sync can be done using Bluetooth or WiFi or by connecting to a cloud service.
- Mobile data plans allow your device to have access at almost any location. Data transfers occur at either 3G or 4G speeds, depending on your device and provider. Fees are tied to the amount of data you transfer each month.
- Viruses can infect smartphones, so using an antivirus software package is important. Check the manufacturer's website frequently for updates and practice safe habits by not downloading or opening files from unknown sources.

Mobile Computing

Objective 8.5 *Demonstrate an understanding of the range of different mobile computing devices.*

- Tablets, ultrabooks, and 2-in-1s each have their own specific place in the range of devices available. Depending on the computing power, screen size and interface you need, one may be a better fit.

Objective 8.6 *Describe how to evaluate which mobile device is appropriate for a specific user.*

- Consider factors including screen size, style of keyboard, weight, and battery life as well as the factors mentioned above when selecting the best device for a specific need.

Impact of Digital Information

Learning Outcome 8.2 You will be able to describe how digital technology is used to produce and distribute digital texts, music, and video.

Digital Publishing

Objective 8.7 *Describe e-readers, and discuss the different types of e-readers that are available.*

- eReaders are devices that store manipulate and transmit textual information digitally. Some use electronic ink for a crisp, sharp grayscale representation of text. Some use backlit monitors.

Objective 8.8 *Explain how to purchase, borrow, and publish e-texts.*

- There are a variety of formats for e-text files including .azw and .epub. E-texts can be purchased from many publishers directly or from online stores.
  Libraries loan e-texts using products like Overdrive.

Digital Music

Objective 8.9 *Describe how digital music is created and stored.*

- Digital music is created by combining pure digital sounds with samples of analog sounds. It has meant changes for the recording industry, for performers, and for music listeners. It's now inexpensive to carry a music library, to create new songs, and to distribute them worldwide. The sampling rate determines the fidelity of the final recorded digital sound.

Objective 8.10 *Summarize how to stream and publish digital music.*

- Digital rights management is a system of access control to digital music. There are many services available for openly sharing and streaming your own content like SoundCloud.

Digital Media

Objective 8.11 *Explain how best to create, print, and share digital photographs.*

- Digital cameras allow you to instantly capture and transfer images to your devices, computers, and cloud storage sites. The camera's resolution is important as it tells the number of data points recorded for each image captured.

Objective 8.12 *Describe how to create, edit, and distribute digital video.*

- Using software for video production, you can create polished videos with titles, transitions, a sound track, and special effects and distribute them on DVDs.
- A codec is a compression/decompression rule, implemented in either software or hardware, that squeezes the same audio and video information into less space.
- You can also use a webcam to stream live video to sites that will "broadcast" it over the Internet.

 Be sure to check out **MyITLab** for additional materials to help you review and learn. And don't forget the Replay Videos.

key terms //

chapter quiz // assessment

For a quick review to see what you've learned, answer the following questions. Submit the quiz as requested by your instructor. If you are using **MyITLab**, the quiz is also available there.

multiple choice

1. A cell phone is cellular because

   a. software can be plugged in or removed.

   b. phones have become so small in size.

   c. it uses a network made up of cells or base transceiver stations.

   d. of the pattern on the screen of the device.

2. Which of the following is *false*?

   a. Bluetooth technology uses radio waves.

   b. An analog-to-digital converter chip converts your voice into digital signals.

   c. Your phone can only be connected to the Internet if there is a WiFi network available.

   d. SMS is an acronym for short message service, also called text messaging.

3. Which of the following is NOT a mobile device?

   a. base transceiver station

   b. 2-in-1

   c. tablet

   d. ultrabook

4. DRM is an acronym for

   a. Digital Role Maker.

   b. Digital Real Movie.

   c. Distribution Regional Media.

   d. Digital Rights Management.

5. Image resolution is

   a. the number of data points recorded in an image.

   b. only important with analog image capture.

   c. the size of the image in bytes.

   d. based on the kind of compression used.

6. A digital camera's resolution

   a. is measured in megapixels (MP).

   b. only matters for analog cameras.

   c. depends on the camera's lens.

   d. tells you how to transfer images to your printing service.

true/false

_____ 1. Sampling rate is important when creating an analog signal from a digital source.

_____ 2. A codec improves digital video resolution.

_____ 3. Digital video can be stored in an .mpg file, an .mpeg file, or an .mp4 file.

_____ 4. HDMI is a single cable that carries both high-definition video as well as audio signals.

critical thinking

1. **Mobile Sensors**

   Smartphones have many built-in sensors, some of which measure acceleration, location, and pressure. What kind of sensors would you add to a smartphone to make it more useful?

2. **Self-Publishing**

   What impact will the availability of self-publication have on the writing and recording industries? Will it promote a greater amount of quality content or a flood of amateur work? How could this be managed?

"And One Will Rule Them All"

Problem

Digital convergence posits the dream of one device that can do it all, for everyone. But there are so many different mobile devices saturating the market that many people are left in a state of confusion.

Task

For each client scenario described as follows, the group will select the minimum set of devices that would support and enhance the client's life.

Process

1. Consider the following three clients:

   - A retired couple who now travels for pleasure a great deal. They want to be involved in their grandchildren's lives and will need support for their health, finances, and personal care as they age.

   - A young family with two children, two working parents, and a tight budget.

   - A couple in which each individual is a physician and each adores technology.

2. Make two recommendations for your clients in terms of digital technologies that will enhance their business or their lifestyle. Discuss the advantages and disadvantages of each technology. Consider value, reliability, computing needs, training needed, and communication needs as well as expandability for the future.

3. As a group, prepare a final report that considers the recommendations you have made for your clients.

Conclusion

Digital information has allowed the development of a new style of living, both at home and at work. With so many digital solutions on the market, recommending digital options needs to focus on converging to the minimum set of tools that will enhance life without adding complication to it.

ethics project //

When Everyone Has a Voice

In this exercise, you'll research and then role-play a complicated ethical situation. The role you play might or might not match your own personal beliefs; in either case, your research and use of logic will enable you to represent the view assigned. An arbitrator will watch and comment on both sides of the arguments, and together the team will agree on an ethical solution.

Background

Much of the world's population is now equipped with Internet-ready camera phones. Sensors on these phones could measure for viruses or compute pollution indexes, while the cameras could be used to document a range of human behavior. This could create changes in political movements, art, and culture as everyone's experience is documented and shared.

Research Areas to Consider

- Evgeny Morozov RSA Animate
- Smartinsights mobile marketing statistics
- The Witness Project
- Center for Embedded Networked Sensing

Process

1. Divide the class into teams.
2. Research the areas cited above and devise a scenario in which mobile access could make an impact politically or environmentally, positively or negatively.
3. Team members should write a summary that provides background information for their character—for example, business owner, politician, reporter, or arbitrator—and that details their character's behaviors to set the stage for the role-playing event. Then team members should create an outline to use during the role-playing event.
4. Team members should arrange a mutually convenient time to meet for the exchange, using a virtual meeting tool or by meeting in person.
5. Team members should present their case to the class or submit a PowerPoint presentation for review by the rest of the class, along with the summary and resolution they developed.

Conclusion

As technology becomes ever more prevalent and integrated into our lives, more and more ethical dilemmas will present themselves. Being able to understand and evaluate both sides of the argument, while responding in a personally or socially ethical manner, will be an important skill.

Estimating Cellular Data Usage

You want to determine how much data you need for your cellular data plan. You have tracked your usage for the past several weeks. You will determine your average weekly usage, then estimate your average monthly usage. Using data guidelines from your local carrier, you determine your total monthly data usage. Lastly, you calculate the percent of total usage each activity uses.

You will use the following skills as you complete this activity:

- Use Absolute Cell References
- Create an IF Function
- Use the ROUNDUP Function
- Apply a Custom Header and Footer
- Insert Dates and Use Date Math
- Use the AVERAGE Function

Instructions:

1. Open *TIA_Ch8_Start* and save as **TIA_Ch8_LastFirst**.

2. In cell B14, use the **TODAY function** to enter today's date. In cell C14, create a formula that adds 7 days to cell B14, then use the **Fill Handle** to copy the results in cell C14 to the range D14:H14. Ensure the results are formatted as Short Date.

3. In the range H15:H21, enter data that reflects an estimate of your own smartphone activity usage. (For example, in cell H15, enter the number of emails you would send in a week, and in cell H16, enter the number of hours you would spend streaming music in a week).

4. In cell B24, use the **AVERAGE function** to compute the average weekly usage for the range B15:H15. Use the **Fill Handle** to copy the results to the range B25:B30.

5. In cell C24, create a formula to compute the average monthly usage by multiplying cell B24 by 4. Use the **Fill Handle** to copy the results to the range C25:C30.

6. In cell D24, create a formula to calculate the estimated usage by multiplying cell C24 by B3. Using the **Fill Handle**, copy the results in cell D24 to the range D25:D30. Select **range B24:D30** and format as **Number with two decimal places**.

7. In cell H8, type **Total Estimated Monthly Data Usage (MB)**. **Bold** and **Right Align** the text. In cell I8, use the **SUM function** to total data in the range D24:D30.

8. In cell H9, type **Total Estimated Monthly Data Usage (GB)**. **Bold** and **Right Align** the text. In cell I9, create a formula to divide cell I8 by 1024 and convert the results in megabytes (MB) to results in gigabytes (GB).

9. In cell H10, type **Minimum Data Required by Plan**. **Bold** and **Right Align** the text. In cell I10, use the **ROUNDUP function** to round the results in cell I9 to a whole number.

   a. Hint: The formula will be = ROUNDUP(I9,0).

10. In cell H11, type **Would selected plan work with 20% increase in usage?**. **Bold** and **Right Align** the text. In cell I11, use the **IF function** to determine whether or not a 20% increase to the results in cell I9 would be greater or equal to the results in cell I10. Use "YES" if the statement is true, and "NO" if the statement is false.

    a. Hint: The formula is: =IF(I9*1.2<=I10,"YES","NO").

11. In cell E23, type **% of Total Usage**, then in **cell E24**, create a formula to divide cell D24 by cell I8 to compute the percentage of total usage. Format results as **Percentage with no decimals**. Use the **Fill Handle** to copy the results to the range E25:E30.

    a. Hint: Use an absolute cell reference for cell I8.

12. Insert a **Header** that displays your First and Last names in the top right header. Use the **Current Date Header & Footer Element** in the bottom left footer, and the **File Name Header & Footer Element** in the bottom right footer.

13. Change the orientation to **Landscape**.

14. Save the workbook and submit based on your instructor's directions.

9

Securing Your System: Protecting Your Digital Data and Devices

Threats to Your Digital Assets

Learning Outcome 9.1 You will be able to describe hackers, viruses, and other online annoyances and the threats they pose to your digital security.

Identity Theft and Hackers   348

Objective 9.1 *Describe how identity theft is committed and the types of scams identity thieves perpetrate.*

Objective 9.2 *List and describe the different types of hackers.*

Objective 9.3 *Describe the various tools hackers use and the types of attacks they might launch against computers.*

Computer Viruses   353

Objective 9.4 *Explain what a computer virus is, why they are a threat to your security, how a computing device catches a virus, and the symptoms it may display.*

Objective 9.5 *List the different categories of computer viruses, and describe their behaviors.*

Online Annoyances and Social Engineering   355

Objective 9.6 *Explain what malware is, and list the common types of malware.*

Objective 9.7 *Define spam, and describe strategies to combat it.*

Objective 9.8 *Explain what cookies are and whether they pose a security threat.*

Objective 9.9 *Describe social engineering techniques, and explain strategies to avoid falling prey to them.*

Protecting Your Digital Property

Learning Outcome 9.2 Describe various ways to protect your digital property and data from theft and corruption.

Restricting Access to Your Digital Assets   366

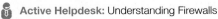

Objective 9.10 *Explain what a firewall is and how a firewall protects your computer from hackers.*

🔒 **Active Helpdesk:** Understanding Firewalls

🔊 **Sound Byte:** Installing a Personal Firewall

Objective 9.11 *Explain how to protect your computer from virus infection.*

🔒 **Active Helpdesk:** Avoiding Computer Viruses

🔊 **Sound Byte:** Protecting Your Computer

Objective 9.12 *Describe how passwords and biometric characteristics can be used for user authentication on computer systems.*

Objective 9.13 *Describe ways to surf the web anonymously.*

Keeping Your Data Safe   377

Objective 9.14 *Describe the types of information you should never share online.*

Objective 9.15 *List the various types of backups you can perform on your computing devices, and explain the various places you can store backup files.*

🔊 **Sound Byte:** Managing Computer Security with Windows Tools

Protecting Your Physical Computing Assets   382

Objective 9.16 *Explain the negative effects environment and power surges can have on computing devices.*

🔊 **Sound Byte:** Surge Protectors

Objective 9.17 *Describe the major concerns when a device is stolen and strategies for solving the problems.*

Make This: MAKE: A Password Generator on **page 365**

All media accompanying this chapter can be found in MyITLab.

For an overview of the chapter, watch the **Preview Video**.

HOW COOL IS THIS?

Biometrics authentication for bank customers has gotten a major upgrade. Banks now use scanners that utilize **finger vein authentication technology**. The scanners read the unique vein patterns inside your finger to **verify your identity**. How does this improve upon fingerprint scans? Fingerprint scanning technology has flaws—impressions of your fingerprints can be left on scanner surfaces and can be duplicated to fool security devices. However, because your veins are inside your body, **they don't leave residue on scanners**. Perhaps your bank will offer this more secure technology soon! *(Nerthuz/Fotolia)*

Threats to Your Digital Assets

Learning Outcome 9.1 **You will be able to describe hackers, viruses, and other online annoyances and the threats they pose to your digital security.**

The media is full of stories about malicious computer programs damaging computers, criminals stealing people's identities online, and attacks on corporate websites bringing major corporations to a standstill. These are examples of *cybercrime*—any criminal action perpetrated primarily through the use of a computer. *Cybercriminals* are individuals who use computers, networks, and the Internet to perpetrate crime. Anyone with a computer and the wherewithal to arm himself or herself with the appropriate knowledge can be a cybercriminal. In this part of the chapter, we'll discuss the most serious types of cybercrime you need to worry about as well as some online annoyances to avoid.

 identity theft and
HACKERS

Every year, the Internet Crime Complaint Center (IC3)—a partnership between the FBI and the National White Collar Crime Center—receives hundreds of thousands of complaints related to Internet crime. Figure 9.1 shows four common categories of complaints the IC3 receives. Government impersonation scams involve people pretending to represent official organizations, such as the FBI, the IRS, or Homeland

Security, to defraud. Nonauction/non-delivery scams involve running auctions (or sales) of merchandise that does not really exist, wherein the perpetrators just collect funds and disappear without delivering the promised goods. Advance fee fraud involves convincing individuals to send money as a "good faith" gesture to enable them to receive larger payments in return. The scammers then disappear with the advance fees. Identity

FIGURE 9.1

Common Types of Cybercrimes Reported to the IC3

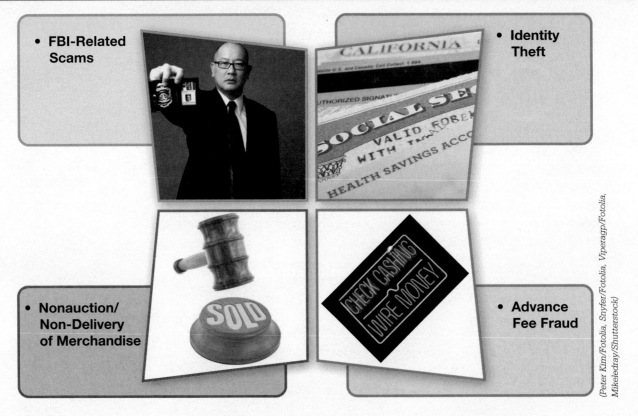

- **FBI-Related Scams**
- **Identity Theft**
- **Nonauction/Non-Delivery of Merchandise**
- **Advance Fee Fraud**

(Peter Kim/Fotolia, Snyfer/Fotolia, Viperagp/Fotolia, Mikeledray/Shutterstock)

theft involves the stealing of someone's personal information for financial gain. Although these complaints relate to some type of fraud, other complaints received involve equally serious matters such as computer intrusions (hacking), extortion, and blackmail. In this section, we'll look at both identity theft and hacking in more detail.

Identity Theft

Objective 9.1 *Describe how identity theft is committed and the types of scams identity thieves perpetrate.*

What is the most financially damaging cybercrime plaguing individuals? Theft of personal data such as bank account numbers and credit/debit card numbers is of most concern to individuals because this information is usually used for fraudulent purposes. As noted above, **identity theft** occurs when a thief steals personal information such as your name, address, Social Security number, birth date, bank account number, and credit card information and runs up debts in your name. Many victims of identity theft spend months, or even years, trying to repair their credit and eliminate fraudulent debts.

What types of scams do identity thieves perpetrate? The nefarious acts cover a wide range:

- Counterfeiting your existing credit and debit cards
- Requesting changes of address on your bank and credit card statements, which makes detecting fraudulent charges take longer
- Opening new credit cards and bank accounts in your name and then writing bad checks and not paying off the credit card balances (ruining your credit rating in the process)
- Obtaining medical services under your name, potentially causing you to later lose coverage if the thief's treatment exceeds the limits of your policy's covered services
- Buying a home with a mortgage in your name, then reselling the house and absconding with the money (leaving you with the debt)

Many people believe that the only way your identity can be stolen is by a computer. However, the Federal Trade Commission (**ftc.gov**) has identified other methods thieves use to obtain others' personal information:

- Stealing purses and wallets, in which people often keep personal information such as their ATM PIN codes
- Stealing mail or looking through trash for bank statements and credit card bills
- Posing as bank or credit card company representatives and tricking people into revealing sensitive information over the phone
- Installing skimming devices on ATM machines that record information, such as account numbers and passcodes

Although foolproof protection methods don't exist, there are precautions that will help you minimize your risk, which we'll discuss later in this chapter.

With all the news coverage about identity theft and other cybercrimes, aren't people being more cautious? Although most people are aware of spam, a survey by the Messaging, Malware and Mobile Anti-Abuse Working Group (M3AAWG) found that half of e-mail users in North America and Europe have opened spam, some of which are designed to trick you into divulging sensitive information. The M3AAWG also discovered that 46% of people who opened spam did so intentionally—out of idle curiosity, to follow links to unsubscribe to unwanted e-mails (which only brings more spam), or because they are interested in the product being offered.

Hacking

Objective 9.2 *List and describe the different types of hackers.*

What exactly defines a hacker? Although there's a great deal of disagreement as to what a hacker actually is, especially among hackers themselves, a **hacker** is most commonly defined as anyone who unlawfully breaks into a computer system—either an individual computer or a network (see Figure 9.2).

Are there different kinds of hackers? Some hackers are offended by being labeled as criminals and therefore attempt to classify different types of hackers as follows:

- **White-hat hackers** (or **ethical hackers**) break in to systems for nonmalicious reasons, such as to test system security vulnerabilities or to expose undisclosed weaknesses.

FIGURE 9.2 Hacking humor. Hackers are a real problem in many instances, but don't let your fears overwhelm you! (© *Andy Singer www.andysinger.com*)

They believe in making security vulnerabilities known either to the company that owns the system or software or to the general public, often to embarrass a company into fixing a problem.

- **Black-hat hackers** break into systems to destroy information or for illegal gain. The terms *white hat* and *black hat* are references to old Western movies in which the heroes wore white hats and the outlaws wore black hats.

- **Grey-hat hackers** are a bit of a cross between black and white—they often illegally break into systems merely to flaunt their expertise to the administrator of the system they penetrated or to attempt to sell their services in repairing security breaches.

Regardless of the hackers' opinions, the laws in the United States and in many other countries consider *any* unauthorized access to computer systems a crime.

Hacking Tools and Attack Types

Objective 9.3 *Describe the various tools hackers use and the types of attacks they might launch against computers.*

Could a hacker steal my debit card or bank account number? Hackers often try to break in to computers or websites that contain credit card information. If you perform financial transactions online, such as banking or buying goods and services, you probably do so using a credit or debit card. Credit card and bank account information can thus reside on your hard drive or an online business's hard drive and may be detectable by a hacker.

Aside from your home computer, you have personal data stored on various websites. For example, many sites require that you provide a login ID and password to gain access. Even if this data isn't stored on your computer, a hacker may be able to capture it when you're online by using a *packet analyzer (sniffer)* or a *keylogger* (a program that captures all keystrokes made on a computer).

What's a packet analyzer? Data travels through the Internet in small pieces called *packets*. The packets are identified with an IP address, in part to help identify the computer to which they are being sent. Once the packets reach their destination, they're reassembled into cohesive messages. A **packet analyzer (sniffer)** is a program deployed by hackers that looks at (or sniffs) each packet as it travels on the Internet—not just those addressed to a particular computer, but all packets coming across a particular network. For example, a hacker might sit in a coffee shop and run a packet sniffer to capture sensitive data

(such as debit/credit card numbers) from patrons using the coffee shop's free wireless network. Wireless networks such as these can be particularly vulnerable to this type of exploitation if encryption of data isn't enabled when the networks are set up. (This topic was covered in more detail in Chapter 7.)

What do hackers do with the information they "sniff"? Once a hacker has your debit/credit card information, he or she can use it to purchase items illegally or can sell the number to someone who will. If a hacker steals the login ID and password to an account where you have your bank card information stored (such as eBay or Amazon), he or she can also use your account to buy items and have them shipped to him- or herself instead of to you. If hackers can gather enough information in conjunction with your credit card information, they may be able to commit identity theft.

Although this sounds scary, you can easily protect yourself from packet sniffing by installing a firewall (which we discuss later in this chapter) and using data encryption on a wireless network (which was covered in Chapter 7).

Trojan Horses and Rootkits

Besides stealing information, what other problems can hackers cause if they break into my computer? Hackers often use individuals' computers as a staging area for mischief. To commit widespread computer attacks, for example, hackers need to control many computers at the same time. To this end, hackers often use Trojan horses to install other programs on computers. A **Trojan horse** is a program that appears to be something useful or desirable, like a game or a screen saver, but while it runs it does something malicious in the background without your knowledge (see Figure 9.3).

What damage can Trojan horses do? Often, the malicious activity perpetrated by a Trojan horse program is the installation of a backdoor program or a rootkit. **Backdoor programs** and **rootkits** are programs (or sets of programs) that allow hackers to gain access to your computer and take almost complete control of it without your knowledge. Using a backdoor program, hackers can access and delete all the files on your computer, send e-mail, run programs, and do just about anything else you can do with your computer. A computer that a hacker controls in this manner is referred to as a **zombie**. Zombies are often used to launch *denial-of-service attacks* on other computers.

Denial-of-Service Attacks

What are denial-of-service attacks? In a **denial-of-service (DoS) attack**, legitimate users are denied access to a computer system because a hacker

FIGURE 9.3 The term *Trojan horse* derives from Greek mythology and refers to the wooden horse that the Greeks used to sneak into the city of Troy and conquer it. Therefore, computer programs that contain a hidden, and usually dreadful, "surprise" are referred to as Trojan horses.
(Ralf Kraft/Fotolia)

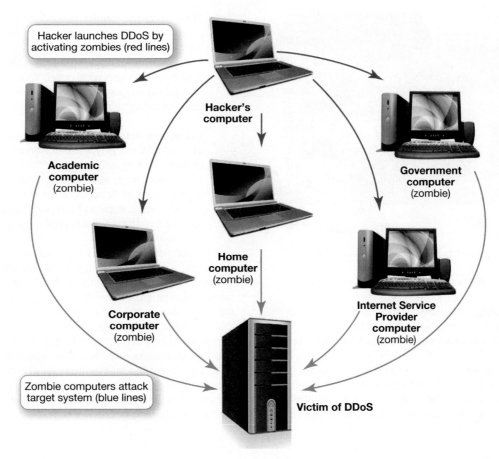

Hacker launches DDoS by activating zombies (red lines)

Hacker's computer

Academic computer (zombie)

Government computer (zombie)

Home computer (zombie)

Corporate computer (zombie)

Internet Service Provider computer (zombie)

Zombie computers attack target system (blue lines)

Victim of DDoS

FIGURE 9.4 Zombie computers are used to facilitate a DDoS attack. *(Vovan/Shutterstock, Nicholas Monu/E+/Getty)*

is repeatedly making requests of that computer system through a computer he or she has taken over as a zombie. A computer system can handle only a certain number of requests for information at one time. When it is flooded with requests in a DoS attack, it shuts down and refuses to answer any requests for information, even if the requests are from a legitimate user. Thus, the computer is so busy responding to the bogus requests for information that authorized users can't gain access.

Couldn't a DoS attack be traced back to the computer that launched it? Launching a DoS attack on a computer system from a single computer is easy to trace. Therefore, most savvy hackers use a **distributed denial-of-service (DDoS) attack**, which launches DoS attacks from more than one zombie (sometimes thousands of zombies) at the same time.

Figure 9.4 illustrates how a DDoS attack works. A hacker creates many zombies and coordinates them so that they begin sending bogus requests to the same computer at the same time. Administrators of the victim computer often have a great deal of difficulty stopping the attack because it comes from so many computers. Often, the attacks are coordinated automatically by botnets. A **botnet** is a large group of software

programs (called *robots* or *bots*) that runs autonomously on zombie computers. Some botnets have been known to span millions of computers.

Because many commercial websites receive revenue from users, either directly (such as via subscriptions to online games) or indirectly (such as when web surfers click on advertisements), DDoS attacks can be financially distressing for the owners of the affected websites.

How Hackers Gain Computer Access

How exactly does a hacker gain access to a computer? Hackers can gain access to computers directly or indirectly. Direct access involves sitting down at a computer and installing hacking software. It's unlikely that such an attack would occur in your home, but it's always a wise precaution to set up your computer so that it requires a password for a user to gain access.

Indirect access involves subtler methods. Many professional hackers use exploit kits. **Exploit kits** are software programs that run on servers and search for vulnerabilities of computers that visit the server. Exploit kits look for security holes in browsers and operating systems that haven't yet been patched by the users. When they detect a vulnerability,

YOUR COMPUTER

FTP (port 21)

E-mail (port 25)

HTTP (port 80)

DNS (port 53)

Telnet (port 23)

WEBSITE REQUEST

FIGURE 9.5 Open logical ports are an invitation to hackers.

they can deliver spyware, bots, backdoor programs, or other malicious software to your computer. Fortunately, most exploit kits take advantage of known vulnerabilities, so if your antivirus software and operating system is up to date, you should be secure. We'll discuss both of these topics later in the chapter.

Hackers also can access a computer indirectly through its Internet connection. Many people forget that their Internet connection is a two-way street. Not only can you access the Internet, but people on the Internet can access your computer.

Think of your computer as a house. Common sense tells you to lock your home's doors and windows to deter theft when you aren't there. Hooking your computer up to the Internet without protection is like leaving the front door to your house wide open. Your computer obviously doesn't have doors and windows like a house, but it does have logical ports.

What are logical ports? Logical ports are virtual—that is, not physical—communications gateways or paths that allow a computer to organize requests for information, such as web page downloads or e-mail routing, from other networks or computers. Unlike physical ports, such as USB ports, you can't see or touch a logical port; it's part of a computer's internal organization.

Logical ports are numbered and assigned to specific services. For instance, logical port 80 is designated for hypertext transfer protocol (HTTP), the main communications protocol for the web. Thus, all requests for information from your browser to the web flow through logical port 80. Open logical ports, like open windows in a home, invite intruders, as illustrated in Figure 9.5. Unless you take precautions to restrict access to your logical ports, other people on the Internet may be able to access your computer through them. Fortunately, you can thwart most hacking problems by installing a firewall, which we discuss later in the chapter. ■

BITS&BYTES

Are Your Photos Helping Criminals Target You?

All cell phones today contain GPS chips. The cameras in phones often use information gathered from the GPS chips to encode information onto photos in the form of geotags. A **geotag** is a piece of data attached to a photo that indicates your latitude and longitude when you took the photo. Geotagging is useful for applications that can take advantage of this information, but problems arise when you share geotagged photos on the web.

If you post a lot of photos, cybercriminals and cyberstalkers can use the information from the geotags on your photos to figure out the patterns of your movements. They may be able to ascertain when you're at work or that you're currently on vacation,

which leads them to determine prime times for burglarizing your home. Some sites such as Facebook and Twitter have measures in place to limit the amount of geotagged information that can be seen in photos in order to prevent their users from unwittingly revealing personal information. However, many photo-sharing sites don't have such protections in place.

The safest thing to do is not tag your photos with geotags in the first place. It's usually easy to disable location tracking on your smartphone in the settings. So stop geotagging your photos, and make it tougher for the cybercriminals to figure out your movements. For photos that already have geotags, you can remove them using software such as BatchPurifier LITE or Pixelgarde.

computer VIRUSES

Creating and disseminating computer viruses is one of the most widespread types of cybercrimes. Some viruses cause only minor annoyances, whereas others cause destruction or theft of data. Many viruses are designed to gather sensitive information such as credit card numbers.

Virus Basics

Objective 9.4 *Explain what a computer virus is, why they are a threat to your security, how a computing device catches a virus, and the symptoms it might display.*

What is a computer virus? A computer **virus** is a computer program that attaches itself to another computer program (known as the *host* program) and attempts to spread to other computers when files are exchanged.

Why are viruses such a threat to my security? Computer viruses are threatening because they are engineered to evade detection. Viruses normally attempt to hide within the code of a host program to avoid detection. And viruses are not just limited to computers. Smartphones, tablet computers, and other devices can be infected with viruses. Viruses such as SpyEye Mobile Banking are used to trick users into downloading an infected file to their phones, which then steals their online banking information.

I have an Apple computer, so I don't need to worry about viruses, do I? This is a popular misconception! Everyone, even Apple users, needs to worry about viruses. As the OS X and iOS operating systems have gained market share, the number of virus attacks against Apple operating systems is on the rise.

What do computer viruses do? A computer virus's main purpose is to replicate itself and copy its code into as many other host files as possible. This gives the virus a greater chance of being copied to another computer system so that it can spread its infection. However, computer viruses require human interaction to spread. Although there might be a virus in a file on your computer, a virus normally can't infect your computer until the infected file is opened or executed.

Although virus replication can slow down networks, it's not usually the main threat. The majority of viruses have secondary objectives or side effects, ranging from displaying annoying messages on the computer screen to destroying files or the contents of entire hard drives.

How does my computer catch a virus? If your computer is exposed to a file infected with a virus, the virus will try to copy itself and infect a file on your computer.

Downloading infected audio and video files from peer-to-peer file-sharing sites is a major source of virus infections.

Shared flash drives are also a common source of virus infection, as is e-mail. Just opening an e-mail message usually won't infect your computer with a virus, although some new viruses are launched when viewed in the preview pane of your e-mail software. Downloading and running (executing) a file that's attached to the e-mail are common ways that your computer becomes infected. Thus, be extremely wary of e-mail attachments, especially if you don't know the sender. Figure 9.6 illustrates the steps by which computer viruses are often passed from one computer to the next:

1. An individual writes a virus program, attaches it to a music file, and posts the file to a file-sharing site.
2. Unsuspecting Bill downloads the "music file" and infects his computer when he listens to the song.
3. Bill sends his cousin Fred an e-mail with the infected "music file" and contaminates Fred's tablet.
4. Fred syncs his phone with his tablet and infects his phone when he plays the music file.
5. Fred e-mails the file from his phone to Susan, one of his colleagues at work. Everyone who copies files from Susan's infected work computer, or whose computer is networked to Susan's computer, risks spreading the virus.

How can I tell if my computer is infected with a virus? Sometimes it can be difficult to definitively tell whether your computer is infected with a virus. However, if your computer displays any of the following symptoms, it may be infected with a virus:

1. Existing program icons or files suddenly disappear. Viruses often delete specific file types or programs.
2. You start your browser and it takes you to an unusual home page (i.e., one you didn't set) or it has new toolbars.
3. Odd messages, pop-ups, or images are displayed on the screen, or strange music or sounds play.
4. Data files become corrupt. (However, note that files can become corrupt for reasons other than a virus infection.)
5. Programs stop working properly, which could be caused by either a corrupted file or a virus.
6. Your system shuts down unexpectedly, slows down, or takes a long time to boot up.

Types of Viruses

Objective 9.5: *List the different categories of computer viruses, and describe their behaviors.*

What types of viruses exist? Although thousands of computer viruses and variants exist, they can be grouped into

STEP 1: Virus creation

STEP 2: Initial virus infection

Hacker's computer

File-sharing server

Bill's computer

STEP 3: Virus spreads to another computer

Susan's work computer

Fred's smartphone

STEP 4: Fred infects his cell phone

Fred's tablet

STEP 5: Other computers susceptible to infection

FIGURE 9.6 Computer viruses are passed from one unsuspecting user to the next. *(Vovan/Shutterstock, Juffin/ DigitalVision Vectors/Getty Images, Denis Rozhnovsky/Alamy, Ian Dagnall/Alamy, Stanca Sanda/Alamy)*

six broad categories based on their behavior and method of transmission.

Boot-Sector Viruses

What are boot-sector viruses? A **boot-sector virus** replicates itself onto a hard drive's master boot record. The **master boot record** is a program that executes whenever a computer boots up, ensuring that the virus will be loaded into memory immediately, even before some virus protection programs can load. Boot-sector viruses are often transmitted by a flash drive left in a USB port. When the computer boots up with the flash drive connected, the computer tries to launch a master boot record from the flash drive, which is usually the trigger for the virus to infect the hard drive.

Logic Bombs and Time Bombs

What are logic bombs and time bombs? A **logic bomb** is a virus that is triggered when certain logical conditions are met, such as opening a file or starting a program a certain number of times. A **time bomb** is a virus that is triggered by the passage of time or on a certain date. For example, the Michelangelo virus was a famous time bomb that was set to trigger every year on March 6, Michelangelo's birthday. The effects of logic bombs and time bombs range from the display of annoying messages on the screen to the reformatting of the hard drive, which causes complete data loss.

Worms

What is a worm? Although often called a virus, a **worm** is subtly different. Viruses require human interaction to spread,

whereas worms take advantage of file transport methods, such as e-mail or network connections, to spread on their own. A virus infects a host file and waits until that file is executed to replicate and infect a computer system. A worm, however, works independently of host file execution and is much more active in spreading itself. Recently developed worms, like The Moon, even attack peripheral devices such as routers. Worms can generate a lot of data traffic when trying to spread, which can slow down the Internet.

Script and Macro Viruses

What are script and macro viruses? Some viruses are hidden on websites in the form of scripts. A **script** is a series of commands—actually, a miniprogram—that is executed without your knowledge. Scripts are often used to perform useful, legitimate functions on websites, such as collecting name and address information from customers. However, some scripts are malicious. For example, you might click a link to display a video on a website, which causes a script to run that infects your computer with a virus.

A **macro virus** is a virus that attaches itself to a document that uses macros. A *macro* is a short series of commands that usually automates repetitive tasks. However, macro languages are now so sophisticated that viruses can be written with them. In 1999, the Melissa virus became the first major macro virus to cause problems worldwide.

E-Mail Viruses

What is an e-mail virus? In addition to being a macro virus, the Melissa virus was the first practical example of an

FIGURE 9.7

Major Categories of Viruses

Boot-sector Viruses
Execute when a computer boots up

Logic Bombs/Time Bombs
Execute when certain conditions or dates are reached

Worms
Spread on their own with no human interaction needed

Script and Macro Viruses
Series of commands with malicious intent

E-mail Viruses
Spread as attachments to e-mail, often using address books

Encryption Viruses
Hold files "hostage" by encrypting them; ask for ransom to unlock them

(Tribalium81/Fotolia, Oleksandr Delyk/Fotolia, DedMazay/Fotolia, Theo Malings/Fotolia, Beboy/Fotolia, Lukas Gojda/Fotolia)

e-mail virus. **E-mail viruses** use the address book in the victim's e-mail system to distribute the virus. In the case of the Melissa virus, anyone opening an infected document triggered the virus, which infected other documents on the victim's computer. Once triggered, the Melissa virus sent itself to the first 50 people in the e-mail address book on the infected computer.

Encryption Viruses

What are encryption viruses? When **encryption viruses** (also known as *ransomware*) infect your computer, they run a program that searches for common types of data files, such as Microsoft Word files, and compresses them using a complex encryption key that renders your files unusable. You then receive a message that asks you to send payment to an account if you want to receive the program to decrypt your files. The flaw with this type of virus, which keeps it from being widespread, is that law enforcement officials can trace the payments to an account and may possibly be able to catch the perpetrators. Figure 9.7 summarizes the major categories of viruses.

Additional Virus Classifications

How else are viruses classified? Viruses can also be classified by the methods they take to avoid detection by antivirus software:

- A **polymorphic virus** changes its own code or periodically rewrites itself to avoid detection. Most polymorphic viruses infect a particular type of file such as .EXE files, for example.
- A **multipartite virus** is designed to infect multiple file types in an effort to fool the antivirus software that is looking for it.
- **Stealth viruses** temporarily erase their code from the files where they reside and then hide in the active memory of the computer. This helps them avoid detection if only the hard drive is being searched for viruses. Fortunately, current antivirus software scans memory as well as the hard drive. ∎

 online annoyances and
SOCIAL ENGINEERING

Surfing the web, using social networks, and sending and receiving e-mail have become common parts of most of our lives. Unfortunately, the web has become fertile ground for people who want to advertise their products, track our browsing behaviors, or even con people into revealing personal information. In this section, we'll look at ways in which you can manage, if not avoid, these and other online headaches.

Malware: Adware and Spyware

Objective 9.6 *Explain what malware is, and list the common types of malware.*

What is malware? Malware is software that has a malicious intent (hence the prefix *mal*). There are three primary forms of

malware: adware, spyware, and viruses. Adware and spyware are not physically destructive like viruses and worms, which can destroy data. Known collectively as *grayware*, most malware are intrusive, annoying, or objectionable online programs that are downloaded to your computer when you install or use other online content such as a free program, game, or utility.

What is adware? Adware is software that displays sponsored advertisements in a section of your browser window or as a pop-up box. It's considered a legitimate, though sometimes annoying, means of generating revenue for those developers who do not charge for their software or information. Fortunately, because web browsers such as Firefox, Chrome, and Edge have built-in pop-up blockers, the occurrence of annoying pop-ups has been greatly reduced.

FIGURE 9.8 Firefox's Allowed Sites - Pop-ups dialog box lets you control which sites you'll allow to display pop-ups. *(Firefox logo® is a registered trademark of the Mozilla Foundation)*

>*To display the pop-up blocker in Firefox, click the* **Open Menu button**, *select* **Options**, *and then select the* **Content option**.

Some pop-ups, however, are legitimate and increase the functionality of the originating site. For example, your account balance may pop up on your bank's website. To control which sites to allow pop-ups on, you can access the pop-up blocker settings in your browser (see Figure 9.8) and add websites for which you allow pop-ups. Whenever a pop-up is blocked, the browser displays an information bar or plays a sound to alert you. If you feel the pop-up is legitimate, you can choose to accept it.

What is spyware? Spyware is an unwanted piggyback program that usually downloads with other software you install from the Internet and that runs in the background of your system. Without your knowledge, spyware transmits information about you, such as your Internet-surfing habits, to the owner of the program so that the information can be used for marketing purposes. Many spyware programs use tracking cookies (small text files stored on your computer) to collect information. One type of spyware program known as a **keystroke logger (key logger)** monitors keystrokes with the intent of stealing passwords, login IDs, or credit card information.

Can I prevent spyware from spying on me? Anti-spyware software detects unwanted programs and allows you to delete the offending software easily. Most Internet security suites now include anti-spyware software. You can also obtain stand-alone anti-spyware software and run it on your computer to delete unwanted spyware. Because so many variants of spyware exist, your Internet security software may not detect all types that attempt to install themselves on your computer. Therefore, it's a good idea to install one or two additional stand-alone anti-spyware programs on your computer.

Because new spyware is created all the time, you should update and run your anti-spyware software regularly. Windows comes with a program called Windows Defender, which scans your system for spyware and other potentially unwanted software. Malwarebytes Anti-Malware, Ad-Aware, and Spybot–Search & Destroy (all available from **download.com**) are other

anti-spyware programs that are easy to install and update. Figure 9.9 shows an example of Windows Defender in action.

Spam

Objective 9.7 *Define spam, and describe strategies to combat it.*

How can I best avoid spam? Companies that send out **spam**—unwanted or junk e-mail—find your e-mail address either from a list they purchase or with software that looks for e-mail addresses on the Internet. Unsolicited instant messages are also a form of spam, called *spim*. If you've used your e-mail address to purchase anything online, open an online account, or participate in a social network such as Facebook, your e-mail address eventually will appear on one of the lists that spammers get.

One way to avoid spam in your primary account is to create a free e-mail address that you use only when you fill out forms or buy items on the web. For example, both Outlook.com and Yahoo! let you set up free e-mail accounts. If your free e-mail account is saturated with spam, you can abandon that account with little inconvenience. It's much less convenient to abandon your primary e-mail address.

Another way to avoid spam is to filter it. A **spam filter** is an option you can select in your e-mail account that places known or suspected spam messages into a special folder (called "Spam" or "Junk Mail"). Most web-based e-mail services, such as Gmail and Yahoo!, offer spam filters (see Figure 9.10). Microsoft Outlook also features a spam filter.

You can also buy third-party programs that provide some control over spam, including SPAMfighter, which you can download at download.com.

How do spam filters work? Spam filters and filtering software can catch as much as 95% of spam by checking incoming e-mail subject headers and senders' addresses against databases of known spam. Spam filters also check

FIGURE 9.9 Routine scans of a computer by Windows Defender will detect and eliminate spyware and other unwanted types of software. *(Microsoft Windows Defender, Microsoft Corporation)*

your e-mail for frequently used spam patterns and keywords, such as "for free" and "over 21." Spam filters aren't perfect, and you should check the spam folder before deleting its contents because legitimate e-mail might end up there by mistake. Most programs let you reclassify e-mails that have been misidentified as spam (see Figure 9.10).

How else can I prevent spam? Here are a few other ways you can prevent spam:

1. Before registering on a website, read its privacy policy to see how it uses your e-mail address. Don't give the site permission to pass on your e-mail address to third parties.

2. Don't reply to spam to remove yourself from the spam list. By replying, you're confirming that your e-mail address is active. Instead of stopping spam, you may receive more.

3. Subscribe to an e-mail forwarding service such as VersaForward (versaforward.com) or Sneakemail (sneakemail .com). These services screen your e-mail messages, forwarding only those messages you designate as being okay to accept.

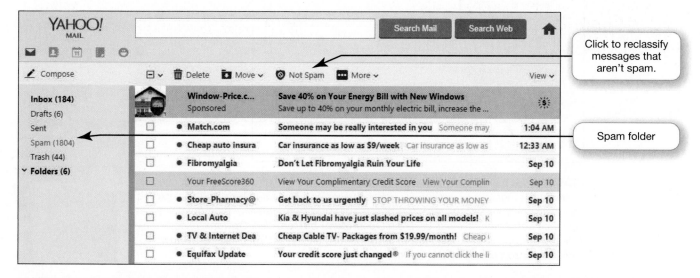

FIGURE 9.10 In Yahoo! Mail, messages identified as spam are directed into a folder called "Spam" for review and deletion. *(Reproduced with permission of Yahoo. ©2015 Yahoo. YAHOO! and the YAHOO! logo are registered trademarks of Yahoo.)*

Cookies

Objective 9.8 *Explain what cookies are and whether they pose a security threat.*

What are cookies? Cookies are small text files that some websites automatically store on your hard drive when you visit them. When you log on to a website that uses cookies, a cookie file assigns an ID number to your computer. The unique ID is intended to make your return visit to a website more efficient and better geared to your interests. The next time you log on to that site, the site marks your visit and keeps track of it in its database.

What do websites do with cookie information? Cookies can provide websites with information about your browsing habits, such as the ads you've opened, the products you've looked at, and the time and duration of your visits. Companies use this information to determine the traffic flowing through their website and the effectiveness of their marketing strategy and placement on websites. By tracking such information, cookies enable companies to identify different users' preferences.

Can companies get my personal information when I visit their sites? Cookies do not go through your hard drive in search of personal information such as passwords or financial data. The only personal information a cookie obtains is the information you supply when you fill out forms online.

Do privacy risks exist with cookies? Some sites sell the personal information their cookies collect to web advertisers who are building huge databases of consumer preferences and habits, collecting personal and business information such as phone numbers, credit reports, and the like. The main concern is that advertisers will use this information indiscriminately, thus invading your privacy. And you may feel your privacy is being violated by cookies that monitor where you go on a website.

Should I delete cookies from my hard drive? Cookies pose no *security* threat because it is virtually impossible to hide a virus or malicious software program in a cookie. Because they take up little room on your hard drive, and offer you small conveniences on return visits to websites, there is no great reason to delete them. Deleting your cookie files could actually cause you the inconvenience of reentering data you have already entered into website forms. However, if you're uncomfortable with the accessibility of your personal information, you can periodically delete cookies (as shown in Figure 9.11) or

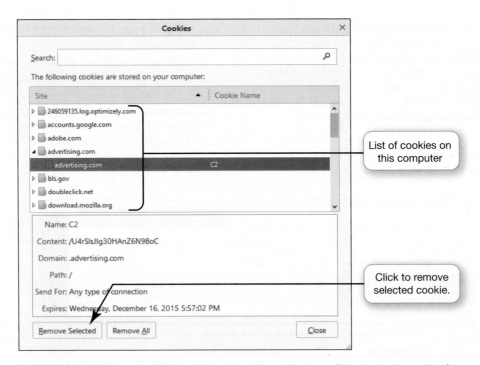

FIGURE 9.11 Tools are available, either through your browser (Firefox is shown here) or as separate programs, to distinguish between cookies you want to keep and cookies you don't want on your system. *(Firefox logo® is a registered trademark of the Mozilla Foundation)* *>On the Firefox menu toolbar, click the **Open Menu button**, click **Options**, choose the Privacy option, choose **Use custom settings for history**, and then click the **Show Cookies button** to display the Cookies dialog box.*

check your understanding // review & practice

For a quick review to see what you've learned so far, answer the following questions.

multiple choice

1. When a hacker steals personal information with the intent of impersonating another individual to commit fraud, it is known as

    a. impersonation theft.

    b. scareware theft.

    c. identity theft.

    d. malware theft.

2. An attack that renders a computer unable to respond to legitimate users because it is being bombarded with data requests is known as a _____ attack.

    a. stealth

    b. backdoor

    c. scareware

    d. denial-of-service

3. A series of commands that are executed without your knowledge is a typical attribute of a _____ virus.

    a. boot-sector

    b. script

    c. time bomb

    d. encryption

4. Software that pretends your computer is infected with a virus to entice you into spending money on a solution is known as

    a. scareware.

    b. spyware.

    c. adware.

    d. trackingware.

5. A technique that uses illegally obtained information about individuals to perform targeted attacks in the hopes of getting them to reveal sensitive information is known as

    a. spear phishing.

    b. pretexting.

    c. keystroke logging.

    d. logic bombing.

MyITLab   Go to **MyITLab** to take an autograded version of the *Check Your Understanding* review and to find all media resources for the chapter.

TECHBYTES WEEKLY
Stay current with TechBytes Weekly Newsletter.

Continue ≫

TRY THIS Testing Your Network Security

A properly installed firewall should keep you relatively safe from wily hackers. But how do you know if your computer system is safe? Many websites help test your security. In this exercise, we'll use tools provided by Gibson Research Corporation (**grc.com**) to test the strength of your protection.

Step 1 Open a web browser and navigate to **grc.com**. From the pull-down Services menu at the top of the screen, select **ShieldsUP!** On the ShieldsUP! welcome screen, click the **Proceed button**. *(Reprinted courtesy of Gibson Research Corporation)*

Step 2 Click the **Common Ports link** to begin the security test. It will take a few moments for the results to appear, depending on the speed of your Internet connection. *(Reprinted courtesy of Gibson Research Corporation)*

Step 3 Hopefully, you'll see a report indicating that your computer has passed the TruStealth analysis test. This means that your computer is very safe from attack. However, don't panic if your results say **failed for true stealth analysis**. Consider these common issues:

- Ports that only report as being closed will result in a TruStealth analysis failure. As long as all common ports are reporting as stealth or closed, you are well protected. However, if any ports report as being open, this means your computer could be exposed to hackers. Consult your firewall documentation to resolve the problem.

- Another common failure on the TruStealth test is ping reply. This means GRC attempted to contact your computer using a method called ping and it replied to the GRC computer. This is not a serious problem. It just means it's a little easier for a hacker to tell your computer network is there, but that doesn't mean that a hacker can break in. Often, your ISP has your home modem configured to reply to ping requests to facilitate remote diagnostics if there is ever a problem with your modem. As long as your ports are closed (or stealthed), your system should still be secure. *(Reprinted courtesy of Gibson Research Corporation)*

Shields UP!!
Port Authority Edition – Internet Vulnerability Profiling
by Steve Gibson, Gibson Research Corporation

Checking the Most Common and Troublesome Internet Ports

This Internet Common Ports Probe attempts to establish standard TCP Internet connections with a collection of standard, well-known, and often vulnerable or troublesome Internet ports on **YOUR** computer. Since this is being done from **our** server, successful connections demonstrate which of your ports are "open" or visible and soliciting connections from passing Internet port scanners.

Your computer at IP:

108.36.157.2

Is being profiled. Please stand by. . .

Total elapsed testing time: 4.995 seconds

| **PASSED** | TruStealth Analysis | **PASSED** |

Your system has achieved a **perfect "TruStealth" rating. Not a single packet** — solicited or otherwise — was received from your system as a result of our security probing tests. Your system ignored and refused to reply to repeated Pings (ICMP Echo Requests). From the standpoint of the passing probes of any hacker, this machine does not exist on the Internet. Some questionable personal security systems expose their users by attempting to "counter-probe the prober", thus revealing themselves. But your system wisely remained silent in every way. Very nice.

Port	Service	Status	Security Implications
0	<nil>	Stealth	There is NO EVIDENCE WHATSOEVER that a port (or even any computer) exists at this IP address!
21	FTP	Stealth	There is NO EVIDENCE WHATSOEVER that a port (or even any computer) exists at this IP address!
22	SSH	Stealth	There is NO EVIDENCE WHATSOEVER that a port (or even any computer) exists at this IP address!
23	Telnet	Stealth	There is NO EVIDENCE WHATSOEVER that a port (or even any computer) exists at this IP address!

Make This ▶ TOOL: AI TinyDB

MAKE: A Password Generator

Want to make sure your passwords are randomly selected so they are more secure, but afraid you'll forget what you chose?

In this exercise, you'll continue your mobile app development by using the TinyDB component in **App Inventor** to store information on your phone so it can be recalled by your application the next time it runs. This is called data persistence and as you'll see, it is very easy to do! *(MIT App Inventor 2, Massachusetts Institute of Technology. Creative Commons Attribution-ShareAlike 3.0 Unported License)*

```
call  TinyDB1 ▾ .StoreValue
                    tag  " Password "
           valueToStore  " 1aB9zqu "
```

The TinyDB component allows you to store data on your device to use the next time the app opens.

For the instructions for this exercise, go to MyITLab.

Learning Outcome 9.2 Describe various ways to protect your digital property and data from theft and corruption.

Often, we can be our own worst enemies when using computing devices. If you're not careful, you might be taken in by thieves or scam artists who want to steal your digital and physical assets. As we'll discuss in this section, protecting yourself is key, and there are many relatively easy measures you can take to increase your level of security.

 restricting access to your
DIGITAL ASSETS

Keeping hackers and viruses at bay is often just a matter of keeping them out. You can achieve this by:

- Preventing hackers from accessing your computer (usually through your Internet connection)
- Using techniques to prevent virus infections from reaching your computer
- Protecting your digital information in such a way that it can't be accessed (by using passwords, for example)
- Hiding your activities from prying eyes

In this section, we explore strategies for protecting access to your digital assets and keeping your Internet-surfing activities from being seen by the wrong people.

Firewalls

Objective 9.10 *Explain what a firewall is and how a firewall protects your computer from hackers.*

What is a firewall? A firewall is a software program or hardware device designed to protect computers from hackers. It's named after a housing construction feature that slows the spread of fires from house to house. A firewall specifically designed for home networks is called a **personal firewall**. By using a personal firewall, you can close open logical ports (communications pathways) to invaders and potentially make your computer invisible to other computers on the Internet.

Which is better, a software firewall or a hardware firewall? Both hardware and software firewalls will protect you from hackers. One type isn't better than the other. Although installing either a software or a hardware firewall on your home

network is probably sufficient, you should consider installing both for maximum protection. This will provide you with additional safety, just as wearing multiple layers of clothing helps keep you warmer in the winter than a single layer.

Types of Firewalls

What software firewalls are there? Both Windows and OS X include reliable firewalls. The Windows Action Center is a good source of information about the security status of your computer. The status of your Windows Firewall is shown in the Windows Firewall dialog box (see Figure 9.16). Security suites such as Norton Security, McAfee Internet Security, and Trend Micro Internet Security Suite also include firewall software. Although the firewalls that come with Windows and OS X will protect your computer, firewalls included in security suites often come with additional features such as monitoring systems that alert you if your computer is under attack.

FIGURE 9.16 The Windows Firewall dialog box provides the status of your firewall. *(Windows 10, Microsoft Corporation)*
>*To view the Windows Firewall dialog box, access **Settings**, select **Network & Internet**, select **Wi-Fi**, and then click the **Windows Firewall link**.*

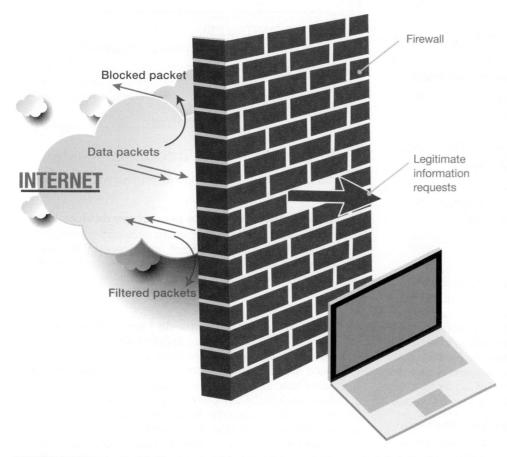

Blocked packet

Data packets

INTERNET

Filtered packets

Firewall

Legitimate information requests

FIGURE 9.17 Firewalls use filtering and blocking to keep out unwanted data and keep your network safe.

logical ports are very popular in hacker attacks. To block access to logical ports, firewalls examine data packets that your computer sends and receives. Data packets contain information such as the address of the sending and receiving computers and the logical port that the packet will use. Firewalls can be configured so that they filter out packets sent to specific logical ports in a process known as **packet filtering**. Firewalls are also often configured to ignore requests that originate from the Internet asking for access to certain ports. This process is referred to as **logical port blocking**. By using filtering and blocking, firewalls keep hackers from accessing your computer (Figure 9.17).

How do firewalls keep your network address secure?

Every computer connected to the Internet has a unique address called an *Internet Protocol address (IP address)*. Data is routed to the correct computer on the Internet based on the IP address. This is similar to how a letter finds its way to your mailbox. You have a unique postal address for your home. If a hacker finds out the IP address of your computer, he or she can locate it on the Internet and try

If you're using a security suite that includes a firewall, the suite should disable the firewall that came with your OS. Two firewalls running at the same time can conflict with each other and cause your computer to slow down or freeze up.

What are hardware firewalls? You can also buy and configure hardware firewall devices. Many routers sold for home networks include firewall protection. Just like software firewalls, the setup for hardware firewalls is designed for novices, and the default configuration on most routers keeps unused logical ports closed. Documentation accompanying routers can assist more-experienced users in adjusting the settings to allow access to specific ports if needed.

How Firewalls Work

How do firewalls protect you from hackers? Firewalls are designed to restrict access to a network and its computers. Firewalls protect you in two major ways:

1. By blocking access to logical ports
2. By keeping your computer's network address secure

How do firewalls block access to your logical ports? As you'll recall, logical ports are virtual communications gateways or paths that allow a computer to organize requests for information from other networks or computers. Certain

to break into it. This is similar to how a conventional thief might target your home after finding out you collect antique cars by using your street address to locate your house.

Your IP address for your home network is assigned to your router by your Internet service provider (ISP), but each device on your home network also has an IP address. Firewalls use a process called **network address translation (NAT)** to assign internal IP addresses on a network. The internal IP addresses are used only on the internal network and therefore can't be detected by hackers. For hackers to access your computer, they must know your computer's internal IP address. With a NAT–capable router/firewall installed on your network, hackers are unable to access the internal IP address assigned to your computer, so your computer is safe. You can use NAT in your home by purchasing a hardware firewall with NAT capabilities. Many routers sold for home use are also configured as firewalls, and many feature NAT.

 ACTIVE HELPDESK
Understanding Firewalls

In this Active Helpdesk, you'll play the role of a helpdesk staffer, fielding questions about how hackers can attack networks and what harm they can cause as well as what a firewall does to keep a computer safe from hackers.

FIGURE 9.18

Common Logical Ports	
PORT NUMBER	**PROTOCOL USING THE PORT**
21	FTP (File Transfer Protocol) control
23	Telnet (unencrypted text communications)
25	SMTP (Simple Mail Transfer Protocol)
53	DNS (domain name system)
80	HTTP (Hypertext Transfer Protocol)
443	HTTPS (HTTP with Transport Layer Security [TLS] encryption)

Knowing Your Computer Is Secure

How can I tell if my firewall is protecting my computer? For peace of mind, you can visit websites that offer free services that test your computer's vulnerability. One popular site is Gibson Research Corporation (**grc.com**). The company's ShieldsUP and LeakTest programs are free and easy to run and can pinpoint security vulnerabilities in a system connected to the Internet. If you get a clean report from these programs, your system is probably not vulnerable to attack. See the Try This section in this chapter (page 00–00) for instructions on how to test your system.

What if I don't get a clean report from the testing program? If the testing program detects potential vulnerabilities and you don't have a firewall, you should install one as soon as possible. If the firewall is already configured and common ports (such as those shown in Figure 9.18) are identified as being vulnerable, consult your firewall documentation for instructions on how to close or restrict access to those ports.

 SOUND BYTE
Installing a Personal Firewall
Firewalls provide excellent protection against hackers on a home network. In this Sound Byte, you'll learn how to install and configure software firewalls to protect your computer.

Preventing Virus Infections

Objective 9.11 *Explain how to protect your computer from virus infection.*

What is the best way to protect my devices from viruses? Earlier in the chapter, we discussed the various viruses that hackers may unleash on your system. There are two main ways to protect your computer from viruses: by installing antivirus software and by keeping your software up to date.

Antivirus Software

What antivirus software do I need? Antivirus software is specifically designed to detect viruses and protect your computer and files from harm. Symantec, Kaspersky, Trend Micro, and McAfee are among the companies that offer highly rated antivirus software packages. Antivirus protection is also included in comprehensive Internet security packages such as Norton Security, Trend Micro Internet Security, and McAfee Total Protection. These software packages also help protect you from threats other than computer viruses. For example, Windows 10 includes Windows Defender, which defends against malware as well as viruses.

How often do I need to run antivirus software? Although antivirus software is designed to detect suspicious activity on your computer at all times, you should run an active virus scan on your entire system at least once a week. By doing so, all files on your computer will be checked for undetected viruses.

Current antivirus programs run scans in the background when your CPU is not being heavily utilized. But you can also configure the software to run scans at times when you aren't using your system—for example, when you're asleep (see Figure 9.19). (However, it's important to note that your computer has to be on and not in sleep mode for these virus scans to take place.) Alternatively, if you suspect a problem, you can launch a scan and have it run immediately.

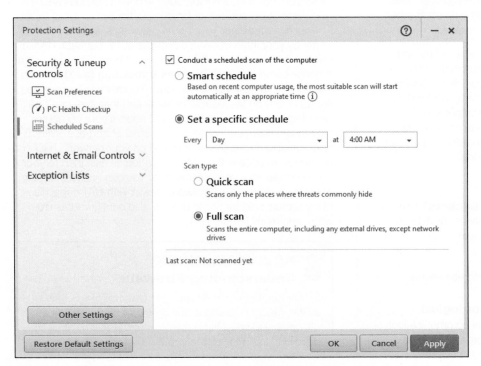

FIGURE 9.19 In Trend Micro Internet Security, you can set up virus scans to run automatically. This computer will be scanned every day at 4 a.m. *(Reprinted courtesy of Trend Micro Incorporated. All rights reserved.)*

How does antivirus software work? The main functions of antivirus software are as follows:

- *Detection*: Antivirus software looks for virus signatures in files. A **virus signature** is a portion of the virus code that's unique to a particular computer virus. Antivirus software scans files for these signatures when they're opened or executed and identifies infected files and the type of virus infecting them.

- *Stopping virus execution*: If the antivirus software detects a virus signature or suspicious activity, such as the launch of an unknown macro, it stops the execution of the file and virus and notifies you that it has detected a virus. It also places the virus in a secure area on your hard drive so that it won't spread to other files; this procedure is known as **quarantining**. Usually, the antivirus software then gives you the choice of deleting or repairing the infected file. Unfortunately, antivirus programs can't always fix infected files to make them usable again. You should keep backup copies of critical files so that you can restore them in case a virus damages them irreparably.

- *Prevention of future infection*: Most antivirus software will also attempt to prevent infection by inoculating key files on your computer. In **inoculation**, the antivirus software records key attributes about your computer files, such as file size and date created, and keeps these statistics in a safe place on your hard drive. When scanning for viruses, the antivirus software compares the attributes of the files with the attributes it previously recorded to help detect attempts by virus programs to modify your files.

Does antivirus software always stop viruses?

Antivirus software catches *known* viruses effectively. However, new viruses are written all the time. To combat unknown viruses, modern antivirus programs search for suspicious virus-like activities as well as virus signatures. To minimize your risk, you should keep your antivirus software up to date.

My new computer came with antivirus software installed, so shouldn't I already be protected?

Most new computers do come with antivirus software preinstalled. However, these are usually trial versions of the software that only provide updates to the software for a limited period of time, usually 90 or 180 days. After that, you have to buy a full version of the software to ensure you remain protected from new viruses. If you have Windows 10 and there is no third-party antivirus software installed, Windows Defender will be active by default so you should have some protection.

How do I make sure my antivirus software is up to date?

Most antivirus programs have an automatic update feature that downloads updates for virus signature files every time you go online. Also, the antivirus software usually shows the status of your update subscription so that you can see how much time you have remaining until you need to buy another version of your software. Many Internet security packages offer bonus features such as cloud storage scanners and password managers (see Figure 9.20) to provide you with extra protection.

FIGURE 9.20 Many protection packages, such as Trend Micro Internet Security, offer other types of security features besides basic malware protection. *(Reprinted courtesy of Trend Micro Incorporated. All rights reserved.)*

What should I do if I think my computer is infected with a virus? Boot up your computer using the antivirus installation disc. This should prevent most virus programs from loading and will allow you to run the antivirus software directly from your disk drive. (*Note*: If you download your antivirus software from the Internet, copy the files to a DVD in case you have problems in the future.) If the software does detect viruses, you may want to research them further to determine whether your antivirus software will eradicate them completely or whether you'll need to take additional manual steps to eliminate the viruses. Most antivirus company websites, such as the Symantec site (**symantec.com**), contain archives of information on viruses and provide step-by-step solutions for removing them.

How do I protect my phone from viruses? Because smartphones and other mobile devices run operating systems and contain files, they are susceptible to infection by viruses. Cybercriminals are now hiding viruses in legitimate-looking apps for download to mobile devices. Most antivirus software companies now offer antivirus software specifically designed for mobile devices. The Google Play store even offers very effective free products to protect your Android devices such

 ACTIVE HELPDESK
Avoiding Computer Viruses

In this Active Helpdesk, you'll play the role of a helpdesk staffer, fielding questions about different types of viruses and what users should do to protect their computer from them.

as 360 Security and Avast! Mobile Security. In addition to providing protection from malware, these apps also provide other useful features such as the ability to wipe your phone's contents if it is lost or stolen.

Software Updates

Why does updating my operating system (OS) software help protect me from viruses? Many viruses exploit weaknesses in operating systems. Malicious websites can be set up to attack your computer by downloading harmful software onto your computer. According to research conducted by Google, this type of attack, known as a **drive-by download**, affects almost 1 in 1,000 web pages. To combat these threats, make sure your OS is up to date and contains the latest security patches.

Do OS updates only happen automatically? Prior to the release of Windows 10, you updated your Windows OS with an automatic update utility called Windows Update. You had the ability to decide when to download updates and when to install them. However, with Windows 10, you no longer have as many choices. Updates are now downloaded automatically whenever they are provided by Microsoft. You do have the choice to allow Windows to automatically schedule a restart of your computer to apply the updates or pick a more convenient

restart time manually (see Figure 9.21). Mac OS X has a similar utility for gathering updates.

The Advanced Options screen for Windows Update provides a few other options (see Figure 9.22). The most notable is the ability to receive updates for other Microsoft products (like MS Office). (Note that the ability to defer upgrades is not available on the Windows 10 Home edition—you must install updates as they are delivered by Microsoft).

Authentication: Passwords and Biometrics

Objective 9.12 *Describe how passwords and biometric characteristics can be used for user authentication on computer systems.*

How can I best use passwords to protect my computer? You no doubt have many passwords you need to remember to access your digital life. However, creating strong passwords—ones that are difficult for hackers to guess—is an essential piece of security that people sometimes overlook. Password-cracking programs have become more sophisticated. In fact, some commonly available programs can test more than one million password combinations per second! Creating a secure password is therefore more important than ever.

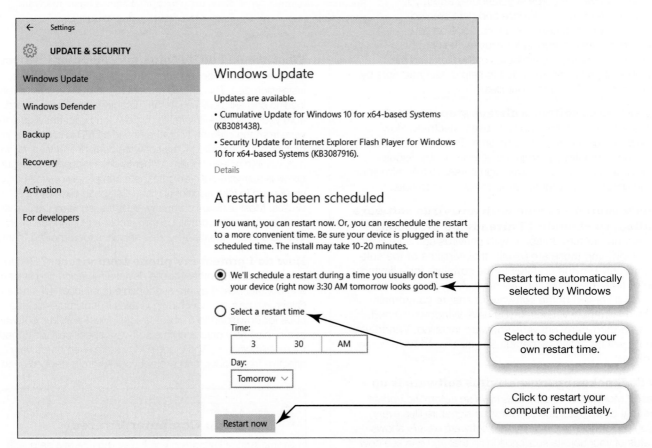

FIGURE 9.21 The Windows Update screen makes it easy for users to stay abreast of software updates and manage restarts.
(Windows 10, Microsoft Corporation)
*>To access the Windows Update screen, from the Start menu, select **Settings**, select **Update & security**, then select* ***Windows Update***.

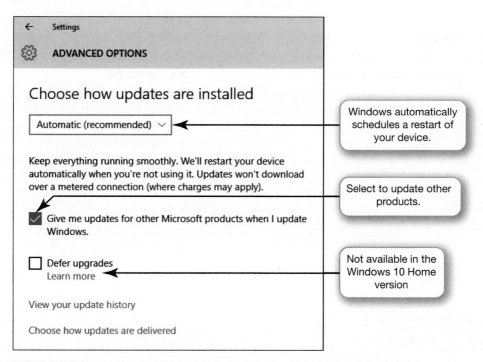

FIGURE 9.22 The Windows Update Advanced Options screen provides a few more user controlled update options. *(Windows 10, Microsoft Corporation)*
*>To access the Windows Update Advanced Options screen, scroll to the bottom of the Windows Update screen (Figure 9.21) and click the **Advanced options link**.*

SOUND BYTE
Protecting Your Computer

In this Sound Byte, you'll learn how to use a variety of tools to protect your computer, including antivirus software and Windows utilities.

Many people use extremely weak passwords. The Imperva Application Defense Center, a computer-security research organization, conducted a review of 32 million passwords that were used at the website **rockyou.com**. More than 345,000 people were using "12345," "123456," or "123456789" as their password. And almost 62,000 people were using "password"! Passwords such as these are easy for hackers to crack.

Websites that need to be very secure, such as those for financial institutions, usually have strong defenses to prevent hackers from cracking passwords. But sites that need less security, such as casual gaming or social networking sites, might have less protection. Hackers attack poorly defended sites for passwords because many people use the same password for every site they use. So if a hacker can get your password from a poorly secured gaming site, they might be able to access your bank account with the same password.

Creating Strong Passwords

What constitutes a strong password? Strong passwords are difficult for someone to guess. Follow these guidelines to create strong passwords (see Figure 9.23):

- Don't use easily deduced components related to your life, such as parts of your name, your pet's name, your street address, or the name of the website or institution for which you are creating the password (i.e., don't use "Citibank" for your online banking password).
- Use a password that is at least 14 characters long. Longer passwords are more difficult to deduce. Consider using a passphrase that is even longer (see the Bits & Bytes on page 375).
- Don't use words found in the dictionary.
- Use a mix of upper- and lowercase letters and symbols (such as # or %).
- Never tell anyone your password or write it down in a place where others might see it, like in your wallet or a sticky note on your computer screen!
- Change your passwords on a regular basis, such as monthly or quarterly. Your school or your employer probably requires you to change your password regularly. This is also a good idea for your personal passwords.
- Don't use the same password for every account you have.

FIGURE 9.23

Strong and Weak Password Candidates

PASSWORD	RATING	GOOD POINTS	BAD POINTS
Joysmithl022	Poor	• Contains upper- and lowercase letters • Contains letters and numbers	• Less than 14 characters • Contains name and birth date
test44drive6car	Mediocre	• 15 characters in length	• Contains three words found in the dictionary • Numbers repeated consecutively
8$RanT%5ydTTtt&	Better	• Good length • Contains upper- and lowercase letters • Contains symbols	• Upper- and lowercase letters repeated consecutively • Still contains one dictionary word (rant)
7R3m3mB3R$5%y38	Best	• All good points from above • Dictionary word (remember) has 3s instead of Es	• None

BITS&BYTES

CAPTCHA: Keeping Websites Safe from Bots

Automated programs called *bots* (or web robots) are used to make tasks easier on the Internet. For example, search engines use bots to search and index web pages. Unfortunately, bots can also be used for malicious or illegal purposes because they can perform some computing tasks faster than humans. For example, bots can be used on ticket-ordering sites to buy large blocks of high-demand concert tickets. They are also often used to post spam in the comment sections of blogs. Fortunately, website owners can deploy CAPTCHA software to prevent such bot activities.

CAPTCHA (Completely Automated Public Turing Test to Tell Computers and Humans Apart) programs used to generate distorted text and require that it be typed into a box. Newer programs, like Google's reCAPTCHA, monitor users' website behavior to determine if you are a human or a bot. reCAPTCHA merely asks you to click a check box (Figure 9.24a) and if it displays a green check (Figure 9.24b), you have passed the bot test. If the app isn't sure if you are a human, it may ask you to type in some distorted text (Figure 9.24c) just like older versions of the program did. If you want to try integrating a CAPTCHA program into your website (to protect your e-mail address), go to **google.com/recaptcha**, which offers free CAPTCHA tools to help you protect your data.

FIGURE 9.24 CAPTCHA programs like reCAPTCHA monitor a user's website behavior and can often determine if a user is human just by having the user check a box. If a green check mark appears, you are human! If the app isn't sure if you're a bot, you may be asked to enter some text. *(Metrue/Shutterstock)*

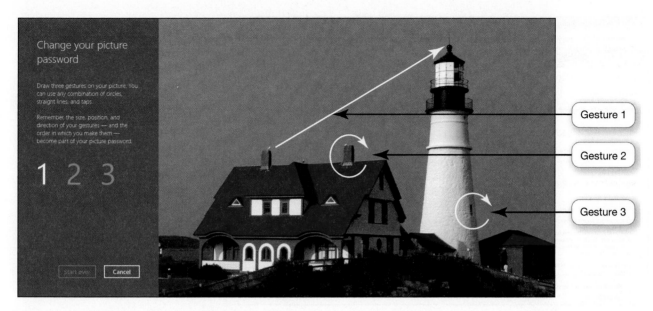

FIGURE 9.25 Drawing three gestures (a swipe and two circles) on this image (and repeating them once) sets your picture password options in Windows. *(Windows 10, Microsoft Corporation)*

If you have trouble thinking of secure passwords, there are many password generators available for free, such as the Strong Password Generator (**strongpasswordgenerator.com**).

How can I check the strength of my passwords? You can use online password strength testers, such as the Password Meter (**passwordmeter.com**), to evaluate your passwords. The Password Meter provides guidelines for good passwords and shows you how integrating various elements, such as symbols, affects the strength score of your password.

How do I restrict access to my computer? Windows, OS X, and most other operating systems have built-in password (or passcode) protection for files as well as the entire desktop. After a certain period of idle time, your computer is automatically password locked, and your password (or PIN) must be entered to gain access to the computer. This provides excellent protection from casual snooping if you need to walk away from your computer for a period of time. If someone attempts to log on to your computer without your password, that person won't be able to gain access. It's an especially good idea to use passwords on laptop computers, smartphones, and tablets because this provides additional protection of your data if your device is lost or stolen.

Windows allows you to use picture passwords. You select a picture and then draw three gestures on it—either straight lines, circles, or taps. This picture then works as an additional method for accessing your computer. You just unlock your computer by repeating the gestures (see Figure 9.25). But if you forget your gestures, you can always access your computer via the conventional password.

Managing Your Passwords

How can I remember all of my complex passwords? Good security practices suggest that you have different passwords for all the different websites that you access and that you change your passwords frequently. The problem with well-constructed passwords is that they can be hard to remember. Fortunately, password-management tools are now available. They take the worry out of forgetting passwords because the password-management software does the remembering for you.

Where can I obtain password-management software? Most current Internet security suites and web browsers make it easy to keep track of passwords by providing password-management tools. For example, Microsoft Edge will remember passwords for you. When you go to a website that requires a login, Microsoft Edge will display a dialog box prompting you to have Microsoft Edge remember the password for the site (see Figure 9.26). Then, when you return to the site and type in your user name, Microsoft Edge will fill in the password information for you using a process known as *auto complete*. However, there are some passwords that you shouldn't have your browser remember, such as your online banking password. So be selective when using this feature.

Biometric Authentication Devices

Besides passwords, how else can I restrict the use of my computer? A **biometric authentication device** is a device that reads a unique personal characteristic such as a fingerprint or the iris pattern in your eye and converts its pattern to a digital code. When you use the device, your pattern is read and compared to the one stored on the computer. Only users having an exact fingerprint or iris pattern match are allowed to access the computer.

Because no two people have the same biometric characteristics (fingerprints and iris patterns are unique), these devices provide a high level of security. They also eliminate the human error that can occur in password protection. You might forget your password, but you won't forget to bring your fingerprints

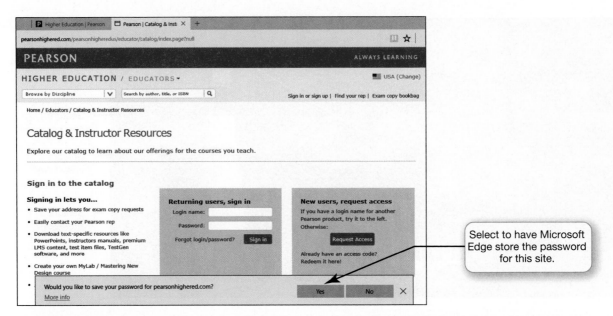

FIGURE 9.26 The password dialog box in Microsoft Edge displays whenever you type in a password for a website for which Microsoft Edge hasn't yet stored the password. *(Screenshot of Pearson Higher Education website, Pearson Education, Inc.)*

when you're working on your computer! Some smartphones, such as the iPhone, now include fingerprint readers. But since Touch ID (the Apple software for fingerprint identification) has already been hacked, you might be safer using a regular password. Other biometric devices, including voice authentication and facial recognition systems, are now widely offered in laptops (see Figure 9.27), tablets, and smartphones (such as the Samsung Galaxy phones).

FIGURE 9.27 Face recognition software is now available on laptops. You might forget your password, but you won't forget to bring your face! *(Jochen Tack/Alamy)*

Anonymous Web Surfing: Hiding from Prying Eyes

Objective 9.13 *Describe ways to surf the web anonymously.*

Should I be concerned about surfing the Internet on shared, public, or work computers? If you use shared computers in public places such as libraries, coffee shops, or student unions, you never know what nefarious tools have been installed by hackers on a public computer. When you browse the Internet, traces of your activity are left behind on that computer, often as temporary files. A wily hacker can glean sensitive information long after you've finished your surfing session. In addition, many employers routinely review the Internet browsing history of employees to ensure workers are spending their time on the Internet productively.

What tools can I use to keep my browsing activities private when surfing the Internet? The current versions of Mozilla Firefox, Microsoft Edge, and Google Chrome include privacy tools (called Private Browsing, InPrivate, and Incognito, respectively) that help you surf the web anonymously (see Figure 9.28). When you choose to surf anonymously, all three browsers open special versions of their browser windows that are enhanced for privacy. When surfing in these windows, records of websites you visit and files you download don't appear in the web browser's history files. Furthermore, any temporary files generated in that browsing session are deleted when you exit the special window.

Are there any other tools I could use to protect my privacy? Portable privacy devices, such as the Ironkey Personal Flash Drives (**ironkey.com**), provide an even higher level of surfing privacy. Simply plug the device into an available

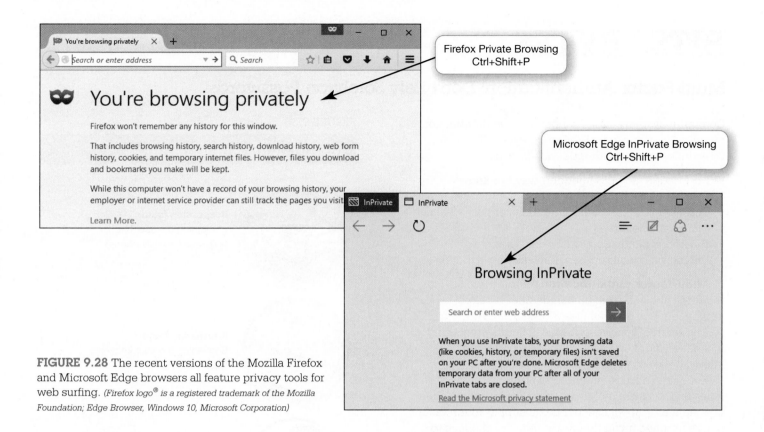

FIGURE 9.28 The recent versions of the Mozilla Firefox and Microsoft Edge browsers all feature privacy tools for web surfing. *(Firefox logo® is a registered trademark of the Mozilla Foundation; Edge Browser, Windows 10, Microsoft Corporation)*

Firefox Private Browsing
Ctrl+Shift+P

Microsoft Edge InPrivate Browsing
Ctrl+Shift+P

USB port on the machine on which you'll be working. All sensitive Internet files, such as cookies, passwords, Internet history, and browser caches, will be stored on the privacy device, not on the computer you're using. Privacy devices such as these often come preloaded with software designed to shield your IP address from prying eyes, making it difficult (if not impossible) for hackers to tell where you're surfing on the Internet. These privacy devices also have password-management tools that store all of your login information and encrypt it so it will be safe if your privacy device falls into someone else's hands.

Is there anything else I can do to keep my data safe on shared computers? Another free practical solution is to take the Linux OS with you on a flash drive and avoid using the public or work computer's OS. The interfaces of many Linux distros look almost exactly like Windows and are easy to use. There are several advantages to using a Linux-based OS on a public or work computer:

- Your risk of picking up viruses and other malicious programs is significantly reduced because booting a computer from a flash drive completely eliminates any interaction with the computer's OS. This, in turn, significantly reduces the chance that your flash drive will become infected by any malware running on the computer.
- Virus and hacking attacks against Linux are far less likely than attacks against Windows. Because Windows has about 90% of the OS market, people who write malware tend to target Windows systems.

- When you run software from your own storage medium, such as a flash drive, you avoid reading and writing to the hard disk of the computer. This significantly enhances your privacy because you don't leave traces of your activity behind.

Pendrivelinux (**pendrivelinux.com**) is an excellent resource that offers many different versions of Linux for download and includes step-by-step instructions on how to install them on your flash drive. If you're a Mac user, the Elementary OS Luna distro of Linux provides a close approximation of OS X, so you can feel right at home.

How can I protect sensitive data transmissions if I have to use a public wireless network? Virtual private networks (VPNs) are secure networks that are established using the public Internet infrastructure. Using specialized software, servers and data transmission protocols, VPNs are used to send information on the public Internet in a such a manner that the data is as secure as sending it on a private network. VPNs used to be only used by businesses. But with public concerns about information security on the rise, many VPN software providers (such as Private Internet Access and Nord VPN) are marketing affordable solutions to individuals. So if you routinely transmit sensitive information, you should consider a personal VPN solution.

Make sure to use some (or all) of these methods to keep your activities from prying eyes and to restrict access to your digital information. ∎

BITS&BYTES

Multi-Factor Authentication: Don't Rely Solely on Passwords!

Computer system security depends on authentication—proving the user is who they say they are. There are three independent authentication factors:

- Knowledge factor: Something the user knows (password, PIN)
- Possession factor: Something the user has (ATM card, mobile phone)
- Inherence factor: Something only the user is (biometric characteristics, such as fingerprints)

Multi-factor authentication requires two of the three above factors be demonstrated before authorization is granted (see Figure 9.30). At the bank's ATM machine, you present an ATM card (something you have) and then use a PIN code (something you know) to access your account.

For online access, multi-factor authentication often relies on the use of mobile phones. For instance, when you register a Google account, you supply your mobile phone number. If you then want to make changes to your account, you supply the password (something you know). The second step of authentication is Google sending an SMS message with a unique code to your mobile phone. Retrieving the code and entering it online proves you have the phone (something the user has) and serves as the second authentication step.

Multi-factor authentication is much safer than single-factor authentication. So make use of it when it is offered to you to enhance your account security.

FIGURE 9.30

Multi-Factor Authentication

Possession factor:
Something the user has
(ATM card, mobile phone)

Knowledge factor:
Something the user knows
(password, PIN)

Inherence factor:
Something only the user is
(biometric characteristics, such as fingerprints)

Strong Authentication:
Two of the three factors

(LoloStock/Fotolia, Jamie/Fotolia, Jamdesign/Fotolia)

keeping your
DATA SAFE

People are often too trusting or just plain careless when it comes to protecting private information about themselves or their digital data. In this section, we discuss ways to keep your data safe from damage, either accidental or intentional.

Protecting Your Personal Information

Objective 9.14 *Describe the types of information you should never share online.*

If a complete stranger walked up to you on the street and asked you for your address and phone number, would you give it to him or her? Of course you wouldn't! But many people are much less careful when it comes to sharing sensitive information online. And often people inadvertently share information that they really only intended to share with their friends. With cybercrimes like identify theft rampant, you need to take steps to protect your personal information.

What information should I never share on websites? A good rule of thumb is to reveal as little information as possible, especially if the information would be available to everyone. Figure 9.31 gives you some good guidelines.

Your Social Security number, phone number, date of birth, and street address are four key pieces of information that identity thieves need to steal an identity. This information should never be shared in a public area on any website.

How can I tell who can see my information on a social network? Social networking sites like Facebook make privacy settings available in your profile settings. If you've never changed your default privacy settings in Facebook, you're probably sharing information more widely than you should.

How can I protect my information on Facebook? To begin, you need to change your privacy settings in your profile from some of the default options. In general, it's a bad idea to make personal information available to the public, although this is a default setting for some items in Facebook. It's a good idea to set most of the options in your profile's Basic Information section to Friends or to Only Me because, presumably, these are personal details you should wish to share only with friends.

In the Contact Information section, restricting this information only to friends or to yourself is imperative. You don't want scammers contacting you via e-mail or snail mail and trying to trick you into revealing sensitive information.

Backing Up Your Data

Objective 9.15 *List the various types of backups you can perform on your computing devices, and explain the various places you can store backup files.*

How might I damage the data on my computer? The data on your computer faces three major threats:

1. Unauthorized access
2. Tampering
3. Destruction

FIGURE 9.31

Internet Information-Sharing Precautions

Information Identity Thieves Crave

STOP

- Social Security Number
- Full Date of Birth
- Phone Number
- Street Address

Never make this information visible on websites!

Other Sensitive Information

CAUTION

- Full Legal Name
- E-mail Address
- Zip Code
- Gender
- School or Workplace

Only reveal this information to people you know—don't make it visible to everyone!

(Mograph/Fotolia, Kevin Largent/Fotolia)

BITS&BYTES

Social Networking: Looking Beyond Facebook

Are the posts you see on Facebook too general for your liking? Do you wish you could participate in a social networking community with more people who share your specific interests or passions? Facebook is the largest social networking site, but it isn't the only option out there. Many social networking sites exist that cater to specific types of users or interests.

Are you a graduate student that needs to monitor progress in a specific field of research? Try **Academia.edu**, which is a site specifically designed to promote the sharing of research papers in the academic community. If cooking is your passion, start your own food blog on **cucumbertown.com** and gain followers who like your recipes. People who love

clubbing can meet at **dontstayin.com** and find out about events at clubs in a specific area. Trying to learn English as a second language? **Englishbaby.com** is a community of ESL students and teachers dedicated to helping members learn conversational English and slang. Free English lessons are posted every day! The Experience Project (**experienceproject.com**) encourages members to post personal experiences and form groups based on people with similar experiences or interests.

So no matter where your interests lie, there is probably a social network that caters to you. If you can't find one that suits you, then use **ning.com** and create your own specialized social network!

As noted earlier, a hacker can gain access to your computer and steal or alter your data. However, a more likely scenario is that you'll lose your data unintentionally. You may accidentally delete files. You may drop your laptop on the ground, causing the hard drive to break and resulting in complete data loss. A virus from an e-mail attachment you opened may destroy your original file. Your house may catch fire and destroy your computer. Because many of these possibilities are beyond your control, you should have a strategy for backing up your files (see Figure 9.32). **Backups** are copies of files that you can use to replace the originals if they're lost or damaged.

What types of files do I need to back up? Two types of files need backups:

1. **Program files** include files used to install software, usually found on DVDs or downloaded from the Internet. As long as you have the DVDs in a safe place, you shouldn't need to back up these program files. If you've downloaded a program file from the Internet, however, you should make a copy of the program installation files on a removable storage device as a backup.

2. **Data files** include files you've created or purchased, such as research papers, spreadsheets, music and photo files, contact lists, address books, e-mail archives, and your Favorites list from your browser.

What types of backups can I perform? There are two main options for backing up files:

1. An **incremental backup** (or **partial backup**) involves backing up only files that have changed or have been created since the last backup was performed. Using backup software that has an option for incremental

FIGURE 9.32

An Effective Backup Strategy

Files to Back Up

- **Program files:** Installation files for productivity software (i.e., Microsoft Office)
- **Data files:** Files you create (term papers, spreadsheets, etc.)

Types of Backups

- **Incremental (partial):** Only backs up files that have changed
- **Image (system):** Snapshot of your entire computer, including system software

Where to Store Backup Files

- Online (in the cloud)
- External hard drives
- Network-attached storage devices or home servers

backups will save time because backing up files that haven't changed is redundant.

2. An **image backup** (or **system backup**) means that all system, application, and data files are backed up, not just the files that changed. Although incremental backups are more efficient, an image backup ensures you capture

changes to application files, such as automatic software updates, that an incremental backup might not capture. The idea of imaging is to make an exact copy of the setup of your computer so that in the event of a total hard drive failure you could copy the image to a new hard drive and have your computer configured exactly the way it was before the crash.

Where should I store my backups? To be truly secure, backups must be stored away from where your computer is located and should be stored in at least two different places. You wouldn't want a fire or a flood destroying the backups along with the original data. You have three main choices for where to back up your files (see Figure 9.33):

1. *Online (in the cloud)*: The beauty of online storage is that you don't need to be at your home computer or lug around your external hard drive to access your data. More importantly, because the information is stored online, it's in a secure, remote location, so data is much less vulnerable to the disasters that could harm data stored in your computer or external hard drive. Free storage options include Microsoft OneDrive (**onedrive.com**) and ADrive (**adrive.com**). However, image backups probably won't fit within the storage limits offered by

free providers. For a fee, companies such as Carbonite (**carbonite.com**) and IBackup (**ibackup.com**) provide larger storage capacity.

2. *External hard drives*: External hard drives, or even large-capacity flash drives, are popular backup options that are usually connected to a single computer. Although convenient and inexpensive, using external hard drives for backups still presents the dilemma of keeping the hard drive in a safe location. Also, external hard drives can fail, possibly leading to loss of your backed-up data. Therefore, using an external hard drive for backups is best done in conjunction with an online backup strategy for added safety.

3. *Network-attached storage (NAS) devices and home servers*: NAS devices are essentially large hard drives connected to a network of computers instead of one computer, and they can be used to back up multiple computers simultaneously. Home servers also act as high-capacity NAS devices for automatically backing up data and sharing files.

How often should I back up my data files? You should back up your data files every time you make changes to them, which can be difficult to remember to do. Fortunately, most backup software can be configured to do backups

FIGURE 9.33

A Comparison of Typical Data Backup Locations

BACKUP LOCATION	PROS	CONS
Online (in the Cloud)	• Files stored at a secure, remote location • Files/backups accessible anywhere through a browser	• Most free storage sites don't provide enough space for image backups
External Hard Drive	• Inexpensive, one-time cost • Fast backups with USB 3.0 devices connected directly to your computer	• Could be destroyed in one event (fire/flood) with your computer • Can be stolen • Slightly more difficult to back up multiple computers with one device
Network-Attached Storage (NAS) Device and Home Server	• Makes backups much easier for multiple computing devices	• More expensive than a stand-alone external hard drive • Could be destroyed in one event (fire/flood) with your computer • Can be stolen

automatically so you don't forget to perform them. For example, with the Windows File History utility, you can have Windows automatically save your data files from your libraries, desktop, contacts, and favorites to an external hard drive or NAS device. The default setting for File History saves files you changed every hour to the backup location you specify. File History even keeps previous versions of the file on the backup drive so you can revert to a previous version of the file if you need to do so.

To set up File History, you first need to connect an external hard drive to your computer or a NAS device (or home server) to your network. You can then access File History through the Control Panel (in the System and Security group) and set it up (see Figure 9.35). Once configured, your data files will be backed up as often as you indicate. You can also restore files that you've backed up from the File History utility.

How often should I create an image backup?
Because your program and OS files don't change as often as your data files, you can perform image backups on a less frequent basis. You might consider scheduling an image backup of your entire system on a weekly basis, but you should definitely perform one after installing new software.

How do I perform an image backup?
Windows includes the System Image Backup utility, which provides a quick and easy way to perform image backups. You can access this utility from the System Image Backup link on the File History screen (see Figure 9.34), which launches the Backup and Restore (Windows 7) screen (see Figure 9.35a). Before starting this utility, make sure your external hard drive or

NAS device is connected to your computer or network and is powered on. To set it up, follow these steps:

1. Click the Create a system image link. Select the location (drive) for your backup files and click Next to proceed.
2. On the second screen (see Figure 9.35b), you can select the drives/partitions from your computer to be backed up. Notice that all the drives/partitions that are required for Windows to run are preselected for you. Windows will back up all data files and system files on all selected drives/partitions. Click Next to proceed.
3. On the third screen, click Start backup to start your system image.

After the system image backup runs for the first time, you will see the results of the last backup and the date of the next scheduled backup on the Backup and Restore (Windows 7) screen (see Figure 9.35a). If the scheduled backup time is not convenient for you, click the Change settings link to select an alternative time.

From the Backup and Restore screen, you can also create a system repair disc. A system repair disc contains files that can be used to boot your computer in case of a serious Windows error.

What about backing up Apple computers? For OS X users, backups are very easy to configure. The Time Machine feature in OS X detects when an external hard drive is connected to the computer or a NAS device is connected to your network. You're then asked if you want this to be your backup drive. If you answer yes, all of your files (including OS files) are automatically backed up to the external drive or NAS device.

Should I back up my files that are stored on my school's network? Most likely, if you're allowed to store files on your school's network, these files are backed up

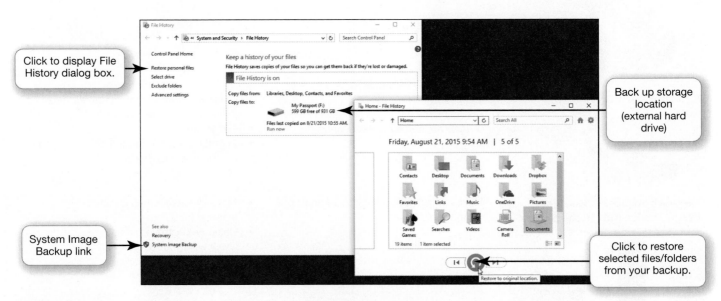

FIGURE 9.34 You can use the Windows File History utility to back up files and restore files from a previous backup. *(Windows 10, Microsoft Corporation)*
>*Right-click **Start**, select **Control Panel**, select **System and Security**, and then click the **File History link**.*

regularly. You should check with your school's network administrators to determine how often they're backed up and how you would request that files be restored from the backup if they're damaged or deleted. But don't rely on these network backups to bail you out if your data files are lost or damaged. It may take days for the network administrators to restore your files. It's better to keep backups of your data files yourself, especially homework and project files, so that you can immediately restore them. ■

SOUND BYTE
Managing Computer Security with Windows Tools

In this Sound Byte, you'll learn how to monitor and control your computer security using features built into the Windows OS.

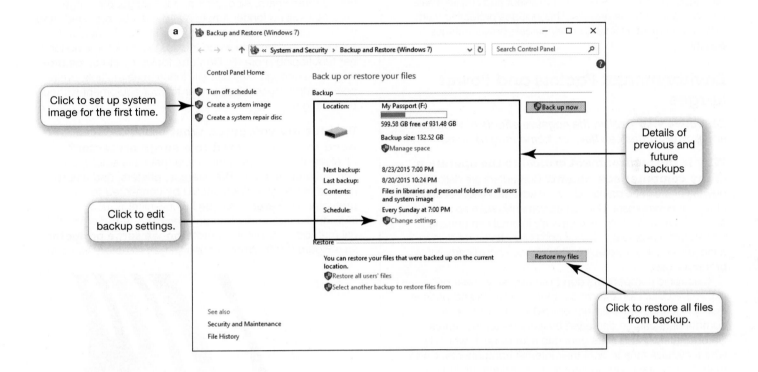

Click to set up system image for the first time.

Click to edit backup settings.

Details of previous and future backups

Click to restore all files from backup.

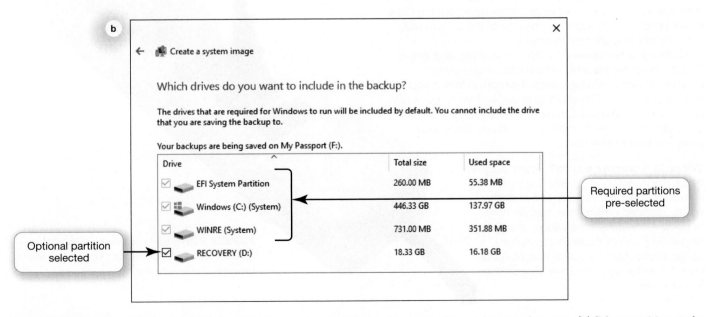

Required partitions pre-selected

Optional partition selected

FIGURE 9.35 (a) The Backup and Restore utility allows you to perform an image backup and restore from one. (b) Select partitions to be included in the system image backup. *(Windows 10, Microsoft Corporation)*

protecting your physical
COMPUTING ASSETS

Your computer, tablet, and phone aren't useful to you if they're damaged. Therefore, it's essential to select and ensure a safe environment for these devices. This includes protecting them from environmental factors, power surges, power outages, and theft.

Environmental Factors and Power Surges

Objective 9.16 *Explain the negative effects environment and power surges can have on computing devices.*

Why is the environment critical to the operation of my computer equipment? Computers are delicate devices and can be damaged by the adverse effects of abuse or a poor environment. Sudden movements, such as a fall, can damage your computing device's internal components. You should make sure that your computer sits on a flat, level surface, and if it's a laptop or a tablet, you should carry it in a protective case.

Electronic components don't like excessive heat or excessive cold. Don't leave computing devices and phones in a car during especially hot or cold weather because components can be damaged by extreme temperatures. Unfortunately, computers generate a lot of heat, which is why they have fans to cool their internal components. Chill mats that contain cooling fans and sit underneath laptop computers are useful accessories for dissipating heat. Make sure that you place your desktop computer where the fan's intake vents, usually found on the rear of the system unit, are unblocked so air can flow inside.

Naturally, a fan drawing air into a computer also draws in dust and other particles, which can wreak havoc on your system. Therefore, keep the room in which your computer is located as clean as possible. Finally, because food crumbs and liquid can damage keyboards and other computer components, consume food and beverages away from your computer.

What is a power surge? Power surges occur when electrical current is supplied in excess of normal voltage. Old or faulty wiring, downed power lines, malfunctions at electric company substations, and lightning strikes can all cause power surges. A **surge protector** is a device that protects your computer against power surges (see Figure 9.36).

Note that you should replace your surge protectors every two to three years. Also, after a major surge, the surge protector will no longer function and must be replaced. And it's wise to buy a surge protector that includes indicator lights, which illuminate when the surge protector is no longer functioning properly. Don't be fooled by old surge protectors—although they can still function as multiple-outlet power strips, they deliver power to your equipment without protecting it.

Besides my computer, what other devices need to be connected to a surge protector? All electronic devices in the home that have solid-state components, such as TVs, stereos, printers, and smartphones (when charging), should be connected to a surge protector. However, it can be inconvenient to use individual surge protectors on everything. A more practical method is to install a **whole-house surge protector** (see Figure 9.37). Whole-house surge protectors function

FIGURE 9.36 Surge protectors such as this one are critical for protecting your electronic devices. *(Aberenyi/Fotolia)*

Surge protector

FIGURE 9.37 A whole-house surge protector is usually installed at the breaker panel or near the electric meter.

like other surge protectors, but they protect *all* electrical devices in the house. Typically, you'll need an electrician to install a whole-house surge protector, which will cost $300 to $500 (installed).

Is my equipment 100% safe when plugged into a surge protector? Lightning strikes can generate such high voltages that they can overwhelm a surge protector. As tedious as it sounds, unplugging electronic devices during an electrical storm is the only way to achieve absolute protection.

Preventing and Handling Theft

Objective 9.17 *Describe the major concerns when a device is stolen and strategies for solving the problems.*

What do I need to worry about if my computing device is stolen? Although theft of computer equipment is not classified as a cybercrime (it is considered larceny), the theft of tablets, smartphones, notebook computers, and other portable computing devices is on the rise. The resale value for used electronic equipment is high, and the equipment can be easily sold online. And because they're portable, laptops, tablets, and phones are easy targets for thieves. You have four main security concerns with mobile devices:

1. Keeping them from being stolen
2. Keeping data secure in case they are stolen
3. Finding a device if it is stolen
4. Remotely recovering and wiping data off a stolen device

Keep Them Safe: Alarms
What type of alarm can I install on my mobile device? Motion alarm software is a good, inexpensive theft deterrent. Free software such as LAlarm (**lalarm.com**) is effective for laptops. Apps such as Motion Alarm and Alarmomatic help secure your iPad or iPhone. Alarm software either detects motion, like your device being picked up, or sounds near your device and then sets off an ear-piercing alarm until you enter the disable code. Thieves normally don't like it when attention is drawn to their activities, so alarms can be a very effective theft deterrent.

Keeping Mobile Device Data Secure
How can I secure the data on my mobile devices? Encrypting the data on your mobile device can make it extremely difficult, if not impossible, for thieves to obtain sensitive data from your stolen equipment. *Encryption* involves transforming your data using an algorithm that can only be unlocked by a secure code (or key). Encrypted data is impossible to read unless it's decrypted, which requires a secure password, hopefully known only to you.

Safe is an app that provides 256-bit encryption, which is very hard to crack, for data and images on your iPhone and iPad. If your password is not entered, no one can access the data and images on your iPhone or iPad. Mobile Strong-Box is a similar app for Android devices. SensiGuard and SafeHouse are available for laptop computers to provide encryption for files or even entire hard drives.

Software Alerts and Data Wipes
How can my computer help me recover it when it is stolen? You've probably heard of LoJack, the theft-tracking device used in cars. Similar systems now exist for computers. Tracking software such as Absolut LoJack (**lojack.absolute.com/en**), PC PhoneHome, and Mac PhoneHome (**brigadoonsoftware.com**) enables your computer to alert authorities to the computer's location if it is stolen. A similar tracking app for Android and iOS devices is iHound.

To enable your mobile device to help with its own recovery, you install the tracking software on your device. The software contacts a server at the software manufacturer's website each time the device connects to the Internet. If your device is stolen, you notify the software manufacturer. The software manufacturer instructs your device to transmit tracking information, such as an IP address, WiFi hotspot, or cell tower location, that will assist authorities in locating and retrieving the mobile device.

What if the thieves find the tracking software and delete it? The files and directories holding the software aren't visible to thieves looking for such software, so they probably won't know the software is there. Furthermore, the tracking software is written in such a way that even if the thieves tried to reformat the hard drive, it would detect the reformat and hide the software code in a safe place in memory or on the hard drive. This works because some sectors of a hard drive are not rewritten during most reformatting. That way, the tracking software can reinstall itself after the reformatting is complete.

What if my device can't be recovered by the authorities? In the event that your laptop can't be recovered, software packages are available that provide for remote recovery and deletion of files. Absolute LoJack has these features and allows you to lock your device to keep the thieves from accessing it or to remotely wipe its contents by deleting all your data from your laptop.

For all iOS devices, Apple offers the Find My iPhone service, which is now part of iCloud. Enabling this service on your device provides you with numerous tools that can assist you in recovering and protecting your mobile devices. Did you forget where you left your iPad? Just sign in with your Apple ID at the iCloud website to see a map showing the location of your iPad (see Figure 9.38). You can send a message to your device, remotely password lock the device, or wipe all data from the device to completely protect your privacy. For Android devices, Where is My Droid? offers similar features, such as texting your device and having it reply with its location. You can even capture images with the front and rear cameras to see what your device is looking at (such as the thief)!

How can I ensure that I've covered all aspects of protecting my digital devices? Figure 9.39 provides a guide to ensure you haven't missed critical aspects of security. If you've addressed all of these issues, you can feel reasonably confident that your data and devices are secure. ■

FIGURE 9.39

FIGURE 9.38 The Find My iPhone app can really help if your iOS device goes astray. You can play a sound to help you find it (if it's misplaced where you are), display a message on the device (Lost Mode), or erase all data on the device. *(LearningStockImages/Alamy)*

Computer Security Checklist

Firewall

- Do all your computers and tablets have firewall software installed and activated before connecting to the Internet?
- Is your router also able to function as a hardware firewall?
- Have you tested your firewall security by using the free software available at grc.com?

Virus and Spyware Protection

- Is antivirus and anti-spyware software installed on all your devices?
- Is the antivirus and anti-spyware software configured to update itself automatically and regularly?
- Is the software set to scan your device on a regular basis (at least weekly) for viruses and spyware?

Software Updates

- Have you configured your operating systems (Windows, OS X, iOS) to install new software patches and updates automatically?
- Is other software installed on your device, such as Microsoft Office or productivity apps, configured for automatic updates?
- Is the web browser you're using the latest version?

Protecting Your Devices

- Are all computing devices protected from electrical surges?
- Do your mobile devices have alarms or tracking software installed on them?

Before moving on to the Chapter Review:
1. **Watch Replay Video 9.2** ▷.
2. **Then check your understanding of what you've learned so far.**

On law enforcement TV shows, you often see computer technicians working on suspects' computers to assist detectives in solving crimes. It may look simple, but the science of computer forensics is a complex, step-by-step process that ensures evidence is collected within the confines of the law.

Forensic means that something is suitable for use in a court of law. There are many branches of forensic science. For example, forensic pathologists provide evidence about the nature and manner of death in court cases involving deceased individuals. **Computer forensics** involves identifying, extracting, preserving, and documenting computer evidence. Computer forensics is performed by individuals known as *computer forensic scientists*, who rely primarily on specialized software to collect their evidence.

Phase 1: Obtaining and Securing Computer Devices

The first step in a computer forensics investigation is to seize the computer equipment that law enforcement officials believe contains pertinent evidence. Police are required to obtain a warrant to search an individual's home or place of business. Warrants must be very specific by spelling out exactly where detectives can search for evidence and exactly what type of evidence they're seeking. If a warrant indicates that the police may search an individual's home for his laptop computer, they can't then confiscate a tablet computer they notice in his car. It is important to specify in the warrant all types of storage devices where potential evidence might be stored, such as external hard drives, flash drives, and servers.

Once permission to collect the computers and devices containing possible evidence has been obtained, law enforcement officials must exercise great care when collecting the equipment. They need to ensure that no unauthorized persons are able to access or alter the computers or storage devices. The police must make sure the data and equipment are safe; if the equipment is connected to the Internet, the connection must be severed without data loss or damage. It's also important for law enforcement officials to understand that they may not want to power off equipment because potential evidence contained in RAM may be lost. After the devices are collected and secured, the computer forensic scientists take over the next phase of the investigation.

Phase 2: Cataloging and Analyzing the Data

It's critical to preserve the data exactly as it was found, or attorneys may argue that the computer evidence was subject to tampering or altering. Because just opening a file can alter it, the first task is to make a copy of all computer systems and storage devices collected (see Figure 9.40). The investigators then work from the copies to ensure that the original data always remains preserved exactly as it was when it was collected.

After obtaining a copy to work from, forensics professionals attempt to find every file on the system, including deleted files. Files on a computer aren't actually deleted, even if you empty the Recycle Bin, until the section of the hard disk they're stored on is overwritten with new data. Therefore, using special forensic software tools such as SIFT, EnCase, and FTK, the forensic scientists catalog all files found on the system or storage medium and recover as much information from deleted files as they can. Forensic software like FTK can readily detect hidden files and perform procedures to crack encrypted files or access protected files and reveal their contents.

The most important part of the process is documenting every step. Forensic scientists must clearly log every procedure performed because they may be required to provide proof in court that their investigations did not alter or damage information contained on the systems they examined. Detailed reports should list all files found, how the files were laid out on the system, which files were protected or encrypted, and the contents of each file. Finally, computer forensic professionals are often called on to present testimony in court during a trial.

Criminals are getting more sophisticated and are now employing anti-forensics techniques to foil computer forensic investigators. Although techniques for hiding or encrypting data are popular, the most insidious anti-forensics techniques

FIGURE 9.40 Portable computer forensic devices make it easy to copy storage devices at crime scenes. *(Lance Mueller/Alamy)*

are programs designed to erase data if unauthorized persons (i.e., not the criminal) access a computer system or if the system detects forensics software in use. When computer forensic investigators detect these countermeasures, they must often use creative methods and custom-designed software programs to retrieve and preserve the data.

Computer forensics is an invaluable tool to law enforcement in many criminal investigations, but only if the correct procedures are followed and the appropriate documentation is prepared.

check your understanding // review & practice

For a quick review to see what you've learned so far, answer the following questions.

multiple choice

1. Firewalls work by closing _____ in your computer.

    a. logical ports

    b. software gaps

    c. logical doors

    d. backdoors

2. _____ involve using a physical attribute such as a fingerprint for authentication.

    a. Backdoors

    b. Rootkits

    c. Biometrics

    d. Trojan horses

3. A backup of only the files on your computing device that have been created (or changed) since the last backup is known as a(n)

    a. total backup.

    b. incremental backup.

    c. image backup.

    d. global backup.

4. Antivirus software looks for _____ to detect viruses in files.

    a. virus artifacts

    b. virus signatures

    c. virus bots

    d. virus VPNs

5. Updating your operating software on a regular basis helps prevent system corruption from _____, which are malicious websites downloading harmful software to your computer.

    a. CAPTCHA

    b. pharming

    c. phishing

    d. drive-by-downloads

(MyITLab)   Go to **MyITLab** to take an autograded version of the *Check Your Understanding* review and to find all media resources for the chapter.

TECHBYTES WEEKLY

Stay current with TechBytes Weekly Newsletter.

Continue >>

9 Chapter Review

summary //

Major Threats to Your Digital Assets

Learning Outcome 9.1 **You will be able to describe hackers, viruses, and other online annoyances and the threats they pose to your digital security.**

Identity Theft and Hackers

Objective 9.1 *Describe how identity theft is committed and the types of scams identity thieves perpetrate.*

- Identity theft occurs when a thief steals personal information about you and runs up debts in your name. Identify thieves can obtain information by stealing mail, searching through trash, or tricking people into revealing information over the phone or via e-mail. Identity thieves counterfeit existing credit cards, opening new credit card and bank accounts, change your address on financial statements, obtain medical services, and buy homes with a mortgage in the victim's name.

Objective 9.2 *List and describe the different types of hackers.*

- White-hat hackers break into systems for nonmalicious reasons such as testing security to expose weaknesses. Black-hat hackers break into systems to destroy information or for illegal gain. Grey-hat hackers often break into systems just for the thrill or to demonstrate their prowess.

Objective 9.3 *Describe the various tools hackers use and the types of attacks they might launch against computers.*

- Packet analyzers (sniffers) are programs used to intercept and read data packets and they travel across a network. Trojan horses are programs that appear to be something else but are really a tool for hackers to access your computer. Backdoor programs and rootkits are tools used by hackers to gain access to and take total control of a computer system. Denial-of-service attacks overwhelm computer systems with so many requests for data that legitimate users can't access the system.

Computer Viruses

Objective 9.4 *Explain what a computer virus is, why they are a threat to your security, and how a computing device catches a virus, and the symptoms it might display.*

- A computer virus is a computer program that attaches itself to another computer program and attempts to spread to other computers when files are exchanged. Computer viruses can display annoying messages, destroy your information, corrupt your files, or gather information about you. Computers catch viruses when exposed to infected files. This can occur from downloading infected files, downloading and running infected e-mail attachments, or sharing flash drives that contain infected files. Symptoms of virus infection include: (1) files or app icons disappear, (2) browser is reset to an unusual home page, (3) odd messages, pop-ups, or images are displayed, (4) data files become corrupt, and (5) Programs stop working properly

Objective 9.5 *List the different categories of computer viruses, and describe their behaviors.*

- Boot-sector viruses copy themselves onto the master boot record of a computer and execute when the computer is started. Logic bombs and time bombs are viruses triggered by the completion of certain events or by the passage of time. Worms can spread on their own without human intervention, unlike conventional viruses. Macro viruses lurk in documents that use macros (short series of commands that automate repetitive tasks). E-mail viruses access the address book of a victim to spread to the victim's contacts. Encryption viruses render files unusable by compressing them with complex encryption keys. Polymorphic viruses periodically rewrite themselves to avoid detection. Stealth viruses temporarily erase their code and hide in the active memory of the computer.

Online Annoyances and Social Engineering

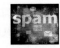

Objective 9.6 *Explain what malware is, and list the common types of malware*

- Malware is software that has a malicious intent. Adware is software that displays sponsored advertisements in a section of your browser window or as a pop-up box. Spyware collects information about you, without your knowledge, and transmit it to the owner of the program.

Objective 9.7 *Define spam, and describe strategies to combat it.*

- Spam is unwanted or junk e-mail. Spim is unsolicited instant messages, which is also a form of spam. Spam filters in e-mail systems forward junk mail to their own folder. Never reply to spam or click on unsubscribe links as this usually just generates more spam.

Objective 9.8 *Explain what cookies are and whether they pose a security threat.*

- Cookies are small text files that some websites automatically store on your hard drive when you visit them. Cookies are usually used to keep track of users and personalize their browsing experience. Cookies do not pose a security threat although some individuals view them as privacy violations.

Objective 9.9 *Describe social engineering techniques, and explain strategies to avoid falling prey to them*

- Social engineering is any technique that uses social skills to generate human interaction that entices individuals to reveal sensitive information. Phishing lures people into revealing personal information via bogus e-mails that appear to be from legitimate sources and direct people to scammer's websites. Pharming occurs when malicious code is planted on your computer, either by viruses or by your visiting malicious websites, which then alters your browser's ability to find web addresses. Scareware attempts to convince you that your computer is infected with a virus and then tries to sell you a "solution." Most Internet security software packages have scareware, phishing and pharming protection built-in.

Protecting Your Digital Property

Learning Outcome 9.2 Describe various ways to protect your digital property and data from theft and corruption.

Restricting Access to Your Digital Assets

Objective 9.10 *Explain what a firewall is and how a firewall protects your computer from hackers.*

- A FIREWALL is a software program or hardware device designed to protect computers from hackers. Firewalls block access to your computer's logical ports and help keep your computer's network address secure. Firewalls use PACKET FILTERING to identify packets sent to specific logical ports and discard them. Firewalls use network address translation to assign internal IP addresses on networks. The internal IP addresses are much more difficult for hackers to detect.

Objective 9.11 *Explain how to protect your computer from virus infection.*

- ANTIVIRUS SOFTWARE is specifically designed to detect viruses and protect your computer and files from harm. Antivirus software detects viruses by looking for VIRUS SIGNATURES: code that specifically identifies a virus. Antivirus software stops viruses from executing and quarantines INfected files in a secure area on the hard drive. Virus software must be constantly updated to remain effective.

Objective 9.12 *Describe how passwords and biometric characteristics can be used for user authentication on computer systems.*

- Secure passwords contain a mixture of upper- and lowercase letters, numbers, and symbols and are at least 14 characters long. Passwords should not contain words that are in the dictionary or easy-to-guess personal information. Utilities built into web browsers and Internet security software can be used to manage your passwords.

- A biometric authentication device is a device that reads a unique personal characteristic to identify an authorized user. Fingerprint readers, iris scanners and facial recognition software are common examples of biometric security devices.

Objective 9.13 *Describe ways to surf the web anonymously.*

- Privacy tools built into web browsers help your surf anonymously by not recording your actions in the history files. USB devices containing privacy tools are available that prevent the computer you are using from storing any information about you on the computer. Virtual private networks (VPNs) are secure networks that can be used to send information securely across the public Internet.

Keeping Your Data Safe

Objective 9.14 *Describe the types of information you should never share online.*

- Reveal as little information as possible about yourself. Your Social Security number, phone number, date of birth, and street address are four key pieces of information that identity thieves need to steal an identity.

Objective 9.15 *List the various types of backups you can perform on your computing devices, and explain the various places you can store backup files.*

- An INCREMENTAL BACKUP involves backing up only files that have changed or have been created since the last backup was performed. An IMAGE BACKUP (or SYSTEM BACKUP) means that all system, application, and data files are backed up, not just the files that changed. You can store backups online (in the cloud), on external hard drives, or on network-attached storage (NAS) devices.

Protecting Your Physical Computing Assets

Objective 9.16 *Explain the negative effects environment and power surges can have on computing devices.*

- Computing devices should be kept in clean environments free from dust and other particulates and should not be exposed to extreme temperatures (either hot or cold). You should protect all electronic devices from power surges by hooking them up through surge protectors, which will protect them from most electrical surges that could damage the devices.

Objective 9.17 *Describe the major concerns when a device is stolen and strategies for solving the problems.*

- The four main security concerns regarding computing devices are (1) keeping them from being stolen, (2) keeping data secure in case they are stolen, (3) finding a device if it is stolen, and (4) remotely recovering and wiping data off a stolen device.

- Software is available for installation on devices that will (1) set off an alarm if the device is moved, (2) help recover the device, if stolen, by reporting the computer's whereabouts when it is connected to the Internet, and (3) allow you to lock or wipe the contents of the device remotely.

MyITLab) Be sure to check out **MyITLab** for additional materials to help you review and learn. And don't forget the Replay Videos.

key terms //

chapter quiz // assessment

For a quick review to see what you've learned, answer the following questions. Submit the quiz as requested by your instructor. If you are using **MyITLab**, the quiz is also available there.

multiple choice

1. Which of the following is NOT a major type of cybercrime reported to the IC3?

    a. Government impersonation scams

    b. identity theft

    c. malware fraud

    d. advance fee fraud

2. Viruses that load from USB drives left connected to computers when computers are turned on are known as

    a. boot-sector viruses.

    b. script viruses.

    c. polymorphic viruses.

    d. encryption viruses.

3. Software designed to close logical ports in your computer is known as a(n)

    a. firewall.

    b. packet filter.

    c. anti-malware blocker.

    d. network address translator.

4. Which is NOT a tool hackers use to gain access to and take control of your computer?

    a. Trojan horse

    b. backdoor programs

    c. rootkits

    d. phishing software

5. A computer that a hacker has gained control of in order to launch DoS attacks is known as a _____ computer.

    a. rootkit

    b. compromised

    c. zombie

    d. breached

6. A backup of all the files on your computer, which essentially creates a "snapshot" of what your computer looks like at that point in time, is known as a(n)

    a. total backup.

    b. incremental backup.

    c. image backup.

    d. modification backup.

true/false

_____ **1.** Password strength is solely determined by the length of the password.

_____ **2.** One of the best and simplest ways to keep hackers out of your computer is to use a firewall.

_____ **3.** Sending e-mails to lure people into revealing personal information is a technique known as phishing.

_____ **4.** Encrypting data is not an appropriate measure for protecting mobile devices such as smartphones.

critical thinking

1. **Protecting Your Data from Data Breaches**

    You most likely have provided personal information to many websites and companies. What information have you provided to companies that you wish you had never disclosed? What types of information have companies asked you to provide that you believe was unnecessary? List specific companies and examples of the extraneous information.

2. **Phishing**

    Have you or anyone you know ever been a victim of a phishing scam? What sorts of scams have you heard about? Research and discuss at least three types of common scams.

Protecting a Network

Problem

Along with easy access to the web comes the danger of theft of digital assets.

Task

A school alumnus is in charge of the county government computer department. The network contains computers running Windows 10, Windows 8, Windows 7, and OS X. He asked your instructor for help in ensuring that his computers and network are protected from viruses, malware, and hackers. He is hoping that there may be free software available that can protect his employees' computers.

Process

1. Break the class into three teams. Each team will be responsible for investigating one of the following issues:

   a. **Antivirus software:** Research alternatives that protect computers from viruses. Find three alternatives and support your recommendations with reviews that evaluate free packages.

   b. **Anti-malware software:** Research three free malware alternatives and determine whether the software can be updated automatically. You may want to recommend that the county purchase software to ensure that a minimum of employee intervention is needed to keep it up to date.

   c. **Firewalls:** Determine if the firewall software provided with Windows 10, Windows 8, Windows 7, and OS X is reliable. If it is, prepare documentation (for all three OSs) for county employees to determine if their firewalls are properly configured. If additional firewall software is needed, research free firewall software and locate three options that can be deployed by the county.

   d. Present your findings to the class and provide your instructor with a report suitable for eventual presentation to the manager of the county office network.

Conclusion

With the proliferation of viruses and malware, it is essential to protect computers and networks. Free alternatives might work, but you should research the best protection solution for your situation.

Content Control: Censorship to Protect Children

In this exercise, you'll research and then role-play a complicated ethical situation. The role you play might or might not match your own personal beliefs; in either case, your research and use of logic will enable you to represent the view assigned. An arbitrator will watch and comment on both sides of the arguments, and together, the team will agree on an ethical solution.

Problem

Many parents use web-filtering software (content-control software) to protect their children from objectionable Internet content. In 2000, the U.S. federal government began requiring libraries to use content-control software as a condition to receiving federal funds under the provisions of the Children's Internet Protection Act (CIPA). Some states, such as Virginia, have passed laws requiring libraries to install filtering software even if they did not receive federal funds. Upon installation of the software, it's up to the library administrators to decide what content is restricted. Therefore, content restriction can vary widely from library to library.

Research Areas to Consider

- U.S. Supreme Court case *United States v. American Library Association* (2003)

- Content-control software and First Amendment rights
- Violation of children's free speech rights
- Children's Internet Protection Act (CIPA)

Process

1. Divide the class into teams. Research the areas above and devise a scenario in which someone has complained about innocuous content that was blocked.

2. Team members should write a summary that provides background information for their character—for example, library patron, library administrator, or arbitrator—and that details their character's behaviors to set the stage for the role-playing event. Then, team members should create an outline to use during the role-playing event.

3. Team members should present their case to the class or submit a PowerPoint presentation for review by the class, along with the summary and resolution they developed.

Conclusion

As technology becomes ever more prevalent and integrated into our lives, more and more ethical dilemmas will present themselves. Being able to understand and evaluate both sides of the argument, while responding in a personally or socially ethical manner, will be an important skill.

Computer Security

You have been asked to prepare a report on computer security using Word 2016. You have written the majority of the report, but you have to make some final modifications and refinements such as adding the results of some research of good antivirus software, adding a cover page, and generating a table of contents.

You will use the following skills as you complete this activity:

- Create and Modify Tables
- Insert Tab Stops
- Add Watermark
- Insert Cover Page

- Create and Update Table of Contents
- Add Footnote
- Use Find and Replace

Instructions:

1. Open *TIA_Ch9_Start* and save as **TIA_Ch9_LastFirst**.
2. Find all instances of *e-mail* and replace with **e-mail**.
   a. Hint: Click **Replace** in the Editing group on the Home tab, type **e-mail** in the Find what box, and type **e-mail** in the Replace with box. Click **Replace All**.
3. Find the first instance of malware. Place the cursor after the word *malware* (before the period) and insert the footnote: **Malware is defined as software that is intended to gain access to, or damage or disable, computer systems for the purposes of theft or fraud.** Close the Navigation pane.
   a. Hint: Use Find in the Editing group on the Home tab to locate malware.
   b. Hint: Click **Insert Footnote** in the Footnotes group on the References tab to insert a footnote.
4. In the section, *Types of Viruses*, highlight the six lines of text that outline the categories of computer viruses and variants. Add a Right Align Tab Stop at 1½" and a Left Align Tab Stop at 2".
   a. Hint: To set tab stop, display ruler, select tab stop style from Select tab box to the left of the ruler, click at the desired position on the ruler.
5. Place cursor at the end of the paragraph in the Antivirus Software section. Press **Enter**, then insert a **3×4 Table**. Type **Product Name, Description/Review**, and **Cost** in the top three cells. Adjust the width of the Description/Review column to **3.5"** and the width of the Cost column to **1"**.
   a. Hint: Click **Table** in the Tables group on the Insert tab, and drag to select the desired grid.
6. Add a row at the top of the table, **Merge Cells**, type **Antivirus Software Reviews**, and **Align Center** the contents. Format the table with **Grid Table 4—Accent 1 style**.
   a. Hint: Click **Insert** above in the Rows & Columns group on the Table Tools Layout tab.
7. Open a browser, and go to **www.pcmag.com/reviews/antivirus**. Research four antivirus software programs and place the software name, review, and cost of the software in the respective columns in the table.
   a. Hint: Press **tab** at the end of the third row to add an additional line to the table to accommodate a fourth review.
8. Press **Ctrl+Home**, then insert the **Banded Cover Page**. Ensure *Computer Security* displays as the title and *your name* displays as the Author. Delete the Company and Address placeholders.
9. Insert **Page Numbers** at the bottom of the page using the **Plain Number 3 format**. Ensure Different First Page is checked. Close Header and Footer.
10. On the page 2 of the document, insert a **Page Break** before the report title, Computer Security.
11. Place the cursor at the top of the new blank page, and insert a **Table of Contents** using the Contents format.
    a. Hint: Click **Table of Contents** in the Table of Contents group on the References tab.
12. Press **Ctrl+End**, scroll up and change the heading style of *Firewalls* to **Heading 2**, change the heading style of *Software Firewalls* and *Hardware Firewalls* to **Heading 3**.
13. Update the Table of Contents to reflect the changes in headings, ensure you update the entire table.
    a. Hint: Click anywhere in the Table of Contents, and click **Update Table**, and then click **Update entire table**.
14. Add a **Draft 1 Watermark** to the report.
    a. Hint: Click **Watermark** in the Page Backgroup group on the Design tab.
15. Save the document and submit based on your instructor's directions.

Technology in Focus

Careers in IT

Learning Outcome 9B.1 **Describe the various categories of IT jobs available, explain why IT jobs are in demand, and discuss various ways to prepare for IT employment.**

It's hard to imagine an occupation in which computers aren't used in some fashion. Even such previously low-tech industries as waste disposal and fast food use computers to manage inventories and order commodities. In this Technology in Focus feature, we explore various information technology (IT) career paths open to you.

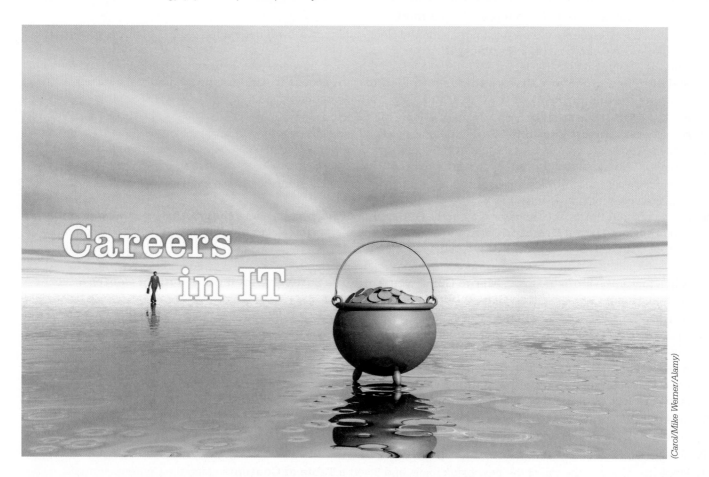

Careers in IT

(Carol/Mike Werner/Alamy)

Rewards of Working in Information Technology

Objective 9B.1 *List the reasons why IT fields are attractive to students pursuing bachelor's degrees.*

There are many great reasons to work in the exciting, ever-changing field of IT. In this section, we'll explore some reasons why IT fields are so attractive to graduates looking for entry-level positions.

IT Workers Are in Demand

If you're investigating a career with computers, the first question you may have is, "Will I be able to get a job?" Consider the following:

- According to projections by the U.S. Department of Labor's Bureau of Labor Statistics, computer-related jobs are expected to be among the fastest-growing occupations through 2022 (see Figure 1).

FIGURE 1

High-Growth IT Jobs*

OCCUPATION	MEDIAN PAY ($)	10-YEAR GROWTH RATE (%)	TOTAL NEW JOBS
Software developers	93,350	22	222,600
Computer systems analysts	79,680	25	127,700
Computer support specialists	48,900	17	123,000
Network and computer systems administrators	72,560	12	42,900
Web developers	62,500	20	28,500
Computer programmers	74,280	8	28,400
Information security analysts	86,170	37	27,400
Computer network architects	91,000	15	20,900
Database administrators	77,080	15	17,900

*Excerpted from Occupational Outlook Handbook, 2014–15 Edition, Bureau of Labor Statistics

- In 2015, *US News and World Report* published a list of the best careers to consider based on employment opportunity, good salary, work–life balance, and job security. Computer systems analyst, software developer, and information security analyst were included among the top 10 careers. Two other IT careers—web developer and IT manager—were in the top 25.

- According to the National Association of Colleges and Employers (NACE) January 2015 Salary Survey, the average starting salary for computer science majors with bachelor's degrees was projected to be $61,287 and was the second highest average salary on the list, trailing only engineering majors.

The number of students pursuing computer science degrees also has been increasing over the past several years. Fields of specialization such as game development, information security, and mobile app development are very popular. Yet, shortages of computing professionals in the United States are still projected over the next 5 to 10 years. What does all this mean? In terms of job outlook, now is a perfect time to consider an IT career.

IT Jobs Pay Well

As you can see from Figure 1, median salaries in IT careers are robust. But what exactly affects your salary in an IT position? Your skill set and your experience level are obvious answers, but the size of an employer and its geographic location are also factors. Large companies tend to pay more, so if you're pursuing a high salary, set your sights on a large corporation. But remember that making a lot of money isn't everything—be sure to consider other quality-of-life issues such as job satisfaction. Of course, choosing a computer career isn't a guarantee you'll get a high-paying job. Just as in any other profession, you'll need appropriate training and on-the-job experience to earn a high salary.

So how much can you expect to start out earning? Although starting salaries for some IT positions such as

computer support specialists are more on the modest side ($48,900), starting salaries for students with bachelor's degrees in IT are fairly robust. But IT salaries vary widely, depending on experience level, the geographic location of the job, and the size of the employer.

To obtain the most accurate information, you should research salaries yourself in the geographic area where you expect to work. **Salary.com** provides a free salary wizard to help you determine what IT professionals in your area are making compared with national averages. You can add information such as your degree and the size of the company to your search selection to fine-tune the figures further.

Figure 2 shows that for an entry-level programming position in Denver, you could expect to earn a salary of between $46,027 and $72,137 with a bachelor's degree. Hundreds of IT job titles are listed in **Salary.com**, so you can tailor your search to the specific job, location, and industry in which you're interested.

IT Jobs Are Not Going "Offshore"

In the global economy in which we now operate, job outlook includes the risk of jobs being outsourced, possibly to other countries. **Outsourcing** is a process whereby a business hires a third-party firm to provide business services (such as customer-support call centers) that were previously handled by in-house employees. **Offshoring** occurs when the outsourcing firm is located (or uses employees) outside the United States.

India, China, and Romania and other former Eastern Bloc countries are major players in providing outsourcing services for U.S. companies. The big lure of outsourcing and offshoring is cost savings: Considering that the standard of living and salaries are much lower in many countries than they are in the United States, offshoring is an attractive option for many U.S. employers.

However, outsourcing and offshoring don't always deliver the cost savings that CEOs envision. Demand for personnel overseas has led to increased costs (primarily due to wage

FIGURE 2 The salary wizard at Salary.com is easy to tailor to your location and experience. *(Salary Wizard/IBM)*

increases) for service providers in foreign markets. Furthermore, other, less-tangible factors can outweigh the cost savings from outsourcing. Communications problems can arise between internal and external employees, for example, and cultural differences between the home country and the country doing the offshoring can result in software code that needs extensive rework by in-house employees. Data also can be less secure in an external environment or during the transfer between the company and an external vendor. Although outsourcing and offshoring won't be going away, companies are approaching these staffing alternatives with more caution and are looking more to U.S. companies to provide resources.

So, many IT jobs are staying in the United States. According to *InformationWeek* magazine, most jobs in the following three categories (see Figure 3) will stay put:

1. *Customer interaction*: Jobs that require direct input from customers or that involve systems with which customers interface daily

2. *Enablers*: Jobs that involve getting key business projects accomplished, often requiring technical skills beyond the realm of IT and good people skills

3. *Infrastructure jobs*: Jobs that are fundamental to moving and storing the information that U.S.-based employees need to do their jobs

In addition, jobs that require specific knowledge of the U.S. marketplace and culture, such as social media managers, are also very likely not to be offshored.

Women Are in High Demand in IT Departments

Currently, women make up about 26% of the IT workforce (per the National Center for Women and Information Technology). This presents a huge opportunity for women who have IT skills, because many IT departments are actively seeking to diversify their workforces. In addition, although a salary gender gap (the difference between what men and women earn for performing the same job) exists in IT careers, it's smaller than in most other professions.

You Have a Choice of Working Location

In this case, location refers to the setting in which you work. IT jobs can be office-based, field-based, project-based, or home-based. Because not every situation is perfect for every individual, you can look for a job that suits your tastes and

FIGURE 3

Jobs That Will Likely Remain Onshore

CUSTOMER INTERACTION	ENABLERS	INFRASTRUCTURE JOBS
Web application developers	Business process analysts	Network security
Web interface designers	Application developers (when customer interaction is critical)	Network installation technicians
Database and data warehouse designers/developers	Project managers (for systems with users who are located predominantly in the United States)	Network administrators (engineers)
Customer relationship management (CRM) analysts		Wireless infrastructure managers and technicians
Enterprise resource planning (ERP) implementation specialists		Disaster recovery planners and responders

FIGURE 4

Where Do You Want to Work?

TYPE OF JOB	LOCATION AND HOURS	SPECIAL CONSIDERATIONS
Office-Based	Report for work to the same location each day and interact with the same people on a regular basis; requires regular hours of attendance (such as 9 a.m. to 5 p.m.)	May require working beyond "normal" working hours; may also require workers to be on call 24/7
Field-Based	Travel from place to place as needed and perform short-term jobs at each location	Involves a great deal of travel and the ability to work independently
Project-Based	Work at client sites on specific projects for extended periods of time (weeks or months)	Can be especially attractive to individuals who like workplace situations that vary on a regular basis
Home-Based (telecommuting)	Work from home	Involves very little day-to-day supervision and requires an individual who is self-disciplined

(Rawpixel/Shutterstock, Muellek Josef/Shutterstock, Maksym Dykha/Shutterstock, Samuel Borges Photography/Shutterstock)

requirements. Figure 4 summarizes the major job types and their locations.

You Constantly Meet New Challenges

In IT, the playing field is always changing. New software and hardware are constantly being developed. You'll need to work hard to keep your skills up to date. You'll spend a lot of time in training and self-study trying to learn new systems and techniques. Many individuals thrive in this type of environment because it keeps their jobs from becoming dull or routine.

You Work in Teams

When students are asked to describe their ideal jobs, many describe jobs that involve working in teams. Despite what some people think, IT professionals are not locked in lightless cubicles, basking in the glow of their monitors and working alone on projects. Most IT jobs require constant interaction with other workers, usually in team settings. People skills are

highly prized by IT departments. If you have good leadership and team-building skills, you'll have the opportunity to exercise them in an IT job.

You Don't Need to Be a Mathematical Genius

Certain IT careers such as programming involve a fair bit of math. But even if you're not mathematically inclined, you can explore many other IT careers. IT employers also value such attributes as creativity, marketing, and artistic style, especially in jobs that involve working on the Internet or with social media.

IT Skills Are Transferable

Most computing skills are transferable from industry to industry. A networking job in the clothing manufacturing industry uses the same primary skill set as a networking job for a supermarket chain. Therefore, if something disastrous happens to the industry you're in, you should be able to switch to another industry without having to learn an entirely new skill set. Combining business courses with IT courses will also make you more marketable when changing jobs. For example, as an accounting major, if you minor in IT, employers may be more willing to hire you because working in accounting today means constantly interfacing with management information systems and manipulating data.

Challenges of IT Careers

Objective 9B.2 *Explain the various challenges of IT careers.*

Although there are many positive aspects of IT careers, there can be some challenges. The discussions that follow aren't meant to discourage you from pursuing an IT career but merely to make you aware of exactly what challenges you might face in an IT department.

Stress

Most IT jobs are hectic (see Figure 5). Whereas the average American works 42 hours a week, a survey by *InformationWeek* revealed that the average IT staff person works 45 hours a week and is on call for another 24 hours. On-call time (hours an employee must be available to work in the event of a problem) has been increasing because most IT systems require 24/7 availability.

Women Are in the Minority

A majority of IT jobs are filled by men, so some women view IT departments as *Dilbert*-like microcosms of antisocial geeks and don't feel like they would fit in. Unfortunately, it is true that in most IT departments, women are underrepresented. As companies begin to push to address this imbalance, new opportunities are emerging for women with technical skill sets.

Lifelong Learning Is Required

Although the constantly changing nature of IT can alleviate boredom, keeping up with the changes can also cause some stress. You'll need to take training courses, do self-study, and perhaps take additional college courses, such as getting a graduate degree, to keep up with the vast shifts in technology.

Choosing Your Realm of IT

Objective 9B.3 *List and describe the various IT careers for which you can train.*

Figure 6 shows an organizational chart for a modern IT department at a large corporation that should help you understand the variety of careers available and how they interrelate. The chief information officer (CIO) has overall responsibility for the development, implementation, and maintenance of information systems and its infrastructure. Usually, the CIO reports to the chief operating officer (COO).

The responsibilities below the CIO are generally grouped into two units:

1. Development and integration (responsible for the development of systems and websites)
2. Technical services (responsible for the day-to-day operations of the company's information infrastructure and network, including all hardware and software deployed)

In large organizations, responsibilities are distinct and jobs are defined more narrowly. In medium-sized organizations, there can be overlap between position responsibilities. At a small company, you might be the network administrator, database administrator, computer support technician, and social media manager all at the same time. Let's look at the typical jobs found in each department.

FIGURE 5 Stress comes from multiple directions in IT jobs. *(Khakimullin Aleksandr/Shutterstock, Monkey Business Images/Shutterstock, Rawpixel/ Shutterstock, VectorLifestylepic/Shutterstock, Ollyy/Shutterstock)*

```
                          ┌─────────────────────────┐
                          │ Chief Information Officer │
                          └─────────────────────────┘
```

Chief Information Officer

Director of Development & Integration

Director of Technical Services

Manager of Web Development

Manager of Systems Development

Manager of Information Systems

Manager of Support Services

Webmaster(s)

Manager of Programming

Manager of Systems Analysis

Manager of Project Management

Network Administrator(s)

Helpdesk Manager

Web Programmer(s)

Senior Programmer(s)

Senior Systems Analyst(s)

Project Manager(s)

Database Administrator(s)

Helpdesk Analyst(s)

Graphic Designer(s)

Junior Programmer(s)

Junior Systems Analyst(s)

Web Server Administrator(s)

Computer Support Technician(s)

Interface Designer(s)

Technical Writer(s)

Telecommunications Technician(s)

Web Content Creator(s)

Database Developer(s)

Customer Interaction Technician(s)

Social Media Director

FIGURE 6 This chart represents a typical structure for an IT department at a large corporation.

Working in Development and Integration

Two distinct paths exist in this division:

1. Web development
2. Systems development

Because everything involves the web today, there's often a great deal of overlap between these paths.

Web Development. When most people think of web development careers, they usually equate them with being a webmaster. Webmasters used to be individuals who were solely responsible for all aspects of a company's website. However, today's webmasters usually are supervisors with responsibility for certain aspects of web development. At smaller companies, they may also be responsible for tasks that other individuals in a web development group usually do, such as the following:

- **Web content creators** generate the words and images that appear on the web. Journalists, other writers, editors, and marketing personnel prepare an enormous amount of web content, whereas **video producers**, **graphic designers**, and **animators** create web-based multimedia. Web content creators have a thorough understanding of their own fields as well as HTML, PHP, and JavaScript.
- **Interface designers** work with graphic designers and animators to create a look and feel for the site and make it easy to navigate.
- **Web programmers** build web pages to deploy the materials that the content creators develop. They wield software tools such as Adobe Dreamweaver and InDesign to develop the web pages. They also create links to databases using products such as Oracle and SQL Server to keep information flowing between users and web pages. They must possess a solid understanding of client- and server-side web languages (HTML, XML, Java, JavaScript, ASP, PHP, Silverlight, and Perl) and of development environments such as the Microsoft .NET Framework.
- **Customer interaction technicians** provide feedback to a website's customers. Major job responsibilities include answering e-mail, sending requested information, funneling questions to appropriate personnel (technical support, sales, and so on), and providing suggestions to web programmers for site improvements. Extensive customer service training is essential to work effectively in this area.
- **Social media directors** are responsible for directing the strategy of the company on all social media sites where the company maintains a presence. Often, while supervising customer interaction technicians, social media directors make sure that customers have a quality experience while interacting with company employees and customers on

sites such as Facebook, Twitter, and Yelp. Responding to comments left on such sites, developing promotional strategies, and designing functionality of the company's social media sites are common job responsibilities.

As you can see in Figure 7, many different people can work on the same website. Web programming jobs often require a four-year college degree in computer science, whereas graphic designers often are hired with two-year art degrees.

Systems Development. Ask most people what systems developers do and they'll answer "programming." However, programming is only one aspect of systems development. Because large projects involve many people, there are many job opportunities in systems development, most of which require four-year college degrees in computer science or management information systems:

- **Systems analysts** gather information from end users about problems and existing information systems. They document systems and propose solutions to problems. Having good people skills is essential to success as a systems analyst. In addition, systems analysts work with programmers during the development phase to design appropriate programs to solve the problem at hand. Therefore, many organizations insist on hiring systems analysts who have solid business backgrounds and programming experience (at least at a basic level).
- **Programmers** attend meetings to document user needs, and they work closely with systems analysts during the design phase of program development. Programmers need excellent written communication skills because they often generate detailed systems documentation for end-user training purposes. Because programming languages are mathematically based, it is essential for programmers to have strong math skills and an ability to think logically.

FIGURE 7 It takes a team to create and maintain a website. *(ChooseMyPlate.gov, United States Department of Agriculture)*

- Programmers build the software that solves problems.

- Project managers supervise, organize, and coach team members.

- Systems analysts document systems and propose solutions.

- Database developers ensure data is accessible when it's needed.

FIGURE 8 There are many important team members in systems development. *(Dmitry Nikolaev/Fotolia, Rob/ Fotolia, Cheekywemonkey/Fotolia, Trueffelpix/Shutterstock)*

- **Project managers** manage the overall systems development process: assigning staff, budgeting, reporting to management, coaching team members, and ensuring deadlines are met. Project managers need excellent time management skills because they're often pulled in several directions at once. They usually have prior experience as programmers or systems analysts. Many project managers obtain master's degrees to supplement their undergraduate degrees.

In addition to these key players, the following people are also involved in the systems development process:

- **Technical writers** generate systems documentation for end users and for programmers who may make modifications to the system in the future.
- **Network administrators** help the programmers and analysts design compatible systems, because many systems are required to run in certain environments (UNIX or Windows, for instance) and must work in conjunction with other programs.
- **Database developers** design and build databases to support the software systems being developed.

Large development projects may have all of these team members on the project. Smaller projects may require an overlap of positions, such as a programmer also acting as a systems analyst. As shown in Figure 8, team members work together to build a system.

Working in Technical Services

Technical services jobs are vital to keeping IT systems running. The people in these jobs install and maintain the infrastructure behind the IT systems and work with end users to make sure they can interact with the systems effectively. There are two major categories of technical services careers:

1. Information systems
2. Support services

Note that these also are the *least likely* IT jobs to be outsourced because hands-on work with equipment and users is required on a regular basis.

Information Systems. The information systems department keeps the networks and telecommunications up and running at all times. Within the department, you'll find a variety of positions.

- **Network administrators** (sometimes called *network engineers*) are involved in every stage of network planning and deployment (see Figure 9). They decide what equipment to buy and what media to use, they determine the network's topology, and they help install the network (by supervising contractors or doing it themselves). Network administrators plan disaster-recovery strategies (such as what to do if a fire destroys the server room). When equipment and cables break, network administrators must fix the problem. They also obtain and install updates to network software and evaluate new equipment to determine whether the network should be upgraded. In addition, they monitor the network's performance and often develop policies regarding network usage, security measures, and hardware and software standards.

FIGURE 9 At smaller companies, network administrators may be fixing a user's computer in the morning, installing and configuring a new network operating system in the afternoon, and troubleshooting a server problem (shown here) in the evening. *(Mikhail Starodubov/Shutterstock)*

The video gaming industry in the United States has surpassed the earning power of the Hollywood movie industry. In 2014, the U.S. video game industry brought in sales of $13.1 billion worth of video game software, hardware and accessories, whereas Hollywood took in just over $10.4 billion. Although some aspects of game development, such as scenery design and certain aspects of programming, are being sent offshore, the majority of game development requires a creative team whose members need to work in close proximity. Therefore, it's anticipated that most game development jobs will stay in the United States.

Consoles such as the Xbox One and the PlayStation 4 generate demand for large-scale games. The popularity of mobile devices such as smartphones and tablets is driving demand for lower-end, casual game applications. Casual games are games that can be played relatively quickly or occasionally, such as MMO (massively multiplayer online) strategy games (see Figure 10). Demand for family-friendly games without violence, sex, and profanity is on the rise. With all this demand, there are many opportunities for careers in game development.

Game development jobs usually are split along two paths: designers and programmers.

- **Game designers** tend to be artistic and are responsible for creating 2-D and 3-D art, game interfaces, video sequences, special effects, game levels, and scenarios. Game designers must master software packages such as Autodesk 3ds Max, Autodesk Maya, NewTek LightWave 3D, Adobe Photoshop, and Adobe Flash.
- **Game programmers** are responsible for coding the scenarios developed by the designers. Using languages and toolsets such as Objective-C, Unity, Apple Xcode, C, C++, Assembly, and Java, programmers build the game and ensure that it plays accurately.

Aside from programmers and designers, play testers and quality-assurance professionals play the games with the intent of breaking them or discovering bugs within the game interfaces or worlds. **Play testing** is an essential part of the game development process because it assists designers in determining which aspects of the game are most intriguing to players and which parts of the game need to be repaired or enhanced.

No matter what job you may pursue in the realm of gaming, you'll need to have a two- or four-year college degree. If you're interested in gaming, look for a school with a solid animation or 3-D art program or a computer game–programming curriculum. Programming requires a strong background in math and physics to enable you to realistically program environments that mimic the real world. Proficiency with math (especially geometry) also helps with design careers.

For more information on gaming careers, check out the International Game Developers Association site (**igda.org**) and the Game Career Guide (**gamecareerguide.com**).

FIGURE 10 Plants vs. Zombies, which has you grow plants to fend off encroaching zombie hordes, is an example of a popular casual game available for many different platforms. *(Stock Experiment/Alamy)*

- **Database administrators (DBAs)** install and configure database servers and ensure that the servers provide an adequate level of access to all users.
- **Web server administrators** install, configure, and maintain web servers and ensure that the company maintains Internet connectivity at all times.

- **Telecommunications technicians** oversee the communications infrastructure, including training employees to use telecommunications equipment. They are often on call 24 hours a day.

Support Services. As a member of the support services team, you interface with users (external customers or employees) and troubleshoot their computer problems. Support service positions include the following:

- **Helpdesk analysts** staff the phones, respond to Internet live chats, or respond to e-mails and solve problems for customers or employees, either remotely or in person. Often, helpdesk personnel are called on to train users on the latest software and hardware.
- **Computer support technicians** go to a user's location and fix software and hardware problems. They also often have to chase down and repair faults in the network infrastructure.

As important as these people are, they may receive a great deal of abuse by angry users whose computers are not working. When working in support services, you need to be patient and not be overly sensitive to insults!

Technical services jobs often require a two-year college degree or training at a trade school or technical institute. At smaller companies, job duties tend to overlap between the helpdesk and technician jobs. These jobs are in demand and require staffing in local markets, so they are staying onshore. You can't repair a computer's power supply if you are located in another country!

Preparing for a Job in It

Objective 9B.4 *Explain the various ways you can prepare for a career in IT.*

A job in IT requires a robust skill set and formal training and preparation. Most employers today have an entry-level requirement of a college degree, a technical institute diploma, appropriate professional certifications, experience in the field, or a combination of these. How can you prepare for a job in IT?

1. **Get educated.** Two- and four-year colleges and universities normally offer three degrees to prepare students for IT careers: computer science, management information systems, and information technology (although titles vary). Alternatives to colleges and universities are privately licensed technical (or trade) schools. Generally, these programs focus on building skill sets rapidly and qualifying for a job in a specific field. The main advantage of technical schools is that their programs usually take less time to complete than college degrees. However, to have a realistic chance of employment in IT fields other than networking or web development, you should attend a degree-granting college or university.

2. **Investigate professional certifications.** Certifications attempt to provide a consistent method of measuring skill levels in specific areas of IT. Hundreds of IT certifications are available, most of which you get by passing a written exam. Software and hardware vendors (such as Microsoft and Cisco) and professional organizations (such as the Computing Technology Industry Association) often establish certification standards. Visit **microsoft.com**, **cisco .com**, **comptia.org**, and **sun.com** for more information on certifications.

3. **Get experience.** In addition to education, employers want you to have experience, even for entry-level jobs. While you're still completing your education, consider getting an internship or part-time job in your field of study.

Many schools will help you find internships and allow you to earn credit toward your degree through internships.

4. **Do research.** Find out as much as you can about the company and the industry it's in before going on an interview. Start with the company's website, and then expand your search to business and trade publications such as *BusinessWeek* and *Inc.* magazines.

Getting Started in an IT Career

Objective 9B.5 *Explain the various ways you can find a career in IT.*

Training for a career is not useful unless you can find a job at the end of your training. Here are some tips on getting a job:

1. **Use the career resources at your school.** Many employers recruit at schools, and most schools maintain a placement office to help students find jobs. Employees in the placement office can help you with résumé preparation and interviewing skills and can provide you with leads for internships and jobs.

2. **Develop relationships with your instructors.** Many college instructors still work in or previously worked in the IT industry. They can often provide you with valuable advice and industry contacts.

3. **Start networking.** Many jobs are never advertised but instead are filled by word of mouth. Seek out contacts in your field and discuss job prospects with them. Find out what skills you need, and ask them to recommend others in the industry with whom you can speak. Professional organizations such as the Association for Computing Machinery (ACM) offer one way to network. These organizations often have chapters on college campuses and offer reduced membership rates for students. Figure 11 lists major professional organizations you should consider investigating.

If you're a woman and are thinking about pursuing an IT career, many resources and groups cater to female

BITS&BYTES

Certifications: How Important Are They?

Employees with certifications generally earn more than employees who aren't certified. However, most employers don't view a certification as a substitute for a college degree or a trade school program. You should think of certifications as an extra edge beyond your formal education that will make you more attractive to employers. To ensure you're pursuing the right certifications, ask employers which certifications they respect, or explore online job sites to see which certifications are listed as desirable or required.

FIGURE 11

Professional Organizations

ORGANIZATION NAME	PURPOSE	WEBSITE
Association for Computing Machinery (ACM)	Oldest scientific computing society; maintains a strong focus on programming and systems development	acm.org
Association for Information Systems (AIS)	Organization of professionals who work in academia and specialize in information systems	aisnet.org
Association of Information Technology Professionals (AITP)	Heavy focus on IT education and development of seminars and learning materials	aitp.org
Institute of Electrical and Electronics Engineers (IEEE)	Provides leadership and sets engineering standards for all types of network computing devices and protocols	ieee.org
Information Systems Security Association (ISSA)	Not-for-profit, international organization of information security professionals and practitioners	issa.org

FIGURE 12

Resources for Women in IT

ORGANIZATION NAME	PURPOSE	WEBSITE
Anita Borg Institute for Women and Technology	Organization whose aim is to "increase the impact of women on all aspects of technology"	anitaborg.org
Association for Women in Computing (AWC)	A not-for-profit organization dedicated to promoting the advancement of women in computing professions	awc-hq.org
The Center for Women in Technology (CWIT)	An organization dedicated to providing global leadership in achieving women's full participation in all aspects of IT	cwit.umbc.edu
Diversity/Careers in Engineering & Information Technology	An online magazine whose articles cover career issues of technical professionals who are members of minority groups, women, or people with disabilities	diversitycareers.com
Women in Technology International (WITI)	A global trade association for tech-savvy, professional women	witi.com

IT professionals and students (see Figure 12). The oldest and best-known organization is the Association for Women in Computing, founded in 1978.

4. **Check corporate websites for jobs.** Many corporate websites list current job opportunities. For example, Google provides searchable job listings by geographic location. Check the sites of companies in which you are interested and then do a search on the sites for job openings or, if provided, click their employment links.

5. **Visit online employment sites.** Most of these sites allow you to store your résumé online, and many sites allow employers to browse résumés to find qualified employees. Begin looking at job postings on these sites early in your education because these job postings detail the skill sets employers require. Focusing on coursework that will provide you with desirable skill sets will make you more marketable. Figure 13 lists employment sites as well as sites that offer other career resources.

The outlook for IT jobs should continue to be positive in the future. We wish you luck with your education and job search.

FIGURE 13

Resources for IT Employment

SITE NAME	URL
CareerBuilder	careerbuilder.com
ComputerJobs.com	computerjobs.com
ComputerWork.com	computerwork.com
Dice	dice.com
Gamasutra	gamasutra.com
JustTechJobs	justtechjobs.com
LinkedIn	linkedin.com
Monster	monster.com
TechCareers	techcareers.com

check your understanding // review & practice

For a quick review of what you've learned, answer the following questions.

multiple choice

1. The individuals responsible for generating images for websites are referred to as
   a. network administrators.
   b. graphic designers.
   c. web programmers.
   d. interface designers.

2. What type of job involves working at client locations and the ability to work with little direct supervision?
   a. field-based
   b. project-based
   c. office-based
   d. home-based

3. Which position is *not* typically a part of the information systems department?
   a. helpdesk analyst
   b. telecommunications technician
   c. network administrator
   d. web server administrator

4. Outsourcing is thought to be an attractive option for many companies because of
   a. the emphasis on employee training.
   b. the cost savings that can be realized.
   c. increased data security.
   d. decreased travel and entertainment costs.

5. Which of the following IT positions is responsible for directing a company's strategy on sites such as Facebook, Twitter, and Yelp?
   a. project manager
   b. customer interaction technician
   c. social media director
   d. social web analyst

6. Which of the following statements about IT careers is *false*?
   a. IT employers typically prefer experience over certification.
   b. Women who have IT skills have ample opportunities for securing IT employment.
   c. Many IT jobs are staying in the United States.
   d. Most IT jobs require little interaction with other people.

7. Which task is *not* typically performed by a network administrator?
   a. developing network usage policies
   b. installing networks
   c. planning for disaster recovery
   d. web programming

8. Interface designers are the people responsible for
   a. orchestrating the company strategy in online venues.
   b. providing feedback to website customers.
   c. creating the look and feel of a website.
   d. deploying the materials prepared by content creators.

9. If you are artistic and have mastered software packages such as Adobe Photoshop, Autodesk 3ds Max, and Autodesk Maya, you might consider a career as which of the following?
   a. game programmer
   b. game designer
   c. game tester
   d. web designer

10. Which position is not a part of the systems development department?
    a. systems analyst
    b. project manager
    c. programmer
    d. database administrator

 Go to **MyITLab** to take an autograded version of the *Check Your Understanding* review and to find all media resources for the chapter.

10 Behind the Scenes: Software Programming

Understanding Programming

Learning Outcome 10.1 **You will be able to describe the life cycle of a software project and identify the stages in the program development life cycle.**

Life Cycle of an Information System   410

Objective 10.1 *Describe the importance of programming to both software developers and users.*

🔊 **Sound Byte:** Programming for End Users

Objective 10.2 *Summarize the stages of the system development life cycle (SDLC).*

Life Cycle of a Program   413

Objective 10.3 *Define programming and list the steps in the program development life cycle (PDLC).*

Objective 10.4 *Describe how programmers construct a problem statement from a description of a task.*

👤 **Active Helpdesk:** Understanding Software Programming

Objective 10.5 *Explain how programmers use flow control and design methodologies when developing algorithms.*

Objective 10.6 *Discuss the categories of programming languages and the roles of the compiler and the integrated development environment (IDE) in coding.*

Objective 10.7 *Identify the role of debugging in program development.*

Objective 10.8 *Explain the importance of testing and documentation in program development.*

Programming Languages

Learning Outcome 10.2 **You will understand the factors programmers consider when selecting an appropriate programming language for a specific problem and will be familiar with some modern programming languages.**

Many Programming Languages   432

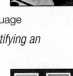

Objective 10.9 *Discuss the driving factors behind the popularity of various programming languages.*

🔊 **Sound Byte:** Programming with the Processing Language

Objective 10.10 *Summarize the considerations in identifying an appropriate programming language for a specific setting.*

Exploring Programming Languages   435

Objective 10.11 *Compare and contrast modern programming languages.*

Objective 10.12 *State key principles in the development of future programming languages.*

🔊 **Sound Byte:** Using the Arduino Microcontroller

Make This: MAKE: A Notepad on **page 431**

All media accompanying this chapter can be found in MyITLab.

For an overview of the chapter, watch the **Preview Video**. ▶

(Dizain/Shutterstock, Dondesigns/DigitalVision Vectors/Getty Images, Corbis, Geozacho/123RF)

HOW COOL IS THIS?

Most major U.S. cities have made a commitment to make the **data** they use to govern **open and transparent**—to human eyes and to your programs. Websites format information so it is useful for communicating with humans, but **web services** format the information in a way that makes it easy to **communicate the data to your program**. Chicago, Philadelphia, and other major cities have opened up thousands of government records through **Open Data initiatives**. Using this data, users can do such things as create a program to **visualize neighborhood crime statistics**, track their city's snowplows, or compare the current school budget expenditures.

It is not just cities becoming more transparent. **Data.gov** opens the U.S. government's data to you. Open government is here. Use it to write a web app or mobile tool that really has an **impact in your community**. Consider your own community. What kind of web app is needed? Get started working on it—the data is waiting for you. *(Nirot Sriprasit/123RF)*

Understanding Programming

Learning Outcome 10.1 You will be able to describe the life cycle of a software project and identify the stages in the program development life cycle.

Every day, we face a wide array of tasks. Some tasks are complex and require creative thought and a human touch. But tasks that are repetitive, work with electronic information, and follow a series of clear steps are candidates for automation with computers—automation achieved through programming. In this part of the chapter, we'll look at some of the basics of programming.

life cycle of an
INFORMATION SYSTEM

A career in programming offers many advantages—jobs are plentiful, salaries are strong, and telecommuting is often easy to arrange. But even if you're not planning a career in programming, knowing the basics of programming is important to help you use computers productively.

Importance of Programming

Objective 10.1 *Describe the importance of programming to both software developers and users.*

Why would I ever need to create a program? Computer programs already exist for many tasks. For example, if you want to write a paper, Microsoft Word has already been designed to translate the tasks you want to accomplish into computer instructions. However, for users who can't find an existing software product to accomplish a task, programming is mandatory. For example, imagine that a farmer needs to have a drone fly a specific pattern inspecting his crops, automatically taking photos and sensor readings at specific points to create a weekly report. No software product exists that will accumulate and relay information in just this manner. Therefore, a team of programmers will have to create smart farming software (see Figure 10.1).

If I'm not going to be a programmer, why should I learn about programming? If you plan to use only existing, off-the-shelf software, having a basic knowledge of programming enables you to add features that support your personal needs. For example, most modern software

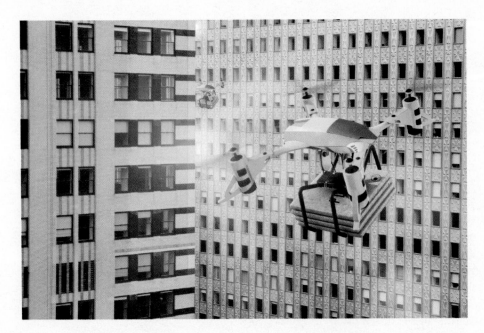

FIGURE 10.1 Unmanned drones are playing a larger role in transportation, videography, agriculture, and other fields. They require programming to integrate sensor and geographic information. *(Miguel Navarro/Getty Images)*

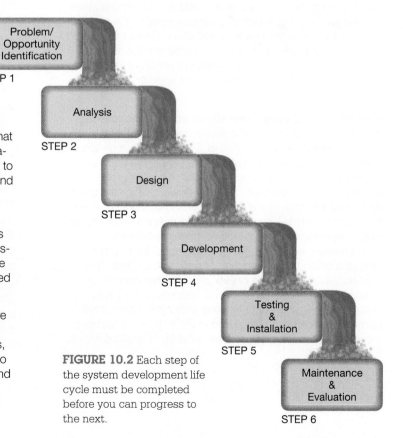

SOUND BYTE
Programming for End Users

In this Sound Byte, you'll be guided through the creation of a macro in the Microsoft Office suite. You'll learn how Office enables you to program with macros in order to customize and extend the capabilities it offers.

applications let you automate features by using custom-built miniprograms called *macros*. By creating macros, you can execute a complicated sequence of steps with a single command. Understanding how to program macros enables you to add custom commands to, for example, Word or Excel and lets you automate frequently performed tasks, providing a huge boost to your productivity. And if you plan to create custom applications from scratch, having a detailed knowledge of programming will be critical to the successful completion of your projects.

System Development Life Cycle

Objective 10.2 *Summarize the stages of the system development life cycle (SDLC).*

What is an information system? Generally speaking, a *system* is a collection of pieces working together to achieve a common goal. Your body, for example, is a system of muscles, organs, and other groups of cells working together. An **information system** includes data, people, procedures, hardware, and software that help in planning and decision making. Information systems help run an office and coordinate online-purchasing systems and are behind database-driven applications used by Amazon and Netflix. But how are these complicated systems developed? Through a particular step-by-step process.

Why do I need a process to develop a system? Because teams of people are required to develop information systems, there needs to be an organized process to ensure that development proceeds in an orderly fashion. Software applications also need to be available for multiple operating systems, to work over networked environments, and to be free of errors and well supported. Therefore, a process often referred to as the **system development life cycle (SDLC)** is used.

What steps constitute the SDLC? There are six steps in a common SDLC model, as shown in Figure 10.2. This system is sometimes referred to as a "waterfall" system because each step is dependent on the previous step being completed before it can be started.

1. *Problem and Opportunity Identification:* Corporations are always attempting to break into new markets, develop new customers, or launch new products. At other times, systems development is driven by a company's desire to serve its existing customers more efficiently or to respond to problems with a current system. Whether solving an existing problem or exploiting an opportunity, large corporations typically form a development committee to

evaluate systems development proposals. The committee decides which projects to take forward based on available resources such as personnel and funding.

2. *Analysis:* In this phase, analysts explore the problem or need in depth and develop a program specification. The **program specification** is a clear statement of the goals and objectives of the project. The first feasibility assessment is also performed at this stage. The feasibility assessment determines whether the project should go forward. If the project is determined to be feasible, the analysis team defines the user requirements and recommends a plan of action.

3. *Design:* The design phase generates a detailed plan for programmers to follow. The proposed system is documented using flowcharts and data-flow diagrams. Flowcharts are visual diagrams of a process, including the decisions that need to be made along the way. **Data-flow diagrams** trace all data in an information system from the point at which data enters the system to its final resting place (storage or output). The data-flow diagram in Figure 10.3 shows the flow of concert ticket information.

   The design phase details the software, inputs and outputs, backups and controls, and processing requirements of the problem. Once the system plan is designed, a company evaluates existing software packages to determine whether it needs to develop a new piece of software or if it can buy something already on the market and adapt it to fit its needs.

4. *Development:* It is during this phase that actual programming takes place. This phase is also the first part of the

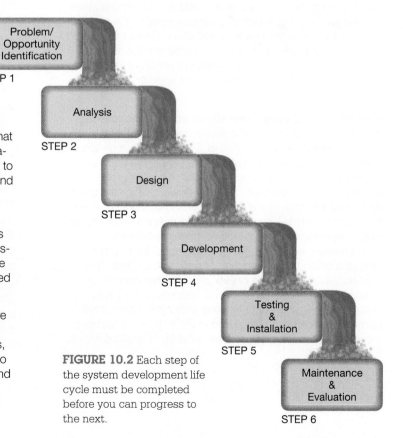

FIGURE 10.2 Each step of the system development life cycle must be completed before you can progress to the next.

FIGURE 10.3 Data-flow diagrams illustrate the way data travels in an information system.

program development life cycle, described in detail later in the chapter. The documentation work is begun in this phase by technical writers.

5. *Testing and Installation:* Testing the program ensures it works properly. It is then installed for official use.

6. *Maintenance and Evaluation:* In this phase, program performance is monitored to determine whether the program is still meeting the needs of end users. Errors that weren't detected in the testing phase but that are discovered during use are corrected. Additional enhancements that users request are evaluated so that appropriate program modifications can be made.

Can the SDLC vary from these steps? The waterfall model is an idealized view of software development. Most developers follow some variation of it. For example, a design team may "spiral," where a group that's supporting the work of another group will work concurrently with the other group on development. This contrasts with workflows in which the groups work independently, one after the other. Often, there is a "back-flow" up the waterfall, because even well-designed projects can require redesign and specification changes midstream.

Some people criticize the waterfall model for taking too long to provide actual working software to the client. This may contribute to **scope creep**, an ever-changing set of requests from clients for additional features as they wait longer and longer to see a working prototype. Other developmental models are being used in the industry to address these issues (see the Bits & Bytes sidebar, "The More Minds, the Better"). ■

BITS&BYTES

The More Minds, the Better

In each phase of the SDLC, a style of interaction called *joint application development (JAD)* can be useful in creating successful, flexible results. JAD is popular because it helps designers adapt quickly to changes in program specifications. In JAD, the customer is intimately involved in the project right from the beginning. Slow communication and lengthy feedback time make the traditional development process extremely time-consuming. In JAD "workshops," there are no communication delays. Such workshops usually include end users, developers, subject experts, observers (such as senior managers), and a facilitator. The facilitator enforces the rules of the meeting to make sure all voices are heard and that agreement is reached as quickly as possible. Also called *accelerated design or facilitated team techniques*, JAD's goal is to improve design quality by fostering clear communication. For more details, search the Internet using keywords like *JAD, JAD methodology,* and *JAD tutorial.*

life cycle of a
PROGRAM

Programming takes place during the fourth step in the SDLC and requires its own step-by-step process.

The Program Development Life Cycle

Objective 10.3 *Define programming and list the steps in the program development life cycle (PDLC).*

How do programmers tackle a programming project? Programming is the process of translating a task into a series of commands that a computer will use to perform that task. It involves identifying which parts of a task a computer can perform, describing those tasks in a highly specific and complete manner, and, finally, translating this description into the language spoken by the computer's central processing unit (CPU).

Programming often begins with nothing more than a problem or a request, such as, "Can you tell me how many transfer students have applied to our college?" A proposal will then be developed for a system to solve this problem, if one does not already exist. Once a project has been deemed feasible and a plan is in place, the work of programming begins.

What are the steps in the programming process? Each programming project follows several stages, from conception to final deployment. This process is sometimes referred to as the **program development life cycle (PDLC)**:

1. *Describing the Problem*: First, programmers must develop a complete description of the problem. The problem statement identifies the task to be automated and describes how the software program will behave.

2. *Making a Plan*: The problem statement is next translated into a set of specific, sequential steps that describe exactly what the computer program must do to complete the work. The steps are known as an **algorithm**. At this stage, the algorithm is written in natural, ordinary language (such as English).

3. *Coding*: The algorithm is then translated into programming code, a language that is friendlier to humans than the *1*s and *0*s

that the CPU speaks but is still highly structured. By coding the algorithm, programmers must think in terms of the operations that a CPU can perform.

4. *Debugging*: The code then goes through a process of debugging in which the programmers repair any errors found in the code.

5. *Testing and Documentation*: The software is tested by both the programming team and the people who will use the program. The results of the entire project are documented for the users and the development team. Finally, users are trained so that they can use the program efficiently.

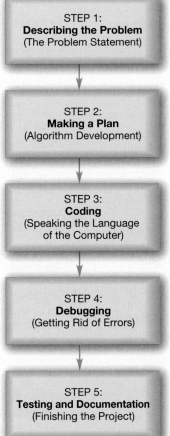

STEP 1:
Describing the Problem
(The Problem Statement)

STEP 2:
Making a Plan
(Algorithm Development)

STEP 3:
Coding
(Speaking the Language of the Computer)

STEP 4:
Debugging
(Getting Rid of Errors)

STEP 5:
Testing and Documentation
(Finishing the Project)

FIGURE 10.4 The stages that each programming project follows, from conception to final deployment, are collectively referred to as the program development life cycle (PDLC).

Figure 10.4 illustrates the steps of a program development life cycle.

Now that you have an overview of the process involved in developing a program, let's look at each step in more detail.

The Problem Statement

Objective 10.4 *Describe how programmers construct a complete problem statement from a description of a task.*

Why is a problem statement necessary? The **problem statement** is the starting point of programming work. It's a clear description of what tasks the computer program must accomplish and how the program will execute those tasks and respond to unusual situations. Programmers develop problem statements so they can better understand the goals of their programming efforts.

What kind of problems can computer programs solve? As noted above, tasks that are repetitive, work with electronic information, and follow a series of clear steps are good candidates for computerization. This might sound as if computers only help us with the dullest and most simplistic tasks. However, many sophisticated problems can be broken down into a series of easily computerized tasks. For example, pharmaceutical companies design drugs using complex computer programs that model molecules. Using simulation software to perform "dry" chemistry, chemists can quickly "create" new drugs and determine whether they will have the desired pharmacological effects.

Scientists then select the most promising choices and begin to test those compounds in the "wet" laboratory.

What kinds of problems can computers not solve? Computers can't yet act with intuition or be spontaneously creative. They can attack highly challenging problems, such as making weather predictions or playing chess, but only in a way that takes advantage of what computers do best—making fast, reliable computations. Computers don't "think" like humans do. They can only follow instructions and algorithms.

How do programmers create problem statements? The goal in creating a useful problem statement is to have programmers interact with users to describe three things relevant to creating a useful program:

1. **Data** is the raw input that users have at the start of the job.
2. **Information** is the result, or output, that the users require at the end of the job.
3. **Method**, described precisely, is the process of how the program converts the inputs into the correct outputs.

For example, say you want to compute how much money you'll earn working at a parking garage. Your salary is $7.50 per hour for an eight-hour shift, but if you work more than eight hours a day, you get time and a half, which is $11.25 per hour, for the overtime work. To determine how much money you will make in any given day, you could multiply this in your mind, write it on a piece of paper, or use a calculator; alternatively, you could create a simple computer program to do the work for you. In this example, what are the three elements of the problem statement?

1. *Data (Input)*: the data you have at the beginning of the problem, which is the number of hours you worked and the pay rate.
2. *Information (Output)*: the information you need to have at the end of the problem, which is your total pay for the day.
3. *Method (Process)*: the set of steps that take you from your input to your required output. In this case, the computer program would check if you worked more than eight hours. This is important because it would determine whether you would be paid overtime. If you didn't work overtime, the output would be $7.50 multiplied by the total number of hours you worked ($60.00 for eight hours). If you did work overtime, the program would calculate your pay as eight hours at $7.50 per hour for the regular part of your shift, plus an additional $11.25 multiplied by the number of overtime hours you worked.

How do programmers handle bad inputs? In the problem statement, programmers also must describe what the program should do if the input data is invalid or just gibberish. This part of the problem statement is referred to as **error handling**.

The problem statement also includes a **testing plan** that lists specific input numbers that the programmers would typically expect the user to enter. The plan then lists the precise output values that a perfect program would return for those input values. Later, in the testing process, programmers use the input and output data values from the testing plan to determine whether the program they created works the way it should. We discuss the testing process later in this chapter.

Does the testing plan cover every possible use of the program? The testing plan can't list every input the program could ever encounter. Instead, programmers work with users to identify the categories of inputs that will be encountered, find a typical example of each input category, and specify what kind of output must be generated. In the parking garage pay example, the error-handling process would describe what the program would do if you happened to enter "–8" (or any other nonsense character) for the number of hours you worked. The error handling would specify whether the program would return a negative value, prompt you to reenter the input, or shut down.

We could expect three categories of inputs in the parking garage example. The user might enter:

1. A negative number for hours worked that day
2. A positive number equal to or less than eight
3. A positive number greater than eight

The testing plan would describe how the error would be managed or how the output would be generated for each input category.

Is there a standard format for a problem statement? Most companies have their own format for documenting a problem statement. However, all problem statements include the same basic components: the data that is expected to be provided (inputs), the information that is expected to be produced (outputs), the rules for transforming the input into output (processing), an explanation of how the program will respond if users enter data that doesn't make sense (error handling), and a testing plan. Figure 10.5 shows a sample problem statement for our parking garage example.

Algorithm Development

Objective 10.5 *Explain how programmers use flow control and design methodologies when developing algorithms.*

How does the process start? Once programmers understand exactly what the program must do and have created the final problem statement, they can begin developing a detailed algorithm—a set of specific, sequential steps that describe in natural language exactly what the computer program must do to complete its task. Let's look at some ways in which programmers design and test algorithms.

ACTIVE HELPDESK
Understanding Software Programming

In this Active Helpdesk, you'll play the role of a help-desk staffer, fielding questions about the life cycle of a program, the role a problem statement plays in programming, how programmers create algorithms and move from algorithm to code to the *1s* and *0s* a CPU can understand, and the steps involved in completing the program.

FIGURE 10.5

Complete Problem Statement for the Parking Garage Example

PROBLEM STATEMENT

Program Goal	Compute the total pay for a fixed number of hours worked at a parking garage.
Input	Number of hours worked (a positive number)
Output	Total pay earned (a positive number)
Process	Total pay earned is computed as $7.50 per hour for the first eight hours worked each day. Any hours worked consecutively beyond the first eight are calculated at $11.25 per hour.
Error Handling	The input (number of hours worked) must be a positive real number. If it is a negative number or another unacceptable character, the program will force the user to reenter the information.

Testing Plan	INPUT	OUTPUT	NOTES
	8	8*7.50	Testing positive input
	3	3*7.50	Testing positive input
	12	8*7.50 + 4*11.25	Testing overtime input
	−6	Error message/ask user to reenter value	Handling error

Do algorithms appear only in programming? Although the term *algorithm* may sound like it would fall only under the domain of computing, you design and execute algorithms in your daily life. For example, say you're planning your morning. You know you need to

1. Get gas for your car,
2. Pick up a mocha latte at the café, and
3. Stop by the bookstore and buy a textbook before your 9 a.m. accounting lecture.

You quickly think over the costs and decide it will take $150 to buy all three. In what order will you accomplish all these tasks? How do you decide? Should you try to minimize the distance you'll travel or the time you'll spend driving? What happens if you forget your credit card?

Figure 10.6 presents an algorithm you could develop to make decisions about how to accomplish these tasks. This algorithm lays out a specific plan that encapsulates all of the choices you need to make in the course of completing a particular task and shows the specific sequence in which these tasks will occur. At any point in the morning, you could gather your current data (your inputs)—"I have $20 and my Visa card, but the ATM machine

is down"—and the algorithm would tell you unambiguously what your next step should be.

What are the limitations of algorithms? An algorithm is a series of steps that's completely known: At each point, we know *exactly* what step to take next. However, not all problems can be described as a fixed sequence of predetermined steps; some involve random and unpredictable events. For example, although the program that computes your parking garage take-home pay each day works flawlessly, programs that predict stock prices are often wrong because many random events (inputs), such as a flood in India or a shipping delay in Texas, can change the outcomes (outputs).

How do programmers represent an algorithm? Programmers have several visual tools at their disposal to help them document the decision points and flow of their algorithms:

- **Flowcharts** provide a visual representation of the patterns the algorithm comprises. Figure 10.6 presents an example of a flowchart used to depict the flow of an algorithm. Specific shape symbols

FIGURE 10.6 An algorithm you might use to plan your morning would include all of the decisions you might need to make and would show the specific sequence in which these steps would occur.

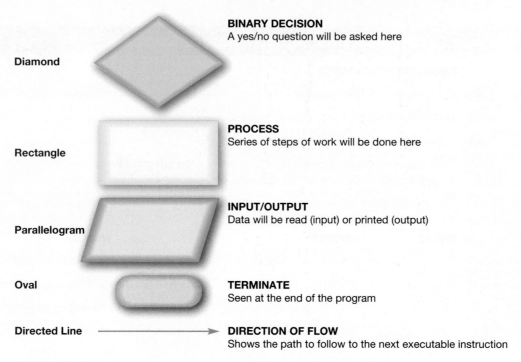

Diamond		**BINARY DECISION** A yes/no question will be asked here
Rectangle		**PROCESS** Series of steps of work will be done here
Parallelogram		**INPUT/OUTPUT** Data will be read (input) or printed (output)
Oval		**TERMINATE** Seen at the end of the program
Directed Line		**DIRECTION OF FLOW** Shows the path to follow to the next executable instruction

FIGURE 10.7 Standard Symbols Used in Flowcharts

indicate program behaviors and decision types. Diamonds indicate that a yes/no decision will be performed, and rectangles indicate an instruction to follow. Figure 10.7 lists additional flowcharting symbols and explains what they indicate. Many software packages make it easy for programmers to create and modify flowcharts. Microsoft Visio is one popular flowcharting program.

- **Pseudocode** is a text-based approach to documenting an algorithm. In pseudocode, words describe the actions that the algorithm will take. Pseudocode is organized like an outline, with differing levels of indentation to indicate the flow of actions within the program. There is no standard vocabulary for pseudocode. Programmers use a combination of common words in their natural language and the special words that are commands in the programming language they're using.

Flow Control

How do programmers handle complex algorithms?
When programmers develop an algorithm, they convert the problem statement into a list of steps the program will take.

Problems that are complex involve choices, so they can't follow a sequential list of steps. Algorithms therefore include **decision points**, places where the program must choose from a list of actions based on the value of a certain input.

Figure 10.8 shows the steps of the algorithm in our parking garage example. If the number of hours

FIGURE 10.8 Decision points force the program to travel down one branch of the algorithm or another.

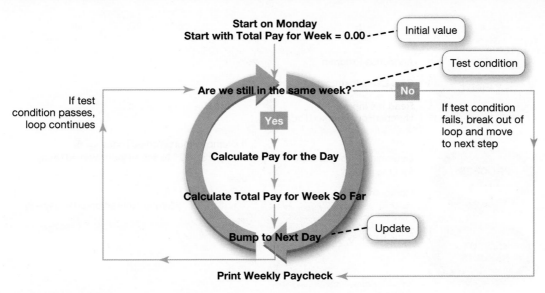

Start on Monday
Start with Total Pay for Week = 0.00 - - - → Initial value

Test condition

Are we still in the same week? - - - - - -

No

If test condition passes, loop continues

If test condition fails, break out of loop and move to next step

Yes

Calculate Pay for the Day

Calculate Total Pay for Week So Far

Bump to Next Day - - - → Update

Print Weekly Paycheck ◄

FIGURE 10.9 We stay in the loop until the test condition is no longer true. We then break free from the loop and move on to the next step in the algorithm, which is outside of the loop.

you worked in a given day is eight or less, the program performs one simple calculation: It multiplies the number of hours worked by $7.50. If you worked more than eight hours in a day, the program takes a different path and performs a different calculation.

What kinds of decision points are there? There are two main types of decisions that change the flow of an algorithm:

1. *Binary decisions:* One decision point that appears often in algorithms is like a "fork in the road." Such decision points are called **binary decisions** because they can be answered in one of only two ways: *yes* (true) or *no* (false). For example, the answer to the question, "Did you work at most eight hours today?" (Is number of hours worked ≤ 8 hours?), shown in Figure 10.8, is a binary decision because the answer can be only *yes* or *no*. If the answer is *yes*, the program follows one sequence of steps; if the answer is *no*, it follows a different path.

2. *Loops:* A second decision point that often appears in algorithms is a repeating loop. In a **loop**, a question is asked, and if the answer is *yes*, a set of actions is performed. Once the set of actions has finished, the question is asked again, creating a loop. As long as the answer to the question is *yes*, the algorithm continues to loop around and repeat the same set of actions. When the answer to the question is *no*, the algorithm breaks free of the looping and moves on to the first step that follows the loop.

In our parking garage example, the algorithm would require a loop if you wanted to compute the total pay you earned in a full week of work rather than in just a single day. For each day of the week, you would want to perform the same set of steps. Figure 10.9 shows how the idea of looping would be useful in this part of our parking garage program. On Monday, the program would set the Total Pay value to $0.00. It would then perform the following set of steps:

1. Read the number of hours worked that day.
2. Determine whether you qualified for overtime pay.

3. Compute the pay earned that day.
4. Add that day's pay to the total pay for the week.

On Tuesday, the algorithm would loop back, repeating the same sequence of steps it performed on Monday, adding the amount you earned on Tuesday to the Total Pay amount. The algorithm would continue to perform this loop for each day (seven times) until it hits Monday again. At that point, the decision "Are we still in the same week?" would become false. The program would stop, calculate the total pay for the entire week of work, and print the weekly paycheck. As you can see, there are three important features to look for in a loop:

1. A beginning point, or **initial value**. In our example, the total pay for the week starts at an initial value of $0.00.
2. A set of actions that will be performed. In our example, the algorithm computes the daily pay each time it passes through the loop.
3. A **test condition**, or a check to see whether the loop is completed. In our example, the algorithm should run the loop seven times, no more and no fewer.

Every higher-level programming language supports both making binary yes/no decisions and handling repeating loops. **Control structures** is the general term used for keywords in a programming language that allow the programmer to direct the flow of the program based on a decision.

How do programmers create algorithms for specific tasks? It's difficult for human beings to force their problem-solving skills into the highly structured, detailed algorithms that computing machines require. Therefore, several different methodologies have been developed to support programmers, including *top-down design* and *object-oriented analysis*.

Design Methodology: Top-Down Design

What is top-down design? Top-down design is a systematic approach in which a problem is broken into a series

FIGURE 10.10 (a) A top-down design is applied to the highest level of task in our parking garage example, (b) the tasks are further refined into subtasks, and (c) subtasks are refined into a sequence of instructions—an algorithm.

of high-level tasks. In top-down design, programmers apply the same strategy repeatedly, breaking each task into successively more detailed subtasks. They continue until they have a sequence of steps that are close to the types of commands allowed by the programming language they'll use for coding. Previous coding experience helps programmers know the appropriate level of detail to specify in an algorithm generated by top-down design.

How is top-down design used in programming? Let's consider our parking garage example again. Initially, top-down design would identify three high-level tasks: Get Input, Process Data, and Output Results (see Figure 10.10a).

Applying top-down design to the first operation, Get Input, we'd produce the more detailed sequence of steps shown in the first step of Figure 10.10b: Announce Program, Give Users Instructions, and Read the Input NumberHours-sWorkedToday. When we try to refine each of these steps, we find that they are just print-and-read statements and that most every programming language will support them. Therefore, the operation Get Input has been converted to an algorithm.

Next, we move to the second high-level task, Process Data, and break it into subtasks. In this case, we need to determine whether overtime hours were worked and to compute the pay accordingly. We continue to apply top-down design on all tasks until we can no longer break tasks into subtasks, as shown in Figure 10.10c.

Design Methodology: Object Oriented Analysis

What is object-oriented analysis? With **object-oriented analysis**, programmers first identify all the categories of inputs that are part of the problem the program is meant to solve. These categories are called **classes**. With the object-oriented approach, the majority of design time

is spent identifying the classes required to solve the problem, modeling them, and thinking about what relationships they need to be able to have with each other. Constructing the algorithm becomes a process of enabling the objects to interact. For example, the classes in our parking garage example might include a TimeCard class and an Employee class.

BITS&BYTES

Hackathons

College hackathons—coding events that take place in a single day or a single weekend—are more popular than ever. The PennApps Hackathon at the University of Pennsylvania sees over 2,000 programmers attend from over 100 universities. Terrific prizes are awarded along with sought-after meetings with engineers at Google, Dropbox, and more. Hackathons to create software with a purpose are appearing more and more as well. The National Day of Civic Hacking (**hackforchange.org**) and Code for America (**codeforamerica.org**) are both examples of hackers working to help develop solutions to local and global needs.

Hackathons can help you build your programming skills incredibly quickly. If you don't have a team, most hackathons link you up with other programmers on the spot. Visit DevPost (**devpost.com**) to find the coding events nearest you—and join in the competition!

Classes are defined by

- Information (data) within the class and
- Actions (methods) associated with the class

For example, as shown in Figure 10.11, *data* for an Employee would include a Name, Address, and Social Security Number, whereas the *methods* for the Employee would be GoToWork(), LeaveWork(), and CollectPay(). The data of the class describes the class, so classes are often characterized as nouns, whereas methods are often characterized as verbs—the ways that the class acts and communicates with other classes.

Programmers may need to create several different examples of a class. Each of these examples is an **object**. In Figure 10.11, John Doe, Jane Doe, and Bill McGillicutty are each Employee objects (specific examples of the Employee class). Each object from a given class is described by the same pieces of data and has the same methods; for example, John, Jane, and Bill are all Employees and can use the GoToWork(), LeaveWork(), and CollectPay() methods. However, because they all have different pay grades (PayGrade 5, PayGrade 10, and PayGrade 4, respectively) and different Social Security numbers, they are all unique objects.

FIGURE 10.11 The Employee class includes the complete set of information (data) and actions (methods or behaviors) that describe an Employee.

Why would a developer select the object-oriented approach over top-down design? An important aspect of object-oriented design is that it leads to **reusability**. Object-oriented analysis forces programmers to think in general terms about their problem, which tends to lead to more general and reusable solutions. Because object-oriented design generates a family of classes for each project, programmers can easily reuse existing classes from other projects, enabling them to produce new code quickly.

How does a programmer take advantage of reusability? Programmers must study the relationships between objects. Hierarchies of objects can be built quickly in object-oriented languages using the mechanism of inheritance. **Inheritance** means that a new class can automatically pick up all the data and methods of an existing class and then can extend and customize those to fit its own specific needs.

The original class is called the **base class**, and the new, modified class is called the **derived class**, as illustrated in Figure 10.12. You can compare this with making cookies. For example, you have a basic recipe for sugar cookies (base class: Sugar Cookies). However, in your family, some people like chocolate-flavored sugar cookies (derived class: Chocolate Sugar Cookies), and others like mini-chip sugar cookies (derived class: Mini-Chip Sugar Cookies). All the cookies share the attributes of the basic sugar cookie. However, instead of creating two entirely new recipes—one for chocolate cookies and one for mini-chip cookies—the two varieties inherit the basic sugar cookie (base class) recipe; the recipe is then customized to make the chocolate and mini-chip sugar cookies (derived classes).

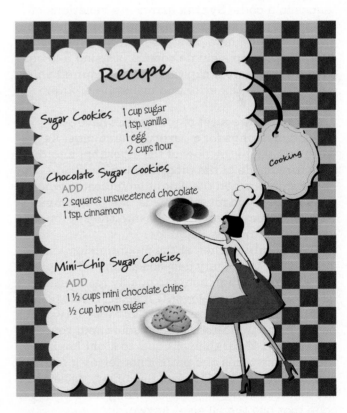

FIGURE 10.12 In object-oriented programming, a single base class—for example, Sugar Cookies—helps you quickly create many additional derived classes, such as Chocolate and Mini-Chip Sugar Cookies. *(Nataliya Dolotko/Fotolia)*

The Building Blocks of Programming Languages: Syntax, Keywords, Data Types, and Operators

Programming languages are evolving constantly. New languages emerge every year, and existing languages change dramatically. Therefore, it would be extremely difficult and time consuming for programmers to learn every programming language. However, all languages have several common elements: rules of syntax, a set of keywords, a group of supported data types, and a set of allowed operators. By learning these four concepts, a programmer will be better equipped to approach any new language.

The transition from a well-designed algorithm to working code requires a clear understanding of the rules (syntax) of the programming language being used. **Syntax** is an agreed-on set of rules defining how a language must be structured. The English language has a syntax that defines which symbols are words (for example, *gorilla* is a word but *allirog* is not) and what order words and symbols (such as semicolons and commas) must follow.

Likewise, all programming languages have a formal syntax that programmers must follow when creating code **statements**, which are sentences in a code. **Syntax errors** are violations of the strict, precise set of rules that define the programming language. In a programming language, even misplacing a single comma or using a lowercase letter where a capital letter is required will generate a syntax error and make the program unusable.

Keywords are a set of words that have predefined meanings for a particular language. Keywords translate the flow of the algorithm into the structured code of the programming language. For example, when the algorithm indicates where a binary decision must be made, the programmer translates that binary decision into the appropriate keyword(s) from the language.

To illustrate further, in the programming language C++, the binary decision asking whether you worked enough hours to qualify for overtime pay would use the keywords **if else**. At this point in the code, the program can follow one of two paths: If you indicated through your input that you worked fewer than or equal to eight hours, the program takes one path; if not (else), it follows another. Figure 10.13 shows this binary decision in the algorithm and the corresponding lines of C++ code that use the "if else" keywords.

Loops are likewise translated from algorithm to code by using the appropriate keyword from

FIGURE 10.13 The binary decision in the algorithm has been converted into C++ code.

the language. For example, in the programming language Visual Basic, programmers use the keywords **For** and **Next** to implement a loop. After the keyword For, an input or output item is given a starting value. Then the statements, or "sentences," in the body of the loop are executed. When the command Next is run, the program returns to the For statement and increments the value of the input or output item by 1. It then tests that the value is still inside the range given. If it is, the body of the loop is executed again. This continues until the value of the input or output item is outside the range listed. The loop is then ended, and the statement that follows the loop is run.

In the parking garage example, the following lines of Visual Basic code loop to sum up the total pay for the entire week:

```
For Day = 1 to 7
    TotalPay = TotalPay + Pay
Next Day
```

In this statement, the starting value of the input item Day is 1, and the program loops through until Day equals 7. Then, when Day equals 8, we move out of the loop, to the line of code that comes after the loop.

Often, a quick overview of a language's keywords can reveal the unique focus of that language. For example, the language C++ includes the keywords *public*, *private*, and *protected*, which indicate that the language includes a mechanism for controlling security.

Each time programmers want to store data in their program, they must ask the OS for storage space at a RAM location. **Data types** describe the kind of data being stored at the memory location. Each programming language has its own data types (although there is some degree of overlap). For example, C++ includes data types that represent integers, real numbers, characters, and Boolean (true–false) values. These C++ data types show up in code statements as *int* for integer, *float* for real numbers, *char* for characters, and *bool* for Boolean values.

Because it takes more room to store a real number such as 18,743.23 than it does to store the integer 1, programmers use data types in their code to indicate to the OS how much memory it needs to allocate. Programmers must be familiar with all the data types available in the language so that they can assign the most appropriate one for each input and output value, without wasting memory space.

Operators are the coding symbols that represent the fundamental actions of the language. Each programming language has its own set of operators. Many languages include common algebraic operators such as +, −, *, and / to represent the mathematical operations of addition, subtraction, multiplication, and division, respectively. Some languages, however, introduce new symbols as operators. The language APL (short for A Programmer's Language) was designed to solve multidimensional mathematical problems. APL includes less familiar operators such as rho, sigma, and iota, each representing a complex mathematical operation. Because it contains many specialized operators, APL requires programmers to use a special keyboard (see Figure 10.14).

Programming languages sometimes include other unique operators. The C++ operator >>, for example, is used to tell the computer to read data from the keyboard or from a file. The C++ operator && is used to tell the computer to check whether two statements are both true. "Is your age greater than 20 AND less than 30?" is a question that requires the use of the && operator.

In the following C++ code, several operators are being used. The > operator checks whether the number of hours worked is greater than 0. The && operator checks that the number of hours worked is simultaneously positive AND less than or equal to 8. If that happens, then the = operator sets the output Pay to equal the number of hours multiplied by $7.50:

```
if (Hours > 0 && Hours <= 8)
    Pay = Hours * 7.50;
```

Knowing operators such as these, as well as the other common elements described earlier, helps programmers learn new programming languages.

FIGURE 10.14 APL requires programmers to use an APL keyboard that includes the many specialized operators in the language.

Coding

Objective 10.6 *Discuss the categories of programming languages and the roles of the compiler and the integrated development environment (IDE) in coding.*

How is a person's idea translated into CPU instructions? Once programmers create an algorithm, they select the best programming language for the problem and then translate the algorithm into that language. Translating an algorithm into a programming language is the act of **coding**. Programming languages are somewhat readable by humans but then are translated into patterns of *1*s and *0*s to be understood by the CPU.

Although programming languages free programmers from having to think in binary language—the *1*s and *0*s that computers understand—they still force programmers to translate the ideas of the algorithm into a highly precise format. Programming languages are quite limited, allowing programmers to use only a few specific keywords, while demanding a consistent structure.

How exactly do programmers move from algorithm to code? Once programmers have an algorithm, in the form of either a flowchart or a series of pseudocode statements, they identify the key pieces of information the algorithm uses to make decisions:

- What steps are required for the calculation of new information?
- What is the exact sequence of the steps?
- Are there points where decisions have to be made?
- What kinds of decisions are made?
- Are there places where the same steps are repeated several times?

Once programmers identify the required information and the flow of how it will be changed by each step of the algorithm, they can begin converting the algorithm into computer code in a specific programming language.

Categories of Programming Languages

What exactly is a programming language? A **programming language** is a kind of "code" for the set of instructions the CPU knows how to perform. Computer programming languages use special words and strict rules so that programmers can control the CPU without having to know all its hardware details.

What kinds of programming languages are there? Programming languages are classified into several major groupings, sometimes referred to as *generations*. With each generation of language development, programmers have been relieved of more of the burden of keeping track of what the hardware requires. The earliest languages—assembly language and machine languages—required the programmer to know a great deal about how the computer was constructed internally and how it stored data. Programming is becoming easier as languages continue to become more closely matched to how humans think about problems.

How have modern programming languages evolved? There are five major categories of languages:

1. A **first-generation language (1GL)** is the actual **machine language** of a CPU, the sequence of bits (*1*s and *0*s) that the CPU understands.

2. A **second-generation language (2GL)** is also known as an **assembly language**. Assembly languages allow programmers to write their programs using a set of short, English-like commands that speak directly to the CPU and that give the programmer direct control of hardware resources.

3. A **third-generation language (3GL)** uses symbols and commands to help programmers tell the computer what to do. This makes 3GL languages easier for humans to read and remember. Most programming languages today, including BASIC, FORTRAN, COBOL, C/C++, and Java, are considered third generation.

4. **Fourth-generation languages (4GLs)** include database query languages and report generators. **Structured Query Language (SQL)** is a database programming language that is an example of a 4GL. The following SQL command would check a huge table of data on the employees and build a new table showing all those employees who worked overtime:

   ```
   SELECT EmployeeName, TotalHours FROM
   EMPLOYEES WHERE "TotalHours" Total
   More Than 8
   ```

5. **Fifth-generation languages (5GLs)** are considered the most "natural" of languages. In a 5GL, a problem is presented as a series of facts or constraints instead of as a specific algorithm. The system of facts can then be queried (asked) questions. PROLOG (PROgrammingLOGic) is an example of a 5GL. A PROLOG program could be a list of family relationships and rules such as "Mike is Sally's brother. A brother and a sister have the same mother and father." Once a user has amassed a huge collection of facts and rules, he or she can ask for a list of all Mike's cousins, for example. PROLOG would find the answers by repeatedly applying the principles of logic instead of following a systematic algorithm that the programmer provided.

Figure 10.15 shows small code samples of examples of each generation of language.

Portability, Variable Declarations, and Commenting

Do programmers have to use a higher-level programming language to solve a problem with a computer? No, experienced programmers sometimes write a program directly in the CPU's assembly language. However, the main advantage of higher-level programming languages—C or Java, for example—is that they allow programmers to think in terms of the problem they're solving rather than having to worry about the internal design and specific instructions available for a given CPU. In addition,

FIGURE 10.15

Sample Code for Different Language Generations

GENERATION	EXAMPLE	SAMPLE CODE
1GL	Machine	**Bits** describe the commands to the CPU. 1110 0101 1001 1111 0000 1011 1110 0110
2GL	Assembly	**Words** describe the commands to the CPU. ADD Register 3, Register 4, Register 5
3GL	FORTRAN, BASIC, C, Java	**Symbols** describe the commands to the CPU. TotalPay = Pay + OvertimePay
4GL	SQL	**More powerful commands** allow complex work to be done in a single sentence. SELECT isbn, title, price, price*0.06 AS sales_tax FROM books WHERE price>100.00 ORDER BY title;
5GL	PROLOG	Programmers can build applications **without specifying an algorithm**. Find all the people who are Mike's cousins as: ?-cousin (Mike, family)

higher-level programming languages have the capability to easily produce a program that will run on differently configured CPUs. For example, if programmers wrote directly in the assembly language for an Intel i7 CPU, they would have to rewrite the program completely if they wanted it to run on a Sun workstation with the SPARC T5CPU. Thus, higher-level programming languages offer **portability**—the capability to move a completed solution easily from one type of computer to another.

What happens first when you write a program?

All of the inputs a program receives and all of the outputs the program produces need to be stored in the computer's RAM while the program is running. Each input and each output item that the program manipulates, also known as a **variable**, needs to be announced early in the program so that memory space can be set aside. A **variable declaration** tells the operating system that the program needs to allocate storage space in RAM. The following line of code is a variable declaration in the language Java:

```
int Day;
```

The one simple line makes a lot of things happen behind the scenes:

- The variable's name is *Day*. The "int" that precedes the Day variable indicates that this variable will always be an integer (a whole number such as 15 or –4).
- The statement "int Day;" asks for enough RAM storage space to hold an integer. After the RAM space is found, it is reserved. As long as the program is running, these RAM cells will be saved for the Day variable, and no other program can use that memory until the program ends. From that point on, when the program encounters the symbol Day, it will access the memory it reserved as Day and find the integer stored there.

Can programmers leave notes to themselves inside a program?

Programmers often insert a **comment** into program code to explain the purpose of a section of code, to indicate the date they wrote the program, or to include other important information about the code so that fellow programmers can more easily understand and update it.

Comments are written into the code in plain English. The *compiler*, a program that translates codes into binary 1s and 0s, just ignores comments. Comments are intended to be read only by human programmers. Languages provide a special symbol or keyword to indicate the beginning of a comment. In C++, the symbol // at the beginning of a line indicates that the rest of the line is a comment.

What would completed code for a program look like?

Figure 10.16 presents a completed C++ program for our parking garage example. We'll discuss later how you would actually enter this program on your system. This program, which is written in a top-down style, does not make use of objects. Each statement in the program is executed sequentially (that is, in order from the first statement to the last) unless the program encounters a keyword that changes the flow. In the figure:

1. The program begins by declaring the variables needed to store the program's inputs and outputs in RAM.
2. Next, the *for* keyword begins a looping pattern. All of the steps between the very beginning bracket ({) and the end one (}) will be repeated seven times to gather the total pay for each day of the week.
3. The next section collects the input data from the user.
4. The program then checks that the user entered a reasonable value. In this case, a positive number for hours worked must be entered.
5. Next, the program processes the data. If the user worked eight or fewer hours, he or she is paid at the rate of $7.50, whereas hours exceeding eight are paid at $11.25.
6. The final statement updates the value of the TotalPay variable. The end bracket indicates that the program has reached the end of a loop. The program will repeat the loop

to collect and process the information for the next day. When the seventh day of data has been processed, the Day variable will be bumped up to the next value, 8. This causes the program to fail the test (Day <= 7?). At that point, the program exits the loop, prints the results, and quits.

Are there ways in which programmers can make their code more useful for the future? One aspect of converting an algorithm into good code is the programmer's ability to design general code that can easily be adapted to new settings. Sections of code that will be used repeatedly, with only slight modification, can be packaged into reusable "containers" or components. Depending on the language,

these reusable components are referred to as *functions, methods, procedures, subroutines, modules,* or *packages*.

In our program, we could create a function that implements the overtime pay rule. As it stands in Figure 10.16, the code works only in situations in which the hourly pay is exactly $7.50 and the bonus pay is exactly $11.25. However, if we rewrote this part of the processing rules as a function, we could have code that would work for any base pay rate and any overtime rate. If the base pay rate or overtime rate changed, the function would use whichever values it was given as input to compute the output pay variable. Such a function, as shown in Figure 10.17, may be reused in many settings without changing any of the code.

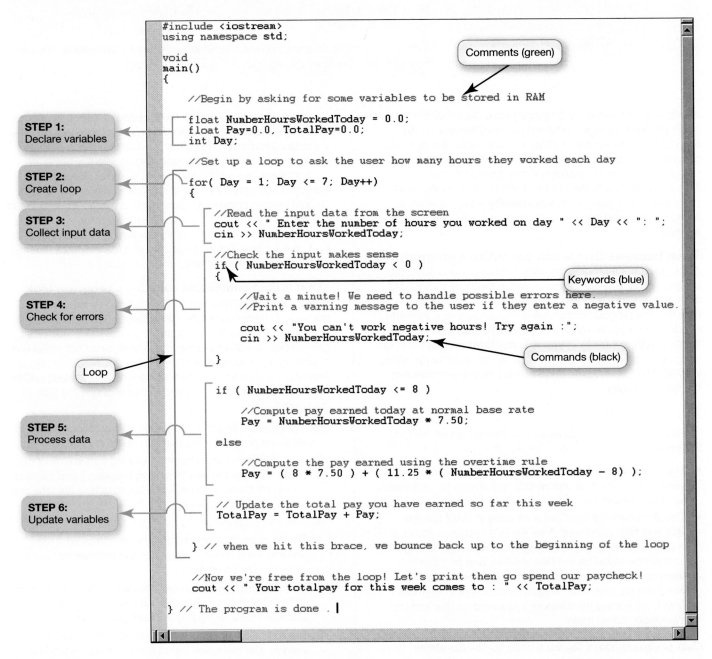

FIGURE 10.16 A Complete C++ Program That Solves the Parking Garage Pay Problem

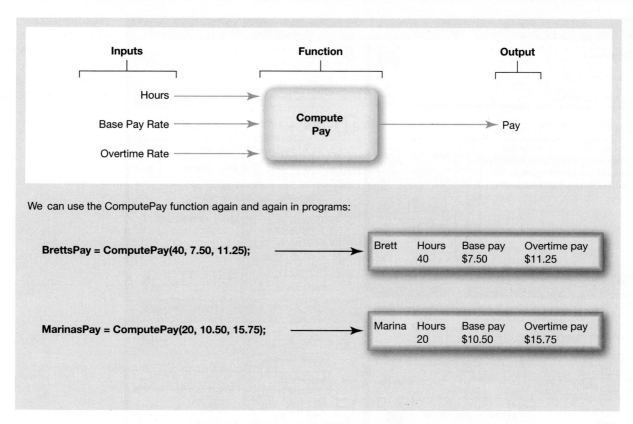

FIGURE 10.17 A function is a reusable component that can be used in different settings.

The Compiler

How does a programmer move from code in a programming language to the 1s and 0s the CPU can understand? Compilation is the process by which code is converted into machine language—the language the CPU can understand. A **compiler** is a program that understands both the syntax of the programming language and the exact structure of the CPU and its machine language. It can "read" the **source code**, which comprises the instructions programmers have written in the higher-level language and can translate the source code directly into machine language—the binary patterns that will execute commands on the CPU. You can learn more about the details of the binary number system in the Technology in Focus section, "Under the Hood."

Each programming language has its own compiler. It's a program that you purchase and install just like any other software on your system. Separate versions of the compiler are required if you want to compile code that will run on separate processor types. One version of a compiler would create finished programs for a Sun SPARC T5 processor, for example, and another version of the compiler would create programs for an Intel i7 CPU.

At this stage, once the compiler has generated the executable program, the programmers have a program to distribute. An **executable program**, the binary sequence that instructs the CPU to run their code, can't be read by human eyes because they're pure binary codes. They're stored as *.exe or *.com files on Windows systems.

Does every programming language have a compiler? Some programming languages don't have a compiler but use an interpreter instead. An **interpreter** translates the source code into an intermediate form, line by line. Each line is then executed as it's translated. The compilation process takes longer than the interpretation process because in compilation, all the lines of source code are translated into machine language before any lines are executed. However, the finished compiled program runs faster than an interpreted program because the interpreter is constantly translating and executing as it goes.

If producing the fastest executable program is important, programmers will choose a language that uses a compiler instead of an interpreter. For development environments in which many changes are still being made to the code, interpreters have an advantage because programmers don't have to wait for the entire program to be recompiled each time they make a change. With interpreters, programmers can immediately see the results of their program changes as they're making them.

Integrated Development Environments

What tools make the coding process easier? Modern programming is supported by a collection of tools that make the writing and testing of software easier. An **integrated development environment (IDE)** is a developmental tool that helps programmers write and test their programs. One IDE can often be configured to support many different

FIGURE 10.18 The jGRASP IDE is a free tool that helps the programmer visualize the code as it runs to help eliminate logical errors. *(Courtesy of Auburn University)*

languages. Figure 10.18 shows the IDE jGRASP working with Java code.

How does an IDE help programmers when they're typing the code? Code editing is the step in which a programmer physically types the code into the computer. An IDE includes an **editor**, a special tool that helps programmers as they enter the code, highlighting keywords and alerting the programmers to typos. Modern IDE editors also automatically indent the code correctly, align sections of code appropriately, and apply color to code comments to remind programmers that these lines won't be executed as code. In addition, IDEs provide auto-completion of code, suggest solutions to common errors, and more.

How does the IDE help programmers after code editing is finished? Editing is complete when the entire program has been keyed into the editor. At that time, the programmer clicks a button in the IDE, and the compilation process begins. The IDE shows how the compilation is progressing, which line is currently being compiled, how many syntax errors have been identified, and how many warnings

have been generated. A warning is a suggestion from the compiler that the code might not work in the way the programmer intended even though there's no formal syntax error on the line.

A syntax error is a violation of the strict, precise set of rules that define the language. Programmers create syntax errors when they misspell keywords (such as typing BEEGIN instead of BEGIN) or use an operator incorrectly (such as typing x = , y + 2 instead of x = y + 2). Once compilation is finished, the IDE presents all of the syntax errors in one list. The programmer can then click any item in the list to see a detailed explanation of the type of error. When the programmer double-clicks an item in the list, the editor jumps to the line of code that contains the error, enabling the programmer to repair syntax errors quickly.

Debugging

Objective 10.7 *Identify the role of debugging in program development.*

What is debugging? Once the program has compiled without syntax errors, it has met all of the syntax rules of

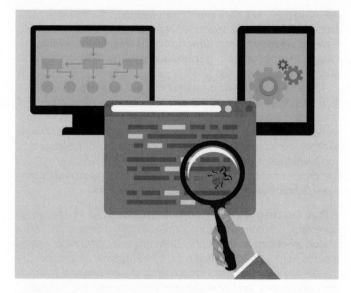

FIGURE 10.19 Debugging—the process of correcting errors in a program—combines logic with an understanding of the problem to be solved. *(Venimo/Fotolia)*

the language. However, this doesn't mean that the program behaves in a logical way or that it appropriately addresses the task the algorithm described. If programmers made errors in the strategy used in the algorithm or in how they translated the algorithm to code, problems will occur. The process of running the program over and over to find and repair errors and to make sure the program behaves in the way it should is termed **debugging** (see Figure 10.19).

How do programmers know the program has solved the problem? At this point in the process, the testing plan that was documented as part of the problem statement becomes critically important to programmers. The testing plan clearly lists input and output values, showing how the users expect the program to behave in each input situation. It's important that the testing plan contain enough specific examples to test every part of the program.

In the parking garage problem, we want to make sure the program calculates the correct pay for a day when you worked eight or fewer hours and for a day when you worked more than eight hours. Each of these input values forces the program to make different decisions in its processing path. To be certain the program works as intended, programmers try every possible path.

For example, once we can successfully compile the example code for the parking garage problem, we can begin to use our testing plan. The testing plan indicates that an input of 3 for NumberHoursWorkedToday must produce an output of Pay = 3 * $7.50 = $22.50. In testing, we run the program and make sure that an input value of 3 yields an output value of $22.50. To check that the processing path involving overtime is correct, we input a value of 12 hours. That input must produce Pay = 8 * $7.50 + (12 − 8) * $11.25 = $105.00.

A complete testing plan includes sample inputs that exercise all the error handling required as well as all the processing paths. Therefore, we would also want to check how the program behaves when NumberHoursWorkedToday is entered as −6.

If the testing plan reveals errors, why does the program compile? The compiler can't think through code or decide whether what the programmer wrote is logical. The compiler can only make sure that the specific rules of the language are followed.

For example, if in the parking garage problem we happened to type the if statement as

```
if (NumberHoursWorkedToday > 88)
//Use the Overtime Pay rule
```

instead of

```
if (NumberHoursWorkedToday > 8)
//Use the Overtime Pay rule
```

the compiler wouldn't see a problem. It doesn't seem strange to the compiler that you only get overtime after working 88 hours a day. These **logical errors** in the problem are caught only when the program executes.

Another kind of error caught when the program executes is a **runtime error**. For example, it's easy for a programmer to accidentally write code that occasionally divides by zero, a big "no-no" mathematically! That kind of forbidden operation generates a runtime error message.

Are there tools that help programmers find logic errors? Most IDEs include a tool called a **debugger** that helps programmers dissect a program as it runs. The debugger pauses the program while it's executing and allows the programmer to examine the values of all the variables. The programmer can then run the program in slow motion, moving it forward just one line at a time. This lets the programmer see the exact sequence of steps being executed and the outcome of each calculation. He or she can then isolate the precise place in which a logical error occurs, correct the error, and recompile the program.

BITS&BYTES

Many Languages on Display

At the 99 Bottles of Beer site **99-bottles-of-beer.net**, you can find a simple program that displays the lyrics to the song "99 Bottles of Beer on the Wall." If you've ever sat through round after round of this song on a long school bus trip, you know how repetitive it is. That means the code to write this song can take advantage of looping statements. This site presents the program in more than 1,500 different languages. Also check out the Rosetta Code wiki (**rosettacode.org/wiki/Rosetta_Code**) to see solutions to many other programming problems in a wide variety of languages.

Testing and Documentation

Objective 10.8 *Explain the importance of testing and documentation in program development.*

What is the first round of testing for a program? Once debugging has detected all the runtime errors in the code, it's time for users to test the program. This process is called *internal testing*. In internal testing, a group within the software company uses the program in every way it can imagine—including how the program was intended to be used and in ways only new users might think up. The internal testing group makes sure the program behaves as described in the original testing plan. Any differences in how the program responds are reported back to the programming team, which makes the final revisions and updates to the code.

The next round of testing is *external testing*. In this testing round, people like the ones who eventually will purchase and use the software must work with it to determine whether it matches their original vision.

What other testing does the code undergo? Before its final commercial release, software is often provided free or at a reduced cost in a **beta version** to certain test sites or to interested users. By providing users with a beta version of software, programmers can collect information about remaining errors in the code and make a final round of revisions before officially releasing the program. Often, popular software packages like Microsoft Windows and Microsoft Office are available for free beta download for months before the official public release.

What happens if problems are found after beta testing? The manufacturer will make changes before releasing the product to other manufacturers, for installation on new machines, for example. That point in the release cycle is called **release to manufacturers (RTM)**. After the RTM is issued, the product is in **general availability (GA)** and can be purchased by the public.

Users often uncover problems in a program even after its commercial release to the public. These problems are addressed with the publication of software updates or **service packs**. Users can download these software modules to repair errors identified in the program code. To make sure you have the latest service pack for your Windows OS, visit the Windows Service Pack Center (**windows.microsoft.com /en-US/windows/downloads/service-packs**).

After testing, is the project finished? Once testing is complete, but before the product is officially released, the work of **documentation** is still ahead. At this point, technical writers create internal documentation for the program that describes the development and technical details of the software, how the code works, and how the user interacts with the program. In addition, the technical publishing department produces all the necessary user documentation that will be distributed to the program's users. User training begins once the software is distributed. Software trainers take the software to the user community and teach others how to use it efficiently. ■

Before moving on to Part 2:
1. Watch Replay Video 10.1 ↻.
2. Then check your understanding of what you've learned so far.

check your understanding // review & practice

For a quick review to see what you've learned so far, answer the following questions.

multiple choice

1. Compiling a program turns
   a. top-down design into object-oriented design.
   b. a first-generation language into a fourth-generation language.
   c. source code into an executable program.
   d. none of the above

2. A dataflow diagram
   a. shows all of the steps of the algorithm.
   b. shows where data is entered and is stored in an information system.
   c. includes the data, people, and hardware needed to help in decision making.
   d. includes design, development, and testing details.

3. The life cycle of a program begins with describing a problem and making a plan. Then the PDLC requires
   a. coding, debugging, and testing.
   b. process, input, and output.
   c. data, information, and method.
   d. an algorithm.

4. A visual representation of an algorithm is represented by a(an)
   a. executable.
   b. compiler.
   c. debugger.
   d. flowchart.

5. In object-oriented analysis, classes are defined by
   a. objects and data.
   b. data and methods.
   c. operators and objects.
   d. behaviors and keywords.

 Go to **MyITLab** to take an autograded version of the *Check Your Understanding* review and to find all media resources for the chapter.

TECHBYTES WEEKLY
Stay current with TechBytes Weekly Newsletter.

Continue ⟫

TRY THIS ▶ Programming with Corona

You've already been doing mobile app development in the Make This activities using App Inventor. In this Try This, we'll use the product Corona to create an application that could be run on either an Android or an iOS device.

(Courtesy of Corona Labs, Inc.)

NOTE: You need to be confident in installing and uninstalling demo software to your system to proceed. Refer to Chapter 4 if you need more support. Also, be aware that you will be asked to provide an e-mail address to qualify for the free trial version of Corona.

Step 1   From **notepad-plus-plus.org**, click **Download** and install the editor Notepad++. Launch Notepad++ and click **File->New**.

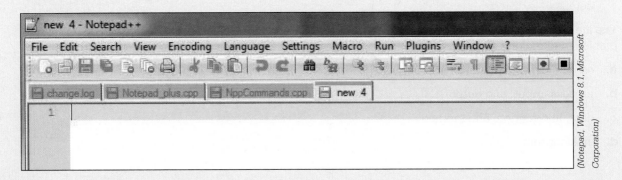

(Notepad, Windows 8.1, Microsoft Corporation)

Step 2   Head to **coronalabs.com/products/corona-sdk**. Select the link for **Download Now** at the bottom of the page, and follow the download instructions.

Step 3   Run the Corona simulator ⬤ (Courtesy of Corona Labs, Inc.). Click the **Continue Trial button.**

Step 4   In Notepad++, type the following:

```
myText = display.newText( "TECH IN ACTION", 20, 40, native.systemFont, 36 )
myText:setTextColor(255,97,3)
```

Step 5   In Notepad++, click **File-> Save As**. In the Save As type dropdown, select **LUA source File (*.lua)** and save this file with the name **main**. The file *main.lua* is now created.

Step 6 Move to the Corona Simulator window and click **File->Open Project**. Then navigate to *main.lua* and open it.

You have just written a complete iPhone application! You can also run it on an iPad or any Android phone or tablet. Click **View->View As** and see how the program output looks on a few different devices.

Step 7 Play with changing the color by altering the values in setTextColor. Try adding the line **myText.rotation = 45**.

Visit **docs.coronalabs.com/api** to see the full set of built-in methods available. Look over the physics library and begin to imagine what you could create!

TECH IN ACTION

(Alan Evans)

Make This   TOOL: AI Canvas, If Block

MAKE: A Notepad

Drawing and writing on a touch device is convenient and creative.

In this exercise, you'll continue your mobile app development by using the Canvas component in App Inventor to build a notepad that lets you switch pen colors and draw shapes.

The Canvas component lets you draw on the screen. Combine that with statements like "if" and "for" and you can make more sophisticated behaviors. *(MIT App Inventor 2, Massachusetts Institute of Technology. Creative Commons Attribution-ShareAlike 3.0 Unported License)*

Use the Canvas component in App Inventor to combine control statements with drawing commands to create your own images.

For the instructions for this exercise, go to MyITLab.

Programming Languages

Earlier in the chapter, you learned about the five main categories (generations) of programming languages. In this section, we discuss the specific programming languages that are members of these different generations.

 many programming

LANGUAGES

In any programming endeavor, programmers want to create a solution that meets several objectives. The software needs to:

- Run quickly
- Be reliable
- Be simple to expand later when the demands on the system change
- Be completed on time
- Be finished for the minimum possible cost

Because it's difficult to balance these conflicting goals, many programming languages have been developed. Although programming languages often share common characteristics, each language has specific traits that allow it to be the best fit for certain types of projects. The ability to understand enough about each language to match it to the appropriate style of problem is an exceptionally powerful skill for programmers.

Need for Diverse Languages

Objective 10.9 *Discuss the driving factors behind the popularity of various programming languages.*

What languages are popular today? One quick way to determine which languages are popular is to examine job postings for programmers. As of this writing, the languages most in demand include C/C++ and Java. In specific industries, certain languages tend to dominate the work. In the banking and insurance industries, for example, the programming language COBOL is still common, although most other industries rarely use it anymore. The TIOBE Index, shown in Figure 10.20, uses a number of different techniques to get a feel for which languages are popular in the software industry at certain times.

Aug 2015	Aug 2014	Change	Programming Language	Ratings	Change
1	2	^	Java	19.274%	+4.29%
2	1	v	C	14.732%	−1.67%
3	4	^	C++	7.735%	+3.04%
4	6	^	C#	4.837%	+1.43%
5	7	^	Python	4.066%	+0.95%
6	3	v	Objective-C	3.195%	−6.36%
7	8	^	PHP	2.729%	−0.14%
8	12	≫	Visual Basic .NET	2.708%	+1.40%
9	10	^	JavaScript	2.162%	−0.01%
10	9	v	Perl	2.118%	−0.10%
11	11		Visual Basic	1.781%	−0.23%
12	24	≫	Assembly language	1.760%	+1.11%
13	13		Ruby	1.416%	+0.17%
14	18	≫	Delphi/Object Pascal	1.407%	+0.49%
15	21	≫	MATLAB	1.232%	+0.50%
16	14	v	F#	1.232%	+0.14%
17	23	≫	Swift	1.179%	+0.51%
18	15	v	Pascal	1.138%	+0.09%
19	20	^	PL/SQL	1.137%	+0.35%
20	30	≫	R	1.010%	+0.49%

FIGURE 10.20 When attacking a problem, you can choose from many different programming languages. This chart of the TIOBE Index shows how popular certain languages are. *(Pearson Education, Inc.)*

How do I know which language to study first? A good introductory programming course will emphasize many skills and techniques that will carry over from one language to another. You should find a course that emphasizes design, algorithm development, debugging techniques, and project management. All of these aspects of programming will help you in any language environment.

Visual languages like App Inventor or Scratch are often used to introduce key programming concepts. Many colleges and universities have opted to have students begin with Java, C++, or Python. Students interested in the arts are often using the language **Processing** as a first experience with coding.

How does anyone learn so many languages? Professional programmers can become proficient at new languages because they've become familiar with the basic components, discussed in this chapter's Dig Deeper feature, that are common to all languages: syntax, keywords, operators, and data types.

Selecting the Right Language

Objective 10.10 *Summarize the considerations in identifying an appropriate programming language for a specific setting.*

How do programmers know which language to select for a specific project? A programming team considers several factors before selecting the language it will use for a specific project:

- *Space available:* Not all languages produce code that takes up the same amount of space. Therefore, the target language should be well matched to the amount of space available for the final program. For example, if the program will be embedded in a chip for use in a cell phone, it's important for the language to create space-efficient programs.

- *Speed required:* Although poorly written code executes inefficiently in any language, some languages can execute more quickly than others. Some projects require a focus on speed rather than size. These projects require a language that produces code that executes in the fastest possible time.

- *Organizational resources available:* Another consideration is the resources available in a manager's group or organization. Selecting a language that's easy to use and that will be easy to maintain if there's a turnover in programmers is an important consideration.

- *Type of target application:* Certain languages are customized to support a specific environment (UNIX or Windows, for instance). Knowing which languages are most commonly used for which environments can be helpful. We'll discuss this more in the next section.

BITS&BYTES

Coding for Zombies

There are an incredible number of free courses available for the latest programming technologies. Rails for Zombies from Code School is one such course. The free interactive coding environment runs right in your browser and teaches you to create a Twitter-like program for Zombies using the Ruby on Rails web application framework. Also, explore course providers like Coursera, Udacity, and Codecademy. They offer courses complete with quizzes, video lectures, and live discussion on topics like Python, Web Programming, and Java.

(Image reprinted courtesy of Code School)

Can I just point and click to create an application? Many languages have a development environment that features a drag and drop-style interface for designing the visual layout of an application. Programmers use a mouse to lay out the screen and position scroll bars and buttons. The code needed to explain this to the computer is then written automatically. **Visual programming languages**, like Scratch and App Inventor, go even further. They use graphical blocks to represent control elements and variables. Programming consists of clicking together these blocks to define program behavior. ∎

In the field of software programming, mistakes can be costly. Consider these examples:

- In 1996, Europe's newest unmanned rocket, the Ariane 5, had to be destroyed seconds after launch, along with its cargo of four scientific satellites. Cost: $500 million. The problem occurred when the guidance computer tried to convert rocket velocity from a 64-bit to a 16-bit value. Programmers had not properly coded for this, and an overflow error resulted. When the guidance system shut down, control passed to the backup unit, which also failed because it was running the same algorithm.
- When one switch in the AT&T network had a minor problem in 1990, system software fired off a message to the other 113 AT&T switching centers. This sparked a cascade of shutdowns, bringing down the entire network for nine hours. An estimated 75 million phone calls were missed, and over 200,000 airline reservations were lost. A single line of code in a large software upgrade was in error and led to the shutdown.
- In 2007, Los Angeles International Airport grounded 17,000 planes. For over eight hours, no one was authorized to enter or leave the United States through LAX. Software on a network card was sending faulty data and brought the entire Customs and Border Protection network to a halt.

Could better software engineering practices have prevented these failures? Many different factors contributed to this set of accidents, including the following:

- Simple programming errors
- Inadequate safety engineering
- Poor human–computer interaction design
- Inadequate or inappropriate testing
- Too little focus on safety by the manufacturing organization
- Inadequate reporting structure at the company level

Who should be held responsible for defective software? Is it the corporate management, who did not institute a defined software process? Is it the production managers, who forced tight schedules that demanded risky software engineering practices? What about the software engineers who wrote the defective code? What about the users of the software? Can they be held responsible for accidents? What if they made changes to the system?

Organizations of engineers and software designers have tried to define ethical standards that will minimize the risk of negative impact from their work. The very first article of the code of ethics of the Institute of Electrical and Electronics Engineers (IEEE) alerts engineers to their responsibility for making decisions that protect the health and safety of others. The Association for Computing Machinery (ACM) and the IEEE have established eight principles for ethical software engineering practices:[1]

1. *Public:* Software engineers shall act consistently with the public interest.
2. *Client and Employer:* Software engineers shall act in a manner that is in the best interests of their client and employer consistent with the public interest.
3. *Product:* Software engineers shall ensure that their products and related modifications meet the highest professional standards possible.
4. *Judgment:* Software engineers shall maintain integrity and independence in their professional judgment.
5. *Management:* Software engineering managers and leaders shall subscribe to and promote an ethical approach to the management of software development and maintenance.
6. *Profession:* Software engineers shall advance the integrity and reputation of the profession consistent with the public interest.
7. *Colleagues:* Software engineers shall be fair to and supportive of their colleagues.
8. *Self:* Software engineers shall participate in lifelong learning regarding the practice of their profession and shall promote an ethical approach to the practice of the profession.

Can you think of other steps the software industry could take to make sure its work contributes positively to our society?

---

[1] "Software Engineering Code of Ethics and Professional Practice," by IEEE-CS/ACM Joint Task Force on Software Engineering Ethics and Professional Practices. Copyright © 2011 by the Institute of Electrical and Electronics Engineers. Reprinted by permission.

exploring programming
LANGUAGES

How are modern programming languages the same and how are they different? What will future programming languages look like? Let's find out.

Tour of Modern Languages

Objective 10.11 *Compare and contrast modern programming languages.*

All programming languages have many features in common. Let's take a tour of many of the popular languages and learn what makes each one special for particular situations.

Visual Basic

Why do programmers choose Visual Basic?
Programmers often like to build a **prototype**, or small model, of their program at the beginning of a large project. Prototyping is a form of **rapid application development (RAD)**, an alternative to the waterfall approach of systems development that was described at the beginning of this chapter. Instead of developing detailed system documents before they produce the system, developers create a prototype first, then generate system documents as they use and remodel the product.

Prototypes for Windows applications are often coded in Microsoft **Visual Basic (VB)**, a powerful programming language used to build a wide range of Windows applications. One strength of VB is its simple, quick interface, which is easy for a programmer to learn and use. It has grown from its roots in the language BASIC (short for Beginner's All-purpose Symbolic Instruction Code) to become a sophisticated and full-featured object-oriented language.

VB is designed for building object-oriented applications for Windows, the web, and mobile devices. The interface of VB makes it easy to drag and drop entire programming components into an application. VB and the .NET Framework are both part of Visual Studio, which provides a complete set of developer tools.

How does the Microsoft .NET Framework help programmers? The Microsoft .NET (pronounced "dot net") Framework is a software development environment designed to let websites "talk" to each other easily. The .NET Framework includes **web services**, programs that a website uses to make information available to other websites. Web services provide a standard way for software to interact. The rules are documented in an **Application Programming Interface (API)**. For example, a web application could use the Google web service to search for information or to check the spelling of a word. The Google web service returns the requested information to your program in a standard format. Figure 10.21 shows just a small list of the many web services available to programmers.

C and C++

What languages do programmers use if the problem requires a lot of "number crunching"?
A Windows application that demands raw processing power to execute difficult, repetitive numerical calculations is most often a candidate for C/C++. For example, applications that simulate human cells and drug interactions have to solve elaborate mathematical equations many thousands of times each second and are, therefore, excellent candidates for programming using C/C++. Several companies sell C/C++ design tools

FIGURE 10.21

Web Services

The New York Times API offers access to articles, book lists, and movie reviews.

Yahoo Finance API provides stock quotes, historic quotes, exchange rates, and company reports.

Wunderground API provides data on tides, forecasts, hurricanes, and weather alerts.

Chicago Open City gives access to plow locations, crime statistics, public school data, and more. Most cities offer a similar API.

(Jin Lee/Bloomberg/Getty Images, Blvdone/Fotolia, James Thew/Fotolia, Jr. Gary Hebding/Alamy) equipped with an environment that makes Windows programming as visual as with VB.

Why was the C language developed? The predecessor of C++, **C**, was originally developed for system programmers. It was defined by Brian Kernighan and Dennis Ritchie of AT&T Bell Laboratories in 1978 as a language that would make accessing the operating system easier. It provides higher-level programming language features (such as *if* statements and *for* loops) but still allows programmers to manipulate the system memory and CPU registers directly. This mix of high- and low-level access makes C highly attractive to "power" programmers. Most modern operating systems (Windows, OS X, and Linux) were written in C.

The C++ language takes C to an object-oriented level. Bjarne Stroustrup, the developer of C++, used all the same symbols and keywords as C, but he extended the language with additional keywords, better security, and more support for the reuse of existing code through object-oriented design.

Are C and C++ natural choices for when I'm looking to learn my first language? Neither C nor C++ was intended as a teaching language. The notation and compactness of these languages make them relatively difficult to master. They're in demand in industry, however, because C/C++ can produce fast-running code that uses a small amount of memory. Programmers often choose to learn C/C++ because their basic components (operators, data types, and keywords) are common to many other languages.

Java and C#

What language do programmers use for applications that need to collect information from networked computers? **Java** would be a good choice

for these types of applications. James Gosling of Sun Microsystems introduced Java in the early 1990s. It quickly became popular because its object-oriented model enables Java programmers to benefit from its large set of existing classes. For example, a Java programmer could begin to use the existing "network connection" class with little attention to the details of how that code itself was implemented. Classes exist for many graphical objects, such as windows and scroll bars, and for network objects such as connections to remote machines. Observing Java's success, Microsoft released a language named **C#** (pronounced "see sharp") that competes with Java.

Can a Java application work on any type of computer? An attractive feature of Java is that it's **architecture neutral**. This means that Java code needs to be compiled only once, after which it can run on many CPUs (see Figure 10.22). The Java program doesn't care which CPU, OS, or user interface is running on the machine on which it lands. This is possible because the target computer runs a Java Virtual Machine (VM), software that can explain to the Java program how to function on any specific system. A Java VM installed with Microsoft Internet Explorer, for example, allows Internet Explorer to execute any **Java applet** (small Java-based program) it encounters on the Internet. Although Java code doesn't perform as fast as C++, the advantage of needing to compile only once before a program can be distributed to any system is extremely important.

Objective C and Swift

What's the most popular language for writing OS X applications? Objective C is the language most often used to program applications to run under OS X. It's

FIGURE 10.22 Java programs can be compiled once and run on many different platforms. *(Anthony Devlin/AP Images, Ifong/Shutterstock, Oleksiy Maksymenko Photography/Alamy)*

FIGURE 10.23 The Xcode IDE tool provides a supportive environment for developing OS X applications. *(Screen shot(s) reprinted with permission from Apple, Inc.)*

an object-oriented style of language, a superset of the C language, so it includes all the keywords of C and then adds more keywords and features. It's often used together with a library called Cocoa. The Cocoa library, or framework, lets users program for the OS X graphical user interface. The Cocoa Touch extension introduces a framework of methods that support gesture recognition for touch devices like the iPhone or iPad.

Swift is a new programming language introduced by Apple for developing for iOS and OS X. Easier to read and maintain, Swift uses a "playground" area where you can quickly write and test ideas before moving the code into the main project.

Is there a favorite IDE for Objective C? Many different IDE tools support Objective C, but OS X ships with a tool named Xcode (see Figure 10.23) that's often used to develop Objective C applications for OS X. Xcode is available free from the online Mac App Store.

HTML

What's the most basic formatting language for web applications? A document that will be presented on the web must be written using special symbols called *tags*. Tags control how a web browser will display the text, images, and other content tagged in **Hypertext Markup Language (HTML)**.

Although knowledge of HTML is required to program for the web, HTML itself isn't a programming language. HTML is just a series of tags that modify the display of text. HTML was the original standard defining these tags. Many good HTML tutorials are available on the web at sites such as Learn the Net (**learnthenet.com**), Webmonkey (**webmonkey. com**), and the World Wide Web Consortium (**w3.org**). These sites include lists of the major tags that can be used to create HTML and XHTML documents.

Are there tools that help programmers write in HTML? Several different programs are available to assist in the generation of HTML. Adobe

Dreamweaver and Microsoft Expression Web present web page designers with an interface that's similar to a word processing program. Web designers can quickly insert text, images, and hyperlinks, as shown in Figure 10.24. The program automatically inserts the corresponding HTML tags. For simple, static web pages, no programming is required.

Will HTML continue evolving? Yes, the current release of HTML is HTML5. HTML standards are discussed and finalized by committee, and HTML5 is a significant advancement. For example <audio> and <video> tags allow pages to easily integrate media and let designers more easily support manipulating those elements. HTML5 eliminates the need to install third-party browser plug-ins and supports features like drag-and-drop elements and document editing.

JavaScript and VBScript

Which programming languages do programmers use to make complex web pages? To make their web pages more visually appealing and interactive, programmers use scripting languages to add more power and flexibility to their HTML code. A **scripting language** is a simple programming language that's limited to performing a set of specialized tasks. Scripts allow decisions to be made and calculations to be performed. Several popular scripting languages work well with HTML, including JavaScript, PHP (Hypertext Preprocessor), and VBScript.

JavaScript is a scripting language that's customized to work with the elements of a web page and is often used to add interactivity to web pages. The syntax, keywords, data types, and operators are subsets of Java. In addition, JavaScript has a set of classes that represent the objects often used on web pages: buttons, check boxes, and drop-down lists.

The JavaScript button class, for example, describes a button with a name and a type—for example, whether it's a regular button or a Submit or Reset button. The language includes behaviors, such as click(), and can respond to user actions. For example, when a user moves his or her mouse over a button and clicks to select it, the button "knows" the user is there and jumps in and performs a special action (such as playing a sound).

FIGURE 10.24 Adobe Dreamweaver is a popular tool for creating web pages. *(Adobe product screenshot(s) reprinted with permission from Adobe Systems Incorporated. Adobe® Dreamweaver® is a registered trademark of Adobe Systems Incorporated in the United States and/or other countries.)*

BITS&BYTES

Your Software Portfolio

Once you begin to program your own projects and make alterations to others' projects, you will want to begin collecting them together in a formal portfolio. Your portfolio should document how you grow as a programmer and should serve as a tool for finding a job, getting into a special course, or attracting others to program with.

Devpost (**devpost.com**) is one site that offers free portfolio management, enabling you to showcase your work and your projects in progress. You can even insert screenshots and videos to explain the story behind the code. And Devpost is also a great site to find your next hackathon, which you can feature in your Devpost portfolio!

Are there other scripting languages besides JavaScript? Programmers who are more familiar with Visual Basic than Java or C++ often use **VBScript**, a subset of Visual Basic, to introduce dynamic decision making into web pages. **Dynamic decision making** means that the page can decide how to display itself based on the choices the reader makes. PHP, discussed in the following section, is another scripting language that has become extremely popular. It's a free, open-source product that runs very efficiently on multiple platforms, including Windows, UNIX, and Linux.

ASP, JSP, and PHP

How are interactive web pages built? To build websites with interactive capabilities, programmers use **Active**

Server Pages (ASP), JavaServer Pages (JSP), or the scripting language **PHP (Hypertext Preprocessor)** to adapt the HTML page to the user's selections. The user supplies information that's translated into a request by the main computer at the company that owns the website, often using a database query language such as SQL. Scripting code in ASP, JSP, or PHP controls the automatic writing of the custom HTML page that's returned to the user's computer.

What does additional programming bring to a web page? The most advanced web pages interact with the user, collecting information and then customizing the content displayed based on the user's feedback. For example, the client/server type application shown in Figure 10.25 shows the web page of the ABC Bike Company collecting a customer bicycle inquiry for red bikes. The program then asks ABC's main server for a list of red bicycles sold by the company. A PHP program running on the server creates a new HTML page and delivers that to the user's browser, telling the customer what red bikes (including details such as model and size) are currently sold by ABC.

Server programs, written in ASP or PHP, can have HTML code as their output. They use what the user has told them (via the list boxes, check boxes, and buttons on the page) to make decisions. Based on those results, the server software decides what HTML to write. A small example of ASP writing its own HTML code is shown in Figure 10.26.

AJAX, XML, and JSON

What if a programmer wants to create a web application that smoothly updates and communicates with other computers? Many websites feature elaborate animations that interact with visitors. They may reach out to several other web resources to gather information or request services like translation. The collection of technologies referred to as **AJAX (Asynchronous JavaScript and XML)** and the continued evolution of HTML5 allow such web applications to update information on a page without requiring the user to do a page refresh or leave the page. By using existing

STEP 1: User requests information on red bikes.

STEP 2: Server sends request to database server.

Customer's computer

ABC Bike Company server

ABC Bike Company database

12345
45678
98764
54321
11223
22334

STEP 4: Server's PHP program writes HTML page.

STEP 3: Database server returns list.

FIGURE 10.25 An online store is an example of the client/server type of Internet application.

a ASP code

```
<%Dim I %>

<%

For I = 1 To 5
        ' Output our HTML and text using the value of I as
        ' the FONT TAG's SIZE attribute.
        %>
        <FONT SIZE="<%= I %>">Hello World</FONT><BR>
        <%
Next ' Continue the loop 5 times
%>
```

> Uses For loops

> Writes five different HTML statements with a different number for font size

b HTML code

```
<FONT SIZE="1">Hello World</FONT><BR>
<FONT SIZE="2">Hello World</FONT><BR>
<FONT SIZE="3">Hello World</FONT><BR>
<FONT SIZE="4">Hello World</FONT><BR>
<FONT SIZE="5">Hello World</FONT><BR>
```

> HTML document in program output

c HTML Displayed on User's Screen

Hello World
Hello World
Hello World
Hello World
Hello World

> HTML document output in web browser

FIGURE 10.26 An ASP program can (a) write HTML code as its (b) output. (c) This image illustrates how the HTML page would show up in a browser.

technologies to do more processing in the browser, users have a more responsive experience.

How do programs gather information from other computers? The markup language called **eXtensible Markup Language (XML)** enables designers to define their own data-based tags, making it much easier for a program running on a server computer (a web service) to transfer the key information on its page to another site. When websites communicate with humans, HTML works well because the formatting it controls is important. People respond immediately to the visual styling of textual information; its layout, color, size, and font design all help to transfer the message of the page to the reader. When computer programs want to communicate with each other, however, all of these qualities just get in the way.

With XML, groups can agree on standard systems of tags that represent important data elements. For example, the XML tags <stock> and </stock> might delimit key stock quote information. Mathematicians have created a standardized set of XML tags named MathML for their work, and biometrics groups continue to refine XML standards to describe and exchange data such as DNA and face scans. Without XML, a website that wanted to look up current stock pricing information at another site would have to retrieve the HTML page, sort through the formatting information, and try to recognize which text on the page identified the data needed. **JavaScript Object Notation (JSON)** is another standard for exchanging information between a server computer process and a client.

The information is delivered as a series of names and their values, making it easy for programs to parse and easy for humans to read.

Figure 10.27 shows a table of popular programming languages and technologies with their features and the typical settings in which they're used.

Mobile Application Development

How do programmers build applications for mobile devices? Special languages and supporting tools are speeding the development of applications for mobile devices like smartphones and tablets. Programmers need to be able to take advantage of specific features like GPS capability, compasses, software keyboards, and touch-sensitive screens. In addition, the user interface has to take the smaller screen size of mobile devices into account.

What development tools are used for creating mobile apps for Apple's iOS platform? To start a complex project like an iPhone app requires a detailed prototype. Each of the many screens, all the user interface elements, and all the content need to be organized and linked smoothly. Often, programmers begin with a prototype, created quickly with drag-and-drop elements using products like Proto. io or Interface Builder. Proto.io (**proto.io**) is a browser-based tool that lets you construct a working simulation of your application. Interface Builder is part of the Apple Xcode development tool; it requires a bit more expertise to use than Proto.io but can also rapidly create a prototype.

FIGURE 10.27

Popular Programming Languages

PROGRAMMING LANGUAGE	FEATURES	TYPICAL SETTING
C/C++ and C#	• Can create compact code that executes quickly • Provides high- and low-level access	• Used in industrial applications such as banking and engineering
Java	• Is architecture neutral • Is object oriented	• Used to create applets that can be delivered over the web
Objective C	• Has a framework for writing iOS applications	• Used to create applications for OS X and Apple mobile devices
Visual Basic	• Is easy to learn and use • Is object oriented • Has a drag-and-drop interface	• Used in prototype development • Used to design graphical user interfaces

WEB TECHNOLOGIES	FEATURES	TYPICAL SETTING
AJAX	• Uses a combination of existing technologies like JavaScript, CSS, and XML	• Creates websites that can update without the user refreshing the page
HTML5	• Latest version of HTML	• Introduces tags like <video> and supports drag and drop
VBScript	• Is similar in syntax to Visual Basic • Has classes that represent buttons, drop-down lists, and other web page components	• Creates code that lives on the client machine and adds interaction to web pages
XML	• Enables users to define their own tags	• Facilitates exchange of information from web services
JSON	• Format defined with name/value pairs	• Very common format for exchange of information from web services

When it's time to begin writing the code for an iOS app, programmers turn to Objective C and use the Apple Xcode development toolset. Xcode lets designers code and debug the behavior of the application and simulate the application in a software version of the target device. After the program is running, its performance can be profiled for speed, memory usage, and other possible problems.

Are there different tools for building apps for Android devices? Yes, the Android software development kit (SDK) is required to build apps targeting Android smartphones and tablets. There are many ways programmers work with the Android SDK, including using well-known IDEs like Eclipse with special plug-ins or using the Android Studio, shown in Figure 10.28. Information on the latest version of the Android SDK, as well as tutorials, guides, and other resources, is available at the Android Developers page (**developer.android.com**).

I'm not a programmer, but can I make a simple app? Absolutely. Tools like Corona and App Inventor produce amazing games and apps quickly (see the Try This on pages 430–431 for more information). Tens of millions of apps constructed using Corona have been downloaded, including the overnight sensation Bubble

FIGURE 10.28 Android Studio integrates all the tools required to program Android applications from scratch. (© 2015 Google Inc, used with permission. Google and the Google logo are registered trademarks of Google Inc.)

trends in IT

Emerging Technologies: Unite All Your Video Game Design Tools

Unity is a game-development environment that supports home video game production by combining many tools into one package, giving you what you need to edit, test, and play your game idea quickly. It can generate real-time shadowing effects, for example, and has preprogrammed scripts integrated. After you've polished your production, Unity allows you to publish for web, mobile, or console platforms. With over 500,000 developers using Unity, and over 60 million installs of the Unity browser plug-in, the potential of this tool is amazing (see Figure 10.29).

You'll start with the built-in Unity editor so you can quickly assemble a 3-D environment. Unity gives you access to its Asset Store right from the editor window. Art assets are supplied so that you instantly have materials to create your own landscape. Tutorials and sample projects are available, as well as character models and textures. Grab a sound effect or some code to simulate a great explosion effect. If you create assets you'd like to distribute, you can put them up for sale within the Asset Store.

Unity incorporates lighting control and shading and the application of textures in order to develop rich terrains. Its built-in physics engine lets objects respond to gravity, friction, and collisions. One example is the "wheel collider," a module that simulates the traction of real car tires. Audio processing is included, with effects like echo, reverb, and a chorus filter, as are tools to make real-time networking available from your game.

Programming is handled through several flexible scripting languages—JavaScript, C#, and an implementation of Python named Boo. It has a visual interface that lets you drag and drop objects to set variables, or you can choose to sync with an external IDE like Visual Studio. There's an integrated debugger so that you can pause your game, check variable values, and quickly repair errors. When it's time to optimize the performance before your final release, you can use the built-in profiler: It reports statistics on where the processing time is being spent so that you can fine tune game play.

Unity is available in a free downloadable version (**unity3d.com**) and in a pay version, Unity 3D Pro. The Pro version adds features but also can be licensed and used by companies. The free version of Unity can be used to create games that can be sold—there is no royalty or revenue sharing required. And there are modules that let you easily port your code to a number of target platforms: PC, iOS, Android, and the web as well as Xbox 360, PS4, and Wii U.

You'll also find an active community to support you as you learn. There are live online training courses offered and forums for community discussion. There is also a dedicated IRC (Internet Relay Chat) channel for live chatting with Unity users. If you need help distributing your finished game, you can join Union, a service that brings your game to new markets for you.

If you're interested in video game development, architectural visualizations, or just creating interactive animations, download Unity and realize the power of programming.

FIGURE 10.29 Unity is a free game engine that can build web, mobile, or console games. *(Screenshot courtesy of Unity Technologies)*

Ball created by 14-year-old Robert Nay (**naygames.com**). The apps you have written using App Inventor in the Make This exercises can be uploaded to the Google Play store for download worldwide.

If your goal is to make a mobile app that's very simple or even specific to one occasion, like a wedding, there are web-based products that make that quick and easy. Magmito (**magmito.com**) supports developing a simple app with text and graphics and requires no programming knowledge.

Does an application need to be rewritten for every kind of mobile device? Programming environments like Corona and Magmito support publishing an application to several different types of devices. Although these tools can be great time savers for very simple applications, for programmers using specific features that make that device unique or for those concerned with extracting ultimate performance, custom programming for each environment still is required.

Future of Programming Languages

Objective 10.12 *State key principles in the development of future programming languages.*

What will the next great language be? It is never easy to predict which language will become the next "great" language. Software experts predict that as software projects continue to grow in size, the amount of time needed to compile a completed project will also grow. It's not uncommon for a large project to require 30 minutes or more to compile. Interpreted languages, however, take virtually no compile time because compilation occurs while the code is being edited. As projects get larger, the capability to be compiled instantaneously will become even more important. Thus, interpreted languages such as Python, Ruby, and Smalltalk could become more important in the coming years.

Will visual programming languages become more popular? Visual programming languages (VPLs) have a history of over 50 years. The idea of "programming without coding," the name of an MIT open-source project to promote VPLs, is maturing but is not yet a tool for most professional software development environments. The future may bring a push for the elegance of visual programming. VPLs use *visual modeling*, creating the code using images to represent each statement, which helps programmers understand complex designs. We have already seen a move toward visual modeling in audio production in the development of software for adding effects like echo or reverse to music snippets. Programming environments like Max 7 are visual and have a growing and enthusiastic user base.

Will all languages someday converge into one? Certain characteristics of modern programming languages correspond well with how programmers actually think. These

FIGURE 10.30 There will always be a variety of languages, each with its own personality. *(Luis Guillermo Restrepo Rivas)*

traits support good programming practices and are emerging as common features of most modern programming languages. The object-oriented paradigm is one example. Both Visual Basic and COBOL have moved toward supporting objects.

There will always be a variety of programming languages, however. Figure 10.30, in which the artist tries to give each language a "personality," illustrates that idea in a lighthearted fashion.

Forcing a language to be so general that it can work for any task also forces it to include components that make it slower to compile, produce larger final executables, and require more memory to run. Having a variety of languages and mapping a problem to the best language create the most efficient software solutions.

So what do I do if I want to learn languages that will be relevant in the future? No particular set of languages is best to learn, and there is no one best sequence in which to learn them. The Association for Computing Machinery (**acm.org**) encourages educators to teach a core set of mathematical and programming skills and concepts, but school and university departments are free to offer a variety of languages.

When you're selecting which programming languages to study, some geographical and industry-related considerations come into play. For example, in an area in which a large number of pharmaceutical companies exist, there may be a demand for Massachusetts General Hospital Utility Multi-Programming System (MUMPS). This language is often used to build clinical databases, an important task in the pharmaceutical industry. Review the advertisements for programmers in area newspapers and investigate resources such as ComputerJobs (**computerjobs.com**) to identify languages in demand in your area.

Regardless of whether you pursue a career in programming, having an understanding of how software is created will help you in many IT careers. Software is the set of instructions that allows us to make use of our hardware. Programming skills give you the power to understand, create, and customize a computer system. ■

 SOUND BYTE
Using the Arduino Microcontroller

In this Sound Byte, you'll use the Arduino microcontroller to control LED lights and motors.

Before moving on to the Chapter Review:
1. **Watch Replay Video 10.2** ▷ .
2. **Then check your understanding of what you've learned so far.**

check your understanding // review & practice

For a quick review to see what you've learned so far, answer the following questions.

multiple choice

1. Selecting the right programming language for a project depends on

    a. who you have working for you and what they know.

    b. the final requirements for performance and space used.

    c. the environment of the finished project.

    d. all of the above

2. An IDE is a tool that facilitates

    a. editing.

    b. debugging.

    c. compiling.

    d. all of the above

3. Which is NOT an advantage of Java?

    a. Java is architecture neutral.

    b. Java needs to compile only once prior to distribution.

    c. Java supports network communications.

    d. Java performs faster than C++.

4. Which is TRUE about XML?

    a. XML supports the development of rich multimedia.

    b. XML makes it possible to update web pages without refreshing.

    c. XML enables designers to define their own data-based tags.

    d. XML has classes that represent drop-down lists and other web elements.

5. Examples of visual programming languages include

    a. Java.

    b. PHP.

    c. JSON.

    d. App Inventor.

MyITLab Go to **MyITLab** to take an autograded version of the *Check Your Understanding* review and to find all media resources for the chapter.

TECHBYTES WEEKLY
Stay current with TechBytes Weekly Newsletter.

Continue »

10 Chapter Review

summary //

Understanding Programming

Learning Outcome 10.1 You will be able to describe the life cycle of a software project and identify the stages in the program development life cycle.

Life Cycle of an Information System

Objective 10.1 *Describe the importance of programming to both software developers and users.*

- Programming skills allow you to customize existing software products to accomplish required tasks. A beginning-level knowledge of programming will let you create macros, customized miniprograms that speed up redundant tasks.

Objective 10.2 *Summarize the stages of the system development life cycle (SDLC).*

- An information system includes data, people, procedures, hardware, and software. The set of steps followed to ensure that development proceeds in an orderly fashion is the system development life cycle (SDLC). There are six steps in the SDLC waterfall model:
  1. A problem or opportunity is identified.
  2. The problem is analyzed, and a program specification document is created to outline the project objectives.
  3. A detailed plan for programmers to follow is designed using flowcharts and dataflow diagrams.
  4. Using the developed plan, programmers develop the program, and the program is then documented.
  5. The program is tested to ensure that it works and that it's installed properly.
  6. Ongoing maintenance and evaluation ensure a working product.

Life Cycle of a Program

Objective 10.3 *Define programming and list the steps in the program development life cycle (PDLC).*

- Programming is the process of translating a task into a series of commands that a computer will use to perform that task. The PDLC involves five steps: describing the problem, developing the algorithm, coding, debugging, and testing and documentation.

Objective 10.4 *Describe how programmers construct a problem statement from a description of a task.*

- The problem statement is an explicit description of what tasks the computer program must accomplish and how the program will execute these tasks and respond to unusual situations. The problem statement describes the input data that users will have at the start of the job, the output that the program will produce, and the exact processing that converts these inputs to outputs. The problem statement identifies potential errors and plans to address these errors.

Objective 10.5 *Explain how programmers use flow control and design methodologies when developing algorithms.*

- Programmers create an algorithm by converting a problem statement into a list of steps and identifying where decision points occur. Yes/no binary decisions are common, and often the pattern of a repeating action loop is recognized. Algorithms are documented in the form of a flowchart or in pseudocode. Programmers use either top-down or object-oriented analysis to produce the algorithm.

Objective 10.6 *Discuss the categories of programming languages and the roles of the compiler and the integrated development environment (IDE) in coding.*

- Computer code uses special words and strict rules to enable programmers to control the CPU without having to know all of its hardware details. Programming languages are classified in several major groupings, sometimes referred to as *generations*, with the first generation being machine language—the binary code of 1s and 0s that the computer understands. Assembly language is the next generation; it uses short, English-like commands that speak directly to the CPU and give the programmer direct control of hardware resources. Each successive generation in language development has relieved programmers of some of the burden of keeping track of what the hardware requires and more closely matches how humans think about problems.

- Compilation is the process by which code is converted into machine language, the language the CPU can understand. A compiler is a program that understands both the syntax of the programming language and the exact structure of the CPU and its machine language. It can translate the instructions written by programmers in the higher-level language into machine language, the binary patterns that will execute commands on the CPU. Each programming language has its own compiler.
- An integrated development environment (IDE) is a developmental tool that helps programmers write and test their programs.

Objective 10.7 *Identify the role of debugging in program development.*

- If programmers make errors in the algorithm or in translating the algorithm to code, problems will

occur. Programmers debug the program by running it constantly to find errors and to make sure the program behaves the way it should.

Objective 10.8 *Explain the importance of testing and documentation in program development.*

- Once debugging has detected all the code errors, users—both within the company and outside the company—test the program in every way they can imagine, both as the program was intended to be used and in ways only new users might think up. Before its commercial release, software is often provided at a reduced cost or at no cost in a beta version to certain test sites or to interested users for a last round of testing.
- Once testing is complete, technical writers create internal documentation for the program and external documentation that will be provided to users of the program. User training, which begins once the software is distributed, teaches the user community how to use the software efficiently.

Programming Languages

Learning Outcome 10.2 You will understand the factors programmers consider when selecting an appropriate programming language for a specific problem and will be familiar with some modern programming languages.

Many Programming Languages

Objective 10.9 *Discuss the driving factors behind the popularity of various programming languages.*

- There are a variety of languages because of the many tradeoffs that must be made between speed of execution, security, ease of programming, interface and ability to grow and support more features later.

Objective 10.10 *Summarize the considerations in identifying an appropriate programming language for a specific setting.*

- A programming team reviews several considerations before selecting the language to be used. Certain languages are best used for certain problems. The target language should be well matched to the amount of space available for the final program. Some projects require the selection of a language that can produce code that executes in the fastest possible time. Selecting a language with which the programmers are familiar is also helpful.

Exploring Programming Languages

Objective 10.11 *Compare and contrast modern programming languages.*

- Visual Basic, C/C++, and Java are languages that enable programmers to include control features such as scroll bars, title bars, text boxes, buttons, and expanding and collapsing menus.
- Objective C is a language used in programming applications for mobile devices using iOS and applications that will run under OS X.
- Programmers use HTML tags to structure web pages. HTML5 includes more advanced tags like .
- For more complex web development, scripting programs such as JavaScript, PHP, and VBScript are popular.
- AJAX is a programming solution that uses a combination of technologies to create websites that can update without the user refreshing the page.
- XML and JSON allow programmers to create their own tags so that web pages can exchange information, not just formatting details.

Objective 10.12 *State key principles in the development of future programming languages.*

in development. Many languages have moved toward the object-oriented paradigm.

- New languages may lean toward being interpreted instead of compiled because of the speed gained

MyITLab) Be sure to check out **MyITLab** for additional materials to help you review and learn. And don't forget the Replay Videos ▷ .

key terms //

chapter quiz // assessment

For a quick review to see what you've learned, answer the following questions. Submit the quiz as requested by your instructor. If you are using **MyITLab**, the quiz is also available there.

multiple choice

1. What is the first step of the SDLC?

   a. Problem identification

   b. Analysis

   c. Development

   d. Design

2. When designing a program, the developer selects a design approach like

   a. if or for

   b. Python or C++

   c. top down or object oriented

   d. IDE or compiler

3. RTM is the point in the software release cycle when

   a. real people are brought into the testing process.

   b. the software is released to programmers.

   c. the software is released to computer manufacturers who install it on the systems they build.

   d. a software update is released to the public.

4. Java is considered to be *architecture neutral* because it

   a. can be recompiled to run on many CPUs.

   b. only needs to be compiled once and can run on many different CPUs.

   c. can run on many different generations of Windows.

   d. can run in any browser.

5. PHP is a scripting language used to

   a. create applications for iOS devices.

   b. program for Android smartphones.

   c. control the automatic generation of HTML pages.

   d. edit text documents.

6. JSON stands for

   a. Just Short Of Notice.

   b. JavaScript Only.

   c. Java Startup Output Naming.

   d. JavaScript Object Notation.

true/false

_____ 1. A logical error can be detected and repaired by the compiler.

_____ 2. An RTM version of software is often released so users can help debug it.

_____ 3. AJAX allows you to create websites that never need to refresh.

_____ 4. XML and JSON are both common formats for the exchange of information between web services.

critical thinking

1. **Key Classes for Shopping**

   Think of the last time you had a big shopping trip facing you. What would key classes be if you were going to design a software program that helped you manage your shopping excursion? What data and methods would belong in each class?

2. **Programming Languages**

   Is there one programming language that can outperform all others? How would you select the first programming language to learn? Will the number of programming languages you need to know as a professional programmer keep increasing or settle down to just few choices?

Working Together for Change

Problem

Your team has been selected to write a program that tells a vending machine how to make change. The program needs to deliver the smallest amount of coins for each transaction.

Task

Divide the class into three teams: Algorithm Design, Coding, and Testing. The responsibilities of each team are outlined as follows.

Process

1. The Algorithm Design team must develop a document that presents the problem as a top-down design sequence of steps, and another document that uses object-oriented analysis to identify the key objects in the problem. Each object needs to be represented as data and behaviors. Inheritance relationships between objects should be noted, as well. You can use flowcharts to document your results.

2. The Coding team needs to decide which programming language would be most appropriate for the project. This program needs to be fast and take up little memory. Use the web to gather information to defend your selection. You may also consider using a product such as Visual Logic (**visuallogic.org**) to develop the code for a prototype of the system.

3. The Testing team must create a testing plan for the program, including a table listing combinations of inputs and correct outputs.

4. As a group, discuss how each team would communicate its results to the other teams. Once one team has completed its work, are the team members finished? How would the tools of a site such as SourceForge (**sourceforge.net**) help your development team?

Conclusion

Any programming project requires teams to produce an accurate and efficient solution to a problem. The interaction of team members is vital to successful programming.

Software That Kills

In this exercise, you'll research and then role-play a complicated ethical situation. The role you play might not match your personal beliefs, but your research and use of logic will enable you to represent the view assigned. An arbitrator will watch and comment on both sides of the argument, and together, the team will agree on an ethical solution.

Problem

The Therac-25 was a computerized radiation-therapy machine. Between 1985 and 1987, six people were killed or badly harmed due to a flaw in its software. The dose that one patient had received was estimated to be in the 15,000- to 20,000- rad range. This is roughly 100 times more than the expected dose and 15 to 20 times more than a fatal dose. The error-prone software remained on the market for months before the problem was recognized, acknowledged, and solved.

Does this situation indicate criminal conduct? Or is it a situation that needs to be resolved in civil court (for monetary damages)? Is this an example of the price society pays for using complex technology so no blame should be assigned?

Research Areas to Consider

- Therac-25 case resolution
- 2010 Toyota recalls for unanticipated acceleration
- Software errors in avionic software systems
- ACM ethical guidelines

Process

1. Divide the class into teams. Research the areas cited above from the perspective of a software developer, the people impacted, or the arbitrator.

2. Team members should write a summary that provides factual support for their character's position regarding the fair and ethical design and use of technology. Then, team members should create an outline to use during the role-playing event.

3. Team members should present their case to the class or submit a PowerPoint presentation for review by the rest of the class, along with the summary and resolution they developed.

Conclusion

As technology becomes ever more prevalent and integrated into our lives, ethical dilemmas will present themselves to an increasing extent. Being able to understand and evaluate both sides of the argument, while responding in a personally or socially ethical manner, will be an important skill.

Time Sheets

You've been asked to automate a time card and to automatically record a log of the weekly payments using Excel 2016. You have made great progress on the time card, and now need to add data validation, VLOOKUPs to automate Employee data entry, an IF function to calculate the daily payments, and a macro to copy the time card data to a payment log.

You will use the following skills as you complete this activity:

- Use Absolute Cell Reference
- Create IF and VLOOKUP Functions
- Record a Macro
- Create a Data Validation
- Fill Date Series
- Use Paste Values

Instructions

1. Open *TIA_Ch10_Start* and save as **TIA_Ch10_LastFirst**.

2. To display the Developer Tab, click **File**, click **Options**, and then click **Customize Ribbon**. In the Customize the Ribbon pane, select the **Developer check box**. Click **OK**.

3. Click the **Time Card worksheet**, in cell B3, type **Ted Hoyt**. In cell B4, create a VLOOKUP function to lookup up the value of cell B3 in the range A2:C16 on the Employee Data worksheet, and return the value in the third column of that range. Use False as the Range_Lookup argument.

    a. Hint: The function will be = VLOOKUP(B3,'Employee Data'!A2:C16,3,FALSE).

4. In cell B5, create a VLOOKUP function to look up the value of cell B3 in the range A2:C16 on the Employee Data worksheet, and return the value from the second column. Use False as the Range_Lookup argument.

5. Click **cell C9** on the Time Card worksheet, type **4/11/2018**, and then use the **Fill Handle** to copy the series of dates in cells C10:C13.

6. Select **range D9:D13**. Click the **Data tab**, select **Data Validation** in the Data Tools group. In the Data Validation dialog box, on the Settings tab, click the **Allow arrow** and select **Decimal**. Click the **Data arrow**, and select **between**; then type **0** in the Minimum box and **12** in the Maximum box. Click the **Error Alert tab**, ensure a Stop style is selected, type the title: **Invalid Entry**, and an Error message: **Total hours worked cannot exceed 12 hours**.

7. In cell D9, type **16** and press **Enter**. The Data Validation Error box displays. Click **Retry**, then type **10** and press **Enter**. In cells D10:D13, type **8**, **12**, **8**, and **9** respectively. Note the Overtime Hours fills in automatically, calculating the hours in excess of 8 hours.

8. In cell F9, use an IF function to test if the value in cell D9 is less than or equal to 8. If this condition is true, then multiply cell D9 times cell E4 (the regular rate). If the condition is false, then multiply 8 times E4 and add to that E9*E5 (the overtime rate). Make sure you use absolute cell references in the formula where needed. Use the **Fill Handle** to copy the formula to range F10:F13.

9. Click the **Payment Log worksheet**. Click **cell A1**.

10. Click the **Developer tab**, click **Record Macro** in the Code group. Name the macro **CopyTimeCard** and assign a shortcut key of Ctrl+t. With the Macro recorder on, complete the following steps: Click the **Time Card worksheet**, select and copy **range A20:F20**, click the **Payment Log worksheet**, and then press **Ctrl + ↓** to go to the last row with values. Click the **Developer tab**, click **Use Relative References** in the Code group, and then press the **↓ key** to move to the first blank cell in the worksheet. Click Use **Relative References** in the Code group to deselect it. Click the **Home tab**, click the **Paste arrow**, and then select **Values**. Click **cell A1**, select the **Time Card worksheet**, press **Esc**, and then click **cell B3**. Click the **Developer tab**, and then click **Stop recording** in the Code group.

11. Test the Macro by typing **Brett Martin** in cell B3. In cells D9:D13, type **8**, **10**, **8**, **8**, and **9**, respectively. Click **cell B3**, then press **Ctrl+T** to run the Macro. Click the **Payment Log worksheet t**o ensure the Brett Martin data was successfully transferred.

12. Click the **Developer tab**, click **Macros** in the Code group, select the **CopyTimeCard macro**, and click **Edit**. Copy the macro code, close the Macro window, add a new worksheet and paste in cell A1 of the new worksheet. Name the worksheet **Macro**.

13. Save the workbook. Note: Answer Yes when asked to save as a Macro-free workbook. Submit based on your instructor's directions.

11

Behind the Scenes: Databases and Information Systems

Database Fundamentals

Learning Outcome 11.1 **You will be able to explain the basics of databases, including the most common types of databases and the functions and components of relational databases in particular.**

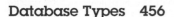

How Businesses Use Databases

Learning Outcome 11.2 **You will be able to explain how businesses use data warehouses, data marts, and data mining to manage data and how business information systems and business intelligence are used to make business decisions.**

Make This: MAKE: A Family Shopping List on **page 471**

All media accompanying this chapter can be found in MyITLab.

For an overview of the chapter, watch the **Preview Video.**

(Marek Uliasz/Alamy, Kheng Ho Toh/Alamy, Juri Samsonov/Fotolia, Mira/Alamy, Fotolia)

HOW COOL IS THIS?

When can **data visualization** not only become more effective but also a **form of art**? When you use **Circos (circos.ca)**—a software package that uses a **circular layout for visualizing data and information**. The data elements (the traditional rows and columns of a table) are represented as segments around the circle and relationships between elements in the data are indicated by ribbon-like links. The color and thickness of each ribbon link represents the element and the magnitude of the relationship, respectively.

The circular layout **emphasizes patterns in connections and data relationships** more readily than traditional linear layouts. This application was originally designed to visualize genome data, but it has also been effectively used to visualize other types of data, including customer loyalty, urban planning, and human migration patterns. Moreover, the **results can just be interesting works of art**. *(Circos: An information aesthetic for comparative genomics Martin I Krzywinski, Jacqueline E Schein, Inanc Birol, Joseph Connors, Randy Gascoyne, Doug Horsman, Steven J Jones, and Marco A Marra Genome Res. Published in Advance June 18, 2009, doi:10.1101/gr.092759.109)*

Database Fundamentals

Learning Outcome 11.1 You will be able to explain the basics of databases, including the most common types of databases and the functions and components of relational databases in particular.

You interact with databases every day—when you retrieve a friend's phone number from your contacts, post to your Facebook page, or add a song to your Spotify playlist. In this part of the chapter, we'll look at the basics of databases and how databases can be used to provide relevant information quickly and easily.

 database

ADVANTAGES

Many actions we frequently perform, such as use an ATM, shop online, and register for classes, generate data that needs to be stored, managed, and used by others. Most likely, a system has been created that receives and stores our generated data and that enables that data to be processed and used by others, effectively turning data into information. In this section, we look at why databases are needed as well as their specific advantages.

The Need for Databases

Objective 11.1 *Explain what a database is and why we need them.*

Why do I need to know about databases? A **database** is a collection of related data that can be stored, sorted, organized, and queried. By creating an organized structure for

data, databases make data more meaningful and therefore more useful. Because you interact with databases every day, understanding how databases work and what you can do with databases will help you use the ones you interact with more effectively. For example, *categorizing*, *sorting*, and *filtering* are key attributes of most databases. If a database isn't set up correctly or if you don't know how to use the database, you may not get the type of information you're looking for.

StubHub, the online ticket-exchange platform (see Figure 11.1), is an example of a database. Sellers list tickets on StubHub. They specify the categories the tickets fall into (sports, concerts, theater) and other details, such as day, time, and seat location of the event, and set a price. Buyers then access the website, using its filters to narrow down to the type of ticket they're looking to purchase. If the database doesn't

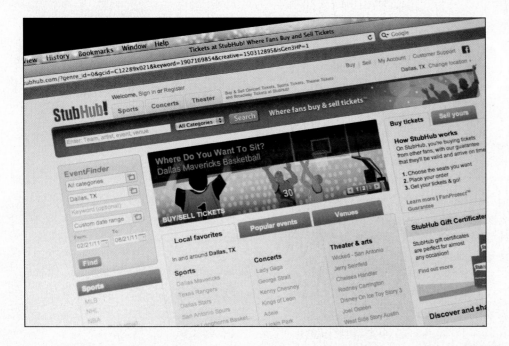

FIGURE 11.1 StubHub is a database that provides for the exchange of tickets between sellers and buyers. *(NetPhotos/ Alamy)*

FIGURE 11.2 A basic list
created as a spreadsheet
in Microsoft Excel or
as a table in Microsoft
Word is often sufficient
to organize simple data.
(Excel 2013, Windows 8.1,
Microsoft Corporation)

	A	B	C	D
2	**Books To Buy**			
3				
4	Class	Title	Author	Bought
5	American Literature 1	Anthology of American Literature, Volume 1	McMichael et al.	
6	American Literature 1	Moby Dick	Melville	Yes
7	American Literature 1	The Last of the Mohicans	Cooper	Yes
8	English Composition 1	The Academic Writer's Handbook	Rosen	
9	English Composition 1	The Write Stuff: Thinking Through Essays	Sims	Yes
10	Intro to Business	Better Business	Solomon, Poatsy, Martin	Yes

have the right categories for sellers to choose from, buyers won't be able to locate the tickets they want.

Do I need databases for managing all types of data?
Not every situation in which related data needs to be turned into organized information demands the complexity of a database. For simple tasks, lists are adequate. Most word processing and spreadsheet applications have tools to help you create simple lists. A table you create in Microsoft Word can serve as a list, as can a spreadsheet you create in Microsoft Excel.

Figure 11.2 shows a simple *Books to Buy* list you might create in Excel before beginning college. This list works well because it's simple and suited to just one purpose: to provide you with a list of

books you need to buy for a particular semester. If all the information that needs to be tracked were as simple as the information in Figure 11.2, there would be little need for databases.

When is a list not sufficient for organizing data?
If complex information needs to be organized or more than one person needs to access it, a list isn't an efficient solution. For example, when you enrolled in college, you provided to a number of people basic information about yourself, including your name and address as well as the classes you wished to take. Your school also tracks other information about you, such as your residence hall assignment and meal plan preferences. Consider the lists shown in Figure 11.3. Figure 11.3a is a list

Class Registration List - Spring Semester

Student ID	Last Name	First Name	Home Address	City	State	Zip	Class Code	Class Name	# of Credits
1234567	Finkel	Susan	645 Pine Street	Philadelphia	PA	19012	CIS 110	Computer Literacy	3
1234567	Finkel	Susan	645 Pine Street	Philadelphia	PA	19012	ENG 101	English Comp 1	3
1234567	Finkel	Susan	645 Pine Street	Philadelphia	PA	19012	HIS 103	Western Civ 1	3
1234567	Finkel	Susan	645 Pine Street	Philadelphia	PA	19012	CHE 140	Chemistry	4
1234567	Finkel	Susan	645 Pine Street	Philadelphia	PA	19012	PSY 101	Intro to Psychology	3
4567890	Garza	Julio	421 West 3rd Street	New Witten	SD	57584	CIS 110	Computer Literacy	3
4567890	Garza	Julio	421 West 3rd Street	New Witten	SD	57584	SOC 101	Intro to Sociology	3
4567890	Garza	Julio	421 West 3rd Street	New Witten	SD	57584	PSY 101	Intro to Psych	3
7890123	O'Connor	Leanne	238 Grant Street	Beverly	MA	01915			
2345678	Stinson	Arthur	345 Ryan Drive	Cedar Falls	IA	50613	MAT 161	Pre-Calculus	3
	Stinson	Arthur	345 Ryan Drive	Cedar Falls	IA	50613	ENG 101	English Comp 1	3
	Stinson	Arthur	345 Ryan Drive	Cedar Falls	IA	50613	SOC 101	Intro to Sociology	3
	Zhang	Mei	457 Blanchard St.	Boston	MA	01901	PSY 101	Intro to Psychology	3
	Zhang	Mei	457 Blanchard St.	Boston	MA	01901	HIS 103	Western Civ 1	3
6789012	Zhang	Mei	457 Blanchard St.	Boston	MA	01901	ENG 102	English Comp 2	3

Data Redundancy: Student name entered multiple times and on different lists

Data Inconsistency: Different data on different lists

Residence Hall and Meal Plan List

Student ID	Last Name	First Name	Home Address	City	State	Zip	Residence Hall	Room Number	Meal Plan
1234567	Finkel	Susan	10 Green Street	Malvern	PA	19355	Fielder Hall	303	1
4567890	Garza	Julio	421 West 3rd Street	New Witten	SD	57584	Bauer Hall	121	3
7890123	O'Connor	Leanne	238 Grant Street	Beverly	MA	01915	Bauer Hall	214	
2345678	Stinson	Arthur	345 Ryan Drive	Cedar Falls	IA	50613	Berger Quad	317	3
6789012	Zhang	Mei	457 Blanchard St.	Boston	MA	01901	Anders Hall	350	2

FIGURE 11.3 (a) A class registration list and (b) a list of residence hall assignments are two lists a college might create to keep track of student information. *(Excel 2013, Windows 8.1, Microsoft Corporation)*

Student Information							
Student ID ▾	Last Name ▾	First Name ▾	Address ▾	City ▾	State ▾	Zip Code ▾
1234567	Finkel	Susan	645 Pine Street	Philadelphia	PA	19012
3456789	Finkel	Susan	25 Maywood Road	Darien	CT	06820
6789012	Zhang	Mei	457 Blanchard Street	Boston	MA	01901
2345678	Stinson	Arthur	345 Ryan Drive	Cedar Falls	IA	50613
4567890	Garza	Julio	421 Western Street	New Witten	SD	05758
2341235	Steuer	James	529 West 3rd Street	McClean	VA	22101

Same name, different Student ID

FIGURE 11.12 The StudentID field makes an ideal primary key field because even students with the same name will not have the same ID number. *(Excel 2016, Windows 10, Microsoft Corporation)*

student ID number is a unique number, most likely generated in some serial manner. Many database programs have a means of automatically generating a unique identifier that has no meaning outside of the database system. In Microsoft Access, the AutoNumber data type provides the means to generate a serial number as each new record is added.

How is the primary key used to establish relationships between tables? Recall that relational databases link tables together to establish a relationship and join the tables through a common field. The common field in one table is that table's primary key and the common field in the related table is called the **foreign key**. When the relationship is established, you have the option of enforcing **referential integrity** for each relationship. Referential integrity ensures that relationships between tables remain constant and guarantees the quality of the data in the database.

Because data is changed continually in a database, it's important to ensure that the data in related tables is synchronized and that a record isn't added or modified in one table and not the other. For instance, going back to our earlier example, you would not be able to enter a student's record in the Residence Assignments table with a StudentID number that doesn't exist in the Student Information table (the primary key table) if referential integrity is being enforced. You first would need to add the student to the Student Information table and then enter the student in the Residence Assignments table.

Inputting and Managing Data

Objective 11.7: *Describe how data is inputted and managed in a database.*

How do I get data into the database? You can key data directly into the database. However, because a great deal of data already exists in some type of electronic format, such as word processing documents, spreadsheets, and web-based sources, most databases can import data electronically from other files, which can save an enormous amount of keying and reduces the amount of data-entry errors.

When importing data, the data must exactly match the format of the database. Most databases usually apply filters to the data to determine whether it's in the correct format as defined by the data dictionary. Nonconforming data is flagged (either on-screen or in a report) so that you can modify the data to fit the database's format.

How can I make manual entry into a database more efficient? Input forms are used to control how new data is entered into a database. Figure 11.13 shows an example of an input form for the Student Information table. Each field has a label that indicates the data to be placed in the field. The data is inputted into the blank boxes. Notes have been added to the form to guide the users. In addition to being used to input new data, input forms are used to make changes to existing data in the database. Because a form can be configured to display individual records, making changes to data by using a form ensures that the change is made to the right record.

Data Validation

How can I ensure that only valid data is entered into a field? Validation is the process of ensuring that data entered into a field meets specified guidelines.

Student Information Input Form

Student ID		Enter a 7 digit Student ID number
Last Name		
First Name		
Address		Student's permanent home address
City		
State		Use the 2 letter state abbreviation
Zip Code		

NOTE: All fields must be completed!

FIGURE 11.13 Input forms are used to enter data into tables. *(Excel 2013, Windows 8.1, Microsoft Corporation)*

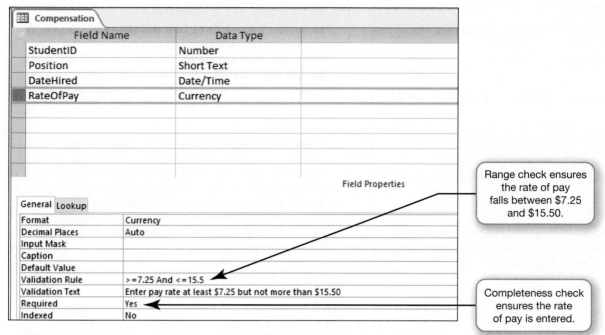

FIGURE 11.14 Validation rules help ensure correct data is entered. *(Excel 2016, Windows 10, Microsoft Corporation)*

A **validation rule** is generally defined as part of the data dictionary and is specified in the field properties. Violations of validation rules usually result in an error message displayed on the screen with a suggested action so that the error can be addressed. Common validation rules include the following:

- *Range check:* A **range check** ensures that the data entered into the field falls within a certain range of values. For instance, you could set a **field constraint** (a property that must be satisfied for an entry to be accepted into the field) to restrict the rate of pay to fall within a certain range. Figure 11.14 shows a range check in the Field Properties pane for an Access database.

  A validation rule restricts the entries for a student's rate of pay for his or her campus job to amounts between $7.25 and $15.50. If users tried to enter a rate of pay less than $7.25 or greater than $15.50, they would be notified of a range error and the input would not be accepted, as shown in Figure 11.15.

- *Completeness:* A **completeness check** ensures that all required fields have been completed. For example, Figure 11.14 shows the Required property set to Yes, so when data is not entered in the field, as is the case in Figure 11.16, the database performs a completeness check, notices the blank RateOfPay field, and displays an error message to alert the user of the omission.

- *Consistency check:* A **consistency check** compares the values of data in two or more fields to see if those values are reasonable. For example, your birth date and the date you enrolled in school are often in a college's database. It's not possible for you to have enrolled in college before

you were born. Furthermore, most college students are at least 16 years old. Therefore, a consistency check on these fields might ensure that your birth date is at least 16 or more years before the date when you enrolled in college.

- *Alphabetic and numeric checks:* An **alphabetic check** confirms that only textual characters (such as Robin) are entered in a field. A **numeric check** confirms that only numbers are entered in the field. With a numeric check in place, $J2.5n would not be accepted as the price of a product. Setting the data type will help ensure that the correct type of data is entered into a field.

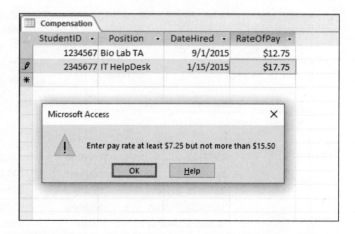

FIGURE 11.15 Access users see this pop-up when they enter a value that falls outside the stated range of acceptable values. The displayed message is generated from the text typed in the Validation Text property. *(Windows 10, Microsoft Corporation)*

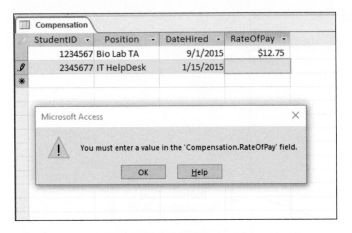

FIGURE 11.16 Access users see this pop-up when they do not enter a value in a field that has been indicated as being required. *(Windows 10, Microsoft Corporation)*

Viewing and Sorting Data

How can I view data in a database? Displaying the tables on-screen and browsing through all the data is an option with most databases. In many instances, you'll only want to view the data one record at a time and not display all the data in an entire table. Forms are used to display individual records, either alone or in conjunction with other related data.

How can I reorder records in a database? You can easily sort data into ascending or descending order. Figure 11.17a shows an Access database table in which the records were inputted in no particular order. By highlighting a column (in this case, Last Name) and then clicking Ascending on the Ribbon, the database displays the records in alphabetical order by last name, as shown in Figure 11.17b.

FIGURE 11.17 (a) Shown is an unsorted table. Notice that the Last Name column is selected (highlighted) for sorting. (b) Selecting the sorting option Ascending produces the sorted output with the records sorted in ascending alphabetical order by last name. *(Access 2016, Windows 10, Microsoft Corporation)*

Extracting or Querying Data

What if I want to display only a certain subset of data in a database? There are two ways to display only those records that match particular criteria:

1. *Use a filter:* A **filter** temporarily displays records that match certain criteria. When you apply a filter, you can't save the results, so filters are useful if you don't need to review the results at another time. Filters can only be applied to fields from the same table, so if you need to combine fields from multiple tables to achieve your subset of data, queries are a better option.

2. *Create a query:* Like a filter, a database **query** is a way of retrieving a particular subset of data that matches certain criteria. However, unlike a filter, a query can be used to extract data from one or multiple tables, and queries can be saved and run again whenever necessary to obtain updated results. When you create a query, you choose the fields that should be included in the results and specify the criteria for selecting records. For example, as shown in Figure 11.18a, if you wanted to create a list of students living in the Boyer 1 dorm and their room numbers, you would pull data from the Student Information table (FirstName and LastName), Residence Halls table (ResidenceName), and Residence Assignments table (RoomNumber). Then you'd need to specify to see only those records pertaining to a specific dorm, in this case Boyer 1. Figure 11.18b displays the results for this query.

Do I have to learn a query language to develop queries for my database? All modern DBMSs contain a query language that the software uses to retrieve and display records. A query language consists of its own vocabulary and sentence structure that you use to frame the requests.

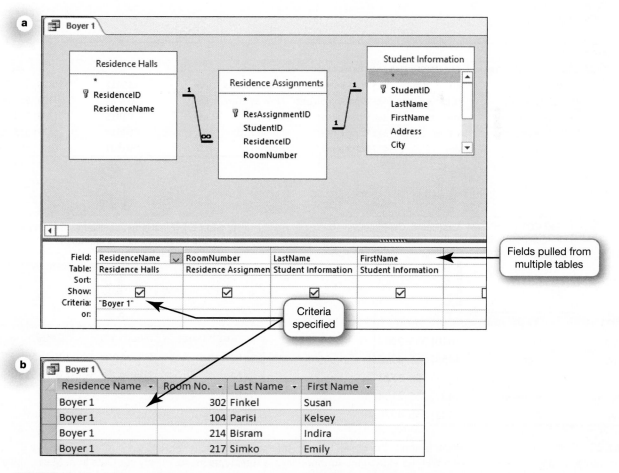

FIGURE 11.18 (a) When creating a query, you can specify fields from multiple tables as well as specific criteria within a field. (b) The outcome reflects those records meeting the specified criteria. *(Microsoft Corporation)*

DIG DEEPER

Structured Query Language (SQL)

To extract records from a database, you use a query language. Almost all relational and object-oriented databases today use Structured Query Language, or SQL. Oracle, Microsoft SQL Server, Microsoft Access, IBM DB2, and MySQL are examples of popular databases that use SQL.

SQL uses relational algebra to extract data from databases. **Relational algebra** is the use of English-like expressions that have variables and operations, much like algebraic equations. Variables include table names, field names, or selection criteria for the data you wish to display. Operations include directions such as *select* (which enables you to pick variable names), *from* (which tells the database which table to use), and *where* (which enables you to specify selection criteria). The two most common queries used to extract data using relational algebra are select queries and join queries.

A **select query** displays a subset of data from a table (or tables) based on the criteria you specify.

A typical select query has the following format:

```
SELECT (Field Name 1, Field Name 2, …)
FROM (Table Name)
WHERE (Selection Criteria)
```

The first line of the query contains variables for the field names you want to display. The FROM statement enables you to specify the table name from which the data will be retrieved. The last line (the WHERE statement) is used only when you wish to specify which records need to be displayed (such as all students with GPAs greater than 3.3). If you wish to display all the rows (records) in the table, then you don't use the WHERE statement (see Figure 11.19).

Suppose you want to create a phone list that includes all students from the Student Information table in Figure 11.19a. The SQL query you would send to the database would look like this:

```
SELECT (FirstName, LastName, CellPhone)
FROM (Student Information Table)
```

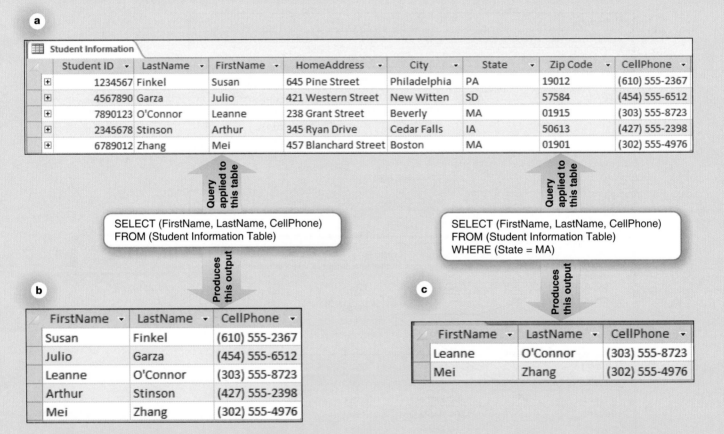

a

Student Information

Student ID	LastName	FirstName	HomeAddress	City	State	Zip Code	CellPhone
1234567	Finkel	Susan	645 Pine Street	Philadelphia	PA	19012	(610) 555-2367
4567890	Garza	Julio	421 Western Street	New Witten	SD	57584	(454) 555-6512
7890123	O'Connor	Leanne	238 Grant Street	Beverly	MA	01915	(303) 555-8723
2345678	Stinson	Arthur	345 Ryan Drive	Cedar Falls	IA	50613	(427) 555-2398
6789012	Zhang	Mei	457 Blanchard Street	Boston	MA	01901	(302) 555-4976

Query applied to this table

```
SELECT (FirstName, LastName, CellPhone)
FROM (Student Information Table)
```

Query applied to this table

```
SELECT (FirstName, LastName, CellPhone)
FROM (Student Information Table)
WHERE (State = MA)
```

Produces this output

Produces this output

b

FirstName	LastName	CellPhone
Susan	Finkel	(610) 555-2367
Julio	Garza	(454) 555-6512
Leanne	O'Connor	(303) 555-8723
Arthur	Stinson	(427) 555-2398
Mei	Zhang	(302) 555-4976

c

FirstName	LastName	CellPhone
Leanne	O'Connor	(303) 555-8723
Mei	Zhang	(302) 555-4976

FIGURE 11.19 When the query on the left is applied to the (a) Student Information table, it restricts the output to (b) only a phone list. The query on the right, which uses a WHERE statement, further restricts the phone list to (c) only students from Massachusetts.
(Windows 10, Microsoft Corporation)

Figure 11.19b shows the output from this query. What if you want a phone list that shows only students from Massachusetts? In that case, you would add a WHERE statement to the query, as follows:

```
SELECT (FirstName, LastName, CellPhone)
FROM (Student Information Table)
WHERE (State = MA)
```

This query restricts the output to students who live in Massachusetts, as shown in Figure 11.19c. Notice that the State field in the Student Information table can be used by the query (in this case, as a limiting criterion) but that the contents of the State field aren't required to be displayed in the query results. This explains why the output shown in Figure 11.19c doesn't show the State field.

When you want to extract data that is in two or more tables, you use a **join query**. The query actually links (or joins) the two tables using the common field in both tables and extracts the relevant data from each. The format for a simple join query for two tables is as follows:

```
SELECT (Field Name 1, Field Name 2)
FROM (Table 1 Name, Table 2 Name)
WHERE (Table 1 Name.Common Field Name =
      Table 2 Name.Common Field Name)
AND (Selection Criteria)
```

Notice how similar this is to a select query, although the FROM statement must now contain two table names. In a join query, the WHERE statement is split into two parts. In the first part (right after WHERE), the relation between the two tables is defined by identifying the common fields between the tables. The second part of the statement (after AND) is where the selection criteria are defined.

The AND means that both parts of the statement must be true for the query to produce results (i.e., the two related fields must exist and the selection criteria must be valid). Figure 11.20 illustrates using a join query for the Student Information and Roster Master tables to produce a class roster for students.

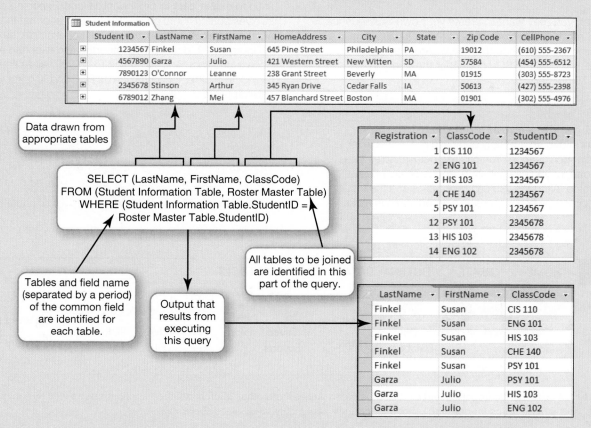

FIGURE 11.20 This join query will display a student roster for each student in the Student Information table. Notice that the WHERE statement creates the join by defining the common field (in this case, StudentID) in each table. *(Windows 8.1, Microsoft Corporation)*

Boyer 1

```
SELECT [Residence Halls].ResidenceName, [Residence Assignments].RoomNumber,
[Student Information].LastName, [Student Information].FirstName
FROM [Student Information]
INNER JOIN ([Residence Halls]
INNER JOIN [Residence Assignments]
ON [Residence Halls].ResidenceID = [Residence Assignments].ResidenceID)
ON [Student Information].StudentID = [Residence Assignments].StudentID
WHERE ((([Residence Halls].ResidenceName)="Boyer 1"));
```

FIGURE 11.21 The SQL View window in Access shows the SQL code for the query in Figure 11.18. Although it's a relatively simple SELECT statement, it's much easier to create the query using the Access tools provided. *(Microsoft Corporation)*
*>To display SQL code for a query, open a query and select **SQL View** from the View drop-down list on the Home tab of the Ribbon.*

Query languages are similar to full-blown programming languages but are usually much easier to learn. The most popular query language used today is SQL. Modern database systems provide wizards or other mechanisms to guide you through the process of creating queries. Figure 11.18a shows an example of an Access query being created in Design View that allows you to easily select query elements. You can also create a query using a Simple Query Wizard in Microsoft Access. When you use the Simple Query Wizard or Design View, you're actually using SQL commands without realizing it.

However, you may want to create your own SQL queries in Access, modify existing queries at the SQL language level, or view the SQL code that the wizard created. Figure 11.21 shows the SQL code that the query in Figure 11.18 created.

Outputting Data

How do I get data out of a database? The most common form of output for any database is a viewable (or printable) electronic report. You can use data in tables to create reports, or you can generate reports based on queries you create. Although you can print tables and the results of queries directly, when you create a report you can make other adjustments to how the information is displayed, such as grouping like information and including aggregate information such as totals. Businesses routinely summarize the data within their databases and compile summary data reports. For instance, at the end of each semester, your school generates a grade report for you that shows the grades you received for the classes you took.

Can I transfer data from a database to another software application? Database systems also can be used to export data to other applications. Exporting data involves putting it into an electronic file in a format that another application can understand. For example, as shown in Figure 11.22, data can be imported and exported among Access and Microsoft Word and Excel, as well as converted to and from other formats such as PDF and XML for use with other applications. ■

> **Before moving on to Part 2:**
> 1. **Watch Replay Video 11.1** ⟳.
> 2. **Then check your understanding of what you've learned so far.**

FIGURE 11.22 Data can be imported and exported between Access and other Microsoft Office applications as well as converted to PDF, XML, and other formats for use with other applications. *(Access 2016, Windows 10, Microsoft Corporation)*

check your understanding // review & practice

For a quick review to see what you've learned so far, answer the following questions.

multiple choice

1. Two lists showing different values for the same data in different places of a database is an example of

   a. data redundancy.

   b. data inconsistency.

   c. data disparity.

   d. data irregularity.

2. Which of the following is NOT a true statement when considering using databases instead of lists?

   a. Data can be easily shared among users.

   b. Data-entry errors can be minimized with databases.

   c. Data integrity can be ensured with a database.

   d. Databases are easier to build and maintain than lists.

3. The field that has a unique entry for each record in a database table is called the

   a. logical key.

   b. master field.

   c. foreign key.

   d. primary key.

4. Which type of database would be best to handle unstructured data?

   a. relational database

   b. object-oriented database

   c. multidimensional database

   d. all of the above

5. Which type of relationship should be used to connect a Password table to a User Account table?

   a. one-to-many relationship

   b. many-to-many relationship

   c. one-to-one relationship

   d. one-to-none relationship

MyITLab Go to **MyITLab** to take an autograded version of the *Check Your Understanding* review and to find all media resources for the chapter.

Continue »

TRY THIS ▶ Using Excel's Database Functions

Databases are great for organizing lots of data, but they can be difficult to understand and to learn how to use. If your data is flat—that is, if it doesn't need to be divided into multiple tables—you can use Excel's database functions to organize your data. Excel is able to work with an enormous amount of data. With any of the recent versions of Excel, you're allowed 1,048,576 rows and 16,384 columns on one worksheet, with a theoretical limit of 255 worksheets. If your computer had enough memory, you could process a lot of data!

Excel includes several useful database functions: sorting one or multiple columns, applying filters, and applying data validation. All the database commands in Excel are on the Data tab.

Sorting in Alphabetical Order

You can sort one column of data in alphabetical or numerical order.

Step 1 Place your cursor anywhere in the column you want to sort.

Step 2 In the Sort & Filter group, click **Sort A to Z** or **Sort Z to A**, depending on whether you want to sort in ascending or descending order. *(Excel 2016, Windows 10, Microsoft Corporation)*

Applying Filters

When you want to isolate a subset of data, you should apply a filter.

Step 1 Click anywhere in the table, then click **Filter** in the Sort & Filter group. Filter arrows will display next to each column heading.

Step 2 Click the filter arrow beside the column heading for the column you want to filter.

Step 3 Remove the checkmark from Select All, and then click the filter value(s) you'd like to apply. Click **OK**. *(Excel 2016, Windows 8.1, Microsoft Corporation)*

Step 4 Review the data to ensure the filter has been applied correctly. (Note: To remove the filter, click **Filter** in the Sort & Filter group to deselect the option.) *(Excel 2016, Windows 8.1, Microsoft Corporation)*

Applying Data Validation

Using the Data Validation tool, you can apply rules to data so that you can ensure the proper data is being entered.

Step 1   Click **Data Validation** in the Data Tools group to display the Data Validation dialog box.

Step 2   On the Settings tab in the Data Validation dialog box, choose the type of data value to be allowed and the value limits in the Data and Maximum boxes. (Note: Depending on the criteria selected in the Allow field, the criteria in the Data box and other limits will vary.)

(Excel 2016, Windows 8.1, Microsoft Corporation)

Step 3   On the Error Alert tab, select the style of error message you want displayed (Stop, Warning, or Information), and then type the title of the error message and the error message text. Click **OK**.

Step 4   Test the data validation by entering an unacceptable value. When an unacceptable value is entered, an error message displays.

Set value limits in Data box.

Other limits (such as Maximum) will vary depending on criteria selected in Allow box.

Set type of data to be allowed.

Make This ▶ TOOL: AI TinyWebDB

MAKE: A Family Shopping List

In this exercise, you'll create an app that allows each family member to add items to a shopping list from their own phone.

This requires the TinyWebDB component in **App Inventor**, which allows you to store information on the Internet so it can be recalled by anyone using your application. Now your app can trade information between all its users! *(MIT App Inventor 2, Massachusetts Institute of Technology. Creative Commons Attribution-ShareAlike 3.0 Unported License)*

Your app can store values on the Internet so they are accessible by everyone using your app.

For the instructions for this exercise, go to MyITLab.

How Businesses Use Databases

Learning Outcome 11.2 You will be able to explain how businesses use data warehouses, data marts, and data mining to manage data and how business information systems and business intelligence are used to make business decisions.

Large organizations accumulate massive amounts of data—both internal and external. By using *data warehousing*, *data marts*, and *data mining*, these organizations can use databases to tap into this wealth of information, improving their internal operations as well as their customer relationships. In this section, we'll look at how they do just that.

 # data warehousing
AND STORAGE

At the simplest level, data is stored in a single database on a database server, and you retrieve the data as needed. This works fine for small databases and simple enterprises where all the data you're interested in is in a single database. Problems can arise; however, when the organization gets much larger and department-specific, data is stored in separate databases. Traditionally, the individual databases are used by different areas of the business and kept separate; however, the benefits of accessing data from all databases are being recognized. The problem with most databases is that they aren't designed to be accessed together to retrieve this type of data. In this section we look at the large storage repositories called *data warehouses* and *data marts* that help solve this problem.

Data Warehouses and Data Marts

Objective 11.8 *Explain what data warehouses and data marts are and how they are used.*

What is a data warehouse? A **data warehouse** is a large-scale collection of data that contains and organizes in one place all the data from an organization's multiple databases. Individual databases contain a wealth of information, but each database's information usually pertains to one area in the organization. For instance, the order database at Amazon.com contains information about book orders, such as the buyer's name, address, and payment information and the book's name. However, the order database doesn't contain information on inventory levels of books, nor does it list suppliers from which out-of-stock books can be obtained. Data warehouses, therefore, consolidate information from various operational systems to present an enterprise-wide view of business operations.

Is data in a data warehouse organized the same way as in a normal database? Data in the data warehouse is organized by *subject*. Most databases focus on one specific operational aspect of business operations. For example, a large electronics retailer sells

many types of electronics, such as TVs and cell phones. Different departments in the retailer are responsible for each type of product and track the products they sell in different databases (one database for TV sales and one for cell phone sales, for example), as shown in Figure 11.23.

FIGURE 11.23 Data from individual databases is drawn together in a data warehouse. Managers can then produce comprehensive reports that would be impossible to create from the individual databases.

These databases capture specific information about each type of electronics. The TV Sales database captures information such as TV features, extended warranty details (and costs), and the cost of the TV because this information is pertinent to determining the ultimate value of TV sales. The Cell Phone Sales database captures information such as data plan details, calling plan features (and costs), and phone costs.

However, data on total electronic devices sold (and the resulting revenue generated) is critical to the management of the electronics retailer no matter what types of products are involved. Therefore, an electronics retailer's data warehouse would have a subject called Electronics Sales Subject (see Figure 11.23) that would contain information about *all* electronic devices sold throughout the company. While the Electronics Sales Subject is a database that contains information from the other databases the company maintains, all data in the Electronics Sales Subject database specifically relates to electronics sales (as opposed to, say, appliances, which the retailer also carries).

From the Electronics Sales Subject database, it's easy for managers to produce comprehensive reports, such as the Total Electronics Sales Report, as shown in Figure 11.23, which can contain information pertaining to all types of electronics sales.

Do data warehouses capture data from only one time period? Data warehouse data is **time-variant data**, meaning it doesn't all pertain to one period in time. The warehouse contains current values, such as amounts due from customers, as well as historical data. If you want to examine the buying habits of a certain type of customer, you need data about both current and prior purchases. Having time-variant data in the warehouse enables you to analyze the past, examine the present in light of historical data, and make projections about the future.

How are data warehouses populated with data? Source data for data warehouses can come from three places:

1. *Internal sources:* Sales, billing, inventory, and customer databases all provide a wealth of information. Spreadsheets and other ad hoc analysis tools may contain data that can be loaded into the data warehouse.

2. *External sources:* Vendors and suppliers often provide data regarding product specifications, shipment methods and dates, billing information, and so on.

3. *Clickstream data:* Software used on company websites to capture information about each click that users make as they navigate through the site is referred to as **clickstream data**. Using clickstream data-capture tools, a company can determine which pages users visit most often, how long users stay on each page, which sites directed users to the company site, and user demographics. Such data can provide valuable clues as to what a company needs to improve on its site to stimulate sales.

Data Staging

Does all source data fit into a data warehouse? Although two source databases might contain similar information (such as customer names and addresses), the format of

BITS&BYTES

Data Warehouses Are Going to the Cloud

Data warehouses provide companies the capability to compile and analyze big data. However, the costs of installing and maintaining the hardware and software required for data warehouses can often be quite expensive. Amazon RedShift is a cloud-based data warehouse service that costs a fraction of traditional on-premise platforms. The cloud-based platform makes it easier for users to increase the size of the data warehouse needs, as well. Redshift is designed to handle petabytes of information, and because it uses parallel processing, it can deliver fast results for virtually any sized dataset.

Other companies have begun to incorporate cloud-based data warehouse capabilities, but none to the scale that Amazon is offering. Big data analytics and data warehouses are becoming the standard. It remains to be seen whether cloud-based data warehouses will also become the standard, or will the traditional on-premise platforms change to meet the quickly increasing demand for data storage and analytics.

the data is most likely different in each database. Therefore, source data must be staged before entering the data warehouse. **Data staging** consists of three steps:

1. Extraction of the data from source databases
2. Transformation (reformatting) of the data
3. Storage of the data in the data warehouse

Many different software programs and procedures may have to be created to extract the data from varied sources and reformat it for storage in the data warehouse. The nature and complexity of the source data determine the complexity of the data-staging process.

How can data stored in the data warehouse be extracted and used? Managers can query the data warehouse in much the same way you would query an Access database. However, because there is more data in the data warehouse, special software is needed to perform such queries. **Online analytical processing (OLAP)** software provides standardized tools for viewing and manipulating data in a data warehouse. The key feature of OLAP tools is that they enable flexible views of the data, which the software user can easily change.

Data Marts

What if a smaller amount of data is needed? Small slices of the data warehouse, each called a **data mart**, are often created so that companies can analyze a related set of data that is grouped together and separated out from the main body of data in the data warehouse. Whereas data warehouses have an enterprise-wide depth, the information in data marts pertains to a single component of the business.

For instance, if you need accurate sales-related information and you don't want to wade through customer service data, accounts payable data, and product shipping data to get it, a data mart that contains information relevant only to the sales department can be created to make the task of finding this data easier. An overview of the data-warehousing process is illustrated in Figure 11.24. Data staging is vital because different data must be extracted and then reformatted to fit the data structure defined in the data warehouse's DBMS. Data can be extracted using powerful OLAP query tools, or it can be stored in specialized data marts for use by specific employee groups.

Data Mining

Objective 11.9 *Describe data mining and how it works.*

What is data mining? Just because you have captured data in an organized fashion and have stored it in a format that seems to make sense doesn't mean that an analysis of the data will automatically reveal everything you need to know. Trends can sometimes be hard to spot if the data isn't organized or analyzed in a particular way. To make data work harder, companies employ data-mining techniques. **Data mining** is the process by which great amounts of data are analyzed and investigated. The objective is to spot significant patterns or trends within the data that would otherwise not be obvious. For instance, by mining student enrollment data, a school may discover that there's been a consistent increase in new engineering-degree students who are women.

Why do businesses mine their data? The main reason businesses mine data is to understand their customers better. If a company can better understand the types of customers who buy its products and can learn what motivates its customers to do so, it can market effectively by concentrating its efforts on the populations most likely to buy. You may have noticed that products are frequently moved around in supermarkets. This is usually the result of data mining. With electronic scanning of bar codes, each customer's purchase is recorded in a database. By classifying the data and using *cluster analysis*, supermarket managers can determine which products people usually purchase with other products. The store then places these products close to each other so that

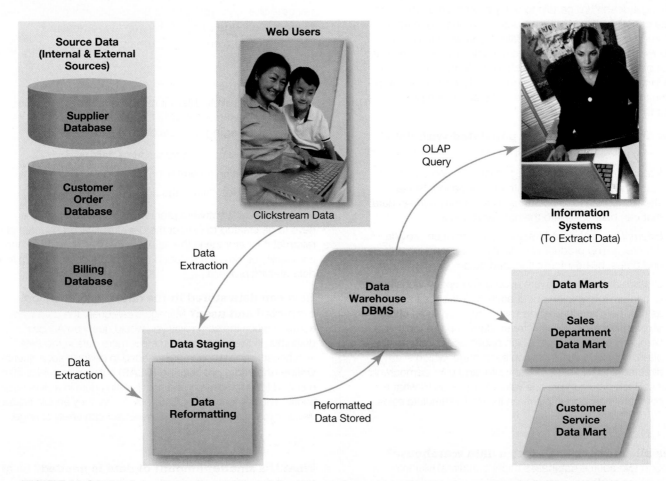

FIGURE 11.24 This figure shows an overview of the data warehouse process. *(Bikeriderlondon/Shutterstock, Redav/Shutterstock)*

FIGURE 11.25

Data-Mining Techniques

Classification
Define data classes to help spot trends, then apply the class definitions to all unclassified data.

Estimation
Assign a value to data based on some criterion.

Affinity Grouping (or Association Rules)
Determine which data goes together.

Clustering
Organize data into similar subgroups, or clusters, without using predefined classes.

Description and Visualization
Describe data so that managers can interpret it in new and different ways.

(Dreaming Andy/Fotolia, Kbuntu/Fotolia, Frank Boston/Fotolia, Gallo Images/Fotolia, Lvnel/Fotolia)

BITS&BYTES

Hadoop: How Big Data Is Being Managed

Hadoop is an open-source platform sponsored by the Apache Software Foundation that makes big, complex, and unstructured data easier to manage. It eliminates the constraints that are placed on how data is traditionally stored and processed by spreading out the data and using many processors that work in parallel. The unique aspects of Hadoop reside in how it stores files and processes data.

- **File Storage:** Hadoop facilitates storing files that are bigger than what can be stored in a centralized database system. Instead of using one server that is common in a centralized database system, Hadoop breaks the data into chunks that it then spreads across to different servers, so it can store many files and very large files.
- **Data Processing:** In addition, Hadoop uses a system called MapReduce for processing big data sets. It makes working with large datasets over a network much more efficient. Rather than moving the data to the software as is done with traditional data processing systems, MapReduce moves the software to the data. MapReduce sends code to each of the dozens of servers that are storing the data, and then each server uses multiple processors to process its set of data. Results then are delivered back in a unified result set.

Hadoop is being used in a variety of industries and markets. For example, Hadoop can be used to conduct accurate portfolio evaluation and risk analysis in the financial industry as well as better organize and manage retail data in order to give customers a better response to their searches.

---

shoppers can find them easily. For instance, if analysis shows that people often buy potato chips with soft drinks, it makes sense to place these items in the same aisle.

How do businesses mine their data? Data mining enables managers to sift through data in several ways. Each technique produces different information on which managers can then base their decisions.

Managers make their data meaningful through the following techniques listed in Figure 11.25.

- *Classification:* Before mining, managers define data classes they think will be helpful in spotting trends. They then apply

these class definitions to all unclassified data to prepare it for analysis. For example, good credit risk and bad credit risk are two data classes managers could establish to determine whether to grant car loans to applicants. Managers would then identify factors, such as credit history and yearly income that they could use to classify applicants as good or bad credit risks.

- *Estimation:* When managers classify data, the record either fits the classification criteria or it doesn't. Estimation enables managers to assign a value to data based on some criterion. For example, assume a bank wants to send out credit card offers to people who are likely to be granted a

trends in IT

Emerging Technologies: Can Your Business Partner Deliver the Goods? Enhanced Databases Can Help You Decide!

Suppose you manufacture T-shirts, and to keep costs low, you'd like to explore Vietnamese T-shirt manufacturers. You could use the terms Vietnamese T-shirt manufacturers in a search engine, and you'd probably find many leads. The information in the leads available online may be factually correct, but how do you determine how reliable these suppliers are? Alibaba.com and Panjiva are two online business-to-business databases that help to navigate these transactions.

Developed to respond to business needs, Alibaba.com (**alibaba.com**) is one of the world's largest online business-to-business databases. Alibaba.com specializes in matching suppliers with buyers for all types of manufactured goods and raw materials. With the global nature of business, databases such as those maintained by Alibaba.com are essential tools that assist businesspeople in managing their global businesses.

Panjiva (**panjiva.com**) is a website that also has a searchable global trade database that tracks the shipments of 10 million companies. The founders of Panjiva decided to make their database different. They gather data that indicates the reliability of suppliers from sources such as government agencies, independent certification companies, nonprofit organizations, and customers. Using the reliability information, Panjiva then creates ratings for companies (on a scale of 1 to 100) based on specific business performance criteria such as number of shipments to the U.S. market, the company's environmental record, and their capability to deliver shipments within promised time frames. Companies such as Home Depot that subscribe to Panjiva's database can feel more comfortable about doing business with suppliers that Panjiva has rated for reliability.

Databases with enhanced information are the wave of the future in the business world. So, before you make that next crucial business decision, ask yourself how much you really know about your prospective business partner. If you don't know enough, then find a database that can make you feel more at ease.

---

credit card. The bank may run the customers' data through a program that assigns a score based on where they live, their household income, and their average bank balance. This provides managers with an estimate of the most likely credit card prospects to target.

- *Affinity grouping (or association rules):* When mining data, managers can determine which data goes together. In other words, they can apply affinity grouping or association rules to the data. For example, suppose analysis of a sales database indicates that two items are bought together 60% of the time. Based on this data, managers might decide that these items should be pictured on the same page of their website.

- *Clustering:* Clustering involves organizing data into similar subgroups, or clusters. It's different from classification in that there are no predefined classes. The data-mining software makes the decision about what to group, and it's up to managers to determine whether the clusters are meaningful. For example, the data-mining software may identify clusters of customers with similar buying patterns. Further analysis of the clusters may reveal that certain socioeconomic groups have similar buying patterns.

- *Description and visualization:* Often, the purpose of data mining is to describe data so that managers can interpret it in new and different ways. For example, if large amounts of data revealed that right-handed women who live in rural environments never take philosophy courses, it would most likely spark a heated discussion about the reasons why. It would certainly provide plenty of opportunities for additional study on the part of psychologists, sociologists, and college administrators!

As we continue to accumulate data, the development of faster and bigger databases will be a necessity. You can expect to interact with more and more databases every year, even if you don't realize you're doing so. While you may never have to create a database, understanding how databases work will enable you to interact with them more effectively. ■

Every organization is generating, acquiring, processing, and storing massive amounts of data every day. Unfortunately, protecting that data from being mishandled is difficult to do. Inadvertently exposing information to inappropriate or unauthorized individuals is known as a *data breach*. According to Identity Theft Resource Center, in the first three quarters in 2015, there were more than 500 data breaches exposing more than 140 million records. The average cost per stolen record is approximately $150. Consider the following:

- In August 2014, JPMorgan Chase and at least four other financial institutions were hacked in a series of coordinated attacks. Hackers broke into the banks' networks from which they stole financial account information of 76 million households and 7 million small businesses.

- In November 2014, a hack of Sony Pictures Entertainment caused private and personal information of over 50,000 current and former Sony employees to be posted online. The data included e-mail exchanges, information about executive salaries, and copies of previously unreleased Sony films.

- In February 2015, more than 2 million users of Anthem, a health insurer in the United States, had their personal information hacked, exposing more than 70 million customer records.

- In June 2015, approximately 22 million records of current, former, and prospective federal employees were exposed when hackers targeted the U.S. Office of Personnel Management.

What responsibility do companies have in safeguarding your data? Should they inform you that your data might be shared with other corporations and obtain your permission before sharing it? How should consumers be compensated (and by whom) if their data is misused?

What Can You Do?

Providing information and having it recorded in databases are part of our way of life now. Ask the following questions related to data you're providing:

- **For what purpose is the data being gathered?** When the clerk at the electronics superstore asks for your zip code, ask why he or she wants it.

- **Are the reasons for gathering the data legitimate or important to you?** You might not want to share your information for marketing purposes, but might want to in order to initiate a product warranty. Similarly, disclosing personal information to your pharmacist may be important for receiving good care and therefore is important to you. If you don't see the advantage, then ask more questions or don't reveal the information.

- **How will the collected information be protected?** Ask about data protection policies before you give information. Most websites provide access to their data protection policies when they ask you for information. If an organization doesn't have a data protection policy, be wary of giving them sensitive information. Data protection doesn't just refer to keeping data secure; it also means restricting access to the data to employees of the organization who need to use that data. A shipping clerk might need to see your address, for example, but doesn't need to see your credit card information.

- **Will the collected information be used for purposes other than the purpose for which it was originally collected?** This might be covered in a data protection policy. If it isn't, ask about it. Will your information be sold to or shared with other companies? Will it be used for marketing other products to you?

- **Could the information asked for be used for identity theft?** Identity thieves usually need your Social Security number and your birth date to open credit card accounts in your name. Be especially wary when asked for this information, and make sure there is a legitimate need for it. And do you really need an e-mail from someone on your birthday advertising a product? It really isn't worth exposing your birth date to potential misuse.

- **Are organizations safeguarding your data?** Don't just consider new requests **for** information. Think about organizations, such as banks, that already have your information. Have they been in the news lately because of a major data breach? You might want to consider switching institutions if yours has a poor record of data security.

Think carefully before providing information and be vigilant about monitoring your data when you can. It may make the difference between invasion of privacy and peace of mind.

using databases to make

BUSINESS DECISIONS

Making intelligent decisions about developing new products, creating marketing strategies, and buying raw materials requires timely, accurate information. In this section, we look at the different types of database systems that are used to help managers make good business decisions.

Business Information Systems

Objective 11.10 *Describe the main types of business information systems and how they are used by business managers.*

What is an information system? An **information system** is a software-based solution used to gather and analyze data. It is made up of the database, application programs, and manual and machine procedures necessary to process data into meaningful information. For example, an information system is used to deliver up-to-the-minute sales data on shoes to the computer of Zappos's president. Databases are integral parts of information systems because they store the information that makes information systems functional.

All information systems perform similar functions, including acquiring data, processing that data into information, storing the data, and providing the user with a number of output options with which to make the information meaningful and useful (see Figure 11.26). There are several types of information systems, including *transaction-processing systems*.

FIGURE 11.26 Information systems acquire data, process that data into information, store the data, and provide the user with a number of output options to make the information useful. *(Wavebreakmedia/Shutterstock, Wavebreakmedia/Shutterstock, Michaeljung/Shutterstock, Raisa Kanareva/Shutterstock)*

What is a transaction-processing system? A **transaction-processing system (TPS)** keeps track of everyday business transactions or activities. For example, colleges have TPSs in place to track transactions that occur frequently, such as registering students for classes, accepting tuition payments, and printing course catalogs. When computers were introduced to the business world, they often were first put to work hosting TPSs.

How are transactions entered into a TPS? Transactions can be entered manually or electronically. When you buy gas at a pay-at-the-pump terminal, the pump captures your credit card data and transmits it to a TPS, which records a sale (gallons of gas and dollar value). Transactions are processed either in batches or in real time. Various departments in an organization then access the TPSs to extract the information they need to process additional transactions, as shown in Figure 11.27.

What is batch processing? Batch processing means that transaction data is accumulated until a certain point is reached and then several transactions are processed at once. Batch processing is appropriate for activities that aren't time sensitive. For example, you may not receive a bill for each charge you make at the bookstore. Instead, the college may collect your charges and batch them together into one monthly billing. It's more efficient to batch and process all requests periodically.

When are TPS transactions processed? For most activities, processing and recording transactions in a TPS occur in real time. **Real-time processing** means that the database is updated while the transaction is taking place. For instance, when you register for classes online, if spots are still available for the classes you want, the database immediately records your registration in the class to ensure you have a

Consumer places
order online

Merchandise arrives
in warehouse

Details of order
- Item #
- Style
- Quantity
- Delivery address

Order
transaction
processing
system

Details of
product
availability
entered

Billing department
extracts information
to process customer
payment

Shipping department
extracts information
to process order

FIGURE 11.27 Transaction-processing systems help capture and track critical business information needed for successful completion of business transactions such as selling merchandise over the Internet. *(Bikeriderlondon/Shutterstock, Penka Todorova Vitkova/Shutterstock, Chuck Rausin/Shutterstock, Natykach Nataliia/Shutterstock)*

spot. This **online transaction processing (OLTP)** ensures that the data in the TPS is current.

Business Intelligence Technologies

Objective 11.11 *Describe business intelligence systems and the types of technologies used to aid in data analysis.*

What is a business intelligence system? Business intelligence (BI) is the ability to improve business decision making with databases and other fact-based support systems. A **business intelligence system** is another form of business information system. A business intelligence system is a set of technologies used to analyze and interpret large sets of data in order to enable managers to make informed

decisions about how best to run a business. Often business intelligence systems use data gathered from data warehouses or data marts because they enable access to information gathered from multiple sources. *Management information systems, decision support systems,* and *enterprise resource planning systems* are classified as business intelligence systems. Increased access to data and the ability to transform it into useful information for business analysis purposes can lead managers to identify new opportunities and implement effective business strategies.

Management Information Systems

What is a management information system? A **management information system (MIS)** provides timely and accurate information that enables managers to make critical business decisions. MISs were a direct outgrowth of TPSs. Managers quickly realized that the data contained in TPSs could be an extremely powerful tool only if the information could be organized and outputted in a useful form. Today's MISs are often included as a feature of TPSs.

What types of reports are generated by MISs? MISs generate three types of reports:

1. A **detail report** provides a list of the transactions that occurred during a certain time period. For example, during registration at your school, the registrar might receive a detail report that lists the students who registered for classes each day. Figure 11.28a shows an example of a detail report on daily enrollment.

2. A **summary report** provides a consolidated picture of detailed data. These reports usually include some calculation (totals) or visual displays of information (such as charts and graphs). Figure 11.28b shows an example of a summary report displaying total daily credits enrolled by division.

3. An **exception report** shows conditions that are unusual or that need attention by system users. The registrar at your college may get an exception report when all sections of a course are full, indicating that it may be time to schedule additional sections. Figure 11.28c shows an example of such an exception report.

Decision Support Systems

What is a decision support system? A **decision support system (DSS)** is another type of business intelligence

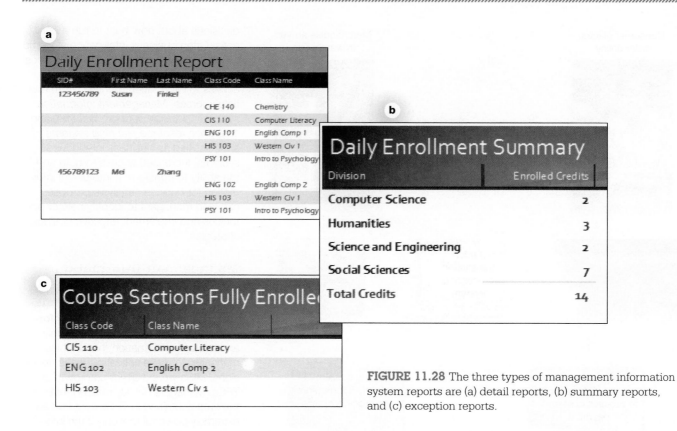

FIGURE 11.28 The three types of management information system reports are (a) detail reports, (b) summary reports, and (c) exception reports.

system designed to help managers develop solutions for specific problems. A DSS for a marketing department might provide statistical information on customer attributes, such as income levels or buying patterns that would assist managers in making advertising strategy decisions. A DSS not only uses data from databases and data warehouses, it also enables users to add their own insights and experiences and apply them to the solution.

What does a DSS look like? DBMSs, while playing an integral part of a DSS, are supplemented by additional software systems in a DSS. In a DSS, the user interface provides the means of interaction between the user and the system. An effective user interface must be easy to learn. The other major components of a DSS are internal and external data sources, model management systems, and knowledge-based systems. As shown in Figure 11.29, these systems work together to provide the user of the DSS with a broad base of information on which to base decisions.

How does a DSS get data? Internal and external data sources provide a stream of data that is integrated into the DSS for analysis. Internal data sources are maintained by the same company that operates the DSS. For example, internal TPSs can provide a wealth of statistical data about customers, ordering patterns, inventory levels, and so on. An external data source is any source not owned by the company that owns the DSS, such as customer demographic data purchased from third parties, mailing lists, or statistics compiled by the government.

What function does a model management system perform? A **model management system** is software that assists in building management models in a DSS. A management model is an analysis tool that, through the use of internal and external data, provides a view of a particular business situation for the purposes of decision making. Models can be built to describe any business situation, such as the classroom space requirements for next semester or a listing of alternative sales outlet locations. Model management systems typically contain financial and statistical analysis tools that are used to analyze the data provided by models or to create additional models.

What is a knowledge-based system, and how is it used in a DSS? A **knowledge-based system** provides intelligence that supplements the user's own intellect and makes the DSS more effective. It could be an **expert system** that tries to replicate the decision-making processes of human experts in order to solve specific problems. For example, an expert system might be designed to take the place of a physician in a remote location. A physician expert system would ask the patient about symptoms just as a live physician would, and the system would make a diagnosis based on the algorithms programmed into it.

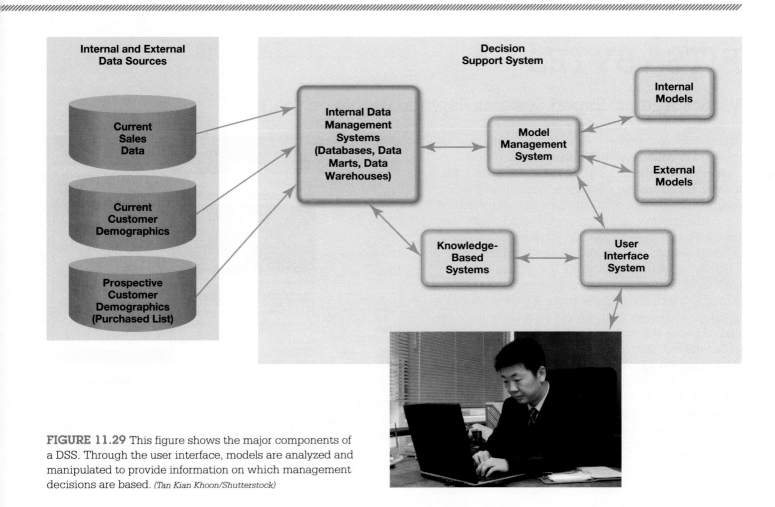

FIGURE 11.29 This figure shows the major components of a DSS. Through the user interface, models are analyzed and manipulated to provide information on which management decisions are based. *(Tan Kian Khoon/Shutterstock)*

Another type of knowledge-based system is a **natural language processing (NLP) system**. NLP systems enable users to communicate with computer systems using a natural spoken or written language instead of using a computer programming language. Individuals just speak to the computer and it understands what they're saying, without users needing to use specific computer commands. Siri, the personal assistant application currently on Apple's iPhone, is an NLP system.

All knowledge-based systems fall under the science of artificial intelligence. **Artificial intelligence (AI)** is the branch of computer science that deals with the attempt to create computers that think like humans. To date, no computers have been constructed that can replicate the thinking patterns of a human brain, because scientists still do not fully understand how humans store and integrate knowledge and experiences to form human intelligence.

How does a knowledge-based system help in the decision-making process? Databases and the models provided by model management systems tend to be extremely analytical and mathematical in nature. If we relied solely on databases and models to make decisions, answers would be derived with a yes or no mentality, allowing no room for human thought. Fortunately, human users are involved in these

systems, providing an opportunity to inject human judgment into the decision-making process.

The knowledge-based system also provides an opportunity to introduce experience into the mix. Knowledge-based systems support the concept of fuzzy logic. Normal logic is highly rigid: If x happens, then y will happen. **Fuzzy logic** enables the interjection of experiential learning into the equation by considering probabilities. Whereas an algorithm in a database has to be specific, an algorithm in a knowledge-based system could state that if x happens, 70% of the time y will happen.

For instance, managers at Best Buy would find it extremely helpful if their DSS informed them that 45% of customers who bought an iPad also bought a Smart Cover for it. This could suggest that designing a discount program for Smart Covers bought with iPads might spur sales. Fuzzy logic enables a system to be more flexible and to consider a wider range of possibilities than would conventional algorithmic thinking.

Enterprise Resource Planning Systems

What does an enterprise resource planning system do? An *enterprise* is any business entity, large or small. All businesses have data and information to manage, and

BITS&BYTES

Virtual Agents: Expert Systems Replace People on the Web

An offshoot of expert systems are the virtual agents that you encounter on the web or on the phone. Virtual agents are frequently used to interface with a database to answer customers' questions. For example, a typical virtual agent on the web features a picture, a name, and a box for entering questions, as shown in Figure 11.30. No virtual agent can be programmed to contain all the possible questions a human might ask. Therefore, the virtual agent software breaks the question down into key words and phrases, which it compares to a database containing question responses. It picks the most likely response and provides the answer. Customers provide feedback as to whether the response adequately answered their question. Usually, if results from the virtual agent aren't satisfactory or if customers need more information, they can connect to a live customer service agent. Virtual agents, although not perfect, save companies money by answering common questions without using expensive human labor.

FIGURE 11.30 Spike, Gonzaga University's sports team mascot, has been transformed into a virtual agent to direct people to the appropriate page of the school's website. *(Courtesy of Gonzaga University)*

large, complex organizations can benefit from managing that information with a central piece of software. An **enterprise resource planning (ERP) system** is a software system that accumulates in a central location all information relevant to running a business and makes it readily available to whoever needs it to make decisions. ERP systems use a common database to store and integrate information. This enables the information to be used across multiple areas of an enterprise.

Human resource functions (such as the management of hiring, firing, promotions, and benefits) and accounting functions (such as payroll) are often the first processes integrated into an ERP system. Historically, human resource records and accounting records were kept in separate databases, but having the information reside in one database makes the management and compensation of employees more streamlined. If manufacturing operations were then integrated into the ERP system, the data that was already in place regarding the employees and payroll could be easily used for determining the cost of running an assembly line or for scheduling workers to run the assembly line. ∎

Before moving on to the Chapter Review:
- **Watch Replay Video 11.2** ▷.
- **Then check your understanding of what you've learned so far.**

The advent of the smartphone brought forth several revolutions that are so standard today that it's hard to remember what life was like before. While entertainment and communication capabilities have been improved by smartphones, tablets, and other mobile devices, so too have business intelligence capabilities. As mentioned above, business intelligence uses databases and other fact-based support systems to improve business decision making. Smartphones, tablets, and more universal access to wireless Internet have enabled business intelligence to go mobile. Using mobile business intelligence systems and technologies, companies have access to data at their fingertips and can interact in real time with customers and business partners. Such capabilities can help to improve service and productivity (see Figure 11.31).

There has always been a huge demand for making data more interesting or useful. Think about how useful transforming a spreadsheet full of values into a chart can be to make trends easier to recognize. However, in earlier models of mobile devices, it was virtually impossible to display data visibly. Early mobile business intelligence systems were limited by small screen sizes and text-based delivery. Most reports were delivered in table format, eliminating the benefit of visual data representation that charts offer. In addition, access to the Internet with mobile devices was limited, making it difficult to interact with real-time data.

Presently, mobile business intelligence solutions makes data not only look good with impressive displays and interactive capabilities, mobile business intelligence systems also makes data completely accessible all the time. Mobile delivery of business intelligence can be accomplished via a mobile web browser or a mobile app. Mobile business intelligence products integrate with business intelligence systems such as knowledge-based and ERP systems to deliver access to key performance indicators, business metrics, and dashboards on mobile devices. Systems such as Oracle's Business Intelligence Enterprise Edition

FIGURE 11.31 Mobile business intelligence applications on smartphones and other mobile devices enable managers to have access to data all the time. *(Charts and BG/Shutterstock)*

and SAP's BusinessObjects Explorer have mobile business intelligence applications that integrates with expansive data sources. Using the capabilities of mobile business intelligence, a corporate executive can, for example, monitor on his or her mobile device a dashboard of key metrics of critical offshore manufacturing facilities while running a meeting thousands of miles away.

Mobile business intelligence solutions are enabling companies to improve business processes, increase employee productivity, and deliver better customer service by providing access to real-time, on-demand access to business critical information. Additionally, mobile business intelligence is expected to make advancements with collaboration and using cloud computing, capturing and capitalizing on social data. However, as great as mobile business intelligence seems, there is room for improvement in many areas, especially security and privacy.

check your understanding // review & practice

For a quick review to see what you've learned so far, answer the following questions.

multiple choice

1. Which best describes a data warehouse?

   a. a building that stores computer servers

   b. a software program that assists with file management

   c. a collection of all the data from an organization's databases

   d. a database that organizes data from multiple organizations

2. The process by which great amounts of data are analyzed and investigated is known as

   a. data mining.

   b. data staging.

   c. online analytical processing.

   d. clustering.

3. A system that is designed to help keep track of everyday business activities is a(n)

   a. management information system.

   b. transaction-processing system.

   c. enterprise resource planning system.

   d. decision support system.

4. Which is a report generated by a management information system?

   a. detail report

   b. summary report

   c. exception report

   d. all of the above

5. Siri, Cortana, and Google Now are examples of which type of knowledge-based system?

   a. artificial intelligence

   b. natural language processing system

   c. expert system

   d. voice management system

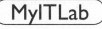 Go to **MyITLab** to take an autograded version of the *Check Your Understanding* review and to find all media resources for the chapter.

TECHBYTES WEEKLY

Stay current with the TechBytes Weekly Newsletter.

 Continue

11 Chapter Review

Summary //

Database Fundamentals

Learning Outcome 11.1 **You will be able to explain the basics of databases, including the most common types of databases and the functions and components of relational databases in particular.**

Database Advantages

Objective 11.1 *Explain what a database is and why we need them.*

- Databases are electronic collections of related data that can be organized so that data is more easily accessed and manipulated. Properly designed databases cut down on data redundancy and duplicate data by ensuring relevant data is recorded in only one place. This also helps eliminate data inconsistency, which comes from having different data about the same transaction recorded in different places. When databases are used, multiple users can share and access information at the same time.

Objective 11.2 *Discuss the benefits of using a database.*

- Some of the main advantages of using databases include that they can manage large amounts of data efficiently, they enable information sharing, and they promote data integrity. Data sharing is made possible because databases provide data centralization—shared source that everyone can access. Data centralization also promotes better data integrity.

Database Types

Objective 11.3 *Describe features of relational databases.*

- A relational database operates by organizing data into various tables based on logical groupings and then creating a relationship between tables by linking through a common field. There are three main types of relationships. A one-to-many relationship has a record appearing only once in a table, while having the capability of appearing many times in a related table. A one-to-one relationship is when there is only one instance of a record in a table, and only one corresponding record in a related table. A many-to-many

relationship has multiple instances of records in both the primary and related tables.

Objective 11.4 *Describe features of object-oriented databases.*

- Object-oriented databases store data in objects rather than in tables, and provide methods for processing or manipulating the data. Object-oriented databases are best for handling unstructured data such as media files and extremely large documents.

Objective 11.5 *Describe features of multidimensional databases*

- Multidimensional databases store data that can be analyzed from different dimensions, or perspectives. Multidimensional databases organize data with three dimensions giving it a cube-like format. In addition to the field and record dimensions of other databases, a measure attribute is also used.

Database Basics

Objective 11.6 *Describe how relational databases organize and define data.*

- Database management systems (DBMSs) are specially designed applications (such as Microsoft Access) that interact with the user, other applications, and the database itself to capture and analyze data. The main operations of a DBMS are creating databases, entering data, viewing (or browsing) data, sorting (or indexing) data, extracting (or querying) data, and outputting data.
- Data is organized using fields, records, and tables. A category of information in a database is stored in a field. Fields are assigned a field name and a data type that indicates what type of data can be stored in the field. Common data types include text, numeric, computational, date/time, memo, object, and hyperlink. A group of related fields is a record. A group of related records is a table or file. Field

properties reflect data dictionary details. Some common field properties include field size, default value, and captions.

- To keep records distinct, each record must have one field that has a value unique to that record. This unique field is a primary key (or a key field).

Objective 11.7 *Describe how data is inputted and managed in a database.*

- Input forms are used to control how new data is entered into a database as well as how changes are made to data. Data validation helps to ensure that only valid data is entered into a field.

Common validation rules include a range check, a completeness check, a consistency check, and an alphabetic or numeric check.

- Queries and filters are used to display a subset of data. A query language is used to extract records from a database. Almost all relational databases today use Structured Query Language (SQL). However, most DBMSs include wizards that enable you to query the database without learning a query language. Reports are used to output data from a database, or data can be transferred to another software application for further distribution or modification.

How Businesses Use Databases

Learning Outcome 11.2 **You will be able to explain how businesses use data warehouses, data marts, and data mining to manage data and how business information systems and business intelligence are used to make business decisions.**

Data Warehousing and Storage

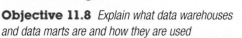

Objective 11.8 *Explain what data warehouses and data marts are and how they are used*

- A data warehouse is a large-scale collection of data that contains and organizes in one place all the relevant data for an organization. Data warehouses often contain information from multiple databases. Because it can be difficult to find information in a large data warehouse, small slices of the data warehouse, called data marts, are often created. The information in data marts pertains to a single department within the organization. Data warehouses and data marts consolidate information from a wide variety of sources to provide comprehensive pictures of operations or transactions within a business.

Objective 11.9 *Describe data mining and how it works.*

- Data mining is the process by which large amounts of data are analyzed to spot otherwise hidden trends. Through processes such as classification, estimation, affinity grouping, clustering, and description (visualization), data is organized so that it provides meaningful information that can be used by managers to identify business trends.

Using Databases to Make Business Decisions

Objective 11.10 *Describe the main types of business information systems and how they are used by business managers.*

- An information system is a software-based solution used to gather and analyze information. All information systems perform similar functions including acquiring, processing, and storing data, and providing the user with a means to output the results into a meaningful and useful information.
- A transaction-processing system (TPS) is used to keep track of everyday business activities.

Objective 11.11 *Describe business intelligence systems and the types of technologies used to aid in data analysis.*

- Business intelligence systems are used to analyze and interpret data in order to enable managers to make informed decisions about how best to run a business. Management information systems, decision support systems, and enterprise resource planning systems are referred to as business intelligence systems.
- A management information system (MIS) provides timely and accurate information that enables managers to make critical business decisions. A decision support system (DSS) is designed

to help managers develop solutions for specific problems. A model management system is software that assists in building analysis tools for DSSs. A knowledge-based system provides intelligence to make the DSS more effective. There are several kinds of knowledge-based systems. An expert system tries to replicate the decision-making process of human experts to solve specific problems. A natural language processing (NLP) system uses natural spoken or written language rather than a computer programming language to communicate with a computer. Artificial intelligence (AI) attempts to create computers that think like humans. An enterprise resource planning (ERP) system is a large software system that gathers information from all parts of a business and integrates it to make it readily available for decision making.

(**MyITLab**) Be sure to check out **MyITLab** for additional materials to help you review and learn. And don't forget the Replay Videos. ⟲

key terms //

chapter quiz // assessment

For a quick review to see what you've learned, answer the following questions. Submit the quiz as requested by your instructor. If you are using **MyITLab**, the quiz is also available there.

multiple choice

1. When is it sufficient to use a list to organize data?
   a. when the data is simple and can be organized in one table
   b. when data needs to be organized into two or more tables
   c. when more than one person needs to access the data
   d. all of the above

2. Which is NOT a component of a database that describes how data is stored?
   a. field
   b. record
   c. table
   d. report

3. The type of database that uses fields, records, and measure as data attributes is
   a. multidimensional.
   b. relational.
   c. object-oriented.
   d. two-dimensional.

4. Which of the following is NOT considered metadata?
   a. data type
   b. table name
   c. field name
   d. field size

5. Data captured from websites as users navigate through a website is called?
   a. staged data
   b. web-user data
   c. clickstream data
   d. time-variant data

6. Which of the following database systems uses artificial intelligence?
   a. office support system
   b. transaction-processing system
   c. knowledge-based system
   d. enterprise resource planning system

True/False

_____ 1. A field labeled PHONE that accepts data such as (610) 555-1212 would use the Number data type.

_____ 2. A query is used to extract a subset of data from a database.

_____ 3. A small slice of a data warehouse is called a data mine.

_____ 4. Data warehouses capture data from only one time period.

Critical Thinking

1. **Auto Repair Database**

   You've been asked to establish a new database for the local auto repair shop. The owner has given you the following data categories that he feels should be in the database. Organize the data categories into two tables, label each table with a name, and identify in each table the primary key field.

Customer ID	Car Make	Last Name
Address	Phone	Vehicle ID
Model Year	Model	City
State	First Name	License Plate

Redesigning Facebook

Problem

Facebook is a database. Facebook management decides what data they require from Facebook account holders and set up specific areas to display what management considers to be a user's pertinent information. But perhaps you as a user would have designed Facebook differently.

Task

Your class has volunteered to work as a focus group for Facebook to assess the usefulness of the information it gathers.

Process

1. Divide the class into small groups.
2. Your group members should examine their individual Facebook accounts. What fields in the profile do you consider to be most useful? Which fields are unnecessary and could be eliminated? What fields are missing from the profile that you think would be useful?
3. Investigate your account settings and application settings. What changes would you make to these settings? Are options missing that you would find helpful?
4. Present your group's findings to the class. Compare your suggestions to those of other groups.
5. Prepare a list of recommendations for improvements to the current Facebook home page and settings pages. Clearly indicate how the proposed changes will benefit both users and the management of Facebook (retaining users, being able to better target advertising to users, and so on).

Conclusion

To remain competitive, Facebook needs to consider the input of users to ensure that it delivers a product with features its customers want and need.

ethics project //

Private Information on Public Databases

In this exercise, you'll research and then role-play a complicated ethical situation. The role you play might not match your own personal beliefs, but your research and use of logic will enable you to represent the view assigned. An arbitrator will watch and comment on both sides of the arguments, and together, the team will agree on an ethical solution.

Problem

A tremendous amount of data is accumulated about us in online databases. Much of this material is accessible in databases that are searchable by anyone with Internet access or to anyone willing to pay a small fee. Websites such as **spokeo.com** and **411.com** comb through publicly accessible databases such as social networking sites, online phone books, as well as business and government websites to compile information on individuals. Your online information may expose you to risks such as identify theft.

Research Areas to Consider

- Electronic information privacy
- Electronic Privacy Information Center (**epic.org)**
- Protecting your online privacy
- Protecting yourself from data breaches

Process

1. Divide the class into teams.
2. Research the areas cited above and devise a scenario in which someone has complained about a website providing information that led to his or her identity being stolen.
3. Team members should write a summary that provides background information for their character—for example, victim of identity theft, website owner, or arbitrator—and that details their character's behaviors to set the stage for the role-playing event. Then, team members should create an outline to use during the role-playing event.
4. Team members should present their case to the class or submit a PowerPoint presentation for review by the rest of the class, along with the summary and resolution they developed.

Conclusion

As technology becomes ever more prevalent and integrated into our lives, ethical dilemmas will present themselves to an increasing extent. Being able to understand and evaluate both sides of the argument, while responding in a personally or socially ethical manner, will be an important skill.

At this time, an auto-graded version of this project is not available in **MyITLab**.

College Database

You help out in the registrar's office at your college. You are being asked to help update the college's database by modifying some of the tables, and creating some queries and reports. You will use Access 2016 to complete this exercise.

You will use the following skills as you complete this activity:

- Create and Modify Data Table
- Import Excel Data
- Create AND Query
- Modify Field Properties
- Establish Table Relationships
- Create Multitable Query

1. Open the *TIA_Ch11_Start.accdb* file and save the database as **TIA_Ch11_LastFirst.accdb**.

2. Open the Faculty table in Design View. Change the Data Type of FullTime to **Yes/No**. Add primary key to the FacultyID field. Move Dept ID field to be after Title field.

3. In the Faculty table, modify the Field Size and Caption properties as follows:

Field Name	Field Size	Caption
FacultyFirst	10	First Name
FacultyLast	15	Last Name
DeptID	3	Dept ID
FullTime		Full Time Status

4. Add a new field with the name **HireDate** and the **Date/Time data type**. Save and close the Faculty table.

5. On the External Data tab, click **Excel** in the Import & Link group. Browse to your student data files and select the *Faculty.xlsx* **file**. In the *Specify how and where you want to store the data in the current database* section, click **Append a copy of the records to the table**: and select the **Faculty table**. Accept all other default options in the wizard. Close the Get External Data – Excel Spreadsheet wizard, and then open the Faculty table to ensure the files were imported correctly. 261 records display. Close the Faculty table.

6. Open the Students table in Datasheet view. Adjust the columns so the column sizes best fit the data in each field. Then, in Design view of the Students table, change the data type for the Email field to **Hyperlink**. Add a Default Value of CT for the State field. Save and close the Students table.

7. Create a form using the Form Wizard using all fields from the Students table. Select a **Columnar layout** and name the form **Students**. In the Students form, click in the **Student Last text box**. Then, using the search box in the Navigation bar at the bottom of the Student form, type **Lopez**. Check that the StudentID is 444096, and then update the address field to **4024 Broad Street** to reflect the student's new address. Save and close the Students form

8. On the Database Tools tab, click **Relationships**. Add the Faculty table, and create a relationship between the Faculty table and the Courses table. Enforce referential integrity. Save and close the Relationships window.

9. Create a query from the Courses table using Query Design. Display CourseID, Building, Room, Days, Start and End fields. Enter criteria to display records for courses meeting in the Park building, on Tuesdays and Thursdays after 12:00 PM. 23 records display. Save the query as **Park TTH**. Close the query.

   a. Hint: Check how Days are displayed in the table, and use the same format for Days in the criteria. Use **>12:00** for the Start criteria.

10. Create a query using Query Design that includes CourseID from the Roster table, Course Description from the Courses table, Faculty Last from the Faculty table, Student Last, Student First, and Email from the Students table. Display only MGT110 IC courses. Save the query as **MGT110 IC Roster**. Close the query.

11. Using the Report Wizard, create a report from the MGT110 IC Roster query. Include all fields except CourseID and FacultyLast. View the data by Courses, do not add additional grouping. Sort Student Last in Ascending order. Accept default layout options, and save the report as Rosters.

12. Save and close the database and submit based on your instructor's directions.

12

Behind the Scenes: Networking and Security in the Business World

Client/Server Networks and Topologies

Learning Outcome 12.1 **You will be able to describe common types of client/server networks, servers found on them, and network topologies used to construct them.**

Client/Server Network Basics   494

Objective 12.1 *List the advantages for businesses of installing a network.*

Objective 12.2 *Explain the differences between a client/server network and a peer-to-peer network.*

Objective 12.3 *Describe the common types of client/server networks as well as other networks businesses use.*

Servers and Network Topologies   499

Objective 12.4 *List the common types of servers found on client/server networks.*

 Active Helpdesk: Using Servers

Objective 12.5 *Describe the common types of network topologies and the advantages and disadvantages of each one.*

Sound Byte: Network Topology and Navigation Devices

Setting Up Business Networks

Learning Outcome 12.2 **You will be able to describe transmission media, network operating system software, and network navigation devices and explain major threats to network security and how to mitigate them.**

Transmission Media   510

Objective 12.6 *Describe the types of wired and wireless transmission media used in networks.*

Network Adapters and Navigation Devices   513

Objective 12.7 *Describe how network adapters help data move around a network.*

Objective 12.8 *Define MAC addresses, and explain how they are used to move data around a network.*

Objective 12.9 *List the various network navigation devices, and explain how they help route data through networks.*

Network Operating Systems and Network Security   516

Objective 12.10 *Explain why network operating systems are necessary for networks to function.*

Objective 12.11 *List major security threats to networks, and explain how network administrators mitigate these threats.*

Sound Byte: A Day in the Life of a Network Technician

Make This: MAKE: An App That Shares on **page 509**

All media accompanying this chapter can be found in MyITLab.

For an overview of the chapter, watch the **Preview Video**. ▶

(Deepadesigns/Shutterstock, Sashkin/Shutterstock, Stuart Ford/Shutterstock, Destina/Fotolia, Paul Velgos/Shutterstock)

HOW COOL IS THIS?

Thinking about installing **solar panels** but not sure how much money you can save? **Google's Project Sunroof** can help! Just enter your address and Google combines information from Google Earth and other sources to determine how much **usable sunlight** hits your roof during a typical year and how many square feet are available on your roof for solar panels. If you enter your average monthly electric bill, the site even suggests the **recommended size of solar installation** you will need to cover your electricity usage. So if you're in one of the areas currently served by Project Sunroof, enter your information and **see how much you could save**! *(slavun/Fotolia)*

Learning Outcome 12.1 You will be able to describe common types of client/server networks, servers found on them, and network topologies used to construct them.

You learned about peer-to-peer networks and home networking in Chapter 7. In this chapter, you'll expand your knowledge about networks by delving into the client/server networks typically used in businesses.

 client/server

NETWORK BASICS

Recall that a *network* is a group of two or more computing devices (or nodes) that are configured to share information and resources such as printers, files, and databases. Businesses such as your school or an insurance company gain advantages from deploying networks, similar to the advantages gained with a home network.

Networking Advantages

Objective 12.1 *List the advantages for businesses of installing a network.*

What advantages do businesses gain from networks? Networked computers have many advantages over individual stand-alone computers (see Figure 12.1):

- **Networks enable expensive resources to be shared.** Networks enable people to share peripherals such as printers or share resources such as an Internet connection. Without a network, each computer would have to be individually connected to a printer and to the Internet. Attaching the computers to a network avoids the cost of providing each computer with duplicate resources.

- **Networks facilitate knowledge sharing.** The databases you learned about in Chapter 11 become especially powerful when deployed on a network. Networked databases can serve the needs of many people at one time and can increase the availability of data. Your college's databases are much more useful when all college employees can look up student records at the same time.

- **Networks enable software sharing.** Installing a new version of software on everyone's desktop in a business with 800 employees can be time-consuming. However, if the computers are networked, all employees can access the same copy of a program from the server. Although the business must still purchase a software license for each user, with a network it can avoid having to install the program on every computer.

- **Networks enable enhanced communication.** Social networking tools, e-mail, and instant messaging are powerful applications when deployed on a network, especially one that's connected to the Internet. Business colleagues can easily exchange information with each other and can share valuable data by transferring files to other users.

Are there disadvantages to using networks?

Because business networks are often complex, additional personnel are usually required to maintain them. These people, called **network administrators**, have training in computer and peripheral maintenance and repair, networking design, and the installation of networking software.

Another disadvantage is that operating a network requires special equipment and software. However, most companies feel that the cost savings of peripheral sharing and the ability to give employees simultaneous access to information outweigh the costs associated with network administrators and equipment.

FIGURE 12.1

Benefits of Business Networks

Enable resource sharing

- Expensive peripherals, such as printers, can be shared.
- Networks can share a single internet connection.

Facilitate knowledge sharing

- Data can be accessed by multiple people.

Enable software sharing

- Software can be delivered to client computers from a server.

Enhance communication

- Information sharing is more effective when employees are connected.

Comparing Client/Server and Peer-to-Peer Networks

Objective 12.2 *Explain the differences between a client/server network and a peer-to-peer network.*

Where do I find client/server networks? Aside from the smallest networks—such as peer-to-peer (P2P) networks, which are typically used in homes and small businesses—the majority of computer networks are based on the client/server model of computing. As you learned in Chapter 7, a **client/server network** (also called a **server-based network**) contains servers as well as client computers. A *server* is a computer that both stores and shares resources on a network, whereas a *client* is a computer that requests those resources.

Recall that in a P2P network, each node connected to the network communicates directly with every other node rather than using a server to exercise central control over the network. Many tasks that individual users must handle on a P2P network can be handled centrally at the server in a client/server network.

For instance, data files are normally stored on a server. Therefore, backups for all users on a business network can be performed by merely backing up all the files on that server. Security, too, can be exercised over the server instead of on each user's computer; this way, the server, not the individual user, coordinates data security. Therefore, client/server networks are said to be **centralized**. P2P networks, on the other hand, are **decentralized**.

Why do businesses use client/server networks? The main advantage of a client/server relationship is that it makes data flow more efficiently than in P2P networks. Servers can respond to requests from a large number of clients at the same time. In addition, servers can be configured to perform specific tasks, such as handling e-mail or database requests, efficiently.

Why aren't P2P networks used more in business settings? P2P networks become difficult to administer when they're expanded beyond 10 users. Each computer may require updating if there are changes to the network, which isn't efficient with large numbers of computers. And as noted previously, security can't be implemented centrally on a P2P network but instead must be handled by each user.

Figure 12.2 shows a small client/server arrangement. The server in this figure provides printing and Internet-connection services for all the client computers connected to the network. The server is performing tasks that would need to be done by each of the client computers in a P2P network. This frees resources on the client computers so that they can more efficiently perform processor-intensive tasks such as viewing a video or accessing a database.

Besides having a server, what makes a client/server network different from a P2P network? Client/server networks also have increased scalability. **Scalability** means that more users can be added easily without

FIGURE 12.2 This small client/server network enables users to share a printer and an Internet connection.

affecting the performance of the other network nodes. Because servers handle the bulk of the printing, Internet access, and other tasks performed on the network, it's easy to accommodate more users by installing additional servers to help with the increased workload. Installing additional servers on a network is relatively simple and can usually be done without disrupting services for existing users.

Types of Client/Server Networks

Objective 12.3 *Describe the common types of client/ server networks as well as other networks businesses use.*

As you learned in Chapter 7, networks are generally classified according to their size and the distance between the physical parts of the network. Figure 12.3 lists the five most common types of client/server network classifications.

What are the most common types of client/server networks encountered in businesses? The two types of client/server networks most commonly encountered in businesses are *local area networks (LANs)* and *wide area networks (WANs)*:

- **Local area network (LAN)**: A LAN is generally a small group of computers and peripherals linked together over a

FIGURE 12.3

Classifications of Client/Server Networks

NETWORK TYPE	DESCRIPTION	WHERE USED IN BUSINESS
PAN (Personal Area Network)	Devices used by one person connected via wireless media	Usually by employees traveling on business
LAN (Local Area Network)	A network consisting of nodes covering a small geographic area	In small businesses or self-contained units of a large business (such as one or more floors of the same office building)
HAN (Home Area Network)	A type of small LAN installed in a home	Not usually deployed by businesses, except small home-based businesses
WAN (Wide Area Network)	Two or more LANs connected together, often over long distances	Connecting business LANs over long distances such as between branches in two cities
MAN (Metropolitan Area Network)	WANs constructed by municipalities to provide connectivity in a specific geographic area	Although not deployed by businesses, employees often use them while traveling

(Drubig Photo/Fotolia, Whitehoune/Fotolia, Maridav/Fotolia, Fotolia, Kamaga/Fotolia)

BITS&BYTES

Your Car Has a Network—So Can It Be Hacked?

Cars today contain multiple microchips (sometime more than 30) that control the vehicle's various systems. For example, some cars use network communications, such as WiFi and Bluetooth, so that parts of the car can communicate with each other. Collision-avoidance systems and anti-theft systems, controlled by microprocessors, make cars safer and tougher to steal. But can your car get hacked?

Hackers have successfully taken over cars' computer systems and caused malfunctions, such as taking control of the cars' entertainment and climate control systems. Fortunately, this hacking has so far been limited to individuals employed by car manufacturers, and to successfully hack the cars usually requires a great deal of time physically accessing the vehicle. Nevertheless, manufacturers have begun to recall cars to patch computer security vulnerabilities when they're discovered.

So is a hacker going to take control of your car? Probably not. Most hacking attacks are aimed at generating financial gain, such as by stealing credit card numbers. There is no real financial incentive for taking control of your car's air conditioning system. But here are a few things you can do to feel more secure about your vehicle's computing systems:

- **Find out if your car has wireless systems:** Ask when buying a new car or read the manual for a car you already own.
- **Inquire whether any systems on your car can be accessed remotely:** Remote shutdown systems on leased or financed vehicles can be activated in the case of repossession by the financing company.
- **Keep your car's computer systems updated:** Dealerships often provide updates during scheduled maintenance, but inquire to see if your vehicle is due for an update.
- **Don't leave password information related to your vehicle systems in the vehicle:** If someone obtains your OnStar password, they could have your car remotely shut down.
- **Don't ignore recall notices:** A recall notice on your car's entertainment system might not sound important, but if it fixes a vulnerability that keeps a hacker out of your vehicle, it could be critical.

---

relatively small geographic area. The computer lab at your school or the network serving the floor of the office building where you work is probably a LAN.

- **Wide area network (WAN)**: A WAN comprises large numbers of users over a wider physical area or separate LANs that are miles apart. Businesses often use WANs to connect two or more geographically distant locations. For example, a college might have a west and an east campus located in two different towns. The LAN at the west campus is connected to the LAN at the east campus, forming one WAN connected either by dedicated telecommunications lines or by satellite links. Students on both campuses can share data and collaborate through the WAN.

What other sort of networks do businesses use? An **intranet** is a private network set up by a business or an organization that's used exclusively by a select group of employees, customers, suppliers, volunteers, or supporters. It can facilitate information sharing, database access, group scheduling, videoconferencing, and other employee collaborations. An intranet isn't accessible by unauthorized individuals; a firewall protects it from unauthorized access through the Internet.

An area of an intranet that only certain corporations or individuals can access is called an **extranet**. The owner of an extranet decides who will be permitted to access it.

For example, a company's customers and suppliers may be permitted to access information on the company's extranet.

Extranets are useful for enabling **electronic data interchange (EDI)**, which allows the exchange of large amounts of business data (such as orders for merchandise) in a standardized electronic format. Walmart has an extranet that allows its employees, vendors, and contractors to easily share information. Other uses of extranets include providing access to catalogs and inventory databases and sharing information among partners or industry trade groups.

How is information kept secure on intranets and extranets? Intranets and extranets often use virtual private networks to keep information secure. A **virtual private network (VPN)** uses the public Internet communications infrastructure to build a secure, private network among various locations. Although WANs can be set up using private leased communications lines, these lines are expensive and tend to increase in price as the distance between points increases. VPNs use special security technologies and protocols that enhance security, enabling data to traverse the Internet as securely as if it were on a private leased line. Installing and configuring a VPN requires special hardware such as VPN-optimized routers and firewalls. In addition, VPN software must be installed on users' computing devices. However, there are many VPN providers (such as Barracuda Networks) that are now offering VPN services to

FIGURE 12.4 Local area networks (LANs) in different cities can communicate securely over the Internet using VPN technology.

businesses and individuals. This alleviates the aggravation and hassle of installing and maintaining VPN equipment.

How do VPNs work? The main technology for achieving a VPN is called **tunneling**. In tunneling, data packets are placed inside other data packets. The format of these external data packets is encrypted and can be understood only by the sending and receiving hardware, which is known as a *tunnel interface*. The hardware is optimized to seek efficient routes of transmission through the Internet. This provides a high level of security and makes information much more difficult to intercept and decrypt. Using a VPN is the equivalent of hiring a limousine and an armed guard to drive a package (your data) through a private tunnel directly to the destination (see Figure 12.4).

What are the key components of a client/server network? The key components of a client/server network are as follows:

- servers
- network topologies (the layout of the components)
- transmission media
- network adapters
- network navigation devices
- a network operating system

Figure 12.5 shows the components of a simple client/server network. In the following sections, we'll explore each component in more detail. ∎

FIGURE 12.5 The Basic Components of a Typical Client/Server Network

servers and
NETWORK TOPOLOGIES

Servers are the workhorses of the client/server network. They interface with many network users and assist them with a variety of tasks. The number and types of servers on a client/server network depend on the network's size and workload. Small networks (such as the one pictured in Figure 12.2 on page 495) would have just one server to handle all server functions. *Network topology* refers to the physical or logical arrangement of computers, transmission media (cables), and other network components. In the following sections, we'll explore the types of servers found in client/server networks and the typical topologies you may encounter.

Servers

Objective 12.4 *List the common types of servers found on client/server networks.*

What types of servers are found on larger client/server networks? A **dedicated server** is a server used to fulfill one specific function, such as handling e-mail. When more users are added to a network, dedicated servers are also added in order to reduce the load on the main server. Once dedicated servers are deployed, the original main server can become a dedicated server.

What functions do dedicated servers handle? Any task that's repetitive or demands a lot of time from a computer's processor (CPU) is a good candidate to relegate to a dedicated server. Common types of dedicated servers are authentication servers, file servers, print servers, application servers, database servers, e-mail servers, communications servers, web servers, and cloud servers. Servers are connected to a client/server network so that all client computers that need to use their services can access them, as shown in Figure 12.6.

FIGURE 12.6

Major Categories of Servers

Print Servers
Manage all printing jobs
for client computers

Application Servers
Serve as a repository for
application software

Database Servers
Provide client computers
with database access

Authentication Servers
Keep track of users logged
onto the network

File Servers
Store and manage
files for network users

E-Mail Servers
Process and deliver incoming
and outgoing e-mail

Communications Servers
Handle all communications
between the network and
other networks

Web/Cloud Servers
Host websites to make them
available through the Internet

(Naypong/Fotolia, Julien Eichinger/Fotolia, Maksym Yemelyanov/Fotolia, Maksim Kabakou/Fotolia, Felix Jork/Fotolia, TAex/Fotolia, AG Visuell/Fotolia, Mariusz Prusaczyk/Fotolia)

Authentication and File Servers

What are authentication and file servers? An **authentication server** is a server that keeps track of who is logging on to the network and which services on the network are available to each user. Authentication servers also act as overseers for the network. They manage and coordinate the services provided by all other dedicated servers located on the network.

A **file server** is a server that stores and manages files for network users. On the network at your workplace or school, you may be provided with space on a file server to store files you create.

Print Servers

How does a print server function? Print servers manage all client-requested printing jobs for all printers on a network, which helps client computers complete more productive work by relieving them of printing duties. When you tell your computer to print a document, it passes off the task to the print server. This frees the CPU on your computer to do other jobs.

How does the printer know which documents to print? A **print queue** (or *print spooler*) is a software holding area for print jobs. When the print server receives a printing request from a client computer, it puts the job into a print queue on the print server. Normally, each printer on a network has its own uniquely named print queue. Jobs receive a number when they enter the queue and go to the printer in the order in which they were received. Thus, print servers organize print jobs into an orderly sequence to make printing more efficient on a shared printer.

Another useful aspect of print servers is that network administrators can set them to prioritize print jobs. Different users and types of print jobs can be assigned different priorities so that higher-priority jobs will be printed first. For instance, in a company in which documents are printed on demand for clients, you would want those print jobs to take precedence over routine employee correspondence.

Application Servers

What function does an application server perform? In many networks, all users run the same application software on their computers. In a network of thousands of personal computers, installing application software on each computer is time-consuming. An **application server** acts as a repository for application software.

When a client computer connects to the network and requests an application, the application server delivers the software to the client computer. Because the software doesn't reside on the client computer itself, this eases the task of installation and upgrading. The application needs to be installed or upgraded only on the application server, not on each client computer.

Database Servers

What does a database server do? A **database server** provides client computers with access to information stored in databases. Often, many people need to access a database at the same time. For example, multiple college advisers can

serve students at the same time because the advisers all have access to the student information database. This is made possible because the database resides on a database server that each adviser's computer can access through the network. If the database were on a stand-alone computer instead of a network, only one adviser could use it at a time.

E-Mail Servers

How is e-mail handled on a large client/server network? The sole function of an **e-mail server** is to process and deliver incoming and outgoing e-mail. The volume of e-mail on a large network could quickly overwhelm a server that was attempting to handle other functions as well. On a network with an e-mail server, when you send or receive an e-mail, it goes through the e-mail server, which then handles the routing and delivery of your message.

Communications Servers

What types of communications does a communications server handle? A **communications server** handles all communications between the network and other networks, including managing Internet connectivity. All requests for information from the Internet and all messages being sent through the Internet pass through the communications server. Because Internet traffic is substantial at most organizations, the communications server has a heavy workload.

The communications server often is the only device on the network connected to the Internet. E-mail servers, web servers, and other devices needing to communicate with the Internet usually route all their traffic through the communications server. Providing a single point of contact with the outside world makes it easier to secure the network from hackers.

Web Servers and Cloud Servers

What function does a web server perform? A **web server** is used to host a website so that it will be available through the Internet. Web servers run specialized software such as Apache HTTP Server or Microsoft Internet Information Services (IIS) that enable them to host web pages. Not every large network has a web server; many businesses use a third-party web-hosting company to host their websites instead.

What is a cloud server? Servers no longer need to be physically located at a company's offices. **Cloud servers** are servers that are maintained by hosting companies, such as Rackspace Hosting, and are connected to networks via the Internet. A company could choose to have any of the server types discussed previously hosted on cloud servers instead of maintaining them locally. Small businesses that don't have a large staff of computer professionals often choose to use cloud servers to save money.

Servers have historically been deployed on client/server networks as dedicated machines that perform one specific task. But today there are good reasons why some businesses may consider having servers perform multiple tasks.

Computers produce a lot of heat and take up physical space. As a company grows, continually adding servers may exceed the available floor space and cooling capacity of a company's data center. And budgets may limit a company's ability to purchase additional dedicated servers when needed.

Dedicated servers are mission critical when those servers handle processor-intensive operations. For instance, a major online retailer would have dedicated web servers handling e-commerce traffic so that customers could purchase items quickly and efficiently. But small businesses don't necessarily require the computing power of a dedicated server for all of their computing needs. In addition, today's powerful multi-core processors allow computers to process data more quickly and efficiently than single-core machines. Sometimes just dedicating a computer to one task, such as an authentication server, might not come close to fully utilizing that server's computing potential. For all of these reasons, *virtualization* was born.

Virtualization involves using specialized software to make individual physical servers behave as though they are more than one physical device (see Figure 12.7). Each virtual server can operate as a separate device and can even run its own operating system (OS). Therefore, you could have a virtual e-mail server running Windows and a virtual web server running Linux on the same physical server.

Creating virtual servers requires running specialized virtualization software on a physical server. The physical server then becomes known as the *host*. Virtual servers running on a host machine are known as *guest servers*. The computing power of the CPU is split between the guests running on the host. Therefore, it wouldn't be practical to run dozens of guest environments on one host because the computing power would become diluted. However, it's very possible to run two or three guest servers on one multi-processor physical server as long as the applications running on the virtual servers aren't overly processor intensive. VMware's vSphere, Microsoft's Hyper-V Server, and XenServer are popular virtualization software packages.

Virtualization is a great way to provide backup servers at a low cost. Mission-critical servers, such as web servers, need to be running and available to customers at all times. If a web server for an e-commerce business fails, the company is unable to sell products until the server is repaired. With virtual servers, you could have a copy of your web server running virtually on two separate physical machines (such as servers 1 and 2). If server 1 breaks, you could immediately have the virtual copy of your web server on physical server 2 take over, and the company could still be processing orders and conducting business.

Although virtualization isn't the perfect solution for every business situation, it does offer intriguing possibilities and effective solutions for specific needs. Even small companies today are actively exploring virtualization as a way to extend their computing resources and save money.

FIGURE 12.7 Virtualization software allows one physical server to appear to be multiple separate servers capable of handling three different processes.

Network Topologies

Objective 12.5 *Describe the common types of network topologies and the advantages and disadvantages of each one.*

Just as buildings have different floor plans depending on their uses, networks have different layouts according to their purpose. As noted above, **network topology** refers to the physical or logical arrangement of computers, transmission media (cables), and other network components. *Physical topology* refers to the layout of the "real" components of the network, whereas *logical topology* refers to the virtual connections among network nodes. Logical topologies usually are determined by network protocols instead of the physical layout of the network or the paths that electrical signals follow on the network.

What are network protocols? A **protocol** is a set of rules for exchanging communications. Although many people think that Ethernet is a type of network topology, it's actually a communications protocol. Therefore, an Ethernet network could be set up using almost any type of physical topology.

In this section, we'll explore the most common network topologies (bus, ring, and star) and discuss when each topology is used. The type of network topology used is important because it can affect a network's performance and scalability. Knowing how the basic topologies work—and knowing the strengths and weaknesses of each one—will help you understand why particular network topologies were chosen on the networks you use.

Bus Topology

What does a bus topology look like? In a **bus** (or **linear bus**) **topology**, all computers are connected in sequence on a single cable, as shown in Figure 12.8. This topology has largely become legacy technology because star topologies are more efficient on Ethernet networks, and a bus topology isn't designed to easily support wireless connections. However, bus topologies are still found in some manufacturing facilities where groups of computer-controlled machines are connected.

Each computer on the bus network can communicate directly with every other computer on the network. **Data collisions**, which happen when two computers send data at the same time and the sets of data collide somewhere in the connection media, are a problem on all networks. When data collides, it's often lost or damaged. A limitation of bus networks is that data collisions can occur fairly easily because a bus network is essentially composed of one main communication medium (a single cable).

Because two signals transmitted at the same time on a bus network may cause a data collision, an **access method** has to be established to control which computer is allowed to use the transmission media at a certain time. Computers on a bus network behave like a group of people having a conversation. The computers "listen" to the network data traffic on the media. When no other computer is transmitting data (that is, when the "conversation" stops), the computer knows it's allowed to transmit data. This means of taking turns "talking" prevents data collisions.

A cable break here cuts off Computer #1 and Computer #2 from the rest of the network.

Computer #1

Terminator

Computer #2

Laser printer

Computer #3

Computer #4

Terminator

FIGURE 12.8 In a linear bus topology, all computers are connected in a sequence.

How does data get from point to point on a bus network? The data is broadcast throughout the network via the media to all devices connected to the network. The data is broken into small segments, each called a *packet*. Each packet contains the address of the computer or peripheral device to which it's being sent. Each computer or device connected to the network listens for data that contains its address. When it "hears" data addressed to it, it takes the data off the media and processes it.

The devices (nodes) attached to a bus network do nothing to move data along the network. This makes a bus network a **passive topology**. The data travels the entire length of the medium and is received by all network devices. The ends of the cable in a bus network are capped off by terminators (as shown in Figure 12.8). A **terminator** is a device that absorbs a signal so that it's not reflected back onto parts of the network that have already received it.

What are the advantages and disadvantages of bus networks? The simplicity and low cost of bus network topology are its key advantages. As shown in Figure 12.8, the major disadvantage is that if there is a break in the cable, the bus network is effectively disrupted because some computers are cut off from others on the network. Also, because only one computer can communicate at a time, adding a large number of nodes to a bus network limits performance and causes delays in sending data.

Ring Topology

What does a ring topology look like? Not surprisingly, given its name, the computers and peripherals in a **ring** (or **loop**) **topology** are laid out in a configuration resembling a circle, as shown in Figure 12.9. Data flows around the circle from device to device in one direction only. Because data is passed using a special data packet called a **token**, this type of topology was once commonly called a *token-ring topology*.

How does a token move data around a ring? A token is passed from computer to computer around the ring until it's grabbed by a computer that needs to transmit data. The computer "holds" on to the token until it has finished transmitting data. Only one computer on the ring can "hold" the token at a time, and usually only one token exists on each ring.

STEP 1: The token travels around the ring until a computer needs to transmit data.

STEP 2: Computer #2 needs to print and grabs the token.

STEP 3: Computer #2 completes the transmission and releases the token.

STEP 4: A cable break stops movement of the token and data transmission.

Computer #1

Computer #4

Computer #2

Computer #3

Token Ring

Printer

FIGURE 12.9 A ring topology provides a fair allocation of resources.

If a node has data to send, such as a document that needs to go to the printer, it waits for the token to be passed to it. The node then takes the token out of circulation and sends the data to its destination. When the receiving node receives a complete transmission of the data (in this example, when the document is received by the printer), it transmits an acknowledgment to the sending node. The sending node then generates a new token and starts it going around the ring again. This is called the **token method** and is the access method that ring networks use to avoid data collisions.

A ring topology is an **active topology**, which means that nodes participate in moving data through the network. Each node on the network is responsible for retransmitting the token or the data to the next node on the ring. Large ring networks have the capability to use multiple tokens to help move data faster.

What are the advantages and disadvantages of a ring topology? A ring topology provides a fairer allocation of network resources than does a bus topology. By using a token, a ring network enables all nodes on the network to have an equal chance to send data. One "chatty" node can't monopolize the network bandwidth as easily as in a bus topology because it must pass the token on after sending a batch of data. In addition, a ring topology's performance remains acceptable even with large numbers of users.

As shown in Figure 12.9, one disadvantage of a ring network is that if one computer fails, the entire network can come to a halt because the failed computer is unavailable to retransmit tokens and data. Another disadvantage is that problems in the ring can be hard for network administrators to find. It's easier to expand a ring topology than a bus topology, but adding a node to a ring causes the ring to cease to function while the node is being installed.

Star Topology

What is the layout for a star topology? A **star topology** is the most widely deployed client/server network topology because it offers the most flexibility for a low price. In a star topology, the nodes connect to a central communications device called a *switch* in a pattern resembling a star, as shown in Figure 12.10. The switch receives a signal from the sending node and retransmits it to the node on the network that needs to receive the signal. Each network node picks up only the transmissions addressed to it. Because the

A cable break here means Computer #1 cannot communicate with the network. However, all other computers and devices can still communicate with each other.

FIGURE 12.10 In a star topology, network nodes are connected through a central switch.

switch retransmits data signals, a star topology is an active topology. The only drawback is that if the switch fails, the network no longer functions. However, it's relatively easy to replace a switch.

How do computers on a star network avoid data collisions?

Because most star networks are Ethernet networks, they use the method used on all Ethernet networks to avoid data collisions: **CSMA/CD** (short for *carrier sense multiple access with collision detection*). With CSMA/CD, a node connected to the network uses carrier sense (that is, it "listens") to verify that no other nodes are currently transmitting data signals. If the node doesn't hear any other signals, it assumes that it's safe to transmit data. All devices on the network have the same right (that is, they have multiple access) to transmit data when they deem it safe. It's therefore possible for two devices to begin transmitting data signals at the same time. If this happens, the two signals collide.

What happens when the signals collide?

As shown in Figure 12.11, when two nodes (#1 and #2) begin transmitting data signals at the same time (Step 1), signals collide, and a node on the network (#3) detects the collision. Node #3 then sends a special signal called a **jam signal** to all network nodes, alerting them that a collision has occurred (Step 2). The original nodes #1 and #2 then stop transmitting and wait a random amount of time before retransmitting their data signals (Step 3). The wait times need to be random; otherwise, both nodes would start retransmitting at the same time and another collision would occur.

What are the advantages and disadvantages of a star topology?

The major advantages of a star network are as follows:

- The failure of one computer doesn't affect the rest of the network. This is extremely important in a large network, where having one disabled computer affect the operations of several hundred other computers would be unacceptable.
- It's easy to add nodes to star networks.
- Performance remains acceptable even with large numbers of nodes.
- Centralizing communications through a switch makes troubleshooting and repairs easier. Technicians can usually pinpoint a communications problem just by examining the switch, as opposed to searching for a particular length of cable that has broken in a ring network.

FIGURE 12.11 Jam signals are used to handle data collisions on an Ethernet network.

FIGURE 12.12

Advantages and Disadvantages of Bus, Ring, and Star Topologies

TOPOLOGY	ADVANTAGES	DISADVANTAGES
Bus	• Uses a minimal amount of cable. • Installation is easy, reliable, and inexpensive.	• Breaks in the cable can disable the network. • Large numbers of users decrease performance because of high volumes of data traffic.
Ring	• Allocates access to the network fairly. • Performance remains acceptable even with many users.	• Adding/removing nodes disables the network. • Failure of one node can bring down the network. • Problems in data transmission can be difficult to find.
Star	• Failure of one node doesn't affect other nodes on the network. • Centralized design simplifies troubleshooting and repairs. • High scalability: Adding computers is easy. • Performance remains acceptable even with many users.	• Requires more cable (and possibly higher installation costs) than a bus or ring topology. • The switch is a single point of failure; if it fails, all computers connected to it are affected.

The disadvantage of star networks used to be cost. Because of the complexity of the layout of star networks, they require more cable and used to be more expensive than bus or ring networks. However, the price of cable has fallen and wireless nodes are replacing many wired nodes on networks, removing cost as a barrier in most cases.

Comparing Topologies

Which topology is the best one? Figure 12.12 lists the advantages and disadvantages of bus, ring, and star topologies. Star topologies are the most common, mainly because large networks are constantly adding new users. The ability to add new users easily—by installing an additional switch—without affecting users already on the network is the deciding factor. Bus topologies have become all but extinct now that most home networks utilize a star topology. Ring topologies are still popular in certain businesses where fair allocation of network access is a major requirement of the network.

Can topologies be combined within a single network? Because each topology has its own unique advantages, topologies are often combined to construct business networks. Combining multiple topologies into one network is known as constructing a **hybrid topology**. For instance, fair allocation of resources may be critical for reservation clerks at an airline (thereby requiring a ring network), but the airline's purchasing department may require a star topology. ■

Before moving on to Part 2:
1. **Watch Replay Video 12.1** ↻ .
2. **Then check your understanding of what you've learned so far.**

check your understanding // review & practice

For a quick review to see what you've learned so far, answer the following questions.

multiple choice

1. Which of the following is not an advantage of installing a network in a business?

   a. enables peripheral sharing

   b. enables software sharing

   c. decentralization of files and data

   d. centralization of files and data

2. Why are client/server networks usually installed in businesses?

   a. Security is weaker on client/server networks.

   b. They do not require dedicated servers like P2P networks.

   c. They are more scalable than P2P networks.

   d. Client/server networks are cheaper to install.

3. To manage authorized connections to external networks, which server would a client/server network include?

   a. database

   b. authentication

   c. communications

   d. application

4. Which type of network topology is most popular?

   a. bus

   b. Ethernet

   c. ring

   d. star

5. A network consisting of two LANs separated by great physical distances is known as a

   a. HAN

   b. WAN

   c. SAN

   d. LAN

 Go to **MyITLab** to take an autograded version of the *Check Your Understanding* review and to find all media resources for the chapter.

TECHBYTES WEEKLY

Stay current with the TechBytes Weekly Newsletter.

Continue >>

TRY THIS

Sharing Folders on a Home Network Using Windows

Creating a HomeGroup in Windows lets you share folders, files, and devices (such as printers) with all computers on a network that belong to that HomeGroup. When you set up a Windows 10, Windows 8, or Windows 7 computer, you're asked to create a HomeGroup and are provided with instructions for having other Windows computers join that HomeGroup. In this tutorial, you'll learn how to share a folder from a Windows 10 machine.

Step 1 Ensure that all the computers on your network are members of the same HomeGroup. (Note: Only Windows 7, 8, and 10 support HomeGroups.) To check if a Windows 10 computer is in a HomeGroup, launch Control Panel, click the **Network and Internet link**, then click the **HomeGroup link**. If you see a screen like the one here, your computer is in a HomeGroup. Note: You may or may not see messages like the one shown here indicating devices found on your home network. To add other computers to the same HomeGroup, click the **View or print the homegroup password link** to display the HomeGroup password. Write it down and use it to have your other computers join the HomeGroup. *(Windows 10, Microsoft Corporation)*

Step 2 Open File Explorer, navigate to the folder you wish to share with your HomeGroup, and left-click to select it. On the File Explorer ribbon, click the **Share tab**, and then select either **Homegroup (view)** or **Homegroup (view and edit)** to share the folder with your HomeGroup. The Homegroup (view) option only allows other members of the HomeGroup the ability to see and open the files in the folder. The Homegroup (view and edit) option gives other members of the HomeGroup the ability to add or delete files from the folder.

(Windows 10, Microsoft Corporation)

Step 3 Launch File Explorer on another computer in the HomeGroup (a Windows 8 computer is shown here). Under Network in the Navigation pane, find the name of the computer on which you shared the folder. Navigate through the directory structure until you find the shared folder. You should now have access to the files.

(Windows 10, Microsoft Corporation)

Make This > TOOL: AI Sharing

MAKE: An App That Shares

Want to share something you have created in an app with others?

In this exercise, you'll continue your mobile app development by using the Sharing component of the Social drawer in **App Inventor** to share information. This component will pull up a list of all the applications on your device that can share a file. Make your work part of a larger community by sharing it! *(MIT App Inventor 2)*

Use the Sharing component to fire up all the ways your users can exchange information.

For the instructions for this exercise, go to MyITLab.

Setting Up Business Networks

Learning Outcome 12.2 You will be able to describe transmission media, network operating system software, and network navigation devices and explain major threats to network security and how to mitigate them.

Setting up business networks is similar to configuring home networks. You need to consider the type of transmission media, ensure all nodes have network adapters, and install the appropriate network communication devices.

transmission
MEDIA

You may only have wireless transmission media in your home network. But businesses have different needs than home users. Let's start by looking at the transmission media used in business networks.

Wired and Wireless Transmission Media

Objective 12.6 *Describe the types of wired and wireless transmission media used in networks.*

What exactly do we mean by transmission media? Transmission media, whether for wired or wireless communications technology, comprise the physical system that data takes to flow between devices on the network. Without transmission media, network devices would be unable to communicate. Most corporate networks contain a combination of wired and wireless media.

Why are wired connections used in business networks? Wired connections are popular in business networks because they generally provide higher throughput and better security than wireless connections. Desktop computers still provide more computing power for less money than laptops, which makes desktop computers popular choices for business networks. Because desktops aren't often moved around, they're usually connected to a network with a wired connection.

What are the important factors in choosing a cable type? For business networks, the three main cable types that are used are *twisted-pair*, *coaxial*, and *fiber-optic*. Although each cable type is different, the same six factors always need to be considered when choosing a cable type (see Figure 12.13): maximum run length, bandwidth, flexibility (bend radius), cable cost, installation cost, and interference.

What causes interference with data signals? Signals traveling down a cable are subject to two types of interference:

1. *Electromagnetic interference (EMI)*, which is caused when the cable is exposed to strong electromagnetic fields, can distort or degrade signals on the cable. Fluorescent lights

FIGURE 12.13

Factors to Consider When Choosing Network Cable

Maximum run length
- How far a cable can run before data signal degrades
- Distance between nodes determines run length needed

Bandwidth
- Amount of data transmitted across medium
- Measured in bits per second (BPS)

Flexibility (bend radius)
- How much a cable can be bent before it is damaged
- Lots of corners? Need cable with a high bend radius.

Cable cost
- Cost is different for each cable type
- Budget may limit choice of cable type

Installation cost
- Twisted-pair and coaxial cable are inexpensive to install (low $)
- Fiber-optic cable requires special training and equipment (high $)

Interference
- Twisted-pair most susceptible to interference
- Fiber-optic immune to interference

(Maridav/Fotolia, Victoria/Fotolia, Nicholas Piccillo/Fotolia, Ion Popa/Fotolia, Auremar/Fotolia, Ermess/Fotolia)

FIGURE 12.14 Anatomy of (a) unshielded twisted-pair (UTP) cable and (b) shielded twisted-pair (STP) cable.

and machinery with motors or transformers are the most common sources of EMI emissions.

2. Cable signals also can be disrupted by *radio frequency interference (RFI)*, which is usually caused by broadcast sources (TV and radio signals) located near the network.

Both coaxial cable and twisted-pair cable send electrical impulses down conductive material to transmit data signals, making them more subject to interference. Fiber-optic cable transmits data signals as pulses of light. Because EMI and RFI don't affect light waves, fiber-optic cable is virtually immune to interference.

In the sections that follow, we'll discuss the characteristics of each of the three major types of cable. We'll also discuss the use of wireless media as an alternative to cable.

Twisted-Pair Cable

Why are the wires in twisted-pair cable twisted? **Twisted-pair cable** consists of pairs of copper wires twisted around each other and covered by a protective sheath (jacket). The twists are important because they cause the magnetic fields that form around the copper wires to intermingle, making them less susceptible to outside interference. The twists also reduce the amount of crosstalk interference (the tendency of signals on one wire to interfere with signals on a wire next to it).

If the twisted-pair cable contains a layer of foil shielding to reduce interference, it's called **shielded twisted-pair (STP) cable**. Most home networks use unshielded twisted-pair (UTP) cable that doesn't have the foil shielding. UTP cable is more susceptible to interference than STP cable. Figure 12.14 shows illustrations of both types of twisted-pair cable. Because of its lower price, UTP is used in business networks unless significant sources of interference must be overcome, such as in a production environment where machines create magnetic fields.

Coaxial Cable

Is coaxial cable still used in business networks? Although not as popular as it once was, coaxial cable is still used in some manufacturing facilities where machinery creates

FIGURE 12.15 Coaxial cable consists of four main components: a core, an insulated covering, a braided metal shielding, and a plastic jacket.

heavy electrical interference. **Coaxial cable** (as shown in Figure 12.15) consists of four main components:

1. A core (usually copper) is in the very center and is used for transmitting the signal.
2. A solid layer of nonconductive insulating material (usually a hard, thick plastic) surrounds the core.
3. A layer of braided metal shielding covers the insulation to reduce interference with signals traveling in the core.
4. An external jacket of lightweight plastic covers the internal cable components to protect them from damage.

Fiber-Optic Cable

What does fiber-optic cable look like? As shown in Figure 12.16, **fiber-optic cable** is composed of the following:

- A glass (or plastic) fiber (or a bundle of fibers called a core) through which the data is transmitted
- A protective layer of glass or plastic cladding is wrapped around the core to protect it
- For additional protection, it has an outer jacket (sheath), which is often made of a durable material such as Kevlar (the substance used to make bulletproof vests)

Data transmissions can pass through fiber-optic cable in only one direction. Therefore, at least two fibers (or cores) are contained in most fiber-optic cables to enable transmission of data in both directions.

FIGURE 12.16 Fiber-optic cable is made up of a glass or plastic fiber (or a bundle of fibers), a glass or plastic cladding, and a protective sheath.

BITS&BYTES

Go Green with Mobile Apps

Many people want to support green initiatives and sustainability. The U.S. Environmental Protection Agency (EPA) hosts the My Green Apps website (**epa.gov/mygreenapps**) to make it easier to find useful apps that support green lifestyles (see Figure 12.17). The site currently lists almost 300 existing apps that can help individuals or groups switch to a greener lifestyle or track progress in daily green living activities.

If you can't locate an app that meets your needs, you can review ideas submitted by previous visitors to the website. For even more ideas, you can visit Eco Libris' green apps website at **ecolibris.net/greenapps.asp**. Eco Libris maintains a list of their top 100 apps, all of which are free or cost less than $2. So visit one of these sites today and find an app to help you live greener.

FIGURE 12.17 The EPA's My Green Apps website provides information about apps that help you go green. *(EPA's My Green Apps website, United States Environmental Protection Agency, http://epa.gov/greenapps/.)*

Wireless Media Options

What wireless media options are there? Most business networks use the same Ethernet standards as home networks. Therefore, the wireless options for business networks are very similar to those available for home networks. *Wireless access points* are installed to provide coverage wherever employees will be working with portable devices, such as in conference rooms.

Comparing Transmission Media

Which medium is best for business networks? Network engineers specialize in the design and deployment of networks and are responsible for selecting the appropriate network topologies and media types. Their decision as to which transmission medium a network will use is based on the topology selected, the length of the cable runs needed, the amount of interference present, and the need for wireless connectivity.

As noted above, most large networks use a mix of media types. For example, fiber-optic cable may be appropriate for the portion of a network that traverses the factory floor, where interference from magnetic fields is significant. However, UTP cable may work fine in a general office area. Wireless media may be required in areas where employees are likely to connect their portable computing devices or where it's impractical or expensive to run cable. ∎

network adapters and
NAVIGATION DEVICES

As mentioned earlier, data flows through the network in packets. Data packets are like postal letters. They don't get to their destinations without some help. In this section, we explore the various conventions and devices that help speed data packets on their way through the network.

Network Adapters

Objective 12.7 *Describe how network adapters help data move around a network.*

What is a network adapter? As noted in Chapter 7, client and server computers and peripherals need an interface to connect with and communicate on the network. **Network adapters** are devices that perform specific tasks to enable nodes to communicate on a network. Network adapters are installed inside computers and peripherals. These adapters are referred to as *network interface cards (NICs)*.

What do network adapters do? Network adapters perform three critical functions:

1. **They generate high-powered signals to enable network transmissions.** Digital signals generated inside the computer are fairly low powered and would not travel well on cable or wireless network media without network adapters. Network adapters convert the signals from inside the computer into higher-powered signals that have no trouble traversing the network media.

2. **They're responsible for breaking the data into packets and transmitting and receiving data.** They also are responsible for receiving incoming data packets and, in accordance with networking protocols, reconstructing them, as shown in Figure 12.18.

3. **They act as gatekeepers for information flowing to and from the client computer.** Much like a security guard in a gated community, a network adapter is responsible for permitting or denying access to the client computer (the community) and controlling the flow of data (visitors).

You should note that there won't always be the same number of response packets as there are request packets. The number of packets depends on the volume of the data being sent. A simple response may have less data than a complex one.

Are there different types of network adapters?
Although there are different types of network adapters, almost without exception Ethernet is the standard communications protocol used on most client/server networks. Therefore, the adapter cards that ship with computers today are Ethernet compliant.

Do wireless networks require network adapters?
A computing device that connects to a network using wireless access needs to have a special network adapter card, called a **wireless network interface card (wireless NIC)**, installed in it. Laptop computers and other portable computing devices contain wireless NICs.

STEP 1: You request information from the network database.

STEP 2: The NIC breaks the request into packets and sends the packets to the server.

Request packet #1

Request packet #2

Request packet #3

Response packet #1

Response packet #2

Server

Network interface card (NIC)

Your computer (client)

STEP 4: The NIC reassembles the response packets and displays information on your screen.

STEP 3: The server executes the request, assembles the response into packets, and sends the packets to the client.

FIGURE 12.18 A network interface card (NIC) is responsible for breaking down data into packets, preparing packets for transmission, receiving incoming data packets, and reconstructing them.

Desktop computer

Cat 6 cable

Laptop computer with wireless NIC

Switch

Smartphone with wireless NIC

Radio waves

Wireless access point

Server

FIGURE 12.19 This small business network has an added wireless access point.

Are MAC addresses the same as IP addresses? MAC addresses and IP (Internet Protocol) addresses are not the same thing. A MAC address is used for identification purposes *internally* on a network. An IP address is the address *external* entities use to communicate with your network. Think of it this way: The postal carrier delivers a package (data packet) to your dorm building based on its street address (IP address). The dorm's mail clerk delivers the package to your room because it has your name on it (MAC address) and not that of your neighbor. Both pieces of information are necessary to ensure that the package (or data) reaches its destination.

How are data packets packaged for transmission? Data packets aren't necessarily sent alone. Sometimes groups of data packets are sent together in a package called a **frame**. A frame is a container that can hold multiple data packets. This is similar to placing several letters going to the same postal address in a big envelope. While the data packets are being assembled into frames, the network operating system (NOS) software assigns the appropriate MAC address to the frame. The NOS keeps track of all devices and their addresses on the network. Much like an envelope that's entrusted to the postal service, the frame is delivered to the MAC address that the NOS assigned to the frame.

What delivers the frames to the correct device on the network? In a small bus network, frames just bounce along the transmission medium until the correct client computer notices that the frame is addressed to it and pulls the signal off the medium. However, this is inefficient in a larger network. Therefore, many types of devices have been developed to deliver data to its destination efficiently. These devices are designed to route signals and exchange data with other networks.

Are MAC addresses useful for anything besides identifying a particular network device? On networks with wireless capabilities, MAC addresses can be used to enhance network security. Because each MAC address is unique, you can input a list of authorized MAC addresses into the router. If someone who is using an unauthorized network adapter attempts to connect to the network, he or she will be unable to make a connection.

To allow wireless connections, a network also must be fitted with devices called wireless access points. A **wireless access point (WAP)** gives wireless devices a sending and receiving connection point to the network.

Figure 12.19 shows an example of a typical small business network with a wireless access point. The access point is connected to the wired network through a conventional cable. When a laptop or other device with a wireless NIC is powered on near a wireless access point, it establishes a connection with the access point using radio waves. Many devices can communicate with the network through a single wireless access point.

Do network adapters require software? Special communications software called a **device driver** is installed on all client computers in the client/server network. Device drivers enable the network adapter to communicate with the server's OS and with the OS of the computer in which the adapter is installed.

MAC Addresses

Objective 12.8 *Define MAC addresses, and explain how they are used to move data around a network.*

How do network adapters know where to send data packets? Each network adapter has a physical address, similar to a serial number on an appliance. This address is called a **media access control (MAC) address**, and it's made up of 6 two-position characters, such as 01:40:87:44:79:A5. (Don't confuse this MAC with the Apple computers of the same name.) The first three sets of characters (in this case, 01:40:87) specify the manufacturer of the network adapter, and the second set of characters (in this case, 44:79:A5) makes up a unique address. Because all MAC addresses must be unique, there is an IEEE (Institute of Electrical and Electronics Engineers) committee responsible for allocating blocks of numbers to network adapter manufacturers.

Switches, Bridges, and Routers

Objective 12.9 *List the various network navigation devices, and explain how they help route data through networks.*

Which devices are used to route signals through a single network? Switches are used to send data on a specific route through the network. A **switch** makes decisions, based on the MAC address of the data, as to where the data is to be sent and rebroadcasts it to the appropriate network node. This improves network efficiency by helping ensure that each node receives only the data intended for it. Figure 12.20 shows a switch being used to rebroadcast a message.

Do all Ethernet networks need a switch?
Switches are needed on Ethernet networks whether they are installed in a home or a business. (Routers sold for home use have switches built in to them.)

Are switches sufficient for moving data efficiently across all sizes of networks?
When a corporate network grows in size, performance can decline because many devices compete for transmission time on the network media. To solve this problem, a network can be broken into multiple segments known as *collision domains*. A **bridge** is a device that's used to send data between different collision domains, depending on where the recipient device is located, as indicated in Figure 12.21. Signals received by the bridge from Collision Domain A are forwarded to Collision Domain B only if the destination computer is located in that domain. (Note that most home networks contain only one segment and therefore do not require bridges.)

What device does a network use to move data to another network?
Whereas switches and bridges perform their functions within a single network, as you learned in

Chapter 7, a **router** is designed to send information between two networks. To accomplish this, the router must look at higher-level network addresses (such as IP addresses), not MAC addresses. When the router notices data with an address that doesn't belong to a device on the network from which it originated, it sends the data to another network to which it is attached or out to the Internet. ■

FIGURE 12.20 Switches rebroadcast messages—but only to the devices to which the messages are addressed.

Message for Computer #3

Switch

Computer #1

Server

Rebroadcast of message for Computer #3

Computer #2

Computer #3

Bridge

Collision Domain A

Collision Domain B

Signal to Computer #2 not passed on to Collision Domain B

Signal to Computer #4

Switch

Signal to Computer #2

Signal to Computer #4 must be passed to Collision Domain B

Signal to Computer #4

Switch

Wireless connection

Signal to Computer #4

Signal to Computer #4

Computer #1

Computer #2

Computer #3

Computer #4

FIGURE 12.21 Bridges are devices used to send data between different network collision domains.

network operating systems and
NETWORK SECURITY

Networks need specialized software so that the devices attached to it can communicate with each other. Business networks need even more security than home networks to protect them from hackers. In this section, we'll explore the software that allows networks to function and discuss security measures that help keep networks safe from prying eyes.

Network Operating Systems

Objective 12.10 *Explain why network operating systems are necessary for networks to function.*

What is a network operating system? Merely using media to connect computers and peripherals does not create a client/server network. Special software known as a **network operating system (NOS)** needs to be installed on each client computer and server that's connected to the network to provide the services necessary for them to communicate. The NOS provides a set of common rules (a *protocol*) that controls communication among devices on the network. Modern operating systems, such as Windows and OS X, include NOS client software as part of the basic installation. However, large networks, such as those found in businesses, require more sophisticated NOS server software.

Why is an NOS needed on large networks? OS software is designed to facilitate communication between the software and hardware components of your computer. NOS software is specifically designed to provide server services, network communications, management of network peripherals, and storage. Popular server software includes Windows Server, Red Hat Enterprise Linux, and SUSE Linux Enterprise Server. NOS software is installed on servers.

To provide network communications, the client computers must run a small part of the NOS in addition to their OS. Windows and OS X contain network communication capabilities; therefore, no other NOS software is usually installed on these client computers.

Do P2P networks need special NOS software? The software that P2P networks require is built into the Windows, Linux, and Macintosh operating systems. So if you have a simple P2P network, there is no need to purchase specialized NOS software.

How does the NOS control network communications? Each NOS has its own proprietary communications language, file-management structure, and device-management structure. The NOS also sets and controls the protocols for all devices wishing to communicate on the network. Proprietary protocols from one vendor's NOS won't work with another vendor's NOS.

However, because the Internet uses an open protocol (called TCP/IP) for communications, most all corporate networks use TCP/IP as their standard networking protocol regardless of the manufacturer of their NOS. All modern NOSs support TCP/IP.

BITS&BYTES

Forget Software as a Service—Lighting as a Service Can Really Save Money

Software as a service (SaaS) is the model of software delivery that is really taking over the industry. But with the Internet of Things (having devices constantly connected to the Internet) picking up momentum, we can use this model to deliver other services efficiently.

Consider smarthomes, which have devices connected through networks to the Internet to control lighting, environmental factors (such as heating and cooling), video surveillance, and door locks. Lighting is estimated to account for 25% of world electricity usage. So how can smart lighting devices be used to help reduce costs?

Enter Lighting as a Service (LaaS). In this approach, energy-efficient light fixtures with integrated motion detectors are installed in your home to detect whether a room is occupied. Light sensors can also be installed to detect when there is adequate sunlight in an area and therefore no artificial light is needed. Lighting is then provided as a service only when required. Why keep the lights on in a room if there is no one in it? It's estimated that LaaS could cut lighting-related electricity usage by up to 90%. Now that's a smart home.

Can a network use two different NOSs? Many large corporate networks use several different NOSs at the same time. This is because different NOSs provide different features, some of which are more useful in certain situations than others. For instance, although the employees of a corporation may be using a Windows environment for their desktops and e-mail, the file servers and web servers may be running a Linux-based NOS.

Client/Server Network Security

Objective 12.11 *List major security threats to networks, and explain how network administrators mitigate these threats.*

What sources of security threats do all network administrators need to watch for? A major advantage that client/server networks have over P2P networks is that they offer a higher level of security. With client/server networks, users can be required to enter a user ID and a password to gain access to the network. The security can be centrally administered by network administrators, freeing individual users of the responsibility of maintaining their own data security, as they must do on a P2P network. Still, client/server networks are vulnerable to threats. These threats can be classified into three main groups:

1. *Human errors and mistakes:* Everyone makes mistakes. For example, a member of the computer support staff could mistakenly install an old database on top of the current one. Even physical accidents fall into this category; for example, someone could lose control of a car and drive it through the wall of the main data center.
2. *Malicious human activity:* Malicious actions can be perpetrated by current employees, former employees, or third parties. For example, a disgruntled employee could introduce a virus to the network, or a hacker could break into the student database server to steal credit card records.
3. *Natural events and disasters:* Some events—such as floods and fires—are beyond human control. All can lead to the inadvertent destruction of data.

Because networks are vulnerable to such security threats, one of the network administrator's key functions is to keep network data secure. Let's explore the challenges network administrators face in keeping a client/server network secure.

Authentication

How do network administrators ensure that only authorized users access the network? Authentication is the process whereby users prove they have authorization to use a computer network. For example, correctly entering the user ID and password on your college network proves to the network that you have authorized access. The access is authorized because the ID was generated by a network administrator when you became an authorized user of the network.

However, authentication can also be achieved through the use of biometric devices (discussed later in this chapter) and through possessed objects. A **possessed object** is any object that users carry to identify themselves and that grants them access to a computer system or computer facility. Examples include identification badges, magnetic key cards, and smart keys (similar to flash drives).

Can hackers use my account to log in to the network? If a hacker knows your user ID and password, he or she can log in and impersonate you. Impersonation can also happen if you fail to log out of a terminal on a network and someone comes along and uses your account. Sometimes network user IDs are easy to figure out because they have a certain pattern, such as your last name and the first initial of your first name.

If a hacker can deduce your user ID, he or she might use a software program that tries millions of combinations of letters and numbers as your password in an attempt to access your account. Attempting to access an account by repeatedly trying different passwords is known as a **brute force attack**. To prevent these attacks from succeeding, network administrators often configure accounts so that they'll disable themselves after a set number of login attempts using invalid passwords have been made.

Access Privileges

How can I gain access to everything on a network? The simple answer is that you can't! When your account is set up on a network, certain access privileges are granted to indicate which systems you're allowed to use. For example, on your college network, your access privileges probably include the ability to access the Internet. However, you definitely weren't granted access to the grade-entering system, because this would enable you to change your grades.

How does restricting access privileges protect a network? Because network-access accounts are centrally administered on the authentication server, it's easy for the network administrator to set up accounts for new users and grant them access only to the systems and software they need. The centralized nature of the network-access creation and the ability to restrict access to certain areas of the network make a client/server network more secure than a P2P network.

Aside from improper access, how else do data theft and destruction occur? A major problem that portable devices such as flash drives pose is theft of data or intellectual property. Because these devices are so easy to conceal and have such large memory capacity, it's easy for a disgruntled employee to walk out the front door with stacks of valuable documents tucked in his or her pocket. Industrial espionage has never been easier—and no spy cameras are needed!

Flash drives can also introduce viruses or other malicious programs to a network, either intentionally or unintentionally. Secure Network Technologies, a security consulting firm, decided to test a client's security procedures by leaving

DIG DEEPER

The OSI Model: Defining Protocol Standards

The Institute of Electrical and Electronics Engineers (IEEE) has taken the lead in establishing worldwide networking protocols, including a standard of communications called the **Open Systems Interconnection (OSI)** reference model. The OSI model, which has been adopted throughout the computing world, provides the protocol guidelines for all modern networks. All modern network operating system (NOS) protocols are designed to interact in accordance with the standards set out in the OSI model.

The OSI model divides communications tasks into seven processes called layers. Each layer of an OSI network has a specific function and knows how to communicate with the layers above and below it. Figure 12.22 shows the layers of the OSI model and their functions.

Application Layer
- Handles all interfaces between the application software and the network
- Translates user information into a format the presentation layer can understand

Presentation Layer
- Reformats data so that the session layer can understand it
- Compresses and encrypts data

Session Layer
- Sets up a virtual (not physical) connection between the sending and receiving devices
- Manages communications sessions

Transport Layer
- Creates packets and handles packet acknowledgment

Network Layer
- Determines where to send the packets on the network

Data Link Layer
- Assembles the data into frames, addresses them, and sends them to the physical layer for delivery

Physical Layer
- Transmits (delivers) data on the network so it can reach its intended address

FIGURE 12.22 Layers of the OSI Model and Their Functions

This layering approach makes communications more efficient because specialized pieces of the NOS perform specific tasks. The layering approach is akin to assembly-line manufacturing. Producing thousands of cars per day would be difficult if one person had to build a car on his or her own. However, by splitting up the work of assembling a car into specialized tasks and assigning the tasks to people who perform them well, greater efficiency is achieved. By handling specialized tasks and communicating only with the layers above and below them, OSI layers make communications more efficient.

Let's look at how each OSI layer functions by following an e-mail you create and send to your friend through the layers:

- *Application layer*: Handles all interaction between the application software and the network. It translates the data from the application into a format that the presentation layer can understand. For example, when you send an e-mail, the application layer takes the e-mail message you created in Microsoft Outlook, translates it into a format your network can understand, and passes it to the presentation layer.
- *Presentation layer*: Reformats the data so that the session layer can understand it. It also handles data encryption (changing the data into a format that makes it harder to intercept and read) and compression, if required. In our e-mail example, the presentation layer notices that you selected an encryption option for the e-mail message and encrypts the data before sending it to the session layer.
- *Session layer*: Sets up a virtual (not physical) connection between the sending and receiving devices. It then manages the communication between the two. In our e-mail example, the session layer would set up the parameters for the communications session between your computer and the Internet service provider (ISP) where your friend has her e-mail account. The session layer then tracks the transmission of the e-mail until it's satisfied that all the data in the e-mail was received at your friend's ISP.

- *Transport layer*: Breaks up the data into packets and sequences them appropriately. It also handles acknowledgment of packets (that is, it determines whether the packets were received at their destination) and decides whether packets need to be sent again. In our e-mail example, the transport layer breaks up your e-mail message into packets and sends them to the network layer, making sure that all the packets reach their destination.
- *Network layer*: Determines where to send the packets on the network and identifies the best way to route them there. In our e-mail example, the network layer examines the address on the packets (the address of your friend's ISP) and determines how to route the packets so they get to the ISP and can ultimately get to the receiving computer.
- *Data link layer*: Responsible for assembling the data packets into frames, addressing the frames, and delivering them to the physical layer so they can be sent on their way. It's the equivalent of a postal worker who reads the address on a piece of mail and makes sure it's sent to the proper recipient. In our e-mail example, the data link layer assembles the e-mail data packets into frames, which are addressed with the appropriate routing information that it receives from the network layer.
- *Physical layer*: Takes care of delivering the data. It converts the data into a signal and transmits it over the network so that it can reach its intended address. In our e-mail example, the physical layer sends the data over the Internet to its ultimate destination (your friend's ISP).

By following standardized protocols set forth by the OSI model, NOS software can communicate happily with the computers and peripherals attached to the network as well as with other networks.

20 flash drives at random locations around the client's office. By the end of the day, employees had picked up 15 of the flash drives and plugged them into computers on the company network. The flash drives contained a simple program to display images as well as a Trojan horse program. While the employees were viewing the images, the Trojan horse program enabled the consultants to access the company network and steal or compromise data. It isn't hard to imagine hackers leaving flash drives around your school that could act as "skeleton keys" to your school's network.

How should network administrators protect their networks from portable storage devices? To head off problems with portable storage devices, the following actions should be taken:

- Educate employees about the dangers posed by portable media devices.
- Create policies regulating the use of portable media devices in the workplace.
- Install security measures such as personal firewalls or antivirus software to protect all computers in the company. The firewalls should be able to prevent malicious programs from running, even if they're introduced to a computer via a flash drive.
- Limit and monitor the use of portable media devices. Microsoft networking software allows network administrators to shut off access to the USB ports on computers, this prevents employees from using flash drives and other USB devices for legitimate purposes.
- Inform employees that their use of portable media devices is being monitored. This alone will often be enough to scare employees away from connecting untrusted devices to the network.

Other software products, such as DeviceLock and Safend Data Protection Suite, can be deployed on a network to provide options such as detailed security policies. Such products can also monitor USB device connections and track which users have connected devices to the network (including devices other than flash drives).

Physical Protection Measures

What physical measures are used to protect a network? Restricting physical access to servers and other sensitive equipment is critical to protecting a network. Where are the servers that power your college network? They're most likely behind locked doors to which only authorized personnel have access. Likewise, the network's switches are securely tucked away in ceilings, walls, or closets, safe from anyone who might tamper with them in an attempt to sabotage the network or breach its security.

Access card reader

Retinal scanning

Fingerprint/palm scanning

Facial recognition

FIGURE 12.23 Access card readers provide a relatively inexpensive solution to security for areas needing low-level security. Biometric authentication devices, such as fingerprint/palm, retinal, and facial-recognition scanners, are used to protect high-security areas, such as a server room. *(Igor/Fotolia)*

As shown in Figure 12.23, a number of different devices can be used to control access:

- An **access card reader** is a relatively cheap device that reads information from a magnetic strip on the back of a credit card–like access card, such as your student ID

 SOUND BYTE

A Day in the Life of a Network Technician

In this Sound Byte, you'll learn firsthand about the exciting, fast-paced job of a computer technician. Interviews with network technicians and tours of networking facilities will provide you with a deeper appreciation for the complexities of the job.

Data breaches occur all too frequently, and it seems we're always seeing reports in the media about yet another hacker obtaining supposedly private information. Many companies have sensitive data about you. But what is their ethical responsibility to protect your data? And what should a company do for its customers when a data breach occurs?

Data Confidentiality

The objective for any company that possesses sensitive data should be **information assurance**, which means ensuring information systems are adequately secured against tampering. The five key attributes of secure information systems are as follows:

1. *Availability:* The extent to which a data processing system is able to receive and process data. A high degree of availability is usually desirable.
2. *Integrity:* A quality that an information system has if the processing of information is logical and accurate and the data is protected against unauthorized modifications or destruction.
3. *Authentication:* Security measures designed to protect an information system against acceptance of a fraudulent transmission of data by establishing the validity of a data transmission or message or the identity of the sender.
4. *Confidentiality:* The assurance that information isn't disclosed to unauthorized persons, processes, or devices.
5. *Nonrepudiation:* A capability of security systems that guarantees that a message or data can be proven to have originated from a specific person and to have been processed by the recipient. The sender of the data receives a receipt for the data, and the receiver of the data gets proof of the sender's identity. The objective of nonrepudiation is to prevent either party from later denying having handled the data.

From your perspective, you are probably the most concerned about authentication and confidentiality. Companies that have your data shouldn't share it with unauthorized parties and should keep unauthorized people out of their databases. Unfortunately, you have very little control over authentication safeguards. That's the responsibility of the company that holds your data.

Authentication Failures

The data breaches that occur usually represent authentication failures—unauthorized people gain access to data. Clearly, when this happens, a corporation has failed in its responsibility to protect its customers' data. No system is ever 100% safe against breaches, but most systems are adequately protected against all but the most determined hackers. But what ethical responsibilities does a company have to its customers after a data breach?

The first thing a company should do is admit the problem and inform its customers. The Federal Trade Commission (FTC) recommends the following course of action for companies who experience data breaches:

1. Notify the appropriate law enforcement agencies.
2. Notify other affected businesses, such as banks and credit card companies. These companies can then monitor the affected accounts for fraudulent activity.
3. Notify the individuals affected. The company should explain what happened, what information was compromised, who to contact in the organization, and what customers should do to protect themselves (which will vary based on the information compromised).

How can you be aware of a data breach if the company that suffered it never tells you that your data was exposed? You should monitor websites such as the Privacy Rights Clearinghouse (**privacyrights.org/data-breach**) and Open Security Foundation's DataLossDB (**datalossdb .org**), which track data breaches. This might be the fastest way to find out if your information has been compromised so you can take action. The FTC website on identity theft (**consumer.ftc.gov /topics/identity-theft**) provides good guidelines to follow when your data has been exposed.

Granting customers free identity-theft protection is one of the more common forms of compensation offered to placate customers after a data breach, but not every company does it. Some companies merely stop at notifying customers and offer nothing in terms of compensation for the inconvenience.

Although companies may behave ethically after a data breach, your best protection is still your own vigilance!

card. The card reader, which can control the lock on a door, is programmed to admit only authorized personnel to the area. Card readers are easily programmed by adding authorized ID card numbers.

- A **biometric authentication device** uses a unique characteristic of human biology to identify authorized users. Some devices read fingerprints or palm prints when you place your hand on a scanning pad. Other devices shine a laser beam into your eye and read the unique patterns of your retina. Facial-recognition systems store unique characteristics of an individual's face for later comparison and identification. When an authorized individual uses a device for the first time, his or her fingerprints, retinal patterns, or face patterns are scanned and stored in a database.

Financial institutions and retail stores are considering using such devices to attempt to eliminate the growing fraud problems of identity theft and counterfeiting of credit and debit cards. If fingerprint authorization were required at the supermarket to make a purchase, a thief who stole your wallet and attempted to use your credit card would be unsuccessful.

What are the problems with biometric devices?
The biometric devices currently on the market don't always function as intended. Facial-recognition and retinal-scanning systems can sometimes be fooled by pictures or videos of an authorized user. Researchers have fooled biometric fingerprint readers by using fingers made out of modeling clay, using the fingers of cadavers, or having unauthorized persons breathe on the sensor, which makes the previous user's fingerprint visible.

Next-generation fingerprint readers will use specially designed algorithms that will detect moisture patterns on a person's fingers. Another approach may involve readers that detect an electrical current when a finger touches the reader, which is possible because the human body conducts electrical current. Future retinal readers may check whether a person blinks or if his or her pupils contract when a bright light shines on them.

Firewalls

Are Internet connections on client/server networks vulnerable to hackers? Just like a home network, any company's network that's connected to the Internet can attract hackers. For this reason, a well-defended business network, just like a well-defended home network, includes a firewall. Firewalls can be composed of software or hardware, and many sophisticated firewalls include both. Routers are often equipped to act as hardware firewalls.

Does a firewall on a client/server network work the same way as a personal firewall installed on a home network? Although a firewall on a business network may contain a few extra security options, making it even harder to breach than a personal firewall, the firewalls for business networks work on the same basic principles as a personal firewall. At a minimum, most firewalls work as packet screeners. **Packet screening** involves having an *external screening router* examining incoming data packets to ensure that they originated from or are authorized by valid users on the internal network. Unauthorized or suspect packets are discarded by the firewall before they reach the network.

Packet screening also can be configured for outgoing data to ensure that requests for information to the Internet are from legitimate users. This is done by an *internal screening router* and helps detect Trojan horse programs that may have been installed by hackers. Trojan horses often try to disguise where they're sending data from by using bogus IP addresses on the packets the programs send instead of using an authorized IP address belonging to the network.

With packet screening in place, packets going into and out of the network are checked to ensure they're either from or addressed to a legitimate IP address on the network. If the addresses aren't valid addresses on the network, the firewall (or the screening routers) discards them.

What other security measures does the firewall on a client/server network use? To increase security even further, most large networks add a **bastion host**, which is a heavily secured server located on a special perimeter network between the company's secure internal network and the firewall.

To external computers, the bastion host gives the appearance of being the internal network server. Hackers can waste a lot of time and energy attacking the bastion host. However, even if a hacker breaches the bastion host server, the internal network isn't vulnerable because the bastion host isn't on the internal network. Moreover, during the time the hackers spend trying to penetrate the bastion host, network administrators can detect and thwart their attacks.

How do bastion hosts help protect systems from hackers? Bastion hosts are a type of honey pot. A **honey pot** is a computer system that's set up to attract unauthorized users by appearing to be a key part of a network or a system that contains something of great value.

Bastion hosts are often configured as proxy servers. A **proxy server** acts as a go-between, connecting computers on the internal network with those on the external network (the Internet). All requests from the internal network for Internet services are directed through the proxy server. Similarly, all incoming requests from the Internet must pass through the proxy server. It's much easier for network administrators to maintain adequate security on one server than it is to ensure that security is maintained on hundreds or thousands of computers in a college network, for example.

FIGURE 12.24 Business firewalls provide sophisticated protection from hackers.

Figure 12.24 shows a network secured by a firewall, a bastion host and proxy server, and a screening router. Now that you know a bit more about business networks, you should be able to comfortably navigate the network at your college or your place of employment and understand why certain security measures have been taken to protect network data. ∎

Before moving on to the Chapter Review:
1. Watch Replay Video 12.2 ▷ .
2. Then check your understanding of what you've learned so far.

check your understanding // review & practice

For a quick review to see what you've learned so far, answer the following questions.

multiple choice

1. Which of the following is used to increase security on a client/server network?

   a. bastion host

   b. bridge

   c. transmission media

   d. database server

2. Fiber-optic cable most likely would be used in a business network when

   a. saving money is more important than speed.

   b. electrical or magnetic interference is present.

   c. very short cable runs are required.

   d. the installation budget is very limited.

3. NOS software is needed

   a. on all computers in a client/server network.

   b. only on the servers in a client/server network.

   c. only if a communications server is deployed on a client/server network.

   d. only when configuring a network in a star topology.

4. On client/server networks, routers

   a. transfer data between two networks.

   b. route data between two collision domains on a single network.

   c. move data efficiently from node to node on the internal network.

   d. are necessary only in networks using the ring topology.

5. Correctly entering the user ID and password on your college network is an example of

   a. authentication.

   b. scalability.

   c. packet screening.

   d. virtualization.

 Go to **MyITLab** to take an autograded version of the *Check Your Understanding* review and to find all media resources for the chapter.

TECHBYTES WEEKLY

Stay Current with TechBytes Weekly Newsletter

 Continue

Chapter Review

summary //

Client/Server Networks and Topologies

Learning Outcome 12.1 You will be able to describe common types of client/server networks, servers found on them, and network topologies used to construct them.

Client/Server Network Basics

Objective 12.1 *List the advantages for businesses of installing a network.*

- Networks enable expensive resources, such as printers, to be shared
- Networks facilitate knowledge sharing as multiple people can access information at the same time
- Software can be shared from network servers thereby reducing the costs of installation on each user's computer
- Information sharing is more effective when employees are connected via networks

Objective 12.2 *Explain the differences between a client/server network and a peer-to-peer network.*

- In a peer-to-peer network, each node connected to the network can communicate directly with every other node on the network. In a client/server network, a separate device (the server) exercises control over the network.
- Data flows more efficiently in client/server networks than in peer-to-peer networks.
- Client/server networks have increased scalability, meaning users can be added to the network easily.

Objective 12.3 *Describe the common types of client/server networks as well as other networks businesses use.*

- Local area networks (LANs) are small groups of computers (as few as two) and peripherals linked together over a small geographic area.
- Wide area networks (WANs) comprise large numbers of users (or of separate LANs) that are miles apart and linked together.
- An intranet is a private network set up by a business or an organization that's used exclusively by a select group of employees, customers, suppliers, volunteers, or supporters.
- Virtual private networks (VPNs) use the public Internet communications infrastructure to build a secure, private network among various locations.

Servers and Network Topologies

Objective 12.4 *List the common types of servers found on client/server networks.*

- Dedicated servers are used on large networks to increase efficiency.
- Authentication servers control access to the network and ensure that only authorized users can log in.
- File servers provide storage and management of user files.
- Print servers manage and control all printing jobs initiated on a network.
- Application servers provide access to application software.
- Database servers store database files and provide access to users who need the information in the databases.
- E-mail servers control all incoming and outgoing e-mail traffic.
- Communications servers are used to control the flow of information from the internal network to outside networks.
- Web servers are used to host websites.
- Cloud servers provide storage and access to data on the Internet.

Objective 12.5 *Describe the common types of network topologies and the advantages and disadvantages of each one.*

- In a bus topology, all nodes are connected to a single linear cable. Installation is easy, reliable and inexpensive. Breaks in the cable disable the network and large numbers of users decrease performance.
- Ring topologies are made up of nodes arranged roughly in a circle. The data flows from node to node in a specific order. Access to the network is allocated fairly among nodes. Failure of one node can bring down the network.
- In a star topology, nodes are connected to a central communication device (a switch) and branch out like points of a star. Failure of one node doesn't affect other nodes and the network is highly scalable. Requires more cable to install and network navigation devices are a single point of failure which can affect many nodes.

Setting Up Business Networks

Learning Outcome 12.2 **You will be able to describe transmission media, network operating system software, and network navigation devices and explain major threats to network security and how to mitigate them.**

Transmission Media

Objective 12.6 *Describe the types of wired and wireless transmission media used in networks.*

- Transmission media comprises the physical systems that data takes to flow between devices on a network. Twisted-pair cable consists of pairs of wires twisted around each other in order to reduce interference. Coaxial cable is the same type of cable used by your cable TV company to run a signal into your house. Fiber-optic cable uses bundles of glass or plastic fiber to send signals using light waves. It provides the largest bandwidth but is expensive and difficult to install. Wireless media uses radio waves to send data between nodes on a network.

Network Adapters and Navigation Devices

Objective 12.7 *Describe how network adapters help data move around a network.*

- A network adapter provides three critical functions: (1) It takes low-power data signals generated by the computer and converts them into higher-powered signals that can traverse network media easily. (2) It breaks the data generated by the computer into packets and packages them for transmission across the network media. (3) It acts as a gatekeeper to control the flow of data to and from the computer.

Objective 12.8 *Define MAC addresses, and explain how they are used to move data around a network.*

- A media access control (MAC) address represents the physical address of a network adapter. It is made up of 6 two-position characters, such as 01:40:87:44:79:A5. A frame is a container that can hold multiple data packets. While the data packets are being assembled into frames, the network operating system (NOS) software assigns the appropriate MAC address to the frame. The NOS keeps track of all devices and their addresses on the network.

Objective 12.9 *List the various network navigation devices, and explain how they help route data through networks.*

- Switches are devices that read the addresses of data packets and retransmit a signal to its

destination instead of to every device connected to the switch. Bridges are devices used to send data between two different segments (collision domains) of the same network. Routers are used to route data between two different networks, such as between a business network and the Internet.

Network Operating Systems and Network Security

Objective 12.10 *Explain why network operating systems are necessary for networks to function.*

- Network operating system (NOS) software needs to be installed on each computer and server connected to a client/server network in order to provide the services necessary for the devices to communicate. The NOS provides a set of common rules (called a protocol) that controls communication between devices on the network.

Objective 12.11 *List major security threats to networks, and explain how network administrators mitigate these threats.*

- Human errors and mistakes, malicious human activity (such as unauthorized access), and natural events and disasters are major categories of security threats.

- Access to most networks requires authentication procedures, such as having users enter a user ID and password, to ensure that only authorized users access the network. The system administrator defines access privileges for users so that they can access only specific files.

- Network equipment is physically secured behind locked doors. Access to equipment is often restricted by biometric devices, which use unique physical characteristics of individuals for identification purposes.

- Firewalls, packet screeners and bastion hosts are employed to keep hackers from successfully attacking networks.

- Data backups help secure data against destruction by natural events and disasters (such as fire).

 Be sure to check out **MyITLab** for additional materials to help you review and learn. And don't forget the Replay Videos ▶ .

key terms //

chapter quiz // assessment

For a quick review to see what you've learned, answer the following questions. Submit the quiz as requested by your instructor. If you are using **MyITLab**, the quiz is also available there.

multiple choice

1. Which of the following is an advantage of installing a client/server network in a business?

   a. centralization of network adapters

   b. centralization of network security protection

   c. decentralization of files and data

   d. decentralization of peripherals

2. Why are P2P networks not usually installed in businesses?

   a. Security is stronger on client/server networks.

   b. They require dedicated servers.

   c. They are more scalable than client/server networks.

   d. Client/server networks are cheaper to install.

3. To ensure only authorized users are logging onto a network, which server would a client/server network include?

   a. Internet   **c.** communications

   b. authentication   **d.** application

4. Which of the following is a private network set up by a business that's used exclusively by a select group of employees and suppliers?

   a. MAN   **c.** HAN

   b. Intranet   **d.** Vendor network

5. Network adapters send data packets based on a(n)

   a. IP address.

   b. router address.

   c. frame address.

   d. MAC address.

6. Providing adequate security on a corporate network involves all of the following issues except

   a. authentication.

   b. restricting access to servers.

   c. proprietary software lockout.

   d. limiting physical access to networking equipment.

true/false

_____ **1.** Client/server networks are generally less secure than P2P networks.

_____ **2.** A web server is used to host websites on a client/server network.

_____ **3.** Bridges are used to route data between two different networks.

_____ **4.** Most modern operating systems include some type of NOS functionality.

critical thinking

1. Acceptable-Use Internet Policies

Most schools have drafted acceptable-use policies for computers and Internet access to inform students and employees of the approved uses of college computing assets. Should college employees be allowed to use their computers and Internet access for personal tasks? If so, how much time per day is reasonable for employees to spend on personal tasks? Should student computer and Internet usage be monitored to ensure compliance with the personal use policies? Should the college inform students that they're being monitored?

2. Monitoring Computer Usage in the Workplace

Software tools for monitoring computer usage are available on the Internet, often for free. In most jurisdictions, it's legal for employers to install monitoring software on computers they provide to employees. It's usually illegal for employees to install monitoring software on computers owned by their employers for purposes of monitoring computer usage of coworkers or bosses. Do you think this double standard is fair? What circumstances do you think would justify an employee monitoring other employees' computer usage?

Developing a Bring-Your-Own-Device Policy

Problem

Employees, especially in developing economies, are often bringing their own computing device (BYOD) to work and using these devices to access company networks, databases, and the Internet. While this can keep equipment costs down, BYOD can present unique challenges for data security.

Task

Cool Tees, a local T-shirt company, has experienced a large rise in BYOD by its employees. It is concerned about the security of data that may be on the devices. The Cool Tees CEO has asked you to assist him in constructing a BYOD policy for his company.

Process

1. Divide the class into small teams. Research BYOD security issues. Review BYOD policies that are in place for businesses and schools. Consider what types of devices (laptops, phones, tablets, etc.) might be used to access company data. Draft a BYOD policy for Cool Tees employees that sets forth the company's expectations with regards to personal devices.

2. Meet as a class to discuss each group's findings. Do you feel most employees are aware of the security issues related to BYOD? Try to obtain a consensus about which precautions are the most important ones for employees to take to protect the company's data.

3. Have each group prepare a multimedia presentation (PowerPoint, video, etc.) to educate employees about the security risks of BYOD.

Conclusion

Having personal computing devices and bringing them to work is fast becoming the norm in the twenty-first century. But the best defense against loss of control of company data is to understand the consequences of accessing data with and storing data on personal computing devices.

Using Wireless Networks Without Permission

In this exercise, you'll research and then role-play a complicated ethical situation. The role you play might not match your own personal beliefs, but your research and use of logic will enable you to represent the view assigned. An arbitrator will watch and comment on both sides of the argument, and together, the team will agree on an ethical solution.

Problem

Piggybacking occurs when people use a wireless network without the owner's permission. Although piggybacking is illegal in many jurisdictions, it's often hard to detect. Piggybacking often happens inadvertently when people trying to connect to their own network accidentally connect to their neighbor's network. And because of the close proximity of many businesses, the potential for piggybacking of business wireless networks also exists. Sharing wireless connections between two entities (whether they be two households or two businesses) may violate the terms of service of the Internet service provider.

Research Areas to Consider

- Detecting wireless piggybacking
- Piggybacking laws (legality of piggybacking)
- Securing wireless networks

Process

1. Divide the class into teams. Research the areas cited above and devise a scenario in which the owner of a coffee shop has accused the proprietor of the sandwich shop next door of encouraging the sandwich shop's patrons to piggyback on the coffee shop's wireless network.

2. Team members should write a summary that provides background information for their character—for example, coffee shop owner, sandwich shop owner, and arbitrator—and that details their character's behaviors to set the stage for the role-playing event. Then, team members should create an outline to use during the role-playing event.

3. Team members should present their case to the class or submit a PowerPoint presentation for review by the rest of the class, along with the summary and resolution they developed.

Conclusion

As technology becomes ever more prevalent and integrated into our lives, ethical dilemmas will present themselves to an increasing extent. Being able to understand and evaluate both sides of the argument, while responding in a personally or socially ethical manner, will be important skills.

Cyber Security Flyer and Mail Merge

You have been asked to modify a flyer that announces an upcoming Cyber-Security presentation to highlight National Cyber Security Awareness Month. Additionally, you have been told to mail the flyer to some key community members. You will use Mail Merge and other features of Word 2016 to complete this task.

You will use the following skills as you complete this activity:

- Apply Picture Style
- Group Objects
- Apply Page Borders

- Create Custom Bullets
- Use Mail Merge
- Use Spell Checker

1. Open *TIA_Ch12_Start* and save as **TIA_Ch12_LastFirst**.

2. Scroll to page 2. Select the image at the top left of the page, click the **Picture Tools Format tab**, click **Artistic Effects** in the Adjust group, and then click the **Film Grain effect**.

3. Click the **Insert tab**, click **Shapes** in the Illustrations group, and then click **Rectangle** from the Rectangles group. Place the cursor in the top left image, and draw a rectangle. In the Size group, modify the size to be 2.2" high and 4.1" wide. Using the arrow keys on the keyboard, nudge the rectangle in any direction so that it is centered within the image.

4. Change the Shape Fill color of the rectangle to **Blue, Accent 5, Lighter 60%**. Type **October is**, press **Enter**, then type **National Cyber Security Awareness Month**. Change the font to **Century Gothic**, change the font color to **Black, Text 1**. Then change the font size of the first line to **14**, and the remaining text to **28**. Center all the text. Click the **Paragraph dialog box launcher**, then change Spacing Before to **12pt**, and Line spacing: At: to **.85**.

5. With the text box still selected, click the **Drawing Tools Format tab**, click **Shape Effects** in the Shape Styles group, then select **Soft Edges, 5 point**.

6. Select **Cyber Security Presentation**. Change the font to **Britannic Bold** and the font color to **Dark Red** in the Standard Colors group.

7. Select the first set of bullets, click the **Bullets arrow** in the Paragraph group, click **Define New Bullet**, and then click **Picture**. Click **Browse** next to From a File, and select **TIA_Ch12_Image1** from your student data files location. Select the second set of bullets, and repeat the process to define a new bullet using **TIA_Ch12_Image2**.

8. Click the **Design tab**, then click **Page Borders** in the Page Background group. Click Box in the *Setting* section, and then click the **triple line** in the *Style* section. Ensure that *Whole document* displays in the Apply to: box.

9. On Page 1, select **National Cyber Security Awareness Month!**. Click **WordArt** in the Text group on the Insert tab, select **Fill – Blue, Accent 1, Shadow**. Click the **Text Fill arrow**, then click **Dark Red** in the Standard Colors group.

10. In the second paragraph, beginning with *You are invited*, **bold** *Springer Auditorium, October 22, from 12 – 2:30 PM* and change the font color to **Dark Red** in the Standard Colors group.

11. On the Mailings tab, click **Start Mail Merge** in the Start Mail Merge group, select **Letters**. Click **Select Recipients**, and click **Use an Existing List**. Navigate to the student data files, and select **TIA_Ch12_MailList**. Ensure Sheet1 is selected, then click **OK**.

12. Click **Edit Recipient List** in the Start Mail Merge group, click the **City header** to sort the files by city, then uncheck the two records from Elk Grove Village. Click **OK**.

13. Place the insertion point at the beginning of the first paragraph. In the Write & Insert Fields group, click **Address Block**. Ensure *Joshua Randall Jr.* is selected in the *Specify address elements* section, and accept all other default settings. Click **OK**. Press **Enter**.

14. Place the insertion point at the beginning of the first paragraph. In the Write & Insert Fields group, click **Greeting Line**, then in the *Greeting line format* section, ensure that *Dear* displays in the first box, select **Joshua** in the second box, and ensure a comma displays in the third box. Click **OK**. Press **Enter**.

15. Click **Preview Results** and click **Next Record** several times to advance through the letters.

16. Save the file and submit based on your instructor's directions.

13

Behind the Scenes:
How the Internet Works

Make This: MAKE: An Earthquake Detector on **page 547**

All media accompanying this chapter can be found in MyITLab.

For an overview of the chapter, watch the **Preview Video**.

(Maksim Pasko/Fotolia, Matthias Pahl/Shutterstock, Olly/Fotolia, Ra2 studio/Fotolia)

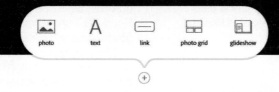

HOW COOL IS THIS?

Want to learn how to **develop websites** that run on all kinds of devices, no matter how the user is holding the device, and use cool popular effects like **parallax scrolling?** Using the free app **Adobe Slate** and an **iPad**, you can create a site in five minutes that gives the **illusion of depth** as multiple layers of, for example, photos scroll by at different rates. This offering from Adobe (**standout.adobe.com/slate**) supports many different **cloud storage options** so you can reach your photos on Dropbox or Creative Cloud. Professional themes and **magazine-style fonts and layout** make your work shine. Hosted for free by Adobe, the final website you have created can be linked to from anywhere. Becoming a web developer has never been so easy. *(Adobe product screenshot(s) reprinted with permission from Adobe Systems Incorporated. Adobe® Slate is a trademark of Adobe Systems Incorporated in the United*

Inner Workings of the Internet

Learning Outcome 13.1 You will be able to explain how the Internet is managed and the details of how data is transmitted across the Internet.

We use the Internet so routinely that it may not have occurred to you to ask some fundamental questions about how it's administered. In this part of the chapter, we'll discuss this and other topics.

 internet management and
NETWORKING

To keep a massive network like the Internet functioning at peak efficiency, it must be governed and regulated. However, no single entity is in charge of the Internet. In addition, new uses for the Internet are created every day by a variety of individuals and companies.

Management

Objective 13.1 *Describe the management of the Internet.*

Who owns the Internet? The local networks that constitute the Internet are owned by different entities, including individuals, universities, government agencies, and private companies. Government entities such as the National Science Foundation (NSF), as well as many privately held companies, own pieces of the communications infrastructure (the high-speed data lines that transport data between networks) that makes the Internet work.

Does anyone manage the Internet? Several nonprofit organizations and user groups, each with a specialized purpose, are responsible for the Internet's management. Figure 13.1 shows major organizations that play a role in the governance and development of the Internet.

Many of the functions handled by these nonprofit groups were previously handled by U.S. government contractors because the Internet developed out of a defense project. However, because the Internet serves the global community, assigning responsibilities to organizations with global membership is the best way to guarantee worldwide engagement in determining the direction of the Internet.

Who pays for the Internet? The National Science Foundation (NSF), which is a U.S. government–funded agency, still pays for a large portion of the Internet's infrastructure and funds research and development for new technologies. The primary source of NSF funding is federal taxes. Other countries also pay for Internet infrastructure and development.

FIGURE 13.1

Major Organizations in Internet Governance and Development

ORGANIZATION	PURPOSE	WEB ADDRESS
Internet Society	Professional membership society that provides leadership for the orderly growth and development of the Internet	internetsociety.org
Internet Engineering Task Force (IETF)	A subgroup of the Internet Society that researches new Internet technologies to improve its capabilities and keep the infrastructure functioning smoothly	ietf.org
Internet Architecture Board (IAB)	Technical advisory group to the Internet Society and an IETF committee; provides direction for the maintenance and development of Internet protocols	iab.org
Internet Corporation for Assigned Names and Numbers (ICANN)	Organization responsible for managing the Internet's domain name system and the allocation of IP addresses	icann.org
World Wide Web Consortium (W3C)	Consortium of organizations that sets standards and develops protocols for the web	w3.org

Networking Components

Objective 13.2 *Explain how the Internet's networking components interact.*

How are computers connected to the Internet?

As a "network of networks," the Internet is similar to the U.S. highway system, where smaller roads feed into larger, faster highways. The main paths of the Internet, along which data travels the fastest, are known collectively as the **Internet backbone**. The Internet backbone is a collection of large national and international networks, most of which are owned by commercial, educational, or government organizations. These backbone providers, which are required to connect to other backbone providers, have the fastest high-speed connections. Figure 13.2 shows a typical Internet backbone provided by a single company. Large U.S. companies that provide backbone connectivity include Verizon, AT&T, and Sprint.

How do the Internet service providers (ISPs) that form the Internet backbone communicate?

A backbone is typically a high-speed fiber-optic line, designated as an **optical carrier (OC) line**. OC lines come in a range of speeds, from 0.052 Gbps for OC-1 to the fastest OC-768, which runs at almost 40 Gbps.

Backbone ISPs initially connected with T lines. A **T line** carried digital data over twisted-pair wires. T-1 lines, which were the first to be used, transmit data at a throughput rate of 1.544 Mbps. T-3 lines, which were developed later, transmit data at 45 Mbps.

The bandwidth of the connections between ISPs and end users depends on the amount of data traffic required. Whereas your home might connect to the Internet with cable or fiber-optic lines, the volume of Internet traffic at your college probably requires it to use an OC line to move data to the school's ISP. Large companies usually must connect to their ISPs using high-throughput OC lines.

How are ISPs connected to each other?

ISPs like Verizon and Comcast are connected together through an **Internet exchange point (IXP)**. A typical IXP is made up of one or more network switches to which ISPs connect. As you'll recall from Chapter 7, *switches* are devices that send data on a specific route through a network. By connecting directly to each other through IXPs, networks can reduce their costs and improve the speed and efficiency with which data is exchanged.

How do individuals connect to an ISP?

Individual Internet users enter an ISP through a **point of presence (POP)**, which is a bank of modems, servers, routers, and switches (see Figure 13.3) through which many users can connect to an ISP simultaneously. ISPs maintain multiple POPs throughout the geographic area they serve.

What type of network model does the Internet use?

The majority of Internet communications follows the **client/server model** of network communications. The clients are devices such as computers, tablets, and smartphones that use browsers to request services such as web pages. Various types of servers from which clients can request services are deployed on the networks that make up the Internet:

- **Web servers:** computers that run specialized operating systems, enabling them to host web pages and other information and to provide requested information to clients.

- **Commerce servers:** computers that host software that enables users to buy goods and services over the web. These servers generally use special security protocols to protect sensitive information, such as credit card numbers, from being intercepted.

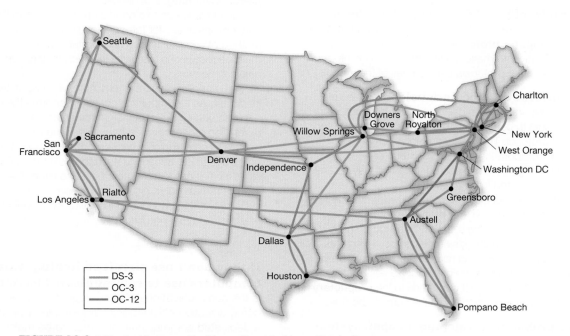

FIGURE 13.2 A Typical Internet Backbone Provided by a Single Company

Wireless connection

Your neighbor's computer

Point of presence (POP)

Networking devices

Broadband connection

Your computer

Your ISP

FIGURE 13.3 Home users connect to their ISPs through a single point of presence that can handle many simultaneous connections.

(Klaus Westermann/Agencja Fotograficzna Caro/Alamy, Ifong/Shutterstock, Robert Hyrons/Alamy, Shashkin/Shutterstock)

- **File servers:** computers that are deployed to provide remote storage space or to act as storehouses for files that users can download. Cloud service providers offering online storage services have a huge collection of file servers.

Data Transmission

Objective 13.3 *List and describe the Internet protocols used for data transmission.*

What is a protocol? Just like any other network, the Internet follows a standard set of rules to send information between computers. A **computer protocol** is the set of rules for exchanging electronic information. If the Internet is the information superhighway, then protocols are the rules of the road.

Why were Internet protocols developed? The idea of a protocol is that anyone can use it on his or her computer system and be able to communicate with any other computer using the same protocol. The most common Internet tasks—communicating, collaborating, creating content, seeking information, and shopping—are all executed the same way on any system following accepted Internet protocols.

When common communication protocols are followed, networks can communicate even if they have different topologies, transmission media, or operating systems. To accomplish the early goals of the Internet, protocols needed to be written and agreed on by users. Each protocol had to be an **open system**, meaning its design would be made public for access by any interested party. This was in direct opposition to the **proprietary system** (private system) model that was the norm at the time.

Were there problems developing an open system Internet protocol? Agreeing on common standards

was relatively easy. The tough part was developing a new method of communication because the technology available in the 1960s—circuit switching—was inefficient for computer communication.

Circuit Switching

Why don't we use circuit switching to connect two computers? Circuit switching has been used since the early days of the telephone for establishing communication. In **circuit switching**, a dedicated connection is formed between two points (such as two people on phones), and the connection remains active for the duration of the transmission. This method of communication is important when communications must be received in the order in which they're sent, like phone conversations.

When applied to computers, however, circuit switching is inefficient. As a computer processor performs the operations necessary to complete a task, it transmits data in a group, or burst. The processor then begins working on its next task and ceases to communicate with output devices or other networks until it's ready to transmit data in the next burst. Circuit switching is inefficient for computers because either the circuit would have to remain open, and therefore unavailable to any other system, with long periods of inactivity, or it would have to be reestablished for each burst.

Packet Switching

If they don't use circuit switching, what do computers use to communicate? Packet switching is the communications methodology that makes computer communication efficient. Packet switching doesn't require a dedicated communications circuit to be maintained. With packet switching, data is broken into smaller chunks called

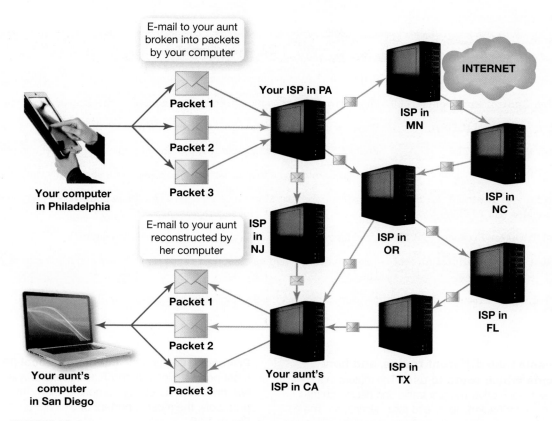

FIGURE 13.4 Each packet sent through the Internet can follow its own route to its final destination. Sequential numbering of packets ensures they're reassembled in the correct order at their destination.
(Baris Simsek/E+/Getty Images, Ifong/Shuttterstock)

packets (or **data packets**). The packets are sent over various routes at the same time. When the packets reach their destination, they're reassembled by the receiving computer. This technology resulted from one of the original goals of creating the Internet: If an Internet node is disabled or destroyed, the data can travel an alternate route to its destination.

What information does a packet contain? Packet contents vary, depending on the protocol being followed. At a minimum, all packets must contain the following:

1. An address to which the packet is being sent
2. The address from where the packet originates
3. Reassembly instructions, if the original data is split between packets, and
4. The data that's being transmitted

Sending a packet is like sending a letter. Assume you're sending a large amount of information in written format from your home in Philadelphia to your aunt in San Diego. The information is too large to fit in one small envelope, so you mail three different envelopes to your aunt. Each envelope includes your aunt's address, your return address, and the information being sent inside it. The pages of the letters in each envelope are numbered so that your aunt will know in which order to read them.

Each envelope may not find its way to San Diego by the same route. However, even if the letters are routed through different post offices, they'll all eventually arrive in your aunt's mailbox. Your aunt will then reassemble the message in the right order and read it. The process of sending a message through the Internet works in much the same way. This process is illustrated in Figure 13.4, which traces an e-mail message sent from a computer in Philadelphia to a computer in San Diego.

BITS&BYTES

Who Opened Your Ports?

If you get curious about what TCP/IP and UDP ports are currently being used on your system, consider trying out the freeware CurrPorts. It displays a listing of all the open TCP/IP ports, along with details like the name of the application that opened it, its current status (Listening, Waiting, etc.), and the time it was created. It also automatically highlights suspicious ports owned by unknown applications.

FIGURE 13.5

TCP/IP Protocol Suite—Main Protocols

Internet Protocol (IP)	Sends data between computers on the Internet
Transmission Control Protocol (TCP)	Prepares data for transmission and provides for error checking and resending of lost data
User Datagram Protocol (UDP)	Prepares data for transmission; lacks resending capabilities
File Transfer Protocol (FTP)	Enables files to be downloaded to a computer or uploaded to other computers
Telnet	Enables user to log in to a remote computer and work on it as if sitting in front of it
Hypertext Transfer Protocol (HTTP) and HTTP Secure (HTTPS)	Transfers Hypertext Markup Language (HTML) data from servers to browsers; HTTPS is an encrypted protocol for secure transmissions
Simple Mail Transfer Protocol (SMTP)	Used for transmission of e-mail messages across the Internet
Dynamic Host Configuration Protocol (DHCP)	Takes a pool of IP addresses and shares them with hosts on a network on an as-needed basis
Real-time Transport Protocol (RTP)	Network protocol for delivering audio and video over IP

Why do packets take different routes, and how do they decide which route to use? The routers that connect ISPs with each other monitor traffic and decide on the most efficient route for packets to take to their destination. The router works in the same way a police officer does while directing traffic. To ensure a smooth flow of traffic, police officers are deployed in areas of congestion, directing drivers along alternate routes to their destinations. The Try This exercise in this chapter uses the Windows utility tracert to show you the details on the exact route your request takes to the destination server.

TCP/IP

What protocol does the Internet use for transmitting data? Although many protocols are available on the Internet, the main suite of protocols used is **TCP/IP**. The suite is named after the original two protocols that were developed for the Internet: the **Transmission Control**

Protocol (TCP) and the **Internet Protocol (IP)**. Although most people think that the TCP/IP suite consists of only two protocols, it actually comprises many interrelated protocols, the most important of which are listed in Figure 13.5.

Which particular protocol actually sends the information? The Internet Protocol (IP) is responsible for sending the information from one computer to another. The IP is like a postal worker who takes a letter (a packet of information) that was mailed (created by the sending computer) and sends it on to another post office (router), which in turn routes it to the addressee (the receiving computer). The postal worker never knows whether the recipient actually receives the letter. The only thing the postal worker knows is that the letter was handed off to an appropriate post office that will assist in completing the delivery of the letter. ■

internet
IDENTITY

Each computer, server, or device connected to the Internet is required to have a unique identification number, or IP address. However, because humans are better at remembering and working with words than with numbers, the numeric IP addresses were given more "human," word-based addresses. Thus, domain names were born. In this section, we'll look at both IP addresses and domain names.

IP Addresses

Objective 13.4 *Explain how each device connected to the Internet is assigned a unique address.*

What is an IP address? You'll recall from Chapter 3 that an **IP address** is a unique identification number that defines each computer, service, or other device connected to the Internet. IP addresses fulfill the same function as street addresses. For example, to send a letter to Rosa Juarez's house in Metamora, Illinois, you have to know her address. Rosa might live at 456 Walnut Street, which isn't a unique address because many towns have a Walnut Street, but 456 Walnut Street, Metamora, IL 61548 *is* a unique address.

The numeric zip code is the unique postal identification for a specific geographic area. IP addresses must be registered with the **Internet Corporation for Assigned Names and Numbers (ICANN)** to ensure they're unique and haven't been assigned to other users. ICANN is responsible for allocating IP addresses to network administrators.

What does an IP address look like? A typical IP address is expressed as follows:

197.169.73.63

An IP address in this form is called a **dotted decimal number** (or a **dotted quad**). The same IP address in binary form is as follows:

11000101.10101001.01001001.00111111

Each of the four numbers in a dotted decimal number is referred to as an **octet**. This is because each number would have eight positions when shown in binary form. Because 32 positions are available for IP address values (four octets with eight positions each), IP addresses are considered 32-bit numbers. A position is filled by either a *1* or a *0*, resulting in 256 (which is 2^8) possible values for each octet, from *0* to *255*. The entire 32-bit address can represent 4,294,967,296 values (or 2^{32}), which is quite a few Internet addresses!

Will we ever run out of IP addresses? When the original IP addressing scheme, **Internet Protocol version 4 (IPv4)**, was created in 1981, no one foresaw the explosive growth of the Internet in the 1990s. Four billion values for an address field seemed like enough to last forever. However, as

the Internet grew, it quickly became apparent that we were going to run out of IP addresses.

Why do we need so many IP addresses? Not only laptops need an IP address. The **Internet of Things (IoT)** is a term for the explosive growth of Internet-enabled devices. Appliances, switches, light bulbs, and smoke detectors all now send and receive messages over the Internet. That means each one needs a unique IP address. As each electronic device begins to have the ability to pull information from the Internet and push out messages, expect changes in our daily lives. Imagine parking lots that know how many spaces are empty and text you directions to a specific free spot. Medical devices will monitor your health and automatically book a doctor appointment when you begin to fall ill. The data we collect will be translated quickly and invisibly into the actions we need to take in the physical world.

How did Internet addresses change to allow more of them? **Internet Protocol version 6 (IPv6)** is an IP addressing scheme developed by the IETF to make

DIG DEEPER

Connection-Oriented Versus Connectionless Protocols

The Internet Protocol is responsible only for sending packets on their way. The packets are created by either the TCP or the **User Datagram Protocol (UDP)**. You don't decide whether to use TCP or UDP. The choice of protocol is made for you by the developers of the computer programs you're using or by the other protocols that interact with your data packet (such as those listed in Figure 13.5).

As explained earlier, data transmission between computers is highly efficient if connections don't need to be established (as in circuit switching). However, there are benefits to maintaining a connection, such as reduced data loss. The difference between TCP and UDP is that TCP is a *connection-oriented* protocol, whereas UDP is a *connectionless* protocol.

A **connection-oriented protocol** requires two computers to exchange control packets, thereby setting up the parameters of the data-exchange session, before sending packets that contain data. This process is referred to as **handshaking**. TCP uses a process called a **three-way handshake** to establish a connection, as shown in Figure 13.7:

1. Your computer establishes a connection to the ISP and announces it has e-mail to send.
2. The ISP server responds that it's ready to receive the e-mail.
3. Your computer then acknowledges the ready state of the server and begins to transmit the e-mail.

A **connectionless protocol** doesn't require any type of connection to be established or maintained between two computers exchanging information. Just like a letter that's mailed, the data packets are sent without notifying the receiving computer or receiving any acknowledgment that the data was received. UDP is the Internet's connectionless protocol.

Besides establishing a connection, TCP provides for reliable data transfer, ensuring that all the data packets are delivered to the receiver free from errors and in the correct order. TCP achieves reliable data transfer by using acknowledgments and providing for the retransmission of data, as shown in Figure 13.8.

Assume that two systems, X and Y, have established a connection. When Y receives a data packet that it can read from X, it sends back a **positive acknowledgment (ACK)**. If X doesn't receive an ACK in an appropriate period of time, it resends the packet. If the packet is unreadable (damaged in transit), Y sends a **negative acknowledgment (NAK)** to X, indicating the packet wasn't received in understandable form. X then retransmits that packet. Acknowledgments ensure that the receiver has received a complete set of data packets. If a packet is unable to get through after being resent several times, the user is generally presented with an error message, indicating the communications were unsuccessful.

Your computer

STEP 1:
I want to send e-mail.

STEP 2:
Okay, I'm ready to receive.

STEP 3:
Here's the e-mail message for Aunt Sally.

Your ISP's server

FIGURE 13.7 Two computers establish communication using a three-way handshake.
(Lfong/Shutterstock, Juffin/DigitalVision Vectors/Getty Images)

Sending computer (X)

Receiving computer (Y)

Packet 1

Packet 1 received and readable. ACK sent.

ACK for packet 1 received. Need to send next packet.

ACK 1

Packet 2

Packet 2 received and unreadable. NAK sent.

NAK for packet 2 received. Must resend packet 2.

NAK 2

Packet 2 resend

Packet 2 received and readable. ACK sent.

FIGURE 13.8 Positive (ACK) and negative (NAK) packet acknowledgments provide reliable data transfer. *(Lfong/Shutterstock, LdF/Getty Images)*

You may wonder why you wouldn't always want to use a protocol that provides for reliable data transfer. On the Internet, speed is often more important than accuracy. For certain applications (such as e-mail), it's important that your message be delivered completely and accurately. For streaming multimedia, it's not always important to have every frame delivered accurately because most streaming media formats provide for correction of errors caused by data loss. However, it's extremely important for streaming media to be delivered at a high rate of speed. Therefore, a protocol such as TCP, which uses handshakes and acknowledgments, would probably not be appropriate for transmitting a movie trailer over the Internet; in this instance, the Real-time Transport Protocol (RTP) would be better.

BITS&BYTES

Internet of Things Goes Shopping

The Amazon Dash button is one example of how the Internet of Things is impacting daily life.

The Dash button (shown here) can be configured to reorder a household product with just a click, so sticking a Dash button in the spot where you'll remember you're running low makes it easy to keep items in stock. You can buy a Dash button from Amazon for a wide range of household and grocery products.

Hacks already have appeared so a Dash button can not only order from Amazon but be used to update your own online spreadsheet, for example. After all, a Dash button is really just a battery and a WiFi radio. When you push the button it wakes up, jumps on your home network, and sends a message to an Amazon server. You can watch for the Dash to join your network and use that as a trigger for your own events, like updating a number in a Google spreadsheet. Want to keep track of how many times you run the dishwasher in a week? Hacks to the Dash button let you do just that.

Amazon Dash buttons order products with a single click.

(Mark Lennihan/AP Images)

IP addresses longer, thereby providing more available IP addresses. IPv6 uses 128-bit addressing instead of 32-bit addressing. An IPv6 address would have the following format:

XXXX:XXXX:XXXX:XXXX:XXXX:XXXX:XXXX:XXXX

Each digit X is a **hexadecimal digit**. Hexadecimal is a base-16 number system, and each hexadecimal digit is one of 16 possible values: 0–9 or A–F. Hex addressing provides a much larger field size, which will make available a much larger number of IP addresses (approximately 340 followed by 36 zeros). This should provide a virtually unlimited supply of IP addresses and will allow many different kinds of non-PC devices such as cell phones and home appliances to join the Internet more easily in the future. All modern operating systems can handle both IPv4 and IPv6 addresses. Although the majority of routing on the Internet still takes place using IPv4 addresses, the conversion to IPv6 addressing should accelerate now that we're running out of IPv4 addresses.

How does my device get an IP address? IP addresses are assigned either statically or dynamically:

- **Static addressing** means that the IP address for a computer never changes and is most likely assigned manually by a network administrator or an ISP.
- **Dynamic addressing**, in which your computer is assigned a temporary address from an available pool of IP addresses, is more common.

A connection to an ISP could use either method. If your ISP uses static addressing, then you were assigned an IP address when you applied for your service and had to configure your computer manually to use that address. More often, though, an ISP assigns a computer a dynamic IP address, as shown in Figure 13.9.

How exactly are dynamic addresses assigned? Dynamic addressing is normally handled by the **Dynamic Host Configuration Protocol (DHCP)**, which belongs to the TCP/IP protocol suite. DHCP takes a pool of IP addresses and shares them with hosts on the network on an as-needed basis. ISPs don't need to maintain a pool of IP addresses for all their subscribers because not everyone is logged on to the Internet at one time. Thus, when a user logs on to an ISP's server, the DHCP server assigns that user an IP address for the duration of the session. Similarly, when you log on to your computer at work in the morning, DHCP assigns an IP address to your computer. These temporary IP addresses may or may not be the same from session to session.

What are the benefits of dynamic addressing? Although having a static address would seem to be convenient, dynamic addressing provides a more secure environment by keeping hackers out of computer systems. Imagine how hard it would be for burglars to find your home if you changed your address every day!

 ACTIVE HELPDESK
Understanding IP Addresses, Domain Names, and Protocols
In this Active Helpdesk, you'll play the role of a helpdesk staffer, fielding questions about which data transmissions and protocols the Internet uses and why IP addresses and domain names are important for Internet communications.

BITS&BYTES

Server in the Cloud

If you want to build a web application (a program that allows a user to send and receive information to a web browser), you may start by buying and maintaining a server computer in your home to host it. That means you have to get up in the middle of the night if the hard drive crashes, or risk angry user e-mails in the morning! What if your site becomes wildly popular and suddenly you need to expand to three or four servers to handle the load?

Using the free Google App Engine service avoids such problems. The server for your application is hosted by Google and is automatically scaled up or down as the demand for it changes. Using App Engine frees you from the worries of maintaining hardware too. And you can test out your ideas and then go live to users at no cost and only pay for services once your usage begins to take off. Your application can live at a domain name you make up, or you can serve your app from an available name off of the **appspot.com** domain. Explore more about Google App Engine at **developers.google.com /appengine**.

Domain Names

Objective 13.5 *Discuss how a numeric IP address is changed into a readable name.*

I've been on the Internet, so why have I never seen IP addresses? As you learned in Chapter 3, a *domain name* is a name that takes the place of an IP address, making it easier for people to remember. For example, **google.com** is a domain name. The server where Google's main website is deployed has an IP address (such as 66.249.64.55), but it's much easier for you to remember to tell your browser to go to **google.com**.

How are domains organized? Domains are organized by level. As you'll recall from Chapter 3, the portion of the domain name after the dot is the *top-level domain (TLD)*. The TLDs are standardized pools such as .com and .org established by ICANN (see Figure 13.10).

Within each top-level domain are many second-level domains. A **second-level domain** is a domain that's directly below a top-level domain. For example, in **dropbox.com**, *dropbox* is the second-level domain to the .com TLD. A second-level domain needs to be unique within its own TLD but not necessarily unique to all top-level domains. For example, mynewIdeaWebsite.com and mynewIdeaWebsite.org could be registered as separate domain names.

Who controls domain name registration? ICANN assigns companies or organizations to manage domain name registration. Because names can't be duplicated within a TLD, one company is assigned to oversee each TLD and to maintain a listing of all registered domains. VeriSign is the current ICANN-accredited domain name registrar for the .com and .net domains. VeriSign provides a database that lists all the registered .com and .net domains and their contact information. You can look up any .com or .net domain at Network Solutions (**networksolutions .com**) to see whether it's registered and, if so, who owns it.

Country-specific domains (such as .au for Australia) are controlled by groups in those countries. You can find a complete list of country-code TLDs on the Internet Assigned Numbers Authority website (**iana.org**).

How does my computer know the IP address of another computer? When you enter a URL in your browser, your computer converts the URL to an IP address. To do this, your computer consults a database maintained on a **domain name system (DNS) server** that functions like a phone book for the Internet.

FIGURE 13.9 With dynamic IP addressing, your IP address changes every time you connect to the Internet. *(Lfong/ Shutterstock, Juffin/DigitalVision Vectors/Getty Images)*

DOMAIN NAMES

FIGURE 13.10 The number of generic top-level domains has grown to include .museum and .job. ICANN is responsible for organizing TLD names. *(Queidea/Fotolia)*

Your ISP's web server has a default DNS server (one that's convenient to contact) that it goes to when it needs to translate a URL to an IP address (illustrated in Figure 13.11). It uses the following steps:

1. Your browser requests information from a website (for example, ABC.com).

2. Your ISP doesn't know the address of ABC.com, so your ISP must request the address from its own default DNS server.

3. The default DNS server doesn't know the IP address of ABC.com either, so it queries one of the 13 root DNS

servers maintained throughout the Internet. Each **root DNS server** knows the location of all the DNS servers that contain the master listings for an entire top-level domain.

4. The root server provides the default DNS server with the appropriate IP address of ABC.com.

5. The default DNS server stores the correct IP address for ABC.com for future reference and returns it to your ISP's web server.

6. Your computer then routes its request to ABC.com and stores the IP address in cache for later use.

How can you make your browser translate IP addresses faster? The **Internet cache** is a section of your hard drive that stores information that you may need again, such as IP addresses and frequently accessed web pages. The caching of domain name addresses also takes place in domain name system (DNS) servers. This helps speed up Internet access time because a DNS server doesn't have to query master DNS servers for top-level domains (TLDs) constantly.

However, caches have limited storage space, so entries are held in the cache only for a fixed period of time and are then deleted. The time component associated with cache retention is known as the time to live (TTL). Without caches, surfing the Internet would take a lot longer.

Remember you can't always tell whether your browser is loading the current version of a page from the web or a copy from your Internet cache. If a website contains time-sensitive information (such as a snow day alert on a college website), clicking the browser's Reload or Refresh button will ensure that the most current copy of the page loads into your browser. ∎

> **Before moving on to Part 2:**
> 1. **Watch Replay Video 13.1** ⟳ .
> 2. **Then check your understanding of what you've learned so far.**

STEP 1: Your browser requests information from ABC.com.

STEP 2: Your ISP's server asks the DNS server to turn that into an IP address.

STEP 3: If the DNS server doesn't know the IP address, it asks the root server for that IP address.

Your computer

Your ISP's web server

Your ISP's default DNS server

Root server for .com domain

STEP 6: Your computer routes request to correct IP address.

STEP 5: The DNS server stores that IP address so it will remember it next time. It then passes it along to the web server.

STEP 4: The root server provides the IP address.

FIGURE 13.11 DNS Servers in Action *(lfong/Shutterstock, Juffin/DigitalVision Vectors/Getty Images, Shashkin/Shutterstock)*

check your understanding // review & practice

For a quick review to see what you've learned so far, answer the following questions.

multiple choice

1. The rise of the Internet of Things has meant
   a. there are more machines with wireless network adapters.
   b. we need longer IP addresses than are available in IPv4.
   c. light bulbs can join your WiFi network at home.
   d. all of the above

2. Packet switching sends information between two points
   a. by breaking it into small chunks and sending the chunks across different routes.
   b. by finding one route between the two points and sending the data.
   c. by encrypting the data, then sending it.
   d. differently for each company using it.

3. In the client–server model, clients are phones or computers and servers are computers
   a. hosting web pages.
   b. with software allowing you to make purchases.
   c. that are storehouses for files.
   d. all of the above

4. The main suite of Internet protocols used to transmit data is called
   a. DNS.
   b. XML.
   c. HTTP.
   d. TCP/IP.

5. A _____ takes the place of an IP address because it's easier for humans to recall than a long string of numbers.
   a. DNS
   b. CGI
   c. domain name
   d. HTML

MyITLab Go to **MyITLab** to take an autograded version of the *Check Your Understanding* review and to find all media resources for the chapter.

TECHBYTES WEEKLY
Stay current with the TechBytes Weekly Newsletter.

Continue ⟫

TRY THIS ▶ Ping Me

Several programs that help you understand networking are part of your Windows operating system but aren't on your desktop. In this Try This, we'll use the **ping command** and the **tracert command** to get some detailed info about the Internet.

Step 1 In Windows, in the search box, type **command**. Click the **Command Prompt icon** from the search results. *(Windows 10, Microsoft Corporation)*

```
Command Prompt                                      —    □    ×

Microsoft Windows [Version 10.0.10240]
(c) 2015 Microsoft Corporation. All rights reserved.

C:\Users\Kendall>
```

Step 2 Type **ping google.com**, and press **Enter**. Ping is a utility that sends a packet of information to a specific computer and measures the time it takes to travel a round trip to the destination and back. You can use ping to test an IP address or a computer name. Ping will send a few packets and then report back to you the minimum, maximum, and average round-trip times in milliseconds, as shown here. *(Windows 10, Microsoft Corporation)*

```
C:\Users\Kendall>ping google.com

Pinging google.com [74.125.228.70] with 32 bytes of data:
Reply from 74.125.228.70: bytes=32 time=15ms TTL=252
Reply from 74.125.228.70: bytes=32 time=17ms TTL=252
Reply from 74.125.228.70: bytes=32 time=14ms TTL=252
Reply from 74.125.228.70: bytes=32 time=16ms TTL=252

Ping statistics for 74.125.228.70:
    Packets: Sent = 4, Received = 4, Lost = 0 (0% loss),
Approximate round trip times in milli-seconds:
    Minimum = 14ms, Maximum = 17ms, Average = 15ms
```

Step 3 Now let's try another utility tracert. Type **tracert google.com**, and press **Enter**. Tracert traces the route that the packet takes from your computer to the destination computer and back. Here, we see it starting off on a home system and jumping on to a computer that ISP Verizon operates in the Philadelphia area. The packet makes one more hop on the Verizon system, then jumps onto backbone network IAD8.ALTER.NET, and then begins to step down to local computers until it reaches Google [74.125.228.6]. Tracert displays the total number of hops to reach the destination. Here, we see it took 10 hops to reach **google.com**. It also shows the round-trip time for a packet to travel to each hop. Tracert sends three packets to each point and reports the round-trip time for each one. Note that the specifics you see when you run tracert will be different because you are starting at a different location. *(Windows 10, Microsoft Corporation)*

```
C:\Users\Kendall>tracert google.com

Tracing route to google.com [74.125.228.6]
over a maximum of 30 hops:

  1    <1 ms    <1 ms    <1 ms  Wireless_Broadband_Router.home [192.168.1.1]
  2     8 ms     6 ms     7 ms  L100.PHLAPA-VFTTP-77.verizon-gni.net [98.114.142
.1]
  3     6 ms     7 ms     7 ms  G0-5-4-7.PHLAPA-LCR-22.verizon-gni.net [130.81.1
82.254]
  4     8 ms     7 ms     7 ms  130.81.199.20
  5    13 ms    12 ms    14 ms  0.xe-3-0-1.XL4.IAD8.ALTER.NET [152.63.3.69]
  6    16 ms    13 ms    15 ms  TenGigE0-5-0-1.GW7.IAD8.ALTER.NET [152.63.37.162
]
  7    15 ms    15 ms    14 ms  google-gw.customer.alter.net [152.179.50.106]
  8    15 ms    14 ms    18 ms  216.239.46.248
  9    17 ms    14 ms    17 ms  72.14.238.173
 10    18 ms    17 ms    14 ms  iad23s05-in-f6.1e100.net [74.125.228.6]

Trace complete.
```

> The packet starts at a home computer, 192.168.1.1.

> Here, the packet has moved onto part of the Internet backbone, IAD8.ALTER.NET.

> The first column tells which hop the packet is on in its journey.

Step 4 Now let's try to reach a location far away from home base. At the prompt, type **tracert www.cityoflondon .gov.uk**, and press **Enter**. Here, a computer in Philadelphia is trying to reach a computer in London, **cityoflondon.gov .uk**. The packet

```
C:\Users\Kendall>tracert www.cityoflondon.gov.uk

Tracing route to www.cityoflondon.gov.uk [86.54.118.84]
over a maximum of 30 hops:

  1    <1 ms    <1 ms    <1 ms  Wireless_Broadband_Router.home [192.168.1.1]
  2     9 ms     7 ms     7 ms  L100.PHLAPA-VFTTP-77.verizon-gni.net [98.114.142
.1]
  3     7 ms     7 ms     7 ms  G0-5-4-6.PHLAPA-LCR-22.verizon-gni.net [130.81.1
83.36]
  4     7 ms     7 ms     8 ms  so-3-1-0-0.PHIL-BB-RTR2.verizon-gni.net [130.81.
22.60]
  5    14 ms    14 ms    14 ms  0.xe-7-3-0.BR1.IAD8.ALTER.NET [152.63.3.125]
  6    14 ms    15 ms    14 ms  ae16.edge1.washingtondc12.level3.net [4.68.62.13
3]
  7    16 ms    21 ms    24 ms  vl-3602-ve-226.ebr2.Washington12.Level3.net [4.6
9.158.38]
  8    17 ms    17 ms    17 ms  4.69.148.49
  9    85 ms    84 ms    85 ms  ae-41-41.ebr2.London1.Level3.net [4.69.137.65]
 10    85 ms    92 ms    84 ms  ae-58-223.csw2.London1.Level3.net [4.69.153.138]
 11     *       86 ms    85 ms  ae-2-52.edge4.London1.Level3.net [4.69.139.106]
 12    84 ms    85 ms    84 ms  195.50.122.126
 13    86 ms    84 ms    87 ms  86.54.118.84
 14     *        *        *     Request timed out.
 15     *        *        *     Request timed out.
```

> Hops 9 and 10 take 85 ms each. These are probably traversing the ocean.

> Here is the destination IP address, 86.54.118.84 (CityofLondon.gov.uk). After that, the firewall of CityofLondon.gov.uk begins to reject the packets.

moves to a Verizon computer in Philadelphia, then travels to Washington. Next, there is a much longer trip time, 85 ms. This is probably as the packet moves across the Atlantic Ocean. The packet finally reaches **cityoflondon.gov.uk** [86.54.118.84]. By using ping and tracert, you can see exactly where a connection is failing. *(Windows 10, Microsoft Corporation)*

Make This ▶ TOOL: AI Web

MAKE: An Earthquake Detector

Want your apps to talk to other computers and grab current information from them? Web services allow you to do just that. Thousands of free web services are available to you, like one that shows current stock prices or one that tells the most recent earthquake activity.

In this exercise, you'll continue your mobile app development by using the Web component of the Connectivity drawer in **App Inventor** to have a conversation with a web service. You will send a request for the specific information you want, then process it with the when **Web.GotText** event handler. *(MIT App Inventor 2, Massachusetts Institute of Technology. Creative Commons Attribution-ShareAlike 3.0 Unported License)*

```
call  Web1 ▼ .BuildRequestData
                            list
```

```
when  Web1 ▼ .GotText
  url   responseCode   responseType   responseContent
  do   set  Stocks ▼ . Text ▼  to   get  responseContent ▼
```

Using web services, your app can talk with other computers and collect useful information.

For the instructions for this exercise, go to MyITLab.

Coding and Communicating on the Internet

Learning Outcome 13.2 You will be able to describe the web technologies used to develop web applications.

The web uses special languages such as *HTML* and protocols such as *HTTP* to facilitate communication between computers that use different system and application software. Communication between any two points on the Internet is possible because of HTML and communication protocols. In this part of the chapter, we'll explore these topics.

 ## web
TECHNOLOGIES

Let's examine in more detail the programming languages and communication protocols that support the Internet. We introduced some of these ideas in Chapter 10. Now we'll explore them in a bit more depth.

Web Development

Objective 13.6 *Compare and contrast a variety of web development languages.*

Websites require more than just simple formatting commands. They are interactive and display high quality audio and video. This is all controlled with a variety of development tools and languages.

HTML

How are web pages formatted? Web pages are text documents formatted using HTML (Hypertext Markup Language). HTML isn't a programming language; rather, it's a set of rules for marking up blocks of text so that a browser knows how to display them.

Blocks of text in HTML documents are surrounded by pairs of **HTML tags** (such as <b> and </b>, which indicate bolding). HTML tags surround and define HTML content. Each pair of tags and the text between them are collectively referred to as an **element**. The elements are interpreted by the browser, and appropriate effects are applied to the text. The following is an element from an HTML document:

```
<i> This should be italicized.</i>
```

The browser would display this element as:

This should be italicized.

The first tag, <i>, tells the browser that the text following it should be italicized. The ending</i> tag indicates that the browser should stop applying italics. Note that multiple tags can be combined in a single element:

```
<b><i>This should be bolded and
italicized.</i></b>
```

The browser would display this element as:

This should be bolded and italicized.

Tags for creating hyperlinks appear as follows:

```
<a href="www.pearsonhighered.com">Pearson
Higher Education</a>
```

The code <a href="www.pearsonhighered.com">defines the link's destination. The</a> tag is the anchor tag and creates a link to another resource on the web. Here, the link is to the **www.pearsonhighered.com** web page. The text between the open and close of the anchor tag, Pearson Higher Education, is the link label. The link label is the text (or image) that's displayed on the web page as clickable text for the hyperlink.

How do I see the HTML coding of a web page? HTML documents are merely text documents with tags applied to them. If you want to look at the HTML coding behind any web page, just right-click and select View Source from the shortcut menu, and the HTML code for that page will display, as shown in Figure 13.12.

What is the current HTML standard? As we discussed in Chapter 10, HTML5 is the current version of the HTML standard. HTML5 modernizes a number of features in HTML such as:

- Reducing the need for external plug-ins (like Flash)
- Supporting better error handling
- Supporting advanced animation and audio effects
- Making it easier to draw graphics.

To see an example of what HTML5 makes possible in a browser, play with the drawing tool at **muro.deviantart.com**.

How can developers easily change the formatting of HTML elements? A **cascading style sheet (CSS)** is a list of rules that defines in one single location how to display HTML elements. Style rules enable a web developer to define a kind of formatting for each HTML element and apply it to all those elements on a set of web pages. Essentially, a template is created on which the formatting for many web pages within a site will be based. When a global change is necessary, the developer only needs to change the style on the style sheet, and all the elements in the web

FIGURE 13.12 You can view the source code of a website by right-clicking and selecting View Source from the shortcut menu. *(Firefox logo® is a registered trademark of the Mozilla Foundation)*

document will update automatically (see Figure 13.13).

For example, a web page has an <h1> heading tag, and all <h1> tags in the web page are formatted with a white background and an orange border. Before cascading style sheets, if you wanted to change the border color from orange to yellow, you had to change the background color of each individual <h1> tag. With cascading style sheets, the change from orange to yellow only needs to happen once on the style sheet; all the <h1> tags on the web pages then update to yellow without individual changes needing to be made.

Where does the cascading come in? In web documents, there are different layers of styles:

- External: stored in a separate file
- Embedded: stored inside the current HTML document
- Inline: stored within a single line inside the HTML document

Therefore, it's possible that different rules can be created for the same type of element located in different places (external, embedded, or inline). In other words, in an external style sheet, there might be

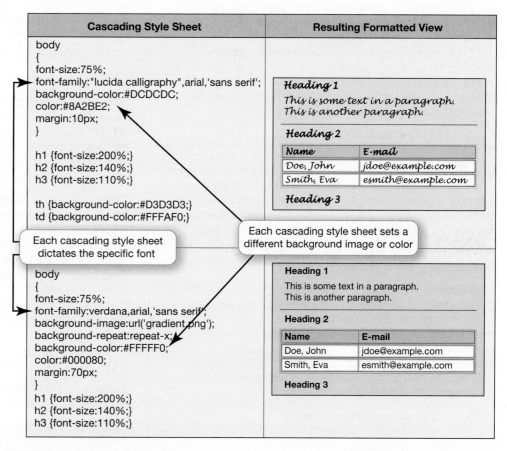

FIGURE 13.13 Cascading style sheets allow developers to create formatting templates. Just as all the pages of this book have a similar look and feel, one style sheet can control the formatting of many web pages.

a rule that defines the background color for all paragraphs as blue. In an embedded style sheet, a rule for the background color for all paragraphs might be white. And in an inline style sheet, the background color might be light pink. Eventually, all these style sheets must be merged to form one style sheet for the document. This creates conflicts among rules. Therefore, each type of rule is understood to have a specific weight so that when the rules are collected and merged, the rule or style with a higher weight overrides the rule or style with a lower weight. This hierarchy of competing styles creates a "cascade" of styles ranked according to their assigned weights.

XML and JSON

How is XML different from HTML? As you learned in Chapter 10, the **eXtensible Markup Language (XML)** describes the content in terms of what data is being described rather than how it's to be displayed. Instead of being locked into standard tags and formats for data, users can build their own markup languages to accommodate particular data formats and needs.

For example, say you want to capture a credit card number. In HTML, the paragraph tags (<p> and </p>) are used to define text and numeric elements. Almost any text or graphic can fall between these tags and be treated as a paragraph. The HTML code could appear as:

```
<p>1234567890123456</p>
```

The browser will interpret the data contained within the <p> and </p> tags as a separate paragraph. However, the paragraph tags tell us nothing about the data contained within them. A better approach lies in creating tags that actually *describe* the data contained within them. Using XML, we could create a "credit card number" tag that's used exclusively for credit card data:

```
<credit_card_number>1234567890123456
</credit_card_number>
```

In addition, HTML tags don't provide any methodology for data validation. If we needed a tag for an age field, we know a person's age can only be between 0 and 120, but any data may be inserted between <p> and </p> tags. How would we know if the age was valid? *XML schema diagrams (XSDs)* allows you to specify all kinds of data validation for a specific XML tag. An XSD schema definition that restricts age to be in the range 0, 120 would read:

```
<xs:simpleType name= "age">
 <xs:restriction base="xs:integer">
   <xs:minInclusive value="0"/>
   <xs:maxInclusive value="120"/>
 </xs:restriction>
</xs:simpleType>
```

FIGURE 13.14

XML Custom Packages

XML CUSTOM PACKAGE	SAMPLE TAGS
MathML	<times>, <power>, <divide>
X3D	<viewpoint>, <shape>, <scene>
MusicXML	<score>, <beat>, <measure>, <clef>

What custom XML packages are available? XML has spawned quite a few custom packages for specific communities. A few examples are listed in Figure 13.14. These packages illustrate the goal of XML—information exchange standards that can be easily constructed and customized to serve a growing variety of online applications.

Is XML the only format websites use to speak to each other? There is another very popular format used to transfer information between computers named **JSON**. It stands for JavaScript Object Notation and is a data interchange standard that is easy for humans to read and write. JSON is faster and easier to use than XML. It consists of name and value pairs like:

```
"firstName" : "Kendall"
```

HTTP

Which Internet protocol does a browser use to send requests? The **Hypertext Transfer Protocol (HTTP)** was created especially for the transfer of hypertext documents across the Internet. (Recall that *hypertext* documents are documents in which text is linked to other documents or media.)

How does a browser safeguard secure information? Hypertext Transfer Protocol Secure (HTTPS) ensures that data is sent securely over the web. HTTPS is actually an acronym that's the combination of HTTP and **Secure Sockets Layer (SSL)**, a network security protocol. **Transport Layer Security (TLS)** is an updated extension of SSL. These protocols provide data integrity and security for transmissions over the Internet. Commerce servers use security protocols to protect sensitive information from interception by hackers.

Application Architecture

Objective 13.7 *Compare and contrast server-side and client-side application software.*

Web application software typically consists of two parts: The client-side software lives on the user's computer while the server-side program lives on the server computer. Let's look more closely at both aspects of web application development.

Server-Side Applications

What are server-side applications? As you'll recall, the web is a client–server network. The type of program that runs on a web server rather than on your computer is referred to as a **server-side program**. Server-side program execution can require many communication sessions between the client and the server to achieve the goal, but server-side programs can perform very complex operations.

What are popular server-side interfaces? Several methods of designing programs are available that execute on the server and give a web page more sophisticated capabilities. Two of the most popular are *CGI (Common Gateway Interface)* and *ASP.NET (Active Server Pages)*.

How does CGI make a web page more interactive? Most browser requests merely result in a file being displayed in your browser. To make a website interactive, you may need to run a program that performs a certain action (such as gathering a name and address and adding it to a database). The **Common Gateway Interface (CGI)** provides a methodology by which your browser can request that a program file be executed instead of just being delivered to the browser. This enables functionality beyond the simple display of information.

What programming language is used to create the programs that run on the server? PHP, Perl, and Python are all languages used to create these server-side programs. One common task is to collect a user's answers in a form and to create and send out an e-mail message with that information.

Let's take an example, as shown in Figure 13.15:

Step 1. A button on bookworlds.com's website may say, "Click Here to Join Mailing List."

Step 2. Clicking the button may execute a script file, called "mailinglist.pl," from the web server hosting the site.

Step 3. This file generates a form that's sent to your browser. The form includes fields for a name and e-mail address and a Submit button.

Step 4. After you fill in the fields and click the Submit button, the mailinglist.pl program sends the information back to the server. The server then records the information in a database.

Client-Side Applications

What are client-side applications? A **client-side program** is a program that runs on the client computer and requires no interaction with a web server. Once a web server processes a web page and sends the page to the client computer that requested it, the receiving computer can't get new data from the server unless a new request is made. If interactivity is required on a web page, this exchange of data between the client and server can make the interactivity inefficient and slow. Often it's more efficient to run programs on your computer (the client). Therefore, client-side programs are created.

How is client-side programming done? There are two main approaches to client-side programming:

1. An **HTML embedded scripting language**, which tucks programming code directly within the HTML of a web page. The most popular embedded language is *JavaScript*.

2. An **applet**, which is a small application actually located on the server. When requested, the applet is downloaded to the client. It's there ready to run when needed without additional data transfers between the client and server. The Java language is the most common language used to create applets for use in browsers.

Isn't there a delay as an applet downloads? You may experience some delay in functionality while waiting for a Java applet to download to your computer, but once the applet arrives, it can execute all its functions without further communication with the server. Let's look at an example, as shown in Figure 13.16:

Step 1. Your browser makes contact with a game on the game site ArcadePod (**arcadepod.com**) and makes your request to play a game.

FIGURE 13.15 Information Flow When a Browser Action Executes a Program on a Web Server *(Ifong/ Shutterstock, Shashkin/Shutterstock)*

Step 2. The web server returns the Java applet that contains all the code to run the game on your computer.

Step 3. Your computer executes the applet code, and the game runs on your computer.

What are some scripting technologies? Dynamic HTML (DHTML) is a combination of technologies—HTML, cascading style sheets, and JavaScript—that's used to create lively and interactive websites. DHTML technologies allow a web page to change (that is, to be dynamic) after it's been loaded. Such change generally occurs in response to user actions, such as when you click your mouse or mouse over objects on a page. DHTML also brings special effects to otherwise static web pages without requiring users to download and install plug-ins or other special software.

What is JavaScript? JavaScript is a commonly used scripting language for creating DHTML effects. JavaScript is often confused with the Java programming language because of the similarity in their names. However, though they share some common elements, the two languages are different.

With JavaScript, HTML documents can be made responsive to mouse clicks and typing. For example, JavaScript is often used to validate the information you input in a web form, for example, to make sure you filled in all required fields.

When JavaScript code is embedded in an HTML document, it's downloaded to the browser with the HTML page. All actions dictated by the embedded JavaScript commands are executed on the client computer. Without JavaScript and other scripting languages, web pages would be lifeless.

How does JavaScript control the components of a web page? Just as cascading style sheets organize and combine the attributes of objects on a web page, JavaScript uses the **Document Object Model (DOM)** to organize the objects and page elements. The Document Object Model defines every item on a web page—including graphics, tables, and headers—as an object. Then with DOM, similar to cascading style sheets, web developers can easily change the look and feel of these objects.

Where is web programming headed? Web pages can interact with servers at times other than when a page is being fetched. Web pages can have an ongoing exchange of information, communicating with the server and updating information on the page without requiring the user to do a page refresh or leave the page. AJAX is the acronym for Asynchronous JavaScript and XML, a group of technologies that facilitates the creation of this style of web applications. There are a huge number of web application frameworks now available, like Ruby on Rails. These packages make it simpler to create an application that talks to a web server, queries a database, and then presents information in a nicely formatted template. ∎

STEP 1: Request from browser for game

STEP 2: Java applet code sent to your computer

Your computer

STEP 3: Computer executes Java applet code and game displays

ArcadePod.com server

FIGURE 13.16 Deployment of a Java Applet on a Computer

communications over
THE INTERNET

In this section, we explore electronic communications media and how to keep your information exchanges efficient and secure.

Types of Internet Communication

Objective 13.8 *Discuss the mechanisms for communicating via e-mail and instant messaging.*

Two of the most common communication methods on the Internet are e-mail and instant messaging.

E-Mail

Who invented e-mail? In 1971, Ray Tomlinson, a computer engineer who worked on the development of the ARPANET, the precursor to the Internet, created e-mail. E-mail grew from a simple program that Tomlinson wrote to enable computer users to leave text messages for each other on a single machine. The logical extension of this was sending text messages between machines on the Internet. E-mail became the most popular application on ARPANET; by 1973, it accounted for 75% of all data traffic.

How does e-mail travel the Internet? Just like other kinds of data that flow along the Internet, e-mail has its own protocol. The **Simple Mail Transfer Protocol (SMTP)** is responsible for sending e-mail along the Internet to its destination. SMTP is part of the Internet Protocol suite. As in most other Internet applications, e-mail is a client/server application. On the way to its destination, your mail will pass through **e-mail servers**—specialized computers whose sole function is to store, process, and send e-mail.

Where are e-mail servers located? If your ISP provides you with an e-mail account, it runs an e-mail server that uses SMTP. For example, as shown in Figure 13.17, say you're sending an e-mail message to your friend Cheyenne. Cheyenne uses Verizon as her ISP. Therefore, your e-mail to her is addressed to Cheyenne@verizon.net.

Let's follow that e-mail:

Step 1. When you send the e-mail message, your ISP's e-mail server receives it.

Step 2. The e-mail server reads the domain name (verizon. net) and communicates with a DNS server to determine the location of verizon.net.

FIGURE 13.17 A Sample Route an E-Mail Takes on the Internet *(Ifong/Shutterstock, Sashkin/Shutterstock, Nebayan Viktoryia/Shutterstock)*

Step 3. The DNS server turns the domain name into the associated IP address.

Step 4. The e-mail message is forwarded to verizon.net, and it arrives at an e-mail server maintained by Cheyenne's ISP.

Step 5. The e-mail is then stored on Cheyenne's ISP's e-mail server. The next time Cheyenne checks her e-mail, she'll receive your message.

How are we able to send files as attachments?
SMTP was designed to handle text messages. When the need arose to send files by e-mail, the **Multipurpose Internet Mail Extensions (MIME)** specification was introduced. All e-mail client software now uses this protocol to attach files. E-mail is still sent as text, but the e-mail client using the MIME protocol now handles the encoding and decoding for the users. When attaching a file, your e-mail client transparently encodes and decodes the file for transmission and receipt.

Instant Messaging

What do you need to run instant messaging?
Instant messaging (IM) requires the use of a client program that connects to an IM service. Yahoo! Messenger and Google Hangouts are two popular IM services in use today.

How does instant messaging work? The client software running on your device makes a connection with the chat server and provides it with connection information for your device (such as the IP address), as shown in Figure 13.18.

Because both your device and your friend's device have the connection information (the IP addresses) for each other, the server isn't involved in the chat session. Chatting takes place directly between the two devices over the Internet.

Is sending an IM secure? Most IM services do not use a high level of encryption for their messages—if they bother to use encryption at all. In addition to viruses, worms, and hacking threats, IM systems are vulnerable to eavesdropping, in which someone using a packet sniffer "listens in" on IM conversations. Although several measures are underway to increase the security of this method of real-time communication, major vulnerabilities still exist. And employers can install monitoring software to record IM sessions. Therefore, it's not a good idea to send sensitive information using IM because it's susceptible to interception and possible misuse by hackers.

FIGURE 13.18 How an Instant Messaging Program Works (*Sashkin/Shutterstock, Tom Wang/Shutterstock, Tyler Olson/Shutterstock*)

BITS&BYTES

Gmail Features You Should Know About

Many individuals use Gmail because it's free. But free doesn't mean it isn't full featured. Gmail has some very useful tricks that can save you time, aggravation, and money. Here are a few to consider:

- **Priority inbox:** Enable this feature and Gmail will predict automatically which e-mails are important by watching which e-mails you read and respond to. You can also downgrade or upgrade the importance of an e-mail so your priority inbox becomes fine-tuned over time.
- **Inbox tabs:** Your inbox can be much more manageable using Inbox tabs. Categories like Promotions automatically catch and sort all the offers that are mailed to you.
- **Free phone calls and video calls:** Install the voice and video chat plug-in for Gmail, and you can call anyone in the United States or Canada directly from Gmail—for free! Just click the Call Phone or Start Video Call options in the Chat section of your Gmail screen to initiate the call.
- **Attach money:** Instead of just attaching a file, how about attaching some money? You can tie your Gmail account to a Google Wallet account and send money with just a click.
- **Big files:** You can insert files directly from your Google Drive account that are up to 1 TB in size.

For even more useful features, click the Labs option on your Gmail settings menu to see the latest and greatest features being tested by Google.

Encryption

Objective 13.9 *Explain how data encryption improves security.*

Can other people read my e-mail? E-mail is highly susceptible to being read by unintended parties because it's sent in plain text. Additionally, copies of your e-mail messages may exist, temporarily or permanently, on numerous servers as the messages make their way through the Internet. To protect your sensitive e-mail messages, encryption practices are available.

How do I encrypt my e-mail? Many e-mail services offer built-in encryption. Hushmail (**hushmail.com**) and Comodo SecureEmail (**comodo.com**) offer free versions of their secure e-mail services. You can sign up on their websites and experiment with sending encrypted e-mail. And you don't

A = C	N = P
B = D	O = Q
C = E	P = R
D = F	Q = S
E = G	R = T
F = H	S = U
G = I	T = V
H = J	U = W
I = K	V = X
J = L	W = Y
K = M	X = Z
L = N	Y = A
M = O	Z = B

The word **C O M P U T E R** using the two-position code at the left now becomes:

E Q O R W V G T

This is difficult to interpret without the code key at the left.

FIGURE 13.19 Writing the word *COMPUTER* using a two-position right-shift encryption code results in *EQORWVGT*.

need to abandon your current e-mail accounts—just use your secure account when you require secure communications.

How does encryption work? Encryption refers to the process of coding your e-mail so that only the person with the key to the code (the intended recipient) can decode (or decipher) the message. There are two basic types of encryption:

1. *Private-key encryption*
2. *Public-key encryption*

What is private-key encryption? In **private-key encryption**, only the two parties involved in sending the message have the code. This could be a simple shift code where letters of the alphabet are shifted to a new position (see Figure 13.19).

For example, in a two-position right-shift code, the letter a becomes c, b becomes d, and so on. Alternatively, it could be a more complex substitution code (*a = h, b = r, c = g*, etc.). The main problem with private-key encryption is key security. If someone steals a copy of the code or is savvy about decoding, the code is broken.

What is public-key encryption? In **public-key encryption**, two keys, known as a **key pair**, are created. You use one key for coding and the other for decoding. The key for coding is generally distributed as a **public key**. You can place this key on your website, for instance. Anyone wishing to send you a message can then download your public key and code the message using your public key.

When you receive the message, you use your **private key** to decode it. You're the only one who ever possesses the private key, and therefore it's highly secure. The keys are generated in such a way that they can work only with each other. The

 ACTIVE HELPDESK
Keeping E-Mail Secure

In this Active Helpdesk, you'll play the role of a helpdesk staffer, fielding questions about how e-mail works and how messages are kept secure.

Encryption has fueled the enormous growth of electronic commerce. Because people feel safe in transmitting private data like credit card numbers across the Internet, online banking, shopping, and communication have exploded. But ardent shoppers are not the only people relying on encryption to keep their information hidden.

Criminals are also increasing their use of encryption. "Going dark" is the term for encrypting the phone and e-mail accounts that carry the details of their illegal transactions. For federal agencies, it becomes more and more difficult to gather the evidence needed for a conviction as easy-to-use encryption software spreads. The encryption standards are now so strong that there is no way to break into some encrypted messages. Apple announced with the release of iOS8 that the default encryption its products support could not be broken by Apple. So if a government agency received a warrant for specific records, Apple could not possibly comply and hand over readable information.

Additionally, phone networks are now

FIGURE 13.20 Should security experts be forced by law to leave a way to break their encryption systems? (*Seanlockephotography/Fotolia*)

switching over to digital so phone companies may not actually be able to comply meaningfully with wiretap requests.

This has created such a level of concern with national security officials and law enforcement agencies that they have lobbied for tech companies to undermine their own encryption schemes (see Figure 13.20). If the encryption were weakened, allowing some mechanism for it to be broken upon request, there would be no information that was completely "secure." This idea of a "backdoor" or a "key under the doormat" allowing every secure message to be broken has been controversial for years, and the debate has been on the front pages once again.

The opposition, which includes many security experts as well as civil libertarians, points to the fact this would be bad for commercial business. Deliberately making security products less secure may be useful to some government agencies but exposes all users to possible security leaks by hackers. Where do you stand on the issue of "going dark"?

BITS&BYTES

Random Numbers: We Wouldn't Have Encryption Without Them!

E-mail encryption, SSL encryption, and just about anything we do to achieve privacy on the Internet requires random numbers. Encryption is accomplished using random number sequences, which are sequences of numbers in which no patterns can be recognized. Even for an e-commerce transaction (say, buying a textbook from **BarnesandNoble .com**) that uses SSL encryption to encode your credit card number, as many as 368 bits of random data might be needed. Only 128 bits are needed for the encryption key, but other random data is needed to create authentication codes and to prevent replay attacks. Replay attacks occur when hackers attempt to copy packets traveling across the Internet and to extract data (such as encryption codes) from them. The hackers then can replay (reuse) the data to gain access to networks or transactions.

So where do all these random numbers come from? Generating true random sequences is more difficult than it sounds. Most random number generators are really pseudo-random because they're all based on some sort of pattern to generate the numbers. However, in 1998, Mads Haahr of the School of Computer Science and Statistics at Trinity College in Dublin created the site **random.org**, which is dedicated to providing true random numbers for web applications such as encryption algorithms. The numbers are generated based on atmospheric noise, which is truly random. The noise is gleaned from radios not tuned to a particular station, so they're broadcasting static. Anyone can access the website and download random numbers to be used for encryption or other vital services such as lottery drawings. For more information, check out **random.org**.

private key is generated first. The public key is then generated using a complex mathematical formula, often using values from the private key. The computations are so complex that they're considered unbreakable. Both keys are necessary to decode a message. If one key is lost, the other key can't be used by itself.

Which type of encryption is used on the Internet? Public-key encryption is the most commonly used encryption on the Internet. Public-key packages such as **Pretty Good Privacy (PGP)** are available for download at sites such as CNET Downloads (download.cnet.com), and you can usually use them free of charge (although there are now commercial versions of PGP). After obtaining the PGP software, you can generate key pairs to provide a private key for you and a public key for the rest of the world.

What does a key look like? A key is a binary number. Keys vary in length, depending on how secure they need to be. A 12-bit key has 12 positions and might look like this:

100110101101

Longer keys are more secure because they have more values that are possible. A 12-bit key provides 4,096 different possible values, whereas a 40-bit key allows for 1,099,511,627,776 possible values. The key and the message are run through a complex algorithm in the encryption program that converts the message into unrecognizable code. Each key turns the message into a different code.

Is a private key really secure? Because of the complexity of the algorithms used to generate key pairs, it's impossible to deduce the private key from the public key. However,

that doesn't mean your coded message can't be cracked. As you learned in Chapter 12, a brute force attack occurs when hackers try every possible key combination to decode a message. This type of attack can enable hackers to deduce the key and decode the message.

What kind of key is considered safe? In the early 1990s, 40-bit keys were thought to be completely resistant to brute force attacks and were the norm for encryption. However, in 1995, a French programmer used a unique algorithm of his own and 120 workstations simultaneously to attempt to break a 40-bit key. He succeeded in just eight days. After this, 128-bit keys became the standard. However, using supercomputers, researchers have had some success cracking 128-bit encryption. Therefore, strong encryption now calls for 256-bit keys. It's believed that even with the most powerful computers in use today, it would take hundreds of billions of years to crack a 256-bit key.

Do corporations use special encryption? Businesses often pay for encryption services that also provide other features such as confirmation of message delivery, message tracking, and overwriting of e-mail messages when they're deleted to ensure that copies don't exist. Companies such as ZixCorp (zixcorp.com) provide these higher levels of service to businesses. ∎

Before moving on to the Chapter Review:
1. Watch Replay Video 13.2 ▷.
2. Then check your understanding of what you've learned so far.

trends in IT

Crowdsourcing: Harnessing the Power of Social Networks

Starting and running a small business involves risk, especially when you're running a merchandising business. Deciding what products to buy and sell to customers is tricky. Will your customers buy the products you think are wonderful? Will they buy them quickly enough so that you can free up your cash to buy more inventory? What quantities should you stock? If you're an entrepreneur, you usually have to make these decisions yourself. Wouldn't it be better to let your customers tell you what to sell?

Many businesses harness the power of their customers (and potential customers) by using the Internet to take advantage of a technique known as **crowdsourcing**. When you crowdsource, you take a task that an employee or a contractor usually performs and instead outsource that task to a large group of people, usually via the Internet. In this way, you can have many individuals work on a task in order to take advantage of aggregated brainpower. Or you can aggregate and analyze the results of feedback from the crowdsourcers to make informed business decisions. A company that exemplifies the crowdsourcing model of customer-driven merchandise buying is ModCloth (**modcloth.com**).

ModCloth is a company founded by two high-school students who were just 17 years old. They started selling only vintage clothing but then expanded to offer vintage-inspired designs by indie designers. When ordering clothing from designers, there's usually a minimum order quantity that often exceeds 100 pieces. Although the buyers for ModCloth feel they have a good eye for what their customers like, it's still risky for a small business to order large quantities of items because they may take a long time to sell.

ModCloth started its Be the Buyer program to involve customers in the buying process. They post clothing they're considering buying on the ModCloth site, and then customers vote to either "Pick It" (stock the item) or "Skip It," as shown in Figure 13.21.

Customers can post comments about the items, which range from humorous to constructive. ModCloth also provides links so that voters can easily share items with their friends on social networks like Facebook and Twitter. Constructive ideas from potential customers can be sent back to designers who might make suggested alterations to items before ModCloth orders them. When ModCloth orders a popular item, customers who indicated they liked it can be contacted via e-mail to stimulate sales.

Be part of the businesses you patronize—look for the chance to be heard through crowdsourcing.

FIGURE 13.21 Customers vote and comment on products that ModCloth is thinking about stocking. *(Modcloth, Inc.)*

check your understanding // review & practice

For a quick review to see what you've learned so far, answer the following questions.

multiple choice

1. JSON, JavaScript Object Notation, is useful because it

   a. uses PGP to encrypt data.

   b. allows web services to exchange information.

   c. makes the Document Object Model usable in HTML.

   d. is hexadecimal codes that execute quickly on computers.

2. The protocol used to send e-mail over the Internet is

   a. HTTP.

   b. DHTML.

   c. DNS.

   d. SMTP.

3. Cascading style sheets allow you to quickly change

   a. from server-side processing to client-side processing.

   b. to a more secure transport protocol.

   c. the rules for applying formatting to an HTML document.

   d. from HTML to XML.

4. HTML5

   a. supports powerful multimedia effects.

   b. is obsolete.

   c. is used to program server-side applications.

   d. provides high-level security for e-mail.

5. MIME is a protocol that's used when you're

   a. sending a video file to YouTube.

   b. encrypting an e-mail message.

   c. executing a CGI script.

   d. sending an e-mail that has a photo attached.

MyITLab Go to **MyITLab** to take an autograded version of the *Check Your Understanding* review and to find all media resources for the chapter.

TECHBYTES WEEKLY

Stay current with the TechBytes Weekly Newsletter.

Continue ≫

13 Chapter Review

summary //

Inner Workings of the Internet

Learning Outcome 13.1 You will be able to explain how the Internet is managed and the details of how data is transmitted across the Internet.

Internet Networking

Objective 13.1 *Describe the management of the Internet.*

- Management of the Internet is carried out by several nonprofit organizations and user groups such as the Internet Society, the Internet Engineering Task Force (IETF), the Internet Architecture Board (IAB), the Internet Corporation for Assigned Names and Numbers (ICANN), and the World Wide Web Consortium (W3C). Each group has different responsibilities and tasks. Currently, the U.S. government funds a majority of the Internet's costs. Other countries also pay for Internet infrastructure and development.

Objective 13.2 *Explain how the Internet's networking components interact.*

- The largest paths of the Internet, along which data travels the most efficiently and quickly, make up the Internet backbone. Homes and all but the largest businesses connect to the Internet through regional or local connections, which then connect to the Internet through the entities that make up the Internet backbone. The largest businesses, educational centers, and some government agencies make up the Internet backbone.

- Optical carrier (OC) lines are high throughput and are used to connect large corporations to their ISPs.

- Service providers use an Internet exchange point (IXP) to connect directly to each other, reducing cost and latency time.

- Individual users enter their ISP through a point of presence (POP), a bank of routers and switches through which many users can connect simultaneously.

Objective 13.3 *List and describe the Internet protocols used for data transmission.*

- Data is transmitted along the Internet using packet switching. Data is broken up into discrete units known as *packets*, which can take independent routes to the destination before being reassembled.

- A computer protocol is a set of rules for exchanging electronic information. Although many protocols are available on the Internet, the main suite of protocols used to move information over the Internet is TCP/IP. The suite is named after the original two protocols that were developed for the Internet: the Transmission Control Protocol (TCP) and the Internet Protocol (IP). TCP is responsible for preparing data for transmission, but IP actually sends data between computers on the Internet.

Internet Identity

Objective 13.4 *Explain how each device connected to the Internet is assigned a unique address.*

- An IP address is a unique number assigned to all computers connected to the Internet. The IP address is necessary so that packets of data can be sent to a particular location (computer) on the Internet.

Objective 13.5 *Discuss how a numeric IP address is changed into a readable name.*

- A domain name is merely a name that stands for a certain IP address and that makes it easier for people to remember it. DNS servers act as the phone books of the Internet. They enable your computer to find out the IP address of a domain by looking up its corresponding domain name.

Coding and Communicating on the Internet

Learning Outcome 13.2 You will be able to describe the web technologies used to develop web applications.

Web Technologies

Objective 13.6 *Compare and contrast a variety of web development languages.*

- The Hypertext Transfer Protocol (HTTP) is the protocol used on the Internet to display web pages in your browser.

- The Hypertext Markup Language (HTML) is a set of rules for marking up blocks of text so that a browser knows how to display them. Most web pages are generated with at least some HTML code. Blocks of text in HTML documents are surrounded by a pair of tags (such as <b> and </b> to indicate bolding). These tags and the text between them are referred to as *elements*. The current HTML standard is HTML5, which offers much better support for media like audio and video.

- Because HTML wasn't designed for information exchange, eXtensible Markup Language (XML) was created. Instead of locking users into standard tags and formats for data, XML enables users to create their own markup languages to accommodate particular data formats and needs. JSON is another standard supporting the exchange of information between web services.

Objective 13.7 *Compare and contrast server-side and client-side application software.*

- Software is developed on both the server and on the client side to make web pages more responsive and interactive. Server-side programming includes CGI and ASP.NET. Client-side programs can run faster because they don't need to wait for information exchanges with the server. Embedded JavaScript and Java applets are two common approaches for writing client-side programs.

Communications Over the Internet

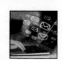

Objective 13.8 *Discuss the mechanisms for communicating via e-mail and instant messaging.*

- Simple Mail Transfer Protocol (SMTP) is the protocol responsible for sending e-mail over the Internet. E-mail is a client/server application. E-mail passes through e-mail servers, whose functions are to store, process, and send e-mail to its ultimate destination. ISPs and portals such as Gmail maintain e-mail servers to provide e-mail functionality to their customers. Your ISP's e-mail server uses DNS servers to locate the IP addresses for the recipients of the e-mail you send.

- Instant messaging (IM) software communicates with a chat server to quickly deliver communications to your friends who are online. It's not secure and can be vulnerable to eavesdropping.

Objective 13.9 *Explain how data encryption improves security.*

- Encryption software, such as Pretty Good Privacy (PGP), is used to code messages so that they can be decoded only by authorized recipients.

(MyITLab) Be sure to check out **MyITLab** for additional materials to help you review and learn. And don't forget the Replay Videos ▶.

key terms //

chapter quiz // assessment

For a quick review to see what you've learned, answer the following questions. Submit the quiz as requested by your instructor. If you are using **MyITLab**, the quiz is also available there.

multiple choice

1. The collection of large national and international network providers used to establish the Internet is called the

  a. T1.

  b. highway system.

  c. OC.

  d. Internet backbone.

2. The information in a data packet includes

  a. the data and the destination.

  b. the data and circuit identifier.

  c. the "To" address, "From" address, data, and reassembly instructions.

  d. different types of information depending on the type of message being sent.

3. IPv6 uses 32 bits to assign a(n)

  a. data packet to each transmission.

  b. memory address to the CPU.

  c. address to every device connected to the Internet.

  d. destination Internet address to each e-mail.

4. A private key is important

  a. to reboot system hardware.

  b. to reset your public key if you lose a password.

  c. to decode an encrypted message.

  d. because it enables you to use MIME.

5. HTTPS is different than HTTP because

  a. of how it transforms or reformats the data.

  b. it is a combination of HTTP and the Secure Sockets Layer (SSL).

  c. it extracts data from source databases.

  d. it stores data in the data warehouse.

6. Encryption is used to

  a. code your e-mail so only one person can decipher it.

  b. shrink the amount of space it takes to store e-mail.

  c. transfer e-mail more quickly.

  d. make shopping on the Internet more available.

true/false

_____ **1.** If you use an Internet cache, then the information displayed in your browser is automatically refreshed.

_____ **2.** Your Internet service provider has a default domain name server to translate a URL into an IP address.

_____ **3.** Instant messaging is secure because of the type of encryption used.

_____ **4.** MIME is the protocol that supports sending files as e-mail attachments.

critical thinking

1. Who's in Charge?

Should there be an agency in charge of the Internet? How would business, government, and education be impacted if the Internet were suddenly no longer available? Does this warrant establishing a governing body to regulate and monitor the Internet?

2. The Future of Web Programming

Where is web programming headed? It will be driven by the needs of users, so think about what kinds of things you need web pages to do for you that they currently cannot do. Should biometric identification replace passwords, for example?

Using Crowdsourcing in a Business

Background

Determining the right merchandise to sell is critical. Having a website that's designed to use crowdsourcing—either to gather information about products you carry, such as customer reviews or to determine what merchandise you're going to stock—provides you with a competitive advantage. In this Team Time, you'll consider how to take advantage of crowdsourcing in running a business.

Task

Three individuals starting new businesses have requested help in designing their websites and customer interaction programs. The businesses are (a) a coffee shop that offers live music; (b) a clothing company; and (c) a company that sells iPhone accessories. You need to help these businesses choose a crowdsourcing strategy.

Process

Break the class into small teams. Each team should select one of the businesses described previously. Each team should prepare a report as follows:

1. Decide on the types of products that will be sold by the company. For each category of product, decide what attributes you feel customers will comment on when giving input on products.

2. Decide if the company will solicit feedback from potential customers on all products or whether the company will offer a core selection of products without soliciting feedback. Divide the products into two lists: core products and products subject to crowdsourcing.

3. Determine a social networking strategy for the company. How will customers be driven to the company website to participate in the crowdsourcing for incentives, discount coupons, contests, and such?

4. Develop a PowerPoint presentation to summarize your findings and present your proposed solution to the class.

Conclusion

E-commerce websites are relatively easy to deploy, but risk exists when financing and stocking products. Crowdsourcing feedback can help businesses minimize the risk of stocking unwanted products.

ethics project //

Privacy at School

In this exercise, you'll research and then role-play a complicated ethical situation. The role you play might not match your own personal beliefs; regardless, your research and use of logic will enable you to represent the view assigned. An arbitrator will watch and comment on both sides of the arguments, and together, the team will agree on an ethical solution.

Problem

Parents are especially concerned about protecting their children's privacy rights. School administrators are quickly learning that they need to craft policies that set appropriate boundaries and guidelines for monitoring students. Should school districts be allowed to monitor students? Should school districts be required to inform students and parents of any monitoring that takes place?

Research Areas to Consider

- Lower Merion school district in Pennsylvania using webcams to monitor students in their homes
- Schools using the Geo Listening service to monitor students' social media posts
- The Family Educational Rights and Privacy Act (FERPA)

Process

1. Divide the class into teams. Research the areas cited above and devise a scenario in which a school district has been monitoring students without their knowledge and has potentially violated their privacy.

2. Team members should write a summary that provides background information for their character—for example, student, parent, school official, or arbitrator—and that details their character's behaviors to set the stage for the role-playing event. Then, team members should create an outline to use during the role-playing event.

3. Team members should present their case to the class or submit a PowerPoint presentation for review by the rest of the class, along with the summary and resolution they developed.

Conclusion

As technology becomes ever more prevalent and integrated into our lives, ethical dilemmas will present themselves to an increasing extent. Being able to understand and evaluate both sides of the argument, while responding in a personally or socially ethical manner, will be an important skill.

Creating an HTML Document

You work part time for a small computer repair and education center. As part of your job you need to be able to edit HTML files. Your boss has started a brief document about the basics of HTML that she'll be using for a training class. She would like you to add the HTML tags so she can put it on the website. You'll be using Notepad to complete this exercise.

You will use the following skills as you complete this activity:

- Apply HTML tags
- View an HTML doc in a browser

Instructions

1. Open Notepad
   - In Windows, click **Start**. Click **All Programs**. Click Accessories. Click **Notepad**.
2. Click **File**, then click **Open**, and navigate to your student data files. Click **TIA_CH13_Start.txt**.
3. Press **CTRL+Home** on your keyboard to place the cursor at the top of the document.
4. Type **<!DOCTYPE html>** and press **Enter**. Type **<html>** and press **Enter**. Type **<body>** and press **Enter**. These tags define the document as an HTML document.
5. Place the cursor at the beginning of the first paragraph that starts with *HTML stands for*, and type **What is HTML?**, then press **Enter**.
6. Place the cursor at the beginning of the second paragraph that starts with *You can easily create* and type **Creating an HTML Document**, then press Enter.
7. At the beginning of the third paragraph, type **Formatting Tags**, then press **Enter**, and at the beginning of the fourth paragraph, type **Viewing an HTML Page**, then press **Enter**.
8. Place the cursor at the beginning of the first header, *HTML Beginning Tutorial*. Add a header start tag by typing **<h1>**. Press **End**, then type the end tag **</h>**.
9. Place the cursor at the beginning of the second header, *What is HTML?*. Add a third level header start tag by typing **<h3>**. Press **End**, then add an end tag by typing **</h1>**.
10. Add third level header tags for the other three headers by repeating step 9 for each.
11. Place the cursor at the beginning of the first paragraph beginning with *HTML stands for*, then add paragraph tags to the beginning and end of the paragraph by typing **<p>** at the start of the paragraph, and **</p>** at the end of the paragraph. Repeat for the remaining three paragraphs.
12. Press **CTRL+Home**, then click **Edit** on the Menu bar, and use Find to locate the first occurrence of the word *tags*. With the cursor at the beginning of *tags*, add a bold formatting start tag by typing ****. Place the cursor at the end of the word *tags*, then add a bold formatting end tag by typing ****.
13. In the same paragraph, add start and end bold tags to the phrases *Start tags* and *end tags*.
14. Place the cursor between the *3* and the *>* in the first <h3> tag. Press **Space**, then type **style="color:blue"**.
15. Repeat step 14 for the remaining three headers.
16. Place the cursor before the paragraph end tag at the end of the third paragraph and type **For more information on creating HTML pages work through this <a href="http://www.w3schools.com/html/">** HTML Tutorial</a>
17. Press **CTRL+End**, then type **</body>**, and press **Enter**.
18. Type **</html>**.
19. Click **File**, click **Save As**, then type **TIA_CH13_LastFirst.html**. (Make sure you type .html). Navigate to where you are saving your student files, then click Save. Close Notepad.
20. Open File Explorer, then navigate to where you saved the *TIA_CH13_LastFirst.html* file. Double click the file to open it in your default browser. Check to ensure all headings have been formatted correctly, select words and phrases have bolding formats applied, and all paragraphs start and end appropriately. Click the hyperlink to ensure that it works.
21. Close the browser and submit the *TIA_CH13_LastFirst.html* file for grading.

Glossary

3-D sound card An expansion card that enables a computer to produce omnidirectional or three-dimensional sounds.

4G The latest mobile communication standard with faster data transfer rates than 3G.

A

access card reader A device that reads information from a magnetic strip on the back of a credit card-like access card.

access method A method to control which computer is allowed to use transmission media at a certain time.

access time The time it takes a storage device to locate its stored data.

accounting software An application program that helps business owners manage their finances more efficiently by providing tools for tracking accounting transactions such as sales, accounts receivable, inventory purchases, and accounts payable.

Active Server Pages (ASP) Programming language used to build websites with interactive capabilities; adapts an HTML page to the user's selections.

active topology In a network, a type of topology where the nodes participate in moving data through the network.

adware A program that downloads on your computer when a user installs a freeware program, game, or utility. Generally, adware enables sponsored advertisements to appear in a section of a browser window or as a pop-up ad.

affective computing A type of computing that relates to emotion or that deliberately tries to influence emotion.

aggregator A software program that finds and retrieves the latest update of web material (usually podcasts) according to your specifications.

AJAX (Asynchronous JavaScript and XML) A collection of technologies that allow the creation of web applications that can update information on a page without requiring the user to refresh or leave the page.

algorithm A set of specific, sequential steps that describe exactly what the computer

program must do to complete the required work.

all-in-one computer A desktop system unit that houses the computer's processor, memory, and monitor in a single unit.

all-in-one printer A device that combines the functions of a printer, scanner, copier, and fax.

alphabetic check In a database, confirms that only textual characters are entered in a field.

analog Waves that illustrate the loudness of a sound or the brightness of the colors in an image at a given moment in time.

analog-to-digital converter chip A chip that converts analog signals into digital signals.

antivirus software Software specifically designed to detect viruses and protect a computer and files from harm.

app marketplace (app store) Online software stores, such as Google Play, where users can purchase and download apps.

applet A small application located on a server; when requested, the applet is downloaded to the client.

application programming interface (API) A set of software routines that allows one software system to work with another.

application server A server that acts as a repository for application software.

application software The set of programs on a computer that helps a user carry out tasks such as word processing, sending e-mail, balancing a budget, creating presentations, editing photos, taking an online course, and playing games.

architecture neutral A feature of Java whereby code needs to be compiled only once, after which the code can be run on many different CPUs.

artificial intelligence (AI) The branch of computer science that deals with the attempt to create computers that think like humans.

aspect ratio The width-to-height proportion of a monitor.

assembly language A computer language that allows programmers to write programs

using a set of short, English-like commands that speak directly to the central processing unit and that give the programmer direct control of hardware resources.

assistive (adaptive) technology Any device, software feature, or app that is designed to improve the functional capabilities of individuals with disabilities.

audio MIDI interface Interface technology that allows a user to connect guitars and microphones to their computer.

audio-editing software Programs that perform basic editing tasks on audio files such as cutting dead air space from the beginning or end of a song or cutting a portion from the middle.

augmentative reality/augmented reality A combination of our normal sense of the objects around us with an overlay of information displayed.

authentication The process of identifying a computer user, based on a login or username and password. The computer system determines whether the computer user is authorized and what level of access is to be granted on the network.

authentication server A server that keeps track of who's logging on to the network and which services on the network are available to each user.

B

backdoor program A program that enables a hacker to take complete control of a computer without the legitimate user's knowledge or permission.

backup A copy of a computer file that can be used to replace the original if it's lost or damaged.

backward compatibility The accommodation of current devices being able to use previously issued software standards in addition to the current standards.

bandwidth The maximum speed at which data can be transmitted between two nodes on a network; usually measured in megabits per second (Mbps). See also *data transfer rate*.

base class In object-oriented analysis, the original class.

base transceiver station A large communications tower with antennas, amplifiers, and receivers/transmitters.

basic input/output system (BIOS) A program that manages the data between a computer's operating system and all the input and output devices attached to the computer; also responsible for loading the operating system (OS) from its permanent location on the hard drive to random access memory (RAM).

bastion host A heavily secured server located on a special perimeter network between the company's secure internal network and its firewall.

batch processing The accumulation of transaction data until a certain point is reached, at which time several transactions are processed at once.

beta version A version of the software that's still under development. Many beta versions are available for a limited trial period and are used to help the developers correct any errors before they launch the software on the market.

Big Data Very large data sets that are analyzed to reveal patterns, trends, and associations.

binary decision A type of decision point in an algorithm that can be answered in one of only two ways: yes (true) or no (false).

binary digit (bit) A digit that corresponds to the on and off states of a computer's switches. A bit contains a value of either 0 or 1.

binary language The language computers use to process data into information, consisting of only the values 0 and 1.

binary large object (BLOB) Audio clips, video clips, pictures, and extremely large documents.

biometric authentication device A device that uses some unique characteristic of human biology to identify authorized users.

black-hat hacker A hacker who uses his or her knowledge to destroy information or for illegal gain.

blog (weblog) A personal log or journal posted on the web; short for *web log*.

Bluetooth technology A type of wireless technology that uses radio waves to transmit data over short distances (approximately 3–300 feet depending on power); often used to connect peripherals such as printers and keyboards to computers or headsets to cell phones.

Blu-ray disc (BD) A method of optical storage for digital data, developed for storing high-definition media. It has the largest storage capacity of all optical storage options.

Bookmarks Features in some browsers that place markers of websites' Uniform Resource Locators (URLs) in an easily retrievable list.

Boolean operators A word used to refine logical searches. For Internet searches, the words AND, NOT, and OR describe the relationships between keywords in the search.

boot process The process for loading the operating system (OS) into random access memory (RAM) when the computer is turned on.

boot-sector virus A virus that replicates itself into the master boot record of a flash drive or hard drive.

botnet A large group of software applications (called *robots* or *bots*) that run without user intervention on a large number of computers.

breadcrumb trail A navigation aid that shows users the path they have taken to get to a web page or where the page is located within the website; it usually appears at the top of a page.

bridge A device that is used to send data between different collision domains in a network, depending on where the recipient device is located.

broadband A high-speed Internet connection such as cable, satellite, or digital subscriber line (DSL).

brute force attack An attempt to access an account by repeatedly trying different passwords.

bus (linear bus) topology A system of networking connections in which all devices are connected in sequence on a single cable.

business intelligence (BI) Systems used to analyze and interpret data in order to enable managers to make informed decisions about how best to run a business.

business intelligence system Systems used to analyze and interpret data in order to enable managers to make informed decisions about how best to run a business.

business-to-business (B2B) E-commerce transactions between businesses.

business-to-consumer (B2C) E-commerce transactions between businesses and consumers.

byte Eight binary digits (bits).

C

C A programming language originally developed for system programmers.

C# A Microsoft programming language developed to compete with Java.

C++ A programming language; takes C to an object-oriented level.

cable Internet A broadband service that transmits data over coaxial cables.

cache memory Small blocks of memory, located directly on and next to the central processing unit (CPU) chip, that act as holding places for recently or frequently used instructions or data that the CPU accesses the most. When these instructions or data are stored in cache memory, the CPU can more quickly retrieve them than if it had to access the instructions or data from random access memory (RAM).

caption A property in a database that enables the field name to display in a more meaningful or readable manner.

cascading style sheet (CSS) A list of rules that defines in one single location how to display HTML elements.

Cat 6 cable A UTP cable type that provides more than 1 Gb/s of throughput.

cellular (cell) phone A telephone that operates over a mobile network. Cell phones can also offer Internet access, text messaging, personal information management (PIM) features, and more.

central processing unit (CPU or processor) The part of the system unit of a computer that is responsible for data processing; it is the largest and most important chip in the computer. The CPU controls all the functions performed by the computer's other components and processes all the commands issued to it by software instructions.

centralized A characteristic of client/server networks where the server, not the individual user, coordinates data security.

Chromebook Any laptop or tablet running the Chrome OS as its operating system.

circuit switching Where a dedicated connection is formed between two points (such as two people on telephones) and the connection remains active for the duration of the transmission.

class A category of input identified in object-oriented analysis; classes are defined by information and actions.

clickstream data Software used on company websites to capture information about each click that users make as they navigate through the site.

client A computer that requests information from a server in a client/server network (such as your computer when you are connected to the Internet).

client/server model A model of network communications where a client device such as a computer, tablet, or smartphone uses browsers to request services from networks that make up the Internet.

client/server network A type of network that uses servers to deliver services to computers that are requesting them (clients).

client-side program A program that runs on the client computer and that requires no interaction with a web server.

clock speed The steady and constant pace at which a computer goes through machine cycles, measured in hertz (Hz).

cloud computing The process of storing data, files, and applications on the web, which allows access to and manipulation of these files and applications from any Internet-connected device.

cloud server A server that is maintained by a hosting company and that is connected to networks via the Internet.

cloud storage A service that keeps files on the Internet (in the "cloud") rather than storing files solely on a local device.

cluster The smallest increment in which data is stored on hard disks; hard disks are divided into *tracks*, then *wedges*, then *sectors*, then clusters.

CMYK A color model in which all colors are described as a mixture of four base colors (cyan, magenta, yellow, and black).

coaxial cable A single copper wire surrounded by layers of plastic insulation, metal sheathing, and a plastic jacket; used mainly in cable television and cable Internet service.

code editing The step of programming in which a programmer types the code to be executed.

codec A rule, implemented in either software or hardware, which squeezes a given amount of audio and video information into less space.

coding Translating an algorithm into a programming language.

cognitive surplus The combination of leisure time and the tools needed to be creative.

cold boot The process of starting a computer from a powered-down or off state.

collaborative consumption Joining together as a group to use a specific product more efficiently.

command-driven interface Interface between user and computer in which the user enters commands to communicate with the computer system.

comment A note left by a programmer in the program code to explain the purpose of a section of code, to indicate the date the program was written, or to include other important information about the code so that other programmers can more easily understand and update it.

commerce server Computers that host software that enables users to buy goods and services over the web.

Common Gateway Interface (CGI) A method of designing programs that provides a methodology by which a browser can request a program file be executed instead of just being delivered to the browser.

communications server A server that handles all communications between the network and other networks, including managing Internet connectivity.

compact disc (CD) A method of optical storage for digital data; originally developed for storing digital audio.

compilation The process by which code is converted into machine language—the language the central processing unit can understand.

compiler A program that understands both the syntax of the programming language and the exact structure of the central processing unit and its machine language.

completeness check In a database, ensures that all required fields have been completed.

computer A data-processing device that gathers, processes, outputs, and stores data and information.

computer forensics The application of computer systems and techniques to gather potential legal evidence; a law enforcement specialty used to fight high-tech crime.

computer literate Being familiar enough with computers that a user knows how to use them and understands their capabilities and limitations.

computer protocol A set of rules for exchanging electronic information.

computer-aided design (CAD) A 3-D modeling program used to create automated designs, technical drawings, and model visualizations.

connectionless protocol A protocol that a host computer can use to send data over the network without establishing a direct connection with any specific recipient computer.

connection-oriented protocol A protocol for exchanging information that requires two computers to exchange control packets, thereby setting up the parameters of the data-exchange session, before sending packets that contain data.

connectivity port A port that enables a computing device to be connected to other devices or systems such as networks, modems, and the Internet.

consistency check In a database, compares the values of data in two or more fields to see if those values are reasonable.

consumer-to-consumer (C2C) E-commerce transactions between consumers through online sites such as eBay.

control structure General term used for a keyword in a programming language that allows the programmer to direct the flow of the program based on a decision.

cookie A small text file that some websites automatically store on a client computer's hard drive when a user visits the site.

copyleft A simplified licensing scheme that enables copyright holders to grant certain rights to a work while retaining other rights.

core A complete processing section from a central processing unit, embedded into one physical chip.

course management software A program that provides traditional classroom tools, such as calendars and grade books, over the Internet, as well as areas for students to exchange ideas and information in chat rooms, discussion forums, and e-mail.

CPU benchmarks Measurements used to compare performance between processors.

CPU usage The percentage of time the central processing unit (CPU) is working.

CPU usage graph Records central processing unit (CPU) usage for several seconds.

crisis-mapping tool A tool that collects information from e-mails, text messages, blog posts, and Twitter tweets and maps them, making the information instantly publicly available.

crowdfunding Asking for small donations from a large number of people, often using the Internet; a style of generating capital to start a business through social media.

crowdsourcing The phenomenon of consumers checking in with the voice of the crowd before making purchases.

CSMA/CD The method used on Ethernet networks to avoid data collisions; short for *carrier sense multiple access with collision detection*. A node connected to the network uses carrier sense to verify that no other nodes are currently transmitting data signals.

custom installation The process of installing only those features of a software program that a user wants on the hard drive.

cyberbullying Using technology to harass or intimidate another individual.

cybercrime Any criminal action perpetrated primarily through the use of a computer.

cybercriminal An individual who uses computers, networks, and the Internet to perpetrate crime.

cyberloafing Doing anything with a computer that's unrelated to a job (such as playing video games) while one's supposed to be working. Also called *cyberslacking*.

D

data Numbers, words, pictures, or sounds that represent facts, figures, or ideas; the raw input that users have at the start of a job.

data breach When sensitive or confidential information is copied, transmitted, or viewed by an individual who is not authorized to handle the data.

data centralization When data is maintained in only one file.

data collision When two computers send data at the same time and the sets of data collide somewhere in the connection media.

data dictionary (database schema) A map of a database that defines the features of the fields in the database.

data file A file that contains stored data.

data inconsistency Data for a record being different in two different lists.

data integrity When the data in a database is accurate and reliable.

data mart Small slices of a data warehouse grouped together and separated from the main body of data in the data warehouse so that related sets of data can be analyzed.

data mining The process by which great amounts of data are analyzed and investigated. The objective is to spot significant patterns or trends within the data that would otherwise not be obvious.

data plan A connectivity plan or text messaging plan in which data charges are separate from cell phone calling charges and are provided at rates different from those for voice calls.

data redundancy Duplicated data in a list.

data staging The act of formatting data from source databases before fitting it into a data warehouse; it consists of three steps: extraction, transformation, and storage.

data transfer rate The maximum speed at which data can be transmitted between two nodes on a network; measured in megabits per second (Mbps) or gigabits per second (Gbps).

data type (field type) (1) Describes the kind of data being stored at the memory location; each programming language has its own data types (although there is some degree of overlap). (2) In a database, indicates what type of data can be stored in a field and prevents the wrong type of data from being entered into the field.

data warehouse A large-scale collection of data that contains and organizes in one place all the data from an organization's multiple databases.

database A digital collection of related data that can be stored, sorted, organized, and queried.

database administrator (database designer) An information technology professional responsible for designing, constructing, and maintaining databases.

database management system (DBMS) A specially designed application software used to create and manage databases.

database server A server that provides client computers with access to information stored in databases.

database software An electronic filing system best used for larger and more complicated groups of data that require more than one table and the ability to group, sort, and retrieve data and generate reports.

data-flow diagram Diagrams that trace all data in an information system from the point at which data enters the system to its final resting place (storage or output).

debugger A tool in an integrated development environment that helps programmers analyze a program as it runs.

debugging The process of running a program over and over to find and repair errors and to make sure the program behaves in the way it should.

decentralized A characteristic of peer-to-peer networks where the individual user coordinates data security.

decision point A place where a program must choose from a list of actions based on the value of a certain input.

decision support system (DSS) A type of business intelligence system designed to help managers develop solutions for specific problems.

dedicated server A server used to fulfill one specific function, such as handling e-mail.

default value The value a database automatically uses for a field unless the user enters another value.

denial-of-service (DoS) attack An attack that occurs when legitimate users are denied access to a computer system because a hacker is repeatedly making requests of that computer system that tie up its resources and deny legitimate users access.

derived class In object-oriented analysis, the modified class.

desktop computer A computer that is intended for use at a single location. A desktop computer consists of a case that houses the main components of the computer, plus peripheral devices.

desktop publishing (DTP) software Programs for incorporating and arranging graphics and text to produce creative documents.

detail report A report generated by a management information system that provides a list of the transactions that occurred during a certain time period.

device driver Software that facilitates the communication between a device and its operating system or between a network adapter and a server's operating system and the operating system of the computer in which the adapter is installed.

digital convergence The use of a single unifying device to handle media, Internet, entertainment, and telephony needs; expressed in the range of devices now on the market.

digital divide The discrepancy between those who have access to the opportunities and knowledge that computers and the Internet offer and those who do not.

digital rights management (DRM) A system of access control that allows only limited use of material that has been legally purchased.

digital signal processor A specialized chip that processes digital information and transmits signals very quickly.

digital subscriber line (DSL) A type of connection that uses telephone lines to connect to the Internet and that allows both phone and data transmissions to share the same line.

digital video (or versatile) disc (DVD) A method of optical storage for digital data that has greater storage capacity than compact discs.

digital video interface (DVI) port: Video interface technology that newer LCD monitors, as well as other multimedia devices

such as televisions, DVD players, and projectors, use to connect to a PC.

digital video-editing software A program for editing digital video.

directory A hierarchical structure that include files, folders, and drives used to create a more organized and efficient computer.

Disk Cleanup A Windows utility that removes unnecessary files from the hard drive.

disk defragmentation The process of regrouping related pieces of files on the hard drive, enabling faster retrieval of the data.

distributed (grid) computing A software system in which components located on networked computers interact to achieve a common goal.

distributed denial-of-service (DDoS) attack An automated attack that's launched from more than one zombie computer at the same time.

distributions (distros) Linux download packages.

Document Object Model (DOM) Used by JavaScript to organize objects and page elements.

documentation Description of the technical details of the software, how the code works, and how the user interacts with the program; in addition, all the necessary user documentation that will be distributed to the program's users.

domain name A part of a Uniform Resource Locator (URL). Domain names consist of two parts: the site's host and a suffix that indicates the type of organization (example: popsci.com, where *popsci* is the domain name and *com* is the suffix).

domain name system (DNS) server A server that maintains a database of domain names and converts domain names to Internet protocol addresses.

dotted decimal number (dotted quad) The form of an Internet protocol address, where sets of numerals are separated by decimals, i.e., 197.169.73.63.

drawing software (illustration software) Programs for creating or editing two-dimensional line-based drawings.

drive bay A special shelf inside a computer that is designed to hold storage devices.

drive-by download The use of malicious software to attack a computer by downloading harmful programs onto a computer, without the user's knowledge, while they are surfing a website.

dynamic addressing A way of assigning Internet protocol addresses where a computer is assigned a temporary address from an available pool of addresses.

dynamic decision making The ability of a web page to decide how to display itself based on the choices the reader makes.

Dynamic Host Configuration Protocol (DHCP) A protocol for assigning dynamic internet protocol addresses.

dynamic HTML (DHTML) A combination of technologies—HTML, cascading style sheets, and JavaScript—used to create lively and interactive websites.

E

e-commerce (electronic commerce) The process of conducting business online for purposes ranging from fund-raising to advertising to selling products.

editor A special tool in an integrated development environment (IDE) that helps programmers as they enter code.

electronic data interchange (EDI) The exchange of large amounts of data in a standardized electronic format.

electronic ink (E Ink) A very crisp, sharp grayscale representation of text achieved by using millions of microcapsules with white and black particles in a clear fluid.

electronic text (e-text) Textual information stored as digital information so that it can be stored, manipulated, and transmitted by electronic devices.

element In HTML, a pair of tags and the text between them.

e-mail (electronic mail) Internet-based communication in which senders and recipients correspond.

e-mail client A software program that runs on a computer and is used to send and receive e-mail through an Internet service provider's server.

e-mail server A server whose sole function is to process and deliver incoming and outgoing e-mail.

e-mail virus A virus transmitted by e-mail that often uses the address book in the victim's e-mail system to distribute itself.

embedded computer A specially designed computer chip that resides inside another device, such as a car. These selfcontained computer devices have their own programming and typically neither receive input from users nor interact with other systems.

encryption The process of coding e-mail so that only the person with the key to the code (the intended recipient) can decode the message.

encryption virus A malicious program that searches for common data files and compresses them into a file using a complex encryption key, thereby rendering the files unusable.

End User License Agreement (EULA) An agreement between the user and the software developer that must be accepted before installing the software on a computer.

enterprise resource planning (ERP) system A business intelligence system that accumulates in a central location all information relevant to running a business and makes it readily available to whoever needs it to make decisions.

e-reader A device that can display e-text and that has supporting tools, like note taking, bookmarks, and integrated dictionaries.

ergonomics How a user sets up his or her computer and other equipment to minimize risk of injury or discomfort.

error handling The part of a problem statement where programmers describe what the program should do if the input data is invalid or just gibberish.

Ethernet network A network that uses the Ethernet protocol as the means (or standard) by which the nodes on the network communicate.

Ethernet port A port that's slightly larger than a standard phone jack and that transfers data at speeds of up to 10,000 Mbps; used to connect a computer to a DSL or cable modem or to a network.

ethics The study of the general nature of morals and the choices individuals make.

event The result of an action, such as a keystroke, mouse click, or signal to the printer, in the respective device (keyboard, mouse, or printer) to which the operating system responds.

exception report A report generated by a management information system that shows conditions that are unusual or that need attention by system users.

executable program The binary sequence that instructs the central processing unit to run the programmer's code.

expansion cards (or adapter cards) A circuit board with specific functions that augment the computer's basic functions and provide connections to other devices; examples include the sound card and the video card.

expert system A system that tries to replicate the decision-making processes of human experts in order to solve specific problems.

exploit kits A software toolkit used to take advantage of security weaknesses found in apps or operating systems, usually to deploy malware.

eXtensible Markup Language (XML) A markup language that enables designers to define their own data-based tags, making it much easier for a website to transfer the key information on its page to another site; it defines what data is being described rather than how it's to be displayed.

extension (file type) In a file name, the three letters that follow the user-supplied file name after the dot (.); the extension identifies what kind of family of files the file belongs to, or which application should be used to read the file.

external hard drive A hard drive that is enclosed in a protective case to make it portable; the drive is connected to the computer with a data transfer cable and is often used to back up data.

extranet An area of an intranet that only certain corporations or individuals can access; the owner of the extranet decides who will be permitted to access it.

F

Favorites A feature in Microsoft Internet Explorer that places a marker of a website's Uniform Resource Locator (URL) in an easily retrievable list in the browser's toolbar. (Called Bookmarks in some browsers.)

feature phone Inexpensive cell phones with modest processors, simple interfaces, and, often, no touch screens.

fiber-optic cable A cable that transmits data at close to the speed of light along glass or plastic fibers.

fiber-optic service Internet access that is enabled by transmitting data at the speed of light through glass or plastic fibers.

field The component of a database in which the database stores each category of information.

field constraint A property that must be satisfied for an entry to be accepted into the field.

field name A way of describing the information in the field.

field properties In an Access database table, the field name, data type, and other data elements.

field size Defines the maximum number of characters that a field can hold in a database.

fifth-generation language (5GL) A computer language in which a problem is presented as a series of facts or constraints instead of as a specific algorithm; the system of facts can then be queried; considered the most "natural" of languages.

file A collection of related pieces of information stored together for easy reference.

file compression utility A program that takes out redundancies in a file in order to reduce the file size.

File Explorer The main tool for finding, viewing, and managing the contents of your computer by showing the location and contents of every drive, folder, and file; called Windows Explorer prior to Windows 8.

File History A Windows utility that automatically creates a duplicate of your libraries, desktop, contacts, and favorites and copies it to another storage device, such as an external hard drive.

file management The process by which humans or computer software provide organizational structure to a computer's contents.

file name The first part of the label applied to a file; generally the name a user assigns to the file when saving it.

file path The exact location of a file, starting with the drive in which the file is located and including all folders, subfolders (if any), the

file name, and the extension (example: C:\
Users\username\Documents\Illustrations\
EBronte.jpg).

file server A server that stores and manages files for network users or that acts as a storehouse for files that users can download.

File Transfer Protocol (FTP) A protocol used to upload and download files from one computer to another over the Internet.

filter In a database, temporarily displays records that match certain criteria.

financial planning software Programs for managing finances, such as Intuit's Quicken, which include electronic checkbook registers and automatic bill-payment tools.

firewall A software program or hardware device designed to prevent unauthorized access to computers or networks.

firmware System software that controls hardware devices.

first-generation language (1GL) The machine language of a central processing unit (CPU); the sequence of bits that the CPU understands.

flash drive (jump drive, USB drive, or thumb drive) A drive that plugs into a universal serial bus (USB) port on a computer and that stores data digitally. Also called a USB drive, jump drive, or thumb drive.

flash memory card A form of portable storage; this removable memory card is often used in digital cameras, smartphones, video cameras, and printers.

flowchart Visual diagram of a process, including the decisions that need to be made along the way.

folder A collection of files stored on a computer.

For In Visual Basic, programmers use the keyword For to implement a loop; after the keyword For, an input or output item is given a starting value, and then the statements in the body of the loop are executed.

foreign key In a relational database, the common field between tables that's not the primary key.

fourth-generation language (4GL) A computer language type that includes database query languages and report generators.

frame Groups of data packets that are sent together in a package.

freeware Any copyrighted software that can be used for free.

full installation The process of installing all the files and programs from the distribution media to the computer's hard drive.

fuzzy logic Enables the interjection of experiential learning into knowledge-based systems by allowing the consideration of probabilities.

G

general availability (GA) The point in the release cycle, where, after release to manufacturers, software is available for purchase by the public.

geolocation The method of identifying the geographical location of a person or device, usually by utilizing information processed through the Internet.

geotag Data attached to a photograph that indicates the latitude and longitude where you were standing when you took the photo.

gigabyte (GB) About a billion bytes.

gigabit Ethernet The most commonly used wired Ethernet standard deployed in devices designed for home networks; provides bandwidth of up to 1 Gbps.

gigahertz (GHz) One billion hertz.

global positioning system (GPS) A system of 21 satellites (plus 3 working spares), built and operated by the U.S. military, that constantly orbit the earth. The satellites provide information to GPS–capable devices to pinpoint locations on the earth.

graphical user interface (GUI) Unlike the command- and menu-driven interfaces used in earlier software, GUIs display graphics and use the point-and-click technology of the mouse and cursor, making them much more user friendly.

graphics double data rate 5 (GDDR5) A standard of video memory.

graphics processing unit (GPU) A specialized logic chip that's dedicated to quickly displaying and calculating visual data such as shadows, textures, and luminosity.

green computing (green IT) A movement that encourages environmentally sustainable computing (or IT).

grey-hat hacker A cross between black and white—a hacker who will often illegally break into systems merely to flaunt his or her expertise to the administrator of the system he or she penetrated or to attempt to sell his or her services in repairing security breaches.

H

hacker Anyone who unlawfully breaks into a computer system (whether an individual computer or a network).

hacktivism Using computers and computer networks in a subversive way to promote an agenda.

handshaking In a connection-oriented protocol, the process of exchanging control packets before exchanging data packets.

hard disk drive (HDD or **hard drive)** The computer's nonvolatile, primary storage device for permanent storage of software and documents.

hardware Any part of a computer or computer system you can physically touch.

head crash Impact of the read/write head against the magnetic platter of the hard drive; often results in data loss.

hexadecimal digit A digit with 16 possible values: 0–9 and A–F.

Hibernate A power-management mode that saves the current state of the current system to the computer's hard drive.

high definition A standard of digital TV signal that guarantees a specific level of resolution and a specific *aspect ratio*, which is the rectangular shape of the image.

high-definition multimedia interface (HDMI) port A compact audio–video interface standard that carries both high-definition video and uncompressed digital audio.

home area network (HAN) A network located in a home that's used to connect all of its digital devices.

home network server A device designed to store media, share media across the network, and back up files on computers connected to a home network.

honey pot A computer system that's set up to attract unauthorized users by appearing to be a key part of a network or a system that contains something of great value.

host The portion of a domain name that identifies who maintains a given website. For example, berkeley.edu is the domain name for the University of California at Berkeley, which maintains that site.

HTML embedded scripting language A programming language that tucks programming code directly within the HTML of a web page; the most popular example is JavaScript.

HTML tag Tags that surround and define HTML content (such as <b> and </b>, which indicate bolding).

hybrid topology Combining multiple topologies into one network.

hyperlink A type of specially coded text that, when clicked, enables a user to jump from one location, or web page, to another within a website or to another website altogether.

Hypertext Markup Language (HTML) A series of tags that define how elements on a website should be displayed in a browser.

Hypertext Transfer Protocol (HTTP) The protocol that allows files to be transferred from a web server so that you can see them on your computer by using a browser.

Hypertext Transfer Protocol Secure (HTTPS) The Internet protocol that ensures data is sent securely over the web.

hyperthreading A technology that permits quicker processing of information by enabling a new set of instructions to start executing before the previous set has finished.

I

identity theft The process by which someone uses personal information about someone else (such as the victim's name, address, and Social Security number) to assume the victim's identity for the purpose of defrauding another.

if else In C++, a binary decision in the code where the program can follow one of two paths: If the decision is made one way, the program follows one path; if made the other way (else), the program follows another path.

image backup (system backup) A copy of an entire computer system, created for restoration purposes.

image-editing software Programs for editing photographs and other images.

impact printer A printer that has tiny hammer-like keys that strike the paper through an inked ribbon, thus making a mark on the paper. The most common impact printer is the dot-matrix printer.

incremental backup (partial backup) A type of backup that only backs up files that have changed since the last time files were backed up.

information Data that has been organized or presented in a meaningful fashion; the result, or output that users require at the end of a job.

information assurance Ensuring that information systems contain accurate information and are adequately secured against tampering.

information system A system that includes data, people, procedures, hardware, and software that help in planning and decision making; a software-based solution used to gather and analyze information.

information technology (IT) The set of techniques used in processing and retrieving information.

inheritance In object-oriented analysis, the ability of a new class to automatically pick up all the data and methods of an existing class and then extend and customize those to fit its specific needs.

initial value A beginning point.

inkjet printer A nonimpact printer that sprays tiny drops of ink onto paper.

inoculation A process used by antivirus software; compares old and current qualities of files to detect viral activity.

input device: A hardware device used to enter, or input, data (text, images, and sounds) and instructions (user responses and commands) into a computer. Some input devices are keyboards and mice.

input forms Used to control how new data is entered into a shared database.

instant messaging (IM) A program that enables users to communicate online in real time with others who are also online.

integrated development environment (IDE) A developmental tool that helps programmers write and test their programs; one IDE can be configured to support many different languages.

intellectual property Refers to products derived from the mind, such as works of art and literature, inventions, and software code.

intelligent personal assistant Software designed to perform tasks or services for individuals.

internal hard drive A hard drive that resides within the computer's system unit and that usually holds all permanently stored programs and data.

Internet A network of networks that's the largest network in the world, connecting billions of computers globally.

Internet backbone The main pathway of high-speed communications lines over which all Internet traffic flows.

Internet cache A section of the hard drive that stores information that may be needed again, such as Internet protocol addresses and frequently accessed web pages.

Internet Corporation for Assigned Names and Numbers (ICANN) The organization that registers Internet protocol addresses to ensure they're unique and haven't been assigned to other users.

Internet exchange point (IXP) A way of connecting Internet service providers (ISPs) that's made up of one or more network switches to which the ISPs connect.

Internet of Things (IoT) The interconnection of uniquely identifiable embedded computing devices that transfer data over a network without requiring human-to-human or human-to-computer interaction.

Internet Protocol (IP) address The means by which all computers connected to the Internet identify each other. It consists of a unique set of four numbers separated by dots, such as 123.45.178.91.

Internet Protocol version 4 (IPv4) The original Internet protocol addressing scheme, created in 1981.

Internet Protocol version 6 (IPv6) An Internet protocol (IP) addressing scheme that makes IP addresses longer, thereby providing more available addresses.

Internet service provider (ISP) A company that specializes in providing Internet access. ISPs may be specialized providers, like Juno, or companies that provide other services in addition to Internet access (such as phone and cable television).

interpreter For a programming language, translates the source code into an intermediate form, line by line; each line is then executed as it's translated.

interrupt A signal that tells the operating system that it's in need of immediate attention.

interrupt handler A special numerical code that prioritizes requests from various devices. These requests then are placed in the interrupt table in the computer's primary memory.

intranet A private network set up by a business or an organization that's used exclusively by a select group of employees, customers, suppliers, volunteers, or supporters.

IP address One of the original two protocols developed for the Internet.

J

jam signal A special signal sent to network nodes alerting them that a data collision has occurred.

Java An object-oriented programming language that has a large set of existing classes.

Java applet A small Java-based program.

JavaScript An Internet protocol (IP) addressing scheme that makes IP addresses longer, thereby providing more available addresses.

Javascript Object Notation (JSON) Stands for Javascript Object Notation; a syntax for exchanging information between computers.

JavaServer Pages (JSP) Programming language used to build websites with interactive capabilities; adapts the HTML page to the user's selections.

join query A query used to extract data that's in two or more tables in a database.

K

kernel (supervisor program) The essential component of the operating system that's responsible for managing the processor and all other components of the computer system. Because it stays in random access memory (RAM) the entire time the computer is powered on, the kernel is called memory resident.

key pair The two keys used in public-key encryption.

keyboard A hardware device used to enter typed data and commands into a computer.

keystroke logger (keylogger) A type of spyware program that monitors keystrokes with the intent of stealing passwords, login IDs, or credit card information.

keyword (1) A specific word a user wishes to query (or look for) in an Internet search. (2) A specific word that has a predefined meaning in a particular programming language.

kilobyte (KB) A unit of computer storage equal to approximately 1,000 bytes.

knowledge-based system A business intelligence system that provides intelligence that supplements the user's own intellect and makes the decision support system more effective.

L

laptop (or notebook) computer A portable computer with a keyboard, a monitor, and other devices integrated into a single compact case.

large format printer A printer that prints on oversized paper. Often used for creating banners and signs.

laser printer A nonimpact printer known for quick and quiet production and high-quality printouts.

latency The process that occurs after the read/write head of the hard drive locates the correct track and then waits for the correct sector to spin to the read/write head.

legacy technology Comprises computing devices, software, or peripherals that use techniques, parts, and methods from an earlier time that are no longer popular.

light-emitting diode (LED) A newer, more energy-efficient technology used in monitors. It may result in better color accuracy and thinner panels than traditional LCD monitors.

Linux An open-source operating system based on UNIX. Because of the stable nature of this operating system, it's often used on web servers.

liquid crystal display (LCD) The technology used in flat-panel computer monitors.

live bookmark A bookmark that delivers updates as soon as they become available, using Really Simple Syndication (RSS).

local apps Apps installed on your computing device that usually do not require an Internet connection to function.

local area network (LAN) A network in which the nodes are located within a small geographic area.

logic bomb A computer virus that runs when a certain set of conditions is met, such as when a program is launched a specific number of times.

logical error An error in a program that produces unintended or undesired output, where the syntax is correct but some other human error has occurred.

logical port A virtual communications gateway or path that enables a computer to organize requests for information (such as web page downloads and e-mail routing) from other networks or computers.

logical port blocking A condition in which a firewall is configured to ignore all incoming packets that request access to a certain port so that no unwanted requests will get through to the computer.

loop A type of decision point in an algorithm. In a loop, a question is asked, and if the answer is yes, a set of actions is performed. Once the set of actions has finished, the question is asked again, creating a loop. If the answer to the question is *no*, the algorithm breaks free of the loop and moves on to the first step that follows the loop.

M

Mac OS The first commercially available operating system to incorporate a graphical user interface (GUI) with user-friendly point-and-click technology.

machine cycle The series of steps a central processing unit goes through when it performs a program instruction.

machine language The machine language of a central processing unit (CPU); the sequence of bits that the CPU understands.

macro A small program that groups a series of commands to run as a single command.

macro virus A virus that's distributed by hiding it inside a macro.

mainframe A large, expensive computer that supports hundreds or thousands of users simultaneously and executes many different programs at the same time.

malware Software that's intended to render a system temporarily or permanently useless or to penetrate a computer system completely for purposes of information gathering. Examples include spyware, viruses, worms, and Trojan horses.

management information system (MIS) A type of business intelligence system that provides timely and accurate information that enables managers to make critical business decisions.

many-to-many relationship In a relational database, records in one table are related to multiple records in a second table, and vice versa.

master boot record A small program that runs whenever a computer boots up.

media access control (MAC) address The physical address, similar to a serial number, of each network adapter.

megabyte (MB) A unit of computer storage equal to approximately 1 million bytes.

memory module (memory card) A small circuit board that holds a series of random access memory (RAM) chips.

menu-driven interface A user interface in which the user chooses a command from menus displayed on the screen.

metadata Data that describes other data.

metasearch engine A search engine, such as Dogpile, that searches other search engines rather than individual websites.

method The process of how a program converts inputs into the correct outputs.

metropolitan area network (MAN) A wide area network (WAN) that links users in a specific geographic area (such as within a city or county).

microphone (mic) A device that allows you to capture sound waves, such as those created by your voice, and to transfer them to digital format on your computer.

Microsoft account Registered user profile with specific user id and password to log into Windows account from any machine and access familiar desktop and applications.

mobile apps Apps installed on mobile computing devices (such as tablets or phones). Usually these apps require an Internet connection to provide full functionality.

mobile broadband Connection to the Internet through the same cellular network that cell phones use to get 3G or 4G Internet access.

mobile hotspot Devices that enable you to connect more than one device to the Internet; they require access to a data plan. Most smartphones have this capability built-in.

mobile switching center A central location that receives cell phone requests for service from a base station.

model management system Software that assists in building management models in decision support systems; an analysis tool that, through the use of internal and external data, provides a view of a particular business situation for the purposes of decision making.

modem A device that connects a network to the Internet.

monitor (display screen) A common output device that displays text, graphics, and video as soft copies (copies that can be seen only on screen).

Moore's Law A prediction, named after Gordon Moore, the co-founder of Intel; states that the number of transistors on a central processing unit chip will double every two years.

motherboard A special circuit board in the system unit that contains the central processing unit, the memory (RAM) chips, and the slots available for expansion cards; all of the other boards (video cards, sound cards, and so on) connect to it to receive power and to communicate.

mouse A hardware device used to enter user responses and commands into a computer.

multidimensional database A database that stores data from different perspectives, called dimensions, and organizes data in cube format.

multi-factor authentication A process that requires two of the three assigned factors be demonstrated before authentication is granted.

multimedia Anything that involves one or more forms of media plus text.

multimedia message service (MMS) A service that allows users to send messages that include text, sound, images, and video clips to other phones or e-mail addresses.

multimedia software Programs that include image-, video-, and audio-editing software, animation software, and other specialty software required to produce computer games, animations, and movies.

multipartite virus Literally meaning "multipart" virus; a type of computer virus that attempts to infect computers using more than one method.

Multipurpose Internet Mail Extensions (MIME) Specification for sending files as attachments to e-mail.

multitask The ability of an operating system to perform more than one process at a time.

multiuser operating system (network operating system) An operating system that enables more than one user to access the computer system at one time by efficiently juggling all the requests from multiple users.

N

natural language processing (NLP) system A knowledge-based business intelligence system that enables users to communicate with computer systems using a natural spoken or written language instead of a computer programming language.

near field communication (NFC) A set of communication protocols that enable devices to communicate with each other when they are held in close proximity. NFC is commonly used for mobile payments.

negative acknowledgment (NAK) In data exchange, the communication sent from one computer or system to another stating that it did not receive a data packet in readable form.

network A group of two or more computers (or nodes) that are configured to share information and resources such as printers, files, and databases.

network adapter A device that enables the computer (or peripheral) to communicate with the network using a common data communication language, or protocol.

network address translation (NAT) A process that firewalls use to assign internal Internet protocol addresses on a network.

network administration Involves tasks such as (1) installing new computers and devices, (2) monitoring the network to ensure it's performing efficiently, (3) updating and installing new software on the network, and (4) configuring, or setting up, proper security for a network.

network administrator Person who maintains networks for businesses.

network architecture The design of a computer network; includes both physical and logical design.

network interface card (NIC) An expansion card that enables a computer to connect other computers or to a cable modem to facilitate a high-speed Internet connection.

network navigation device A device on a network such as a router or switch that moves data signals around the network.

network operating system (NOS) Software that handles requests for information, Internet access, and the use of peripherals for the rest of the network node, providing the services necessary for the computers on the network to communicate.

network topology The physical or logical arrangement of computers, transmission media (cable), and other network components.

network-attached storage (NAS) device A specialized computing device designed to store and manage network data.

network-ready device A device (such as a printer or an external hard drive) that can be attached directly to a network instead of needing to attach to a computer on the network.

Next In Visual Basic, programmers use the keyword Next to implement a loop; when the Next command is run, the program returns to the For statement and increments the value of the input or output item by 1 and then runs a test cycle.

node A device connected to a network such as a computer, a peripheral (such as a printer), or a communications device (such as a modem).

nonimpact printer A printer that sprays ink or uses laser beams to make marks on the paper. The most common nonimpact printers are inkjet and laser printers.

nonvolatile storage Permanent storage, as in read-only memory (ROM).

normalization A process to ensure data is organized most efficiently in a database.

numeric check In a database, confirms that only numbers are entered in a field.

O

object An example of a class in objectoriented analysis.

Object Query Language (OQL) A query language used by many object-oriented databases.

Objective C The programming language most often used to program applications to run under OS X.

object-oriented analysis A type of analysis in which programmers first identify all the categories of inputs that are part of the problem the program is meant to solve.

object-oriented database A database that stores data in objects rather than in tables.

octet A reference to each of the four numbers in a dotted decimal number internet protocol address, so called because each number would have eight numerals in binary form.

offshoring When outsourcing is done by a company located in a country other than the one in which the firm procuring the services is physically located.

one-to-many relationship In a relational database, a record appears only once in one table while having the capability of appearing many times in a related table.

online analytical processing (OLAP) Software that provides standardized tools for viewing and manipulating data in a data warehouse.

online transaction processing (OLTP) The real-time processing of database transactions online.

open source software Program code made publicly available for free; it can be copied, distributed, or changed without the stringent copyright protections of proprietary software products.

open system A system having the characteristic of being public for access by any interested party; as opposed to a *proprietary system*.

Open Systems Interconnection (OSI) A networking protocol established by the Institute of Electrical and Electronics Engineers (IEEE) that provides guidelines for modern networks.

operating system (OS) The system software that controls the way in which a computer system functions, including the management of hardware, peripherals, and software.

operator A coding symbol that represents a fundamental action of the programming language.

optical carrier (OC) line A high-speed fiber-optic line.

optical drive A hardware device that uses lasers or light to read from, and even write to, CDs, DVDs, or Blu-ray discs.

optical media Portable storage devices, such as CDs, DVDs, and Blu-ray discs, that use a laser to read and write data.

optical mouse A mouse that uses an internal sensor or laser to control the mouse's movement. The sensor sends signals to the computer, telling it where to move the pointer on the screen.

organic light-emitting diode (OLED) displays Displays that use organic compounds to produce light when exposed to an electric current. Unlike LCDs, OLEDs do not require a backlight to function and therefore draw less power and have a much thinner display, sometimes as thin as 3 mm.

output device A device that sends processed data and information out of a computer in the form of text, pictures (graphics), sounds (audio), or video.

outsourcing A process whereby a business hires a third-party firm to provide business services that were previously handled by in-house employees.

overclocking Running the central processing unit at a speed faster than the manufacturer recommends.

P

packet (data packet) A small segment of data that's bundled for sending over transmission media. Each packet contains the address of the computer or peripheral device to which it's being sent.

packet analyzer (sniffer) A computer hardware device or software program designed to detect and record digital information being transmitted over a network.

packet filtering A process in which firewalls are configured so that they filter out packets sent to specific logical ports.

packet screening Having an external screening router examine incoming data packets to ensure they originated from or are authorized by valid users on the internal network.

packet switching A communications methodology that makes computer communication efficient; in packet switching, data is broken into smaller chunks called packets.

paging The process of swapping data or instructions that have been placed in the swap file for later use back into active random access memory (RAM). The contents of the hard drive's swap file then become less active data or instructions.

passive topology In a network, a type of topology where the nodes do nothing to move data along the network.

path (subdirectory) The information after the slash that indicates a particular file or path (or subdirectory) within the website.

path separator The backslash mark (\) used by Microsoft Windows and DOS in file names. Mac files use a colon (:), and UNIX and Linux use the forward slash (/) as the path separator.

peer-to-peer (P2P) network A network in which each node connected to the network can communicate directly with every other node on the network.

peer-to-peer (P2P) sharing The process of users transferring files between computers.

peripheral device A device such as a monitor, printer, or keyboard that connects to the system unit through a data port.

personal area network (PAN) A network used for communication among devices close to one person, such as smartphones, laptops, and tablets, using wireless technologies such as Bluetooth.

personal ethics The set of formal or informal ethical principles that an individual uses to guide their ethical decisions.

personal firewall A firewall specifically designed for home networks.

personal information manager (PIM) software Programs such as Microsoft Outlook or Lotus Organizer that strive to replace the various management tools found on a traditional desk such as a calendar, address book, notepad, and to-do lists.

petabyte 10^{15} bytes of digital information.

pharming Planting malicious code on a computer that alters the browser's ability to find web addresses and that directs users to bogus websites.

phishing The process of sending e-mail messages to lure Internet users into revealing personal information such as credit card or Social Security numbers or other sensitive information that could lead to identity theft.

PHP (Hypertext Preprocessor) Programming language used to build websites with interactive capabilities; adapts the HTML page to the user's selections.

physical memory The amount of random access memory (RAM) that's installed in a computer.

piggybacking The process of connecting to a wireless network without the permission of the owner of the network.

pinning The process through which you choose which applications are visible on the Windows Start screen.

pixel A single point that creates the images on a computer monitor. Pixels are illuminated by an electron beam that passes rapidly back and forth across the back of the screen so that the pixels appear to glow continuously.

platform The combination of a computer's operating system and processor. The two most common platform types are the PC and the Apple.

platter A thin, round, metallic storage plate stacked onto the hard drive spindle.

Plug and Play (PnP) The technology that enables the operating system, once it is booted up, to recognize automatically any new peripherals and to configure them to work with the system.

podcast A clip of audio or video content that's broadcast over the Internet using compressed audio or video files in formats such as MP3.

point of presence (POP) A bank of modems, servers, routers, and switches through which Internet users connect to an Internet service provider.

polymorphic virus A virus that changes its virus signature (the binary pattern that makes the virus identifiable) every time it infects a new file. This makes it more difficult for antivirus programs to detect the virus.

port An interface through which external devices are connected to the computer.

portability The capability to move a completed solution easily from one type of computer to another.

positive acknowledgment (ACK) In data exchange, the confirmation sent from one computer or system to another saying that the computer has received a data packet that it can read.

positive psychology A field that attempts to discover the causes of happiness rather than to address the treatment of mental dysfunctions.

possessed object Any object that users carry to identify themselves and that grants them access to a computer system or facility.

power supply A power supply regulates the wall voltage to the voltages required by computer chips; it's housed inside the system unit.

power-on self-test (POST) The first job the basic input/output system (BIOS) performs, ensuring that essential peripheral devices are attached and operational. This process consists of a test on the video card and video memory, a BIOS identification process (during which the BIOS version, manufacturer, and data are displayed on the monitor), and a memory test to ensure memory chips are working properly.

preemptive multitasking When the operating system processes the task assigned a higher priority before processing a task that has been assigned a lower priority.

presentation software An application program for creating dynamic slide shows, such as Microsoft PowerPoint or Apple Keynote.

pretexting The act of creating an invented scenario (the pretext) to convince someone to divulge information.

Pretty Good Privacy (PGP) A public-key package for encryption available for download on the Internet.

primary key field In a database, a field that has a value unique to a record.

print queue A software holding area for print jobs. Also called a print spooler.

print server A server that manages all client-requested printing jobs for all printers on a network.

printer A common output device that creates tangible or hard copies of text and graphics.

private key The key for decoding retained as private in public-key encryption.

private-key encryption A type of encryption where only the two parties involved in sending the message have the code.

problem statement The starting point of programming work; a clear description of what tasks the computer program must accomplish and how the program will execute those tasks and respond to unusual situations.

processing Manipulating or organizing data into information.

productivity software Programs that enable a user to perform various tasks generally required in home, school, and business. Examples include word processing, spreadsheet, presentation, personal information management, and database programs.

program A series of instructions to be followed by a computer to accomplish a task.

program development life cycle (PDLC) The process of performing a programming project, which consists of five stages: describing the problem, making a plan, coding, debugging, and testing and documentation.

program file Files that are used in the running of software programs and that do not store data.

program specification A clear statement of the goals and objectives of the project.

programming The process of translating a task into a series of commands a computer will use to perform that task.

programming language A kind of "code" for the set of instructions the central processing unit knows how to perform.

project management tools Software designed to help assess the progress of a project as it moves towards completion.

projector A device that can project images from your computer onto a wall or viewing screen.

proprietary (commercial) software Custom software application that's owned and controlled by the company that created it.

proprietary system A system having the characteristic of being closed to public

access (private), as opposed to an *open system*.

protocol A set of rules for exchanging communications.

prototype A small model of a program built at the beginning of a large project.

proxy server A server that acts as a go-between, connecting computers on the internal network with those on the external network (the Internet).

pseudocode A text-based approach to documenting an algorithm.

public key The key for coding distributed to the public in public-key encryption.

public-key encryption A type of encryption where two keys, known as a *key pair*, are created. One key is used for coding and the other for decoding. The key for coding is distributed as a public key, while the private key is retained for decoding.

Q

quarantining The placement (by antivirus software) of a computer virus in a secure area on the hard drive so that it won't spread infection to other files.

query In a database, a way of retrieving information that defines a particular subset of data; can be used to extract data from one or more tables.

query language A specially designed computer language used to manipulate data in or extract data from a database.

quick response (QR) code Technology that lets any piece of print in the real world host a live link to online information and video content.

QWERTY keyboard A keyboard that gets its name from the first six letters on the top-left row of alphabetic keys on the keyboard.

R

RAID 0 The strategy of running two hard drives in one system, cutting in half the time it takes to write a file.

RAID 1 The strategy of mirroring all the data written on one hard drive to a second hard drive, providing an instant backup of all data.

random access memory (RAM) The computer's temporary storage space or shortterm memory. It's located in a set of

chips on the system unit's motherboard, and its capacity is measured in megabytes or gigabytes.

range check Ensures that the data entered into the field of a database falls within a certain range of values.

rapid application development (RAD) An alternative program-development method; instead of developing detailed system documents before they produce the system, developers first create a prototype, then generate system documents as they use and remodel the product.

read/write head The mechanism that retrieves (reads) and records (writes) the magnetic data to and from a data disk.

read-only memory (ROM) A set of memory chips, located on the motherboard, which stores data and instructions that cannot be changed or erased; it holds all the instructions the computer needs to start up.

Really Simple Syndication (RSS) An XML–based format that allows frequent updates of content on the World Wide Web.

real-time operating system (RTOS) A program with a specific purpose that must guarantee certain response times for particular computing tasks or else the machine's application is useless. Real-time operating systems are found in many types of robotic equipment.

real-time processing The processing of database transactions in which the database is updated while the transaction is taking place.

record A group of related fields in a database.

Recycle Bin A folder on a Windows desktop in which deleted files from the hard drive are held until permanently purged from the system.

redundant array of independent disks (RAID) A set of strategies for using more than one drive in a system.

referential integrity In a relational database, a condition where, for each value in the foreign key table, there's a corresponding value in the primary key table.

registry A portion of the hard drive containing all the different configurations (settings) used by the Windows operating system as well as by other applications.

relational algebra The use of English like expressions that have variables and operations, much like algebraic equations, to extract data from databases using Structured Query Language.

relational database A database type that organizes data into related tables based on logical groupings.

relationship In a relational database, a link between tables that defines how the data is related.

release to manufacturers (RTM) The point in the release cycle, where, after beta testing, a manufacturer makes changes to the software and releases it to other manufacturers, for installation on new machines, for example.

Reset this PC A utility program in Windows 10 that attempts to diagnose and fix errors in Windows system files that are causing a computer to behave improperly.

resolution The clearness or sharpness of an image, which is controlled by the number of pixels displayed on the screen.

reusability In object-oriented analysis, the ability to reuse existing classes from one project for another project.

ring (loop) topology A type of network topology where computers and peripherals are laid out in a configuration resembling a circle.

root directory The top level of the filing structure in a computer system. In Windows computers, the root directory of the hard drive is represented as C:\.

root DNS server A domain name system (DNS) server that contains the master listings for an entire top-level domain.

rootkit Programs that allow hackers to gain access to your computer and take almost complete control of it without your knowledge. These programs are designed to subvert normal login procedures to a computer and to hide their operations from normal detection methods.

rotational delay The process that occurs after the read/write head of the hard drive locates the correct track and then waits for the correct sector to spin to the read/write head.

router A device that routes packets of data between two or more networks.

runtime error An error in a program that occurs when a programmer accidentally writes code that divides by zero, a mathematical error.

S

sampling rate The number of times per second a signal is measured and converted to a digital value. Sampling rates are measured in kilobits per second.

satellite Internet A way to connect to the Internet using a small satellite dish, which is placed outside the home and is connected to a computer with coaxial cable. The satellite company then sends the data to a satellite orbiting the Earth. The satellite, in turn, sends the data back to the satellite dish and to the computer.

scalability A characteristic of client/server networks where more users can be easily added without affecting the performance of other network nodes.

scanner A type of input device that inputs images into computers.

scareware A type of malware that's downloaded onto your computer and that tries to convince you that your computer is infected with a virus or other type of malware.

scope creep An ever-changing set of requests from clients for additional features as they wait longer and longer to see a working prototype.

script A list of commands (mini-programs or macros) that can be executed on a computer without user interaction.

scripting language A simple programming language that's limited to performing a set of specialized tasks.

search engine A set of programs that searches the web for specific words (or keywords) you wish to query (or look for) and that then returns a list of the websites on which those keywords are found.

second-generation language (2GL) A computer language that allows programmers to write programs using a set of short, English-like commands that speak directly to the central processing unit and that give the programmer direct control of hardware resources; also called *assembly language*.

second-level domain A domain that's directly below a top-level domain.

sector A section of a hard drive platter, wedge-shaped from the center of the platter to the edge.

Secure Sockets Layer (SSL) A network security protocol that provides for the encryption of data transmitted using the

Internet. The current versions of all major web browsers support SSL.

seek time The time it takes for the hard drive's read/write heads to move over the surface of the disk to the correct track.

select query In Structured Query Language, displays a subset of data from a table (or tables) based on the criteria specified.

semantic web (Web 3.0) An evolving extension of the World Wide Web in which information is defined in such a way as to make it more easily readable by computers.

server A computer that provides resources to other computers on a network.

server-side program A type of program that runs on a web server rather than on a computer.

service pack A software update.

service set identifier (SSID) A network name that wireless routers use to identify themselves.

shielded twisted-pair (STP) cable Twisted-pair cable that contains a layer of foil shielded to reduce interference.

short message service (SMS) Technology that enables short text messages (up to 160 characters) to be sent over mobile networks.

Simple Mail Transfer Protocol (SMTP) The protocol responsible for sending e-mail along the Internet to its destination; part of the Internet Protocol suite.

simulation programs Software, often used for training purposes, which allows the user to experience or control an event as if it's reality.

Sleep mode A low-power mode for electronic devices such as computers that saves electric power consumption and saves the last-used settings. When the device is "woken up," work is resumed more quickly than when cold booting the computer.

smart home A house in which devices and appliances are automated or controlled by apps.

smartphone A device with features of a computer including a wide assortment of apps, media players, high-quality cameras, and web connectivity.

social commerce A subset of e-commerce that uses social networks to assist in marketing and purchasing products.

social engineering Any technique that uses social skills to generate human interaction for the purpose of enticing individuals to reveal sensitive information.

social media Websites or apps that allow users to create and share content and/or participate in social networking with others.

social media directors People who are responsible for directing the company strategy on all social media platforms where the company has a presence.

social networking A means by which people use the Internet to communicate and share information among their immediate friends and to meet and connect with others through common interests, experiences, and friends.

software The set of computer programs or instructions that tells the computer what to do and that enables it to perform different tasks.

Software as a Service (SaaS) Software that's delivered on demand over the Internet.

software license An agreement between the user and the software developer that must be accepted before installing the software on a computer.

software piracy Violating a software license agreement by copying an application onto more computers than the license agreement permits.

software suite A collection of software programs that have been bundled together as a package.

solid-state drive (SSD) A storage device that uses the same kind of memory that flash drives use but that can reach data in only a tenth of the time a flash drive requires.

solid-state hybrid drive (SSHD) A drive that is a combination of both a mechanical hard drive and an SSD into a single device.

sound card An expansion card that attaches to the motherboard inside the system unit and that enables the computer to produce sounds by providing a connection for the speakers and microphone.

source code The instructions programmers write in a higher-level language.

spam Unwanted or junk e-mail.

spam filter An option you can select in your e-mail account that places known or suspected spam messages into a folder other than your inbox.

speakers Output devices for sound.

spear phishing A targeted phishing attack that sends e-mails to people known to be customers of a company. Such attacks have a much greater chance of successfully getting individuals to reveal sensitive data.

spooler A program that helps coordinate all print jobs being sent to the printer at the same time.

spreadsheet software An application program such as Microsoft Excel or Lotus 1-2-3 that enables a user to do calculations and numerical analyses easily.

spyware An unwanted piggyback program that downloads with the software you want to install from the Internet and then runs in the background of your system.

stakeholders People or entities who are affected by the operations of a business.

star topology The most widely deployed client/server network topology, where the nodes connect to a central communications device called a switch in a pattern resembling a star.

Start menu A feature in Windows 10 that provides access to all applications in one convenient screen.

statement A sentence in a code.

static addressing A way of assigning internet protocol addresses where the address for a computer never changes and is most likely assigned manually by a network administrator or an Internet service provider.

stealth virus A virus that temporarily erases its code from the files where it resides and hides in the active memory of the computer.

streaming media Multimedia (audio and video) that is fed continuously fed to the browser to avoid waiting for the entire file to download completely before listening to or watching it.

structured (analytical) data Data such as "Bill" or "345," as opposed to *unstructured data*.

Structured Query Language (SQL) A database programming language used to construct queries to extract data from relational databases; one example of a fourth-generation language.

stylus A pen-shaped device used to tap or write on touch-sensitive screens.

summary report A report generated by a management information system that provides a consolidated picture of detailed data; these reports usually include some calculation or visual displays of information.

supercomputer A specially designed computer that can perform complex calculations extremely rapidly; used in situations in which complex models requiring intensive mathematical calculations are needed (such as weather forecasting or atomic energy research).

SuperFetch A memory-management technique used by Windows 7. Monitors the applications you use the most and preloads them into your system memory so that they'll be ready to go.

surge protector A device that protects computers and other electronic devices from power surges.

surround sound A type of audio processing that makes the listener experience sound as if it were coming from all directions.

surround-sound speaker A system of speakers set up in such a way that it surrounds an entire area (and the people in it) with sound.

swap file (page file) A temporary storage area on the hard drive where the operating system "swaps out" or moves the data or instructions from random access memory (RAM) that haven't recently been used. This process takes place when more RAM space is needed.

Swift A new programming language introduced by Apple for developing for iOS and OS X.

switch A device for transmitting data on a network. A switch makes decisions, based on the media access control address of the data, as to where the data is to be sent.

synchronizing (or syncing) The process of updating data on portable devices (such as a cell phone or iPod) and a computer so that they contain the same data.

syntax An agreed-on set of rules defining how a language must be structured.

syntax error A violation of the strict set of rules that define the programming language.

system development life cycle (SDLC) A process used to develop information systems; it consists of the following six steps: problem and opportunity identification, analysis, design, development, testing and installation, and maintenance and evaluation.

system evaluation The process of looking at a computer's subsystems, what they do, and how they perform to determine whether the computer system has the right hardware components to do what the user ultimately wants it to do.

system files The main files of an operating system.

system requirements The set of minimum storage, memory capacity, and processing standards recommended by the software manufacturer to ensure proper operation of a software application.

System Restore A utility in Windows that restores system settings to a specific previous date when everything was working properly.

system restore point In Windows, a snapshot of your entire system's settings used for restoring your system to a prior point in time.

system software The set of programs that enables a computer's hardware devices and application software to work together; it includes the operating system and utility programs.

system unit The metal or plastic case that holds all the physical parts of the computer together, including the computer's processor (its brains), its memory, and the many circuit boards that help the computer function.

T

T line A communications line that carries digital data over twisted-pair wires.

table (file) A group of related records in a database.

tablet (2-in-1) PC A laptop computer designed specifically to work with handwriting recognition technology.

tablet computer A mobile computer, such as the Apple iPad or Samsung Galaxy Tab, integrated into a flat multitouch-sensitive screen. It uses an onscreen virtual keyboard, but separate keyboards can be connected via Bluetooth or wires.

tagging (social bookmarking) A keyword or term that Internet users assign to a web resource such as a web page, digital image, or video.

Task Manager A Windows utility that shows programs currently running and permits you to exit nonresponsive programs when you click End Task.

taskbar In later versions of Windows operating systems, a feature that displays open and favorite applications for easy access.

tax preparation software An application program, such as Intuit's TurboTax or H&R Block's At Home, for preparing state and federal taxes. Each program offers a complete set of tax forms and instructions as well as expert advice on how to complete each form.

TCP/IP The main suite of protocols used for transmitting data over the Internet. Named after Transmission Control Protocol (TCP) and the Internet Protocol (IP).

telephony The use of equipment to provide voice communications over a distance.

template A form included in many productivity applications that provides the basic structure for a particular kind of document, spreadsheet, or presentation.

terabyte (TB) 1,099,511,627,776 bytes or 2^{40} bytes.

terminator A device that absorbs a signal so that it's not reflected back onto parts of the network that have already received it.

test condition A check to see whether the loop in an algorithm is completed.

testing plan The part of the problem statement that lists specific input numbers the programmers would typically expect the user to enter; the plan then lists the precise output values that a perfect program would return for those input values.

tethering Approach which makes sure that as long as you have a 3G signal, your computer can access the Internet even when it tells you there are no available wireless networks. Several smartphones offer this capability.

thermal printer A printer that works either by melting wax-based ink onto ordinary paper (in a process called *thermal wax transfer printing*) or by burning dots onto specially coated paper (in a process called *direct thermal printing*).

third-generation language (3GL) A computer language that uses symbols and commands to help programmers tell the computer what to do, making 3GL languages easier for humans to read and remember; examples of 3GL languages include BASIC, FORTRAN, COBOL, C/C++, and JAVA.

thrashing A condition of excessive paging in which the operating system becomes sluggish.

three-way handshake In Transmission Control Protocol, the process used to establish a connection between two computers before exchanging data. The steps in a three-way handshake are as follows: One computer establishes a connection to the Internet service provider (ISP) and announces it has e-mail to send, the ISP server responds that it's ready to receive, and the computer acknowledges the ready state of the server and begins to transmit the e-mail.

throughput The actual speed of data transfer that's achieved. It's usually less than the data transfer rate and is measured in megabits per second (Mbps).

Thunderbolt port A high speed input/output port; Thunderbolt 2 provides two channels of 20 Gbps capacity on one port.

time bomb A virus that's triggered by the passage of time or on a certain date.

time-variant data Data that doesn't pertain to one period in time.

token A special data packet used to pass data in a ring topology network.

token method The access method used by ring networks to avoid data collisions.

top-down design A systematic approach in which a problem is broken into a series of high-level tasks.

top-level domain The suffix, often of three letters (such as .com or .edu), in the domain name that indicates the kind of organization the host is.

touch pad (trackpad) A small, touchsensitive screen at the base of a laptop keyboard that's used to direct the cursor.

touch screen A type of monitor (or display in a smartphone or tablet computer) that accepts input from a user touching the screen.

track A concentric circle that serves as a storage area on a hard drive platter.

transaction-processing system (TPS) A type of business intelligence system for keeping track of everyday business activities.

Transmission Control Protocol (TCP) One of the original two protocols developed for the Internet.

transmission media The radio waves or the physical system (cable) that transports data on a network.

Transport Layer Security (TLS) An updated extension of *Secure Sockets Layer*.

Trojan horse A computer program that appears to be something useful or desirable (such as a game or a screen saver), but at the same time does something malicious in the background without the user's knowledge.

tunneling The main technology for achieving a virtual private network; the placement of data packets inside other data packets.

twisted-pair cable Cables made of copper wires that are twisted around each other and are surrounded by a plastic jacket (such as traditional home phone wire).

U

ultrabook A full-featured but lightweight laptop computer that features a low-power processor and a solid-state drive; it tries to reduce its size and weight to extend battery life without sacrificing performance.

Uniform Resource Locator (URL) A website's unique address; an example is microsoft.com.

universal serial bus (USB) port A port that can connect a wide variety of peripheral devices to the computer, including keyboards, printers, mice, smartphones, external hard drives, flash drives, and digital cameras.

UNIX An operating system originally conceived in 1969 by Ken Thompson and Dennis Ritchie of AT&T's Bell Labs. In 1974, the UNIX code was rewritten in the standard programming language C. Today there are various commercial versions of UNIX.

unshielded twisted-pair (UTP) cable The most popular transmission media option for Ethernet networks. UTP cable is composed of four pairs of wires that are twisted around each other to reduce electrical interference.

unstructured data Audio clips, video clips, pictures, and extremely large documents. Also called *binary large object (BLOB)*.

User Datagram Protocol (UDP) An Internet Protocol that creates data packets across the Internet.

user interface Part of the operating system that enables individuals to interact with the computer.

utility program A small program that performs many of the general housekeeping tasks for the computer, such as system maintenance and file compression.

V

validation rule In a database, generally defined as part of the data dictionary and specified in the field properties for each field; violations result in an error message and a suggested action.

validation The process of ensuring that data entered into a field of a database meets specified guidelines.

variable Each input and output item the program manipulates.

variable declaration Tells the operating system that the program needs to allocate storage space in RAM.

VBScript A subset of Visual Basic, used to introduce dynamic decision making into web pages.

vertical market software Software that's developed for and customized to a specific industry's needs (such as a wood inventory system for a sawmill) as opposed to software that's useful across a range of industries (such as word processing software).

video card (video adapter) An expansion card that's installed inside a system unit to translate binary data (the *1*s and *0*s the computer uses) into the images viewed on the monitor.

video graphics array (VGA) port: A port to which a cathode ray tube monitor connects.

video log (vlog or video blog) A personal online journal that uses video as the primary content in addition to text, images, and audio.

video memory Random access memory that's included as part of a video card.

virtual desktops A Windows 10 feature that allows you to organize groups of windows into different displays.

virtual memory The space on the hard drive where the operating system stores data if there isn't enough random access memory to hold all of the programs you're currently trying to run.

virtual private network (VPN) A network that uses the public Internet communications infrastructure to build a secure, private network among various locations.

virtualization Using specialized software to make individual physical servers behave as though they are more than one physical device.

virus A computer program that attaches itself to another computer program (known as the host program) and attempts to spread itself to other computers when files are exchanged.

virus signature A portion of the virus code that's unique to a particular computer virus and that makes it identifiable by antivirus software.

Visual Basic (VB) A programming language used to build a wide range of Windows applications.

visual programming languages Programming language that uses graphical blocks to represent control elements and variables.

Voice over Internet Protocol (VoIP) A technology that facilitates making telephone calls across the Internet instead of using conventional telephone lines.

voice recognition software Software that allows you to control your computing devices by speaking into the microphone instead of using a keyboard or mouse.

volatile storage Temporary storage, such as in random access memory. When the power is off, the data in volatile storage is cleared out.

W

warm boot The process of restarting the system while it's powered on.

Web 2.0 Tools and web-based services that emphasize online collaboration and sharing among users.

web authoring software Programs you can use to design interactive web pages without knowing any HyperText Markup Language (HTML) code.

web browser (browser) Software installed on a computer system that allows individuals to locate, view, and navigate the web.

web server A computer running a specialized operating system that enables it to host web pages (and other information) and to provide requested web pages to clients.

web service Part of the Microsoft .NET Framework, programs that a website uses to make information available to other websites.

web-based apps A program that is hosted on a website and that doesn't require installation on the computer.

web-based e-mail A type of e-mail system that's managed by a web browser and that allows access to e-mail from the web.

webcam A small camera that sits on top of a computer monitor (connected to the computer by a cable) or that's built into a laptop computer and is usually used to transfer live video.

webcast A location on the web.

whistle-blowers: People who report businesses to regulatory agencies for committing illegal acts, or who expose unethical (but still legal) acts committed by their employers by publicizing unethical behavior.

white-hat hacker (ethical hacker) A hacker who breaks into systems just for the challenge of it (and who doesn't wish to steal or wreak havoc on the systems). Such hackers tout themselves as experts who are performing a needed service for society by helping companies realize the vulnerabilities that exist in their systems.

whole-house surge protector A surge protector that's installed on (or near) the breaker panel of a home and that protects all electronic devices in the home from power surges.

wide area network (WAN) A network made up of local area networks (LANs) connected over long distances.

wiki A type of website that allows anyone visiting the site to change its content by adding, removing, or editing the content.

Windows 10 Newest release of Microsoft's operating system that provides an interface optimized for touch-screen devices and is designed to run across all devices: phones, tablets, laptops, and desktops.

Windows Microsoft's operating system that incorporates a user-friendly, visual interface.

wireless access point (WAP) Gives wireless devices a sending and receiving connection point to the network.

wireless fidelity (WiFi) The 802.11 standard for wireless data transmissions established by the Institute of Electrical and Electronics Engineers (IEEE).

wireless Internet service provider (wireless ISP): An ISP that provides service to wireless devices such as smartphones.

wireless network interface card (wireless NIC) A special network adapter card that allows a computing device to connect to a network using wireless access.

wireless range extender A device that amplifies your wireless signal to get it out to parts of your home that are experiencing poor connectivity.

wizard A step-by-step guide that walks a user through the necessary steps to complete a complicated task.

word processing software Programs used to create and edit written documents such as papers, letters, and résumés.

World Wide Web (WWW or the web) The part of the Internet used the most. What distinguishes the web from the rest of the Internet are (1) its use of common communication protocols (such as Transmission Control Protocol/Internet Protocol, or TCP/IP) and special languages (such as the HyperText Markup Language, or HTML) that enable different computers to talk to each other and display information in compatible formats and (2) its use of special links (called hyperlinks) that enable users to jump from one place to another in the web.

worm A program that attempts to travel between systems through network connections to spread infections. Worms can run independently of host file execution and are active in spreading themselves.

Z

zombie A computer that is controlled by a hacker who uses it to launch attacks on other computer systems.

sample requirements, 236
solid-state drive, 52
storing data on, 233
Hardware
basic network, 267–268
coordination, 168
defined, 31
firewalls, 367
Harvard Mark I, 118
HDDs (hard disk drives). *See* Hard disk drives
(HDDs)
HDMI (high-definition multimedia
interface), 57
HDMI ports, 242
HD (high definition) signal, 336
HDTV
described, 336
types of connectivity, 336
Head crash, 235
Health care, technology and, 5
Hearing aids, 64
Helpdesk analysts, 405
Hexadecimal digit, 542
Hexadecimal notation, 299
Hibernate option, 59
High-definition multimedia interface
(HDMI), 57
High definition (HD) signal, 336
High-level formatting, 235
Hollerith, Herman, 117
Hollerith Tabulating Machine, 117–118
Home area network (HAN), 262, 496
configuring software for, 281–282
connecting devices to networks for,
277–278
connecting DVRs to, 279
connecting gaming consoles to, 280
digital entertainment devices on, 279
home network servers for, 279
for home security, 280
installing and configuring, 276–284
network-attached storage devices, 278
network software for, 268
planning, 276–277
smart TVs and, 279
Homegroups
creating in Windows, 283
defined, 281
in Windows, 508–509
Home networks servers, 279
Hopper, Grace, 118
Host servers, 501
Hotspots, mobile, 271–272
H&R Block Tax Software, 133
HTML5, 437, 548
HTML (Hypertext Markup Language), 437,
548–550
HTML embedded scripting language, 551
HTTP (Hypertext Transfer Protocol), 77,
94, 550
HTTPS (Hypertext Transfer Protocol
Secure), 550
Hulu, 87, 336
Human-implanted data chips, 212–213
Hybrid topology, 506
Hyperlinks, 94

Hypertext Markup Language (HTML), 437,
548–550
Hypertext Preprocessor (PHP), 438
Hypertext Transfer Protocol (HTTP), 77,
94, 550
Hypertext Transfer Protocol Secure
(HTTPS), 550
Hyperthreading, 227

I
IBackup, 379
IBM PC, 114
IC3 (Internet Crime Complaint Center), 348
ICANN (Internet Corporation for Assigned
Names and Numbers), 534, 539, 543–544
iCloud, 166
IDE (integrated development environment),
425–426
for Objective C, 436–437
Identity theft, 349
defined, 349
and hackers, 348–352
methods used for, 349
types of scams, 349
IEEE (Institute of Electrical and Electronics
Engineers), 264, 406, 434, 514, 518
If else keyword, 420
IFTTT (If This Then That) app, 284
Illustration software, 141–142
IM (instant messaging), 84
security, 554
summary, 83
Image backups, 378–379
frequency for, 380
method for, 380–381
Image-editing software, 140–141
Images
input devices for, 37, 39
search engines for, 98
Impact printers, 43
Imperva Application Defense Center, 371
Incremental backups, 378
Indiegogo, 332
Information
assurance, 521
data *vs.*, 30
storing, 52, 54–55
Information systems, 410–412, 478–479
defined, 478
types used by business managers,
478–483
Information Systems Security Association
(ISSA), 406
Inheritance, 419
Initial values, 417
Inkjet printers, 43–44
Inoculation, 369
Input devices
for games, 37
for images and sound input, 37, 39–40
keyboards and touch screens, 34–36
mice/pointing devices, 36–37
Input forms, 463–464
Instant messaging (IM), 84, 554
security, 554
summary, 83

Institute of Electrical and Electronics
Engineers (IEEE), 264, 406, 434,
514, 518
Instruction set, 303
Integrated circuits (chips), 120, 297
Integrated development environment (IDE),
422, 425–426
for Objective C, 436–437
Intel, 305–306
Intellectual property, 102, 210–211
and cyberbullying, 102
ethics and, 207
Intelligent personal assistant, 39
Interface designers, 402
Interference, types of, 510
Internal drive bays, 52
Internal hard drives, 52, 55
Internal testing, 428
International Game Developers
Association, 404
Internet
backbones, 78, 533
cable, 270
cache, 544
communication, 553–555
connecting to, 269–271
data routes, 535–536
data transmission, 536–538
free and uncensored access to, 216–217
management of, 534
networking components, 535–536
network model of, 535–536
origin of, 76–77
process of, 77–78
protocols, 536–538
satellite, 270
testing connection speed, 274–275
Internet2, 78
Internet Corporation for Assigned Names and
Numbers (ICANN), 534, 539, 543–544
Internet Crime Complaint Center (IC3), 348
Internet exchange points (IXPs), 535
Internet Explorer, 117
Internet of Things (IoT), 268, 401, 539
ethical challenges of, 269
shopping, 542
Internet Protocol (IP) address, 78, 539,
542–543
Internet Protocol version 4 (IPv4), 539
Internet Protocol version 6 (IPv6), 539, 542
Internet service providers (ISPs), 269–270
Interpreters, 425
Interrupt, 168
Interrupt handler, 168
Intranets, 497
Intuit QuickBooks, 134
Intuit TurboTax, 133
IP (Internet Protocol) address, 78, 539,
542–543
iPads, 31, 38
iPods, operating systems for, 164
IPv4 (Internet Protocol version 4), 539
IPv6 (Internet Protocol version 6), 539, 542
Ironkey Personal Flash Drive, 364–375
ISSA (Information Systems Security
Association), 406